THE GENESIS FLOOD

The Biblical Record and Its Scientific Implications

John C. Whitcomb

and

Henry M. Morris

Foreword by

John C. McCampbell

BAKER BOOK HOUSE

Grand Rapids, Michigan 49506

THE BOOK

THE GENESIS FLOOD presents a new and powerful system for unifying and correlating scientific data bearing on the earth's early history. Frankly recognizing the inadequacies of uniformitarianism and evolutionism as unifying principles, the authors propose a Biblically-based system of creationism and catastrophism. They stress the philosophic and scientific necessity of the doctrine of "creation of apparent age," as well as the importance in terrestrial history of geologic and hydrologic "catastrophes," especially that of the great Deluge inscribed in the records of the Bible and in the legends of early peoples all over the world. The book is careful and courteous in its treatment of opposing viewpoints, and is thoroughly documented and up-to-date.

The uniformist approach to the study of earth history has proved unable to explain many of the most important physical structures and phenomena, a fact which has become of increasing concern to geologists and other scientists in recent years. At the same time, archaeological discoveries in the Near East have stimulated a growing confidence in the reliability of the historical data recorded in the Bible. These two important facts amply warrant a serious study of the possibility of reorienting the pertinent scientific data within the framework of Biblical Creationism and Catastrophism.

The authors, each of recognized scholarship in his own field, contend that this approach will ultimately provide a more satisfactory basis for the correlation of all pertinent scientific data than does the present uniformist-evolutionist approach. Consideration of their evidence will make an intensely fascinating and thought-provoking study for the open-minded reader. The publishers believe that *The Genesis Flood* will prove to be one of the most widely-discussed and possibly one of the most significant books of our times.

Contents

Contents

APPENDIX I. PALEONTOLOGY AND THE EDENIC CURSE

List of Illustrations and Diagrams

xiii

Foreword

by

JOHN C. McCAMPBELL, PH.D.
Professor & Head, Department of Geology
University of Southwestern Louisiana
Lafayette, Louisiana

In the beginning God created the heavens and the earth. So the Bible teaches, and so we believe, for God has given us the Bible not only to guide our faith but also to provide a framework of revelation within which to interpret the mysteries of the earth's origin and destiny. The Biblical record states that all things were created in six days, in an original condition of divine perfection. It also records that this original creation was cursed because of the entrance of sin into the world through Adam, and that the resultant moral and spiritual deterioration eventually brought on the judgment of the great Flood. The Genesis Flood is said in the Bible to have been of such magnitude that it covered the whole globe for an entire year, destroying all living things on the face of the earth, except those preserved in the Ark.

For many centuries, men in Christian lands accepted these Biblical teachings in their literal sense, with little question. The earth was assumed to be only some six thousand years old, and most of the sedimentary rocks of its crust, especially those containing fossils, were believed to have been formed during the catastrophic conditions of the Noachian Deluge. These are the obvious inferences to be drawn on the basis of the assumption of the literal and historical reliability of the Biblical records.

But there has been a gradual change in outlook during the past two centuries. With more intensive study of the earth's rock strata,

xv

along with the development of a more inquisitive and rationalistic spirit among scholars, a completely different explanation of origins has been worked out. As a result especially of the studies and theories of men like Hutton, Lyell and Smith, climaxed one hundred years ago by the publication of Charles Darwin's theory of evolution, the study of geologic history has been dominated by the concept of uniformitarianism. The sedimentary rocks, sometimes many thousands of feet in thickness, are thus assumed to have been laid down by ordinary processes of deposition, at rates similar to those in effect at present. This concept of course implies that the earth must be tremendously old, its age now believed on the basis of evidence from radioactivity to be some 4½ billion years, instead of the traditional six thousand or so years.

The serious-minded Christian, desiring of course to accept both the truths revealed in Scripture and the findings of science as well, thus finds himself on the horns of a dilemma. The decision as to which position is to be accepted has too often been made simply on the basis of expediency. The uniformitarian concept has, by the mere fact of its being more modern and spectacular, and because of the strong pressure toward conformity even in scientific attitudes, been uncritically accepted today by the great majority of modern geologists.

But to reach a truly logical and correct conclusion, especially on such important and fundamental problems as these, an individual should certainly be willing to make a careful and open-minded study of both types of explanations. The fact is, however, that very few modern scientists in recent years have made any kind of serious attempt to evaluate the facts of geology and other sciences in terms of their possible harmonization with the Biblical revelation of the Creation and the Flood.

This book is an exception to such conformist thinking. *The Genesis Flood* places before the reader in clear and comprehensive fashion the theological and scientific basis for a literal acceptance of the Biblical account. The authors have carefully considered and developed their arguments, supporting each of them with an abundance of recent and authoritative documentation.

The reader who desires to accept the Biblical account literally and without reservation will discover that the authors have shown such a position to be supported by excellent proof and sound interpretation. They have clearly shown that the Bible teaches a unique Creation and subsequent worldwide Deluge, and that the major facts of geology and other sciences can be satisfactorily oriented within this framework.

The reader who respects the Bible but prefers to interpret it in non-literal terms, as well as the skeptic who rejects it altogether, should carefully study and evaluate the authors' position—certainly not ignore or summarily reject it. The authors have advanced strong arguments against the validity of uniformitarianism and evolutionism as controlling principles in historical geology, and in favor of what they call Biblical catastrophism. The various methods of geological time-measurement are analyzed and their basic assumptions adjudged inadequate by them, whenever these assumptions lead to results in contradiction to Biblical inferences. Furthermore, a number of the important unsolved problems in geology, such as the causes of past climatic change (including both universal warm climates and ice ages), the formation of geosynclines, the problem of orogenesis, the origin of petroleum, and numerous others, are believed by the authors to be more amenable to their framework of interpretation than to that of uniformitarianism.

From the writer's viewpoint, as a professional geologist, these explanations and contentions are difficult to accept. For the present at least, although quite ready to recognize the inadequacies of Lyellian uniformitarianism, I would prefer to hope that some other means of harmonization of religion and geology, which retains the essential structure of modern historical geology, could be found.

Nevertheless, the authors have made a strong case and this volume offers a serious challenge to the uniformitarian position. They have in no way distorted this position, but have opposed it in a courteous, fair and scholarly manner. I would suggest that the skeptical reader, in like fashion, before he dismisses the Biblical-literal viewpoint of this book as unworthy of notice, should at least give it a careful reading and evaluation. He will find that the essential differences between Biblical catastrophism and evolutionary uniformitarianism are not over the factual data of geology but over the interpretations of those data. The interpretation preferred will depend largely upon the background and presuppositions of the individual student.

But in either case, whether one prefers the Biblical framework or that of modern historical geology, he should in fairness to himself and others consider both sides of the question with equal diligence. He will find great personal satisfaction from such careful analysis and interpretation. In these days of intellectual and cultural conformity, real independent thinking seems to be becoming a lost art. A volume such as this offers us the challenge to begin to think carefully and creatively concerning the great issues with which it deals.

Introduction

The question of the historicity and the character of the Genesis Flood is no mere academic issue of interest to a small handful of scientists and theologians. If a worldwide flood actually destroyed the entire antediluvian human population, as well as all land animals, except those preserved in a special Ark constructed by Noah (as a plain reading of the Biblical record would lead one to believe), then its historical and scientific implications are tremendous. The great Deluge and the events associated with it necessarily become profoundly important to the proper understanding of anthropology, of geology, and of all other sciences which deal with historical and prehistorical events and phenomena.

But of even greater importance are the implications of the mighty Flood of Genesis for Christian theology. For that universal catastrophe speaks plainly and eloquently concerning the sovereignty of God in the affairs of men and in the processes of nature. Furthermore, it warns prophetically of a judgment yet to come, when the sovereign God shall again intervene in terrestrial events, putting down all human sin and rebellion and bringing to final fruition His age-long plan of creation and redemption.

But we have come to a day when the world of science and scholarship no longer regards the witness and warnings of the Flood with any seriousness. Men instead have adopted a philosophy of uniformity and evolution with which to interpret both cosmic and human history and with which even to predict and plan the future. Even evangelical Christians, though still professing belief in the divine validity of Scripture, have often capitulated to uniformitarian[1] scholarship, denying the universality of the Flood and, with the denial, thereby sacrificing its mighty evangelistic witness to a world in rebellion against its Creator.

Our present study therefore has a twofold purpose. In the first place, we desire to ascertain exactly what the Scriptures say concerning the Flood and related topics. We do this from the perspective of full belief in the complete divine inspiration and perspicuity of Scripture, believing that a true exegesis thereof yields determinative Truth in all matters with which it deals.

We accept as basic the doctrine of the verbal inerrancy of Scripture, to which Benjamin B. Warfield has given admirable expression in the following words:

> The Church has held from the beginning that the Bible is the Word of God in such a sense that its words, though written by men and bearing indelibly impressed upon them the marks of their human origin, were written, nevertheless, under such an influence of the Holy Ghost as to be also the words of God, the adequate expression of His mind and will. It has always recognized that this conception of co-authorship implies that the Spirit's superintendence extends to the choice of the words by the human authors (verbal inspiration), and preserves its product from everything inconsistent with a divine authorship . . . thus securing, among other things, that entire truthfulness which is everywhere presupposed in and asserted for Scripture by the Biblical writers (inerrancy).[2]

The second purpose is to examine the anthropological, geological, hydrological and other scientific implications of the Biblical record of the Flood, seeking if possible to orient the data of these sciences within this Biblical framework. If this means substantial modification of the principles of uniformity and evolution[3] which currently control the interpretation of these data, then so be it.

---

[1] Uniformitarianism is the belief that existing physical processes, acting essentially as at present, are sufficient to account for all past changes and for the present state of the astronomic, geologic and biologic universe. The principle of uniformity in *present* processes is both scientific and Scriptural (Gen. 8:22), but comes into conflict with Biblical revelation when utilized to deny the possibility of *past* or *future* miraculous suspension or alteration of those processes by their Creator.

[2] Benjamin B. Warfield, "The Real Problem of Inspiration," in *The Inspiration and Authority of the Bible*, edited by Samuel G. Craig (Philadelphia: The Presbyterian and Reformed Publishing Co., 1948), p. 173. See also, Edward J. Young, *Thy Word is Truth* (Grand Rapids: Wm. B. Eerdmans Pub. Co., 1957).

[3] We use the term "evolution" in the broadest sense; namely, the theory that all

We realize, of course, that modern scholarship will be impatient with such an approach. Our conclusions must unavoidably be colored by our Biblical presuppositions, and this we plainly acknowledge.

But uniformitarian scholarship is no less bound by *its* own presuppositions and these are quite as dogmatic as those of our own! The assumptions of historical continuity and scientific naturalism are no more susceptible of genuine scientific *proof* than are Biblical catastrophism[1] and supernaturalism. Furthermore, we believe that certain of the assumptions implicit in evolutionary theory (e.g., tacit denial of the two universal laws of thermodynamics)[2] are much farther removed from scientific actualities than are our own premises. We believe that a system founded squarely on full confidence in the Scriptures will be found ultimately to be much more satisfying than any other, in its power to correlate scientific data and to resolve problems and apparent conflicts.

We recognize, certainly, that a work of this nature cannot deal comprehensively with all the problems entailed in the formulation of a truly Biblical and scientific catastrophism. The scope of these problems is vast, bearing really upon the whole spectrum of the sciences. The background and special interests of the authors are, on the one hand, the fields of Old Testament interpretation and Biblical criticism and, on the other, the fields of hydraulics, hydrology, and geomorphology. It is hoped that this combination will serve as well as any for a preliminary study[3] of the Genesis Flood and its implications.

organisms, man included, have been derived by gradual diversification from common ancestral forms of life, through innate processes of variation and selection, forms which in turn originally were derived by spontaneous generation from inanimate matter.

[1] Biblical catastrophism is the doctrine that, at least on the occasions mentioned in Scripture, God has directly intervened in the normal physical processes of the universe, causing significant changes therein for a time. At the same time, such miraculous intervention acquires significance only against the backdrop of a basic pattern of uniformity.

[2] Evolution, in the broad sense, implies increasing organization and complexity in the universe and is in effect a doctrine of continuous creation; conversely, the first law of thermodynamics affirms that creation is no longer normally occurring, and the second that the original creation is decreasing in organization and complexity. See pp. 222f.

[3] We emphasize, as strongly as possible, that this can only be an exploratory sketch of a vast and complex field of study. It will necessarily be subject to extensive modification and amplification, but we trust that such difficulties of detail as may occur to the reader will not deter him from a genuinely candid consideration of the picture as a whole.

The advice of many others, specialists in different pertinent disciplines, has also been very helpful.

Nevertheless, we are realistic concerning the reception this work may expect, by and large, from evolutionary scientists. We believe that most of the difficulties associated with the Biblical record of the Flood are basically religious, rather than scientific. The concept of such a universal judgment on man's sin and rebellion, warning as it does of another greater judgment yet to come, is profoundly offensive to the intellectual and moral pride of modern man and so he would circumvent it if at all possible.

We hope, however, that those whose confidence, like ours, is centered in the revelation of God, will be encouraged herein to see that a truly Biblical approach will eventually correlate all the factual data of science in a much more harmonious and satisfying way than the uniformitarian assumption can ever do. Because the Creator is also the true Author of Scripture, we believe that the more faithfully we believe His Word, the more effectively shall we be able to advance the frontiers of true knowledge concerning His Creation, exercising in the process the functions of the image of God in man.

Preface to the Second Printing

The authors wish to take this opportunity to thank God for the large measure of favorable response He has seen fit to grant to this volume. Letters have been received from pastors, missionaries, and Christian men of science all over the world, which indicate that the book has helped to meet an urgent need in the realm of Christian apologetics. There are many who agree with us that the time has come when the false presuppositions and implications of organic evolution and geologic uniformitarianism need to be challenged in the name of holy Scripture. We hope that THE GENESIS FLOOD has made a positive contribution in this direction.

Of about twenty published reviews that we have seen thus far, only two have been unfavorable. Certain important implications of these two critical reviews call for clarification at this time. In the first place, the basic argument of this volume is based upon the presupposition that the Scriptures are true (being verbally inspired by God—II Timothy 3:16, II Peter 1:21, John 10:35, etc.). We believe it has been proved that they consistently teach the universality of the great Flood of the days of Noah. It is quite significant, in the light of this, that neither review alluded to above attempted to deal with this Biblical doctrine of the Flood.

In the second place, it seems quite obvious that a misrepresentation of the authors' position on the doctrine of uniformitarianism continues to persist in some quarters. So far from holding that this doctrine, which underlies much of modern scientific theory, is totally invalid, the authors have insisted that "the principle of uniformity in *present* processes is both scientific and Scriptural (Gen. 8:22), but comes into conflict with Biblical revelation when utilized to deny the possibility of *past* or *future* miraculous suspension or alteration of those processes by their Creator" (xx, note 1).

In the third place, we have made every effort to quote our sources in proper context and to avoid attributing our own views to those whom we have quoted. Having observed these precautions, however, one has a perfect right in polemical writings to quote from one's opponent in order to expose the inconsistency of his position. Full documentation has been given in THE GENESIS FLOOD for each reference, and any reader who may question the propriety or pertinence of any of them is urged to look them up for himself. True Christian scholarship thrives on an open Bible and on fair and open debate.

Finally, we emphasize again that many minor details of our analysis of these problems may require modification in the light of further study, but these will not affect the major conclusions. We therefore urge the reader not to be overly swayed by minor difficulties, but rather to consider candidly the tremendous accumulated weight of Biblical and scientific evidence validating the universal Flood and its geological implications.

In this second printing of THE GENESIS FLOOD, a few minor errors have been corrected, mostly typographical in nature. The general format and pagination remains unchanged.

It is our sincere prayer that God may continue to use this volume for the purpose of restoring His people everywhere to full reliance on the truth of the Biblical doctrine of origins. We are convinced that it is only through a proper understanding of God's Word that men can understand the mysteries of God's world. "With thee is the fountain of life: in thy light shall we see light" (Psa. 36:9).

Henry M. Morris
John C. Whitcomb

November 15, 1961

Preface to the Sixth Printing

The authors wish to take this opportunity to thank God for the large measure of favorable response He has seen fit to grant to this volume. Letters have been received from pastors, missionaries, and Christian men of science all over the world, which indicate that the book has helped to meet an urgent need in the realm of Christian apologetics. There are many who agree with us that the time has come when the false presuppositions and implications of organic evolution and geologic uniformitarianism need to be challenged in the name of holy Scripture. We hope that THE GENESIS FLOOD has made a positive contribution in this direction.

Of the forty-five published reviews that we have seen thus far, only a few have been unfavorable. The few critical reviews seem to focus upon two main objections. *One* is the supposed impropriety of questioning the authority of those geologists and other scientists who have concluded that the earth and its life forms have been developing into their present state for billions of years. The *second* is a complaint against our use of documented quotations from various authorities, who themselves would disagree with our basic position, as evidence in support thereof. The *first* criticism implies that no one but a geologist has the right to evaluate a geological theory; the *second* would in effect preclude the use of statements from anyone except authors already in agreement with our position, as this would be "quoting out of context."

Rather than attempting to answer the various specific examples of these objections selected by the reviewers, it will be more to the point to deal with these basic charges in their totality. We believe, of course, that the reviewers have misunderstood what we were saying in the specific examples cited. A more careful reading of the whole book, instead of isolated portions lifted out for criticism, we believe would show that every one of the objections raised is without foundation. However, it is more important to get at the basic issues, and so we confine our attention to the two fundamental objections noted above.

The first point has been discussed at considerable length in the book, and since the reviewers have chosen to ignore our references to this matter, we must emphasize again several things. In the first place, we do not presume to question any of the data of geological *science*. Science (meaning "knowledge") necessarily can deal only with *present* processes, which can be measured and evaluated at the present time; the "scientific method" by definition involves experimental reproducibility. Thus, extrapolation of present processes into the prehistoric past or into the eschatalogical future is not really science. Such extrapolation necessarily involves assumptions and presuppositions and is therefore basically a philosophy, or even a faith. The assumption of uniformity is one such assumption that can be made, but it is not the only one, and there is no way of *proving* that it is the correct one. The very same data can also be explained in terms of the assumption of Biblical creationism and catastrophism, and it is mainly a matter of one's own judgment and preferences as to which he chooses. We frankly prefer the latter presupposition, on the basis of what we consider wholly adequate grounds centered in the revelation of God in Christ. We believe that the Bible, as the verbally inspired and completely inerrant Word of God, gives us the true framework of historical and scientific interpretation, as well as of so-called religious truth. This framework is one of special creation of all things, complete and perfect in the beginning, followed by the introduction of a universal principle of decay and death into the world after man's sin, culminating in a worldwide cataclysmic destruction of "the world that then was" by the Genesis Flood. We take this revealed framework of history as our basic datum, and then try to see how all the pertinent data can be understood in this context. It would be salutary for the "uniformitarians" to recognize that this is exactly the procedure they follow too, except that they start with the assumption of uniformity (and therefore, implicitly, evolution) and then proceed to interpret all the data to fit into *that* context. Neither procedure is scientific, since we are not dealing with present and reproducible phenomena. Both approaches are matters of faith. It is not a scientific decision at all, but a spiritual one.

In the second place, we emphatically do not question uniformity of the basic laws of physics (e.g., the two laws of thermodynamics) as charged by the reviewers. We strongly emphasized that these laws have been in operation since the *end* of the creation period. The first teaches that no creation is now taking place, and the second enunciates the universal law of decay. These laws are basic in geology and in all science, and are clearly set forth in Scripture. This is the *true* principle of uniformity. We only question the assumption of uniformity of *rates* of geological and other processes, and even here essentially only as required by Biblical revelation. It is well known that the second law of thermodynamics implies decay but does not say anything about the *rate* of decay. There is nothing fundamentally inviolable about even rates of *radioactive* decay.

Geologists, therefore, must leave the strict domain of *science* when they become *historical* geologists. We repeat that we have *no quarrel whatever* with geological *science,* which in its many disciplines is contributing most significantly to our understanding and utilization of our terrestrial environment and resources. The so-called historical geology, on the other hand, has not changed or developed in any essential particular for over a hundred years, since the days when its basic philosophical structure was first worked out by such non-geologists as Charles Lyell (a lawyer), William Smith (a surveyor), James Hutton (an agriculturalist), John Playfair (a mathematician), George Cuvier (a comparative anatomist), Charles Darwin (an apostate divinity student turned naturalist), and various theologians (Buckland, Fleming, Pye Smith, and Sedgwick). Might we respectfully suggest that, if non-geologists were allowed to develop the standard historical geology, non-geologists might also be permitted to evaluate and criticize it? Historical geology, with its evolutionary implications, has had profound influence on nearly every aspect of modern life, especially in its fostering of an almost universal rejection of the historicity of Genesis and of Biblical Christianity generally. It is not reasonable, therefore, to expect Bible-believing Christians to acquiesce quietly when, in the name of "science," historical geologists attempt to usurp all authority in this profoundly important field of the origin and history of the earth and its inhabitants.

It is at this point that the authors feel that these critical reviewers have been most unfair. As we have stressed repeatedly in our book, the real issue is not the correctness of the interpretation of various details of the geological data, but simply what God has revealed in His Word concerning these matters. This is why the first four chapters and the two appendixes are devoted to a detailed exposition and analysis of the Biblical teachings on creation, the Flood, and related topics. The last three chapters attempt then, in an admittedly preliminary and incomplete manner, to explain the pertinent geological and other scientific data in the light of these teachings. The criticisms, however, have almost always centered upon various details of the latter, and have ignored the former and more important matters. The very strong and detailed Biblical evidences for a recent Creation, the universal effects of the Curse, and the worldwide destructive effects of the Deluge, have evidently been neglected as peripheral and inconsequential as far as these reviewers are concerned. Of course, they cite opinions to the effect that various interpretations are possible, etc., but *none ever deals with the actual Biblical evidence.*

The only conclusion that one can draw from this is that the authors and their critics seem to be operating on two entirely different sets of presuppositions. On the one hand, scientific data are interpreted in the light of Biblical revelation; on the other hand, both revelation and the scientific data are interpreted in the light of the philosophic assumption of uniformity.

The second basic criticism of these reviewers is the charge that we have supported our position by quotations taken out of context, and that these quotations are consequently misleading. To this we would only suggest that skeptical readers look up the references for themselves. We have been careful to give full documentation for every reference, for just this reason. We flatly reject the innuendo that we have tried to give the impression that the authorities cited agree with our basic position or even with the particular argument we are attempting to illustrate by each quotation. We are of course trying to show in each case that the actual scientific data can be interpreted just as well or better in terms of the creation-catastrophe framework. Since it would be unrealistic to expect most readers to accept our description of the particular phenomenon under discussion simply on our own authority, we use instead the works of recognized geologists of the orthodox school. No implication is intended, unless explicitly so stated, concerning the beliefs of the particular writer quoted. We believe the quotation in each case speaks for itself concerning the issue at hand. This, of course, is standard procedure in scientific dialogue and argumentation. The latter would be quite impossible were writers expected to limit their citations to recognized authorities who already agreed with their position.

Space does not permit a detailed discussion of the specific examples which the reviewers give in support of their charge of misleading quotations. However, we deny not only the general charge but also the validity of the individual examples. We believe a *careful* reading of both the original articles and our use of portions of them in our discussions will verify their pertinence and contextual soundness as they stand. We of course readily acknowledge our fallibility. When and if legitimate weaknesses or mistakes are pointed out, we hope that we shall be willing to acknowledge and revise them. As we have tried repeatedly to stress in the book, our specific discussions of individual geologic problems are tentative and subject to continuing re-evaluation with further study, but these problems do not, and cannot be allowed to, raise questions concerning the basic framework of Biblical revelation within which they must be understood.

It is our sincere prayer that God may continue to use this volume for the purpose of restoring His people everywhere to full reliance on the truth of the Biblical doctrine of origins. We are convinced that it is only through a proper understanding of God's Word that men can understand the mysteries of God's world. "With thee is the fountain of life: in thy light shall we see light" (Psa. 36:9).

Henry M. Morris
John C. Whitcomb

May 25, 1964

Acknowledgments

The manuscript for this volume has been reviewed, in full or in part, by a large number of men who are specialists in different branches of science or theology. The writers wish to acknowledge with genuine gratitude the suggestions and assistance of these men and to thank them for their interest and encouragement.

We have endeavored to follow their suggestions insofar as it was feasible, either in correcting our own presentation or in attempting to answer more effectively the questions raised. Of course, the fact must be emphasized that we assume full responsibility for the volume; probably no single reviewer would concur with *everything* in it.

Nevertheless, we desire to mention the names and connections of these friends and colleagues in appreciation of their generous help and encouragement. The subject treated involves vital contact with many different disciplines, so that the criticisms and suggestions of those who are active in these fields have been invaluable to us.

The following men read the entire manuscript and should be recognized in a special way: *Oswald T. Allis*, Ph.D., D.D., formerly a member of the Old Testament Department at Princeton Theological Seminary and Professor of Old Testament at Westminster Theological Seminary; *Warren Driver*, M.A., B.D., Assistant Professor of Education and Science, Grace College; *Thomas Gilmer*, Ph.D., Professor of Physics, Virginia Polytechnic Institute; *C. Lowell Hoyt*, B.D., postgraduate student, Grace Theological Seminary; *Homer A. Kent, Jr.*, Th.D., Professor of New Testament and Greek, Grace Theological Seminary; *John W. Klotz*, Ph.D., Professor of Natural Science, Concordia Senior College; *Wilbert H. Rusch, Sr.*, M.A., Professor of Science, Concordia Teachers College, Seward, Nebraska; *Rousas J. Rushdoony*, M.A., pastor and author, Santa Cruz, California.

We especially thank John C. McCampbell, Ph.D., Professor and Head of the Department of Geology at the University of Southwestern Louisiana (a rapidly-growing state university of six colleges and over

5,000 students, situated in the heart of the south's petroleum industrial expansion), who not only reviewed the entire manuscript but also graciously consented to write the Foreword. This was in spite of his many duties as head of a large and active geology department and in spite of his natural reservations concerning many of the implications of geological catastrophism advocated herein.

The following have read the first draft of our Chapters 1 through 7 (not including the Appendixes), and their suggestions contributed substantially to our final revisions of the manuscript: *David K. Blake,* B.S., an industrial engineer with the General Electric Company, Schenectady, New York; *R. Laird Harris,* Ph.D., Professor of Old Testament, Covenant Theological Seminary; *Walter E. Lammerts,* Ph.D., Horticultural Consultant, Germaine's, Inc., Livermore, California; *Frank L. Marsh,* Ph.D., Professor of Biology, Emmanuel Missionary College; *Edwin Y. Monsma,* Ph.D., Professor and Head, Department of Biology, Calvin College; *Harold S. Slusher,* M.S., Assistant Professor of Physics and Astronomy, Texas Western College; *William J. Tinkle,* Ph.D., formerly Head of the Biology Department, Taylor University; and *Merrill F. Unger,* Ph.D., Th.D., Professor of Old Testament, Dallas Theological Seminary.

In addition, a number of men have reviewed either Chapters 1-4 (the geographical extent of the Flood) or Chapters 5-7 (the geologic implications of the Flood). Those who reviewed only the first four chapters are as follows: *Arthur C. Custance,* Ph.D., F.R.A.I., Toronto, Canada; *Herman A. Hoyt,* Th.D., Dean and Professor of New Testament and Greek, Grace Theological Seminary; *Homer A. Kent, Sr.,* Th.D., Registrar and Professor of Church History and Practical Theology, Grace Theological Seminary; *Alva J. McClain,* Th.M., D.D., President and Professor of Christian Theology, Grace Theological Seminary; *Allan A. MacRae,* Ph.D., President and Professor of Old Testament, Faith Theological Seminary; *John Rea,* M.A., Th.D., Professor of Bible and Archaeology, Grace Theological Seminary.

Chapters 5 through 7 were reviewed in their original form by the following: *L. A. M. Barnette,* Ch.E., petroleum geologist, Humble Oil Company, Houston, Texas; *Clifford L. Burdick,* M.A., consulting mining geologist, Tucson, Arizona; *Harold W. Clark,* M.A., formerly Professor of Biology at Pacific Union College; *Wayne M. Frair,* M.A., Assistant Professor of Biology, King's College; *Elbert H. Hadley,* Ph.D., Professor of Chemistry. Southern Illinois University; *H. Clay*

Hudson, B.S., formerly a soil scientist with the U.S. Soil Conservation Service; *George McCready Price*, M.A., formerly Professor of Geology and Philosophy, Walla Walla College; and *Lloyd D. Vincent*, Ph.D., Professor and Head, Department of Physics, Sam Houston College.

Miss Elener Norris, M.A., Assistant Professor of English and Journalism, Grace College, reviewed the entire manuscript for style and grammar. *Miss Ava Schnittjer*, M.A., M.R.E., Professor of English and Speech, Grace College, also read parts of the manuscript for this purpose.

It has been a pleasure to work with Mr. Charles H. Craig, Director of the Presbyterian and Reformed Publishing Company. His encouragement and helpful counsel in the preparation of this volume for publication have been deeply appreciated by the authors.

Finally, special thanks are due to Mrs. Mary Morgan, Civil Engineering Department secretary at Virginia Polytechnic Institute, who typed the manuscript, and to the writers' families, without whose patience and prayerful encouragement this project could never have been completed.

Henry M. Morris
Blacksburg, Virginia
John C. Whitcomb
Winona Lake, Indiana

December 15, 1960

Chapter I

Basic Arguments for a
Universal Flood

In harmony with our conviction that the Bible is the infallible Word of God, verbally inspired in the original autographs, we begin our investigation of the geographical extent of the Flood with seven Biblical arguments in favor of its universality. The first six of these arguments are briefly stated, but the seventh is more complex and requires a number of supporting arguments. The major objections to these seven arguments will be considered in Chapter II and Chapter III.

THE DEPTH OF THE FLOOD

One of the most important Biblical arguments for a universal Flood is the statement of Genesis 7:19-20:

And the waters prevailed exceedingly upon the earth; and all the high mountains that were under the whole heaven were covered. Fifteen cubits upward did the waters prevail; and the mountains were covered.[1]

One need not be a professional scientist to realize the tremendous implications of these Biblical statements. If only *one* (to say nothing of *all*) of the high mountains[2] had been covered with water, the Flood

---

[1] Unless otherwise noted, all Scripture quotations are taken from the American Standard Version of 1901.

[2] The present Mt. Ararat, on or near which the Ark was said to have grounded,

would have been absolutely universal; for water must seek its own level—and must do so quickly! Herbert C. Leupold makes the following statement concerning the exegesis and interpretation of this crucial text of Scripture:

A measure of the waters is now made by comparison with the only available standard for such waters—the mountains. They are said to have been "covered." Not merely a few but "all the high mountains under all the heavens." One of these expressions alone would almost necessitate the impression that the author intends to convey the idea of the absolute universality of the Flood, e.g., "all the high mountains." Yet since "all" is known to be used in a relative sense, the writer removes all possible ambiguity by adding the phrase "under all the heavens." A double "all" (*kol*) cannot allow for so relative a sense. It almost constitutes a Hebrew superlative. So we believe that the text disposes of the question of the universality of the Flood.[1]

The phrase "fifteen cubits upward did the waters prevail" does not mean that the Flood was only fifteen cubits (22 feet) deep, for the phrase is qualified by the one which immediately follows: "and the mountains were covered." Nor does it necessarily mean that the mountains were covered to a depth of *only* fifteen cubits, for this would require that all antediluvian mountains be exactly the same altitude.

The true meaning of the phrase is to be found in comparing it with Genesis 6:15, where we are told that the height of the Ark was thirty cubits. Nearly all commentators agree that the phrase "fifteen cubits" in 7:20 must therefore refer to the draught of the Ark. In other words, the Ark sank into the water to a depth of fifteen cubits (just one-half of its total height) when fully laden. Such information adds further support to this particular argument for a universal Flood, because it tells us that the Flood "prevailed" over the tops of the highest mountains to a depth of *at least* fifteen cubits. If the Flood had not covered the mountains by at least such a depth, the Ark could not have floated over them during the five months in which the waters "prevailed" upon the earth.

is some 17,000 feet in elevation! Of course, unless uniformitarianism be presupposed, it is not necessary to assume that antediluvian mountains were this high. See below, pp. 266-270.

[1] H. C. Leupold, *Exposition of Genesis* (Columbus: The Wartburg Press, 1942), p. 301.

Fig. 1. THE CHRONOLOGY OF THE FLOOD[a]

There were forty days during which the rain fell 40

Throughout another 110 days the waters continued to rise, making 150 days in all for their "prevailing" (7:24) 110

The waters occupied 74 days in their "going and decreasing" (AV margin). This was from the 17th day of the seventh month to the 1st day of the tenth month (8:5). There being 30 days to a month, the figures in days are 13 plus 30 plus 30 plus 1 74

Forty days elapsed before Noah sent out the raven (8:6-7) 40

Seven days elapsed before Noah sent out the dove for the first time (8:8). This period is necessary for reaching the total and is given by implication from the phrase "other seven days" (8:10) 7

Seven days passed before sending out the dove for the second time (8:10) 7

Seven days more passed before the third sending of the dove (8:12) 7

Up to this point 285 days are accounted for, but the next episode is dated the 1st of the first month in the 601st year. From the date in 7:11 to this point in 8:13 is a period of 314 days; therefore an interval of 29 days elapses 29

From the removal of the covering of the ark to the very end of the experience was a further 57 days (8:14) 57

TOTAL 371

---

[a] This table appears in E. F. Kevan's commentary on Genesis in *The New Bible Commentary*, ed. F. Davidson (Grand Rapids: Wm. B. Eerdmans Pub. Co., 1953), pp. 84-85. As is pointed out in our discussion below (p. 4), the Flood probably reached its maximum depth after the first forty days, instead of rising throughout the 150 days as Kevan indicates.

THE DURATION OF THE FLOOD

A careful study of the Biblical data reveals the fact that the Flood lasted for 371 days, or a little over a year (see the accompanying chronology chart, Fig. 1). That the Flood continued for more than a year is entirely in keeping with the doctrine of its universality but cannot properly be reconciled with the local-Flood theory. While there may be a difference of opinion among Christian scholars as to the general depth of the Flood (depending upon the altitude of antediluvian mountains), there can be no question as to its duration.

Twenty-one Weeks of "Prevailing"

Now some commentators have assumed that the waters continued to rise during the 150 days that the waters "prevailed upon the earth," because "the windows of heaven were stopped, and the rain from heaven was restrained" (8:2) only after the end of the 150-day period (8:3). This is certainly a possible interpretation of the text, but it is better to conclude with Leupold[1] that the Flood attained its maximum depth after the first forty days and continued to maintain this level for an additional 110 days before beginning to assuage (7:24, 8:3). Our basis for assuming this is found in 7:4 and 7:12, where we read that the rains came "upon the earth forty days and forty nights"; and 7:17 where we are told that "the flood was forty days upon the earth." Most of "the waters which were above the firmament" (Gen. 1:7) must have fallen through "the windows of heaven" during the first period of forty days; and although "the windows of heaven" were not stopped for another 110 days (8:2), the rainfall during this second period may have contributed only to the maintaining of the Flood at its maximum height.

Thirty-one Weeks of "Assuaging"

One's imagination is indeed staggered at the thought of a Flood so gigantic as to overwhelm the high mountains of the earth within a period of *six weeks* and then to continue prevailing over those mountains for an additional *sixteen weeks,* during which time the sole survivors of the human race drifted upon the face of a shoreless ocean! But if the Biblical concept of a deluge covering the tops of mountains for sixteen consecutive weeks is hard to reconcile with the local-Flood theory, what are we to say of the fact that *an additional thirty-one weeks* were required for the waters to subside sufficiently for Noah to disembark safely in the mountains of Ararat?

[1] Leupold, *op. cit.,* pp. 300, 306. Cf. Alexander Heidel, *The Gilgamesh Epic and Old Testament Parallels* (2nd Ed.; Chicago: University of Chicago Press, 1949), p. 246.

Arthur C. Custance has recently published a booklet in defense of the local-Flood theory, in which he attempts to deal with this problem:

> There are certain figures indicated in the text which, if we are rightly interpreting them, provide some rather surprising information about the rate at which the waters receded. In Gen. 8:4 we are told that the Ark came to rest, i.e., grounded, on the 17th day of the 7th month . . . The record states then that the waters receded (Gen. 8:5) until the first day of the 10th month, at which time apparently it became possible to *see* dry land. Before this, the raven released from the Ark had not found any resting place within easy flying distance so that we must assume that the peak on which the Ark was actually grounded had not appeared above the water up to this time. Obviously, if land could be *seen,* the raven would have found a place to alight instead of wandering to and fro as depicted in Gen. 8:7. In this interval, therefore, from the 17th day of the 7th month to the 1st day of the 10th month the water level had fallen perhaps 25 or 30 feet. It is clear that as soon as the level had fallen by the amount equal to the draught of the vessel dry land would appear . . . and 25 feet in 74 days is the equivalent of a drop in level of about 4 inches per day.[1]

Custance then proceeds to demonstrate that a drop in water level of only a few inches a day would be more appropriate for a limited flood than a universal one.

When we turn to the text of Genesis, however, we discover that this could not have been the case. For 8:4-7 indicates that "the tops of the mountains" were seen as much as forty days *before* the raven was sent forth. Custance assumes that the raven was released forty days after the Ark was grounded and that the 74-day period described in 8:5 overlapped the 40-day period mentioned in 8:6. But if this were true, the entire bird episode, including the plucking of the fresh olive leaf, would have been completed two weeks before the tops of the mountains were seen![2] Noah did *not* send forth the raven to determine

---

[1] Arthur C. Custance, *The Extent of the Flood: Doorway Papers #41* (Ottawa: Published by the author, 1958), pp. 8-9. Earlier in the century, George Frederick Wright wrote in a similar fashion: "The duration of the Deluge, according to Genesis, affords opportunity for a gradual progress of events which best accords with scientific conceptions of geological movements. If, as the most probable interpretation would imply, the water began to recede after 150 days from the beginning of the Flood and fell 15 cubits in 74 days, that would only be 3⅔ inches per day—a rate which would be imperceptible to an ordinary observer." *International Standard Bible Encyclopedia,* ed. James Orr (Grand Rapids: Wm. B. Eerdmans Pub. Co., reprint, 1946), II, 824.

[2] Even if one were to adopt/E. F. Kevan's theory that the tops of the mountains "were not then just beginning to emerge, but had been hidden by the mists which such a downpour of rain must have created" (*The New Bible Commentary,* p. 84)

whether any mountain peaks had emerged as yet, as Custance assumes, but to gain information about the nature of these exposed areas. Alexander Heidel explains:

> Forty days after the tops of the other mountains had become visible, Noah opened the window of the ark and sent forth a raven (8:5-7). The wild, omnivorous bird went flying back and forth, sometimes away from the ark and sometimes back to it again, until the waters had dried off the earth, but he did not again go into the ark. He presumably found some carrion meat floating in the water or deposited on the mountaintops, or some aquatic creatures trapped on the mountain peaks as the water receded, and this provided sufficient sustenance for the unclean raven with his carrion-eating propensities. The raven's failure to return into the ark does not show that he proved himself useless for the intended purpose and that the experiment was unsuccessful. To the contrary, it was a *good* sign; for it proved that the waters had declined considerably and that even though the outside world was still very unfriendly or inhospitable, it was no longer too inhospitable for so sturdy and unfastidious a bird as the raven.[1]

Furthermore, it can hardly be emphasized too strongly that it was not merely the top of the high mountain on which the Ark rested that was seen on the first day of the tenth month. The Scriptures inform us that on that day "were the *tops* of the *mountains* seen." In other words, the Flood waters must have subsided hundreds of feet in order for *various mountain peaks of different altitudes* to be seen by then.

Nor does the Bible teach that the tops of the mountains were still submerged on the last day of the ninth month and then suddenly emerged on the first day of the tenth month. With equal justification,

it would still not be permissible to overlap the 74 days and the 40 days, for this would call for an interval of 103 days instead of 29 days between 8:12 and 8:13 (see Figure 1). But Kevan's theory (which is similar to the "phenomenal" theory of Ramm discussed on pp. 58-59) is contradicted by the fact that the Scriptures do not speak of *mists fading away* until the tops of the mountains were seen, but rather of *the waters decreasing continually* until the tops of the mountains were seen (8:5). It should be noted that Custance is not appealing to any "mists" to confuse the picture, as others have done, but is claiming that not even the mountain peak on which the Ark rested emerged from the waters until the first day of the tenth month.

[1] Heidel, *op. cit.*, pp. 251-252. Similarly, Robert Jamieson commented that the raven "went forth going and returning; i.e., roving on the heights that had emerged from the waters, or perched on the external covering of the ark, so that he was at no loss for a resting-place, and his voracious appetite would find plenty of carrion floating on the slimy hillsides on which, after so long an abstinence, he would greedily prey." *Critical and Experimental Commentary* (Grand Rapids: Wm. B. Eerdmans Pub. Co., reprinted, 1948), I, 102. The dove, on the other hand, would not be satisfied until it found a clean and dry resting-place. For a discussion of the significance of the olive leaf, see pp. 104-106.

one might argue that the ground was still soaked on the twenty-*sixth* day of the second month because we are told that the ground was dry on the twenty-*seventh* day of the second month. It is obvious that the Scripures speak of definite stages of drying in verses 11, 13, and 14, with the implication of a uniform process between the stages. In like manner, from the day that the Ark grounded on the highest peak in the mountains of Ararat, more and more of the lower peaks emerged from the waters as they gradually subsided. Doubtless during much of the ninth month the tops of various mountains were seen. But it is also true that on the first day of the tenth month "were the tops of the mountains seen." It just so happens that God chose this date, rather than a slightly earlier one, to mark a stage in the abating of the waters.

The order of events as set forth in the first part of the eighth chapter of Genesis would seem, then, to be as follows: (1) After the waters had "prevailed upon the earth" 150 days, the waters began to assuage. (2) The Ark rested upon the mountains of Ararat the same day that the waters began to assuage, for the 17th day of the 7th month was exactly 150 days after the Flood began. (3) The waters continued to subside, so that by the 1st day of the 10th month (74 days later), the tops of various lower mountains could be seen. This would suggest a drop of perhaps fifteen or twenty feet a day, at least during the initial phase of this assuaging period. (4) The Flood level continued to fall for forty more days, so that Noah, no longer fearing that the Flood would return, sent forth a raven to investigate the conditions outside the Ark. These events are sketched in Figure 2.

Instead of constituting an objection to the universal Flood concept, the rate of decline of the water level thus becomes a strong argument in its favor. For if nothing could be seen but the tops of mountains after the waters had subsided for 74 days, we are left with no other alternative than to conclude that the Flood covered the whole earth. The duration of the Flood in its assuaging, as well as in its prevailing, compels us to think of it as a global, not merely a local, catastrophe.

THE GEOLOGY OF THE FLOOD

Since so many arguments against the universality of the Flood have been based upon supposed geological objections, it is very important to realize that the Scriptures have something to say about the geo-

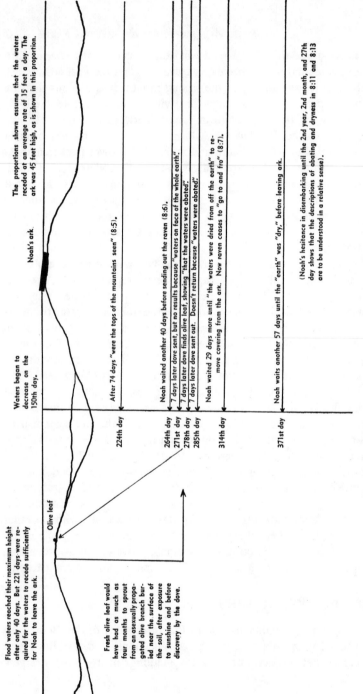

The proportions shown assume that the waters receded at an average rate of 15 feet a day. The ark was 45 feet high, as is shown in this proportion.

Noah's ark.

Waters began to decrease on the 150th day.

After 74 days "were the tops of the mountains seen" (8:5).

Noah waited another 40 days before sending out the raven (8:6).

7 days later dove sent, but no results because "waters on face of the whole earth".

7 days later dove finds olive leaf, showing "that the waters were abated".

7 days later dove sent out. Doesn't return because "waters were abated."

Noah waited 29 days more until "the waters were dried from off the earth" to re-move covering from the ark. Now raven ceases to "go to and fro" (8:7).

Noah waits another 57 days until the "earth" was "dry," before leaving ark.

(Noah's hesitance in disembarking until the 2nd year, 2nd month, and 27th day shows that the descriptions of abating and dryness in 8:11 and 8:13 are to be understood in a relative sense).

224th day

264th day
271st day
278th day
285th day

314th day

371st day

Olive leaf

Flood waters reached their maximum height after only 40 days. But 221 days were re-quired for the waters to recede sufficiently for Noah to leave the ark.

Fresh olive leaf would have had as much as four months to sprout from an asexually propa-gated olive branch bur-ied near the surface of the soil, after exposure to sunshine and before discovery by the dove.

Figure 2. THE ABATING OF THE FLOOD WATERS.

logical factor too. In fact, the first recorded event of the Flood is that "on the same day were all the fountains of the great deep broken up" (7:11). According to Brown, Driver, and Briggs, the word *tᵉhôm* (translated "deep" in this verse) has the primary meanings of (1) "deep, of subterranean waters," (2) "sea," and (3) "primeval ocean, deep."[1] There can be little question, then, that the phrase *tᵉhôm rabbâh* ("great deep") points back to the *tᵉhôm* of Genesis 1:2 and refers to the oceanic depths and underground reservoirs of the antediluvian world. Presumably, then, the ocean basins were fractured and uplifted sufficiently to pour waters over the continents, in conjunction with those waters which were above the "firmament" (expanse) and which poured down through the "windows of heaven."

The close connection that exists between Genesis 7:11 and 1:2-10 must be evident to all who have studied the text with care. For example, Franz Delitzsch calls our attention to the fact that "it was by a cooperation of subterranean and celestial forces, which broke through the restraints placed upon the waters on the second and third days of creation, that the Deluge was brought to pass."[2]

But the most significant fact to be observed is that these geological phenomena were not confined to a single day. In fact, the Scriptures state that this breaking up of "the fountains of the great deep" continued for a period of *five months;* for it was not until after the 150 days had passed that "the fountains of the deep . . . were stopped" (8:2). Such vast and prolonged geologic upheavals in the oceanic depths cannot be reconciled with the theory that the Flood was merely a local inundation in some part of the Near East. Instead, this Biblical information gives substantial support to the concept of a geographically universal Deluge.[3]

[1] Francis Brown, S. R. Driver, and Charles A. Briggs, *A Hebrew and English Lexicon of the Old Testament* (Boston, New York, and Chicago: Houghton, Mifflin, & Co., 1906), p. 1062. Ludwig Koehler and Walter Baumgartner, *Lexicon in Veteris Testamenti Libros* (Grand Rapids: Wm. B. Eerdmans Pub. Co., 1953), II, 1019, give the first two meanings of *tᵉhôm* as (1) the primeval ocean, and (2) the subterranean water.

[2] Franz Delitzsch, *A New Commentary on Genesis,* trans. Sophia Taylor (New York: Scribner & Welford, 1899), p. 267. J. P. Lange was much impressed by the geological argument: "the flood itself may, perhaps, have been partial, but the earthcrisis, on which it was conditioned, must have been universal. With the opening of the fountains of the deep stands the opening of the windows of heaven in polar contrast . . . As an earth-crisis, the flood was probably universal." *A Commentary on the Holy Scriptures: Genesis,* ed. J. P. Lange (Grand Rapids: Zondervan Publishing House, n.d.), p. 296.

[3] See below, pp. 122, 127, for further discussion of this point.

THE SIZE OF THE ARK

According to Genesis 6:15, Noah was commanded to make "the length of the ark three hundred cubits, the breadth of it fifty cubits, and the height of it thirty cubits." The first question to be considered, of course, is the length of the cubit as used in this passage. The Babylonians had a "royal" cubit of about 19.8 inches, the Egyptians had a longer and a shorter cubit of about 20.65 inches and 17.6 inches respectively, while the Hebrews apparently had a long cubit of 20.4 inches (Ezek. 40:5) and a common cubit of about 17.5 inches.[1]

While it is certainly possible that the cubit referred to in Genesis 6 was longer than 17.5 inches, we shall take this shorter cubit as the basis for our calculations. According to this standard, the Ark was 437.5 feet long, 72.92 feet wide, and 43.75 feet high. Since it had three decks (Gen. 6:16), it had a total deck area of approximately 95,700 square feet (equivalent to slightly more than the area of twenty standard college basketball courts), and its total volume was 1,396,000 cubic feet. The gross tonnage[2] of the Ark (which is a measurement of cubic space rather than weight, one ton in this case being equivalent to 100 cubic feet of usable storage space) was about 13,960 tons, which would place it well within the category of large metal ocean-going vessels today.[3]

Arthur Custance questions whether the Ark could really have been this huge and suggests, without evidence, that the cubit of those days may have been much shorter than eighteen inches. Then he goes on to say:

I think anyone who tries to visualize the construction of a vessel 450 feet long by four men will realize that the size of the timbers alone for a "building" 45 feet high (analogous to a four story apartment building) would seem by their sheer massiveness to be beyond the powers of four

[1] R. B. Y. Scott, "Weights and Measures of the Bible," *The Biblical Archaeologist,* Vol. XXII, No. 2 (May, 1959), pp. 22-27.

[2] The displacement tonnage of the Ark (defined as the weight of sea water displaced by the structure when submerged to its design draught, assumed at $\frac{1}{2}5$ cubits), is:

$$\frac{(300)(50)(15)\left(\dfrac{17.5}{12}\right)^3(64)}{2240} = 19,940 \text{ tons}$$

[3] The U.S.S. Mariposa is 14,512 tons, the U.S.S. Constitution is 23,719 tons, and the U.S.S. United States (the largest American ocean liner) is 53,329 tons. (New York, *1960 World Almanac,* N. Y. World Telegram Co., p. 680). See below, p. 103, for a discussion of the structure and stability of the Ark.

men to handle. With all the means later at their disposal, subsequent builders for 4000 years constructed seaworthy vessels that seldom seem to have
exceeded 150 to 200 feet at the most. The Queen Mary has a total length
of 1018 feet which is not very much more than twice the length of the
Ark. It was not until 1884 apparently that a vessel, the Eturia, a Cunard
liner, was built with a length exceeding that of the Ark.[1]

The Scriptures, however, do not suggest that Noah and his three
sons had to construct the Ark without the help of hired men. Nevertheless, we agree that the sheer massiveness of the Ark staggers the
imagination. In fact, this is the very point of our argument: for Noah
to have built a vessel of such magnitude simply for the purpose of
escaping a local flood is inconceivable. The very size of the Ark
should effectively eliminate the local-Flood view from serious consideration among those who take the Book of Genesis at face value.

THE NEED FOR AN ARK

Not only would an ark of such gigantic proportions have been
unnecessary for a local flood, but there would have been no need
for an ark at all! The whole procedure of constructing such a vessel,
involving over a century of planning and toiling, simply to escape a
local flood, can hardly be described as anything but utterly foolish
and unnecessary. How much more sensible it would have been for
God merely to have warned Noah of the coming destruction, so that
he could move to an area that would not have been affected by the
Flood, even as Lot was taken out of Sodom before the fire fell from
heaven. Not only so, but also the great numbers of animals of all
kinds, and certainly the birds, could easily have moved out also, without having to be stored and tended for a year in the Ark! The entire
story borders on the ridiculous if the Flood was confined to some section of the Near East.

The writers have had a difficult time finding local-Flood advocates
that are willing to face the implications of this particular argument.
Arthur Custance, however, has recently suggested that the Ark was
simply an object-lesson to the antediluvians:

It would require real energy and faith to follow Noah's example and
build other Arks, but it would have required neither of these to pack up a
few things and migrate. There is nothing that Noah could have done to

[1] Custance, *op. cit.*, p. 20.

stop them except by disappearing very secretly. Such a departure could hardly act as the kind of warning that the deliberate construction of the Ark could have done. And the inspiration for this undertaking was given to Noah by leaving him in ignorance of the exact limits of the Flood. He was assured that all mankind would be destroyed, and probably supposed that the Flood would therefore be universal. This supposition may have been quite essential for him.[1]

But how can one read the Flood account of Genesis 6-9 with close attention and then arrive at the conclusion that the Ark was built *merely* to warn the ungodly, and not *mainly* to save the occupants of the Ark from death by drowning? And how can we exonerate God Himself from the charge of deception, if we say that He led Noah to believe that the Flood would be universal, in order to encourage him to work on the Ark, when He knew all the time that it would *not* be universal?

With respect to the animals in the Ark, Custance takes the view that they were only domesticated varieties that would prove to be useful to man:

> To begin with, there is plenty of evidence to show that the domestication of animals was first undertaken somewhere in this general area. Assuming that such species as had been domesticated in the centuries between Adam and Noah were confined to the areas settled by man and had not spread beyond this, any Flood which destroyed man would also wipe out these animals. The process of domestication would then have to be begun all over again, and probably under far less ideal conditions . . . It is almost certain that domesticated animals could not have migrated alone . . . For this reason, if for no other, some animals at least would have to be taken on board . . . but these were probably of the domesticated varieties.[2]

But where does the Book of Genesis suggest that Noah was to take only domesticated animals into the Ark? The purpose of the Flood was to destroy "both man, and beast, and creeping things, and birds of the heavens" (6:7), and "to destroy all flesh, wherein is the breath of life, from under heaven" (6:17, cf. 6:12-13, 19-21, 7:2-4, 8, 14-

---

[1] Custance, *op. cit.,* p. 18. Custance feels that the Ark was not overly large (see above, p. 10) and that it did not take over a century to build. The 120 years of Gen. 6:3, in his opinion, refers to man's future life-span. But where is the evidence that man's life span after the Flood was to be 120 years? Many men lived much longer than this (11:11, 13, 15, 17, 19, 21, 23, 25; 25:7; 35:28; 47:9). See Heidel, *op. cit.,* p. 230, and Leupold, *op. cit.,* pp. 256-257.

[2] Custance, *op. cit.,* p. 19. For further discussion on the problem of animals in the Ark, see below, pp. 63 ff.

16; 8:1, 17-19; 9:8-17). And this was accomplished when "all flesh died that moved upon the earth, both birds, and cattle, and beasts, and every creeping thing that creepeth upon the earth, and every man: all in whose nostrils was the breath of the spirit of life, of all that was on the dry ground, died. And every living thing was destroyed that was upon the face of the ground, both man, and cattle, and creeping things, and birds of the heavens; and they were destroyed from the earth" (7:21-23). These are exactly the same terms used in the first chapter of Genesis to describe the various kinds of land animals which God created. If only domesticated animals were to be taken into the Ark, are we to assume that only domesticated animals were created by God in the first chapter of Genesis? The fact of the matter is that no clearer terms could have been employed by the author than those which he did employ to express the idea of *the totality of air-breathing animals in the world.* Once this point is conceded, all controversy as to the geographical extent of the Deluge must end; for no one would care to maintain that all land animals were confined to the Mesopotamian Valley in the days of Noah! Joseph P. Free, Professor of Archaeology at Wheaton College, concludes:

The fact that every living creature was to be destroyed would indicate that the whole earth was subject to the flood (Gen. 7:4). Probably the animals had scattered over much of the earth; a universal flood would have been needed to destroy them . . . Certainly all the main groups of animals were represented on the ark. The variations which we observe today within the main groups of animals could have developed in the few thousand years (more or less) since the flood.[1]

---

[1] Joseph P. Free, *Archaelogy and Bible History* (5th ed. rev.; Wheaton, Ill.: Scripture Press, 1956), p. 42. Some defenders of the local-Flood theory claim to have found in Genesis 9:10 support for their view that only a few land animals were affected by the Flood. They claim that a literal reading of this verse calls for two groups of animals: "from all going out of the ark to every beast of the earth." It is highly questionable, however, whether this is the correct translation. Brown, Driver, and Briggs cite this verse as an example of the special usage of *l^ekol* at the close of a description or enumeration, and translate it as follows: "all that go out of the ark *as regards* (=namely, even) all the beasts of the earth." *A Hebrew and English Lexicon of the Old Testament,* p. 514. See also Franz Delitzsch and August Dillmann *in loco.* The ASV thus improves over the AV by translating: "of all that go out of the ark, even every beast of the earth." Thomas Whitelaw, who believed that the Flood was local, admitted that this verse is "not necessarily implying . . . , though in all probability it was the case, that there were animals which had never been in the ark; but simply an idiomatic phrase expressive of the totality of the animal creation (Alford)." *The Pulpit Commentary,* ed. H. D. M. Spence (Grand Rapids: Wm. B. Eerdmans Pub. Co., reprinted 1950), p. 143.

The fact that Noah was commanded to built an ark "to the saving of his house" (Heb. 11:7) and was commanded to bring in two of every kind of animal "to keep seed alive upon the face of the earth" (7:3) proves conclusively that the Flood was universal in scope.

THE TESTIMONY OF THE APOSTLE PETER

One of the most important Biblical passages relating to the magnitude of the Deluge is to be found in II Peter 3:3-7:

> . . . knowing this first, that in the last days mockers shall come with mockery, walking after their own lusts, and saying, Where is the promise of his coming? for, from the day that the fathers fell asleep, all things continue as they were from the beginning of the creation. For this they willingly forget, that there were heavens from of old, and an earth compacted out of the water and amidst water, by the word of God; by which means the world that then was, being overflowed with water, perished; but the heavens that now are, and the earth, by the same word have been stored up for fire, being reserved against the day of judgment and destruction of ungodly men.

In this passage of Scripture, Peter speaks of a day, yet future from his standpoint, when men would no longer think seriously of Christ's Second Coming as a cataclysmic, universal intervention by God into the course of world affairs. And the reason for this skeptical attitude would be none other than a blind adherence to the doctrine of uniformitarianism—a doctrine which maintains that natural laws and processes have never yet been interrupted (or newer and higher laws introduced) so as to bring about a total destruction of human civilization through the direct intervention of God. And since this has never been the case in past history, there should be no cause to fear that it will ever occur in the future!

In answering these skeptics of the end-time, the Apostle Peter points to two events in the past which cannot be explained on the basis of uniformitarianism. The first of these events is the creation of the world: "there were heavens from of old, and an earth . . . *by the word of God"*; and the second event is the Flood: "the world [*kosmos*] that then was, being overflowed with water, perished [*apōleto*]."

But it is the second of these two events, the Flood, which serves as the basis of Peter's comparison with the Second Coming and the final destruction of the world. For even as "the world that then was" perished by *water,* so "the heavens that now are, and the earth," protected as they are, by God's eternal promise, from another aqueous cataclysm (Gen. 9:11-19), have, nevertheless, "been stored up for *fire,* being reserved against the day of judgment and destruction of ungodly men."

Let us now consider the implications of this passage with respect to the geographical extent of the Flood. In speaking of the events of the second and third days of creation, Peter uses the terms "heavens *from of old,* and an earth" in a sense that is obviously universal. By the same token, no one can deny that Peter also uses the terms "heavens *that now are,* and the earth" in the strictly universal sense. Otherwise, Peter would be speaking of the creation and final destruction of only a part of the earth!

Now the one event which Peter sets forth as having brought about a transformation, not of the earth only but also of the very *heavens,* is the Flood! It was the Flood that constituted the line of demarcation between "the heavens from of old" and "the heavens that now are" in the thinking of the Apostle Peter. It was the Flood that utilized the vast oceans of water out of which and amidst which the ancient earth was "compacted," unto the utter destruction of the *kosmos* "that then was."[1] It was the Flood to which Peter appealed as his final and incontrovertible answer to those who chose to remain in willful ignorance of the fact that God had *at one time* in the past demonstrated His holy wrath and omnipotence by subjecting "all things" to an overwhelming, cosmic catastrophe that was on an absolute par with the final day of judgment, in which God will yet consume the earth with fire and will cause the very elements to dissolve with fervent heat (II Peter 3:10).

[1] Henry Alford's comments on the use of *kosmos* in this passage are important: ". . . *kosmos,* as an indefinite common term, takes in the *ouranoi kai ge* [heavens and earth], which were then instrumental in, and purified by, the destruction, if not altogether swept away by it." (*The Greek Testament,* 5th ed.; London: Longmans, Green, & Co., 1895, IV, 414).

Of special significance also is this comment by Joseph B. Mayor: "It is evident from [II Peter 3:7, 10, 12] that the writer looked forward to a fundamental metamorphosis of the existing universe through the final conflagration, and this naturally leads him to take an exaggerated [*sic!*] view of the deluge, which he regards as a parallel destruction. Hence the present heavens and earth are distinguished from the antediluvian in the next verse [v. 7]" (*The Epistle of St. Jude and the Second Epistle of St. Peter,* London, Macmillan & Co., 1907, p. 153). It would be appropriate for a uniformitarian to describe Peter's reference to the Flood as "exaggerated." True Biblical exegesis simply cannot be harmonized with this philosophy of earth-history.

If the Flood was limited to the region of Mesopotamia, it is difficult to see how Peter's appeal to the Flood would have any value as a contradiction to the doctrine of uniformitarianism, which assumes that "all things" have *never yet* been upset by a universal cataclysm. Nor is it easy to excuse Peter of gross inaccuracy when he depicts the Flood in such cosmic terms and in such an absolutely universal context, if the Flood was only a local inundation after all.

Merrill F. Unger, Professor of Old Testament at Dallas Theological Seminary, emphasizes the crucial significance of Peter's statements in determining the magnitude and effects of the Deluge:

That the antediluvian era, described by Peter as "the world that then was," was obviously different climatically and geologically from the "heavens" and "the earth . . . that now are" (II Peter 3:7), is clearly implied in the Apostle's stern warning to naturalistic skeptics, who mock at the idea of Christ's supernatural Second Advent on the ground that "all things continue as they were from the beginning of the creation" (II Peter 3:4). Against the false naturalistic theory of uniformity, the Apostle urges the truth of supernatural catastrophism as evidenced by the Noahic Flood.[1]

Thus, the third chapter of Second Peter provides powerful New Testament support for the geographical universality of the Flood. Anything less than a catastrophe of such proportions would upset the entire force of Peter's argument and would give much encouragement to those whom he so solemnly warned.

THE TOTAL DESTRUCTION OF A WIDELY-DISTRIBUTED HUMAN RACE

Our seventh and final basic argument for a universal Flood is founded upon the Biblical testimony of a total destruction of the human race outside of the Ark. Such an argument, to be conclusive in demonstrating a geographically universal Flood, must include two sub-arguments: (1) the Bible teaches that all mankind perished in

---

[1] Merrill F. Unger, *Archaeology and the Old Testament* (3rd. Ed., Grand Rapids: Zondervan Publishing House, 1956), p. 62. There are some writers who have applied II Peter 3:6 ("the world that then was, being overflowed with water, perished") to Genesis 1:2 instead of to Genesis 6-9. See J. Sidlow Baxter, *Explore the Book* (London: Marshall, Morgan, & Scott, Ltd., 1951), I, 42; and Kenneth S. Wuest, *In These Last Days* (Grand Rapids: Wm. B. Eerdmans Pub. Co., 1954), p. 67.

But such an application is impossible for three reasons: (1) Genesis 1:2 does not speak of a world perishing by being overflowed with water, whereas four entire chapters of Genesis are devoted to a description of the great Noahic Deluge which

the Flood and (2) the human race had spread far beyond the Near East, if not around the earth, by the time of the Flood. In the development of this argument, we shall set forth four major reasons for believing that the Bible teaches a total destruction of the race and two major reasons for believing that the antediluvians had become widely distributed by the time of the Flood.

The Total Destruction of Humanity

From the very beginning of the Flood controversy, there has been little question among conservative Christian scholars as to the total destruction of the human race by the Flood. In the year 1845, Charles Burton could say, without fear of contradiction:

> Among the Christian philosophers who dispute on this arena, there is a perfect agreement on the most important point, viz., that by the Flood, the *whole* population of the world was destroyed. With the Mosaic narrative before them, no other opinion could be entertained.[1]

The same situation prevails today, more than a century later, with only very rare exceptions.[2] The reasons for this remarkable unanimity of opinion among evangelical scholars must now be presented.

The moral purpose of the Flood. The Flood must have destroyed the entire human race outside of the Ark, because the Scriptures clearly state that the purpose of the Flood was to wipe out a sinful and degenerate humanity; and this purpose could not have been accomplished by destroying only a portion of the race. Turning our attention now to the most important passages of Scripture that shed light on this question, we read in the sixth chapter of Genesis:

> And Jehovah saw that the wickedness of man was great in the earth, and that every imagination of the thoughts of his heart was only evil con-

fits Peter's description perfectly; (2) II Peter 3:5 describes the earth's condition during the second and third days of the creation week (Gen. 1:6-10), and the catastrophe of II Peter 3:6 obviously follows this; (3) Peter has already referred to the Noahic Deluge twice before (I Pet. 3:20, II Pet. 2:5), and therefore the context would demand that II Peter 3:6 refer to the same Deluge. Neither Baxter nor Wuest offers proof for his interpretation, and the vast majority of commentators agree that Peter is referring to the Flood.

[1] Charles Burton, *Lectures on the Deluge and the World After the Flood* (London: Hamilton, Adams, & Co., 1845), p. 21.

[2] Bernard Ramm (*The Christian View of Science and Scripture*, Grand Rapids: Wm. B. Eerdmans Pub. Co., 1954) is one modern evangelical writer who believes that only a part of the human race was destroyed by the Flood. Because of the important implications of this view, we shall devote most of Chapter II to an examination of his arguments.

tinually. And it repented Jehovah that he had made man on the earth, and it grieved him at his heart. And Jehovah said, I will destroy man whom I have created from the face of the ground; both man, and beast, and creeping things, and birds of the heavens; for it repenteth me that I have made them (6:5-7) . . . And the earth was corrupt before God, and the earth was filled with violence. And God saw the earth, and, behold, it was corrupt; for all flesh had corrupted their way upon the earth. And God said unto Noah, The end of all flesh is come before me; for the earth is filled with violence through them; and, behold, I will destroy them with the earth (6:11-13).

The constant, almost monotonous repetition of phrases depicting the utter depravity of antediluvian humanity has filled the minds of believers with a sense of awe and astonishment. Every statement seems calculated to impress upon its readers the idea of *universal sin;* not just the exceptional sins of this group or of that region, nor even of specific times or occasions, but rather the sin of an entire age and an entire race that had utterly corrupted its way upon the earth and was now ripe for the judgment of a holy God. W. Graham Scroggie has skillfully and graphically sketched the Biblical picture of antediluvian humanity:

The appalling condition of things is summed up in a few terrible words, words which bellow and burn: *wickedness, evil imagination, corruption,* and *violence;* and these sins were *great, widespread,* "in the earth," *continuous,* "only evil continually," *open* and *daring,* "before God," *replete,* "filled," and *universal,* "all flesh."

. . . .

This is an astounding event! After over 1,600 years of human history the race was so utterly corrupt morally that it was not fit to live; and of all mankind only four men and four women were spared, because they did not go with the great sin drift.[1]

In the light of these facts, the conclusion seems to be self-evident that God's stated purpose of destroying "man whom I have created," because of his hopeless depravity and in order to start afresh with Noah, could not have been accomplished by destroying only a part of the race and allowing the rest of Adam's descendants to continue in their sinful ways.

The exceptional case of Noah. The fact that all mankind, rather

[1] W. Graham Scroggie, *The Unfolding Drama of Redemption* (London: Pickering & Inglis, Ltd., 1953), I, 74, 77. Italics are his.

than just a part of the race, was destroyed in the Flood is emphasized in the Scriptures by repeated statements to the effect that Noah and his family were the *only* ones who escaped the judgment waters. The pertinent passages in Genesis read as follows:

> But Noah found favor in the eyes of Jehovah . . . *Noah* was a righteous man and perfect *in his generations: Noah* walked with God (6:8-9) . . . *everything* that is in the earth shall die. But I will establish my covenant with *thee;* and thou shalt come into the ark, thou, and thy sons, and thy wife, and thy sons' wives with thee (6:17-18) . . . And Jehovah said unto Noah, Come thou and all thy house into the ark; for *thee* have I seen righteous before me *in this generation* (7:1) . . . and they were destroyed from the earth: and *Noah only was left,* and they that were with him in the ark. And the waters prevailed upon the earth a hundred and fifty days. And God remembered *Noah* . . . (7:23,24; 8:1).

And lest there might remain some lingering doubt in the minds of Bible students as to whether or not Noah's family constituted the *sole* survivors of the Flood, we have two emphatic statements by the Apostle Peter on this matter:

> . . . the longsuffering of God waited in the days of Noah, while the ark was a preparing, wherein *few,* that is, *eight souls,* were saved through water (I Pet. 3:20).
>
> God spared not the ancient world [*kosmos*], but preserved *Noah with seven others,* a preacher of righteousness, when he brought a flood upon the world [*kosmos*] of the *ungodly* (II Pet. 2:5).

Now it would seem to be perfectly evident from studying these passages that Noah was spared because of his righteous character. By the same token, the Flood came to destroy others because they were unrighteous. Now if it should actually turn out to have been the case that only a portion of the human race outside of the Ark was destroyed by the Flood, then we must conclude one of two things: (1) there were people outside of the Ark who were as righteous as Noah and thus were permitted by God to escape the Flood waters also; or (2) having a righteous character was not the only factor that determined who was to escape the Flood.

As we consider these two alternatives, we must admit that the first one is quite inconceivable, for the exceptional and unique righteousness of Noah is emphasized over and over again throughout the entire Bible (Gen. 5:29; 6:8,9,18; 7:1; 9:1; Ezek. 14:14,20; Heb.

11:7 and II Pet. 2:5). Also, the abysmal and universal wickedness of the antediluvians has been affirmed by an astonishing array of Scriptural testimony (Gen. 6:1-6, 11-13; Luke 17:26-27; I Pet. 3:20; II Pet. 2:5 and Jude 14-15). To deny this is simply to deny the Word of God.

But the second alternative is equally untenable, for the Scriptures give no hint anywhere that men were destroyed for any other reason than for their ungodliness. Now if any ungodly people actually did escape the Flood, they must have done so by virtue of the fact that they didn't happen to live in that particular area where the Flood came (assuming that the Flood was local); or else they were stronger or more ingenious than other sinners and thus, in one way or another, managed to escape the onrushing Flood waters. But if this had been the case, then those who died in the waters did so only because they were unfortunate enough to be living in the wrong place or because they were not sufficiently strong or clever, and not simply because they were ungodly!

We pause at this point to ask the question: can sane and sensible hermeneutics tolerate for one moment such an interpretation of the Biblical doctrine of the Flood? We may disagree on various methods of interpretation or even on whether the Biblical record is to be accepted as authentic and trustworthy and credible. But when mature and trained scholars can examine the Scriptural account of the Flood, in both Old and New Testaments, and conclude that the Bible *does not really intend to teach* that the Flood was sent to destroy *all ungodly men,* then Biblical hermeneutics, in our opinion, ceases to be a scientific and scholarly discipline.

Consequently, both of the above-mentioned alternatives must be rejected without hesitation. The Scriptures *do* teach that the Flood destroyed all mankind outside of the Ark, because none outside of the Ark were godly and the Flood was sent by God to destroy the ungodly.[1]

The testimony of the Lord Jesus Christ. It almost seems that our Lord made a special point of choosing His illustrations and warnings

[1] William Sanford LaSor claims that the Flood was sent as a judgment upon the godly Sethite line for intermarrying with the ungodly Cainite line. Thus, the Flood needed to be only as extensive as the Sethite line ("Does the Bible Teach a Universal Flood?" *Eternity,* Vol. XI, No. 10 [December, 1960]). But how could the Flood have destroyed the Sethites only, if they were living with Cainites? Even more important, the Scriptures emphasize everywhere that God brought the Flood not to destroy sinning saints, but rather to destroy "the world of the *ungodly"* (II Pet. 2:5).

from those portions of the Old Testament that would become objects of unbelieving scorn and ridicule throughout the coming centuries. For example, in Matthew 19:4 He referred to the creation of Adam and Eve in the Garden of Eden; in Luke 17:29 to the destruction of Sodom by fire and brimstone from heaven; in Luke 17:32 to the transformation of Lot's wife into a pillar of salt; in Matthew 12:40 to the experience of Jonah in the belly of the great fish; in Luke 11:32 to the repentance of the Ninevites at the preaching of Jonah. And in addition to all of these, our Lord made special reference to Noah and the Flood in the seventeenth chapter of Luke. For the sake of our subsequent discussion, we must include part of the context in our quotation of this passage:

And as it came to pass in the days of Noah, even so shall it be also in the days of the Son of man. They ate, they drank, they married, they were given in marriage, until the day that Noah entered into the ark, and the flood came, and destroyed them *all*. Likewise even as it came to pass in the days of Lot; they ate, they drank, they bought, they sold, they planted, they builded; but in the day that Lot went out from Sodom it rained fire and brimstone from heaven, and destroyed them *all:* after the same manner shall it be in the day that the Son of man is revealed (Luke 17:26-30. Cf. Matt. 24:39).

Now it is very important that we observe the context into which our Lord places the Flood-destruction. It is placed alongside the destruction of Sodom and the destruction of the ungodly at the time of Christ's Second Coming. This fact is of tremendous significance in helping us to determine the sense in which the word "all" is used in reference to those who were destroyed by the Flood.

Our argument proceeds in the following manner: the force of Christ's warning to the ungodly concerning the doom which awaits them at the time of His Second Coming, by reminding them of the destruction of the Sodomites, would be *immeasurably weakened* if we knew that *some* of the Sodomites, after all, had escaped. This would allow hope for the ungodly that some of *them* might escape the wrath of God in that coming day of judgment. But we have, indeed, no reason for thinking that any Sodomite did escape destruction when the fire fell from heaven.

In exactly the same manner, Christ's warning to future generations, on the basis of what happened to the ungodly in the days of Noah, would have been pointless if part of the human race had escaped the judgment waters. In fact, the only characterization which our Lord made of those who perished in the Flood was that they ate and drank and married and were given in marriage. Thus, if it should be argued that people living in other parts of the world might not have been as wicked as those who lived in the area that was flooded, it would be sufficient reply to point out that our Lord's characterization did not have to do with degrees of ungodliness, but rather with the utter absence of that positive godliness which was essential to salvation.

Therefore, we are persuaded that Christ's use of the word "all" in Luke 17:27 must be understood in the absolute sense; otherwise the analogies would collapse and the warnings would lose their force. A heavy burden of proof rests upon those who would maintain that only a part of the human race was destroyed in the Flood, in view of the clear statements of the Lord Jesus Christ.

God's Covenant with Noah After the Flood. One of the most difficult problems to be faced by those who deny that the Flood was anthropologically universal is the covenant which God made with Noah after the Flood had ended. For if the Flood destroyed only a part of the human race, then those who escaped the Flood waters were not included in the Covenant of the Rainbow.[1] Only toward the descendants of Noah would the birds, beasts, and fishes show fear and dread (Gen. 9:2); they only would be prohibited from eating flesh with the blood (9:3-4); and they only would have the authority to take life (9:5-6).

If God's covenant with Noah means anything at all, it must be a covenant with the entire human race. But the Scriptures repeatedly state that God made this covenant with Noah and his sons (Gen. 9:1-17). Therefore the whole of humanity has descended from Noah's family and the Flood destroyed the entire antediluvian race. Samuel J. Schultz of Wheaton College has reached a similar conclusion on this crucial question:

[1] God's thrice-repeated promise never to wipe out "everything living" and "all flesh" again by a Flood (Gen. 8:21; 9:11,15) makes it quite impossible to accept the view that only a part of the human race was destroyed by the Flood. And if it be insisted that these terms are to be understood in a limited sense, then we must say that God has broken His promise repeatedly; for millions have perished in vast and destructive local floods in many parts of the earth. The same argument is decisive against the view that the Flood was geographically local though anthropologically universal, for God promised not only to spare the human race (to say nothing of "every thing living") from another Flood but also *the earth itself* (Gen. 8:21; 9:11, Isa. 54:9).

Had any part of the human race survived the flood outside of Noah and his family they would not have been included in the covenant God made here. The implication seems to be that all mankind descended from Noah so that the covenant with its bow in the cloud as a reminder would be for all mankind.[1]

The Extensive Distribution of the Antediluvian Race

Those who acknowledge the tremendous weight of Biblical testimony concerning the total destruction of the human race outside of the Ark, and yet who are still unwilling to admit that the Flood was geographically universal, usually maintain that the race had not spread beyond the region of Mesopotamia during the period from Adam to Noah.[2] But it is our conviction that such a position cannot be successfully defended and that for at least two reasons which must now be considered.

Longevity. In the first place, the vast possibilities for population growth due to longevity among the antediluvians must be recognized. Even a rather cursory examination of Genesis 5 brings to light some rather startling statistics in this respect. In that chapter we read that Adam lived 930 years, Seth 912, Enosh 905, Kenan 910, Mahalalel 895, Jared 962, Enoch 365 (who did not die, but was translated to God's presence without dying), Methuselah 969, Lamech 777, and Noah 950. The average of these ages, omitting Enoch, is 912.[3]

William R. Vis has prepared a graph to indicate the contrast between the ages of patriarchs before and after the Flood (see Fig. 3). He explains:

A study of this chart shows in a striking way that *something extremely*

---

[1] Samuel J. Schultz, "The Unity of the Race: Genesis 1-11," *Journal of the American Scientific Affiliation,* VII (September, 1955), p. 52. LaSor (*loc. cit.*) argues that the Flood did not destroy all men outside the Ark because the New Testament consistently traces the human race to Adam rather than to Noah! It hardly seems necessary to point out, however, that Noah could not have been the federal head of postdiluvian humanity because neither his wife nor his three daughters-in-law owed their physical existence to him in the same sense that Eve owed hers to Adam.

[2] Another possibility would be that antediluvians in other parts of the earth died or were driven back into Mesopotamia just in time to drown in a local Flood. See below, pp. 32-33.

[3] C. F. Keil says concerning Genesis 5: "Every attack upon the historical character of its numerical statements has entirely failed, and no tenable argument can be adduced against their correctness." *Biblical Commentary on the Old Testament,* trans. James Martin (Grand Rapids: Wm. B. Eerdmans Pub. Co., reprinted 1951), I, 123.

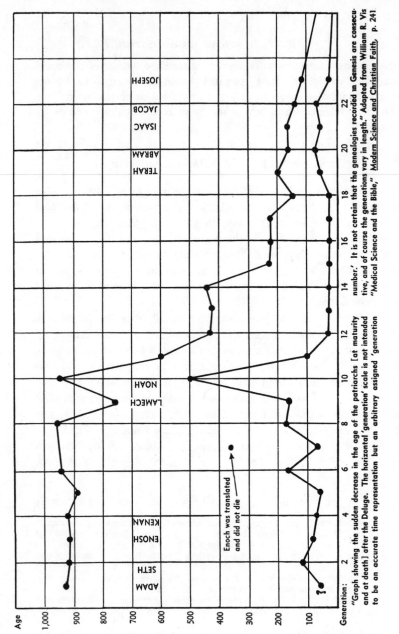

Figure 3. PATRIARCHAL AGES AT MATURITY AND DEATH.

Generation:

"Graph showing the sudden decrease in the age of the patriarchs [at maturity and at death] after the Deluge. The horizontal 'generation' scale is not intended to be an accurate time representation but an arbitrary assigned 'generation number.' It is not certain that the genealogies recorded in Genesis are consecutive, and of course the generations vary in length." Adopted from William R. Vis "Medical Science and the Bible," Modern Science and Christian Faith, p. 241

Enoch was translated and did not die

24

significant happened to the earth and to man at the time of the flood. It would seem that whatever this was, it probably removed the dominant factor for the long life of the patriarchs. The spiritual message of the Bible is clear: the length of life decreased because of the entrance of sin into the human family. However, the scientific explanation is not evident. Could some antediluvian climatic or other condition have been extremely favorable for long life in man? Perhaps future scientific research will cast some light on this.[1]

That there is nothing inherently impossible about such long ages is believed by many modern students of the phenomenon of biologic aging and maturity. One of the researchers on these problems is Dr. Hans Selye, Director of the Institute of Experimental Surgery at the University of Montreal. Dr. Selye has recently said:

Medicine has assembled a fund of knowledge that will now serve, I believe, as a point of departure for studying the causes of old age. If the causes of aging can be found, there is no good medical reason to believe that it will not be possible for science to find some practical way of slowing the process down or even bringing it to a standstill.[2]

Possible physical explanations of antediluvian longevity, and its decline after the Flood, will be discussed later.[3] We merely accept the *fact* at this point and note the important consequences of this fact with respect to the world population before the Flood.

The record in Genesis 5 clearly implies that men had large families in those days. Although in most cases only one son is named in each family (apparently for the purpose of tracing the line of descent from Adam to Noah), it is also said that each "begat sons and daughters," so that each family must have had at *least* four children, and probably many more. Furthermore, the age of the fathers at the birth of each of the *named* sons ranged from 65 years (in the case of Mahalalel and Enoch) to 500 years (in Noah's case). Consequently the Bible implies that: (1) men typically lived for hundreds of years, (2) their procreative powers persisted over hundreds of years also, and (3) through the combined effects of long lives and large families, mankind was rapidly "filling the earth" (Gen. 1:28; 6:1,11).

All things considered, it is certainly very conservative to estimate

---

[1] William R. Vis, "Medical Science and the Bible," *Modern Science and Christian Faith* (2d ed.; Wheaton: Van Kampen Press, 1950), p. 242. Italics are ours.

[2] Hans Selye: "Is Aging Curable?" *Science Digest*, Vol. 46, December 1959, p. 1.

[3] See pages 399-405.

that each family had, say, six children, and that each new generation required ninety years on the average. That is, assume the first family (Adam and Eve) had six children; the three families that could be established from these had six children each; and the nine families resulting from these each had six children, and so on. Actually, each probably had far more than six children, but this figure will allow for those who did not marry, who died prematurely, etc. At an average figure of ninety years per generation, which seems far higher than was probably actually the case, one can calculate that there were some eighteen generations in the 1,656 years from Adam to the Flood.

The total number of people in the nth generation can be calculated on this basis as equal to $2(3)^n$. Thus, at the end of the first generation (n equals one), the number in the family was $2(3)$, or 6. At the end of two generations, it was $2(3)^2$, or 18. Finally, at the end of 17 generations, the number was 258 million and, at the end of 18 generations, it was 774 million! If, at this time, only one previous generation was still living, the total population of the earth would have been over 1,030 million! And we believe that anyone would agree that these calculations are extremely conservative, assuming only that the Biblical statements are true.

Lest anyone regard such rates of population increase as unreasonable, listen to the following:

During the first half of the nineteenth century, world population reached 1 billion; in 1930 the figure was about 2 billion. In 1957 and 1958 alone, the earth's population increased by 90 million, a figure twice the population of France, and the world is expected to have 3 billion inhabitants by 1962. The acceleration of population growth in underdeveloped countries is especially spectacular. Annual increases of 2 percent or more are usual in most of these countries, and in some there is a growth of 3 percent. . . .[1]

The present rate of world population increase is thus approximately 2 per cent per year. But the rate of population growth we have supposed for the antediluvian period is less than 1.5 per cent per year!

Of course, the modern population "explosion," as it is sometimes called, is not believed to be typical of increase rates during earlier periods of history. Theorists usually say that earlier population in-

---

[1] "Population Growth," News item in *Science*, Vol. 129, April 3, 1959, p. 882, referring to a recent report *The Future Growth of World Population*, published by the United Nations' Bureau of Social Affairs.

creases were lower due to the effects of war, disease and starvation. But as Fairfield Osborn points out:

It must be remembered that the numerical loss of human life in the last two great wars was relatively inconsequential when measured against the total populations of the countries at war. In fact, the wars of the last century have had virtually no influence in restraining population increase in the countries engaged.[1]

Similarly, there is little real evidence to support the opinion that either disease or starvation, although they have occasionally taken great toll of human life, have had any very significant influence in restraining population increase, on a percentage basis. And especially is this true with respect to the antediluvian period, when the very fact that men lived to such great ages would indicate that famine and disease were not serious problems.

We are confident, therefore, that our estimate of a population of one billion people on the earth at the time of the Deluge is very conservative; it could well have been far more than this. A population of this order of magnitude would certainly have spread far beyond the Mesopotamian plains—in fact, for all practical purposes, would have "filled the earth," as the Scripture says. In fact, this very figure is the estimated population of the earth in 1850,[2] the earliest date for which there is any really accurate estimate of world population, and the entire earth was certainly "filled" at that time.

In the early days of the controversy over the geographical extent of the Deluge (1840-1860), the most common arguments for a limited antediluvian population, as set forth, for example, by John Pye Smith,[3] Edward Hitchcock,[4] and Hugh Miller,[5] were that the extreme sinfulness of the race made rapid population growth impossible and that the patriarchs did not beget children until late in life, with only a few children being mentioned even then.

[1] Fairfield Osborn: "Our Reproductive Potential," *Science,* Vol. 125, March 22, 1957, p. 531.

[2] V. E. McKelvey: "Resources, Population Growth, and Level of Living," *Science,* Vol. 129, April 3, 1959, p. 878. See also our discussion on post-diluvian populations, pages 396-398.

[3] John Pye Smith, *The Relation Between The Holy Scriptures and Some Parts of Geological Science* (5th ed.; London: Henry G. Bohn, 1854), pp. 269-270.

[4] Edward Hitchcock, *The Religion of Geology and Its Connected Sciences* (Boston: Phillips, Sampson & Co., 1852), p. 132.

[5] Hugh Miller, *The Testimony of the Rocks* (New York: Robert Carter and Brothers, 1875), pp. 316-319.

With regard to the first of these arguments, it needs only to be pointed out that while the Scriptures *do* say that the earth was filled with *"violence"* (Gen. 6:11,13), they say, at the same time, that *"the earth"* was *"filled"* with violence![1] In other words, the very proof text which these men put forward in support of the limited-population view, turns out upon closer examination to be an even more effective argument for the universal distribution of antediluvian populations. Furthermore, if analogies with postdiluvian history are at all valid in such a study, they certainly prove beyond any question that extreme sinfulness and a tendency to strife and violence in human society are factors that have favored the scattering, rather than the centralizing, of populations. The history of Indian tribes in the Americas and of the Gothic and Germanic tribes in Europe illustrates this fact clearly. And finally, the nations which boast the highest birth rates in the world today (India, China, and Russia) are not necessarily the most righteous!

The second objection commonly urged against a large antediluvian population was that children were not born until the patriarchs were well advanced in years and that even then few children are named in the genealogies of Genesis. For example, it was observed that Noah lived 500 years before he begat any sons, and then only three are named.

But such an argument is refuted by the following considerations: (1) Noah must have been the exception to the rule, because in the case of *every other patriarch* the phrase "begat sons and daughters" is used; (2) if Noah did not have any children until he was 500 years old (which cannot be proved), then he was also exceptional in this regard; for all the other patriarchs had children when they were less than 200 years old, and most of them (if we include Adam) when less than 130 years of age; (3) the fact that Noah was 500 years old when he begat three sons is important, for it proves that the patriarchs were capable of begetting children for hundreds of years; (4) it is possible that the sons who are named in Genesis 5 were *not* the first-born sons in each case, because we know that Adam had sons and daughters (Cain, Abel, and Cain's wife, at the very least) long before

[1] The Hebrew word for "earth" (*'ares*) can sometimes be translated "land." Except in rare instances, the context clearly indicates which translation is preferable. *'ares* appears 79 times in the first nine chapters of Genesis, but in only four cases can it be legitimately translated "land" (Gen. 2:11,12,13; 4:16). For a discussion of the limited usage of universal terms, see below, pp. 55-62.

we read the formula of Genesis 5:3, "And Adam lived a hundred and thirty years, and begat a son in his own likeness, after his image; and called his name Seth";[1] (5) God's command to Adam and his descendants was to "be fruitful and multiply, and replenish [fill] the earth" (1:28), and this command was obeyed: "men began to multiply on the face of the ground" (6:1).

A well-known German writer of the present day has expressed the matter as follows:

> Already in the time of Cain, apparently in his advanced age, a city could be built (probably at first simply an established colony), Gen. 4:17. This is the less astonishing, since the life-energy of the youthful race must at the beginning have been very powerful. Also, with the long lives of the parents, the number of children must have been much greater than later on; and, for the same reason, many generations must have lived alongside of each other at the same time. With an average of only six children per family, by the time Cain was only 400 years old he would have had far more than 100,000 descendants.[2]

C. F. Keil agreed with Franz Delitzsch that one explanation for the amazing longevity of these patriarchs was "that the after-effects of the condition of man in paradise would not be immediately exhausted"; to which Keil added these words: "This longevity, moreover, necessarily contributed greatly to the increase of the human race."[3] A contemporary Catholic scholar comes to the following conclusion as to what the Bible teaches concerning the geographical distribution of antediluvian humanity:

> In view of the insistence shown by the sacred writer on the multiplication of the race by the repeated declaration that each of the patriarchs begat "sons and daughters," and that he allows so much time between Adam and the flood (MT 1656 years, Samaritan text 1307, LXX 2256), it is hardly to be assumed that he thought all men could still be living in one region. In fact, the text indicates to the contrary, for God not only gave the command to increase and multiply, but also to "fill the earth," 1:28.[4]

Robert Jamieson, prominent nineteenth century defender of the local-Flood theory, must have realized the inherent weakness of Pye

---

[1] For further discussion of this point, see below, pp. 479-480.

[2] Erich Sauer, *The Dawn of World Redemption,* trans. G. H. Lang (Grand Rapids: Wm. B. Eerdmans Pub. Co., 1952), p. 67.

[3] C. F. Keil, *op. cit.,* pp. 123-124.

[4] Edmund F. Sutcliffe, S.J., "Genesis," *A Catholic Commentary on Holy Scripture* (New York; Thomas Nelson & Sons, 1953), p. 190.

Smith's arguments for a limited distribution of humanity in the days of Noah, for he did not use them in his lengthy defense of the local-Flood theory in the *Jamieson, Fausset, and Brown Commentary* (1870). In fact, his only remark on the subject was this: "The human race as yet occupied a small tract of western Asia, their members being comparatively few, as is evident from the single fact that the preaching of Noah was within the hearing of all that generation."[1] Since this argument is still being echoed today,[2] we do well to examine it more closely.

We must first of all recognize that nowhere in Scripture are we told that "the preaching of Noah was within the hearing of all that generation." Peter says that Noah was "a preacher of righteousness" (II Peter 2:5), and the author of Hebrews tells us that Noah by faith "prepared an ark to the saving of his house; through which he condemned the world" (Heb. 11:7). But this is not equivalent to saying that Noah preached directly to all the people of his generation!

While it is true that multitudes of people may have heard Noah's impassioned warnings directly, Noah's condemnation of the world probably consisted mainly in the very contrast of his godly and believing life with the lives of all others in his time. To him only God could say: "Come thou and all thy house into the ark; for thee have I seen righteous before me in this generation" (Gen. 7:1). The fact that no other human beings of that time had Noah's faith and righteousness was the condemnation of the world. The kind of faith that produced *obedience* (Gen. 6:22), even unto the building of the Ark, was the only kind of faith that could bring deliverance from judgment. No one else had the kind of faith that produced obedience; therefore the world was condemned. In like manner, only a relatively few persons of the world ever saw the Lord Jesus Christ during his earthly ministry; but it is true, nevertheless, that "the world knew him not" (John 1:10) and "this is the judgment, that the light is come into the world, and men loved darkness rather than the light; for their works were evil" (John 3:19).

But even if the fact that Noah's ark-building faith "condemned the world" should mean that everyone in the world heard the warnings of

---

[1] Jamieson, *op. cit.,* p. 99.

[2] Custance, *op. cit.,* p. 18: "The very method by which God forewarned men implies a situation in which the population of the world was still fairly well congregated." Ramm, *op. cit.,* p. 239, uses the same argument to prove that the Flood was anthropologically local, affecting only a small part of the human race!

Noah, it would by no means follow that the human race had to be confined to one small region of the earth. During that 120-year period of grace "when the long-suffering of God waited in the days of Noah, while the ark was a preparing" (Gen. 6:3, I Pet. 3:20), the news of Noah's remarkable activities and alarming warnings could easily have spread throughout the entire earth.[1]

To summarize briefly, it is easier to understand how the earth could have been filled with people by the time of the flood if we realize the greatness of antediluvian longevity, fecundity, and strife and the command of God to "fill the earth" (Gen. 1:28). The sinfulness of the antediluvians and the characteristics of patriarchal family life are objections that can easily be turned into supporting arguments, and the fact that Noah was a preacher who condemned the world can be made to harmonize perfectly with the concept of a widely scattered antediluvian race.[2]

Paleontology. Our second reason for believing that man had travelled far beyond the confines of the Near East by the time of the Flood is based upon evidence from paleontology. It is not our purpose here to enter into a discussion of the absolute age of the various "fossil men." Nor are we attempting to settle here the difficult question of which, if any, of these human remains are antediluvian. Our purpose in appealing to such evidence in this chapter is simply to show how devastating to the limited-distribution theory would be the discovery that even *one* human fossil from Africa, Europe, Asia, or America antedated the Flood.

[1] Civilization may very well have reached great heights before the Flood, and thus communication systems may have been efficient. "Vast strides must have been made in knowledge and civilization in such a lapse of time. Arts and sciences may have reached a ripeness of which the record, from its scantiness, conveys no adequate conception. The destruction caused by the Flood must have obliterated a thousand discoveries, and left men to recover again by slow and patient steps the ground they had lost" (J. J. Stewart Perowne, "Noah," *Dr. William Smith's Dictionary of the Bible,* ed., H. B. Hackett and Ezra Abbot. Boston: Houghton, Mifflin, & Co., 1896, III, p. 2178). See also below pp. 40-41.

If, in addition, we allow for a possible uniformity of language before the Flood, more than a hundred years during which the report of Noah's words could have been spread abroad, and the sensational nature of his ark-building enterprise, we have more than enough reasons for assuming that everyone in the world had an opportunity to hear directly or indirectly the warnings of this mighty "preacher of righteousness."

[2] Many Old Testament scholars believe that the period from Adam to the Flood lasted much more than 1656 years, because of gaps in the genealogy of Genesis 5. If this be true, how much more impossible it would be to insist that the human race did not spread out beyond Mesopotamia by the time of the Flood! See pp. 474-477.

Now the important fact to be observed with regard to these ancient fossils is that practically all of them have been found hundreds, and even thousands, of miles from the Mesopotamian Valley! In view of this fact, the advocates of the limited-distribution theory are forced to maintain one of two possible positions: (1) no human fossils that ever have or ever will be discovered outside of the Mesopotamian Valley can be considered antediluvian, or (2) if men actually did migrate to distant regions before the Flood, they must have been driven back into Mesopotamia by some universally compelling force, whether natural or supernatural, in order to be drowned in a limited Flood.

George Frederick Wright, a geologist of two generations ago, seeing the futility of defending the first of these two alternatives, wrote as follows:

An insuperable objection to this theory is that the later discoveries have brought to light remains of prehistoric man from all over the northern hemisphere, showing that long before the time of the flood, he had been widely scattered.[1]

He then proceeded to defend the second alternative, by suggesting that:

in connection with the enormous physical changes in the earth's surface during the closing scenes of the glacial epoch, man had perished from off the face of the earth except in the valley of the Euphrates, and that the Noachian Deluge is the final catastrophe in that series of destructive events.[2]

But this second alternative is also faced with insuperable objections: (1) if we are to follow the modern scientific theory of Pleistocene ice ages, then we must also follow the scientists when they tell us that the ice sheets never covered the major part of the earth at any time;[3] (2) even if an ice age could have succeeded in confining mankind to the Mesopotamian Valley, it would not help the limited-distribution theory, because the Flood must have come at a later time when temperatures had risen sufficiently to cause a sudden melting of the ice sheets (as Wright himself suggests), and (3) the Scriptures

[1] George F. Wright, "The Deluge of Noah," *International Standard Bible Encyclopedia*, II, 824. Cf. Ramm, *op. cit.*, p. 239.

[2] Wright, *loc. cit.*

[3] Richard F. Flint of Yale University claimed that "glaciers have covered nearly one-third of the land area of the world." *Glacial Geology and the Pleistocene Epoch* (New York: John Wiley & Sons, Inc., 1947), p. 10.

give no hint whatever of any natural or supernatural gathering of humanity back into Mesopotamia to be drowned by melting ice sheets!

Wright's hypothesis has received little support in the twentieth century, and we must concur with Byron C. Nelson's verdict that "it was a fruitless effort to combine the theory of the Flood with the theories of modern geology."[1]

In conclusion, it must be admitted that evidence from paleontology presents some very embarrassing problems for those who believe that the entire human race was confined to the region of Mesopotamia at the time of the Flood. If it should ever be proved that any of the ancient human fossils discovered in Java, China, South Africa, or Western Europe were antediluvian, then the universality of the Flood could be proven by paleontology alone.[2] For it would be quite futile to defend the theory that a mountain-covering, year-long deluge extended from Mesopotamia to Western Europe, South Africa, China, or Java, without at the same time covering the entire earth.

SUMMARY AND CONCLUSION

In this chapter we have attempted to establish the geographical universality of the Flood on the basis of seven major Biblical arguments: (1) the Bible says that the waters of the Flood covered the highest mountains to a depth sufficient for the Ark to float over them; (2) the Bible also informs us that this situation prevailed for a period of five months and that an additional seven months were required for

[1] Byron C. Nelson, *The Deluge Story in Stone* (Minneapolis: Augsburg Publishing House, 1931), p. 134. As late as 1950, however, Dr. R. C. Stone defended this view: "The Biblical account does not preclude mass migration to S. America, Java, Northern Europe, and the Far Eastern Asia mainland before Noah's day, providing such men had become extinct before the Flood or were killed by the flooding of these areas." ("Exegesis of the Biblical Account of the Flood," Unpublished Paper, Wheaton College, Nov. 11, 1950).

[2] This argument seriously undermines the popular local-Flood view. Wright's bizarre theory would not be affected by it, of course; nor would Ramm's theory of an anthropologically local Flood. In fact, Ramm uses this same argument to defend his own view: "Some assert that man never spread beyond the Mesopotamian Valley. This is impossible to defend in that it is so well proven that men were to be found outside of the Mesopotamian area long before the Flood." *Op. cit.,* p. 239. Then, in a footnote, he adds: "Rehwinkel admits this. *Op. cit.,* pp. 32-40."

But this is a strange way to express it, since Rehwinkel, a defender of the universal flood view, cited those numerous instances of human fossils in various parts of the world for the very reason that they constitute supporting evidence for the universal Flood view!

the waters to subside sufficiently for Noah to disembark in the mountains of Ararat; (3) the expression "fountains of the great deep were broken up" points unmistakably to vast geological disturbances that are incompatible with the local-Flood concept, especially when these disturbances are said to have continued for five months; (4) the construction of the Ark with a capacity of at least 1,400,000 cubic feet, merely for the purpose of carrying eight people and a few animals through a local inundation is utterly inconceivable; (5) if the Flood had been limited in extent, there would have been no need for an ark at all, for there would have been plenty of time for Noah's family to escape from the danger-area, to say nothing of the birds and beasts; (6) Peter's use of the Flood as a basis for refuting uniformitarian skeptics in the last days would have been pointless if the Flood had been merely a local one, especially when we consider the cosmic setting into which he placed that cataclysm (II Pet. 3:3-7), and (7) a widely distributed human race could not have been destroyed by a local Flood.

In support of our seventh argument, we presented four Biblical reasons for the necessity of a total destruction of humanity in the days of Noah: (1) since the stated purpose of the Flood was the punishment of a sinful race, such a purpose could not have been accomplished if only a part of humanity had been affected; (2) the fact that the Flood destroyed the rest of mankind is greatly strengthened by repeated statements in Genesis, I Peter, and II Peter, to the effect that *only* Noah and his family were spared; (3) the Lord Jesus Christ clearly stated that all men were destroyed by the Flood (Luke 17:26-30), and (4) the covenant which God made with Noah after the Flood becomes meaningless if only a part of the human race had been involved.

In addition to these arguments for a total destruction of the human race except for Noah's family, we gave two reasons for believing that the human race could not have been confined to the Mesopotamian Valley at the time of the Flood: (1) the longevity and fecundity of the antediluvians would allow for a very rapid increase in population even if only 1,656 years elapsed between Adam and the Flood; and the prevalence of strife and violence would have encouraged wide distribution rather than confinement to a single locality; (2) evidence of human fossils in widely-scattered parts of the world makes it very difficult to assume that men did not migrate beyond the Near East before the time of the Flood.

The writers are firmly convinced that these basic arguments, if carefully weighed by Christian thinkers, would prove to be sufficiently powerful and compelling to settle once and for all the long-debated question of the geographical extent of the Flood. This is not to say, of course, that a universal Flood presents no serious scientific problems; for the remaining chapters of this volume are devoted largely to an examination of such problems. But we do believe that no problem, be it scientific or philosophical, can be of sufficient magnitude to offset the combined force of these seven Biblical arguments for a geographically universal Flood in the days of Noah.

Chapter II

Basic Arguments Against an Anthropologically Universal Flood

INTRODUCTION

As part of the seventh major argument for a universal flood, in the preceding chapter, four reasons were presented for believing that the entire human race outside of the Ark perished in the Flood. It was observed that conservative Christians have been practically unanimous in their adherence to this view. In recent years, however, an evangelical scholar has taken pen in hand to deny, on supposedly scientific grounds, that the Flood could have destroyed the entire human race except for Noah's family.

In his controversial volume, *The Christian View of Science and Scripture*, Bernard Ramm, as Director of Graduate Studies in Religion at Baylor University,[1] has challenged the evangelical world to abandon its "hyperorthodox" attitude toward uniformitarian science and to surrender the notion that the Flood was universal in either a geographical or anthropological sense.[2] There are other

[1] Now Professor of Systematic Theology and Christian Apologetics at California Baptist Theological Seminary.

[2] Among the many reviews of this book that have been written, the following may be mentioned: James O. Buswell, Robert D. Culver, and Russell L. Mixter, *Journal of the American Scientific Affiliation*, Vol. 7, No. 4 (Dec., 1955); Meredith G. Kline, *The Westminster Theological Journal*, Vol. 18, No. 1 (Nov., 1955); Joseph T. Bayly, *Eternity*, Vol. 6, No. 8 (August, 1955); Arthur W. Kuschke, *The Presbyterian Guardian* (March 15, 1955); Edwin Y. Monsma, *Torch and Trumpet* (Sept., 1955); and John Theodore Mueller, *Concordia Theological Monthly*, Vol. 26, No. 3 (March, 1955).

evangelical scholars today who look with favor upon this view; but there can be little question that Dr. Ramm is one of the most prominent and outspoken representatives of this school of thought at the present time.

It is necessary that we devote one chapter to a consideration of Dr. Ramm's objections to an *anthropologically* universal Flood before we turn our attention to the major objections that have been raised against a *geographically* universal Flood; for if it can be shown on scientific grounds that the Flood could not have destroyed the entire human race in the days of Noah, then efforts to defend a geographically universal Flood would be pointless.

INDIANS WERE IN AMERICA BEFORE THE FLOOD

The first argument against the doctrine that all men outside of the Ark were destroyed has been expressed as follows:

If the evidence is certain that the American Indian was in America around 8,000 B.C. to 10,000 B.C., then a universal flood or a destruction of man, must be before that time, and due to Genesis and Babylonian parallels there is hardly an evangelical scholar who wishes to put the flood as early as 8,000 B.C. to 10,000 B.C.[1]

It will be observed that this argument rests upon a question of relative chronology. In order for it to have validity, both of its premises must be proven true: (1) scientific dating methods for early man are reliable and, therefore, it is certain that the direct ancestors of the American Indians were living in the Western Hemisphere around 10,000 B.C.; and (2) because of parallels between the Babylonian and Biblical Flood accounts, the Flood itself could not have occurred as early as 10,000 B.C.

The Babylonian Flood Account

First of all, we must turn our attention to the second of Dr. Ramm's premises in order to determine exactly why it is that parallels between the Babylonian and Biblical Flood accounts preclude the possibility of a pre-10,000 B.C. Flood.

[1] Ramm, *op. cit.,* p. 336. For the sake of convenience, we have isolated from Dr. Ramm's discussions what we feel are his major arguments, for he has not arranged them in any particular order.

There seems to be general agreement among Semitic scholars that the date of the composition of the Gilgamesh Epic, at least in its twelve-tablet Akkadian poetic form, was approximately 2000-1700 B.C.[1] The Flood narrative, which is found in Tablet XI of the epic, probably existed in independent written form long before it was incorporated into the completed Gilgamesh Epic. The Semitic Babylonians, who produced this amazing epic, may have borrowed many elements of their Flood narrative from the Sumerians whose culture they adopted.[2] That the Sumerians also had a legend of the Flood has been proven by the discovery of a fragment of a clay tablet at Nippur dating around 2000 B.C. or earlier. Because the Babylonian Flood account contains closer parallels to the Biblical account, we may assume either that the Sumerians had more than one version and that the Babylonians copied the most accurate one, or that the Babylonians received their Flood tradition directly from their Amorite ancestors who apparently had closer ties with Abram's ancestors than did the Sumerians.[3]

It is indeed astonishing to see how large are *the areas of general agreement* between the Biblical and Babylonian Flood accounts. As Unger points out, both accounts (1) state that the Deluge was divinely planned, (2) agree that the impending catastrophe was divinely revealed to the hero of the Deluge, (3) connect the Deluge with defection in the human race, (4) tell of the deliverance of the hero and his family, (5) assert that the hero of the Deluge was divinely instructed to build a huge boat to preserve life, (6) indicate the physical causes of the Flood, (7) specify the duration of the Flood, (8) name the landing place of the boat, (9) tell of the sending forth of birds at certain intervals to ascertain the decrease of the waters, (10) describe acts of worship by the hero after his deliverance, and (11) allude to the bestowment of special blessings upon the hero after the disaster.[4]

On the other hand, it must be recognized that there are so many important *differences in detail* between the two accounts (the Biblical being far more rational and consistent than the Babylonian), that it

---

[1] James B. Pritchard, ed., *Ancient Near Eastern Texts Relating to the Old Testament* (Princeton: Princeton University Press, 1950), p. 73.

[2] Alexander Heidel, *The Gilgamesh Epic and Old Testament Parallels,* (2nd. Ed., Chicago, University of Chicago Press, 1949), p. 14.

[3] See John Bright, *A History of Israel* (Philadelphia: The Westminster Press, 1959), pp. 43, 49.

[4] Merrill F. Unger, *Archaeology and the Old Testament* (3rd ed.; Grand Rapids: Zondervan Publishing House, 1956), pp. 55-65.

is quite impossible to assume that Genesis in any way depends upon the Gilgamesh Epic as a source. Alexander Heidel has carefully analyzed a number of these differences, among which are the following:

(1) *The Authors of the Flood.* In Genesis it is the one and only true God who brings the Flood because of the moral depravity of mankind; in the Babylonian account the Flood is sent because of the rashness of Enlil and in opposition to the will of other gods.

(2) *The Announcement of the Flood.* In Genesis God Himself warns Noah to build an ark and gives mankind 120 years to repent; in the Babylonian account the Flood is kept a secret by the gods, but Utnapishtim (the Babylonian Noah) is given a hint of the coming disaster by Ea without the knowledge of Enlil.

(3) *The Ark and its Occupants.* In Genesis the Ark is 300 x 50 x 30 cubits with three decks and carries eight people, two of each unclean animal and seven of the clean, and food; in the Babylonian account the Ark is 120 x 120 x 120 cubits with nine decks and carries all of Utnapishtim's family and relations, the boatman, all the craftsmen (or learned men), "the seed of all living creatures," and all his gold and silver.

(4) *Causes and Duration of the Flood.* In Genesis the Flood is caused by the breaking up of the fountains of the great deep and the opening of the windows of heaven, and these conditions continue for 150 days followed by an additional 221 days during which the waters abate; in the Babylonian account rain is the only cause mentioned and it ceases after only six days. After an unspecified number of days, Utnapishtim and the others leave the Ark.

(5) *The Bird Scene.* In Genesis a raven is sent out first and then a dove three times at intervals of seven days; in the Babylonian account a dove is sent out first, then a swallow, and finally a raven, at unspecified intervals. The Babylonian account does not mention the olive leaf.

(6) *The Sacrifice and Blessings.* In Genesis the Lord graciously receives Noah's sacrifice, gives him and his family power to multiply and fill the earth, emphasizes the sanctity of human life, and promises not to destroy the earth again by a flood. In the Babylonian account hungry gods "gathered like flies over the sacrificer" because they had been deprived of sacrifices for so long. A quarrel ensues between the gods Enlil and Ea, and Enlil finally blesses Utnapishtim and his wife after being rebuked by Ea for his rashness in bringing the Flood.

Utnapishtim and his wife are rewarded by being made gods and are taken to the realm of the gods.[1]

The gross polytheism and confusion of details in the Babylonian account seem to indicate a long period of oral transmission. Nevertheless, since the Book of Genesis contains God's inspired record of the great Flood, the remarkable similarities of the two accounts make it extremely difficult to assume that the Babylonians received their Flood account from *a tradition that was transmitted orally for over seven thousand years* from the time of the dispersion of nations from Babel to the late fourth millennium B.C., when, at long last, it could be written down for future inclusion in the eleventh tablet of the Gilgamesh Epic. But this is exactly what we would have to assume if Indians have been inhabiting North America continually since around 10,000 B.C. and if writing was not invented until around 3000 B.C.![2]

It must be realized that the insertion of 7,000 years between Babel and Abraham creates more problems than it solves. Since these problems are discussed in Appendix II (485-488), it will suffice merely to mention them here: (1) the analogy of Biblical chronology; (2) the proximity of at least half of the postdiluvian patriarchs to the Flood because of the comparative shortness of the time-span between the Flood and Babel; and (3) the absurdity of spacing Reu, Serug, and Nahor thousands of years apart, especially in view of the fact that various Mesopotamian towns are named after them.

Furthermore, it is difficult to harmonize the early chapters of Genesis with the concept of a seven-thousand-year period of universal *illiteracy* between the judgment of Babel and the rise of Near Eastern civilizations in the fourth millennium B.C. As a matter of fact, the Scriptures seem to imply that written records were made and kept by at least a portion of the human race during the entire period from Adam to Abraham. With respect to the *antediluvian* period, Ramm admits:

> In the fourth and fifth chapters of Genesis we have lists of names, ages of people, towns, agriculture, metallurgy, and music. This implies the abil-

[1] Alexander Heidel, *The Gilgamesh Epic and Old Testament Parallels* (2d ed.; Chicago: The University of Chicago Press, 1949), pp. 224-258. Especially significant is Heidel's discussion of Utnapishtim's blunder in sending out the raven last. *Ibid.,* p. 253.

[2] It is generally believed that the earliest form of writing was invented after 3500 B.C., as represented by the Sumerian pictographic script discovered at Erech. Cf. Jack Finegan, *Light From the Ancient Past* (2d ed.; Princeton, N. J.: Princeton University Press, 1959), pp. 26, 29; and John Bright, *op. cit.,* pp. 22-24.

ity to write, to count, to build, to farm, to smelt, and to compose. Further, this is done by the immediate descendants of Adam.[1]

Now if it be granted that the Scriptures imply that men could read and write before the Flood, is it not reasonable to assume that Noah and his sons could have provided an accurate written account of the Flood for *postdiluvian humanity?* And may we not also assume that a large number of people possessed the ability to read and write down to the judgment of Babel, perhaps as much as 1,000 years after the Flood?[2] This seems to be indicated by the unity of their speech (Gen. 11:1), the unity of their purpose in defying God's direct commands to fill the earth (Gen. 11:3-4; cf. 1:28; 9:1), and, above all, the magnitude of their building project ("let us build us a city, and a tower, whose top may reach unto heaven"—11:4) which presupposes a knowledge of mathematics and engineering.

That literacy and written records did not vanish from the earth even *after* the judgment of Babel is suggested by the fact that the Bible provides us with a list of patriarchs and their ages, not only for the pre-Flood and the pre-Babel periods, but also for *the post-Babel period down to Abraham.* Probably these patriarchs (Peleg, Reu, Serug, Nahor, and Terah) were widely separated links in the long line of Messiah's human ancestors between the confusion of tongues at Babel and the birth of Abraham.[3] But whether or not we have a complete list of the human links in this portion of the Messianic line, the fact that we have the names of *some* of these men, together with their ages at the birth of their first sons and their total life-spans, indicates that a genealogical record was kept somewhere throughout the entire period.[4]

[1] Ramm, *op. cit.,* p. 327.

[2] See page 486, note 1, for a discussion of the length of the period between the Flood and the judgment of Babel.

[3] Biblical evidences for the existence of gaps in the genealogy of Genesis 11 are set forth in Appendix II.

[4] It is conceivable, of course, that God may have supernaturally sustained a *pure oral tradition* of the details of Genesis 1-11 within the line of post-Babel patriarchs; or that He may have revealed all these details to Moses directly, apart from any oral or written sources. Neither hypothesis would clear the way for an unlimited stretching of the postdiluvian period, however, for the problems discussed in Appendix II (pp. 485-488) would still have to be faced. It is important to remember that whatever may have been the sources employed by Moses in the composition of Genesis—whether written records, oral traditions, or direct revelation—verbal inspiration guarantees its absolute authority and infallibility (Matt. 5:18, Luke 24:25-27, John 5:46, 10:35). Cf. Unger, *op. cit.,* p. 71.

Thus, the early chapters of Genesis imply that there was at least a small pocket of civilization in the Near East linking the civilization of Babel with that of the Sumerians and Babylonians (cf. Gen. 10:6-14). The memory of the "golden age" which preceded the confusion of tongues and the scattering of peoples at Babel must have lingered long afterward in the minds of men, providing fertile seed for the rise of a new civilization in the fourth millennium B.C., even as the so-called "dark ages" which followed the fall of Rome were merely a transition to the even higher cultural achievements of the Renaissance period.

Under these circumstances, it is very difficult to conceive of more than four or five thousand years intervening between the judgment of Babel and the time of Abraham; for if writing were known in any part of the Near East during those thousands of years, it is strange that the earliest form of writing known consists of pictographs dating no earlier than the middle of the fourth millennium B.C. It would be more in line with the Biblical evidence to suppose that the Amorites (and possibly the Sumerians) received their superior account of the Flood from the direct ancestors of Abraham who had kept written records since the time of Babel. Thus, even though the Sumerians independently invented their own form of script, the Flood tradition (and doubtless traditions of the Creation and the Fall) would have been kept pure for many generations after Babel in written records that have long since disappeared.

In bringing this part of our discussion to a conclusion, we find ourselves in agreement with Dr. Ramm's second premise, namely, that because of parallels between the Babylonian and Biblical Flood accounts, the Flood itself (and the judgment of Babel) could not have occurred before 10,000 B.C. We found this premise to be true, not only because of the problem of accounting for the remarkable Babylonian Flood tradition as the end product of millenniums of purely oral transmission but, even more important, because of the impossibility of fitting the Biblical picture of postdiluvian civilization and the line of post-Babel patriarchs into such a chronological framework. Genesis 11 can hardly be stretched to cover a period of eight to ten thousand years.

The Presuppositions of Age Determination Methods

If the Flood did not occur earlier than 10,000 B.C., are we to conclude with Dr. Ramm that North America and the American Indians were not affected by the Deluge? By no means, for we deny his first premise that scientific dating methods for early man are completely reliable and that the direct ancestors of American Indians were living in North America around 10,000 B.C. To be sure, the new radiocarbon method of determining the age of dead organic substances has been widely acclaimed in recent years, and many have insisted that dates obtained by this method are valid (within a certain margin of error) back to 70,000 years or more.

However, the fact that this method rests upon doubtful presuppositions and needs to be used with great caution may be illustrated by a recent incident. Dr. Stuart Piggott, a British archaeologist, reports that two radiocarbon tests on a sample of charcoal indicated a date of 2620-2630 B.C. for an ancient structure at Durrington Walls in England. But absolutely compelling archaeological evidences called for a date approximately 1,000 years later! Dr. Piggott concludes that the radiocarbon date is "archaeologically unacceptable."[1] Dr. Glyn Daniel, the editor of the journal in which the problem is presented, comments on this contradictory evidence:

It is very important to realize that doubts about the archaeological acceptability of radiocarbon dates is not obscurantism nor another chapter in the battle of Science versus the Arts. It is an attempt to evaluate all the available evidence, physical and non-physical . . . We are at a moment when some of us at least are uncertain how to answer the question: when is a Carbon 14 reading an archaeological fact? We certainly need reassurance beyond all reasonable doubt at the present moment that scientists know all about the variables involved, that Elsasser, Ney, and Winckler are wrong in supposing that there was variation in the intensity of cosmic-ray formation and that others are wrong in supposing that there were fluctuations in the original C-14 content.[2]

Since the entire question of age determination methods and their

[1] Stuart Piggott, "The Radio-Carbon Date from Durrington Walls," *Antiquity*, XXXIII, No. 132 (Dec., 1959), p. 289. Another prominent archaeologist, Professor V. Milojčić, states that some radio carbon dates from south-eastern Europe are 1,000 years too high. H. T. Waterbolk, "The 1959 Carbon-14 Symposium at Groningen," *Antiquity*, XXXIV, No. 133 (March, 1960), pp. 14-18; cf. pp. 4-5.

[2] Glyn Daniel, *loc. cit.*, p. 239.

presuppositions will be discussed at length in later chapters,[1] we will only state at this point that the radiocarbon method cannot be applied to periods in the remote past, because the Biblical doctrine of a universal Deluge calls for a non-uniformitarian history of the earth's atmosphere and thus of cosmic-ray activity and radiocarbon concentrations. Since the assumptions of this and similar methods of dating the remains of early man are clearly contradicted by the testimony of God's Word (e.g., II Pet. 3:3-7), we may conclude that American Indians migrated to this continent following the confusion of tongues at Babel, even though the Flood occurred after 10,000 B.C.

ALL MANKIND NOT DESCENDED FROM NOAH'S FAMILY

This is a rather complex argument, which Ramm sets forth in an effort to discredit the anthropologically universal Flood view from a Biblical as well as from a scientific standpoint.

The derivation of all races from Noah is only possible if one accepts a universal flood or a flood as universal as man. It is pious fiction to believe that Noah had a black son, a brown son, and a white son.

.   .   .   .

As far as can be determined the early chapters of Genesis center around that stream of humanity (part of the Caucasoid race) which produced the Semitic family of nations of which the Hebrews were a member. The sons of Noah were all Caucasian as far as can be determined, and so were all of their descendants. The Table of Nations gives no hint of any Negroid or Mongoloid peoples . . . Suffice it to say that the effort to derive the races of the entire world from Noah's sons of the Table of Nations is not necessary from a Biblical standpoint, nor possible from an anthropological one.[2]

Before attempting to answer this argument, we must first analyze it into component parts: (1) Noah could not have had a black son, a brown son, and a white son; (2) the Table of Nations in Genesis 10 speaks only of Caucasian peoples; (3) it is not necessary to derive all nations from Noah's family from a Biblical standpoint; and (4) it is impossible to do so from an anthropological standpoint.

[1] See below, pp. 296-303; 370-379, and 405-438.
[2] Ramm, *op. cit.*, pp. 336-337.

The Sons of Noah

The first of these arguments certainly falls wide of the mark, for it suggests that advocates of an anthropologically universal Flood are committed to the absurd hypothesis that Noah's three sons were racially distinct. R. Laird Harris of Covenant Theological Seminary has some very helpful comments on this matter, which we submit as our answer to this argument:

> We need not adopt the view that has sometimes been expressed that the three sons were black, yellow, and white. If they were so, what were their wives? Rather we would say that in these six people were all the genes which have separated out into the modern races . . . Shem may have had the genes for kinky hair and yellow skin, Ham for white skin and Mongoloid eyes, etc. But the genes we would have to say were all there whether in evidence in the body characteristics or not.[1]

The Table of Nations

The second part of this argument against a Flood that destroyed all mankind, namely, that the Table of Nations in Genesis 10 speaks only of Caucasian peoples, is at best merely an argument from silence. Since the tenth chapter of Genesis doesn't claim to speak of races at all but rather of nations and families and languages,[2] it would be rash indeed to insist that the ancestors of the Negroid and Mongoloid peoples are not included in this chapter. The racial differences we know of today were probably brought about by mutations that "occurred in small, isolated groups which, because of their small size and isolation at rather extreme positions in the Europe-Asia-Africa land area, inbred the new factor. Both cultural and environmental selection could have operated."[3] Negroes are considered by anthropologists to have migrated from southern Asia into Africa in

---

[1] R. Laird Harris, "Racial Dispersion," *Journal of the American Scientific Affiliation,* Vol. 7, No. 3 (Sept., 1955), p. 52.

[2] Harris points out that "race is a physical term. The A.S.A. Symposium quotes Boas' definition that race is the 'assembly of genetic lines represented in a population' (p. 105). With this in mind we are at a disadvantage in ancient racial studies based upon literary sources. Men were more often described according to language and culture than according to physical characteristics" (*loc. cit.*).

[3] William A. Smalley, "A Christian View of Anthropology," *Modern Science and Christian Faith,* (2nd Ed., Wheaton, Ill., Van Kampen Press, 1950), p. 114.

comparatively recent times.[1] According to Genesis 10, descendants of all three sons of Noah were living in Western Asia after the Tower of Babel. Therefore it is impossible to say from which son or sons of Noah the Negroid and Mongoloid peoples have descended.

Furthermore, the geographical outreach of Genesis 10 does not leave one with the impression that only the peoples of the Mesopotamian Valley were affected by the Flood. The sons of Japheth are depicted as moving into various parts of Europe including Tarshish (probably Spain), and some of Ham's descendants settle in northern and eastern Africa (Cush, Mizraim, and Put). Are we to suppose then, on the basis of Ramm's theory, that all of Europe, northern Africa, and the Near East were completely lacking in human population until the "Caucasian" descendants of Noah moved into those areas around 5000 B.C.? If the inhabitants of those areas had been wiped out by the Flood, we are faced with the problem of explaining how the Flood could have covered such a vast area of the globe without at the same time covering the whole earth. But to say that people were already living in all of those regions when the descendants of Noah were scattered abroad after the judgment of the Tower of Babel would be to contradict the clear statement of Genesis, that "of them was the whole earth overspread" (9:19; cf. 10:5,32; 11:1,9).[2]

The Bible and Racial Distribution

In the third place, Ramm asserts that "the effort to derive the races of the entire world from Noah's sons of the Table of Nations is not

---

[1] William Howells, *Mankind So Far* (New York: Doubleday and Co., Inc., 1947), p. 299. See below, p. 47, for the full quotation. It is worth noting that Cush, at least, must have had descendants with very dark skins: "Can the Ethiopian [Cushite] change his skin, or the leopard his spots?" (Jer. 13:23, cf. Num. 12:1, Jer. 38:7, Amos 9:7, Acts 8:27). Racial differences may have occurred very quickly after the judgment of the Tower of Babel because of the sudden dispersion and isolation of families and nations.

[2] While Ramm traces only the *Caucasian* languages back to Babel (*op. cit.*, p. 340), LaSor (*loc. cit.*) takes an even more extreme view by suggesting that the dispersion of peoples in Genesis 10 took place *before* the judgment of Babel and that this judgment involved only the *Semites* (descendants of Shem). Such a view fails to take into account the Old Testament characteristic of chronological overlapping (e.g., Gen. 1 and 2; 4 and 5; 7:6-12 and 7:13-17, etc.); or the necessity of interpreting the term "earth" in 11:1,4,9, in the light of 10:32; or the incongruity of having the Scriptures explain the origin of Semitic tongues without explaining the origin of Japhetic and Hamitic tongues (10:5,20); or the fact that Babel became a Hamitic rather than a Semitic city (10:10). See the standard commentaries on Genesis 10-11.

necessary from a Biblical standpoint." But this is most definitely a begging of the question, for we have already shown in the preceding chapter that (1) the very purpose of the Flood would have been frustrated if only a part of sinful humanity had been destroyed; (2) many passages in the Old and New Testaments emphasize that *only* Noah and his family were spared; (3) the Lord Jesus Christ clearly stated that *all* men were destroyed except those in the Ark, and (4) the Covenant of the Rainbow would have been utterly meaningless if only a part of the human race was involved. If these Biblical arguments are cogent, then it *is* necessary to derive all the races of the world from Noah's sons, from a Biblical standpoint.

Anthropology and Racial Dispersion

Ramm's fourth point requires more detailed consideration, because it appeals to the science of anthropology for proof that the present distribution of humanity could not have been accomplished since the Flood. If such proof could be adduced from anthropology, it would indeed present a serious problem. But where is such proof? Once again we seem to have an argument from silence, for Ramm does not support his statements with positive evidence.

Recent migrations from Asia. Does anthropological evidence actually point to a very gradual distribution of modern races during hundreds of thousands of years? Not at all. In his well-known textbook, *Mankind So Far,* Professor William Howells says that the Australian aborigines probably reached their island continent "at roughly the time that the Indians were going to America, perhaps 10,000 B.C."[1] In discussing the problem of the original distribution of Negroes and Negritoes, Howells has this to say:

> They are doubtless "newer" races than the Australian, because they are specialized, particularly in hair . . . Their final outward spread, however, would have been recent, because the Negritoes would have needed true boats to arrive in the Andamans or the Philippines. The Negroes would have made their Asiatic exit still later, with a higher (Neolithic) culture, and probably also with boats. A relatively recent arrival of Negroes in Africa should not shock anthropologists . . . And there are no archaeolog-

[1] Howells, *op. cit.,* pp. 297-298.

ical signs of pre-Neolithic people in the Congo at all, and it might have been empty when the Negritoes and the Negroes came.[1]

After emphasizing the "stupendous growth of the last 10,000 years," and "the recent spread of man," Howells states: "If we look, first of all, for that part of the world which was the hothouse of the races, we can make only one choice. All the visible footsteps lead away from Asia."[2]

In view of all this vast dispersion of races from Asia during the past several thousand years (even on the basis of time-reckonings commonly employed by evolutionary anthropologists), what becomes of Ramm's assertion that the derivation of modern races from Noah's sons is impossible from an anthropological standpoint?

Universal flood traditions. But an even more interesting line of evidence than that of racial diversification and migration is to be found in the universal flood traditions. Scores and even hundreds of such traditions have been found in every part of the world, in both the Eastern and Western hemispheres; and common to most of them is the recollection of a great flood which once covered the earth and destroyed all but a tiny remnant of the human race. Many of them, even those which have been found among the American Indians, tell of the building of a great ark which saved human and animal seed from total destruction by the Flood and which finally landed upon a mountain. Lengthy discussions of flood traditions from nearly every nation under heaven, together with suggestions for further research, may be found in any of the large Bible dictionaries and encyclopedias.[3]

---

[1] *Ibid.*, p. 299. We have omitted Howell's claim that "the Grimaldi skeletons of Europe indicate that Negroes existed in the Upper Paleolithic," because A. L. Kroeber says this can no longer be sustained. *Anthropology* (New York: Harcourt, Brace & Co., 1948), pp. 104, 114, 663.

[2] Howells, *op. cit.*, p. 295. Similar testimony has been given by William A. Smalley: "The Scriptural record is of the spread of peoples from their origin in the approximate center of the great Europe-Asia-Africa land mass. The Biblical picture is so close to the best anthropological reconstructions of the original dispersion and divergences of races that it is used as the allegorical picture of scientific findings by Dr. Ruth Benedict and Miss Gene Weltfish in their population booklets combating race prejudice, and is basic in their map." *Op. cit.*, p. 116.

[3] Sir James George Frazer, *Folk-Lore in the Old Testament* (London: Macmillan & Co., Ltd. 1918), Vol. I, pp. 104-361, describes over 100 flood traditions from Europe, Asia, Australia, the East Indies, Melanesia, Micronesia, Polynesia, South America, Central America, North America, and East Africa. Frazer acknowledges his main source to be the large work by the German geographer and anthropologist,

It could not be expected, of course, that non-Christian scholars would acknowledge such traditions as constituting confirmatory evidence for the historicity of the Genesis account, because that portion of the Bible (among others) has been assigned, on the basis of antitheistic presuppositions, to the realm of myth and legend.

The astonishing manner in which modern scholarship has misinterpreted the true significance of the Gilgamesh Epic is an example of this antisupernaturalistic bias. Conservative Christian scholars have considered the eleventh tablet of that epic, which contains the Babylonian flood account, to be one of the most remarkable confirmations of Genesis ever discovered in ancient literature. In spite of polytheistic elements, the Babylonian account contains parallels to the Genesis account, even in matters of detail, that are nothing less than amazing. The Genesis account of the Flood, being free from any of the corrupting elements which abound in the Babylonian version, is based upon written records that were kept pure and accurate down through the centuries by the providence of God.[1]

But critical scholarship, instead of admitting that the Babylonian is a highly corrupted cognate of the pure Genesis account, has deliberately perverted the true relationship of these records by making Genesis a corruption of the Gilgamesh Epic! The following quotation will serve to illustrate the absurdities to which this type of reasoning must ultimately lead:

> Just at this time [the 1870's] the traditional view of the Deluge received its death-blow, and in a manner entirely unexpected. By the investigations of George Smith among the Assyrian tablets of the British Museum, in 1872, and by his discoveries just afterward in Assyria, it was put beyond a reasonable doubt that a great mass of accounts in Genesis are simply adaptations of earlier and especially of Chaldean myths and legends . . . Other devoted scholars followed in the paths thus opened—Sayce in England, Lenormant in France, Schrader in Germany—with the result that the Hebrew account of the Deluge, to which for ages theologians had obliged all geological research to conform, was quietly relegated, even by the most eminent Christian scholars, to the realm of myth and legend. Sundry feeble attempts to break the force of this discovery, and an evi-

---

Richard Andree, *Die Flutsagen* (Brunswick, 1891). An interesting chart representing the principal ideas of the Biblical account of the Deluge in non-Biblical traditions may be found in Byron C. Nelson, *The Deluge Story in Stone* (Minneapolis: Augsburg Pub. House, 1931, p. 169.

[1] See our earlier discussion of the Babylonian Flood account, pp. 37-42.

dently widespread fear to have it known, have certainly impaired not a little the legitimate influence of Christian clergy.[1]

Unfortunately, the situation has remained unchanged during the sixty years that have passed since Andrew White wrote these words; and, as Merrill F. Unger has pointed out, the idea that the Hebrews borrowed their flood story from the Babylonians "is the most widely accepted explanation at the present."[2] Practically all evangelical scholars unite their voices in denunciation of this bland and uncritical prejudice on the part of liberal and secular scholarship.[3]

But if such men have failed to hide their anti-Biblical prejudices in the relatively simple case of Babylonian and Genesis parallels, what confidence can we place in their dogmatic assertions that the vast multitude of flood traditions throughout the world offer no evidence whatever of an original Flood of the magnitude described in the Book of Genesis?

One excuse which anthropologists have often used for denying the significance of universal flood traditions in this connection is that other traditions, obviously fictitious, have been found among primitive peoples in widely separated areas, having several elements in common. A. L. Kroeber describes the Magic Flight legend as follows:

> There is one folklore plot with a distribution that leaves little doubt as to its diffusion from a single source. This is the incident known as the magic flight or the obstacle pursuit. It recounts how the hero, when pursued, throws behind him successively a whetstone, a comb, and a vessel of oil or other liquid. The stone turns into a mountain or a precipice, the comb into a forest or a thicket, the liquid into a lake or a river. Each of these obstacles impedes the pursuer and contributes to the hero's final escape.[4]

---

[1] Andrew D. White, *A History of the Warfare of Science With Theology in Christendom* (New York: George Braziller, reprinted 1955), pp. 237-238. Recently, Edward A. White has noted that this volume "more than any other kept the battle raging for the next generation." *Science and Religion in American Thought* (Stanford University Press, 1952), p. 2.

[2] Merrill F. Unger, *Archaeology and the Old Testament*, p. 69.

[3] Bernard Ramm comments: "It is typical of radical critics to play up the similarity of anything Biblical with the Babylonian, and omit the profound differences or gloss over them." *Op. cit.*, p. 102. Cf. p. 248. A recent example of such prejudice against the historicity of the Genesis account is found in Jack Finegan's discussion of the Gilgamesh Epic: "Such is the ancient flood story of Babylonia which, purified of its polytheistic elements, survived among the Israelites in two sources, now woven together into a single moving story in Genesis 6:5 to 9:17." *Light From the Ancient Past* (2nd ed. Princeton: Princeton University Press, 1959), p. 36.

[4] Kroeber, *op. cit.*, p. 544.

Since this legend was told by primitive peoples from Europe across Asia to North America, it has been used by anthropologists as an example of how the flood legends spread from a common center from tribe to tribe around the world, without the people themselves necessarily having carried the story with them as they migrated to their present areas of distribution.

But while we must readily grant the possibility of explaining universal flood legends on the principle of *diffusion,* we do insist that it is equally possible, from an anthropological standpoint, to explain them on the principle of *tradition:*

> Whatever may be the truth—universal or local Flood—memory of the Flood transmitted from generation to generation as a tradition or from people to people by diffusion—the problems are there and the data are anthropological. Anthropology cannot do much to orient the prehistory of man in relation to the Flood until the geological flood questions are settled, or until a lead presents itself, but the questions and data are anthropological from there on.[1]

Thus, anthropology has no right to decide one way or the other concerning *the true significance of these flood legends.* All it can do is describe them and give some cautious guesses as to how they might be explained, such guesses being unavoidably colored by the presuppositions of the one who makes them. Even Kroeber admits as much in his introduction to the chapter which contains his discussion of the flood legends.

> A considerable part of the endeavors of anthropology consists of a groping into these dimly lit realms, of collecting shreds of evidence and partial orientations, and of construing them into the best probability attainable . . . This chapter accordingly reviews a number of problems to which only partial or probable answers can be given—reviews them as a sample of the type of approach that anthropology mobilizes in avowedly inferential situations.[2]

Such professions of humility and scientific objectivity are to be commended in men whose investigations grope "in avowedly inferential situations." But we fail to notice this spirit of impartiality and objectivity in Kroeber's discussion of the flood legends in relation to Genesis:

[1] Smalley, *op. cit.,* p. 189.
[2] Kroeber, *op. cit.,* pp. 538-539.

Flood myths are told by probably the majority of human nations. Formerly this wide distribution was thought to prove the actuality of the Biblical Flood, or to be evidence of the descent of all mankind from a single nation that had once experienced it. Refutation is hardly necessary.[1]

Statements like this, however, are quite misleading; for conservative scholars do not look upon the flood traditions as constituting *proof* of the Noahic Deluge. Instead, they look upon these traditions as providing important *circumstantial evidence*[2] for a flood that was at least anthropologically universal; for such evidence, while perhaps inconclusive in itself, gains new significance when combined with the overwhelming Biblical evidence for such a catastrophe far back in human history and has been legitimately used by Christians through the centuries as corroboration for the Book of Genesis. In other words, if there actually was a Flood that destroyed mankind, as the Bible teaches, then universal flood traditions would be exactly what one would *expect* to find. Some nations would perpetuate the story of the Ark, the favored family, the landing on a mountain, and the sending forth of the birds; others would remember only the Flood itself and the purpose for which it was sent, and still others would have retained only the barest outline of events connected with that most stupendous crisis in human history.

But the real question is this: what would non-Christian anthropologists say about the Genesis Flood account if there were *no* legends or traditions anywhere in the world of such a Flood? Would they not use this very lack of circumstantial evidence as a weighty objection to the veracity of the Biblical account? Allan A. MacRae of Faith Theological Seminary has put his finger upon the heart of the matter when he writes:

If a universal flood occurred centuries after the creation, it would be natural to expect that all humanity would recall many of its details for a long time, even though some points would tend to become quite garbled, as people more and more forgot the cause and purpose of the catastrophe.[3]

In discussing the evidence of flood traditions, Ramm fails to delineate the issues clearly. Apparently realizing the strength of these

[1] *Ibid.*, p. 545.

[2] According to Webster, circumstantial evidence is "evidence that tends to prove a fact in issue by proving circumstances which afford a basis for a reasonable inference of the occurrence of the fact."

[3] Allan A. MacRae, "The Relation of Archaeology to the Bible," *Modern Science and Christian Faith*, p. 234.

traditions as circumstantial evidence for an *anthropologically* universal Flood (which is the entire question at issue in this particular chapter), he centers his attack upon those who would use such traditions as evidence for a *geographically* universal Flood. He writes:

> We must carefully distinguish between what is certainly related to the Biblical accounts; what is probably related; what is conscious or unconscious assimilation of flood data as related by missionaries and merged into local flood stories; and what are purely local affairs having no connection at all with the Bible . . . The data are not such that from a wide spread of flood legends a *universal* flood may be properly inferred.[1]

In addition to sidestepping the main issue, Ramm is guilty of minimizing the amazing similarities of detail among these flood traditions by suggesting that a large number of them may have arisen out of "purely local affairs" or from the preaching of missionaries! In our opinion, it is scientifically absurd to place the flood traditions in such a light. John Bright, a well-known contemporary scholar, discusses the "local inundations" view and confesses that "it is difficult to believe that so remarkable a coincidence of outline as exists between so many of these widely separated accounts can be accounted for in this way."[2]

It hardly seems necessary to refute the notion that *missionaries* were responsible for the spread of flood legends in any appreciable way.[3] Byron C. Nelson attacks this theory from three different directions: (1) there are no universal legends of other great miracles re-

---

[1] Ramm, *op. cit.*, pp. 242-243. Italics are his. This is part of Ramm's refutation of a geographically universal Flood.

[2] John Bright, "Has Archaeology Found Evidence of the Flood?" *The Biblical Archaeologist* V, No. 4 (Dec., 1942), pp. 56, 58, 59. Similarly, Marcus Dods observed that "local flood happenings at various times in different countries could not give birth to the minute coincidences found in these traditions, such as the number of persons saved, and the sending out of birds." W. Robertson Nicoll, ed., *The Expositor's Bible.* Vol. I: *The Book of Genesis* (4th ed.; London: Hodder and Stoughton, 1890), p. 55.

[3] Sir James Frazer doubted whether "a single genuinely native tradition of a great flood has been recorded" in all of Africa. After describing in detail two remarkable flood traditions discovered by German scholars in East Africa, he summarily dismisses them because "the stories are plainly mere variations of the Biblical narrative, which has penetrated to the savages through Christian or possibly Mohammedan influence." *Op. cit.*, pp. 329-332. One can only marvel at the naïveté of such a statement! Additional efforts to explain Flood traditions as the product of Christian missionary work may be found in the article "Deluge," *Encyclopaedia of Religion and Ethics,* James Hastings, ed. (New York, Charles Scribner's Sons, 1928), III, pp. 546-547.

corded in the Bible, such as the crossing of the Red Sea; (2) if missionaries were responsible for flood traditions, it is difficult to explain the many important differences of emphasis and detail in these traditions, and (3) the vast majority of flood traditions have been gathered and recorded, not by Christian missionaries, but by secular anthropologists who had no interest in verifying the Genesis account. "Thatcher, Catlin, Emmerson, Bancroft, and Kingsborough, by whom the American legends were collected, were students of the native races and nothing more."[1] To these arguments we may add the fact that Christian missionaries have never in the past reached all these remote tribes of the world; and even if they had, they would have preached the Gospel of salvation instead of concentrating all of their teaching upon the Genesis Flood.

SUMMARY AND CONCLUSION

Bernard Ramm's two basic arguments against an anthropologically universal Flood really come down to this: the Flood was too recent to allow for the present population of the world, in its racial types and geographical distribution, to have descended from Noah's family. In answer to this, we have shown: (1) *negatively,* that there is no way of proving scientifically that the present distribution of mankind occurred at a date prior to that which the Bible suggests for the Flood, and (2) *positively,* that the relatively recent distribution of races from the Asiatic mainland, together with the circumstantial evidence from universal Flood traditions, is more favorable to the concept of an anthropologically universal Flood than it is to the concept of an anthropologically local Flood. Thus we must conclude that Ramm's arguments against a Flood that destroyed the human race in the days of Noah are inadequate, being sustained by neither science nor Scripture.

[1] Byron C. Nelson, *The Deluge Story in Stone,* p. 168.

Chapter III

*Basic Non-Geological Arguments
Against a Universal Flood*

In the first two chapters evidence has been presented to show that the Flood was universal in both the geographical and anthropological sense of the term. But many Christian scholars who readily assent to the Biblical teaching of an anthropologically universal Flood deny that the Scriptures teach a geographically universal Flood also. In taking this stand, they join forces with those who deny that the entire human race was involved in the Flood and even with non-Christian thinkers in formulating arguments against the doctrine of an earth-covering Deluge. Most objections to the universal Flood concept are based upon supposed geological evidences and will be considered in later chapters. However, there are several major objections to this doctrine that are not strictly geological in nature, and it is the purpose of this chapter to examine these objections. In so doing, it is well to keep firmly in mind the seven basic arguments for a geographically universal Flood as set forth in the first chapter, for the force of these Biblical evidences is so clear and compelling that the burden of proof really rests upon any who would deny that the Flood could have covered the earth.

UNIVERSAL TERMS USED IN A LIMITED SENSE

The argument which Christian scholars have most frequently used against the universal Flood concept is one which purports to find its support in the Bible itself. It is that universal terms, such as "all" and "every," need not always be understood in the strictly literal sense. For example, when we read in Genesis 41:57 that *"all* countries came into Egypt to buy grain," we are not to interpret this as meaning that people from America and Australia came to Egypt for grain. And thus, by the same token, the statement of Genesis 7:19, that *"all* the high mountains that were under the *whole* heaven were covered," may be interpreted as referring to only *some* high mountains under *part* of the heavens.

Most Universal Terms Are to Be Interpreted Literally

But in spite of the seeming logic of this argument, there are several important considerations that render it untenable. In the first place, not even the most fervent local-Flood advocates would deny that there are many places in the Bible where the words "all" and "every" must be understood in the literal sense. For example, let us observe the wording of Matthew 28:18-20.

Jesus came to them and spake unto them saying, *All* authority hath been given unto me in heaven and on earth. Go ye therefore, and make disciples of *all* nations . . . teaching them to observe *all* things whatsoever I have commanded you . . .

Are we at liberty to substitute the words "much" and "many" for the word "all" in this passage, just because there are some passages in the Bible that employ universal terms in a limited sense? Obviously not; for there are *many* passages, and we believe they are in the vast majority, where universal terms must be interpreted literally. Thus, as Ramm himself admits, "there are cases where all means all, and every means every, but *the context tells us where this is intended.*"[1]

The Context Determines the Meaning

But this leads us into our second point, namely, that it is *the context* in which such terms are used that determines the sense in which they are to be understood. And it is this fact which gives us one of our greatest arguments for interpreting *literally* the universal terms of Genesis 6-9. M. M. Kalisch, a leading Hebrew scholar of the nine-

---

[1] Ramm, *op. cit.,* p. 241. Italics are ours.

teenth century, strongly opposed those who tried to tone down the universal terms of the Genesis Flood account:

> They have thereby violated all the rules of a sound philology. They have disregarded the spirit of the language, and disregarded the dictates of common sense. It is impossible to read the narrative of our chapter [Genesis 7] without being irresistibly impressed that the *whole* earth was destined for destruction. This is so evident throughout the whole of the description, that it is unnecessary to adduce single instances . . . In our case *the universality does not lie in the words merely, but in the tenor of the whole narrative.*[1]

Thus, the analogy with Genesis 41:57 utterly breaks down because *the constant repetition of universal terms* throughout the four chapters of Genesis 6-9 shows conclusively that the question of the magnitude and geographical extent of the Flood was not a merely incidental one in the mind of the writer, but was rather one of primary importance to the entire Flood narrative. In fact, so frequent is the use of universal terms and so tremendous are the points of comparison ("high mountains" and "whole heaven"), that it is impossible to imagine what more could have been said than actually was said to express the concept of a *universal* Deluge![2]

The Book of Genesis is clearly divided into two main sections: chapters 1-11 deal with *universal* origins (the material universe, the plant and animal kingdoms, the human race, sin, redemption, and the nations of the earth); chapters 12-50, on the other hand, concentrate upon the *particular* origin of the Hebrew nation and its tribes, mentioning other nations only insofar as they came into contact with Israel.[3] This sheds much light on the problem of the magnitude of the

---

[1] M. M. Kalisch, *Historical and Critical Commentary on the Old Testament* (London: Longman, Brown, Green, et al., 1858), pp. 209-210. Italics are ours. According to the estimate of one historian, Kalisch's commentaries on the Old Testament "at the time of publication were the best commentaries on the respective books in the English language and are not yet wholly superseded, having especial value as the work of a learned Jew." *The New Schaff-Herzog Encyclopedia of Religious Knowledge,* ed. Samuel M. Jackson (Grand Rapids: Baker Book House, reprinted 1950), VI, 293.

[2] The very nature of the Hebrew language accentuates the importance of context for the full understanding of terms. Thus, *ha-'ares* (the earth) in Gen. 7:19 must be understood to mean the entire globe because the following words speak of "all the high mountains that were under the whole heaven." Alexander Heidel concludes that the Biblical account "plainly asserts the universality of the Deluge." *The Gilgamesh Epic and Old Testament Parallels,* p. 250.

[3] See W. H. Griffith Thomas, *Genesis: A Devotional Commentary* (Grand Rapids: Wm. Eerdmans Pub. Co., 1946), pp. 18-19.

Deluge, for the Biblical account of the Deluge occupies *three and a half chapters* in the midst of these eleven chapters on universal origins, while only *two chapters* are devoted to the creation of all things!

From a purely literary and historical perspective, therefore, we are perfectly justified in coming to the account of the Noahic Deluge in Genesis 6-9 with the expectation of reading about a catastrophe of *universal* proportions. And if we thus approach the Flood narrative from the perspective which the Bible itself supplies for us, unemcumbered with scientific and philosophical presuppositions, we shall not be surprised to discover that the number of Hebrew superlatives used to describe the magnitude of the Flood are entirely proportional to the amount of space allotted to it in the first eleven chapters of Genesis.

Most advocates of the local-Flood view would maintain that "the deluge was universal *in so far as the area and observation and information of the narrator extended.*"[1] But even if we were to assume, for the sake of argument, that the mountain ranges of the world were as high before the Flood as they are now (as most local Flood advocates would claim[2]), then what are we to say of the idea that Noah's "observation and information" about geography was limited to the Mesopotamian valley? Even if he were a man of only average intelligence, he could have learned a great deal about his own continent of Asia (where the world's highest mountains are found today) during the six centuries that he lived before the Flood came. And assuming again, for the sake of argument, that Genesis 6-9 depicts the Flood from Noah's standpoint, and not from God's,[3] could he have been so ignorant of the topography of southwestern Asia as to think that the Flood covered "all the high mountains that were under the whole heaven" when, as a matter of fact, it covered only a few foothills?[4]

---

[1] Ramm, *op. cit.*, p. 240. Italics are his.

[2] See below, pp. 122, 267-270, 286 for further discussion of this point.

[3] Actually, there is nothing in the entire passage to indicate that Noah is recording his personal impressions of the Flood. Instead, it is all seen from God's viewpoint. *God* looks down upon mankind and sees that it is corrupt; *God* chooses Noah and commands him to build the Ark; *God* calls him into the Ark and shuts the door; *God* remembers Noah and the animals and gradually brings the Flood to an end, and *God* commands them to leave the Ark and gives them His special covenant. In fact, Noah does not speak a single word in the entire passage, until the very end of the ninth chapter, when *God* puts into his mouth the remarkable prophecy concerning his three sons.

[4] To illustrate the extent to which some scholars will go in this direction, we quote from a paper read by Lt. Col. F. A. Molony, O.B.E., before the Victoria Institute in London in 1936: "Now the part of the great Mesopotamian plain which lies be-

Some have tried to shield Noah from the accusation of childish ignorance by asserting that the terrific downpour of rain prevented him from making clear distinctions between mountains and foothills and, therefore, that "the entire record must be interpreted phenomenally."[1] But to say that the record must be interpreted "phenomenally" is only a polished way of saying that Noah *thought* the high mountains were covered, when actually they were not. Whether such impressions were due to his ignorance of how high the mountains in the Near East really were, or to his inability to evaluate the situation properly because of adverse weather conditions, makes little difference. Such an interpretation must be rejected without qualification, because it does to the entire Flood narrative exactly what John Pye Smith's local-creation theory did to the creation account. Concerning this theory, Ramm enters the following protest:

> The weakness of the theory is that it essentially cheapens Genesis 1. The majestic language, the chaste and factual terminology, and the celestial-terrestrial scope of the passage lose so much of their import and force if restricted to a small patch of the earth. Rather than having the six majestic acts of creation of the world and all its life, we have a small scale remodeling job.[2]

And we maintain that the "limited observation and information" theory and the "phenomenal" theory do the very same thing to the "majestic language, the chaste and factual terminology, and the celestial-terrestrial scope" of the Flood account. They cheapen it and reduce it to a small-scale disaster. Perhaps the famous agnostic, T. H. Huxley, was not far from the truth when he said:

low the 500′ contour is as large as England without Wales. Hence it is probable that *Noah and his sons never saw a mountain in their lives* . . . Fifteen cubits is only about 23 feet, so it would seem that the word we translate 'mountains' would be better rendered *mounds,* probably raised by human labor . . . The chronicler knew that the artificial mounds were very seldom more than 15 cubits high. He saw that they were all covered, so he wrote 'Fifteen cubits upward did the waters prevail; and the mountains were covered'." ("The Noachian Deluge and Its Probable Connection With Lake Van," *Journal of the Transactions of the Victoria Institute,* LXVIII [1936], pp. 44, 51, 52. Italics are ours.)

Col. Molony went on to explain that the Flood was caused by a sudden emptying of Lake Van (in eastern Turkey) into the Mesopotamian Valley. Lifting the Ark above the artificial mounds, the lake water threatened to sweep it out into the Persian Gulf. But in order to avoid such a fate, Noah "may have rigged jury masts and sails, and anchored when the wind was northerly." Comment hardly seems necessary!

[1] Ramm, *op. cit.,* p. 239.
[2] *Ibid.,* p. 192.

If we are to listen to many expositors of no mean authority, we must believe that what seems so clearly defined in Genesis . . . as if very great pains had been taken that there should be no possibility of mistake . . . is not the meaning of the text at all . . . A person who is not a Hebrew scholar can only stand aside and admire the marvelous flexibility of a language which admits of such diverse interpretations.[1]

Universal Terms Are Literal in Genesis 6-9 Because of the Physical Phenomena

But our third and most impelling reason for interpreting the universal terms of Genesis 6-9 literally is that *the physical phenomena* described in those chapters would be quite inconceivable if the Flood had been confined to one section of the earth. While it would be entirely possible for a seven-year famine to have gripped the Near East without at the same time affecting Australia and America (cf. Gen. 41:57), it would *not* have been possible for water to cover even *one* high mountain in the Near East without inundating Australia and America too! Another famous Hebrew scholar of modern times who wrote a commentary on Genesis was Samuel R. Driver, Professor of Hebrew at Oxford University and co-author with F. Brown and C. A. Briggs of *A Hebrew and English Lexicon of the Old Testament.* Driver insists that the local-Flood theory "does not satisfy the terms of the narrative of Genesis" and then goes on to say:

It is manifest that a flood which would submerge Egypt as well as Babylonia must have risen to at least 2000 ft. (the height of the elevated country between them), *and have thus been in fact a universal one . . .* a flood, on the other hand, which did less than this *is not what the Biblical writers describe,* and would not have accomplished what is represented as having been the entire *raison d'etre* of the Flood, the destruction of all mankind.[2]

---

[1] Quoted in O. T. Allis, *God Spake By Moses* (Philadelphia: The Presbyterian and Reformed Pub. Co., 1951), p. 158. Dr. Allis is firmly convinced that the Book of Genesis teaches a geographically universal Deluge. *Ibid.,* p. 24.

[2] Samuel R. Driver, *The Book of Genesis* (London: Methuen & Co., 1904), p. 101. For a similar conclusion, see John Skinner, *A Critical and Exegetical Commentary on Genesis,* Vol. I of *The International Critical Commentary,* p. 165. Driver, Skinner, and Kalisch (quoted above, p. 57) were of the old liberal school of theology. Such scholars did not believe, of course, that there ever was a Flood of such magnitude, an Ark of such dimensions, or a patriarch named Noah who was 600 years old. In fact, they did not really accept the historicity of the Book of Genesis at all. But they had little patience for those who professed to accept the historicity of Genesis and yet did not hesitate to take the plain statements of the text and mold them into conformity with their own scientific presuppositions.

Advocates of the local-Flood theory have long felt the force of such reasoning; and many of them, doubtless in desperation, have resorted to Hugh Miller's bizarre hypothesis that the Near East sank as fast as the Flood waters rose, in order that the Flood might cover the mountains of Ararat and still not be universal! Miller calculated that if the Near East had suddenly begun to sink at the rate of 400 feet a day, reaching a depth of over 16,000 feet in forty days, the oceanic waters could have poured into the resulting basin, covering the mountains that were in it.[1] Robert Jamieson perpetuated this fantastic theory in the *Jamieson, Fausset and Brown Commentary*,[2] and Bernard Ramm seems to have been influenced by it too (he quotes Jamieson at length), although he is careful to omit any reference to the rate at which the Near East must have been lowered to make it into a "natural saucer."[3]

Delitzsch, on the other hand, defended the local-Flood view by assuming that the waters could have covered mountains in one region without at the same time flowing into other regions: "the waters could, just where the extermination of the numerous population who would have fled to the mountains was to be effected, *stand at such a height, without reaching a similar height elsewhere or uniformly covering the whole earth.*"[4] Perhaps this learned commentator was appealing to the supernatural power of God, as an invisible wall, to hold the Flood within the Near East. But if he was appealing to the laws of physics and hydrostatics, he committed a serious scientific blunder;

[1] Hugh Miller, *The Testimony of the Rocks* (New York: Robert Carter and Brothers, 1875), p. 358. This volume was first printed in 1857 and proved to be immensely popular during the last half of the nineteenth century when the local-Flood view was so much in vogue.

[2] Jamieson, *op. cit.,* p. 100.

[3] Ramm, *op. cit.,* pp. 238-239. He claims that "some sort of geological phenomenon . . . caused the ocean waters to creep up the Mesopotamian valley. The waters carried the ark up to the Ararat range . . . By the reversal of the geological phenomenon, the water is drained back from the valley." After quoting Jamieson's statement that "the Caspian Sea . . . and the Sea of Aral occupy the lowest part of a vast space, whose whole extent is not less than 100,000 square miles, hollowed out, as it were, in the central region of the great continent, and no doubt formerly the bed of the ocean," Ramm asserts that "into this natural *saucer* the ocean waters poured," and "from this natural saucer the waters were drained." Ramm accepts the conclusions of modern uniformitarian geology. But what would modern geologists say about such a "geological phenomenon" as this, supposedly occurring about 5,000 or 6,000 B.C.?

[4] Franz Delitzsch, *A New Commentary on Genesis,* trans. Sophia Taylor (New York, Scribner & Welford, 1899), p. 270. Italics are ours.

for such a condition, continuing throughout an entire year, would contradict all known laws of water action.[1] Albertus Pieters, a more recent advocate of the limited-Flood view, frankly admits the problems that this view entails:

> If the relative elevation of the continents above the sea level was as at present, and if the "mountains of Ararat" mentioned as the resting place of the ark are the table land now known by that name, the flood must have been universal or nearly so; for that region is now 5,000 feet above sea level, and an inundation sufficient to cover it would cover the whole world, with the exception of the highest mountain ranges. But it is not at all certain that the levels have not changed.[2]

Therefore, we conclude that the argument based upon a limited usage of universal terms must be rejected. It does not do justice to the context of the Flood narrative, it fails to cope with the physical phenomena described in those chapters, and it has encouraged Christian thinkers to take utterly unwarranted liberties with the text of Scripture. Our main concern, as honest exegetes of the Word of God, must not be to find ways of making the Biblical narratives conform to modern scientific theories. Instead, our concern must be to discover exactly what God has said in the Scriptures, being fully aware of the fact that modern scientists, laboring under the handicap of non-Biblical philosophical presuppositions (such as materialism, organic evolution, and uniformitarianism), are in no position to give us an accurate reconstruction of the early history of the earth and its inhabitants.

---

[1] It is of interest to note that his co-worker, C. F. Keil, was strongly opposed to the local-Flood concept: "A flood which rose 15 cubits above the top of Ararat could not remain partial, if it only continued a few days, to say nothing of the fact that the water was rising for 40 days, and remained at the highest elevation for 150 days. To speak of such a flood as partial is absurd. Even if it broke out at only one spot, it would spread over the earth from one end to the other, and reach everywhere to the same elevation. However impossible, therefore, scientific men may declare it to be for them to conceive of a universal flood of such height and duration in accordance with the known laws of nature, this inability on their part does not justify anyone in questioning the possibility of such an event being produced by the omnipotence of God." *Op. cit.*, p. 146.

[2] Pieters, *op. cit.*, p. 119. J. J. Stewart Perowne, another advocate of a limited Flood, was embarrassed by the same problem: "On reading this narrative it is difficult, it must be confessed, to reconcile the language employed with the hypothesis of a partial deluge . . . The real difficulty lies in the connecting of this statement [7:19] with the district in which Noah is supposed to have lived, and the assertion that the waters prevailed fifteen cubits upward." *Loc. cit.*, pp. 2181-2182. Not until Christian scholars show a willingness to break completely with uniformitarian geology will they begin to understand the full significance of the Genesis Flood.

NOAH AND THE ANIMALS

Another familiar cluster of objections to the doctrine of a universal Flood gathers around the problem of how the animals were brought into the Ark and cared for during the 371 days of the Flood. Conservative Christians of the local-Flood school believe that collecting a few domesticated animals in Mesopotamia and caring for them in the Ark would have been a relatively simple matter. But to gather and care for two of *every* kind of land animal in the world would be a different matter. It has been repeatedly asserted by these men that even if Noah could have collected such a vast number of animals, the Ark could not have contained them, nor could they have been properly cared for by eight persons for an entire year.

Gathering the Animals to the Ark

Since the year 1840, when John Pye Smith first set forth these objections,[1] writers of the limited-Flood school have outdone one another in an effort to depict the supposed absurdities of such a situation. For example, Robert Jamieson wrote in 1870:

On the hypothesis, therefore, of a universal flood, we must imagine motley groups of beasts, birds, and reptiles, directing their way from the most distant and opposite quarters to the spot where Noah had prepared his ark—natives of the polar regions and the torrid zones repairing to sojourn in a temperate country, the climate of which was unsuited alike to arctic and equatorial animals. What time must have been consumed! what privations must have been undergone for want of appropriate food! what difficulties must have been encountered! what extremes of climate must have been endured by the natives of Europe, America, Australia, Asia, Africa, and the numerous islands of the sea! They could not have performed their journeys unless they had been miraculously preserved.[2]

Twenty years later, Marcus Dods added some finishing touches to this caricature of Genesis by suggesting that the animals of Australia, "visited by some presentiment of what was to happen many months after, selected specimens of their number, and that these specimens

[1] John Pye Smith, *The Relation Between the Holy Scriptures and Some Parts of Geological Science*, p. 145.
[2] Robert Jamieson, *Critical and Experimental Commentary*, I, 99.

. . . crossed thousands of miles of sea . . . singled out Noah by some inscrutable instinct, and surrendered themselves to his keeping."[1]

However, by the time the Flood controversy had reached this stage, several important fallacies became apparent in the arguments which Marcus Dods and others were setting forth in refutation of the universal Flood view. For one thing, it was recognized on all sides that there was definite danger involved in carrying this type of logic too far—the danger of removing every supernatural element from the Genesis Flood and explaining everything on a purely naturalistic basis. One defender of a limited Flood who clearly saw this danger was J. Cynddylan Jones. In his "Davies Lecture" for 1896, he took occasion to rebuke Marcus Dods:

> That doubtless is the way Dr. Dods would set about it . . . "get the animals to select specimens of their number," though the learned divine does not condescend to tell us whether it would be by ballot or by show of hands. However, the Supreme Being is not necessarily confined to Dr. Dods' methods. Even if the Deluge were universal, the difficulties enumerated would not prove insuperable to the Almighty . . . Such writing ignores the supernatural character of the episode, endeavors to explain it on naturalistic principles, and thereby comes very near holding up to ridicule Him who is God blessed for evermore.[2]

An equally serious fault in this type of reasoning is that it begs the question of the extent and effects of the Deluge. It assumes, for example, that climatic zones were exactly the same before the Flood as they are now, that animals inhabited the same areas of the world as they do now, and that the geography and topography of the earth continued unchanged. But on the assumption of a universal Deluge, all these conditions would have been profoundly altered.[3] Arctic and desert zones may never have existed before the Flood; nor the great intercontinental barriers of high mountain ranges, impenetrable jungles, and open seas (as between Australia and Southeast Asia, and between Siberia and Alaska). On this basis, it is quite probable that animals were more widely distributed than now, with representatives

[1] Marcus Dods, *The Book of Genesis*, Vol. I of *The Expositor's Bible*, ed. W. Robertson Nicoll (4th ed.; London: Hodder and Stoughton, 1890), p. 55.

[2] J. Cynddylan Jones, *Primeval Revelation: Studies in Genesis I-VIII* (New York: American Tract Society, 1897), p. 356.

[3] See discussion of antediluvian geography and climate, pp. 121-122; 240-245; 287-293.

of each created kind of land animal living in that part of the earth
where Noah was building the Ark.

The Capacity of the Ark

Another aspect of this problem is the capacity of the Ark for
carrying two of every kind of land animal and seven of every "clean
beast" (Gen. 7:2-3).[1] Realizing full well that the Ark was a gigantic
structure, advocates of a local Flood have had to resort to various
methods of "multiplying the species" in order to make it impossible
for any ark, however large, to carry two of each kind. One method
has been to take the phrase "seven and seven" (Gen. 7:2-3) to mean
fourteen, instead of "by sevens," and to classify all the birds of the
heavens as "clean." Jan Lever, Professor of Zoology at the Free University of Amsterdam, has done this and comes to the conclusion that
"of the clean animals and of the birds there were seven pairs, of the
unclean one pair. There are known at present about 15,000 species of
birds. This means that there were 210,000 birds in the ark."[2]

But even assuming that there *were* 15,000 different species of birds
in the days of Noah,[3] Dr. Lever has put 180,000 too many birds into
the Ark! The Hebrew phrase "seven and seven" no more means
fourteen than does the parallel phrase "two and two" (Gen. 7:9,15)
mean four! Furthermore, the context demands that the birds were
to be classified into "clean" and "unclean" just like the other animals. Leupold explains:

> The Hebrew expression "take seven seven" means "seven each" (Koe-
> nig's *Syntax* 85; 316b; Gesenius' *Grammatik* rev. by Kautzsch 134q). He-
> brew parallels support this explanation. In any case, it would be a most
> clumsy method of trying to say "fourteen." Three pairs and one super-
> numerary make the "seven." As has often been suggested, the super-
> numerary beast was the one Noah could conveniently offer for sacrifice
> after the termination of the Flood. In verse 3 the idea of "the birds of the
> heavens" must, of course, be supplemented by the adjective "clean," ac-
> cording to the principle laid down in verse 2. The birds are separately

---

[1] See above, pp. 12-13, for discussion of which animals were to be included in
the Ark.

[2] Jan Lever, *Creation and Evolution* (Grand Rapids: Grand Rapids International
Publications, 1958), p. 17.

[3] But see Mayr's tabulation, below, p. 68, listing only 8,600 species of birds.

mentioned so that Noah might not be left to his own devices in fixing the limits of what verse 2 included.[1]

Another common method of "multiplying the species" has been to identify the "species" of modern taxonomy with the "kinds" of Genesis. John Pye Smith seemed to find much delight in pointing out that the Ark was too small for such a cargo, for "the innumerable millions upon millions of animalcules must be provided for; for they have all their appropriate and diversified places and circumstances of existence."[2]

But a hundred years of further study in the science of zoology has brought to light some interesting facts concerning the amazing potentialities for diversification which the Creator has placed within the Genesis kinds. These "kinds" have never evolved or merged into each other by crossing over the divinely-established lines of demarcation;[3] but they have been diversified into so many varieties and subvarieties (like the races and families of humanity) that even the greatest taxonomists have been staggered at the task of enumerating and classifying them.[4]

Frank Lewis Marsh has prepared a diagram (see Fig. 4) to illustrate his conception of how some of the typical *baramins* (from *bara*—"created," and *min*—"kind") might have become diversified before and after the Flood. He points out that over 500 varieties of the sweet pea have been developed from a single type since the year 1700; and that over 200 distinct varieties of dogs, as different from each other as the dachshund and the collie, have developed from a very few wild dogs. In further discussing the matter, Dr. Marsh writes:

In the field of zoology a very good illustration of descent with variation is furnished by the domestic pigeon. The diversity in form and temperament to be found among strains of pigeons would stagger our belief in their com-

[1] Leupold, *op. cit.*, p. 290. Birds are specifically divided into "clean" and "unclean" kinds in Leviticus 11, along with the other animals.

[2] John Pye Smith, *op. cit.*, p. 144.

[3] Robert E. D. Clark has recently concluded: "Every theory of evolution has failed in the light of modern discovery and, not merely failed, but failed so dismally that it seems almost impossible to go on believing in evolution!" *Darwin: Before and After* (Grand Rapids: Grand Rapids International Publication, 1958), p. 145.

[4] See Theodosius Dobzhansky, *Genetics and the Origin of Species* (3rd ed.; New York: Columbia University Press, 1951), pp. 3-10.

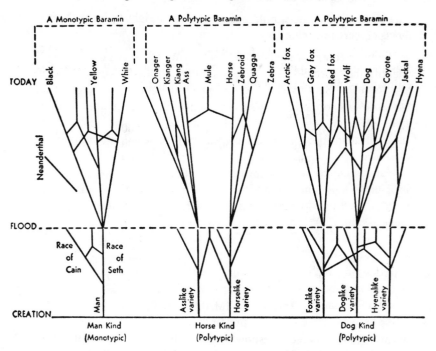

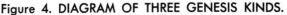

Figure 4. DIAGRAM OF THREE GENESIS KINDS.

(From Frank L. Marsh, *Evolution, Creation, and Science*, p. 179.

mon origin if we did not know that they have all been developed from the wild rock pigeon of European coasts, *Columbia livia*. It is extremely interesting to see the variations from the ancestral form which are exhibited in such strains as the pouter, the leghorn runt, the fantail, the tumbler, the owl, the turbit, the swallow, the carrier, the nun, the jacobin, and the homer. Different "species" names and possibly even different "generic" names would certainly be assigned to some of these if it were not known that they are merely strains of a common stock.[1]

It is unwarranted to insist that all the present species, not to mention all the varieties and sub-varieties of animals in the world today, were represented in the Ark. Nevertheless, as a gigantic barge, with a volume of 1,396,000 cubic feet (assuming one cubit = 17.5 inches), the Ark had a carrying capacity equal to that of 522 standard stock

[1] Frank L. Marsh, *Evolution, Creation, and Science* (Washington: Review and Herald Pub. Assoc., 1947), pp. 29, 351.

cars as used by modern railroads or of eight freight trains with sixty-five such cars in each![1]

Ernst Mayr, probably the leading American systematic taxonomist, lists the following numbers for animal species according to the best estimates of modern taxonomy:[2]

Mammals	3,500
Birds	8,600
Reptiles & Amphibians	5,500
Fishes	18,000
Tunicates, etc.	1,700
Echinoderms	4,700
Arthropods	815,000
Mollusks	88,000
Worms, etc.	25,000
Coelenterates, etc.	10,000
Sponges	5,000
Protozoans	15,000
TOTAL ANIMALS	1,000,000

In the light of this recent estimate, one wonders about "the innumerable millions upon millions of animalcules" which Pye Smith insisted the Ark had to carry, especially when we consider that of this total there was no need for Noah to make any provision for *fishes* (18,000 "species"), *tunicates* (marine chordates like sea squirts—1,700), *echinoderms* (marine creatures like starfishes and sea urchins—4,700), *mollusks* (mussels, clams, oysters, etc.—88,000), *coelenterates* (corals, sea anemones, jelly fishes, hydroids—10,000), *sponges* (5,000), or *protozoans* (microscopic, single-celled creatures, mostly marine—15,000). This eliminates 142,000 "species" of marine creatures. In addition, some *mammals* are aquatic (whales, seals, porpoises, etc.); the *amphibians* need not all have been included; a large number of the *arthropods* (815,000 "species"), such as lobsters, shrimps, crabs, water fleas, and barnacles, are marine creatures, and the insect "species" among arthropoda are usually very small; and

---

[1] Lionel S. Marks, ed., *Mechanical Engineers' Handbook* (New York: McGraw-Hill Book Co., Inc., 1958, p. 11:35), states that the standard stock car contains 2670 cu. ft. effective capacity. Also see the *"Car Builders' Cyclopedia of American Practice,"* Simmons-Boardman Pub. Co., 1949-51, p. 121.

[2] Cited in Dobzhansky, *op. cit.*, p. 7.

many of the 25,000 "species" of *worms,* as well as many of the insects, could have survived outside of the Ark. When we consider further that Noah was not required to take the largest or even adult specimens of each "kind" and that comparatively few were classified as "clean" birds and beasts, the problem vanishes. Jan Lever completely misses the mark when he states that "the lowest estimate of the number of animals in the ark then would be fully 2,500,000."[1]

For all practical purposes, one could say that, at the outside, there was need for no more than 35,000 individual vertebrate animals on the Ark. The total number of so-called species of mammals, birds, reptiles and amphibians listed by Mayr is 17,600, but undoubtedly the number of original "kinds" was less than this. Assuming the average size of these animals to be about that of a sheep (there are only a very few really large animals, of course, and even these could have been represented on the Ark by young ones), the following will give an idea of the accommodations available:

> The number of animals per car varies greatly, depending on the size and age of the animals. . . . . Reports of stock cars and railroads show that the average number of meat animals to the carload is for cattle about 25, hogs in single deck cars about 75, and sheep about 120 per deck.[2]

This means that at least 240 animals of the size of sheep could be accommodated in a standard two-decked stock car. Two trains hauling 73 such cars each would thus be ample to carry the 35,000 animals.[3] We have already seen that the Ark had a carrying capacity equivalent to that of 522 stock cars of this size! We therefore find that a few simple calculations dispose of this trivial objection once and for all.

With respect to the survival of plants through the Flood, we have this comment from Walter E. Lammerts, consultant in the Horticultural Research Division of Germain's, Inc.:

[1] Lever, *op. cit.,* p. 17.

[2] H. W. Vaughan: *Types and Market Classes of Live Stock* (Columbus, Ohio: College Book Co., 1945) p. 85.

[3] Lest anyone be concerned about the space occupied by the insects, worms, and similar small creatures, let it be noted that, if the space occupied by each individual averaged 2 inches on the side, only 21 more cars of this size would suffice for over a million individuals. Extinct animals such as the dinosaurs may also have been represented on the Ark, probably by very young animals, only to die out because of hostile environmental conditions after the Flood; it seems more likely, however, that animals of this sort were not taken on the Ark at all, for the very reason of their intended extinction.

I am convinced that many thousands of plants survived either as floating vegetation rafts or by chance burial near enough to the surface of the ground for asexual sprouting of new shoots. I am, of course, aware that objections could be raised on the idea that long exposure to salt water would be so harmful to any vegetation as to either kill it or so reduce its vitality as to make root and new shoot formation impossible. However, I see no reason at all to postulate that the salt content of the ocean at the time of the flood was as high as it is now. In fact, on the basis of the canopy theory, we would most certainly expect that the salt content of the ocean before the flood would be diluted, perhaps by one-half. Naturally, during the first few hundred years after the flood the salt content of the ocean would again be rather rapidly raised because of the much above normal drainage of the land surface.[1]

Marsh further suggests that:

There was doubtless a considerable number of plants which were carried through the Flood in the form of seeds which composed a portion of the large store of food cached in the ark. But most of the vegetation sprang up here and there wherever the propagules were able to survive the Flood.[2]

Caring for the Animals in the Ark

Granting, then, that the Ark was large enough to carry two of every kind of land animal, how could Noah and his family have cared for them during the year of the Flood? Ramm fears that "the task of carrying away the manure, and bringing food would completely overtax the few people in the ark," and quotes F. H. Woods in the *Hastings Encyclopedia of Religion and Ethics* to the effect that not even the most skilled modern zoologists could have coped with such a task.[3] Arthur Custance multiplies the difficulties even more:

Many commentators have calculated the size of the Ark and the total number of species in the world, and spoken freely of its capacity to carry them. What they do not always remember is that such animals need attention and food, the carnivorous ones, if they existed as such, requiring meat which would have to be stored up for one whole year. In any case, a sufficient supply of water for drinking would probably have to be taken on board since the mingling of the waters in a worldwide Flood would presumably render it unfit to drink . . . It is rather difficult to visualize a

[1] Letter from W. E. Lammerts, Livermore, Calif., Nov. 27, '57.
[2] Marsh, *op. cit.*, p. 213.
[3] Ramm, *op. cit.*, p. 246.

Flood of worldwide proportions but with so little turbulence that four men (perhaps helped by their womenfolk) were able to care for such a flock. It would take very little unsteadiness to make the larger animals almost unmanageable. It becomes even more difficult to conceive how proper provision could have been made for many animals which spend much of their time in the water, such as crocodiles, seals, and so forth.[1]

Since the Bible does not give us details on these points, we are of course unable to speak dogmatically as to the methods which were used in caring for the animals. We suggest the reasonable possibility, however, that the mysterious and remarkable factor of animal physiology known as *hibernation* may have been involved. There are various types of dormancy in animals, with many different types of physiologic and metabolic responses, but it is still an important and widespread mechanism in the animal kingdom for surviving periods of climatic adversity.

Hibernation and estivation occur in every group of vertebrates save birds, and its pre-disposing causes, immediate and remote, are by no means uniform.[2]

Hibernation is usually associated with "winter sleep," estivation with escape from summer heat and drought. Other factors also apparently are often involved, such as food shortage, carbon dioxide in the environment, and accumulation of fat. Practically all reptiles and amphibians have the capacity of hibernation. Mammals, being warm-blooded, do not have as great a need for it, and so at present, relatively few practice it. Nevertheless, it is probable that the latent ability to do so is present in practically all mammals.

The zoological dispersion of hibernation among mammals is not especially illuminating, since closely allied forms may differ radically in this

---

[1] Custance, *op. cit.*, pp. 19-20. May we suggest at least that Noah may have obtained drinking water from the rain that fell? Custance imagines another difficulty when he says that the "rarified atmosphere" at elevations above that of Mount Everest, if the Flood covered the mountains, would "render all but a few creatures insensible in a very few moments for lack of oxygen" (*op. cit.*, p. 9). He particularly expresses concern about Noah and his sons having to climb between the ark's three decks at such high elevations! He of course has overlooked the elementary fact that atmospheric pressure depends on elevation *relative to sea level*. The air column above the raised sea level during the Flood was just as high, and the resulting sea level atmospheric pressure just as great, as the present sea level pressure.

[2] W. P. Pycraft: "Hibernation," article in *Encyclopedia Britannica*, 1956, Volume 11, p. 539.

respect. Hibernation is reported for the orders Monotremata, Marsupiala, Insectivora, Chiroptera, Rodentia, and Carnivora.[1]

Similarly, many of the invertebrates hibernate in some fashion for long periods. Although it is sometimes said that birds do not hibernate, it is now known that at least one bird, the poor-will, does so, and the humming-bird also exhibits nightly many of the characteristics of hibernation,[2] so that fundamentally it can be said that birds also possess the latent capacity of hibernation. Apparently, the reason more of them do not practice it is that their power of flight makes long migrations a more effective means of coping with adverse weather and other conditions.

It is well known that many species of birds migrate thousands of miles, with unerring accuracy, between their summer and winter homes. It is not so well known, but is true, that many kinds of mammals also migrate long distances to escape unfavorable weather. The homing instinct also seems strongly developed in many mammals. Both for birds and mammals, however, the mechanism of the migratory instinct is one of the greatest unsolved puzzles in biology.

We know, therefore, something of the facts about the migration of some mammals, but the means whereby migration is carried out still remain completely unknown; many theories have been tried, but none of them has been capable of experimental proof. It is all very puzzling; as far as we know, the bodies of the other mammals are essentially similar to our own, and we flatter ourselves that our brains are more highly developed. And yet these animals that we classify as lower than ourselves can do something, and presumably with their brains too, that we cannot; something so far outside our own experience and abilities that we cannot even conceive how they do it.[3]

Similarly, the phenomena of hibernation and estivation are still not understood. Two of the most active researchers on the subject, professors at Harvard University, say:

Mammalian hibernation interested many of the earlier zoologists, and

[1] W. C. Alee, A. E. Emerson, Orlando Park, Thomas Park, and K. P. Schmidt: *Principles of Animal Ecology* (Philadelphia: W. B. Saunders Co., 1949) p. 106.

[2] L. H. Matthews: "The Hibernation of Mammals," 1955 Report of the Smithsonian Institution, 1956, pp. 410-11.

[3] L. H. Matthews: "The Migration of Mammals," 1954 Report of the Smithsonian Institution, 1955, p. 284.

sporadic research on the subject has been going on for at least 100 years. Yet the fundamental causes of the condition are still a mystery.[1]

Another authority, Marston Bates, of the Rockefeller Foundation, says:

> Our knowledge of this mechanism is very incomplete, perhaps because it represents a field on the border line between physiology and ecology and is consequently neglected by both sciences. Various theories have been proposed to account for hibernation, and it seems likely that the controlling stimuli may vary with different animals.[2]

And still more recently, a prominent evolutionist, Joseph Wood Krutch, in a popular account of the most recent thinking on the subject, says:

> Evolution gives part of the answer when it stresses "adaptation." But why, in a given instance, this adaptation rather than another? It can hardly be just to make the world more interesting. But that is exactly what it does.[3]

It appears, therefore, that the animal world has two powerful means for coping with unfavorable environmental conditions, hibernation and migration. It is likely that all animals possess these powers in latent form, some of them still in active form. And thus far, at least, science has been utterly unable to explain them, in spite of their great importance in animal physiology and ecology.

It was pointed out that an organism has but three choices available when exposed to adversity: it may die, adjust or migrate. Hibernation and estivation are broad adjustments to adverse weather or climate. Migration or emigration are still different ways of avoiding unfavorable conditions.[4]

We suggest that these remarkable abilities of animals were unusually intensified during the Deluge period. In fact, it may well have been at this time that these powers were first imparted to the animals by God. It seems rather likely that climatic conditions before the Flood were so equable that these particular abilities were not needed then. Perhaps it is significant that, after the Flood, God's pro-

---

[1] C. P. Lyman and P. O. Chatfield: "Hibernation," *Scientific American,* Dec. 1950, p. 19.

[2] Marston Bates: "Hibernation," article in *Collier's Encyclopedia,* 1956, Vol. 7, p. 11.

[3] J. W. Krutch: "Now the Animal World Goes to Sleep," *New York Times Magazine,* Jan. 4, 1959.

[4] W. C. Allee, et al., *op. cit.,* p. 539.

nouncement that "cold and heat, and summer and winter" (Gen.
8:22) would henceforth come in regular cycles is immediately followed by statements concerning the animals that seem to imply
changes in animal natures and relationships to mankind (Gen. 9:2-5).
Even as God instructed Noah, by specific revelation, concerning
the coming Flood and his means of escape from it, so He instructed
certain of the animals, through impartation of a migratory directional
instinct which would afterward be inherited in greater or less degree
by their descendants, to flee from their native habitats to the place of
safety. Then, having entered the Ark, they also received from God
the power to become more or less dormant, in various ways, in order
to be able to survive for the year in which they were to be confined
within the Ark while the great storms and convulsions raged outside.

Hibernation is generally defined as a specific physiological state in an
animal in which normal functions are suspended or greatly retarded, enabling the animal to endure long periods of complete inactivity.[1]

This ability has also been inherited, in greater or less degree, by the
descendants of those animals that, in the Ark, survived the Flood.

The mechanistic scientist, of course, will deride these suggestions
with the epithet of "supernaturalistic." Exactly so! The Bible plainly
says that God directed the animals to come to Noah, not Noah to go
in search of the animals (Gen. 6:20, 7:9, 15). It also indicates that
God continued to keep special watch over the occupants of the Ark
during the Flood (Gen. 8:1).

But if the uniformitarian decries our ascription of the migration
of the animals to the Ark and their dormancy in the Ark to powers
imparted to them by God, let him offer a better explanation of these
same powers even as they exist today! As we have seen, no explanation has yet been forthcoming, and one might even be justified in saying that the marvelous migratory instinct and the equally remarkable
power of hibernation can only be explained teleologically.

We do not deny, of course, that some truly physiological explanation of these capacities may some day be developed, although none is
in sight as yet, but even this would only constitute a description of
that which God Himself originally endowed. Again we say that we do
not really *know* how all this was accomplished, since the Bible is

[1] Marston Bates, *op. cit.,* p. 11.

silent on these matters, but this is a very possible and plausible explanation, so that there is no longer any justification for the critic to profess incredulity about the animals on the Ark!

The "Natural-Supernatural" Philosophy of Miracles

But strange as it may seem, evangelical defenders of the limited-Flood concept have sought to win the victory in this controversy by denying us the right to appeal to God's overruling power in the events related to the Flood catastrophe! Notice carefully, for example, the line of reasoning which is involved here:

One point must be clearly understood before we commence these criticisms: *the flood is recorded as a natural-supernatural occurrence*. It does not appear *as a pure and stupendous* miracle. The natural and supernatural work side by side and hand in hand. If one wishes to retain a universal flood, it must be understood that a series of stupendous miracles are required. Further, one cannot beg off with pious statements that God can do anything.

. . . .

Rehwinkel constantly solves his difficulties by recourse to the miraculous or to the sheer omnipotence of God. With this type of argumentation any theory, no matter how feeble, can be *ad hoc* patched up.

. . . .

There is no question what Omnipotence can do, but the simplicity [?] of the flood record prohibits the endless supplying of miracles to make a universal flood feasible.[1]

Since this type of objection is very common in discussions concerning the magnitude of the Deluge, we must stop to examine it before proceeding to our next section. Our first criticism of this attitude is that it fails to take into account the fact that the Word of God makes ample provision for miraculous elements in connection with the gathering and keeping of the animals. For example, God told Noah that "two of every sort *shall come unto thee*" (6:20); and then we read that *"they went in unto Noah into the ark,* two and two of all flesh, wherein is the breath of life" (7:15), and finally that *"Jehovah shut him in"* (7:16).

Furthermore, we must not underestimate the implications of 8:1, "God *remembered* Noah, and all the beasts, and all the cattle that

[1] Ramm, *op. cit.*, pp. 243, 244, 247. Italics are his.

were with him in the ark." This statement refers to a time when the waters were still at their height and the fountains of the deep had not yet been stopped (8:2). It is important to realize that the word "remember" (*zākar*) in this context does not imply that God had forgotten the Ark and its occupants during the first five months of the Flood! According to Hebrew usage, the primary meaning of *zakar* is "granting requests, protecting, delivering," when God is the subject and persons are the object.[1]

But the inconsistency of these who teach a limited Flood becomes more evident when we discover that they, too, must acknowledge God's special control over the animals at the time of the Flood. Thus, we find Ramm saying that the animals which came to Noah were "prompted by a divine instinct."[2] But once we grant God's power in bringing the animals *to* the Ark, we have no right to deny His power over the animals while they were *in* the Ark. The simple fact of the matter is that one cannot have *any* kind of a Genesis Flood without acknowledging the presence of supernatural elements.[3]

On the other hand, the writers do not find it necessary to indulge in an "endless supplying of miracles to make a universal flood feasible." That God intervened in a supernatural way to gather the animals into the Ark and to keep them under control during the year of the Flood is explicitly stated in the text of Scripture. Furthermore, it is obvious that the opening of the "windows of heaven" in order to allow "the waters which were above the firmament" to fall upon the earth, and the breaking up of "all the fountains of the great deep" were supernatural acts of God.

But throughout the entire process, "the waters which were above the firmament" and "the waters which were under the firmament" *acted according to the known laws of hydrostatics and hydrodynamics*. They churned up, carried away, and deposited sediments ac-

---

[1] Brown, Driver, and Briggs, *A Hebrew and English Lexicon of the Old Testament*, p. 270. Cited by Leupold, *op. cit.,* p. 308.

[2] Ramm, *op. cit.,* p. 249. Jamieson also (*op. cit.,* p. 95) concludes that "they must have been prompted by an overruling Divine direction, as it is impossible, on any other principles, to account for their going in *pairs.*"

[3] This statement finds full support in Psalm 29:10, which definitely speaks of the Noahic Deluge (*mabbûl*): "Jehovah sat as King at the Flood; yea, Jehovah sitteth as King for ever." The entire Psalm emphasizes the *omnipotence* of God and is climaxed by this reference to His greatest manifestation of omnipotence. J. P. Lange notes that "the history of the Flood is an *hapax legomenon* in the world's history, analogous to the creation of Adam, the birth and history of Christ, and the future history of the world's end." *Op. cit.,* p. 295.

cording to natural hydraulic processes, moving at velocities and in directions that were perfectly normal under such conditions. To be sure, the sudden and powerful upsetting of the delicate balances of antediluvian nature brought into play hitherto unknown tectonic and aqueous movements while new sets of balances and adjustments were being achieved. But such adjustments must be described as natural and not supernatural.[1]

An example of the basic misconceptions underlying this entire controversy is the assertion on the part of Dr. Ramm that a universal flood would necessitate "a great creation of water" because "all the waters of the heavens, poured all over the earth, would amount to a sheath seven inches thick" and "to cover the highest mountains would require eight times more water than we now have."[2] For such an objection to be valid we would have to assume that there were no waters "above the firmament" before the Flood, and that the earth's topography was unaltered by the Flood. In other words, we would be assuming the truth of uniformitarianism in order to prove the impossibility of catastrophism! But if we accept the Biblical testimony concerning an antediluvian canopy of waters (Gen. 1:6-8, 7:11, 8:2, II Peter 3:5-7), we have an adequate source for the waters of a universal Flood. Furthermore, such passages as Genesis 8:3 and Psalm 104:6-9 suggest that ocean basins were deepened after the Flood to provide adequate storage space for the additional waters that had been "above the firmament" from the second day of creation to the time of the Flood, while mountain ranges rose to heights never attained during the antediluvian era.[3]

It is a mistake, therefore, to assume that the concept of a universal Flood involves "an endless supplying of miracles." A few Biblical analogies may be helpful at this point. When the Israelites crossed the Red Sea and the Jordan, God held back the waters supernaturally in both cases.[4] But once His hand was released, the waters hurried back

---

[1] We read in Genesis 8:1 that "God made a wind to pass over the earth, and the waters assuaged." Judging from the effects produced (see below, note #4), it seems that this must have been more than a merely natural wind. Leupold, *op. cit.*, pp. 309-310, states: "We are sure, as an element of the miraculous entered into the matter of the coming of the Flood, so a similar element contributed to its abatement." But see the discussion below, pp. 266-269, for the non-miraculous aspects of the post-Deluge winds and their possible effects.

[2] Ramm, *op. cit.*, p. 244.

[3] See below, pp. 121-122, 266-271, for further discussions of this important point from the scientific standpoint.

[4] The "strong east wind" of Exodus 14:21 could hardly have been a merely natural

to their appointed bounds in accordance with the normal laws of gravity. Likewise, the stones in the walls of Jericho fell to the ground by gravitational force; but it was evidently the unseen hand of God that first shook the foundations.

We may agree with Dr. Ramm that the Flood was "a natural and supernatural occurrence," with "the natural and the supernatural working side by side and hand in hand." But how this militates against its universality we fail to see. One cannot help but suspect that the real thrust of Dr. Ramm's objection lies at a deeper level than that of a mere demand for "natural" as well as "supernatural" elements in the Flood. What he really seems to be demanding is a removal of anything in the Flood narrative that might offend modern uniformitarian geologists. In other words, God is permitted to intervene supernaturally for the purpose of destroying some godless men; but in this supernatural intervention, He is not permitted to go so far as to upset the general processes of nature as we know them today!

If this be the underlying motivation of Dr. Ramm's "natural-supernatural" argument, he is not only completely at variance with the Biblical testimony concerning the Flood, but also may be accused of inconsistency in his approach to the problem of Biblical miracles in general. For in the case of Jonah's being swallowed by the great fish Dr. Ramm clearly "solves his difficulties by recourse to the miraculous or to the sheer omnipotence of God," as he accuses Rehwinkel of doing in connection with the Flood. In speaking of Jonah and the fish, Ramm states:

> The record clearly calls the creature a *prepared fish* and if this means a special creature for a special purpose we need not search our books on sea creatures to find out the most likely possibility. *It would be a creature created by God especially for this purpose, and that is where our investigation ends.* The evangelical accepts a supernatural theism, and the centrality of redemption and moral values. The necessity of getting the message of redemption to Nineveh *is sufficient rationale for God to have made such a creature.*[1]

wind, for it must have blown in opposite directions at the same time to make the waters "a wall unto them on their right hand, and on their left" (Ex. 14:22, 29; cf. 15:8 and Psa. 78:13), and yet not hinder the people as they walked. And it is important to note that the Jordan waters were stopped at flood-time (Joshua 3:15). It is most unlikely that blockage by a mere landslide upstream could have done this.

[1] Ramm, *op. cit.*, p. 297. Italics are ours. We agree with Ramm's analysis of this problem but wonder how it would impress uniformitarian biologists. The fact of the matter is that consistent uniformitarianism can allow for *no* Biblical miracles whatever.

Now if getting Jonah to Nineveh to preach the message of redemption was "sufficient rationale" for God to create a special fish, then what right do we have to question God's "rationale" in bringing into operation forces of destruction and providence never before seen by man, for the purpose of wiping out a hopelessly corrupt race and preserving the Messianic line through Noah? Since God's *thoughts* (or "rationale") and God's *ways* (including miracles) are higher than ours, even the employment of a universal Deluge and an ark to accomplish these purposes could have been wholly in accord with the mind of God, even though they might cause offense to the mind of modern man.

It must be recognized, then, that the efforts which some evangelical Christians have exerted to write off the universality of the Flood by appealing to supposed *a priori* principles of divine methodology in the performing of miracles, stand condemned by the testimony of the Word of God itself. Whether or not such a concept can be adjusted harmoniously into one's theological or philosophical presuppositions, it happens to be true nonetheless that the Flood was an utterly unique and never-to-be-repeated phenomenon, a year-long demonstration of the omnipotence of a righteous God which mankind has never been permitted to forget, and a crisis in earth-history that is comparable in Scripture only to the creation and to the final renovation of the earth by fire at the end of the age. It is because the Bible itself teaches us these things that we are fully justified in appealing to *the power of God,* whether or not He used means amenable to our scientific understanding, for the gathering of two of every kind of animal into the Ark and for the care and preservation of those animals in the Ark during the 371 days of the Flood.

POSTDILUVIAN ANIMAL DISTRIBUTION

A problem which is closely related to the one just discussed, and yet one which demands separate attention, is that of animal distribution throughout the earth since the time of the Flood. If the Flood was geographically universal, then all the air-breathers of the animal kingdom which were not in the Ark perished; and present-day animal distribution must be explained on the basis of migrations from the mountains of Ararat.

In order to have this problem set clearly before us, we shall mention here just two groups of animals, the *edentates* and the *marsupials*. The edentates are slow-moving, nearly toothless animals, some of which are to be found in the jungles of South America (tree sloths, armadillos, and anteaters). How could they have travelled so far from the Near East? The marsupials, or pouched-mammals, are found only in Australia and the Western Hemisphere. How is this peculiarity of animal distribution to be explained?

Three Major Views

There are three generally accepted views as to how such animal distribution came about. First, we have the evangelical advocates of a local Flood, who claim that most of these animals were probably created in the ecological niches where they are now found. Secondly, we have the advocates of a universal Flood, who believe that these animals must have reached their present locations by waves of migration during the centuries that followed the Flood.[1] And thirdly, we have the evolutionary school of modern science, which explains such distribution on the basis of gradual processes of migration over millions of years, together with the evolution of totally new kinds of animals in geographically isolated areas.

An unusual feature of this division of opinion is that, in certain respects, most advocates of a universal Flood join the evolutionists in contending for the migration of animals from distant areas, as opposed to the theory of a special creation of animals in their *present* (postdiluvian) ecological zones. Both the evolutionist and the universal Flood advocate claim that inter-continental land bridges have aided animals in their migratory movements across the face of the earth. There are, however, two important differences between these two schools of thought: (1) the evolutionist allows for millions of years, rather than merely thousands, for the present distribution of animals, and (2) the evolutionist allows for the development of different *kinds* of animals instead of holding to the fixity of kinds throughout the entire period of animal distribution.

The controversy increases in complexity when we find local-Flood

---

[1] Another possible theory is that the animals were re-created after the Flood, in their present ecological niches. This has been advocated by D. J. Whitney, who is also a strenuous proponent of the Universal Flood. However, this expedient would eliminate the need of an ark to preserve the animals through the Flood, and of course is not suggested in the Biblical account.

advocates appealing to the evolutionary time-scale to emphasize the impossibility of a universal distribution of animals since the Flood. They are willing to use inter-continental land bridges to explain the distribution of some animals but claim that others, such as the edentates of South America and the marsupials of Australia, were created in the continents where we now find them.

One evangelical scientist of the local-Flood persuasion who has written on this problem is Russell L. Mixter, Professor of Zoology at Wheaton College. In his discussion of the kangaroo, Mixter writes:

> If kangaroos were in the ark and first touched land in Asia, one would expect fossils of them in Asia. According to Romer, the only place where there are either fossil or living kangaroos is in Australia. What shall we conclude? If the fossil evidence means that there never have been kangaroos in Asia, then kangaroos were not in the ark or if they were, they hurried from Australia to meet Noah, and as rapidly returned to their native land. Is it not easier to believe that they were never in the ark, and hence were in an area untouched by the flood, and that the flood occurred only in the area inhabited by man?[1]

Since arguments of this type, based upon problems of zoogeography, have been considered by many evangelicals to be conclusive, we must examine them at some length. It should be observed at the outset, however, that our purpose cannot be to *prove* that all modern animals have migrated from the Near East; for little is known about the movements of animals in the past from either science or Scripture. It is necessary to show only that a general migration of animals from the Near East since the Flood is reasonable and possible.

Australian Marsupials

The marsupials of Australia consist of very distinct types which find their parallels among the placental animals. For example, there are marsupial *moles,* marsupial *anteaters,* marsupial *mice,* marsupial *squirrels* (flying phalangers), marsupial *sloths* (koalas), marsupial *gophers* (wombats), marsupial *cats* (dasyures), marsupial *wolves* (thylacines), marsupial *monkeys,* marsupial *badgers* (Tasmanian devils), strange *lizard-like* marsupials called bandicoots, and the *rabbit-like* kangaroos and wallabies. In addition, Australia boasts the

---

[1] Russell L. Mixter, *Creation and Evolution* (American Scientific Affiliation, Monograph Two, 1950), p. 15.

only monotremes (egg-laying mammals) in the world: the duck-billed platypus and the spiny anteater.[1]

On the assumption that the animals of the present world trace their ancestry back to those within the Ark, how can we explain the facts that these marsupials and monotremes are found nowhere in the world except in Australia and that the placentals never succeeded in reaching that sub-continent?[2] John W. Klotz, Professor of Natural History at Concordia Senior College, suggests:

> It may be that these forms have become extinct in Asia and along the Malay Peninsula. Possibly they were able to live in some of these areas for only a very short time and travelled almost immediately to those places included in their present range. The evolutionary scheme itself requires that animals have become extinct in many areas in which they once lived.[3]

A. Franklin Shull, Professor of Zoology at the University of Michigan, has touched upon a very plausible solution to this problem:

> The marsupials spread over the world, in all directions. They could not go far to the north before striking impossible climate, but the path south was open all the way to the tips of Africa and South America and through Australia . . . The placental mammals proved to be superior to the marsupials in the struggle for existence and drove the marsupials out . . . that is, forced them southward. Australia was then connected by land with Asia, so that it could receive the fugitives . . . Behind them the true mammals were coming; but before the latter reached Australia, that continent was separated from Asia, and the primitive types to the south were protected from further competition.[4]

Since fossil marsupials have been found in Europe, as well as in Australia and the Western Hemisphere, it seems evident that they have migrated rather widely in the past. Mixter quotes A. M. Davies as saying that "they probably reached Europe from North America, but whether they originated in the Northern or Southern Hemisphere,

---

[1] M. W. de Laubenfels, *Life Science* (4th ed.; New York: Prentice Hall, Inc., 1949), p. 285; and Paul Amos Moody, *Introduction to Evolution* (New York: Harper & Brothers, 1953), pp. 242-244.

[2] The only placentals that reached Australia were bats, rats, and mice. Perhaps dingos (dogs) were introduced by aborigines.

[3] John W. Klotz, *Genes, Genesis, and Evolution* (St. Louis: Concordia Publishing House, 1955), p. 226.

[4] *Evolution* (2d ed.; New York: McGraw-Mill Book Co., Inc., 1951), p. 60. It should be noted that Shull is an evolutionist.

whether in Australia or South America is a matter for guesswork in view of the small amount of evidence."[1]

But what right does one have to map out trans-Asiatic migrations for some marsupials (from North America to Europe) in spite of a lack of fossil evidence for such animals in Asia and then insist that other marsupials could not have migrated from Asia to Australia because of a lack of fossil evidence for marsupials in Asia? Since we have such "a small amount of evidence" to explain marsupial migrations anyway, who can say that marsupials could not have migrated into Australia? The Old Testament informs us that Palestine was infested with lions for centuries (Judges 14:5, I Sam. 17:34, II Sam. 23:20, I Kings 13:24, 20:36, and especially II Kings 17:25), but where is the fossil evidence for their having been in Palestine?[2] It is a well-known fact that animals leave fossil remains only under rare and special conditions. Therefore, the lack of fossil evidence for marsupials in southern Asia cannot be used as proof that they have never been in that region of the world.[3]

Dr. Mixter certainly has no warrant for his assertion that if kangaroos were in the Ark, "they hurried from Australia to meet Noah, and as rapidly returned to their native land." The universal Flood concept by no means involves such absurdities. In the first place, no one can prove that the Ark was built in the same region of the world as that in which it landed.[4] As a matter of fact, if the Flood was universal, antediluvian geography may well have been different from that of the present earth. In the second place, no one can prove that kangaroos and the other Australian marsupials were confined to Australia *before* the Flood.[5] And if not, then none of the chosen pairs

[1] Mixter, *op. cit.,* p. 17.

[2] In a personal communication dated April 20, 1959, Nelson Glueck, Palestinian archaeologist, states: "I do not believe that any fossils of lions have ever been found in Palestine, although the fossils of elephants and other animals have been discovered."

[3] An even more familiar example is that of the American bison or buffalo. "The buffalo carcasses strewn over the plains in uncounted millions two generations ago have left hardly a present trace. The flesh was devoured by wolves or vultures within hours or days after death, and even the skeletons have now largely disappeared, the bones dissolving and crumbling into dust under the attack of the weather." Carl O. Dunbar, *Historical Geology* (New York, Wiley, 1949), p. 39.

[4] The fact that Genesis 2:14 mentions the Tigris (Hiddekel) and the Euphrates rivers is certainly not conclusive evidence to the contrary, for these and other geographical names could have been perpetuated by Noah's family into "the new world" even as happens in modern times.

[5] Since no fossil kangaroos have been found in Australia earlier than the Pleistocene, no one can prove that any of them are antediluvian. See Alfred S. Romer,

of marsupials would have had to "hurry" to get to the Ark during the 120 years that it was under construction. In the third place, it is not necessary to suppose that the very same pair of kangaroos that were in the Ark had to travel all the way to Australia after the Ark landed in the mountains of Ararat. Frank Lewis Marsh has made some helpful observations in this connection:

> The journeys from the mountains of Ararat to their present habitats were made in an intermittent fashion, each generation sending representatives a little farther from the original home. The presence of tapirs today only in South America and the Malayan islands, opposite sides of the earth, is indicative of the fact that animals migrated in more than one direction. The creationist holds that there is no reason for believing that this distribution of animals was accomplished by any other processes than those employed in distribution today . . . Increase in number of individuals of any one kind causes a necessity for spreading outward toward the horizon in search of food and homes . . . Their arrival in new areas may be a result of deliberate individual endeavor or it may be that they arrive as wave-tossed survivors of some coastal accident.[1]

Rapid Animal Dispersion

Furthermore, it is quite unnecessary to assume that hundreds, or even scores, of thousands of years were required for animals to attain their present geographical distribution. In fact, there is some evidence available to show that animals could have reached their present habitats with astonishing speed, crossing vast continents and even wide stretches of open sea on their way. In the year 1883, the island of Krakatoa in the Sunda Strait, betweeen Java and Sumatra, was almost destroyed by a volcanic explosion that shook that entire part of the world. For twenty-five years practically nothing lived in the remnant of that volcanic island. But "then the colonists began to arrive—a few mammals in 1908; a number of birds, lizards, and snakes; various mollusks, insects, and earthworms. Ninety percent of

Vertebrate Paleontology (2d ed.; Chicago: University of Chicago Press, 1955), p. 320, and Edwin H. Colbert, *Evolution of the Vertebrates* (New York: Wiley, 1955), p. 245. Furthermore, as we have already pointed out, the absence of kangaroo fossils in Asia does not prove that they have never been there. It must be kept in mind, throughout this entire discussion, that the question of paleontological dating methods is being held in suspension. On the hypothesis of a universal Flood, we have no assurance whatever that the fossil-bearing strata must be dated according to the uniformitarian scheme.

[1] Marsh, *op. cit.,* p. 291.

Krakatoa's new inhabitants, Dutch scientists found, were forms that could have arrived by air."[1] Professor Paul A. Moody of the University of Vermont tells how large land animals have been able to cross oceans on natural rafts and "floating islands":

> In times of flood large masses of earth and entwining vegetation, including trees, may be torn loose from the banks of rivers and swept out to sea. Sometimes such masses are encountered floating in the ocean out of sight of land, still lush and green, with palms twenty to thirty feet tall. It is entirely probable that land animals may be transported long distances in this manner. Mayr records that many tropical ocean currents have a speed of at least two knots; this would amount to fifty miles in a day, 1000 miles in three weeks.[2]

Professor Shull makes the interesting observation that "the fauna of Madagascar is most similar, not to that of its continental neighbor Africa, but to that of Asia, the gap being bridged over by the Seychelles Islands whose animals are similar to those of Madagascar."[3] But when we look at the map of the Indian Ocean, our astonishment increases, for the Seychelles Islands are 700 miles north of Madagascar, and the Asiatic mainland is another 1500 miles beyond the Seychelles! The monkey-like *lemur* is practically the only mammal found on Madagascar, so it would seem that lemurs found their way across 2,200 miles of the Indian Ocean in order to reach the island which is now their home.[4]

While it is true that even the open sea has proven to be no final barrier to the onrushing migrations of animals, we must look to the land bridges as the principal means of animal distribution around the world. Marsh summarizes the significance of these continental connections:

[1] Rachel L. Carson, *The Sea Around Us* (New York: Oxford University Press, 1951), pp. 91-92. ". . . riding on the winds, drifting on the currents, or rafting in on logs, floating brush, or trees, the plants and animals . . . arrive from the distant continents." *Ibid.,* p. 89.

[2] Moody, *op. cit.,* p. 262. Alfred S. Romer of Harvard University also states: "It seems certain that land animals do at times cross considerable bodies of water where land connections are utterly lacking . . . Floating masses of vegetation, such as are sometimes found off the mouths of the Amazon, may be one means of effecting this type of migration. Even the case of the entry of the hystricoids [porcupine-like rodents] into South America may be a case of this sort . . . and one successful crossing might populate a continent." *Op. cit.,* p. 513.

[3] Shull, *op. cit.,* p. 70.

[4] See Paul Almasy, "Madagascar: Mystery Island," *The National Geographic Magazine,* LXXXI (June, 1942), pp. 798, 802.

One glance at a world map will show that, with the exception of the narrow break at the Bering Strait, a dry-land path leads from Armenia to all lands of the globe except Australia. In the case of the latter the East Indies even today form a fairly continuous bridge of stepping-stones to that southern continent. As regards the Bering Strait, there is no doubt that a land connection once existed between Asia and North America. With the strait closed, the cold waters of the Arctic would have been prevented from coming south, and the Japan Current would have curved around the coast line farther north than today. The washing of those shores by the warm waters of this current would have produced a dry-land route that even tropical forms could have used.[1]

The more we study the fascinating story of animal distribution around the earth, the more convinced we have become that this vast river of variegated life forms, moving ever outward from the Asiatic mainland, across the continents and seas, has not been a chance and haphazard phenomenon. Instead, we see the hand of God guiding and directing these creatures in ways that man, with all his ingenuity, has never been able to fathom, in order that the great commission to the postdiluvian animal kingdom might be carried out, and "that they may breed abundantly in the earth, and be fruitful, and multiply upon the earth" (Gen. 8:17).

SUMMARY AND CONCLUSION

In this chapter we have discussed three of the most commonly used non-geological arguments against a universal Flood. The first of these was the argument based upon the limited use of universal terms. In answering this argument, we submitted three reasons for maintaining a literal interpretation of the universal terms employed in Genesis 6-9: (1) in most cases the Bible uses such terms in a literal sense; (2) the context of Genesis 6-9, including the tenor of the entire Flood narrative, demands a literal interpretation of the universal terms; and (3) the physical phenomena described in these chapters would be meaningless if the universal terms were not taken in the literal sense.

[1] Marsh, *op. cit.*, pp. 291-292. "Geological and paleontological evidence indicates that this land bridge was never glaciated. For a time, at least, much of it seems to have been open grassland . . ." Ralph Linton, "New Light on Ancient America," *The Scientific Monthly*, LXXII (May, 1951), pp. 314-315. Even more recently, David M. Hopkins has pointed out that "glaciers may have barred access to the central parts of North America and Asia, but they have never constituted a barrier to migration between eastern Siberia and central Alaska." ("Cenozoic History of the Bering Land Bridge," *Science*, Vol. 129, No. 3362 [June 5, 1959], p. 1526).

The second argument against a universal Flood was that Noah and his family could neither have gathered nor cared for the animals if two of *every* Genesis kind were to be included in the Ark. In answer, we pointed to the probable difference of climatic and zoogeographical conditions before the Flood as compared to the postdiluvian area; the tremendous capacity of the Ark; the large number of marine creatures for which no provision in the Ark need have been made; the possibility of extensive diversification within kinds since the Flood, and the possible impartation of migratory instincts and powers of hibernation to the animals by God with respect to the gathering and caring for the animals during that year of cosmic crisis.

Finally, in the argument concerning postdiluvian animal distribution, we showed why it is by no means unreasonable to assume that all land animals in the world today have descended from those which were in the Ark. In spite of the lack of evidence of marsupials having lived in Asia, it is quite conceivable that marsupials could have reached Australia by migration waves from Asia, before that continent became separated from the mainland. Comparatively little is known of the migrations of animals in the past; but what we do know indicates very clearly the possibility of rapid colonization of distant areas, even though oceans had to be crossed in the process. It would not have required many centuries even for animals like the edentates to migrate from Asia to South America over the Bering land bridge. Population pressures, search for new homes, and especially the impelling force of God's command to the animal kingdom (Gen. 8:17) soon filled every part of the habitable earth with birds, beasts, and creeping things.

The teaching of the Scriptures concerning the Flood is clear. Except for the family of Noah, the entire antediluvian race of mankind, widespread and hopelessly wicked, was destroyed by water. Sharing in this destruction were all the air-breathing animals of the world, except those which were gathered into the Ark and sustained there by the power of God. Heaven and earth joined forces in this cosmic cataclysm, which submerged all the highest mountains for 110 days and finally left the Ark stranded upon the mountains of Ararat.[1] From

---

[1] Rumors of the reported discovery of the Ark, preserved high on the snow-covered slopes of Mt. Ararat, have been published from time to time. These have never been confirmed, however, and more than one expedition to the area has failed in the attempt to locate it. We fear that any hope of its preservation for the thou-

the occupants of the Ark have descended all men and land animals in the world today.

However complex and obscure the problems may seem to be, with respect to the date of the Flood, the exact nature of racial distribution, the number of "kinds" of land animals in the days of Noah, and the distribution of animals from the Ark to the ends of the earth, the fact remains that the Genesis Flood was geographically universal. "The world that then was, being overflowed with water, perished" (II Pet. 3:6); and it is in the light of this tremendous Biblical truth that all of our investigations into the past history of this planet and its inhabitants must be carried on.

sands of years of post-diluvian history is merely wishful thinking. Even if it *had* been preserved, through burial and freezing, it would be so hard to find that nothing less than divine direction could ever lead explorers to its true location.

Chapter IV

Uniformitarianism and the Flood: A Study of Attempted Harmonizations

INTRODUCTION

The hostility of modern uniformitarians toward geological catastrophism in general and the concept of a universal Deluge in particular is a striking phenomenon of contemporary scientific thought. In spite of the fact that actual observation of geologic processes is strictly limited to those now in operation, uniformitarians have assumed that these, and only these, acted in the past and therefore must be applied to the study of origins. They thus have presumed to speak with finality upon matters which can be understood properly only in the light of God's revelation in Scripture. Geologic evidences for the great Flood are ignored, and even the possibility of such a catastrophe in the past is ruled out on the basis of *a priori* philosophical reasoning.

L. Merson Davies, a prominent British field and laboratory paleontologist and for many years a vigorous opponent of the theory of organic evolution, read a paper before the Victoria Institute in which he pointed to this remarkable antipathy on the part of geologists to the subject of the Biblical Deluge:

> Here, then, we come face to face with a circumstance which cannot be ignored in dealing with this subject . . . namely, the existence of a marked *prejudice* against the acceptance of belief in a cataclysm like the Deluge.

89

Now we should remember that, up to a hundred years ago, such a prejudice did not exist . . . as a general one, at least. Belief in the Deluge of Noah was axiomatic, not only in the Church itself (both Catholic and Protestant) but in the scientific world as well. And yet the Bible stood committed to the prophecy that, in what it calls the "last days," a very different philosophy would be found in the ascendent; a philosophy which would lead men to regard belief in the Flood with disfavor, and treat it as disproved, declaring that "All things continue as from the beginning of the creation" (2 Peter 3:3-6). In other words, a doctrine of Uniformity in all things (a doctrine which the apostle obviously regarded as untrue to fact) was to replace belief in such cataclysms as the Deluge.[1]

Davies then proceeded to show how this remarkable prophecy of Peter has begun to find its fulfillment in the last century, with the doctrines of uniformitarianism, as set forth by Hutton and Lyell, supplanting those of earlier thinkers. In bringing his introductory remarks to a conclusion, he said:

And so, after eighteen centuries, we at last find the ancient prophecy fulfilled before our eyes; for here is, as foretold, where opposition to belief in the Flood lies today. There is no mistaking the fact. It stares us in the face. *Anyone, today, who argues in favor of belief in the Flood, at once encounters opposition upon these long-foretold lines.*[2]

Before 1800, some of the outstanding theologians of the Church were of the opinion that the Genesis Flood not only was universal in extent but also was responsible for the reshaping of the earth's surface, including the formation of sedimentary strata. Among those who held this view were Tertullian, Chrysostom, Augustine, and Luther.[3]

It is somewhat surprising to learn, however, that the Flood theory of geology had to overcome serious opposition in the seventeenth century before it became generally accepted by scientists and theologians in the western world. John Ray (1692), John Arbuthnot (1697), and Edward Lhwyd (1698), among others, insisted that fossils were not the remains of plants and animals from an earlier age but were freaks of nature, "produced by a certain 'fatty matter,' set

---

[1] L. Merson Davies, "Scientific Discoveries and their Bearing on the Biblical Account of the Noachian Deluge," *Journal of the Transactions of the Victoria Institute* LXII (1930), pp. 62-63. Italics are his.

[2] *Loc. cit.* Italics are ours.

[3] See Byron C. Nelson, *The Deluge Story in Stone*, pp. 7-10, for quotations from the writings of these men on the subject of the Flood.

into fermentation by heat, giving birth to fossil shapes," or the seeds and germs of living things which "sank down into the rocks through pores, and there grew into fossil forms," or even that the fossils had been created by God just to puzzle men and to test their faith![1]

During the last twenty years of the seventeenth century, however, a new enthusiasm for the Flood theory of geology swept England and the Continent, through the influence of three Cambridge scholars: Thomas Burnet, *A Sacred Theory of the Earth* (1681); John Woodward, *An Essay Toward A Natural Theory of the Earth* (1693); and William Whiston, *A New Theory of the Earth* (1696).[2] So great was the impact of these volumes upon the thinking of western Europeans in those days that the older theory of fossils vanished forever, and John Harris could write in 1697 that "all sober and judicious men are now convinced that the exuviae of sea animals, so plentifully found at this day in the strata of the earth, and in the most hard and solid stone and marble, are the lasting proof of the Deluge itself and of its universality."[3]

Throughout the entire eighteenth century, and well into the nineteenth, an imposing list of scientists and theologians produced works in support of the Flood theory of geology. That the Flood was universal and that it was responsible for the major geologic formations of the earth was accepted almost without question in the western world during that period. In the words of Charles Coulston Gillispie:

> There was no question about the historical reality of the flood. When the history of the earth began to be considered geologically, it was simply assumed that a universal deluge must have wrought vast changes and that it had been a primary agent in forming the present surface of the globe. Its occurrence was evidence that the Lord was a governor as well as a creator.[4]

Opposition to this generally accepted Flood theory of geology gave

[1] *Ibid.*, p. 31. For lengthy excerpts from Edward Lhwyd's letter to John Ray, setting forth objections to the Flood theory in favor of the "seed" or "germ" theory, see Edwin T. Brewster, *Creation: A History of Non-Evolutionary Theories* (Indianapolis: The Bobbs-Merrill Co., 1927), pp. 132-140.

[2] Don Cameron Allen, *The Legend of Noah* (Urbana: University of Illinois Press, 1949), pp. 66-112, provides a thoroughly documented history of the Flood controversy during the Middle Ages.

[3] Quoted in Nelson, *op. cit.*, p. 51.

[4] Charles C. Gillispie, *Genesis and Geology* (Cambridge: Harvard University Press, 1951), p. 42.

birth to the three greatest harmonization efforts of modern times: the *diluvium theory,* the *tranquil theory,* and the *local-Flood theory.* To each of these we must now turn our attention.

CUVIER'S CATASTROPHISM AND THE DILUVIUM THEORY

It is not without significance that the first major attack upon eighteenth-century Flood. geology came from a man who was thoroughly convinced that the Genesis Flood had left unmistakable evidences of its magnitude and destructive power upon the surface of the entire globe. By accepting these basic tenets of the Flood theory of geology, he gained the confidence of a large number of Christian people; but by introducing other elements that were essentially fatal to Flood geology, he unintentionally opened the door to a veritable host of theories that threatened to drive that concept from the intellectual scene by the middle of the nineteenth century.

Cuvier's Multiple Catastrophism

The man to whom we refer was Georges Cuvier (1769-1832), Professor of Comparative Anatomy in the Museum of Natural History at Paris and the founder of modern vertebrate paleontology—a man of immense learning and reputation. Cuvier's opposition to Flood geology was subtle, because while he insisted that the *superficial* deposits of the earth had beeen laid down by the Flood, he also taught that the *major* fossiliferous strata of the earth had been laid down by a series of great floods, separated by immense periods of time, and long before the creation of man. After each of these catastrophes, the few surviving animals spread out over the earth again, only to be nearly annihilated by another great flood. The last of these aqueous catastrophes was the Noahic Deluge, concerning which he wrote: "If there be a fact well ascertained in geology, it is this, that the surface of our globe has suffered a great and sudden revolution, the period of which cannot be dated further back than 5 or 6,000 years."[1]

Cuvier's theory of catastrophism, or better, of successive catastro-

[1] Georges Cuvier, *Discours sur les Revolutions de la Surface du Globe* (3rd ed; Paris, 1836), p. 133. Quoted in William T. Hamilton, *The Friend of Moses* (New York: M. W. Dodd, 1852), p. 332.

phes, became so popular throughout western Europe that it is credited with having postponed the general acceptance of the theory of organic evolution for many years.[1] His successor at the Paris museum, Alcide d'Orbigny (1802-1857), went a step farther and taught that each of these catastrophes had been followed by an entirely new creation of animal life. As early as 1814, Cuvier's views were being propounded in England by Dr. Thomas Chalmers, who found room between Genesis 1:1 and 1:2 for this succession of pre-Adamic catastrophes and thus became the popularizer of the now famous "gap theory."[2] Many of the greatest English geologists of this period, such as Adam Sedgwick, Roderick Murchison, and William Buckland, adopted Cuvier's theory because it seemed to offer an easy explanation for the fossil strata.

Buckland's Diluvium Theory

William Buckland, Professor of Geology at Oxford University, was a key figure during the period of transition we are now considering. Even as early as 1820, when, as reader on geology at Oxford, he published his *Vindiciae Geologicae, or the Connection of Geology with Religion Explained,* his views were essentially those of Cuvier. His abandonment of the older Flood geology was expressed as follows: "It seems . . . impossible to ascribe the formation of these strata to . . . the single year occupied by the Mosaic deluge . . . The strata . . . must be referred . . . to periods of much greater antiquity."[3]

In 1823, Buckland's fame was secured by the publication of his *Reliquiae Diluvianae* (Relics of the Flood), in which he set forth the thesis that evidences of the Genesis Flood, which he named *diluvium,* are to be found in the great deposits of "drift" and in the bones of tropical animals such as elephants, hippopotami, and tigers, which he had found jumbled together in a Yorkshire cave at Kirkdale. Cuvier, in turn, adopted Buckland's evidence for the Deluge and incorporated it into his last and greatest work, *Discours sur les Revolu-*

---

[1] George Gaylord Simpson, *Life of the Past: An Introduction to Paleontology* (New Haven: Yale University Press, 1953), p. 141.

[2] Hugh Miller, *The Testimony of the Rocks,* p. 143. See also Ramm, *op. cit.,* p. 196, and Francis C. Haber, *The Age of the World: Moses to Darwin* (Baltimore: The Johns Hopkins Press, 1959), pp. 201-204.

[3] Quoted in Harold W. Clark's *The New Diluvialism* (Angwin, California: Science Publications, 1946), p. 9.

tions de la Surface du Globe (1826). In discussing the Kirkdale discoveries, Cuvier wrote:

> Most carefully described by Professor Buckland, under the name of *diluvium,* and exceedingly different from those other beds of similarly rolled materials, which are now constantly deposited by torrents and rivers, and containing only bones of animals existing in the country, and to which Mr. Buckland gives the name *alluvium,* they now form, in the eyes of all geologists, the fullest proof to the senses, of that immense inundation (the Noachian flood) which came last in the catastrophes of our globe.[1]

For much of the nineteenth century, the "diluvium theory" of Buckland, which was based upon the "successive catastrophes theory" of Cuvier, gripped the imaginations of theologians who were happy to have such positive evidence of the universality of the Flood, even if it meant relegating the vast majority of fossils to pre-Adamic catastrophes. After all, they reasoned, it was important to keep in step with the very latest geological theories, especially because the "diluvium" deposits of Buckland and Cuvier still gave them plenty of ammunition against deists who had never been willing to admit God's power to destroy mankind by a universal Deluge![2]

Encouraged by the scientific favor accorded this new "harmonization" of Genesis and geology, many theologians of that period proceeded to denounce the older Flood theory of geology in the name of "modern" geology. To be sure, the older view did not lack its defenders in subsequent decades; but increasingly, the views of prominent geologists became the criteria for exegeting the early chapters of Genesis, and the great Flood began a slow but steady retreat from its recognized position as the greatest catastrophe of geologic history.[3]

---

[1] Cuvier, *op. cit.,* p. 141 (quoted by Hamilton, *op. cit.,* p. 332).

[2] Francis H. Haber has pointed out that this "quest for harmony between the Word of God and the Works of God was an attempt to make room in the traditional outlook for the new science. In retrospect, we can see that this was accomplished by the geologists, with the unwitting help of some of the orthodox, by drawing through the gate of Biblical chronology a Trojan horse, thought to be laden with glorious scientific proofs of the universal Noachian Deluge and the history of nature given in Genesis. Accidentally perhaps, the chief architect of the stratagem was Baron Cuvier . . . Cuvier's vigorous espousal of the Deluge as an actual geological event mollified some of the orthodox into thinking it was now safe to interpret Biblical chronology as applying to man only. Thus Cuvier provided a safety valve between the irrefutable proofs of an ancient earth and Mosaic history, between the push of geology and the drag of theology." *The Age of the World: Moses to Darwin,* pp. 194, 199.

[3] See Charles Burton, *Lectures on the Deluge and the World After the Flood*

LYELL'S UNIFORMITARIANISM AND
THE TRANQUIL THEORY

The Rise of Uniformitarianism

Strange to relate, no sooner had the theologians scrapped the Flood theory of geology in favor of Cuvier's theory of successive catastrophes, than the professional geologists began to abandon Cuvier! For Cuvier's views were now being eclipsed by the Lyellian school of uniformitarian geology, and within half a generation sank into almost complete oblivion.[1]

Charles Lyell (1797-1875), "the high priest of uniformitarianism," and author of the famous textbook, *Principles of Geology,* was a young English attorney who had enthusiastically accepted the doctrine of gradual geological changes which had been advocated at the end of the eighteenth century by James Hutton (1726-1797). Hutton, a Scottish geologist, had taught that many of the geologic processes now operating in the earth had been active for extremely long periods in the past, and that such gradual processes could account for the world as we see it today, with its mountains and valleys and fossiliferous strata, without the need of appealing to sudden and stupendous catastrophes. In other words, "the present is the key to the past."

Lyell also adopted the theories of William ("Strata") Smith (1769-1839), "the father of stratigraphic geology," who believed that rock layers always occur in the same sequence, depending on the type of fossils they contain, and that any particular stratum can be traced over a vast area simply by noting its "index fossils."[2]

But Lyell went even farther than his predecessors, in his insistence that all geologic processes had been very gradual in the past, and in his utter abhorrence for anything suggestive of sudden catastrophes.

(London: Hamilton, Adams & Co., 1845), pp. 16-17; and James M. Olmstead, *Noah and His Times* (Boston: Gould and Lincoln, 1854), p. 154.

[1] A remarkable defense of Cuvierian catastrophism may be found in N. Heribert-Nilsson's *Synthetische Artbildung* (Lund, Sweden: Verlag CWE Gleerup, 1953), an 1130-page, two-volume work in German, with a 100-page English summarization. Heribert-Nilsson was Professor of Botany at Lund University.

[2] Cf. O. D. von Engeln and Kenneth E. Caster, *Geology* (New York: McGraw-Hill Book Co., Inc., 1952), pp. 20-25.

The following quotation from his textbook on geology clearly reveals his basic attitude on this question:

The earlier geologists had not only a scanty acquaintance with existing changes, but were singularly unconscious of the amount of their ignorance. With the presumption naturally inspired by this unconsciousness, *they had no hesitation in deciding at once that time could never enable the existing powers of nature to work out changes of great magnitude, still less such important revolutions as those which are brought to light by Geology* . . . Never was there a dogma more calculated to foster indolence, and to blunt the keen edge of curiosity, than this assumption of discordance between the ancient and existing causes of change. It produced a state of mind unfavourable in the highest degree to the candid reception of the evidence of those minute but incessant alterations which every part of the earth's surface is undergoing . . . *For this reason all theories are rejected which involve the assumption of sudden and violent catastrophes and revolutions of the whole earth, and its inhabitants*—theories which are restrained by no reference to existing analogies, and in which a desire is manifested to cut, rather than patiently to untie, the Gordian knot.[1]

This was surely uniformitarianism with a vengeance. But it was suited to the times, when men were weary of the eruptions of revolution and political turmoil, and were ready for doctrines which spoke in terms of peace and tranquility, whether in government or in geology.[2]

The fact that Lyellian uniformitarianism has been accepted as the true philosophy of geology in all major centers of scientific learning in the world today may be attributed partially to the fact that Charles Darwin, a disciple of Lyell, built his theory of organic evolution upon the uniformitarian foundation which Lyell had laid. Nor was Darwin reluctant to acknowledge his debt of gratitude to Lyell when he pointed out, in *The Origin of Species,* that

He who can read Sir Charles Lyell's grand work on the *Principles of*

[1] Charles Lyell, *Principles of Geology* (11th ed. rev.; New York: D. Appleton & Co., 1892), I, 317-318. Italics are ours.

[2] In 1896, William Brown Galloway looked back upon the sweeping triumph of uniformitarianism and commented: ". . . they had settled it that the universal Deluge was to be rejected, Scripture notwithstanding. Away with catastrophes! Let us have only the present rate of change, the gradual operation of present known causes, however slow; and give them plenty of time! A hundred thousand or a million or a few millions of years can be created at will for the purpose. Truth shall be what we make it, and they who do not so accept it shall be held comparable to the persecutors of the great Galileo." *The Testimony of Science to the Deluge* (London: Sampson Low, Marston, & Co., 1896), p. 22.

Geology, which the future historian will recognize as having produced a revolution in natural science, and yet does not admit how vast have been the past periods of time, may at once close this volume.[1]

The Tranquil Theory

Although Lyell's first blast of the uniformitarian trumpet was sounded as early as 1830, it required many years for Cuvier's theory of successive catastrophes to be dislodged from the minds of English geologists. In the meantime, however, a new theory was rapidly gaining acceptance in Great Britain, which was intended to dislodge completely the Genesis Flood as a factor to be taken into consideration by geologists in explaining Buckland's "diluvium" deposits. This was the "tranquil theory," which maintained that the universal Flood was far too "tranquil" a phenomenon to leave any deposits whatever. Although first suggested by the Swedish botanist, Carolus Linnaeus (1707-1778), the "tranquil theory" was introduced to the British public in 1826 by a Scottish minister named John Fleming.

I entertain the same opinion as Linnaeus on this subject; nor do I feel, though a clergyman, the slightest reason to conceal my sentiments, though they are opposed to the notions which a false philosophy has generated in the public mind. I have formed my notions of the Noachian deluge, not from Ovid, but from the Bible. *There the simple narrative of Moses permits me to believe, that the waters rose upon the earth by degrees . . . that the flood exhibited no violent impetuosity, displacing neither the soil nor the vegetable tribes which it supported . . .* With this conviction in my mind, I am not prepared to witness *in nature* any remaining *marks* of the catastrophe, and I find my respect for the authority of revelation heightened, when I see, on the present surface, *no memorials* of the event.[2]

Charles Lyell eagerly grasped at this new theory as being in perfect harmony with his uniformitarian philosophy of nature:

[1] Charles Darwin, *The Origin of Species by Means of Natural Selection,* Vol. XLIX of *Great Books of the Western World,* ed. Robert M. Hutchins (Chicago: Encyclopedia Britannica, Inc., 1955), p. 153. Francis C. Haber concludes: "There can be little doubt that it was through Lyell's *Principles* that Darwin's mind was emancipated from the shackles of Biblical chronology, and had this step not taken place, it seems unlikely that the *Origin of Species* could ever have fermented out of the *Voyage of the Beagle,* for Darwin's theory of evolution required for its foundation far more historical time than even the uniformitarian geologists were accustomed to conceiving." *Op. cit.,* p. 268.

[2] *Edinburgh Philosophical Journal,* XIV (April, 1826), pp. 214-215. Quoted by John Pye Smith, *op. cit.,* p. 101. Only the italics of the third sentence are ours.

I agree with Dr. Fleming that *in the narrative of Moses there are no terms employed that indicate the impetuous rushing of the waters, either as they rose, or when they retired* upon the restraining of the rain and the passing of the wind over the earth. On the contrary, the olive branch brought back by the dove seems as clear an indication to us that the vegetation was not destroyed, as it was to Noah that the dry land was about to appear.[1]

Although Buckland's "diluvium" theory had enjoyed an immense popularity in Britain during the 1820's and continued to attract theologians for many years afterwards, it was well on the way to being totally abandoned by geologists by the middle of the 1830's. These British men of science were greatly attracted to Fleming's and Lyell's new "harmonization" of Genesis and geology, whereby the Genesis Flood, though still universal in extent, was not to be thought of as having any geological significance whatever. Not that they were ready to give up Cuvier in favor of Lyell immediately, for they still thought in terms of Cuvier's theory of successive catastrophes. But the so-called "diluvium" deposits which Buckland had attributed to the Flood must have been deposited instead by the last of the great geologic catastrophes of the pre-Adamic ages. The universal Flood of Noah was so "tranquil" in its movements that it didn't even disturb olive trees, to say nothing of soil and rocks! Uniformitarianism won its first great victory by divorcing geology from Genesis!

That this had become the scientific mood of Great Britain during the 1830's is evident from the following statement by Adam Sedgwick of Cambridge University, in his last address as president of the Geological Society in 1831:

I think it right, as one of my last acts before I quit this Chair, thus publicly to read my recantation. We ought, indeed, to have paused before we adopted the diluvian theory, and referred all our old superficial gravel to the action of the Mosaic Flood. For of man, and the works of his hands, we have not yet found a single trace among the remnants of a former world entombed in these deposits.[2]

And five years later, William Buckland of Oxford, the author of

---

[1] Charles Lyell, *Principles of Geology*, IV, 216. Quoted in Olmstead, *op. cit.*, p. 169. Italics are ours. For further discussion on the olive tree problem, see below, pp. 104-106.

[2] Adam Sedgwick, "Presidential Address" (1831), *Proceedings of the Geological Society*, I, 313. Quoted by Immanuel Velikovsky, *Earth in Upheaval* (Garden City, New York: Doubleday & Co., 1955), p. 235.

Reliquiae Diluvianae (1823) and popularizer of the "diluvium" theory, finally wrote his recantation of earlier views concerning the identification of superficial deposits with the Genesis Flood. In the sixth of the series of "Bridgewater Treatises," delivered in 1836, Buckland admitted:

> Discoveries which have been made since the publication of this work [the *Reliquiae Diluvianae*], show that many of the animals therein described, existed during more than one geological period preceding the catastrophe by which they were extirpated. Hence it seems more probable that the event in question was the last of the many geological revolutions that have been produced by violent irruptions of water, *rather than by the comparatively tranquil inundation described in the Inspired Narrative*. It has been justly argued, against the attempt to identify these two great historical and natural phenomena, that, *as the rise and fall of the waters of the Mosaic deluge are described to have been gradual and of short duration, they would have produced comparatively little change on the surface of the country they overflowed.*[1]

Thus, within one generation in the early nineteenth century, recognized geologists had abandoned the Flood theory of geology in favor of Cuvier's successive catastrophes and Buckland's "diluvium" deposits; and then, before the Christian public had time to adjust its thinking to the new theory, the geologists had fallen under the spell of the "tranquil theory," which removed the Flood from the category of geologic catastrophes and left it without any visible traces. Because this theory still claims its followers in the mid-twentieth century, it is important that we examine its implications in the light of science and Scripture.[2]

The Language of Scripture

We have already observed how Fleming, Lyell, and Buckland insisted that "the rise and fall of waters of the Mosaic deluge are described to have been gradual and of short duration" and that "they

---

[1] William Buckland, *Geology and Minerology Considererd With Reference to Natural Theology* (Bridgewater Treatises, 1836), p. 94. Quoted by Olmstead, *op. cit.*, p. 159. Italics are ours.

[2] Thus, J. Laurence Kulp, a Christian geologist, feels that "insofar as geology is concerned, one would not expect much of a record of the flood of Noah, even if it had covered, as apparently it did, the entire earth . . . A thousand years later, subsequent erosion may have removed all traces of such an event." *Journal of the American Scientific Affiliation*, Vol. 1, No. 3 (June, 1949), p. 25.

would have produced comparatively little change on the surface of the country they overflowed." But what do the Scriptures have to say about the movements and effects of the Flood waters? Are they depicted in Genesis in terms of "tranquility"? At this point we do well to ponder the words of Byron C. Nelson. After giving a literal translation of Genesis 8:3 ("and the waters were going and returning from off the earth"), he adds:

Here is described some ebb and flow, some notable back and forth movement of the Deluge waters, as they slowly retreated into the ocean depths. Whether the ebb and flow was that of tides, or some other extraordinary movements, the Scriptures do not say . . . But that there were sufficient movements, tidal or otherwise, to stir up immense quantities of the soil, which perhaps covered the old earth to an enormous depth, certainly seems plain. And a little forward in the Scriptural account, in brief yet expressive narrative, it says, "And the waters decreased continually," or "were going and decreasing" (Genesis 8:5).[1]

Nelson then goes on to point out two other passages of Scripture which he feels must constitute "the *coup de grace* to the objection that physical violence and disaster in the Flood is foreign to the Bible itself." The first of these passages is Genesis 6:13, "The end of all flesh is come before me; for the earth is filled with violence through them; and, behold, I will destroy them *with the earth*." H.C. Leupold observes here that

in order to make the sweeping nature and the dread earnestness of this destruction more clearly apparent, it is His purpose to destroy men "together with the earth." Thus, when man is wiped away and his habitations with him, men realize more fully how serious the nature of the misdeeds is. The critics did not expect the phrase "with the earth" and so subject it to severe criticism. It makes too good sense to call for criticism.[2]

The other passage referred to by Nelson is II Peter 3:6 ("the world that then was, being overflowed with water, perished"), which we have already discussed at length in Chapter I.

Today, when the continents and oceans are in a state of equilibrium, there are tremendous oceanic currents. One of these, the south equatorial current, carries *six million tons of water a second north-*

---

[1] Nelson, *The Deluge Story in Stone*, p. 5.
[2] Leupold, *op. cit.*, p. 269.

ward across the Equator.[1] But how much more powerful must the currents have been when the oceanic waters, impelled onward by the breaking up of the fountains of the great deep and suddenly swollen by the opening of "the windows of heaven," rose above the highest mountains of the earth within a period of forty days and then after five months began to return "from off the earth continually."

Nelson clearly indicates the impossibility of the tranquil theory:

As the sea began to rise, each twice-daily current could come higher and higher up the rivers and valleys, spreading farther and wider inland each time, and would then recede. In places, doubtless, the incoming movements would be as fierce and violent as in the Bay of St. Michael or the mouth of the Amazon, and even more so. The directions of the tidal currents and their violence would change with the changing contours of the surfaces being encroached upon. We do not say that the Flood was brought on by the gradual raising of the sea bottoms, though it may have been. But that being the gentlest manner in which a universal Deluge could be brought about, shall we, in view of what we know of tides, say there could be a universal flood and no violence be done to the earth? Can we think it possible there were no currents, no movements, no motions of the waters back and forth and hither and yon?[2]

Even if it were not for the fact that the Bible gives clear indications of the movement and destructive effects of the Flood waters, it would be impossible to imagine a universal Flood that could be so tranquil as to leave the surface of the earth unaltered. Even the relatively small amounts of water involved in river floods have caused damage that staggers the imagination.[3] Bridges, houses, immense boulders, and trees are torn up and swept along as mere pebbles and matchsticks. Such floods seldom attain a depth of more than a few dozen feet and their main force is expended within a few days or hours. But when we begin to speak in terms of a Flood that "grew mightily upon the earth" and "prevailed upon the earth one hundred and fifty days" and covered "all the high mountains which

---

[1] Map of the Atlantic Ocean, *The National Geographic Magazine* (Washington, D.C., December, 1955). See also, Henry Chapin and F. G. Walton Smith, *The Ocean River* (New York: Charles Scribner's Sons, 1954), pp. 138-139.

[2] Nelson, *op. cit.,* p. 4.

[3] For an enlightening collection of testimonies concerning the destructive force of modern river floods, see A. M. Rehwinkel, *The Flood* (St. Louis: Concordia Publ. House, 1951), pp. 329-340. See also discussion below, pp. 259-261.

are under all the heavens,"[1] we must face the fact that we are no longer dealing with phenomena that are familiar to modern science.

It therefore cannot be denied that a universal Flood must, of absolute necessity, have accomplished a vast amount of geologic work in a relatively short period. Erosion and sedimentation must have taken place on a gigantic scale. Previous isostatic adjustments, of whatever sort they were, must have been entirely unbalanced by the great complex of hydrostatic and hydrodynamic forces unleashed in the floodwaters, resulting very likely in great telluric movements. Associated with the volcanic phenomena and the great rains must also have been tremendous tidal effects, windstorms, and a great complexity of currents, cross-currents, whirlpools, and other hydraulic phenomena. After the floodgates were restrained and the fountains of the great deep stopped, there must still, for a long time, have been much more geologic work accomplished as the masses of water were settling into new basins and the earth was adjusting itself to new physiographic and hydrologic balances.

Leupold insists that "note should be taken of the tremendous geological possibilities that lie behind the breaking open of the fountains of the great deep. The vastness of these eruptions must be in proportion to the actual depth of the Flood."[2] And he adds further, with regard to the significance of Genesis 7:18-20 for modern science:

> What opportunity for working vast geologic changes lie dormant in these "mighty" waters! The native force of *gabhar* is enhanced by one *me'odh,* "exceedingly" in verse 18 and by the doubling of the same adverb . . . a Hebrew superlative . . . in verse 19. *When will geologists begin to notice these basic facts?*[3]

The Imperiling of the Ark

One argument that has frequently been advanced against the idea that the Flood waters moved rapidly back and forth across the earth is that the Ark would have been in danger of capsizing and its occupants would not have been able to survive under such conditions for a year.

---

[1] A literal translation of the Hebrew text of Genesis 7:18, 19, and 24, by H. C. Leupold, *op. cit.,* p. 300.

[2] *Ibid,* p. 296.

[3] *Ibid.,* p. 301. Italics are ours.

In answer to this objection, we would suggest two important considerations. In the first place, the Ark was not a ship, but a barge. The Biblical evidence indicates that the Ark was built specifically for the purpose of withstanding the terrific impact of the waves that would dash against it. It is interesting that the local-Flood school has provided us with some of the most helpful information in this connection. Robert Jamieson discusses the matter at length, and some of his points are summarized by Ramm:

> The ark had a door and three stories. The stories functioned the same as the staterooms in providing a division of animals and a bracing of the structure. The shape of the ark was boxy or angular, and not streamlined nor curved. With this shape it increased its carrying capacity by one third. It was a vessel designed for floating, not for sailing. A model was made by Peter Jansen of Holland, and Danish barges called *Fleuten* were modeled after the ark. These models proved that the ark had a greater capacity than curved or shaped vessels. They were very seaworthy and almost impossible to capsize. . . . The stability of such a barge is great and it increases as it sinks deeper into the water. The lower the center of gravity the more difficult it is to capsize. If the center of gravity were low enough the ark or barge could only be capsized if violently rolled over. Wherever the center of gravity may have been in the ark, it certainly was a most stable vessel.[1]

In the second place, we must not make the mistake of underestimating the implications of Genesis 8:1, "God *remembered* Noah, and all the beasts, and all the cattle that were with him in the ark." This statement refers to a time when the waters were still at their height and the fountains of the great deep had not yet been stopped (Gen. 8:2). It is important to remind ourselves that the word "remembered" (*zākar*) in this context does not imply that God had forgotten the Ark and its occupants for a time! According to Hebrew usage, the meaning of *zākar* is "granting requests, protecting, delivering," when God is the subject and persons are the object.[2] In fact, as

---

[1] Ramm, *op. cit.*, pp. 230-231. Cf. Jamieson, *op. cit.*, p. 92. Alexander Heidel points out that the Hebrew term for ark is *tēbâ* and is related to the Egyptian *db't,* meaning "chest," "box," "coffin." Outside of the Flood account, it is used only of Moses' ark in the Nile (Exodus 2:3,5). Heidel concludes: "Noah's ark, as evidenced by its dimensions and the names by which it is designated in Greek and Hebrew, was of flat-bottomed, rectangular construction, square on both ends and straight up on the sides." *The Gilgamesh Epic and Old Testament Parallels,* pp. 233-235.

[2] Brown, Driver, and Briggs, *A Hebrew and English Lexicon of the Old Testament,* p. 270. Cited by Leupold, *op. cit.*, p. 308. See above p. 76.

Leupold observes, "God's power in keeping the ark amid such dangers stands out the more distinctly."[1]

Thus, when we take into account the divinely-planned structure of the Ark and the ever-watchful care of God for His creatures in that Ark, it is entirely gratuitous to insist that the Flood must have been a tranquil affair for Noah's family and the animals to have survived that year-long ordeal unscathed.

The Olive Leaf

Another argument in support of the "tranquil theory" that often appears in the literature of the past century and a quarter is based upon the episode of the dove and the olive leaf. The Scriptures tell us that "the dove came in to him at eventide; and lo, in her mouth an olive-leaf plucked off [A.S.V. margin: a fresh olive leaf]: so Noah knew that the waters were abated from off the earth" (Gen. 8:11).

Now it must be admitted that this olive leaf could not have been an old one floating on the surface of the water, for the Hebrew word *taraph* means "plucked off" or "fresh"; and furthermore, it would not have given Noah any indication that "the waters were abated from off the earth." J. P. Lange quotes Delitzsch as saying:

The olive tree has green leaves all the year through, and appears to endure the water, since Theophrastus, *Hist. Plant.* IV, 8, and Pliny, *Hist. Nat.* XIII, 50, give an account of olive trees in the Red Sea. It comes early in Armenia (Strabo), though not on the heights of Ararat, but lower down, below the walnut, mulberry, and apricot tree, in the valleys on the south side.[2]

It is upon the basis of these facts that some argue for a Flood so gentle in its movements that not even the trees were disturbed, and the fact that the dove brought back the freshly-plucked leaf of an olive tree was supposedly an indication to Noah that the waters had subsided to the level where olive trees were accustomed to growing.

Charles Lyell, in advocating the "tranquil theory," had claimed that "the olive branch brought back by the dove seems as clear an indication to us that the vegetation was not destroyed, as it was to Noah that the dry land was about to appear."[3] But in refutation of

---

[1] Leupold, *op. cit.*, p. 301.

[2] J. P. Lange, *op. cit.*, pp. 310-311.

[3] Charles Lyell, *Principles of Geology*, IV, 216. Quoted by Olmstead, *op. cit.*, p. 169.

this, L. Vernon Harcourt, writing in 1838, pointed out that the Bible does not say that a dove brought back an "olive *branch*," but merely an olive *leaf*. To Harcourt, this was "a clear indication, that he [Lyell] has not examined the sacred narrative with the same attention and accuracy, as he bestowed upon the strata of the earth."[1] The importance of this distinction may be seen from the fact that "even if every olive tree in Armenia had been uprooted and covered with diluvium, it is evident, that sufficient time had elapsed to allow for the germination of the seed on the rising grounds, although the plains were still lying under water."[2]

Nor is it necessary to suppose, as Harcourt did, that the new olive plant would have to have grown from a seedling. Just as much of modern horticulture is carried on by the use of cuttings from older plants, so also much of the postdiluvian plant life probably began from broken branches buried near the surface. It is significant that the olive leaf is mentioned, since it is well known that this is one of the hardiest of all plants and would be one of the first to sprout again from such a cutting after the Flood. Even full-grown trees can be subjected to extremely harsh treatment and yet survive.

So indestructible that it can survive in the poorest soil through drought, pests, grass fires, or years of neglect, it revives when fed and irrigated and pruned, and yields prodigious crops. . . . By pruning back the branches to blunt stubs, chopping off the roots and digging out the burl, an olive grower can lift and transplant a full-grown tree anytime. After a year to recover from this shocking treatment, the burl sends out new roots for moisture, grows new roots, and bears crops anew. . . ."[3]

Neither does the tree have to grow in the plains; it could have sprouted high on the barren hillsides long before the Flood waters retreated to the lowlands.

The adaptable nature of the trees permits them to be grown in soils of high lime content and on rocky hills unsuited for other crops.[4]

That only a few months would be needed from the time of implanta-

---

[1] L. Vernon Harcourt, *The Doctrine of the Deluge.* (London: Longman, *et al*, 1838), p. 5.

[2] *Ibid.*, p. 8.

[3] F. J. Taylor: "California's Strangest Crop," *Saturday Evening Post*, October 2, 1954, p. 56.

[4] Arnold Krochmal: "Olive Growing in Greece," *Economic Botany*, July-Sept., 1955, p. 228. It must be kept in mind that even mountain peaks would have been

tion of cuttings until the sprouting of leaves is indicated by the following:

> Cuttings are therefore almost universally used for olive tree propagation. These may be of branches several inches in diameter and five to six feet long, planted in the ground where the tree is to remain, or of shorter and smaller pieces planted in nursery rows. The large knots or ovoli which naturally grow at the base of olive trees are sometimes chiselled off and planted, their sprouts being planted as cuttings. In California the trees are grown either from hard- or soft-wood cuttings. Cuttings of mature wood placed in sand with bottom heat in February form roots and make a short growth by fall. Softwood olive cuttings are made in October of mature terminal twigs about five inches long, and placed close together in sand for rooting. The following May the rooted cuttings are set in nursery rows. . . ."[1]

Thus the record of the dove and the olive leaf harmonizes perfectly with what is known of the nature of the olive tree and with the Biblical account of a great world-destroying Flood.

Thus we see that the really fatal weakness of the objection based on the episode of the olive leaf is that it tries to prove too much. That a universal Flood could have left trees undisturbed is simply inconceivable. The fact that 135 days elapsed *after* the waters began to assuage before the dove could find a living leaf is eloquent testimony in itself to the vast destructiveness of the Flood. Many Englishmen would have agreed with L. Vernon Harcourt when he wrote in 1838: "It is to be lamented that Mr. Lyell should have carried his theory of tranquility to a degree which borders upon ridicule."[2]

only a few hundred feet above sea level during the weeks immediately following the grounding of the Ark. Consequently, climatic conditions could have been most favorable at that time for the rapid sprouting of leaves from an olive tree cutting even on the highest mountain.

[1] I. J. Condit: Article "Olive," in *Encyclopedia Britannica,* Vol. 16, 1956, p. 774. The California horticulturist, Dr. Walter Lammerts, in a personal communication, (Nov. 27, 1957), says that "Sections of olive branches placed in trenches about ten inches deep and covered with soil and watered will sprout shoots very rapidly. Actually, therefore, all you need to postulate is that branches of olive trees happened to be buried near enough to the surface of the soil in certain areas for sprouting of shoots and thus you would have a new generation of trees from asexually propagated plants" (See Fig. 2.).

[2] Harcourt, *op. cit.,* p. 5.

JOHN PYE SMITH AND THE LOCAL FLOOD THEORY

The Birth of the Theory

Though the "tranquil theory" appealed to many theologians as a remarkable harmonization of Genesis and geology, it soon became evident to the majority that it was scientifically preposterous. It was an interesting but hopeless effort to ward off the inevitable, and now the handwriting was on the wall. Once the process of "harmonization" had fairly gotten under way, there was nothing to stop it short of total capitulation of the Genesis Flood to the demands of uniformitarian speculation. A new era of harmonization was about to dawn, and the herald of this new era was at hand.

John Pye Smith's long and active life (1774-1851) paralleled the entire history of transition in scientific and theological thought with regard to the extent and effects of the Flood. Not only was he alert to the intellectual trends of his day but he also frequently engaged in oral and written controversy, producing a number of works on theological subjects.

Toward the end of his teaching career at Homerton College in London, Smith became enamoured of the new science of geology; and he began to give lectures on the harmonization of Genesis and geology. According to one of his biographers:

> Relying on EVIDENCE, the only valuable ally in scientific investigation, our author arrived at the conclusion . . . that the Noachian deluge was not, and could not have been, universal; and that the affirmation could not be maintained, except by the wretched subterfuge of supposing a stupendous miracle throughout the whole continuance of that Deluge.[1]

The first edition of his famous work, *On The Relation Between the Holy Scriptures and Some Parts of Geological Science,* was published in 1839. The fifth edition, which was published posthumously in 1854, contained sixty pages of arguments against the universality of the Flood (pp. 109-149; 264-283), many of which have been used by advocates of the local-Flood theory ever since.

The publication of Smith's lectures in 1839 aroused a veritable storm of protest from evangelical Christians in Great Britain. Before

---

[1] John Hamilton Davies, "Sketch of the Literary Life of Dr. John Pye Smith, F.R.S.," in Smith, *op. cit.,* pp. liii-liv.

1839, discussions concerning the Flood and its geologic effects had been carried on with comparative equanimity, although the recantations of Adam Sedgwick in 1831 and William Buckland in 1836 on the identification of superficial deposits with the Deluge had produced uneasiness in the minds of many. But *now*, for the first time since the seventeenth century, an English theologian arose to denounce in no uncertain terms *the geographical universality of the Flood* and to support his assertions with eloquent and lengthy arguments from science and Scripture.[1]

If Pye Smith's biographer had been able to foresee the controversies that are raging throughout conservative Christian circles on the subject of the Genesis Flood in the mid-twentieth century, he would not have written so optimistically about Smith's victory in the first round of the modern debate on the geographical extent of the Deluge:

> Undaunted either by the insinuations or by the outcry of those who were sceptical of the facts of science, Dr. Smith, with yet louder voice, maintained for geology a perfect harmony both with Scripture and with reason; and those sentiments which, at their first publication, caused alarm in some quarters, are now admitted and familiar truths with all but those who, with narrowmindedness and bigotry, "love the darkness" of ignorance "rather than the light" of knowledge.[2]

But it is true that the bitter outcry which accompanied the publication of Smith's book soon subsided, and the spirit of the times was

---

[1] The first advocate of the local-Flood view on record was a Frenchman, Isaac de la Peyrere, author of *Prae-Adamitae* (Amsterdam, 1655). Far more influential were Isaac Vossius, *Dissertatio de vera aetate mundi* (Hague, 1659) and George Kaspar Kirchmaier, *De diluvii universalitate dissertatio prolusoria* (Geneva, 1667). These continental works produced the Flood geology reaction of Burnet, Woodward, and Whiston, discussed above, p. 91.

But Vossius and Kirchmaier succeeded in gaining two disciples in Great Britain: Matthew Poole, *Latin Synopsis of Critical Writers upon the Bible* (1670); and Bishop Stillingfleet, *Origines Sacrae* (London, 1709): "the Flood was universal as to Mankind; but from thence follows no necessity at all of asserting the universality of it, as to the Globe of the Earth, unless it be sufficiently prov'd that the whole Earth was Peopled before the Flood: Which I despair of ever seeing prov'd." (p. 337, quoted in Allen, *op. cit.,* p. 89).

Two other continentals of the local-Flood persuasion were an Italian named Quirini (1676), and Dathe, in a commentary on the Pentateuch (1791). As far as Great Britain was concerned, however, the local-Flood view never really took root. It was only mentioned in passing by Poole and Stillingfleet and then disappeared for over a century until the publication of John Pye Smith's work in 1839. Don Cameron Allen, *op. cit.,* pp. 66-112, provides the most thoroughly documented discussion of early Flood controversies. See above, p. 91, note #2.

[2] J. H. Davies, *op. cit.,* p. lvi.

such that a multitude of geologists and theologians fell quickly into line with the new theory. After all, if there were no universal geologic evidences of the Flood, it must have been because the Flood was not universal!

William Buckland and his fellow geologists were greatly relieved to learn that Biblical exegesis did not require the universality of the Flood, for the "tranquil theory" had long since become logically and scientifically intolerable to them. By 1863, one Scottish geologist could speak for practically all the others in his profession, as well as for most theologians, when he said:

> At the present day it seems altogether superfluous to raise the ghosts of the old floods and debacles, which, after playing so active a part in the early history of geology, have now for a good many years been quietly consigned to oblivion. Few now seriously hold the belief, that the phenomena of the drift are due to a vast cataclysmic deluge, or to any number of deluges, how enormous soever in power and long continued in operation.[1]

Thus, well before the mid-nineteenth century, the local-Flood theory was launched upon the sea of Biblical and scientific controversy. Older harmonizations quietly faded out, and Pye Smith's contention that the Flood was anthropologically universal though geographically local had become one of the greatest harmonization schemes ever devised. Within the span of a single generation, geologists had led the Church to change its views on the Flood three times; but it has already taken over a century of controversy and investigation to evaluate the full significance of that triple compromise for exegesis and science, and the end is not yet in sight.

Sir Leonard Woolley and the "Flood Stratum" at Ur

Many theologians since the days of John Pye Smith have seen very clearly the futility of trying to reconcile the doctrine of a universal Flood with uniformitarian geology. But not being willing to place themselves in the unpleasant position of opposing the conclusions of eminent geologists, they have accepted the alternative of the local-Flood theory under the assumption that "a local flood could come and go and leave no trace after a few thousand years."[2]

---

[1] Archibald Geikie, "On the Phenomena of the Glacial Drift of Scotland," *Transactions of the Geological Society of Glasgow*, Vol. I, Part II (1863), 1-190. Quoted by Harold W. Clark, *op. cit.*, p. 10.

[2] Ramm, *op. cit.*, p. 243.

Nevertheless, the vast majority of local-Flood advocates were discontent with the thought that a population-destroying Flood could have covered the Near East or even Mesopotamia for over a year without leaving a single discernible trace. This sense of uneasiness was clearly evidenced by the eagerness with which such theologians accepted Sir Leonard Woolley's claims to have found incontrovertible evidence of the Genesis Flood in an eight-foot stratum of clean clay under the ancient city of Ur in lower Mesopotamia.[1]

When this discovery was made in 1929 and when Professor Stephen Langdon announced a few months later that he had made a similar discovery at Kish, several hundred miles to the north, there was great rejoicing everywhere among those who had adopted the local-Flood theory. Here, at last, was evidence for the historicity of the Noahic Deluge (as against those who denied the Genesis account); and also, here was evidence that the Flood was no more than a Mesopotamian inundation (as against those who maintained that it was geographically universal).

This startling and unexpected "evidence" for the Genesis Flood caused many local-Flood advocates to repent of their former opinion that such a Flood need not have left any visible traces. This may be seen in a statement by André Parrot, Curator-in-Chief of the French National Museum, Director of the Mari Archaeological Expedition, and a supporter of the local-Flood theory:

> It seems probable, *a priori,* that *a disaster whose magnitude cannot be in doubt must have left traces in the soil of Mesopotamia. One ought to find there the thick deposits of alluvium which would be left by the unleashing of great masses of water.* Granted the antiquity of the event, which must have been at least prior to the year 2000 B.C. (the oldest narrative, the Sumerian, must go back to that date), such traces would be found only at a considerable depth, that is to say *beneath* recent historical strata, which the pick finds almost at the surface.[2]

But the joy which many experienced in this newly-discovered "harmony" of Genesis and geology was soon to fade. For the embarrassing announcement was shortly to be made that the "flood deposits" at Ur and Kish were not even contemporaneous; and furthermore, the Ur

---

[1] Sir Leonard Woolley, *Excavations at Ur* (London: Ernest Benn, Ltd., 1954), pp. 27-36. Woolley concludes (p. 36): "The Genesis version says that the waters rose to a height of twenty-six feet, which seems to be true" [!].

[2] André Parrot, *The Flood and Noah's Ark* (Eng. tr., London: SCM Press Ltd., 1955), p. 45. Italics are ours.

"flood" did not even inundate the entire city! George A. Barton, writing later of the "flood deposits" at Ur and Kish, said that "Henri Frankfort, indeed, has shown that, from the evidence of the pottery found above and below the strata of silt on the two sites, the two inundations did not occur at the same time, and were not even in the same century!"[1]

Francis R. Steele, who at the time of writing was Assistant Professor of Assyriology in the Department of Oriental Studies at the University of Pennsylvania Graduate School, as well as Assistant Curator of the Babylonian Section of the University Museum, and who participated in several archaeological expeditions to Iraq, strongly denounced the identification of such strata with "the tremendous catastrophe which God brought to destroy a sinning race of men." He insisted that "the presumed 'evidence' has nothing whatever to do with the flood recorded in the Bible."[2]

The Local Flood Theory and Uniformitarian Geology

Now if a minor inundation in just one section of an ancient Mesopotamian city could have left an eight-foot stratum of clay that is clearly distinguishable after 5,000 years, who would be so bold as to claim that the Biblical Deluge could wipe out the entire human population of Mesopotamia (to say nothing of the entire human race), lift a gigantic ark off the earth for a period of months, and yet leave behind it no geological evidences whatever? The time has now passed

[1] George A. Barton, *Archaeology and the Bible* (7th ed.; Philadelphia, 1937), p. 71. G. E. Wright, *Biblical Archaeology* (Philadelphia: Westminster Press, 1957), p. 119, observes: "Woolley seems to have dug some five pits through the early strata of occupation at Ur, but in only two of them did he find deposits of water-borne debris. The logical inference from this is that the flood in question did not cover the whole city of Ur, but only part of it. Furthermore, the site showed no break in occupation, as a result of the flood, which we should expect if there had been a major catastrophe."
[2] Francis R. Steele, "Science and the Bible," *Eternity*, Vol. III, No. 3 (March, 1952), p. 44. It is indeed disappointing to see how many scholars have been deceived into thinking that the Ur stratum gives evidence of the Genesis Flood. Among these have been Harold Peake, *The Flood: New Light on an Old Story* (New York, 1930), p. 114; Sir Charles Marston, *The Bible is True* (London, 1934), pp. 67ff; James Muir, *His Truth Endureth* (Philadelphia, 1937), p. 19; Stephen Caiger, *Old Testament and Modern Discovery* (London, 1938), p. 34; Sir Frederick Kenyon, *The Bible and Archaeology* (London, 1940), p. 140; A. Rendle Short, *Modern Discovery and the Bible* (London, 1942), p. 98; Alfred Rehwinkel, *The Flood* (St. Louis, 1951), pp. 47-54, 174-176; E. F. Kevan, "Genesis" in *The New Bible Commentary* (Grand Rapids, 1953), p. 84; Fred Wight, *Highlights of Archaeology in Bible Lands* (Chicago, 1955), p. 57; Werner Keller, *The Bible as History* (London, 1956), pp. 48-51,

when scholars can set aside such questions as irrelevant; those who take the Biblical account of the Flood seriously consider this to be one of the most devastating arguments against the entire effort to harmonize Genesis and uniformitarian geology.

If modern geologists claim to be able to date with reasonable accuracy even such minute strata as lake varves and confidently correlate these and other minor deposits, glacial and otherwise, into a chronological series that stretches back for millions of years,[1] then Christians who accept such dating methods need not be surprised when geologists utterly reject the possibility of a year-long, population-destroying Flood, even within the confines of the Near East.

As we have previously noted (p. 61), Bernard Ramm seeks to accommodate Genesis to uniformitarian geology by advocating Hugh Miller's theory that ocean waters poured into the "natural saucer" of Western Asia, comprising 100,000 square miles of territory including Mesopotamia and the Caspian Sea, and then drained out again without leaving any visible marks in that region. Ramm concludes:

> From this natural saucer the waters are drained. The purpose of the flood was to blot out the wicked civilization of Mesopotamia, and being a local flood of short duration [*sic!*] we would not expect to find any specific evidence of it, especially after the minimum of another six thousand years of weathering.[2]

and Nelson B. Keyes, *Story of the Bible World* (Maplewood, N. J.: C. S. Hammond & Co., 1959), pp. 19-21.

On the other hand, there is an increasing number of scholars who admit the impossibility of connecting the Genesis Flood with the Ur stratum. Among these are John Bright, "Has Archaeology Found Evidence of the Flood?" *The Biblical Archaeologist*, Vol. V, No. 4 (December, 1942), pp. 55-60; R. Laird Harris, "The Date of the Flood and the Age of Man," *The Bible Today*, Vol. XXXVII, No. 9 (June-Sept., 1943), pp. 575ff; Byron C. Nelson, *Before Abraham* (Minneapolis, 1948), p. 108; Merrill F. Unger, *Archaeology and the Old Testament* (Grand Rapids, 1954), p. 47; Allan A. MacRae, "Archaeology," *Journal of the American Scientific Affiliation*, Vol. 8, No. 4 (December, 1956), p. 16; and R. K. Harrison, *A History of Old Testament Times* (Grand Rapids, 1957), pp. 34-35. Emil G. Kraeling, *Rand McNally Bible Atlas* (Chicago, 1956), p. 44, notes that "some uncertainty" attaches to Woolley's claims; and G. Ernest Wright, *Biblical Archaeology* (Philadelphia, 1957), p. 119, feels that "the Flood story is an old tradition, going back to the end of the Stone Age [c. 4000 B.C.] before the present bounds of the oceans were fixed. To place the tradition this early would make it possible for us to account for the widespread diffusion over the earth of so many different versions of a catastrophe by flood."

[1] Richard Foster Flint, *Glacial Geology and the Pleistocene Epoch* (New York: John Wiley & Sons, 1955), pp. 389-406, claims that the Ice Ages lasted over a million years. For evidence in support of a very brief "Pleistocene epoch" see below, pp. 296-303.

[2] Ramm, *op. cit.*, p. 239.

But in accordance with what principles of modern uniformitarian geology may one assert that such a vast body of water could have covered the entire Near East for a year? And further, by what principles of geology may one assert that six thousand years of weathering would be sufficient to eradicate the specific evidences for such a flood? Assuming that uniformitarian geologists could be persuaded that a flood of such magnitude occurred at all, they would never concede that it came within the past million years, to say nothing of the six thousand years suggested by Ramm.

Thus, the local-Flood theory, which thousands of Christians have accepted in order to be in step with modern geologists, is altogether incompatible with the uniformitarian presuppositions of modern geologists! The only kind of "harmonization" of Genesis and geology that can satisfy a consistent uniformitarian geologist is one which eliminates entirely any flood that even faintly resembles the one described in Genesis. There can be no concord between Moses and Lyell, in spite of the wishful thinking of all too many Christians today.

SUMMARY AND CONCLUSION

In this chapter we have traced the influence of geological theories of the early nineteenth century upon Christian views of the Flood. Throughout the eighteenth century, and well into the nineteenth, most theologians and scientists of the western world believed that the Deluge was responsible for the major fossiliferous strata of the earth. But the rise of Cuvier's theory of successive catastrophes, which assigned most of the fossil strata to ages long before the creation of man, caused many to abandon the older Flood theory of geology. William Buckland led the way in Great Britain by pointing to "diluvium" deposits as positive evidence of the last and greatest catastrophe in the history of the earth—the Genesis Flood.

But no sooner had a large number of Christians accepted the "successive catastrophes" view than Buckland and Sedgwick, along with other geologists, began to make public recantations of their former views. The "diluvium" deposits were no longer attributed to the Flood, but to the last of a series of pre-Adamic catastrophes. The Flood, though still regarded as universal, was now depicted as a comparatively "tranquil" affair, which left no discernible geologic effects.

By now, the Church was ready for the final stage of the harmonization process; for in 1839 John Pye Smith set forth his theory that the Flood was nothing but a local inundation in the Mesopotamian Valley. Freed at long last from the necessity of harmonizing geology with Genesis, scientists dismissed the Genesis Flood from their minds and joined Sir Charles Lyell in his efforts to "patiently untie the Gordian knot" of fossiliferous strata according to the uniformitarian principles which he had enunciated as early as 1830.

Thus it was that under the steadily increasing blows of geological theorizing the Biblical Flood faded from the intellectual horizon of the western world to a mere shadow of its former awe-inspiring grandeur—from a world-engulfing cataclysm to a mere Mesopotamian inundation. Many theologians of the nineteenth century, nurtured by a somewhat anemic philosophy of revelation, fell into line with the latest scientific speculations, fearing lest they might be found at odds with Copernicus and Galileo again (as the geologists were always ready to remind them). Since the books of nature and revelation cannot ultimately contradict each other, it was assumed that the new discoveries of the geologists and the interpretations which they were giving to these discoveries were God's own clues for exegeting the early chapters of Genesis and that men like Buckland and Lyell were the inspired prophets of God's Book of Nature.

The viewpoint that science rather than Scripture must speak the final word on the magnitude of the Flood certainly did not die with the nineteenth century, as the wholehearted acceptance by evangelical theologians of the "evidence" of Sir Leonard Woolley's "Flood stratum" so clearly demonstrates. Nevertheless, a significant minority of Christians have continued to look upon these "harmonizations" of Genesis and geology with profound misgivings and would concur with the judgment of Andrew D. White that "each mixes up more or less of science with more or less of Scripture, and produces a result more or less absurd."[1]

From this study we may draw one vitally important lesson for the present hour: *the Biblical doctrine of the Flood cannot be harmonized with the uniformitarian theories of geology.* A careful examination of the various "blind alleys" into which evangelical Christians have been led should serve as a solemn warning to those who are

[1] White, *op. cit.*, p. 234.

still persisting in the hopeless task of harmonizing two mutually exclusive philosophies of nature and history. It is the conviction of the writers, at least, that a true historical geology will never be formulated until the Genesis Flood, as a universal aqueous catastrophe, is granted its rightful and vital place in the thinking of Christian men of science.

Chapter V

Modern Geology and the Deluge

INTRODUCTION

It has been shown clearly in the first four chapters that the Biblical account of the Flood describes it as of global extent, both anthropologically and geographically. All non-geological objections to this plain teaching of Scripture have been considered and, we believe, thoroughly discredited. There seems to be no reasonable question that, if language can at all be used to convey sensible meanings, the writer of the account of the Deluge (supported by many later writers of Scripture and especially by the Lord Jesus Himself) definitely intended to record the great fact of a universal, world-destroying Flood, of absolute uniqueness in the entire history of this planet.

But we have also seen that, over the past century and more, the development of historical geology has been accompanied by a gradual rejection of the Scriptural revelation of the early history of the earth, at least in its geological implications. Except for occasional abortive attempts to harmonize the sequences of creation week with those of the geological ages, modern geology has all but universally repudiated the book of Genesis, as far as any geological significance is concerned. The attitude of Dorsey Hager, in his recent presidential address before the Utah Geological Society, is typical:

The most important responsibilities of the geologists involve the effect of their findings on the mental and spiritual lives of mankind. Early geologists fought to free people from the myths of Biblical creation. Many mil-

116

lions still live in mental bondage controlled by ignorant ranters who accept the Bible as the last word in science, and accept Archbishop Ussher's claim that the earth was created 4004 B.C. Attempts to reconcile Genesis with geology lead to numerous contradictions. Also the theory of evolution greatly affects modern thinking. Man's rise from simple life forms even today causes much controversy among "fundamentalists" who cling to a literal belief in the Bible.[1]

In similar fashion, the Harvard paleontologist, George Gaylord Simpson, in an important speech delivered in connection with the Darwinian Centennial Convocation at the University of Chicago, said:

With the dawning realization that the earth is extremely old, in human terms of age, came the knowledge that it has changed progressively and radically but usually gradually and always in an orderly, a natural, way. The fact of change had not earlier been denied in Western science or theology—after all, the Noachian Deluge was considered a radical change. But the Deluge was believed to have supernatural causes or concomitants that were not operative through earth's history. The doctrine of geological uniformitarianism, finally established early in the 19th century, widened the recognized reign of natural law. The earth has changed throughout its history under the action of material forces, only, and of the *same* forces as those now visible to us and still acting on it. The steps that I have so briefly traced reduced the sway of superstition in the conceptual world of human lives.[2]

The Flood was once believed to be the explanation for most of the phenomena of geology; later it was regarded as one of a series of geological cataclysms which were the key features in geologic interpretation; then it was thought to explain only certain of the superficial deposits of the earth's surface; finally it was either dismissed as legendary or interpreted as a local flood in Mesopotamia, thus stripping it of all geological consequence. One may search modern geological textbooks or reference works from one end of the library to the other and find in every work consulted either no mention of the Noachian Flood at all or else perhaps a patronizing reference in some historical note on the rise of modern geology.

A Bible-believing Christian thus faces a serious dilemma. When

---

[1] Dorsey Hager: "Fifty Years of Progress in Geology," *Geotimes*, Vol. II, No. 2, (August 1957), p. 12.

[2] George Gaylord Simpson: "The World Into Which Darwin Led Us," *Science*, Vol. 131, April 1, 1960, p. 967.

many thousands of trained geologists, most of them sincere and honest in their conviction of the correctness of their interpretation of the geological data, present an almost unanimous verdict against the Biblical accounts of creation and the Flood, he must of course feel very reluctant to oppose such a tremendous array of scholarship and authority.

On the other hand, when confronted with the Biblical evidence for a global Flood, of tremendous geological potency, he is still more reluctant to reject the Bible's testimony. This is no problem, of course, to men who do not accept the inspiration of the Bible or the authority of Jesus Christ. But the instructed Christian knows that the evidences for full divine inspiration of Scripture are far weightier than the evidences for any fact of science. When confronted with the consistent Biblical testimony to a universal Flood, the believer must certainly accept it as unquestionably true.

Christians have attempted to escape this dilemma by various stratagems of harmonization of the Genesis record of creation and the Flood with the scheme of uniformitarian historical geology. As far at least as the Flood is concerned, the foregoing chapters have demonstrated these attempts to be quite sterile.

The decision then must be faced: either the Biblical record of the Flood is false and must be rejected or else the system of historical geology which has seemed to discredit it is wrong and must be changed. The latter alternative would seem to be the only one which a Biblically and scientifically instructed Christian could honestly take, regardless of the "deluge" of scholarly wrath and ridicule that taking such a position brings upon him.

But this position need not mean at all that the actual observed data of geology are to be rejected. It is not the facts of geology, but only certain interpretations of those facts, that are at variance with Scripture. These interpretations involve the principle of uniformity and evolution as a framework for the historical evaluation of the geological data. But, historical geology is only one of the many branches of geologic science and is, for the most part, of scant practical interest to the commercial geologist, who finds it of little use in his search for oil or mineral deposits. Dr. Walter Bucher, Professor of Geology at Columbia University, and past president of the Geological Society of America admits as much when he says:

The habit of looking up from the pressing detail of an ore body or an oil pool and seeing it in its regional setting is by no means general among the "practical" men of our profession; . . . Professional geologists working in the petroleum industry are apt to lose sight of the importance of fossils, for within the confines of one oil field and even one sedimentary basin, bed tracing by lithologic characters and by electric logging makes fossils appear superfluous.[1]

In context, Dr. Bucher is deploring this lack of practical geologic interest in fossils, because of their presumed necessity for inter-regional or international geologic time correlations, but he is unintentionally thereby admitting that these "correlations" have little genuine scientific value for the understanding of geology. They are not really fundamental; and it is, therefore, possible that entirely different schemes of correlation may be worked out which will be found to fit the facts of geologic science as well as or better than those heretofore in fashion.

It becomes very important, therefore, for Christians to re-study and re-think the great mass of geologic and paleontologic data, with two main purposes in view. The first aim should be to examine carefully the currently accepted scheme of historical geology and its guiding principles, in order to determine clearly wherein and to what degree it is at variance with the Biblical record of creation and the Flood. If this scheme is basically fallacious, as we have had to decide it must be, then we need to try to understand why it could be that such a great body of responsible scientists has accepted it as true. It will be necessary also to discover and point out the inadequacies of the scheme from a strictly scientific viewpoint and to show that it is unable to correlate satisfactorily all the available geologic data. This chapter will attempt to deal primarily with questions of this sort.

The second aim, which will be that of the following chapter, will be to develop, if possible, a new scheme of historical geology, which would not only be true to the Biblical revelations that are pertinent to it but also would serve as a better basis of correlation for the available scientific data than does the present one.

These goals are, to put it very mildly, not easily attainable. It will likely have to be attempted, if at all, largely by men outside the camp of professional geologists. It is unlikely that many students majoring

[1] Walter H. Bucher: "International Responsibilities of Geologists," *Geotimes,* Vol. I, No. 3, 1956, p. 6.

in the field could survive several years of intensive indoctrination in the uniformitarian interpretation of geology without becoming immune to any other interpretation and still less likely that they would ever be granted graduate degrees in this field without subscribing wholeheartedly to it. There is an immense amount of data available that must be restudied and re-evaluated, enough to require the attention of many experts for a very long period of time. Considering the dual limitations imposed on the present writers by their lack of broad training in this field and by the lack of available space in this volume, all that is hoped for at present is to develop and present a plausible preliminary outline study which will stimulate others to further study along the same lines.

GEOLOGICAL IMPLICATIONS OF THE BIBLICAL RECORD

The only proper place to start in this study is with the Bible record of the Flood itself. The following appear to be legitimate inferences from the account:

(1) Tremendous Erosion from Rainfall

Great quantities of water were poured down on the earth from the skies, not in the form of a gentle drizzle but as a torrential downpour continuing without ceasing for forty days and nights, all over the world. Speaking metaphorically, the Scriptures say that the "floodgates of heaven were opened." This pounding rain would first, by its own impact, begin the work of soil and rock erosion. Modern hydrology has proved that raindrop impact is a very significant factor in the initiation of the erosion phenomenon.[1] As the waters begin to run off to lower levels, already containing a certain amount of sedimentary load to aid in further erosive action by the mechanisms of turbulence and attrition,[2] it would begin to form rivulets. These would run finally to the nearest stream but in the process would deepen their own channels by further erosion. This is the way in which great gullies are formed, often to great depths in a single rainstorm, in the

---

[1] W. D. Ellison: "Protecting the Land Against the Raindrop's Blast," *Scientific Monthly*, Vol. 68, April 1949, pp. 241-51.

[2] Linsley, Kohler, and Paulhus: *Applied Hydrology* (New York, McGraw-Hill, 1949), p. 322.

present day.[1] For the uniquely intense rainstorm of the Deluge, the combined processes of raindrop impact, sheet erosion and gully erosion would necessarily have excavated and transported prodigious quantities of earth and rock, even if no other agencies had been available for sediment transfer.

(2) Clouds Not the Source of the Deluge Rains

A global rain continuing for forty days, as described in the Bible, would have required a completely different mechanism for its production than is available at the present day. If all the water in our present atmosphere were suddenly precipitated, it would only suffice to cover the ground to an average depth of less than two inches.[2] The process of evaporation could not have been effective during the rain, of course, since the atmosphere immediately above the earth was already at saturation level. The normal hydrologic cycle would, therefore, have been incapable of supplying the tremendous amounts of rain the Bible record describes. The implication seems to be that the antediluvian climatology and meteorology were much different from the present. There seems to have been an atmospheric source of water of an entirely different type and order of magnitude than now exists.

(3) Enlarged Ocean Basins

Whatever the source of the Deluge rain, the mass of waters which descended to the earth could hardly have been elevated back into the heavens, because it is not there now. This can only mean that much of the waters of our present oceans entered the oceans at the time of the Flood. This in turn implies that the proportion of land area to water area was larger before the Flood, perhaps very much larger, than at present. Much of the present sea-bottom was once dry land. Very likely, in order to accommodate the great mass of waters and permit the land to appear again, great tectonic movements and isostatic adjustments would have to take place, forming the deep ocean

[1] Harry R. Leach: "Soil Erosion," in *Hydrology,* O. E. Meinzer, Ed., (New York, Dover, 1942), p. 609.

[2] C. S. Fox: *Water* (New York, Philosophical Library, 1952), p. xx. Recent measurements indicate the water in the atmosphere over the United States averages only ¾ inches. (Clayton H. Reitan: "Distribution of Precipitable Water Vapor over the Continental United States," *Bulletin of the American Meteorological Society,* Vol. 41, February 1960, p. 86).

basins and troughs and elevating the continents. This seems to be specifically implied in the poetic reflection of the Deluge in Psalm 104:5-9:

> Who laid the foundations of the earth,
> That it should not be moved for ever.
> Thou coveredst it with the deep as with a vesture;
> The waters stood above the mountains.
> At thy rebuke they fled;
> At the voice of thy thunder they hasted away
> (The mountains rose, the valleys sank down)
> Unto the place which thou hadst founded for them.
> Thou hast set a bound that they may not pass over;
> That they turn not again to cover the earth.

That this passage refers to the Flood rather than to the initial Creation is evident from the last verse, which refers to God's promise that a world-covering flood would never again be visited upon the earth.[1] Certainly, therefore, the Bible makes it abundantly plain that the events associated with the Deluge were of immense geologic potency and must have caused profound geologic changes.

(4) Volcanic and Seismic Upheavals

Great volcanic explosions and eruptions are clearly implied in the statement that "all the fountains of the great deep [were] broken up."[2] This must mean that great quantities of liquids, perhaps liquid rocks or magmas, as well as water (probably steam), had been confined under great pressure below the surface rock structure of the earth since the time of its formation and that this mass now burst forth through great fountains, probably both on the lands and under the seas. By analogy with present phenomena associated with volcanism, there must also have been great earthquakes and tsunamis (popularly known as tidal waves) generated throughout the world. These eruptions and waves would have augmented the Flood waters as well as accomplished great amounts of geologic work directly.

[1] Genesis 9:11.
[2] Genesis 7:11.

(5) Unprecedented Sedimentary Activity

The entire account plainly yields the inference that tremendous quantities of earth and rock must have been excavated by the waters of the Flood. Many factors must have contributed to this—the driving rains, the raging streams resulting from them, the earthquakes and volcanic eruptions, the powerful tidal waves, then later the waves and other currents generated by the rising of the lands and sinking of the basins, and perhaps many other factors which we cannot now even guess. Never since the world was formed could there ever have been such extensive erosion of soil and rock beds, on a global scale, as during the Genesis Flood. And the materials that were eroded must eventually have been redeposited somewhere, and necessarily in stratified layers, such as we find everywhere around the world today in the great sedimentary rock systems.

(6) Ideal Conditions for Formation of Fossils

Antediluvian fauna and flora seem to have been richer and more varied than in our present world. This is inferred from our deduction that the land areas were much more extensive than at present and also from the implication that the pre-Deluge climate was vastly different. This probability will be discussed in more detail later. Suffice to note at present that, with the primary purpose of the Deluge being to destroy all life on the earth (at least on the dry land) except the Ark's passengers, there must have been uncounted multitudes of living creatures, as well as plants, trapped and eventually buried in the moving masses of sediments, and of course under conditions eminently conducive to fossilization. Never before or since could there have been such favorable conditions for the formation of fossiliferous strata.

(7) Uniformitarianism Undermined by the Flood

Finally, in view of the global nature of the catastrophe and the magnitude of the geophysical phenomena accompanying it, it follows that the Flood constitutes a profound discontinuity in the normal processes of nature. Any deposits formed before the Flood would almost certainly have been profoundly altered by the great complex of hydrodynamic and tectonic forces unleashed during the Deluge period. The fundamental principle of historical geology, that of uniformitarianism, however valid it may be for the study of deposits formed *since* the Deluge, can therefore not legitimately be applied before that time. This factor is of special importance in the consideration of the so-called absolute geological chronometers, which have been interpreted as giving ages for the various strata and for the earth itself.

BASIC HARMONY OF THE FIELD DATA AND THE BIBLICAL INFERENCES

The Nature of Sedimentary Strata

All of these Biblical inferences from the Flood record are clearly supported in at least a general way by the actual records of the rocks. Almost all of the sedimentary rocks of the earth, which are the ones containing fossils and from which the supposed geologic history of the earth has been largely deduced, have been laid down by moving waters. This statement is so obvious and so universally accepted that it needs neither proof nor elaboration. Sedimentary rocks by definition are those that have been deposited as sediments, which the Oxford Universal Dictionary defines as "earthy or detrital matter deposited by aqueous agency." Obviously these great masses of sediments must first have been eroded from some previous location, transported, and then deposited (perhaps, of course, more than once) —exactly the sort of thing which occurs in any flood and which we have seen must have occurred on a uniquely grand scale during the great Flood of Genesis.

More Water in the Present Oceans

There is, also, much evidence that sea level was once much lower relative to the land surfaces than it is at present, implying either that the amount of water in the ocean was much smaller, or that some parts of the sea bottom have dropped, or both. In the past decade have been discovered great numbers of "seamounts," which are nothing but drowned islands out in the middle of the ocean. These are flat-topped, and therefore non-volcanic in formation, and are now in many cases more than 1,000 fathoms below the surface. Yet they give abundant evidence of having once been above the surface. Dr. Edwin L. Hamilton, the marine geologist, says concerning them:

> They are fossil landforms preserved in the depths of the sea, where they are disturbed only by light currents and the slow rain of pelagic material from the waters above.[1]

Submarine canyons constitute another very intriguing indication that the ocean level was once much lower relative to the present sea-coast than at present. These are great canyons, similar in every respect to the great river canyons of the land surface but extending under the ocean far out on the continental shelves. Usually they project seaward from a river valley on the land. One of the best known is the submarine canyon extending out some 300 miles to the deep sea floor from the mouth of the Hudson River. These canyons exist in great numbers around every continent of the world.[2]

Their striking similarity to canyons on land certainly would seem to favor the view that they were formed above the ocean. However, this would require a differential lowering of the ocean by at least several thousand feet, and therefore other explanations have been assiduously sought. There have been some geologists who strongly maintained the sub-aerial origin of the canyons, accounting for the sea-level lowering by means of the storage of water in the glacial ice-sheets of the Pleistocene. In a recent review of the problem, W. D. Thornbury, Professor of Geology at Indiana University, says:

> The difficulties encountered in explaining the lowering of sea level necessary for the canyons to have been cut by streams seem insurmountable. . . . If Tolstoy's conclusion that Hudson Canyon extends down to a depth of 15,000 feet is correct, the magnitude of lowering of sea level to permit subaerial canyon cutting seems beyond any possibility of realization.[3]

It is thus primarily the difficulty of accounting for the much lower former sea level that has caused most geologists to attempt to find ways of explaining the origin of the canyons while under the sea, the

---

[1] Edwin L. Hamilton: "The Last Geographic Frontier: The Sea Floor," *Scientific Monthly,* Vol. 85, December 1957, p. 303.

[2] Francis P. Shepard: *Submarine Geology* (New York, Harper's, 1948), pp. 231-233.

[3] Wm. D. Thornbury: *Principles of Geomorphology,* (New York, Wiley, 1954), p. 472.

most generally accepted hypothesis at present being that they were formed by "turbidity currents" or flows of mixtures of water and sediment under water. This theory also has many difficulties, so that Thornbury says, after reviewing all the theories:

> The origin of submarine canyons remains a perplexing problem. The theory that they were cut by turbidity currents aided by submarine landsliding, slumping, and creep holds a slightly favored position, not so much because it answers all the questions connected with them but because it encounters fewer difficulties than any other theory.[1]

It would seem, on the other hand, that Deluge conditions, as inferred from the Scriptural record, could give a reasonable explanation for their origin. As the lands were uplifted and the ocean basins depressed at the close of the Deluge period, the great currents streaming down into the ocean depths would quickly have eroded great gorges in the still soft and unconsolidated sediments exposed by the sinking of the basins. Then, as these gorges were themselves submerged by the continuing influx of waters from the rising continental blocks, it may well have been that the turbidity currents entering the canyons may have deepened and extended them still further, a process which has continued on a smaller scale throughout the centuries since.

These and other evidences prompted Dr. K. K. Landes, Head of the Geology Department at Michigan University, to say recently:

> Can we, as seekers after truth, shut our eyes any longer to the obvious fact that large areas of sea floor have sunk vertical distances measured in miles?[2]

Volcanism

Further inferences from the Biblical record of the Deluge are that there were great amounts of volcanism and great earth movements, both in the early and later stages of the Flood period. That these inferences are supported by the field evidence, at least in a general way, is unquestionable. A great part of the earth's land surface is covered with material originally ejected from volcanic cones or vents.

Rocks formed by volcanic action are called *igneous,* from a Latin term

[1] *Ibid.,* p. 475.
[2] Kenneth K. Landes, "Illogical Geology," *Geotimes,* Vol. III, No. 6 (March 1959), p. 19.

for "fire." Without them, no continent would have assumed anything like its present features. During past geological ages, lava flowed much more freely than now; it not only spouted from craters, but also pushed upward from immense cracks in the planet's crust. Earth's most stupendous rock formation, stretching for more than a thousand miles along the shores of Canada and Alaska, was squeezed out in such fashion. Oozing lava built great plateaus which now cover 200,000 square miles in Washington, Oregon, Idaho and northern California. An even larger eruption created India's famous Deccan Plateau, whose once molten rock extends as much as 2 miles below the surface. Argentina, South Africa and Brazil have similar plateaus.[1]

It is significant, too, that volcanic rocks are found interbedded with sedimentary rocks of all supposed geologic ages, which would correlate with the Biblical implication that the "fountains of the great deep" continued to pour out their contents throughout the entire Flood period (see Genesis 8:2). It is not only on the land, of course, that evidences of volcanic action are found.

The present status of knowledge of the sea floor in the Pacific Ocean area is such that a surprising amount of evidence of large-scale faulting, mountain-building, volcanic activity, and large-scale crustal movements is known; this is a marked departure from earlier assumptions, which, because of lack of information, held that this vast area had been relatively calm during geologic time.[2]

It is well known, of course, that most of the oceanic islands, both above and below present ocean level, were primarily of volcanic origin.

Earth Movements

With regard to earth movements, it is likewise common knowledge that the rock formations of the earth exhibit everywhere profound evidence of great tectonic activity. Most of the sedimentary strata (not to mention the still more disturbed igneous and metamorphic rocks) have been tilted, folded and faulted on a tremendous scale. It is extremely interesting, in light of the Biblical suggestion of uplift of the lands at the conclusion of the Deluge period, to note that most of the present mountain ranges of the world are believed to have been

[1] Gary Webster: "Volcanoes: Nature's Blast Furnaces," *Science Digest,* Vol. 42, Nov. 1957, p. 5.

[2] Edwin L. Hamilton, *op. cit.,* p. 299.

uplifted (on the basis of fossil evidence) during the Pleistocene or late Pliocene. Flint makes this fact the basis for his "topographic control" theory of continental glaciation.

Despite the fact that references are scattered and the data have never been fully assembled, the worldwide distribution of these movements is striking. In North America late Pliocene or Pleistocene movements involving elevations of thousands of feet are recorded in Alaska and in the Coast Ranges of southern California. . . . In Europe the Scandinavian Mountains were created from areas of very moderate relief and altitude in "late Tertiary" time. . . . The Alps were conspicuously uplifted in Pleistocene and late pre-Pleistocene time. In Asia there was great early Pleistocene uplift in Turkestan, the Pamira, the Caucasus, and central Asia generally. Most of the vast uplift of the Himalayas is ascribed to the "latest Tertiary" and Pleistocene. In South America the Peruvian Andes rose at least 5000 feet in post-Pliocene time. . . . In addition to these tectonic movements many of the high volcanic cones around the Pacific border, in western and central Asia and in eastern Africa, are believed to have been built up to their present great heights during the Pliocene and Pleistocene.[1]

Since the Pliocene and Pleistocene are supposed to represent the most recent geological epochs, except that of the present, and since nearly all of the great mountain areas of the world have been found to have fossils from these times near their summits, there is no conclusion possible other than that the mountains (and therefore the continents of which they form the backbones) have all been uplifted essentially simultaneously and quite recently. Surely this fact accords well with the Biblical statements.

Fossilization

Another Biblical implication is that great numbers of living creatures must have been entrapped and buried in the swirling sediments. Under ordinary processes of nature as now occurring, fossils (especially of land animals and even marine vertebrates) are very rarely formed. The only way they can be preserved long enough from the usual processes of decay, scavenging and disintegration is by means of

---

[1] R. F. Flint: *Glacial Geology and the Pleistocene Epoch* (New York, Wiley, 1947), pp. 514-15. See also an extensive listing of Pliocene-Pleistocene uplifts in Flint's more recent work, *Glacial and Pleistocene Geology* (New York, Wiley, 1957), pp. 501-502.

quick burial in aqueous sediments. William J. Miller, Emeritus Professor of Geology at U.C.L.A., points this out:

> Comparatively few remains of organisms now inhabiting the earth are being deposited under conditions favorable for their preservation as fossils. . . . It is, nevertheless, remarkable that so vast a number of fossils are embedded in the rocks. . . .[1]

That the rock formations of the earth are veritably rich in fossils is a fact hard to reconcile with the paucity of potential fossils being formed under present conditions. Geologists sometimes speak of the "incompleteness of the fossil record," but this is only because of the absence of the anticipated missing links in the supposed evolutionary sequences of development. There is an abundance of fossils known, of all kinds of creatures. Practically all modern families, and most genera, are represented in the fossil record, as well as great numbers of extinct creatures. An outstanding Swedish scientist, late Director of the Botanical Institute at Lund, Sweden, says:

> It has been argued that the series of paleontological finds is too intermittent, too full of "missing links" to serve as a convincing proof. If a postulated ancestral type is not found, it is simply stated that it has not so far been found. Darwin himself often used this argument and in his time it was perhaps justifiable. But it has lost its value through the immense advances of paleobiology in the twentieth century. . . . The true situation is that those fossils have not been found which were expected. Just where new branches are supposed to fork off from the main stem it has been impossible to find the connecting types.[2]

The late Dr. Richard Goldschmidt, of the University of California, one of the world's outstanding geneticists, said in similar vein:

> In spite of the immense amount of the paleontologic material and the existence of long series of intact stratigraphic sequences with perfect records for the lower categories, transitions between the higher categories are missing.[3]

We shall consider the fossil deposits again later, in more detail. The point to be made here is that they are very rich, both in num-

[1] William J. Miller: *An Introduction to Historical Geology* (6th Ed., New York, Van Nostrand, 1952), p. 12.

[2] N. Heribert-Nilsson: *Synthetische Artbildung* (Verlag CWH Gleerup, 1953), p. 1188.

[3] Richard Goldschmidt: "Evolution, as Viewed by One Geneticist," *American Scientist,* Vol. 40, Jan. 1952, p. 98.

bers and variety, in spite of having yielded up very few, if any, forms that might be considered as transitional between distinct kinds of creatures, whether living or extinct. The richness of the deposits fits well with the Genesis record of the character and magnitude of the great Flood but accords very poorly with the uniformitarian notion that the relatively quiescent sedimentary processes of the present day, forming almost no fossils, can account for the extensive fossil-bearing strata.

It seems evident, therefore, that the major geological inferences that can be derived from the Biblical record of the Flood are in good agreement with the actual geological facts as seen in the field. But this does not mean, of course, that these facts have been thus interpreted. They have rather been fitted as well as possible into the uniformitarian scheme of historical geology. In fact, the sedimentary strata with their entombed fossils have been made the very basis of this system of interpretation. These rocks have been divided into chronologic sequences based on the types of fossils contained in them, the resulting synthesis being the generally accepted "geological ages," with the fossil sequences supposedly demonstrating the evolutionary history of life on the earth.

THE UNIFORMITARIAN INTERPRETATION OF GEOLOGY

As was pointed out in Chapter IV, the Lyellian method of geologic interpretation has now for over a hundred years been the generally accepted method. Geologists almost universally have accepted his principle of uniformity as the only proper basis of geologic analysis.

This is the great underlying principle of modern geology and is known as the *principle of uniformitarianism.* . . . Without the principle of uniformitarianism there could hardly be a science of geology that was more than pure description.[1]

The Present: the Key to the Past

This principle is commonly stated in the Huttonian catchword that "the present is the key to the past." That is, geomorphic processes which can be observed in action at present, such as erosion, sedimentation, glaciation, volcanism, diastrophism, etc.—all operating

[1] W. D. Thornbury, *op. cit.*, pp. 16, 17.

in essentially the same fashion as at present—can be invoked to explain the origin and formation of all the earth's geologic deposits.

The doctrine of uniformity thus is supposed to render unnecessary any recourse to catastrophism, except on a minor scale. Great geologic features once attributed to geologic cataclysms or "revolutions" can presumably be explained instead by ordinary processes operating over long periods of time. As R. W. Fairbridge, Professor of Geology at Columbia University, points out:

> In their effort to establish natural causes for the grand-scale workings of nature they spurned the Scriptural concept of catastrophe. Under the leadership of the Scottish pioneers, James Hutton and Charles Lyell, they advanced the principle of uniformitarianism, which held that the events of the past could be explained in the light of processes at work in the present.[1]

It should be obvious that this principle can never actually be *proved* to be valid. To be sure, it *seems* eminently reasonable, because the same principle is basic in other sciences. The uniform and dependable operation of natural processes is the foundation of modern experimental science, without which, indeed, modern science as we know it would be quite impossible.

But historical geology is unique among the sciences in that it deals with events that are past, and therefore not reproducible. Since presumably no human observers were present to record and study these events of the past (actually, the only human observers—Noah and his family—recorded that the events were catastrophic!), it thus is impossible ever to prove that they were brought about by the same processes of nature that we can measure at present. The uniformitarian assumption is certainly a reasonable assumption, provided there is no sufficiently valid evidence to the contrary, but it must always remain merely an assumption.

Organic Evolution

A second great principle of historical geology as currently developed is that of organic evolution. This is implicit in the fossil identification method of determining the geological ages of specific rocks. It is assumed that, at any given period in the past history of the earth,

[1] Rhodes W. Fairbridge: "The Changing Level of the Sea," *Scientific American,* Vol. 202, May 1960, p. 70.

there was only one assemblage[1] of organisms on the earth and that, therefore, when these organisms are found as fossils in the rock stratum, the latter is thereby identified as belonging to that age. It is believed that, through evolution, these creatures, and the assemblages thereof, became progressively more developed and specialized in the course of the ages. The fossils contained in the rocks, therefore, are considered the best means (and indeed the only completely reliable means) of assigning a geologic date to the rocks.

Geologic dating and correlation are thus based upon the two assumptions of uniformity and evolution. The importance of the so-called "index fossils" in the geologic identification and dating of rocks is indicated by the Yale geologists, Charles Schuchert and Carl Dunbar, as follows:

> A trained paleontologist can identify the relative geologic age of any fossiliferous rock formation by a study of its fossils almost as easily and certainly as he can determine the relative place of a sheet of manuscript by looking at its pagination. Fossils thus make it possible to correlate events in different parts of the world and so to work out the history of the earth as a whole.[2]

In similar vein, a leading European paleontologist writes:

> The only chronometric scale applicable in geologic history for the stratigraphic classification of rocks and for dating geological events exactly is furnished by the fossils. Owing to the irreversibility of evolution, they offer an unambiguous time scale for relative age determinations and for worldwide correlations of rocks.[3]

The Geologic Time-Table

The rock systems of geology and their corresponding geologic ages have for many years been worked up in the form of a geologic timetable. For a typical example, see Figure 5 (p. 133). Such a presentation obviously indicates a gradual progression of life from the

---

[1] By "assemblage" is meant the entire number of species living at the time. It is the group of species, rather than any individual species, that is considered typical of the particular age, although certain individual species are also used as "index fossils" in many cases.

[2] Schuchert and Dunbar: *Outlines of Historical Geology* (4th Ed., New York, Wiley, 1941), p. 53.

[3] O. H. Schindewolf: "Comments on Some Stratigraphic Terms," *American Journal of Science* (Vol. 255, June 1957), p. 394.

Figure 5. GEOLOGIC TIME TABLE.

MAIN DIVISIONS AND EVENTS OF GEOLOGICAL TIME

ERAS	PERIODS	CHARACTERISTIC LIFE	ESTIMATED YEARS AGO
CENOZOIC	Quaternary: Recent Epoch Pleistocene Epoch	Rise of modern plants and animals, and man	25,000 975,000
	Tertiary: Pliocene Epoch Miocene " Oligocene " Eocene " Paleocene "	Rise of mammals and development of highest plants	12,000,000 25,000,000 35,000,000 60,000,000 70,000,000
MESOZOIC	Cretaceous	Modernized angiosperms and insects abundant. Foraminifers profuse. Extinction of dinosaurs, flying reptiles, and ammonites.	70,000,000 to 200,000,000
	Jurassic	First (reptilian) birds. First of highest forms of insects. First (primitive) angiosperms.	
	Triassic	Earliest dinosaurs, flying reptiles, marine reptiles, and primitive mammals. Cycads and conifers common. Modern corals common. Earliest ammonites.	
PALEOZOIC	Permian	Rise of primitive reptiles. Earliest cycads and conifers. Extinction of trilobites. First modern corals.	200,000,000 to 500,000,000
	Pennsylvanian	Earliest known insects. Spore plants abundant.	
	Mississippian	Rise of amphibians. Culmination of crinoids.	
	Devonian	First known seed plants. Great variety of boneless fishes. First evidence of amphibians.	
	Silurian	Earliest known land animals. Primitive land plants. Rise of fishes. Brachiopods, trilobites, and corals abundant.	
	Ordovician	Earliest known vertebrates. Graptolites, corals, brachiopods, cephalopods, and trilobites abundant. Oldest primitive land plants.	
	Cambrian	All subkingdoms of invertebrate animals represented. Brachiopods and trilobites common.	
PROTEROZOIC	Keweenawan Huronian	Primitive water-dwelling plants and animals.	500,000,000 to 1,000,000,000
ARCHEOZOIC	Timiskaming Keewatin	Oldest known life (mostly indirect evidence).	1,000,000,000 to 1,800,000,000

simple to the complex, from lower to higher, and therefore implies organic evolution. This is considered by geologists to be a tremendously important key to the interpretation of geologic history. Modern biologists in turn regard the geologic record as the cornerstone of their hypothesis of organic evolution. It is common to read statements in biologic literature to the effect that, although modern biologic research has been unable to agree on the method by which evolution is brought about genetically or to provide examples of evolution occurring on any large scale today, it is nevertheless proved to be a fact by the paleontologic record.

Evolution of the animal and plant world is considered by all those entitled to judgment to be a fact for which no further proof is needed. But in spite of nearly a century of work and discussion there is still no unanimity in regard to the details of the means of evolution.[1]

It is true that nobody thus far has produced a new species or genus, etc., by macromutation. It is equally true that nobody has produced even a species by the selection of micromutations. In the best-known organisms, like *Drosophila,* innumerable mutants are known. If we were able to combine a thousand or more of such mutants in a single individual, this still would have no resemblance whatsoever to any type known as a species in nature.[2]

Although the comparative study of living animals and plants may give very convincing circumstantial evidence, fossils provide the only historical documentary evidence that life has evolved from simpler to more complex forms.[3]

These quotations, from outstanding evolutionary authorities both in geology and biology, demonstrate the great importance of the paleontological record to the theory of evolution. In turn, the principles of evolution and uniformity are seen to be of paramount importance in the correlation of the geologic strata. These principles are absolutely basic, both from the point of view of the history of the development of modern geology and from that of present interpretation of geologic field data. The circular reasoning here should be evident and indeed *is* evident even to many historical geologists. For example, R. H. Rastall, Lecturer in Economic Geology at Cambridge University, says:

[1] Richard Goldschmidt: "Evolution, as Viewed by One Geneticist," *American Scientist,* Vol. 40, January 1952, p. 84.
[2] *Ibid.,* p. 94.
[3] Carl O. Dunbar: *Historical Geology* (New York, Wiley, 1949), p. 52.

It cannot be denied that from a strictly philosophical standpoint geologists are here arguing in a circle. The succession of organisms has been determined by a study of their remains embedded in the rocks, and the relative ages of the rocks are determined by the remains of organisms that they contain.[1]

Methods of Resolving Contradictions

Of course, it is maintained by many stratigraphers that other factors, especially that of superposition of the strata, are also important in geologic correlation and that, in general, these factors justify the usual assignment of ages to strata on the basis of their fossil contents.[2] The usual situation, however, is that only a few formations are ever superposed in any one locality and that it is very difficult or impossible to correlate strata in different localities by this principle of superposition. The fossils must be resorted to, and the fossil sequence is assumed to accord with the principle of evolution. Furthermore, even where superposed strata *are* exposed, it rather often happens that the fossils appear to be in reverse order from that demanded by the evolutionary history, which paradox is commonly explained by the assumption that the strata have been folded or faulted out of their original sequence.

In any particular region the sequence of geologic events is clearly shown by the order of superposition of undeformed sedimentary formations. . . . Of course, there are many places where the succession has been locally inverted by folding or interrupted by faulting, but such exceptions will betray themselves in the evidences of disturbance and in the unnatural succession of the fossils.[3]

The sedimentary rocks by themselves, however, do not yield any specific time marks, setting aside the old law of superposition, which can provide relative age indicators only in a restricted manner, and which is unfit for age correlations. Moreover, it may be misleading in some cases: the beds

[1] R. H. Rastall article, "Geology," in *Encyclopedia Brittannica*, 1956, p. 168, Vol. 10. In similar vein, though in a slightly different connection, E. I. White says: "Paleogeography is anything but an exact science, largely owing to our limited knowledge but also to subjective interpretation, and moreover, there is also the danger of circular argument, since the geography of these early times is based at least in part on the distribution and supposed habitat of the very fossils with which we are dealing." ("Original Environment of the Craniates," in *Studies on Fossil Vertebrates*, ed. by T. S. Westoll, London, Athlone Press, 1958).

[2] In most cases, the "index fossils" are marine organisms.

[3] Schuchert and Dunbar, *op. cit.*, p. 5.

in a section may be overturned or, owing to a hidden thrust plane, older beds may overlie younger ones.[1]

The basis for the apparent great strength of the present system of historical geology is here clearly seen. Provision is made ahead of time for any contrary evidence that might be discovered in the field. The geologic time sequence has been built up primarily on the tacit assumption of organic evolution, which theory in turn derives its chief support from the geologic sequence thus presented as actual historical evidence of the process. Fragments of the sequences thus built up often appear legitimately superposed in a given exposure, but there are never more than a very few formations exposed at any one locality, occupying only a small portion of the geologic column. Formations from different localities are integrated into a continuous sequence almost entirely by means of the principle of organic evolution.[2]

And when, as frequently occurs, strata are found superposed but with the fossils in the inverse order, this paradox is resolved by saying that the strata must have been inverted through faulting or folding, whether or not there is any physical evidence thereof. When superposed strata are found with intervening systems missing, this is explained by the assumption of a corresponding period of erosion rather than deposition.

This neatly packaged system of geologic interpretation has the effect of making it practically impossible ever to dislodge it by any amount of contrary evidence. Nevertheless, the writers are convinced that this uniformitarian, evolutionary scheme of historical geology is basically fallacious and that extensive contrary evidence against it *does* exist. We have reference now to scientific evidence, of course, since it has already been demonstrated that the Biblical evidence is strongly opposed to it.

THE INADEQUACY OF UNIFORMITY
TO EXPLAIN THE STRATA

Historical geology purports to explain all of the earth's geologic formations in terms of the essentially uniform operation of processes

---

[1] Schindewolf, *loc. cit.*

[2] In the historical development of the phylogenies of the paleontologic record, much use was made of anticipated analogies with the ontogenies revealed by embryologic studies, and with the studies of comparative anatomy.

of nature that are now occurring and can be studied at the present time. This is the basic philosophy behind the rejection of the earlier catastrophism in geologic interpretation, it being held unreasonable to postulate geologic phenomena outside the range of present experience to explain the strata. Thus it is now believed that the present-day geomorphic processes (including erosion, deposition, volcanism, diastrophism, etc.), acting essentially in the same manner and at the same rates as at present, can suffice to account for all the earth's physiographic features when properly studied and correlated. The philosophy that has dominated the development of historical geology as currently understood is revealed by the following quotation from an early and very influential textbook:

> It is the triumph of geology as a science to have demonstrated that we do not need to refer to vast, unknown and terrible causes the relief features of the earth, but that the known agencies at work today are competent to produce them, provided they have time enough.[1]

This statement is significant in its implication that an understanding of the earth's surface is possible in terms of either intense processes acting over short times or slow processes acting over long times. The claim is merely made that it is *possible* to interpret geology in terms of slow processes acting over long time periods—not that it is *necessary* to do so. One may, in fact, read at length in Lyell and in works of the other early uniformitarian geologists without finding more than essentially this claim. *Uniformitarianism, in other words, has simply been assumed, not proved. Catastrophism has simply been denied, not refuted.*

But as a matter of fact it is not even true that uniformity is a *possible* explanation for most of the earth's geologic formations, as any candid examination of the facts ought to reveal.

Volcanism and Igneous Rocks

For example, a great part of the earth's surface rocks are igneous in origin, in many different forms, and are often of tremendous extent, sometimes on the surface, sometimes intruded between sedimentary rocks, sometimes forming the base of a sedimentary series. Their magnitude is indicated by the following:

[1] Pirsson, L. V., and C. Schuchert: *Textbook of Geology* (New York, Wiley, 1920), Vol. I, p. 5.

Sills and interformational sheets may range in thickness from a fraction of a millimeter to over 1000 feet, and in lateral extent from a few millimeters to many miles. Laccoliths vary in thickness from a fraction of an inch to several miles; they are commonly thicker than sills. They may be over 100 miles in length and nearly as wide, although they are usually smaller. . . . A batholith may be exposed over thousands of square miles. Individual flows are generally several feet thick and they may be over 100 feet thick. If successive flows have been poured out upon one another, the total thickness may amount to many hundreds of feet.[1]

These igneous rocks are found all over the world in great profusion. Often they are found intruding into previously deposited sedimentary rocks or on the surface covering vast areas of earlier deposits. The Columbia Plateau, of the northwestern United States, is a tremendous lava plateau of almost incredible thickness covering about 200,000 square miles.

The physiographic history of this province begins with the ancient surface before the lavas were erupted. This is known to have been locally rough, even mountainous, partly by the fact that some of the old peaks rose above the lava flood, *which was at least several thousand feet deep*.[2]

The great shields of the world, notably in this continent the great Canadian shield, are mainly granites and other igneous rocks. Says Hussey:

Two million square miles of the great Canadian Shield region are covered by Pre-Cambrian rocks composed in part of pink granite-gneiss that was originally intruded in the form of batholiths during vast mountain-making upheavals.[3]

Space precludes further multiplication of examples, but these phenomena are common all over the world and account for a substantial percentage of the earth's surface rocks, in addition to the intrusive rocks found in every part of the geologic column and the igneous masses underlying the sedimentaries.

But the only modern process at all pertinent to these phenomena is that of volcanism, which in its present character could not possibly have produced these great igneous formations. There are perhaps 500

[1] F. H. Lahee: *Field Geology* (Fifth Ed., New York, McGraw-Hill, 1952), p. 139.
[2] N. M. Fenneman: *Physiography of the Western United States* (New York, McGraw-Hill, 1931), p. 229. Italics are ours.
[3] R. C. Hussey: *Historical Geology* (New York, McGraw-Hill, 1947), p. 54.

active volcanoes in the world,[1] and possibly three times that many extinct volcanoes.[2] But nothing ever seen by man in the present era can compare with whatever the phenomena were which caused the formation of these tremendous structures. The principle of uniform-- ity breaks down completely at this important point of geologic inter- pretation. Some manifestation of catastrophic action alone is suffi- cient.

Earth Movements

Another major geologic phenomenon, encountered all over the world, is the evidence of tremendous crustal movements that must have occurred in the past. Great thicknesses of rocks have apparently been uplifted thousands of feet; strata have buckled, folded, some- times been thrust laterally or completely overturned on a gigantic scale.

The great Rocky Mountain chain, especially as developed in the Southern Rockies, is essentially a series of great folds. In the eastern part of this country, the Appalachian system of mountains is believed to be the uplifted and eroded remnant of a great geosynclinal trough, in which a thickness of some 40,000 feet of sedimentary rocks was deposited.[3] These mountains reveal a very involved assortment of gigantic faults, folds, and thrusts. Similar phenomena are found in nearly every region of the world. The crust of the earth seems to have been distorted, fractured, elevated, depressed and contorted in almost every conceivable way at some time or times in the past. This is fur- ther attested by the great areas of metamorphism, in which the orig- inal sedimentary or crystalline rocks have been completely changed in form as a result of the gigantic stresses acting in the crust. Schis- tosity in crystalline rocks is also attributed to these causes.

Nor are these phenomena, which are too familiar to everyone even to require documentation, limited to the land surfaces.

It was once supposed that the deep oceans had remained dark, life- less, and unchanged, save for the finest rain of sediment, since the world

[1] A list of 450 volcanoes that have erupted in historic times is given by B. Guten- berg and C. F. Richter in their *Seismicity of the Earth* (Princeton, N. J., University Press, 1949), pp. 253-267.

[2] It is interesting that Mt. Ararat itself is an old volcanic cone 17,000 ft. high.

[3] Charles Schuchert: *Stratigraphy of the Eastern and Central United States* (New York, Wiley, 1943), pp. 117-122.

began; but new knowledge has quite dispelled this view. Across the ocean floor geophysicists have now traced great fractures, scarps and rifts, have found scattered volcanic peaks and ranges, and have charted canyons cut by slumps and flows of mud on the continental margins.[1]

Most, if not all, of these diastrophic features of the earth's crust are believed to be associated with orogenies; that is, periods of "mountain-building." Says Dr. W. H. Bucher:

> The most conspicuous and perhaps also the most significant structural features of the face of the earth are the great belts of folded mountains, like those of the Himalayas, the Andes, the Urals and the Appalachians, the so-called orogenic belts. Along these long and relatively narrow zones, great thicknesses of dominantly marine sediments have been squeezed together and thrust one upon the other to form highly elongated folds with axes essentially parallel to that of the belt.[2]

It is here that the principle of uniformity would appear to be most inadequate. If it were valid, surely a feature of such prime importance in the interpretation of earth history as diastrophism and orogeny should be explainable in terms of some sort of present-day observable and measurable process which is now producing incipient earth movements of similar kind. But so far is this from being the case that geologists are still utterly unable to agree on even a satisfactory hypothesis of mountain-building! L. H. Adams, of the Carnegie Institute, said some years ago in his retiring address as president of the American Geophysical Union, concerning these problems of orogeny:

> Many attempts to answer these questions have engaged the attention of the best minds, but the existing answers leave much to be desired. Complicated mechanisms in great variety have been adduced, but in all instances cogent objections have been raised.[3]

In general, there are currently two main hypotheses of mountain-building. One depends on thermal contraction of the crust, the other on subcrustal convection currents. Another, the theory of continental drift, is at present running a poor third. None of them is based on present measurable processes, but solely on hypothetical speculations

[1] J. Tuzo Wilson: "The Crust," in *The Earth and Its Atmosphere*, D. R. Bates, ed., (New York, Basic Books, Inc., 1957), p. 63.

[2] W. H. Bucher: "Fundamental Properties of Orogenic Belts," *Transactions, American Geophysical Union*, Vol. 32, August 1951, p. 514.

[3] L. H. Adams: "Some Unsolved Problems of Geophysics," *Transactions, American Geophysical Union*, Vol. 28, October, 1947, p. 673.

which may or may not be meaningful. Proponents of the two leading hypotheses have each advanced arguments showing the inadequacies of the other. One of the leading modern authorities, Dr. J. Tuzo Wilson, says:

> When the cause of orogenesis can be stated in precise physical terms and when the result of repeated application of the fundamental orogenetic process can be shown to be adequate to produce the complexities of geology, then geology and physics of the earth will have merged. This has not yet been achieved, but there appears to be a reasonable expectation that it can be achieved and that fairly soon.[1]

This hope seems no closer to realization today. In a recent Sigma Xi National Lecture, Dr. A. J. Eardley says:

> The internal structure of mountains is fairly well understood, and the erosional processes that fashion the details of their outward appearance are no longer great mysteries. Yet the cause of the deformation of the earth's outer layers and the consequent building of mountains still effectively evades an explanation."[2]

All attempted explanations of orogeny thus still seem to have unreconciled difficulties, and none is yet generally accepted.[3] The only modern force of possibly similar character is the earthquake. These sometimes are of terrific intensity but obviously provide no real explanation of orogeny or of other diastrophic phenomena. In fact, earthquakes are believed to be merely the result of slippage along fault planes or planes of weakness already formed.[4]

---

[1] J. Tuzo Wilson: "Orogenesis as the Fundamental Geologic Process," *Transactions, American Geophysical Union,* Vol. 33, June, 1952, p. 445.

[2] Armand J. Eardley: "The Cause of Mountain Building—an Enigma," *American Scientist,* Vol. 45, June, 1957, p. 189.

[3] Three recent theories of considerable interest are those of J. Tuzo Wilson ("Geophysics and Continental Growth," *American Scientist,* Vol. 47, March 1959, pp. 1-24), who assumes that the continents have been developed entirely by volcanism through geologic time, with the escaping magmas leading to much contraction and fracturing in the crust; Charles H. Hapgood (*Earth's Shifting Crust,* Pantheon, 1958), who visualizes the earth's crustal structure as slipping over semi-fluid or plastic rock in the mantle in response to centrifugal forces on the heterogeneously distributed masses of rock and ice on the continents, and George C. Kennedy ("The Origin of Continents, Mountain Ranges, and Ocean Basins," *American Scientist,* Vol. 47, December 1959, pp. 491-504), who explains uplift and subsidence in terms of decrease or increase in rock densities at great depths as a result of changes in physical state. Each of these authors claims a good degree of correlation of the structural implications of his theory with observed crustal features. Each theory, of course, is highly speculative.

[4] L. Don Leet: *Causes of Catastrophe* (New York, McGraw-Hill, 1948), p. 31.

All this, again, bears very heavily against the notion of uniformity. Furthermore, these orogenic processes cannot be shoved back into the dim recesses of early terrestrial history but must very recently have been immensely potent. All the major mountain ranges of the present world evidently were uplifted within the most recent eras of geologic history. It has already been pointed out that fossil evidence indicates most of the great mountain chains date from the Pleistocene or late Pliocene at the earliest. The geologic and archaeologic chronologies of the fossil beds which have yielded remains and artifacts of human beings likewise date in many instances from the Pleistocene and even perhaps the Pliocene. After considering all the human fossil evidence, Zeuner concludes:

> One point is apparent from the table, that the evolution of *Homo* is not entirely confined to the Pleistocene. We find the definitely human Pithecanthropus group in the lower Pleistocene, and there is some suggestive evidence for the Sapiens-stock going back to this time. If this proves to be true, the Homo-stock as a whole must date from well within the Pliocene.[1]

Of course, we are not subscribing to the evolutionary interpretation of these evidences, but it is significant that the geologic and paleontologic data seem to prove that man lived during the times when deposits were being laid down which are now found capping the mountains and thus that the mountain-making processes, with all their associated phenomena—the faults, folds, rifts, thrusts, etc.— have been active within geologically very recent times. *But they are not active now,* at least not measurably so! And yet the processes associated with mountain-building, and their results, are considered by all geophysicists and geomorphologists to be absolutely basic to the interpretation of earth history. Here, then, is another extremely important gap in the range of applicability of the so-called law of uniformity, whereby present processes are supposed to suffice to explain all geologic phenomena!

Continental Ice Sheets

And what about the phenomenon of continental glaciation, about which so much has been written and so many theories developed? There are many present-day glaciers, of course, and even two great

[1] F. E. Zeuner: *Dating the Past* (2nd Ed., London, Methuen & Co., Ltd., 1950), p. 303.

ice-caps, in Greenland and Antarctica; but nothing occurring in the present is at all comparable to the great ice sheets of the past, which have supposedly molded so much of the earth's present surface geology:

> Some 4,000,000 square miles of North America, 2,000,000 square miles or more of Europe, and an as yet little known but possibly comparable area in Siberia were glaciated. In addition, many lesser areas were covered by local ice caps. Thousands of valley glaciers existed in mountains where today there are either no glaciers or only small ones. . . . There seems to be agreement that the Pleistocene epoch consisted of four glacial ages separated by interglacial ages of probably far greater duration than the glacial.[1]

Without attempting for the present[2] to discuss the validity of the evidence for these ice ages (the evidence for which is circumstantial, rather than direct as in the case of the evidence for extensive vulcanism and diastrophism), let it merely be noted that, if they ever actually existed, the principle of uniformity is once again woefully inadequate to account for them.

If they could be explained so readily in terms of present processes, as uniformitarianism would teach, then it should easily be possible to point to those present processes and show how the continental glaciers are explained thereby. This has certainly not yet been accomplished. A great many theories have been advanced, almost as many as the number of those who have written upon the subject. Says one such recent writer, Dr. Wm. L. Stokes, who is Chairman of the Geology Department at the University of Utah:

> The recognition of widespread glaciation as an explanation for numerous details of topography, geology, and biological distribution ranks with the greatest achievements of scientific observation and reasoning. The underlying cause of glaciation, however, remains in doubt. . . . At least 29 "explanations" have been advanced to account for widespread glaciations. Most of these had little chance of survival from the first, but others enjoyed some degree of success until they were rendered untenable by subsequently accumulated information.[3]

---

[1] W. D. Thornbury: *Principles of Geomorphology* (New York, Wiley, 1954), p. 354.

[2] See pp. 288-303.

[3] Wm. L. Stokes: "Another Look at the Ice Age," *Science,* Vol. 122, October 28, 1955, p. 815.

Dr. Stokes then proceeds, as have many others, to offer a theory of his own, but he is frank to admit, in conclusion:

Serious and perhaps fatal objections to an ocean-control theory of glaciation [that is, his own hypothesis] will probably have already occurred to some who have read the foregoing summary.[1]

There seems no need here to labor the point, which is obvious: that the dogma of uniformity has thus far completely failed to account for this additional very important aspect of accepted geologic history.

Phenomena of Sedimentation

We have briefly considered three of the most important agencies of geologic work, those of volcanism, diastrophism and glaciation, and have seen that they were in the past utterly different, not only quantitatively but qualitatively, from their corresponding phenomena in the modern era. We shall now see that this is no less true of even the most important geologic agency of all, that of sedimentation.

Most of the sedimentary rocks of the earth's crust, which are the ones containing fossil remains and which therefore provide the chief basis of geologic interpretation of earth history, have been laid down as sediments by moving water (some have apparently been formed by wind, glaciers, or other agencies, but by far the largest part of sedimentary rocks are aqueous in origin). It is even possible[2] that many metamorphic (including "granitized" rocks, ordinarily classed as igneous) were originally sedimentaries.

Sedimentary rocks have been formed through a process of erosion, transportation, deposition, and lithification of sediments. The deposition occurs, of course, when the running water containing the sediments enters a quiescent or less rapidly moving body of water, the lowered velocity resulting in a dropping out of part or all of its load

---

[1] *Ibid.,* p. 820. A still more recent theory is that of Maurice Ewing and W. L. Donn ("A Theory of Ice Ages," *Science,* Vol. 127, May 16, 1958, pp. 1159-1162). The theory is somewhat similar to that of Stokes but is highly speculative, involving among other things wandering poles. It has been sharply criticized by D. A. Livingstone (*Science,* Feb. 20, 1959, pp. 463-4) and others. An explanation in terms of wandering continents is given by Charles H. Hapgood in his book *Earth's Shifting Crust* (Pantheon, 1958).

[2] W. H. Bucher: "Megatectonics and Geophysics," *Transactions American Geophysical Union,* Vol. 31, August 1950, p. 500-501. Also see Matt Walton: "Granite Problems," *Science,* Vol. 131, March 4, 1960, pp. 635-645.

of moving sediment. If the sediment happens to contain organic remains, and these are buried by the sands or silts accompanying them, it may be possible over the years for the organic remains to become fossilized and to be preserved in form in the stratum. The remains of such plant and animal forms, as discovered in the present sedimentary rocks of the earth, have of course served as the basis of our modern divisions of the strata into units of geologic time and have provided paleontology with the materials upon which the bulk of the evidence for organic evolution rests today.

Here is where the principle of uniformity is applied most insistently. To be consistent with uniformitarianism, the various types of sedimentary rocks must all be interpreted in terms of so-called environments of deposition exactly equivalent to present-day situations where sediments are being laid down. Rocks are thus said to have been deposited in "deltaic," "lacustrine," "lagoonal," or other environments.

The many different methods of attempting to classify depositional environments have become more complex with the passing of time. One very ambitious modern classification is due to Krumbein and Sloss,[1] who postulate eight basic geographical environments, each of which is divided into several dynamically controlled sub-environments based on tectonic activity at the time in the particular area. This is their so-called "tectono-environmental" classification of depositional environments, comprising a total of some twenty-five distinct types of sedimentary environments.

It is of course quite impractical to attempt to discuss each of these postulated environments individually. It is pertinent to note, however, that the *tectonic* basis of the classification is actually non-uniformitarian in principle, since there is no present-day observational basis for the tectonic processes assumed in the identification of the environments (that is, processes such as subsidence, oscillation, etc.). The very fact that so many different environments are postulated, and indeed so many different systems of classifying environments suggested by different authorities, plainly would indicate that it is impossible to apply, successfully, strictly uniformitarian principles to modern processes and environments of deposition with the hope of arriving at a satisfactory and workable means of classifying ancient

---

[1] W. C. Krumbein & L. L. Sloss: *Stratigraphy and Sedimentation* (San Francisco, W. H. Freeman & Co., 1951), pp. 388-389.

sediments. Of course, the device of adding environmental types as needed, to fit each type of deposit found, will itself guarantee that some sort of "explanation," couched in highly technical terminology, can be offered to explain anything. However, Krumbein and Sloss admit:

The classification [that is, their very complicated tectono-environmental classification] was developed mainly for the analysis of stratigraphic sections, rather than as a means for analyzing present-day deposits.[1]

The method, therefore, is admittedly inapplicable to *present-day processes* of sediment deposition and is only a means of pigeon-holing the rock strata! As a taxonomic device, this is quite legitimate if convenient. But it is *not* legitimate to use a mere classification system for stratigraphic systems as a basis for time-correlation as well, unless it is made plain that such is strictly hypothetical, in view of the fact that it is based in large part on *assumed* processes, rather than *observed* processes.[2] The geologic dogma of uniformity has once again proved inadequate to explain the geologic data.

Criticizing the classification scheme of Krumbein and Sloss, as well as others (and of course presenting another of his own), another leading geologist admits that:

Process is, again, something that apparently no worker in the field of geotectonism has been able, up to the present, to express with much clarity, or at least with pragmatic usefulness. The large number of structural publications dealing with the supposed details of the final operative mechanisms of local crustal deformation or conversely covering the more hypothetical aspects of the broad final causes of crustal deformation in general have not suggested as yet any simple and effective way of gaging (that is, comparing effectively) the actions of the processes responsible for the formation of geotectonic elements, such as geosynclines. . . . Per-

---

[1] *Ibid.*, p. 386.

[2] Francis P. Shepard, a leading marine geologist, points out the fact that, despite the dogma of uniformitarianism, geologists have actually paid little heed even to *present* processes of sedimentation in building up their interpretations of the sedimentary rocks. He says: "Most sedimentary rocks are believed to have been deposited in the seas of the past. One of the primary purposes in geological investigations has been to interpret the conditions under which these ancient sediments were deposited. One of the obvious places to look for guidance in these interpretations is in the deposits of the present. It is, therefore, rather surprising to find how little attention geologists had paid to these recent marine sediments until very recent years." ("Marine Sediments," *Science*, Vol. 130, July 17, 1959, p. 141).

haps workers in this field have been too concerned with effects and have not given sufficient thought to causes in terms of dynamic processes.[1]

This statement contains a perhaps unintended admission that the processes that formed the great sedimentary beds of the geosynclines are not yet understood and, thus, certainly have not been accounted for on the basis of uniformity and continuity with present processes. This is especially significant in light of the fact that the most spectacular and quantitatively significant sedimentary rock deposits of the world are found in these geosynclines, which are supposed to have been great troughs of continuing subsidence in shallow seas. The concept has been that large masses of sediments were being more or less continuously deposited at shallow depths as rivers entered the seas and that the region subsided at a rate just sufficient to balance the incoming sediments. Then later, the entire geosyncline was somehow uplifted to form one of our present mountain ranges, thus supposedly accounting for the tremendous beds of sedimentary, stratified rock found in all the continents. The tremendous mass of sediments contained in the geosynclines is indicated by the following:

> The original dimensions of a typical major geosyncline must have been of the order of magnitude of 100 to 200 km. wide, 1000 to 2000 km. long, and 4 to 12 km. deep.[2]

This means that 40,000 feet of sediments or more have accumulated in these great troughs. That great thicknesses of sediments have accumulated is unquestioned, but the problem is how to account for the origin of the geosyncline in the first place, then how to explain the continued subsidence (for which, incidentally, there is little or no *direct* evidence—only the fact that the sediments were all deposited in shallow waters and, therefore, there *must* have been subsidence or else gradually rising water levels), how to account for the source areas from which these great volumes of sediments must have been eroded, and lastly, how to account for the uplift and deformation of these geosynclines to form the present mountain ranges. None of these basic questions has yet been solved on the basis of uniformity. Dr. L. H. Adams, only a decade ago, called this problem of the origin

[1] Paul D. Krynine: "A Critique of Geotectonic Elements," *Transactions, American Geophysical Union*, Vol. 32, October 1951, p. 743-44.
[2] W. H. Bucher: "Fundamental Properties of Orogenic Belts," *Transactions, American Geophysical Union*, Vol. 32, August 1951, p. 514.

of geosynclines one of the major unsolved problems of geology,[1] and there has been nothing significant accomplished in the intervening period to solve it. Dr. George C. Kennedy, Professor of Geology at U.C.L.A., has said recently:

"These deep troughs filled with sediments may contain 50,000 to 100,-000 feet of sediments and may be 1000 or more miles long and 100 miles in width. . . . The mystery, then, of the downsinking of the sedimentary troughs, in which low density sediments apparently displace higher density rocks, is heightened when we note that these narrow elongate zones in the Earth's crust, downwarped the most, with the greatest accumulation of rock debris, shed by the higher portions of the continents, become in turn the mountain ranges and the highest portions of the continents."[2]

And what is true concerning the geosynclines is equally true with respect to most of the other important sedimentary features of the earth. For example, there is evidence that in the past there were great peneplains at various places and times. These were vast surfaces of erosion which had been worn down almost to flat, plain surfaces, as the word means. They are conceived as the ultimate product of the work of erosion, accomplished by natural land drainage over long ages. Speculative geologic history is full of these peneplains (or "peneplanes," as some writers call them). However, there are no true peneplains of any consequence in the present surface. This is admitted, for example, by Thornbury:

Admittedly there are few good examples of peneplains at the present base level of erosion, but their scarcity may be attributed to Pliocene-Pleistocene diastrophism. Locally, limited areas have been reduced to or nearly to base level, but they can hardly be called more than local or incipient peneplains.[3]

Once again, assuming that there actually have been in the past many of these extensive plains of sub-aerial erosion, as the evidence seems to indicate in some places, the lack of anything in the present to correspond to them shows that the present is *not* the key to the past!

Other striking erosional features unmatched by modern equivalents

---

[1] L. H. Adams, *op. cit.,* p. 676.
[2] George C. Kennedy: "The Origin of Continents, Mountain Ranges, and Ocean Basins," *American Scientist,* Vol. 47, December 1959, p. 495.
[3] W. D. Thornbury: *Principles of Geomorphology* (New York, Wiley, 1954), p. 180.

would include the great numbers of dry canyons and falls. Particularly picturesque are the so-called "scabland" areas, of which the best known in this country is in the Columbia Plateau. Here, vast and intricate dry canyons or coulees, hanging valleys, dry waterfalls, rock-rimmed basins and other bizarre features are found in profusion. These things are obviously not being formed anywhere at the present time, so there is much disagreement among geologists as to their explanation. The man who has made the most thorough study of the area is Harlan Bretz, whose theory envisaged a sudden vast flood as being the only agency capable of creating these forms. Thornbury's comment here is interesting:

> (Bretz) has been unable to account for such a flood but maintained that field evidence indicated its reality. This theory represents a return to catastrophism which many geologists have been reluctant to accept.[1]

Nor are the geosynclines the only depositional features of physiography which seem unrelated to any sort of deposits being formed at the present time. The large central region of the United States, known as the Great Plains, stretching roughly from the Rockies to the Mississippi and from Canada to Mexico, consists largely of remnants of a single great fluviatile plain or alluvial slope. Describing the origin of these plains, Fenneman says:

> The Fluviatile mantle was laid down by overloaded streams after the manner of alluvial fans, or of flood plains when the streams are building so many bars and shoals that the water is subdivided into many channels, each of which is in turn filled, and the stream shifted. . . . Near where the streams issued from the mountains, each stream built its own alluvial fan but farther out the fans merged into a single broad alluvial slope. Such deposits were made in this region in late Tertiary time and are frequently referred to as the Tertiary mantle."[2]

The above description applies especially to the so-called "High Plains" of Kansas, New Mexico and Texas. Concerning the remarkable aspect of these features, Fenneman says:

---

[1] Thornbury, *op. cit.*, p. 401. More recent studies in the area by Bretz and others have further confirmed the catastrophic diluvial origin of the scablands. See the article: "Channeled Scabland of Washington: New Data and Interpretations," by J. H. Bretz, H. T. V. Smith, & G. E. Neff, *Bulletin of the Geological Society of America,* Vol. 67, August 1956, pp. 957-1049.

[2] N. M. Fenneman: *Physiography of Western United States* (New York, McGraw-Hill, 1931), p. 11.

The surface produced by this alluviation is as flat as any land surface in nature. Many thousands of square miles still retain this flatness. In the Llano Estacado or Staked Plains of Texas and New Mexico an area of 20,000 square miles is almost untouched by erosion.[1]

There is no reason to question the general correctness of the nature of the geomorphic origin of these plains, as attributable to widespread and overlapping alluvial fans formed by heavy-laden rivers coming down from the recently uplifted mountains to the west. The significant thing, however, is that here again one must visualize a phenomenon for which there is no parallel in the modern world except on a much smaller scale. The principle of uniformity is misnamed if, to interpret ancient phenomena on the basis of the present, the expedient of extrapolation must so continually be employed and to such a great degree. The example chosen is one taken almost at random from many similar deposits around the world. It seems that almost everywhere one looks, he can find evidence of widespread deposition, either alluvial or deltaic in nature, of magnitude quite beyond that of any deposits being formed in the present.

These phenomena are not confined to lowland areas. Certain peculiar stream courses are often explained as due to streams cutting down through alluvial sediments which had once completely covered the mountains. Concerning one such location, in the Uinta Mountains of Utah, Fenneman says:

A simple hypothesis to explain the anomalous course of all the streams is that, after the mountains were made and were being eroded, sediments were deposited in and around the basin to such a depth that they rose above the ranges at the places where streams now cross them. The streams were thus superposed. This is believed to be the only hypothesis adequate to explain the wholesale disregard of present-day mountains by the streams.[2]

These mountain-burying sediments are believed to have been derived from the wearing down of more than 7,000 cubic miles from the summit of a great fold, filling in the surrounding area to a depth of at least several thousand feet, up almost to the summits of the remaining mountains themselves! After the formation of the now-anomalous rivers on these tremendous alluvial deposits, another up-

---

[1] *Ibid.*, p. 14. Note that this is not an erosional surface and therefore not a peneplain.

[2] *Ibid.*, p. 147.

lift is postulated, permitting a new cycle of dissection to begin. This sort of phenomenon is frequently encountered in the study of geomorphology and provides still another evidence that present-day rates of erosion and deposition cannot account for the ancient deposits as they are found.

Another major difficulty of the uniformitarian concept of sedimentary processes is found in those great areas of very thick deposits which have gone through one or more cycles of uplift and submergence and yet remain marvelously horizontal and continuous. A good example is found in the Colorado plateaus. Describing this province, Fenneman says:

> The first distinguishing feature is approximate horizontality of its rocks. . . . The second distinguishing feature of the province is great elevation. Aside from canyon bottoms, no considerable portion of it is lower than 5,000 feet. Between this and 11,000 ft., there are plateaus of all altitudes, some of them being higher than the nearby mountain ranges.[1]

This region occupies some 250,000 square miles, including most of Utah and Arizona, with large segments of Colorado and New Mexico. The Grand Canyon and many other spectacular canyons have been excavated through thousands of feet of these flat-lying sedimentary rocks.

The remarkable thing is that this entire region has somehow been uplifted from far below sea level, since most of its sediments are of marine origin, to over a mile above sea level, without disturbing the horizontality of the strata or summit levels! See Figure 6. And this has happened not once, but many times, since there are several disconformities in the stratigraphic sequences of these sediments, each supposedly representing a period of uplift and erosion followed by subsidence and deposition. No wonder Kennedy says:

> The problem of the uplift of large plateau areas is one that has puzzled students of the Earth's crust for a very long time.[2]

After describing the Colorado Plateau uplift, Kennedy continues:

> The Tibetan plateaus present a similar problem, but on a vastly larger scale. There, an area of 750,000 square miles has been uplifted from approximately sea level to a mean elevation of roughly three miles, and the Himalayan mountain chain bordering this region has floated upward some

[1] *Ibid.*, p. 274.
[2] George C. Kennedy, *op. cit.*, p. 493.

Figure 6. GRAND CANYON OF THE COLORADO.

five miles, and rather late in geologic time, probably within the last 20,-000,000 years.[1]

Although various theories, all highly speculative and none as yet generally accepted, have been devised in an attempt to account for these phenomena, we merely point out that uniformist concepts have apparently proved incapable of providing a satisfactory solution. It seems much more likely that the sediments all were deposited more or less rapidly and continuously, followed by a single great regional uplift. Subsequent rapid canyon downcutting then ensued while the sediments were still relatively soft and the rivers were carrying much larger discharges.

The canyons in these plateau regions present another mystery, for which uniformitarian explanations have proved inadequate. Many of them are strongly sinuous and meandering in their courses, looking very much like the typically meandering mature rivers winding across alluvial plains, except that the canyons are hundreds of feet deep and the meander patterns are even sharper than in alluvial rivers. These are called incised, or entrenched, meanders, in view of their presumed "entrenchment" in the regional bedrocks during the process of uplifting. That is, it is supposed that the entire area was once near sea level, with an alluvial blanket on its surface. On this surface flowed typical alluvial rivers with typical meandering patterns.

Then, according to the theory, the process of regional uplift was initiated. The rivers, which before had been eroding laterally, now began to erode vertically, but in the process maintained their same meandering course, thus incising the pattern deep into the rocks of the plateau.

[1] *Ibid.*, p. 494.

FIGURE 6.

Spectacular exposures of flat-lying sedimentary rocks such as in the Grand Canyon provide ample visible evidence of Deluge deposition. In this area, there are thousands of square miles of horizontal strata, thousands of feet thick, supposed to have been deposited over about half a billion years! The strata include limestones, shales, and sandstones. According to uniformist concepts, numerous changes of environment, with great regional subsidences and uplifts, must have been involved, but this would appear quite impossible. The strata simply could *not* have remained so nearly uniform and horizontal over such great areas and great periods of time, while undergoing such repeated epeirogenic movements. By far the most reasonable way of accounting for them is in terms of relatively rapid deposition out of the sediment-laden water of the Flood. Following the Flood, while the rocks were still comparatively soft and unconsolidated, the great canyons were rapidly scoured out as the waters rushed down from the newly-uplifted peneplains to the newly-enlarged ocean basins.

Much study has been devoted to the subject of the mechanics of meandering rivers, since it involves engineering problems of considerable importance. In particular, extensive model tests have demonstrated that the phenomenon of meandering is associated only with non-resistant banks.[1] If the bed is subject to down-cutting at all, *it* will be eroded rather than the banks, since the greatest tractive stresses are directed along the bed rather than at the sides of a stream. A stream which is degrading its bed tends to straighten its course, with sharp-radius bends being eliminated by "cut-offs." This would happen, in fact, even before the alluvial blanket was eliminated and, certainly, no substantial amount of lateral shifting could be initiated once the stream had cut down into bedrock. Intense meandering, when slopes and velocities are high, would require that the bed rock be extremely resistant to erosion, so that excess energy could be dissipated in no other way than by lateral cutting. But if this be so, then the deep meandering gorges could never be cut. See Fig. 7.

Nevertheless, such incised meanders are a common phenomenon in uplifted plateau or other mountainous regions. It would seem that some sort of avulsive origin for them must be postulated. Great systems of vertical fissures might be imagined, which have been widened, deepened, and rounded by subsequent drainage through them. If erosion processes must account for the complete excavations, however, then it would seem necessary to postulate much greater volumes of water in the streams than now present, together with much less resistant walls than the rocks of which they now consist.

Fossil Graveyards

And if the inorganic sediments bear so hard on the concept of continuity with present-day conditions, what should be said about the organic deposits which are found in such profusion around the world? The great deposits of fossils of all kinds, and especially the vast coal and oil beds of the world, have proved exceedingly difficult to explain on the basis of uniformity. And yet these very organic deposits, especially the so-called "index fossils," have been made the basis for the standard geologic time-scale, and this in turn has been the pillar of the structure of evolutionary theory!

[1] Joseph F. Friedkin: *"A Laboratory Study of the Meanderings of Alluvial Rivers"* (Vicksburg, U.S. Waterways Experiment Station, Mississippi River Commission, 1945).

Figure 7. INCISED MEANDERS.

The familiar meandering pattern of streams in alluvial valleys primarily results from a small stream gradient, inhibiting further down-cutting, and weak banks, permitting side-cutting by local curvilinear water motions. Occasionally, however, strong meander patterns are found in valleys of steep gradients and strong rock banks, such as in the San Juan River in Colorado, as shown here. This anomaly is commonly attributed by geologists to a former alluvial blanket that supposedly once overlaid the rocks and since has been eroded away; the meander pattern is said to have developed in the normal way on the alluvium, and then "entrenched" in the underlying rocks when the region was uplifted. However, such an explanation is highly questionable in terms of known principles of stream mechanics. It would seem that the only way in which such strong lateral cutting could take place simultaneously with down-cutting would be for the banks to be less resistant than the bed, and this implies that most of the meander formation must have taken place when the horizontal beds were still soft and unconsolidated, soon after deposition during the Flood period.

Although the occasional anti-uniformist claim that *no* fossils are *now* being formed is not strictly valid, it is nevertheless certainly true that no modern parallels can be cited of great fossil beds such as are found in the geologic column, and this is doubly true for oil and coal beds.

The significance of this evidence can only be appreciated when it is first realized just what conditions must be present in order for fossils to form and be preserved. We shall consider this situation by noting the six ways listed by Miller[1] in which fossil remains can be preserved, adding a few comments of our own about each.

(1). *Preservation of the entire organism by freezing.* It is unnecessary to point out that very few, if any, animals are now being fossilized by this process. Yet it is well known that many extinct animals have been found preserved in just this way, especially in Siberia. Numerous animals have been found preserved whole, with flesh and even hair intact. The fact that these cannot be explained as due to freak accidents, as often suggested, is obvious from the great numbers of bones interred with them in the same strata. Estimates have run as high as 5,000,000 mammoths, whose remains are buried all along the coast line of northern Siberia and into Alaska.[2] Abundant remains of many other animals (only rarely the entire organism of course) have been found in these northern lands, especially of the rhinoceros, bear, horse and other mammals.

(2). *Preservation of only the hard parts*[3] *of the organisms.* This is the most common type of fossil found, especially bones and shells. At first one would suppose that fossil deposits of shells or bones would be easily formed and that such deposits are commonly being formed now. However it is very difficult to point to specific present-day deposition areas which are analogous to those found in the rocks. Bones of land animals, or of amphibians or even of fishes, may occasionally be trapped in some sediment and buried, but this is not the normal or frequent situation. Usually, the bones remain on the surface until gradually disintegrated. Never does one find, in the present era, great "graveyards" of organisms buried together and waiting fossilization. But this is exactly the sort of thing that is encountered in fossil deposits in many, many places around the world. Space precludes any adequate discussion of those remarkable deposits, but a few examples, taken at random, will be mentioned. For instance, reference may be made to the deposits found in Lincoln County, Wyoming.

[1] William J. Miller: *Introduction to Historical Geology* (New York, Van Nostrand, 1952), pp. 12-16.

[2] For the most detailed description of these remarkable deposits, see *The Mammoth and the Flood*, by the prominent nineteenth-century archaeologist, Sir Henry Howorth (London; Sampson Low, Marston Searle, & Risington, 1887). Also see our discussion, pp. 288-291.

[3] As will be seen, the soft parts also have often been preserved.

Today, this oddity of nature is not only a tourist curiosity, but is furnishing some of the most perfect specimens of fossil fish and plants in the world. The removed items have been placed in museums throughout the world, and many even appear in famous private collections. . . . Other than the fish, palm leaves, from 6 to 8 feet in length and from 3 to 4 feet wide have been uncovered. The occurrence of these confirms the geological theory that the climate was tropical and quite unlike the blizzard-ridden mountains of Wyoming today. This theory was further substantiated in 1890 when an alligator was found. . . . Several Gar-pike, ranging in size from 4 to 6 feet, have been disentombed, as have birds of about the size of the domestic chicken and resembling the snipe or plover in general conformation. In addition, specimens of sunfish, rasp-tongues, deep sea bass, chubs, pickerel and herring have been found, not to mention mollusca, crustaceans, birds, turtles, mammals and many varieties of insects.[1]

It is not easy to imagine any kind of "uniform" process by which this conglomeration of modern and extinct fishes, birds, reptiles, mammals, insects and plants could have been piled together and preserved for posterity. Fish, no less than other creatures, do not naturally become entombed like this but are usually quickly devoured by other fish after dying.

When a fish dies its body floats on the surface or sinks to the bottom and is devoured rather quickly, actually in a matter of hours, by other fish. However, the fossil fish found in sedimentary rocks is very often preserved with all its bones intact. Entire shoals of fish over large areas, numbering billions of specimens, are found in a state of agony, but with no mark of a scavenger's attack.[2]

An entirely different type of deposit, but one also containing a wealth of fossils, is that near Florissant, Colorado, where myriads of a wide variety of insect fossils are preserved in rocks of volcanic shale, with a minute perfection of detail that is truly remarkable, interspersed with layers of other types of fossils. Dr. R. D. Manwell, Professor of Zoology at Syracuse University, a specialist in the study of fossil insects, says in describing these deposits:

Although insect remains are by far the most numerous of the animal

---

[1] "Fishing for Fossils," Vol. 63, *Compressed Air Magazine,* March 1958, p. 24.
[2] I. Velikovsky: *Earth in Upheaval,* (New York, Doubleday and Co., 1955), p. 222. M. Brogersma-Sanders says: "The life of most animals in the sea is terminated by their capture by other animals; those that die in other ways are sooner or later eaten by scavengers" (*Treatise on Marine Ecology and Paleoecology,* Vol. I, Geological Society of America Memoir 67, 1957, p. 972).

fossils preserved at Florissant, other groups are also represented. The shells of tiny fresh-water mollusks are not difficult to find entombed in the rock and occasionally even the skeletons of fish and birds are seen. Several hundred species of plants have been identified from these shales, usually from leaves, but fruits (that is, nuts) and even blossoms have also been found. . . . Insect life around and above Lake Florissant must have been abundant, for it is not unusual to find on a single piece of shale from one of the richer fossiliferous layers several individuals within 2 to 3 inches of each other. This life was also extremely varied, with the total number of species running into the hundreds.[1]

Again, one must realize the difficulty of trying to account for such phenomena on the basis of continuity with present processes. The general sort of explanation postulated for the Florissant deposits has to do with volcanic dust showers over a body of water, but no one can point to similar phenomena creating similar deposits today!

Many rich fossil deposits have been found in caves, one of the outstanding being the Cumberland Bone Cave in Maryland. Remains of dozens of species of mammals, ranging from bats to mastodons, are found in the cave, together with some reptiles and birds—from different types of climates and habitats.

In this one cave have been found such types as the wolverine, grizzly bear, and Mustelidae, which are native to Arctic regions. Peccaries, the most numerous type represented, tapirs, and an antelope possibly related to the present-day eland are indigenous to tropical regions. Ground-hogs, rabbits, coyotes, and hare remains are indicative of dry prairies, but on the other hand such water-loving animals as beaver and muskrat suggest a more humid region.[2]

This kind of thing does not lend itself well to uniformitarian interpretation but strongly suggests some sort of very unusual catastrophe(s). Other caves in the same region, within three miles of Cumberland, are barren of fossils.

This mixing of organisms from entirely different habitats and even different climatic regimes in one great mass is characteristic of many of the most important fossil deposits. Perhaps the only place in the world more important for the study of fossil insects than the Florissant shales already mentioned is in the famous Baltic amber de-

[1] R. D. Manwell: "An Insect Pompeii," *Scientific Monthly,* Vol. 80, June 1955, p. 357-358.

[2] Brother G. Nicholas: "Recent Paleontological Discoveries from Cumberland Bone Cave," *Scientific Monthly,* May 1953, Vol. 76, p. 301.

posits, where multitudes of insects and other organisms are preserved with an unsurpassed exquisiteness of detail. Dr. Heribert-Nilsson, late Director of the Swedish Botanical Institute and as familiar as anyone with these deposits, says concerning them:

In the pieces of amber, which may reach a size of 5 kilos or more, especially insects and parts of flowers are preserved, even the most fragile structures. The insects are of modern types and their geographical distribution can be ascertained. It is then quite astounding to find that they belong to all regions of the earth, not only to the Paleoarctic region, as was to be expected. . . . The geological and paleobiological facts concerning the layers of amber are impossible to understand unless the explanation is accepted that they are the final result of an allochthonous process, including the whole earth.[1]

An allochthonous process is one which transports the materials to their final deposition locality, probably by flooding waters. Nilsson thus is saying that these deposits could not have been formed in the region where the organisms lived but must have been transported there from great distances in a violent cataclysm of some sort and that no other explanation can account for the facts as they are observed. He further describes the lignite beds of Geiseltal, Germany, as follows:

Exactly the same picture as the one just given is offered by the well-known studies of certain fossil-carrying strata of the lignite in Geiseltal. Here, too, there is a complete mixture of plants and insects from all climatic zones and all recognized regions of the geography of plants or animals.

It is further astonishing that in certain cases the leaves have been deposited and preserved in a fully fresh condition. The chlorophyll is so well preserved that it has been possible to recognize the alpha and beta types. . . .

An extravagant fact, comparable to the preservation of the chlorophyll, was the occurrence of preserved soft parts of the insects: muscles, corium, epidermis, keratin, colour stuffs as melanin and lipochrome, glands, and the contents of the intestines. Just as in the case of the chlorophyll we are dealing with things that are easily destroyed, disintegrating in but a few days or hours. The incrustation must therefore have been very rapid.[2]

Dr. N. D. Newell, paleontologist of the American Museum of Natural History, has recently discussed these same deposits in even more remarkable detail, as follows:

---

[1] N. Heribert-Nilsson: *Synthetische Artbildung,* pp. 1194-1195.
[2] *Ibid.,* pp. 1195-1196.

One of the most remarkable examples of preservation of organic tissues in antiseptic swamp waters is a "fossil graveyard" in Eocene lignite deposits of the Geiseltal in central Germany. . . . More than six thousand remains of vertebrate animals and a great number of insects, molluscs, and plants were found in these deposits. The compressed remains of soft tissues of many of these animals showed details of cellular structure and some of the specimens had undergone but little chemical modification. . . . Well-preserved bits of hair, feathers and scales probably are among the oldest known examples of essentially unmodified preservation of these structures. The stomach contents of beetles, amphibia, fishes, birds and mammals provided direct evidence about eating habits. Bacteria of two kinds were found in the excrement of crocodiles and another was found on the trachea of a beetle. Fungi were identified on leaves and the original plant pigments, chlorophyll and coproporphyrin, were found preserved in some of the leaves.[1]

That these, though striking, are not unique instances of fossil preservation is substantiated also by Newell.

There are innumerable well-documented records of preservation of tissues of animals and plants in pre-Quaternary rocks.[2]

It is inconceivable that deposits of this sort could be really due to normal, slow, autochthonous processes. Unusual transportation and rapid burial mechanisms are plainly indicated.

The great numbers of fossils entombed in the rocks are stressed repeatedly by Newell; for example:

Robert Broom, the South African paleontologist, estimated that there are eight hundred thousand million skeletons of vertebrate animals in the Karroo formation.[3]

The examples cited are merely random samplings of phenomena which are found in great numbers of places all around the world. They are not by any means the most spectacular or impressive examples but merely typical illustrations of what is quite commonly encountered in the fossiliferous deposits of the world. One might, for

[1] N. O. Newell: "Adequacy of the Fossil Record," *Journal of Paleontology,* Vol. 33, May 1959, p. 496.

[2] *Ibid.,* p. 495.

[3] *Ibid.,* p. 492. Harry S. Ladd, of the U. S. Geological Survey, describing beds of herring fossils in the Miocene shales of California says that "more than a billion fish, averaging 6 to 8 inches in length, died on 4 square miles of bay bottom" ("Ecology, Paleontology, and Stratigraphy," *Science,* Vol. 129, January 9, 1959, p. 72).

(Photo from American Museum of Natural History)

Figure 8. FOSSIL GRAVEYARD.

This rock slab was taken from the well-known "bone bed" at Agate Springs, Nebraska, a stratum in which thousands of bones of fossil mammals have been found. The bone layer runs horizontally for a large distance in the limestone hill, and has evidently been water-laid. Fossils of the rhinoceros, camel, giant boar, and numerous other exotic animals are found jumbled together in this stratum.

example, discuss at length such marvels as the La Brea Pits in Los Angeles, which have yielded tens of thousands of specimens of all kinds of living and extinct animals (each of which, by the unbelievable uniformitarian explanation, fell into this sticky graveyard by accident—one at a time!); the Sicilian hippopotamus beds, the fossils of which are so extensive that they have actually been mined as a source of commercial charcoal; the great mammal beds of the Rockies; the dinosaur beds of the Black Hills and the Rockies, as well as in the Gobi Desert; the astounding fish beds of the Scottish Devonian strata, and on and on.

To attempt to account for these vast graveyards in terms of present-day processes and events, except via the most extreme and unscientific extrapolation, is absolutely impossible! And yet it is in deposits such as these that most of the fossils are found on which is based much of the generally accepted uniformitarian scheme of historical geology.

(3). *Preservation of carbon only (carbonization)*. This is the third way listed by Professor Miller whereby fossil remains can be preserved, having reference to the formation especially of coal, in which the hydrogen and oxygen largely disappear from the organic remains, leaving only the carbon but often also leaving the original structure beautifully preserved. The coal deposits of the world are of course tremendous in magnitude, with the exact amount quite uncertain, but somewhere around 7 trillion tons.

About all we really know about coal reserves is that there appears to be lots of coal in the world. . . . Instead of 7 trillion tons, there may be double that. On the other hand, there may be less than half that.[1]

Coal is the end product of the metamorphism of tremendous quantities of plant remains under the action of temperature, pressure and time. Coal has been found throughout the geologic column and in all parts of the world, even in Antarctica. Many coal fields contain great numbers of coal-bearing strata, interbedded with strata of other materials, each coal seam having a thickness which may vary from a few inches to several feet. And each foot of coal must represent many feet—just how many, no one knows—of plant remains, so that the coal measures testify of the former existence of almost unimaginably massive accumulations of buried plants.

Coal geologists have long been divided into two camps, those favoring the autochthonous (growth-in-place) theory of coal origin and those favoring the allochthonous (transportation and deposition) theory. Consistent uniformitarianism, of course, tends to favor the former and attempts to picture the coal-forming processes in terms of modern peat deposits forming under swamplands, such as in the Dismal Swamp of Virginia. The great thickness of the coal beds is accounted for on this theory by assuming a continuous subsidence of the land more or less keeping up with the slow accumulation of plant remains. The interbedded strata of non-carbonaceous deposits are explained by alternating marine transgressions and resulting periods of sediment deposition. A wide variety of types of these intervening sediments have been noted and attempts made to explain them in terms of "cyclothems" or recurring cycles of deposition of different kinds of materials corresponding to the different stages of marine

---

[1] Eugene Ayres and Charles A. Scarlott: *Energy Sources: the Wealth of the World* (New York, McGraw-Hill Book Co., 1952), p. 53.

transgression and regression. The exact cycle, however, found at any one locality is always different from the cycle at any other locality. This is admitted by Krumbein and Sloss:

> The concept of the ideal cyclothem was developed to represent the optimum succession of deposits during a complete sedimentary cycle. The ideal cyclothem has not been observed fully developed in any one locality. . . .[1]

If the autochthonous theory of coal bed origin is correct, it is testimony to quite a marvelous sequence of circumstances. One or two or three coal seams formed by alternate stages of swamp growth, peat accumulation, marine transgression and emergence, etc., might be believable, but the assertion that this cycle was repeated scores of times on the same spot, over a period of perhaps millions of years, is not so easy to accept. And yet there are many sites where 75 or more such coal seams are found. Some seams, too, are up to 30 or 40 feet in thickness, representing perhaps an accumulation of 300 or 400 feet of plant remains for the one seam.

This theory, which is purportedly uniformitarian in essence, is actually anything but that, as there is no modern parallel for any of its major features. The peat-bog theory constitutes a very weak attempt to identify a modern parallel, but it will hardly suffice. One of the most respected modern authorities says:

> Though a peat-bog may serve to demonstrate how vegetal matter accumulates in considerable quantities it is in no way comparable in extent to the great bodies of vegetation which must have given rise to our important coal seams. . . . There is sufficient peat in the temperate regions of the world today to form large amounts of coal, if it were concentrated into coal seams, but no single bog or marsh known would supply sufficient peat to make a large coal seam.[2]

The Dismal Swamp of Virginia, perhaps the most frequently cited case of a potential coal bed, has formed only an average of 7 feet of peat, hardly enough to make a single respectable seam of coal. Furthermore, there is no actual evidence that peat is now being transformed into coal anywhere in the world. *No locality is known where the peat bed, in its lower reaches, grades into a typical coal bed.* All

[1] Krumbein and Sloss: *Stratigraphy and Sedimentation* (San Francisco, W. H. Freeman & Co., 1951), p. 376.
[2] E. S. Moore: *Coal: Its Properties, Analysis, Classification, Geology, Extraction, Uses and Distribution* (New York, 2nd Ed., Wiley, 1940), p. 146.

known coal beds, therefore, seem to have been formed in the past and are not continuing to be formed in the present, as the principle of uniformity could reasonably be expected to imply.

As a matter of fact, except for uniformist preconceptions, it would seem that the actual physical evidence of the coal beds strongly favors the theory that the plant accumulations had been washed into place. The coal seams are almost universally found in stratified deposits. The non-carbonaceous sediments intervening between the coal seams are always said to have been water-deposited, and it would seem that consistency alone would warrant the conclusion that the coal seams were likewise water-borne and deposited. The great thickness of some seams and the great numbers of seams in a given locality also constitute *prima facie* evidence of rapid and cyclic currents carrying and depositing heavy burdens of organic material.

The most important reason given for believing the coal seams to have been deposited *in situ* rather than after aqueous transport is the evidence of the so-called *stigmaria*. These are root-like fossils that project out under the coal seams into the "underclay" and have been interpreted as the roots of the trees which formerly grew in the peat-bog. This is held to prove that the vegetation actually grew in the place where its remains now rest. However, other explanations are possible. It is conceivable that they were rhizomes rather than true roots and were thus able to develop under water, independently of the plants to which they were attached. Or they may have simply been transported along with the plants and deposited together with them. That their true origin is not by any means a settled problem is indicated by Professor Arnold of the University of Michigan, who says, in connection with a lengthy review of the problem:

> The true morphology of *Stigmaria,* and its relation to the stem, remain, even after more than a century of research, one of the great unsolved problems of paleobotany. . . . Modern research has thrown little additional light on the *Stigmaria* problem and the remains are generally ignored by present-day paleobotanists. . . . On purely morphological grounds *Stigmaria* cannot be regarded as a true root, and probably not as a rhizome.[1]

Related to the nature of the *Stigmaria* has been the question of the "underclays," which are supposed to be the fossil soils in which the coal-swamp vegetation grew. However, recent careful studies on

[1] C. A. Arnold: *Introduction to Paleobotany* (New York, McGraw-Hill, 1947), p. 124.

the chemical and physiological nature of the underclays show this to be highly improbable.

The relationships between underclays and coals indicate that the underclays formed before the coals were deposited. Furthermore, lack of a soil profile similar to modern soils and similarity of the mineralogy of all rock types below the coals indicate that underclay materials were essentially as they were transported into the basin. . . . The underclays were probably deposited in a loose, hydrous, flocculated state, and slickensides developed during compaction.[1]

Space precludes further discussion of the question of coal formation, although many more evidences could be marshalled in favor of the allochthonous theory, such as the frequent splitting of coal seams into two or more independent seams, the many fossil trunks that have been found extending through two or more seams, the "coal balls" of matted and exceptionally well-preserved fossils, the great boulders often found in coal beds,[2] the frequent grading of coal seams into stratified layers of shale or other sedimentary rock, etc.

Regardless of the exact manner in which coal was formed, it is quite certain that there is nothing corresponding to it taking place in the world today. This is one of the most important of all types of geologic formations and one on which much of our supposed geologic history has been based. Nevertheless, the fundamental axiom of uniformity, that the present is the key to the past, completely fails to account for the phenomena.

(4). *Preservation of original form only, in casts or molds.* This is another means of fossil preservation, whereby the original organic substance entombed in the sediments dissolves away, either leaving a cavity having the form of the original organism, or else being replaced by some sort of mineral water which is then cast into the form of the original organism. Once again this sort of preservation requires sudden or catastrophic burial, followed by rather rapid cementation of the surrounding sediments, in order for the mold to be preserved. The remains at the Roman cities of Pompeii and Herculaneum, entombed

[1] Leonard G. Schultz: "Petrology of Underclays," *Bulletin, Geological Society of America,* Vol. 69, April 1958, pp. 391-392.

[2] Otto Stutzer says: "Numerous theories have been advanced to explain the transportation of these boulders to their positions. Phillips' (1855) explanation that the boulders were floated in, held by the roots of floating trees, has still the greatest support among geologists" (*Geology of Coal,* transl. by A. C. Noe, Chicago, University of Chicago Press, 1940, p. 277).

by volcanic materials, offer an excellent illustration of this type of fossilization. The principle of uniformity again fails to provide modern examples of this type of process except in terms of intense aqueous or volcanic action.

(5). *Petrifaction.* This process is similar to that of the formation of a mold and subsequent cast in that it consists of detailed replacement of the organic material by mineral water, usually brought about by the action of underground water. The famous petrified forests of the Yellowstone Park region and of Arizona are familiar examples of this process. The exact details of the process of petrifaction are not known, although the usual associations of petrified wood and other materials indicate that volcanic action has been a contributing factor. The petrified forest of Arizona, as well as other regions, also shows action of subsequent flood waters as a probable agent of deposition of the materials in their present location. In any case, some sort of catastrophic agent is again necessary for at least the burial of the materials before the agencies of petrification can begin their work.

(6). *Preservation of tracks of animals.* This is Professor Miller's last category of means of fossil preservation. Many thousands of tracks of animals of all kinds have been found preserved in stone, including many tracks of dinosaurs and other creatures now extinct. Says Professor Miller:

> Footprints of animals, made in moderately soft mud or sandy mud which soon hardens and becomes covered with more sediment, are especially favorable for preservation. Thousands of examples of tracks of great extinct reptiles have been found in the red sandstone of the Connecticut River Valley alone.[1]

This sort of thing has been found so frequently that it has been considered more or less normal. Dinosaur footprints discovered in Texas are shown in Fig. 9 and Fig. 10. Related to animal tracks that have been thus preserved are the many instances of preservation of ancient ripple marks or raindrop impressions. But that such ephemeral markings could have been preserved in such great numbers and in such perfection is truly a remarkable phenomenon and one for which there is little if any modern parallel. It is a matter of common experience that impressions of this sort in soft mud or sand are very quickly obliterated. It seems clear that the only way in which

[1] Miller, *op. cit.,* p. 16.

Figure 9. FOOTPRINTS IN CRETACEOUS RIVER BED.

These dinosaur tracks were supposedly made over 100,000,000 years ago, in a river bed now identified as formed in the Cretaceous Period. Aside from the remarkable and hardly believable claim that such ephemeral markings could have been preserved in such fine detail for such a long time, it is particularly significant that in this same bed have been found what appear to be human footprints!

such prints could be preserved as fossils is by means of some chemical action permitting rapid lithification and some aqueous action permitting rapid burial. Some sudden and catastrophic action is again necessary for any reasonable explanation of the phenomena.

One rather strange fact in this connection is that while there seem to be many cases known of ancient ripple marks and ancient raindrop splash marks being preserved as fossils, there do not seem to be any clearcut cases of ancient hail imprints preserved. Says Twenhofel:

> Hail may make larger and deeper impressions than those made by rain, and some should be very deep and large, considering that hail as large as grapefruit has fallen and hail 2 cm. or more in diameter is common. Impressions made by hail should be common in the column, but beyond a possible occurrence in Triassic red shale of New Jersey none have been recorded.[1]

Would this fact imply that whatever the unknown conditions were that caused the "freezing" of ancient current ripple marks and raindrop splash marks in the sands, such conditions were inadequate to fix the much larger hail imprints or else that hail conditions (and, therefore, atmospheric conditions inducing thunderstorms) were not present when the fossil prints were formed?

In summary, we have seen that the preservation of organic materials as fossils, *by whatever means,* requires some sort of catastrophic condition, some kind of quick burial by engulfing sediments, usually followed by some abnormal chemical means of rapid solidification. There is little wonder, then, that it is so difficult to find any remains of the modern era which could be said to be in the process of "becoming" fossils. Those that *are* found are invariably so situated as to indicate that they, too, have been buried by some sudden flood or volcanic eruption or some other catastrophe.[2] But even such modern deposits as these are few and lean in comparison with the great extent and prodigious richness of the world's fossiliferous rocks.

---

[1] W. H. Twenhofel: *Principles of Sedimentation* (2nd Ed., New York, McGraw-Hill, 1950), p. 621.

[2] "Where catastrophes occur the situation is different. . . . It is questionable whether the hundreds of vertebrates killed by storms leave evident traces in the sediment, but if killing attains catastrophic proportions, the chance is much greater." (M. Brongersma-Sanders: "Mass Mortality in the Sea," Ch. 29 in *Marine Ecology and Paleoecology*, Vol. I, Joel Hedgpeth, Ed., Geological Society of America Memoir 67, 1957, p. 972). "The similarity of sediments in regions where catastrophes occur with certain fossil deposits indicates that catastrophic killing has played a part in geology" (*Ibid.,* p. 973).

And so again we have seen that the principle of uniformity is utterly inadequate to explain the geologic phenomena, even in its most important aspect—that of the fossil deposits on which the entire structure of evolutionary historical geology is built!

CONTRADICTIONS IN THE UNIFORMITARIAN SYSTEM

We have now seen that the major geologic agencies—erosion, deposition, volcanism, glaciation, diastrophism, etc.—do not suffice to explain on uniformist principles the rock formations of the earth's crust. Each of them must, at some time or times in the past, have acted on a scale and with an intensity far greater than manifested in the present, if the geologic phenomena are to be explained thereby. And this is especially true of those rocks and other deposits containing fossil remains of living organisms of the past, which we have seen to be utterly unaccountable in terms of normal processes.

But the main buttress of the uniformity theory, together with its evolutionary implications, is the supposed fact that the strata everywhere exhibit the same order, thus permitting the development of a worldwide system of identification and correlation. Paleontologists maintain that the strata can be divided into a series of identifiable units corresponding to definite geologic ages and that these units always are in the same order and thus testify to their chronologic equivalence. This is the standard system of geologic ages, as found in any textbook on historical geology. A typical chart of the geologic ages is shown on page 133. The importance of this supposed historical evidence and its dependence upon the fossils is indicated by the following quotation, typical of many:

> The part of geology that deals with the tracing of the geologic record of the past is called *historic geology*. Historic geology relies chiefly on paleontology, the study of fossil organisms. . . . The geologist utilizes knowledge of organic evolution, as preserved in the fossil record, to identify and correlate the lithic records of ancient time.[1]

Such identification of age by means of contained fossils obviously requires that there be only one assemblage of organisms corresponding to each age. Any particular animal, or at least those animals used as index fossils, should correspond to only one time period. Further-

[1] O. D. von Engeln and K. E. Caster: *Geology* (New York, McGraw-Hill, 1952), p. 423.

more, any particular assemblage of organisms should always occupy the same relative position with respect to organisms which either preceded or succeeded it in history, with the rocks identified by the assemblage therefore always occupying the same position in the superposed sequence of rock formations. It is claimed by uniformitarians that these relationships actually do always exist and therefore that the geologic time scale is valid and that the indicated evolutionary progression of organisms is an actual fact of history.

It may of course be granted that the principle of stratigraphic correlation by means of fossils, in terms of the accepted sequence, is supported by much evidence. Any theory that could have obtained almost universal acceptance by geologists is obviously not founded solely on wishful thinking.

On the other hand, it is possible that some other theory may explain the same evidence more effectively. This process has often been true in the history of science, whenever a new generalization has been developed to incorporate within its framework not only the facts supporting the previous theory but also those facts contradicting the previous theory.

And in spite of the general validity of the standard and accepted geologic stratigraphic succession, there are many exceptions and contradictions to it, which have been very unsatisfactorily explained in terms of the accepted theory. One prominent geologist says:

> Because of the sterility of its concepts, historical geology, which includes paleontology and stratigraphy, has become static and unreproductive. Current methods of delimiting intervals of time, which are the fundamental units of historical geology, and of establishing chronology are of dubious validity. Worse than that, the criteria of correlation—the attempt to equate in time, or synchronize, the geological history of one area with that of another—are logically vulnerable. The findings of historical geology are suspect because the principles upon which they are based are either inadequate, in which case they should be reformulated, or false, in which case they should be discarded. Most of us refuse to discard or reformulate, and the result is the present deplorable state of our discipline.[1]

These contradictions are many, but we shall only discuss two main categories, instances of individual fossils being found out of proper context and instances of entire formations being found out of proper

---

[1] Robin S. Allen: "Geological Correlation and Paleoecology," *Bulletin of the Geological Society of America,* Vol. 59, January 1948, p. 2.

sequence with those above and below. Before citing specific instances of these phenomena, the methods by which uniformitarianism attempts to reconcile them may be noted.

When a fossil is found in a stratum to which it theoretically does not belong, several means of explaining the discrepancy are possible. If it is supposed to be older than the containing bed, it can be said to have been redeposited from an earlier eroded deposit or to indicate the survival of its particular species longer than had been previously believed. If it is supposed to be younger than its stratum, it can be again explained as due to the reworking and mixing of two originally distinct deposits or else as showing that the animal dates from earlier antiquity than previously thought. Often, discovery of such an anomalous fossil has been deemed sufficient justification for redating the entire formation, to conform to the supposed age of the particular fossil. With so many speculative devices conveniently at hand for reconciling these discrepancies, it is obvious that all but the most flagrant cases of mislocation can be quickly and easily explained away. In cases that simply *cannot* be explained in such a manner, it is still possible to ignore them, on the assumption that there must have been some mistake in the field evidence or its description.

When an entire formation seems out of place in the standard sequence, on the basis of either lithologic or paleontologic evidence, it is not so easy to conceive explanatory mechanisms. However, as we have seen, these cases are usually handled in terms of supposed great earth movements, faulting, folding, thrusting, etc., whether or not there is any actual physical evidence of such movement.

As already noted, systems of rocks are quite often found with the intervening systems omitted. Even more paradoxically, formations are often found actually in reverse order, with presumed older rocks lying on top of younger rocks. In the first case, the missing rocks are accounted for as periods of erosion; in the second, the theory of the thrust fault is commonly advanced, according to which rocks which originally were flat-lying and contiguous were suddenly separated by a vertical or sloping fault, the rocks on one side of the fault rising with respect to those on the other. Then the upper rocks were thrust horizontally over the lower. In time, the top layers were eroded away, leaving then only the older rocks on the bottom of the faulted portion resting on top of the younger rocks over which they were supposed to move.[1] As we have already pointed out, if such phenomena as this have ever taken place on the earth, it is thereby proved that the principle of uniformity is invalid as a guiding geologic principle, since there are no demonstrably comparable phenomena now occurring.

But on the other hand, is it not possible that all of the many paradoxes and exceptions, with which the geological formations abound, can be better explained by means of some other principle than that of uniformity and evolution? Except for these philosophies, there is no reason to be greatly surprised when a fossil is found out of place or even when an entire formation is out of place. The concept of catastrophe, which we have already seen to be necessary to account for many of the geologic formations, may quite possibly suffice not only to account for the deposition of the rocks and organisms in their usual sequences but also for occasional deposits in unusual orders.

For, in spite of all the devices which are available for harmonizing the contradictory cases with the accepted system, there still exist many examples which seem much more difficult to explain in terms of uniformity and evolution than in terms of creation and subsequent catastrophe(s).

Misplaced Fossils

For example, there is the case of the human footprints that have frequently been found in supposedly very ancient strata. Man, of course, is supposed to have evolved only in the late Tertiary, at the earliest, and therefore to be only about one million years old. But what appear to be human footprints have been found in rocks from as early as the Carboniferous Period, supposedly some 250,000,000 years old. Says Ingalls:

> On sites reaching from Virginia and Pennsylvania, through Kentucky, Illinois, Missouri and westward toward the Rocky Mountains, prints similar to those shown above [referring to several accompanying pictures],

---

[1] "How can we be so sure that these great masses of rock, weighing untold millions of tons, have really been moved across the surface of the earth for distances that may range up to 25 miles? . . . Where ages of erosion have stripped away enough of the overlying rocks, geologists can look through the resulting erosion openings, or "windows," and see the younger rocks below, with their younger fossils—a contradiction of one of the established rules of the science of geology." (P. M. Tilden, "Mountains That Moved," *Science Digest*, Vol. 44, June 1959, p. 74).

and from 5 to 10 inches long, have been found on the surface of exposed rocks, and more and more keep turning up as the years go by.[1]

These prints give every evidence of having been made by human feet, at a time when the rocks were soft mud. As indicated in the quotation, this sort of thing is not a rare occurrence but is found rather frequently. However, geologists refuse to accept the evidence at face value, because it would mean either that modern man lived in the earliest years of the postulated evolutionary history or that this history must be condensed to a duration measured by the history of man. Neither alternative is acceptable. Ingalls says:

> If man, or even his ape ancestor, or even that ape ancestor's early mammalian ancestor, existed as far back as in the Carboniferous Period in any shape, then the whole science of geology is so completely wrong that all the geologists will resign their jobs and take up truck driving. Hence for the present at least, science rejects the attractive explanation that man made these mysterious prints in the mud of the Carboniferous Period with his feet.[2]

Ingalls and others have tried to explain the prints as modern Indian carvings or as prints made of some as yet undiscovered Carboniferous amphibian. Such explanations illustrate the methods by which the uniformitarians can negate even the most plain and powerful evidence in opposition to their philosophy. Nevertheless, it is obvious that it is only the philosophy, and not the objective scientific evidence, that would prevent one from accepting these prints as of true human origin.

In Figures 10 and 11 are shown some remarkable footprints found in a Cretaceous limestone formation near Glen Rose, Texas, photographed by Mr. Clifford L. Burdick, a practicing mining geologist. Roland T. Bird, a paleontologist from the American Museum of Natural History, carefully examined the rocks pictured in Figure 11 and reported as follows:

> Yes, they apparently were real enough. Real as rock could be . . . the strangest things of their kind I had ever seen. On the surface of each was

---

[1] Albert C. Ingalls: "The Carboniferous Mystery," Vol. 162, *Scientific American*, January 1940, p. 14.
[2] *Ibid.*

(Photo by C. L. Burdick)

Figure 10. CONTEMPORANEOUS FOOTPRINTS OF MAN AND DINOSAUR.

These tracks were both cut from the Paluxy River Bed near Glen Rose, Texas, in supposedly Cretaceous strata, plainly disproving the evolutionist's contention that the dinosaurs were extinct some 70 million years before man "evolved." Geologists have rejected this evidence, however, preferring to believe that the human footprints were carved by some modern artist, while at the same time accepting the dinosaur prints as genuine. If anything, the dinosaur prints look more "artificial" than the human, but the genuineness of neither would be questioned at all were it not for the geologically sacrosanct evolutionary time-scale.

splayed the near-likeness of a human foot, perfect in every detail. But each imprint was 15 inches long![1]

[1] Roland T. Bird, "Thunder In His Footsteps," *Natural History,* May, 1939, p. 255. Bird personally investigated the river bed from which these footprints had reportedly been cut and was told by James Ryals, a property owner, that a whole trail of these "man tracks" had been washed away recently. "My surprise was partly overcome by Ryals' casual reference to them as human footprints. I smiled. No man had ever existed in the Age of Reptiles . . ." (p. 257). Ryals could only show him one such track, 15 inches long, "but the track lacked definition on which to base conclusions." However, he insisted that dinosaur tracks could still be found in the river bed. To his utter amazement, Bird discovered not only the trails of large three-toed carnivorous dinosaurs, but also the footprints of a gigantic sauropod, 24 x 38 inches, twelve feet apart, and sunk very deeply in the mud! (See also, R. T. Bird, "We Captured a 'Live' Brontosaur," *National Geographic Magazine,* May, 1954, pp. 707-722). In spite of all this, Bird dismissed the large human footprints as clever carvings.

(*Photo by C. L. Burdick*)

Figure 11. GIANT HUMAN FOOTPRINTS IN CRETACEOUS STRATA.

These are more of the apparently human footprints found in the Paluxy River Bed. Note the tremendous size, which immediately reminds one of the Biblical statement that there were "giants in the earth in those days" (Genesis 6:4). Similar giant human footprints have been found in Arizona, near Mt. Whitney in California, near the White Sands in New Mexico, and in other places.

Burdick has published some of the results of his investigations[1] in this region, and it certainly appears from his description of the evidence that dinosaurs and giant humans must have lived at the same time.

Another amazing find was reported many years ago, that of a fossilized human skull in the coal measures. The outstanding authority on coal geology, Otto Stutzer, says concerning this mysterious fossil:

[1] C. L. Burdick, in *The Naturalist*, Vol. 16, Spring 1957. Also, in *Signs of the Times*, July 22, 1950.

In the coal collection in the Mining Academy in Freiberg [Stutzer was Professor of Geology and Mineralogy in the School of Mines at Freiberg, in Saxony], there is a puzzling human skull composed of brown coal and manganiferous and phosphatic limonite, but its source is not known. This skull was described by Karsten and Dechen in 1842.[1]

The coal was presumably Tertiary in age but at any rate is supposed to have far antedated the first appearance of man. The evidence again seems mostly to have been ignored, although it has been suggested that someone must have carved the skull!

Living Fossils

The above examples illustrate the occurrence of the supposedly most recent creature (man) in supposedly ancient deposits. Almost equally anomalous are the many instances of supposedly ancient and long extinct creatures which have suddenly and unexpectedly turned up living in the modern world. An example of this is the odd creature known as the tuatara, which now lives only in New Zealand, shown in Fig. 12. It is the sole living representative of that order of reptiles known as the "beakheads."

Today it is of no economic importance. Why, then, should this reptile attract so much attention? The answer lies in the eventual realization that the tuatara is a relic, a living fossil—another way of saying that it is the lone survivor of a group of animals that had its heyday in the distant past.[2]

The remarkable thing is that a creature which is so apparently out of place in the modern world and which has apparently little selection value in the struggle for existence could have survived the countless vicissitudes of the millions of years that are supposed to have elapsed since all its relatives perished. A few thousands of years of survival under adverse circumstances might be possible, but hardly millions!

Despite the present-day existence of the tuatara, not one bone identifiable as that of a beakhead has been discovered in the rocks laid down since the early Cretaceous Period, some 135 million years ago.[3]

[1] Otto Stutzer: *Geology of Coal* (Transl. by A. C. Noe, Chicago, University of Chicago Press, 1940), p. 271.
[2] Charles M. Bogert: "The Tuatara: Why Is It a Lone Survivor?" *Scientific Monthly*, Vol. 76, March 1953, p. 165.
[3] *Ibid.*, p. 166.

(Photo by Chas. M. Bogert, Am. Mus. Natl. Hist.)

Figure 12. THE TUATARA.

This is a true "living fossil," the sole survivor of the reptilian order of beakheads, which otherwise became extinct some 135 million years ago, according to the standard evolutionary time scale. Fossils of these creatures are found in Cretaceous and older rocks, but none whatsoever in more recent strata. Yet they are still living in the modern world! And the tuatara is only one of numerous examples of such living fossils. It is strange that no remains of this creature have been found in the rocks representing this 135 million-year gap, if such a gap actually exists.

The skeleton of a reptile found in the Jurassic deposits of Europe is so nearly identical with that of the living tuatara that very little change in the bony structure must have taken place during a period of 150,000,000 years.[1]

Another recent discovery, quite amazing to the evolutionists, was that of the coelecanth, a supposedly long-extinct fish whose fossils are abundant in the Paleozoic and Mesozoic strata. The Harvard paleontologist, Dr. A. S. Romer, remarks concerning this discovery:

The coelecanths are a marine offshoot of the Crossopterygii, a group essentially ancestral to land vertebrates and, hence, of evolutionary importance. Typical crossopterygians have been extinct since the Paleozoic; the fossil record of the coelecanths extends to the Cretaceous, some 70 million years ago, and then stops. In consequence, I (like many another lecturer) used to tell my class, emphatically, that "there are no living crossopterygians." And I can well remember my amazement, in the winter

[1] *Ibid.*, p. 167.

of 1939, at seeing in the *London Illustrated News* a photograph of a living—or rather recently living—coelecanth.[1]

Even more remarkable than the discovery of the coelecanth was the recent dredging-up of several specimens of a living segmented mollusk (at a depth of 11,700 feet in the Acapulco Trench off Central America), representing a primitive type that supposedly became extinct in the Devonian period. The biologist Bentley Glass, reporting on this find, says:

> To zoologists the recently reported discovery by the Galathea Expedition of the extraordinary deep-sea mollusk *Neopilina galatheae* will seem even more incredible than the famous discovery in recent times of *Latimeria,* the living coelecanth, . . . the new-found mollusk represents a class that existed in the Cambrian to Devonian periods of the Paleozoic, and was supposed to have become extinct about 280 million years ago.[2]

280 million years is a long time and one cannot help but wonder about its reality. Fossils of this class of mollusk were apparently plentiful in the early Paleozoic strata and it is amazing that none have been found in the marine strata of the Mesozoic or Tertiary, if indeed these actually represent the hundreds of millions of years following the Paleozoic that they are supposed to.

Harry S. Ladd, a paleoecologist with the U. S. Geological Survey, has called attention to a number of these "living fossils" recently discovered.

> In the same year that the first coelecanth was caught, in fairly deep water, a series of primitive crustaceans was found inhabiting the interstitial waters of beach sands in New England. . . . (It) was regarded as the most primitive living crustacean yet discovered. It held this significant position only until 1953, at which time a still more primitive crustacean was dredged from the mud beneath the shallow waters of Long Island Sound. . . . Its closest known relative, *Lepidocaris,* lived in Middle Devonian time, some 300 million years ago.[3]

In view of these and many similar discoveries, one also wonders whether or not many more of the supposedly extinct creatures of

---

[1] A. S. Romer, review of "The Search Beneath the Sea," by J. L. B. Smith, *Scientific Monthly,* Vol. 84, February 1957, p. 101.

[2] Bentley Glass: "New Missing Link Discovered," *Science,* Vol. 126, July 26, 1957, p. 158.

[3] Harry S. Ladd: "Ecology, Paleontology and Stratigraphy," *Science,* Vol. 129, January 9, 1959, p. 74.

geologic history might not also be living in some unexplored region of the globe,[1] especially in the deep oceans. It would not be surprising if even the famous trilobite, perhaps the most important "index fossil" of the earliest period of the Paleozoic, the Cambrian, should turn up one of these days. A creature very similar to it has already been found.

A specimen of a "living fossil," perhaps the most primitive extant member of one of the major classes of animals, has recently been added to the collections of the Smithsonian Institution. This is a crustacean that has certain characters of the long-extinct trilobites, the earth's dominant animals of a half-billion years ago, fossils of which are among the earliest traces of a high order of life on this planet. . . . Presumably it is exclusively an inhabitant of the mud bottoms of shallow inshore waters and never comes to the surface or has a free-swimming existence. This may account for the fact that it has remained unknown so long.[2]

In the plant kingdom, it has not been many years since quite a sensation was created among paleobotantists by the discovery of living specimens of the tree *Metasequoia,* in a remote region of China.

The conifer genus Metasequoia was widely distributed over the northern hemisphere in past ages. Its fossil remains have been found in Alaska, Greenland, Spitzbergen and northern Siberia, in rocks of Eocene age (60,-000,000 years old); in rocks of Miocene age (30,000,000 years old) in Oregon and California, Germany and Switzerland, Manchuria and Japan. It was considered to have become extinct some 20 million years ago, since its fossil remains did not occur in rocks younger than Miocene.[3]

Chaney, who is paleobotantist at the University of California and who made an expedition to study the trees, proceeds to tell about one which was nearly 100 feet high and one stand of over 100 of the trees, still thriving. Evidently something must have been wrong with

[1] See Bernard Heuvelmans, *On the Track of Unknown Animals* (Hill and Wang, Inc., 1959, 558 pp.) for an interesting discussion of many such possibilities.

[2] "Living Fossil Resembles Long-Extinct Trilobite," *Science Digest,* Vol. 42, December 1957. A recent note says that Scripps Institute scientists have initiated an intense search for living trilobites. "Deeply interested in the living-fossil hunt, are Robert H. Parker, a Scripps ecologist, and Dr. Henning Lemche, a zoologist from Denmark, who say they do not believe the trilobite is extinct and are planning to go out and look for the organism" ("Start Search for Living Trilobites," *Science Digest,* September 1959, p. 81).

[3] Ralph W. Chaney: "Metasequoia Discovery," *American Scientist,* Vol. 36, October 1948, p. 490.

the geological record deduced from the Pliocene and Pleistocene strata, which failed to reveal the continued existence of the trees, in spite of their great abundance in the supposedly earlier strata.

Formations Out of Sequence

But if this is the import of individual creatures which are found out of place in the sequences, what should be said of the many examples of entire formations being out of place in the standard geologic time-table? In every mountainous region on every continent, there seem to be numerous examples of supposedly "old" strata superimposed on top of "young" strata.[1] In the absence of definite structural evidence to the contrary, one would naturally suppose that the lowermost strata must necessarily have been first deposited and, therefore, be "older." But the fossils often seem to belie this assumption, and it is the fossils which govern the assigned formation age.

As noted previously, the official explanation of this sort of anachronism is in terms of what is variously called an "overthrust," "thrust-fault," "low-angle fault," "nappe," "detachment thrust," or similar term. The concept is of a large section of stratified rock being elevated and slid over on top of the adjacent rocks, so that the "older" rocks on the bottom of the moving mass will then be on top of the "younger" rocks on the top of the stationary rocks. Subsequent erosion then is usually assumed to have worn off the younger rocks on top of the displaced topography.

It is recognized that phenomena of this sort have taken place on a small scale, in certain localities where there is ample evidence of intense past faulting and folding. However, these visible confirmations of the concept are definitely on a small scale, usually in terms of a few hundreds of feet, *whereas many of the great overthrust areas occupy hundreds or even thousands of square miles*. It seems almost fantastic to conceive of such huge areas and masses of rocks really behaving in such a fashion, unless we are ready to accept catastrophism of an intensity that makes the Noachian Deluge seem quiescent by comparison! Certainly the principle of uniformity is inadequate to

---

[1] See a recent article by M. King Hubbert and Wm. W. Rubey, "Role of Fluid Pressure in Mechanics of Overthrust Faulting," (*Bulletin of Geological Society of America*, Vol. 70, Feb. 1959, pp. 115-166) for an extensive listing of areas of this type, pp. 119-122.

account for them. Nothing we know of present earth movements—
of rock compressive and shearing strengths, of the plastic flow of
rock materials, or of other modern physical processes—gives any
observational basis for believing that such things are happening now
or ever could have happened, except under extremely unusual conditions. As Hubbert and Rubey admit:

> Since their earliest recognition, the existence of large overthrusts has
> presented a mechanical paradox that has never been satisfactorily re-
> solved.[1]

To illustrate the character of these important areas, we might consider the well-known Heart Mountain Thrust of Wyoming. This supposed thrust occupies roughly a triangular area, 30 miles wide by 60
miles long, with its apex at the northeast corner of Yellowstone Park.
It consists of about 50 separate blocks of Paleozoic strata (Ordovician, Devonian and Mississippian) resting essentially horizontally
and conformably on Eocene beds, some 250,000,000 years younger!
This formation is shown in Fig. 13.

Although there are some brecciated sections near the contact line,
the supposed thrust blocks certainly give every appearance visually of
having been deposited more or less normally on top of the beds beneath. A recent author who has made an extensive study of the area
says:

> Although the normal sequence of beds above the Heart Mountain thrust
> is in ascending order Bighorn, Jefferson, Three Forks, and Madison
> formations, in many places this sequence is broken, and one or more of the
> lower formations may be absent. . . . Were it not for the broken sequence
> and absence of some formations at places such as these just mentioned,
> the presence of a fault might not be recognized in the northwestern part
> of the area.[2]

Pierce shows many pictures of the "fault-line." all of them looking

---

[1] Hubbert and Rubey, *op. cit.*, p. 122. In like manner, Philip B. King says: "It
seems mechanically implausible that great sheets of rock could have moved across
nearly flat surfaces for appreciable distances, although recent papers by Rubey and
Hubbert have shed new light on how this might have been accomplished" ("The
Anatomy and Habitat of Low-Angle Thrust Faults," *American Journal of Science*,
Vol. 258-A, 1960, p. 115).

[2] William G. Pierce: "Heart Mountain and South Fork Detachment Thrusts of
Wyoming," *Bulletin of the American Association of Petroleum Geologists*, Vol. 41,
April 1957, p. 596.

(Photo by Wm. G. Pierce)

Figure 13. HEART MOUNTAIN THRUST.

All appearances to the contrary, uniformitarianism insists that the Mississippian limestone formation (designated Cm in the picture) was not deposited directly above the
Cambrian rocks below (Ggc), but was slid into place by gravity from another region!
Ordovician and Devonian strata are also frequently found in the thrust block, but
for some reason were not included here. Furthermore, in many areas of the Heart
Mountain Thrust, this thrust block is resting conformably upon Eocene strata, supposedly some 250,000,000 years younger! At least, that is the theory, but it would
appear quite obvious physically that this whole sequence has been normally deposited,
and that the great "thrust" is really a normal bedding plane.

for all the world like any other normal contact between chronologically deposited strata (See Fig. 14). An even more mysterious factor
is that there appear to be no source beds from which the thrust blocks
could have broken off.

The Heart Mountain thrust has long been structurally perplexing because
there are no known structural roots or source from which it could have
been derived. Furthermore, there is no known surface fault or fault zone
within or adjoining the region from which the thrust sheet could have been
derived.[1]

Not only is there no indication of where the superposed rocks could
have come from (unless of course they were normally deposited on

[1] *Ibid.*, p. 592.

(Photo by Wm. G. Pierce)

Figure 14. SUPPOSED THRUST CONTACT LINE.

Here a close-up of the Heart Mountain thrust plane plainly reveals a lack of any real evidence of thrusting. The formation designated (Tebb) is known as the "early basic breccia" and is frequently found at the base of the supposed thrust block, here lying on top of the Cambrian Grove Creek Formation (Cgc). But, as Pierce says: "There is no clear indication, however, of any fault movement between the 'early basic breccia' and the Grove Creek formation or other beds on which it may lie." (op. cit., p. 607).

top of the underlying Eocene strata, as all appearances indicate), but there is no physical or mechanical explanation of how the fifty-odd blocks could all have individually slid into place. Pierce's best guess is simply "gravity," but he acknowledges this explanation to be essentially inadequate. As far as the fault-lines are concerned, he says:

The fault contact or fault plane is usually concealed or at best is poorly exposed where it is an erosion thrust or a shear thrust, but the bedding thrust contact is well-exposed in places. The fault contact of the bedding thrust may either be clean-cut and sharp, with essentially no brecciation of the beds above or below the fault, as observed at several places, or it may have a line of broken limestone and limestone debris, such as observed at the northwest end of Sugarloaf Mountain.[1]

[1] *Ibid.*, p. 598.

Uniformitarians will say that these brecciated areas at the fault plane are evidence that movement has actually occurred and, therefore, that the "thrust-fault" concept of these Heart Mountain blocks is valid. However, it should be remembered that breccias occur widely, usually in places where no such phenomenon is in question at all. They might easily have been produced by means other than this hypothetical sliding. On the other hand, the really pertinent question is: Why is not the *entire* fault-plane heavily brecciated and distorted? The fact that there are many places where the contact line is clean-cut and sharp, looking very like a normal bedding plane, is seemingly inexplicable if the plane is in reality a thrust-plane.

Of course, if the contact plane *is* a normal bedding plane, as it certainly appears to be, that means that, at least at this locality, the Eocene series was laid down before the strata of the Ordovician, Devonian, and Mississippian. Uniformitarians and evolutionists of course absolutely refuse even to consider such a possibility and so will continue to call this the Heart-Mountain "thrust," all physical evidence to the contrary notwithstanding.

Let no one think that this is an exceptional example. Pierce says:

> The Heart Mountain and South Fork thrusts are by no means the only thrusts without roots. Particularly in the Jura Mountains of Switzerland and France, but in other places also, there are more widely known examples of the decollement or detachment type of structure.[1]

Space does not permit discussion of many of these areas. Long ago, George McCready Price made an extensive study of areas of this type around the world. He discussed these in many books written by him on the general theme of deluge geology.[2] Although his examples were very impressive and well-documented, his writings were largely ignored by geologists, ostensibly because of his largely self-made geologic education.[3]

The only half-serious attempt that was ever made to refute Price's examples of this serious geological contradiction was by J. L. Kulp, of Columbia University's Lamont Geological Laboratory.[4] Kulp

---

[1] *Ibid.*, p. 625.

[2] See especially, *Evolutionary Geology and the New Catastrophism* (Mountain View, California, Pacific Press Publishing Association, 1926), pp. 105-146.

[3] We feel that Price was *really* ignored because of his strong case against uniformitarianism, a case more easily ridiculed or ignored than refuted.

[4] J. L. Kulp: "Flood Geology," *Journal of the American Scientific Affiliation*, Vol. 2, January 1950, pp. 1-15.

dealt with only one of his examples, though certainly one of the most spectacular, namely that of a large section of the Canadian Rockies in Alberta extending down into Montana, where an extensive area of Pre-Cambrian limestone is resting in apparent conformity upon Cretaceous shale beds. Other areas in the same general region have Paleozoic limestones superposed on the Cretaceous. Many of these phenomena are said to be attributable to the "Lewis Overthrust," one view of which appears in Fig. 15. Thornbury says concerning it:

> The Lewis overthrust of Montana has a length of approximately 135 miles and a horizontal displacement of about 15 miles. Its fault plane dips to the southwest at an angle of about 3 degrees.[1]

The overthrust includes the Glacier National Park area, and one of the most spectacular features is that of Chief Mountain, which is an entirely isolated outlier of Algonkian limestone, resting on a Cretaceous base (see Fig. 16). Kulp insisted that the fault-plane frequently gave evidence of the overriding action of the thrust block, evidence of a physical nature, and therefore that Price's contention that the thrust concept was based only on fossil evidence was invalid.

It is quite true that the entire area (as is true of mountainous areas in general) gives much evidence of faulting, folding, and general tectonic activity, both at the so-called fault planes and at many other locations, including planes which are supposed to be normal bedding planes. Such activity is to be expected in connection with mountain-uplift processes, whatever the nature or cause of those processes may be. On a small scale, it is evident that overthrusting has actually occurred in many places.

Nevertheless, it requires a tremendous and entirely unwarranted extrapolation to infer from these small-scale folds and thrusts that over-thrusting can occur on the infinitely greater scale required to account for the Lewis "overthrust" and others like it. If such had occurred, it would seem that every part of the overriding block would be intensely deformed and that the fault plane especially would everywhere be brecciated, deformed and perhaps metamorphosed. But although there is evidence of disturbance at many points of the

---

[1] Wm. D. Thornbury: *Principles of Geomorphology* (New York, Wiley, 1954), p. 268. More recent studies indicate the thrust block to have been 350 miles wide, with a displacement of at least 35 or 40 miles and about 6 miles thick! (C. P. Ross and Richard Rezak: *The Rocks and Fossils of Glacier National Park*, U. S. Geological Survey Professional Paper 294-K, 1959, pp. 422, 424, plate 53C).

Figure 15. THE LEWIS OVERTHRUST.

supposed fault-plane, and above, there are also many points where there seems to be no physical evidence whatever of the tremendous sliding that is supposed to have taken place. Fig. 17 shows a close-up view of the contact line.

Kulp, in quoting from an early report of the Canadian Geological Survey on the region, emphasizes that portion of the report describing physical evidences of possible sliding. On the other hand, he also quotes a statement acknowledging that the underlying shales appear undisturbed, as follows:

The fault plane here (in the Bow valley) is nearly horizontal and the two formations, viewed from the valley, appear to succeed one another conformably. The Cretaceous shales are bent sharply toward the east in a number of places, but with this exception have suffered little by the sliding of the limestone over them, and their comparatively undisturbed condition seems hardly compatible with the extreme faulting which was necessary to bring them into their present position.[1]

The undisturbed condition of the underlying shales is attributed by Kulp to their softness, but it is not explained just how this property would inhibit deformation or grinding of the shales. The overlying limestones are said to have been much deformed. If this deformation were caused by sliding over the shales, the latter must have been competent to transmit the necessary shearing stresses and therefore not too soft to undergo distortion by those same stresses. This is basic mechanics.

Another difficulty with the concept of the Lewis overthrust is that it should have produced a large mass of broken rock in front of it and along the sides. But this has not been found.

[1] J. L. Kulp, *op. cit.*, quoting R. G. McConnell, *Annual Report, Canadian Geological Survey*, 1886, Part D, p. 34. Ross and Rezak say: "Most visitors, especially those who stay on the roads, get the impression that the Belt strata are undisturbed and lie almost as flat today as they did when deposited in the sea which vanished so many years ago" (*op. cit.*, p. 420).

FIGURE 15.

This is one of the most famous (and unbelievable) of the supposed overthrust regions, being, according to recent estimates, some 350 miles wide and six miles thick, with an inferred horizontal displacement of at least 35 or 40 miles! The black rocks on the upper half of the mountain in the photo are Pre-Cambrian, the lighter-colored rocks below Cretaceous, about 500,000,000 years younger. Although there are slight indications of folding, both above and below the contact line, these are certainly no greater than at any other normal unconformity. It is clearly only uniformist assumption that says the upper beds were deposited *before* the lower beds were laid down.

Figure 16. CHIEF MOUNTAIN.

The absence of rubble or breccia is among the compelling reasons that have forced the abandonment of the long-held idea that the Lewis overthrust emerged at the surface and moved over a plain near the front of the present mountains. . . . Such a slab moving over ground as is now believed to have existed should have scarred and broken the hills and have itself been broken to a greater or less extent, depending on local conditions. No evidence of either of these things has been found.[1]

This does not mean, of course, that belief in the idea of the overthrust itself has been abandoned! This could not be the case unless the standard system of geologic ages also could be rejected. Nevertheless, it is plain that there is no physical indication of where the overthrust came from or how it moved or where it ended. This entire problem is thus still unsettled.

A California scientist, Dr. Walter Lammerts, recently made a trip to the area for the specific purpose of examining the fault line. Dr. Lammerts is a horticulturist and rose breeder whose hobby is geology. He is a careful scientist, formerly on the University of California faculty and now a nationally-known horticultural consultant, and is well able to make careful observations of a geologic nature. After examining the fault plane in the Glacier National Park area, he says:

After careful observation I am convinced Price is even more right than he thought—at the actual contact line very thin layers of shale were always present. Furthermore these were cemented both to the upper Altyn limestone (oldest of the Pre-Cambrian series) and lower Cretaceous shale layers. In fact, in some places along the almost one-quarter mile line of exposed contact the limestone and Cretaceous have split apart at the contact line. Often where this has occurred the thin band of soft shale sticks to the upper block of Altyn limestone.

This seems to clearly indicate that just before the Altyn limestone was deposited and after the tilting of the Cretaceous beds (tilting in some areas

[1] C. P. Ross and Richard Rezak, *op. cit.,* p. 424.

FIGURE 16.

Another remarkable part of the Lewis Overthrust is Chief Mountain, which is composed of Algonkian (Precambrian) limestone resting conformably on Cretaceous shales. Furthermore, the massive limestone of the mountain is an entirely isolated outlier of the thrust block, surrounded by and resting on top of Cretaceous strata. On top of the mountain are found no remnants of Cretaceous shales as might be supposed but only a few granitic boulders. At the bottom is a talus slope, formed of broken pieces of the soft and easily eroded Cretaceous shales.

(Photo by Walter E. Lammerts)

Figure 17. LEWIS OVERTHRUST CONTACT LINE.

The almost perfectly horizontal nature of the Lewis Overthrust contact line (indicated by arrow) is revealed in this photograph. There is certainly no apparent indication of any substantial amount of shearing distortion along this surface. Slight differential movements on the two sides of the *bedding* plane, due to differences in the structural characteristics of shale and limestone, have caused some slight distortion, particularly opening up a clear-cut split along the contact. All along this contact line, for at least a half mile, a very thin ($\frac{1}{16}''$ to $\frac{1}{8}''$) layer of shale-like material made of fine clay particles is found, adhering in some places to the upper Algonkian limestone and in some to the underlying Cretaceous shales, which are lithologically quite distinct from the layer itself. It seems inconceivable that this very fine layer would have been left so intact if the limestone had actually been thrust over the shale as the Lewis "Overthrust" interpretation demands.

only—others have perfectly conformable level contact lines) a thin wafer-like one-eighth to one-sixteenth inch layer of shale was deposited.

Careful study of the various locations showed no evidence of any grinding or sliding action or slicken-sides such as one would expect to find on the hypothesis of a vast overthrust.

Another amazing fact was the occurrence of two four-inch layers of Altyn limestone intercalated with Cretaceous shale. These always occurred *below* the general contact line of Altyn limestone and shale. Likewise careful study of these intercalations showed not the *slightest* evidence of abrasive action such as one would expect to find if these were shoved forward in between layers of shale as the overthrust theory demands.[1]

The phenomena noted by Lammerts are shown in the photographs in Figs. 18 and 19. In the light of such physical evidence as cited above, how is it possible to defend any longer the grand fiction of the "Lewis overthrust"? There ought to be no reasonable doubt that the limestones were actually deposited *after* the shales on which they lie and, therefore, that they are younger in geologic age!

The problem of overthrusting becomes still more difficult when an attempt is made to understand it from the viewpoint of engineering mechanics. The mass of rock in the Lewis overthrust slab, for example, must have weighed approximately eight hundred thousand billion tons! Assuming for the sake of argument that sufficient force could somehow be generated in the earth's crust to start such a mass moving with both a vertical and lateral component (moving vertically against the force of gravity and laterally against the frictional force along the sliding plane), it still does not follow that really large blocks could be moved in this manner. It can be calculated, on the basis of known friction coefficients for sliding blocks, that so much frictional (shearing) stress would be developed in a large block that the material itself would fail in shear or compression and, therefore, could not be transported as a coherent block at all. As Hubbert and Rubey point out:

> Consequently, for the conditions assumed, the pushing of a thrust block, whose length is of the order of 30 km. or more, along a horizontal surface, appears to be a mechanical impossibility.[2]

The impossibility is compounded, of course, when it is noted that the block does not simply move along a horizontal plane but must also move vertically in order to ride up over the strata on the other side of the fault plane. Some theorizers have attempted to avoid these difficulties by assuming that the fault plane sloped *downward,* with the underlying strata somehow sinking ahead of it, thus getting an "assist" from gravity in overcoming the friction. As noted before, this was the suggestion that was made by Pierce in trying to explain the Heart Mountain Thrust. This mechanism, however, requires that the lateral compression be relieved and the thrust be accomplished en-

---

[1] Walter E. Lammerts, Personal Communication, November 27, 1957.
[2] Hubbert and Rubey, *op. cit.,* p. 126.

(Photo by Walter E. Lammerts)

Figure 18. INTERCALATION AT CONTACT PLANE.

tirely by gravity. Calculations reveal, however, that in order to permit sliding in this fashion the fault plane would have to dip at an angle of at least 30 degrees, whereas all of the great thrust faults have inclinations much less than this.

In thus substituting a body force for the originally supposed surface force, [i.e., gravity for lateral compression] the limitation imposed by the insufficient strength of the rock is eliminated, but what appears to be an equally insuperable difficulty still remains in the form of the measured values of coefficient of friction of rock on rock.[1]

The only apparent way out of these difficulties heretofore has seemed to be to assume that rocks completely change their properties when subjected to such huge stresses acting over millions of years of time. In discussing the vexed question of the mechanics of orogenies (which, of course, are basically involved in the phenomena of faulting and folding), the geodynamicist Scheidegger concludes:

The difficulties inherent in finding the proper rheological conditions applicable to the Earth arise from two causes. First, the state of the material in all but the uppermost few kilometers of the Earth's crust is not easy to envisage. Pressures and temperatures are such that it is unlikely that they can be duplicated in the laboratory in the near future, leaving only theoretical guessing to determine the behaviour of the material under consideration. Second, the time elements involved are for the greater part such that, even if experiments involving the correct temperatures and pressures could be performed, the human life span would be millions of times too short to obtain the desired answers. This, again, forces one to speculate.[2]

All of which is one way of admitting that the principle of uniformity is unable to yield a real understanding of the processes by which the great tectonic structures of the earth have been produced. And this is exactly what we have been contending. It may be possible by various speculative devices to develop a hypothesis in terms of long

[1] *Ibid.*, p. 128.
[2] Adrian E. Scheidegger: *Principles of Geodynamics* (Berlin, Springer-Verlag, 1958), p. 103.

FIGURE 18.

Below the usual contact surface along the Lewis Overthrust appears in some places this limestone intercalation, about four inches in width, shown in the picture by the grayish band (see arrow) interposed between the lighter-colored shales above and below it. The limestone (Precambrian) could not have been intruded in the thrusting process because the shales (Cretaceous) show no evidence of abrasion or distortion, either above or below.

(Photo by Walter E. Lammerts)

Figure 19. DOUBLE INTERCALATION AT CONTACT PLANE.

ages and altered rock properties, but surely this is, if anything, less consistent with uniformitarianism than even the Deluge hypothesis. In the latter, it is postulated that the earth's great complex of faults and folds was produced fairly rapidly when the strata were still soft and plastic. No mysterious and unknown properties of the materials or extravagant attributes of the time dimension need to be invented at all!

Because of the physical and mathematical difficulties inherent in any attempt to make an analysis of the mechanics of faults and folds, geologists have been placing much confidence in model tests which are supposed to have duplicated these structures in the laboratory. Using sand or clay or other soft materials, it is claimed that all the various types of structural phenomena including overthrusting have been fully duplicated in the laboratory. But it should be realized that even if the laboratory results seem to resemble the phenomena in the rocks, this does not explain the mechanics of the phenomena or prove that they occurred in similar fashion or even prove that it was possible for the rocks themselves to be formed in the assumed manner.

The mechanism of producing the folds is not any better understood in the model than it is in nature. Nevertheless, the duplication of natural phenomena on a small scale shows that the evident geological effects of crustal shortening are nothing supernatural or catastrophic, but the reasonable outcome of a reasonable process.[1]

The last sentence above is a choice example of a *non sequitur.* Model tests of this sort may appear to duplicate qualitatively the natural phenomena, but there is nothing inherent in them to identify them with uniformitarian rather than catastrophic causes! They could, with equal propriety, be said to represent on a model scale the crustal phenomena during the Deluge period. In fact, in order to

[1] *Ibid.,* p. 243.

FIGURE 19.

In this photograph, the limestone intercalation occurs in two phases, with a layer of shale in between, as well as above and below the limestone. It seems quite impossible to understand this phenomenon in terms of the overthrusting concept. The several layers were apparently deposited as normal sedimentary layers, one above the other in order. The rock above the arrow is the Pre-Cambrian limestone (1); below this is a layer of Cretaceous shale strata (2), then an intercalation of limestone (3), then more shale (4) and, at the bottom of the picture, another limestone intercalation. (5) Below this is continuous Cretaceous shale, which is crumbled and forms the usual talus slope at the base of the mountain.

make the model studies at all, the factor of *time* specifically must be excluded from consideration![1]

A further important limitation on the significance of such model tests is the very situation offered as an excuse for postulating changed mechanical properties for the rocks at great depths; namely, that such conditions and properties cannot be produced in the laboratory! Model testing is a legitimate means of determining data for engineering design, of course, and is often used in the structural and hydraulic design of dams and many other structures. But model analysis can be extremely misleading if not carried out acccording to true principles of mechanics and similitude! For example, the assumption that sand or clay behaves similarly to solid rock under the model conditions is entirely unwarranted by any reasonable criteria of dynamic similarity. As a matter of fact, the model could only be expected to behave similarly to a prototype material of the same basic character (elastic, plastic, homogeneous, heterogeneous, etc.). Thus the model results prove, if they prove anything, that the rock materials were still soft and plastic, like those in the model, when they were deformed. To discuss this question more thoroughly at this point would require a rather extended and technical digression, so that we shall only say here that model tests of this sort, though often cited as evidence of the validity of the uniformitarian concept of thrust faulting, really prove nothing whatever about the physical characteristics or possibilities of such phenomena under present conditions of rock properties and tectonics.

A very recent theory purporting to explain the phenomena of thrust faulting is that of Hubbert and Rubey.[2] These two outstanding geologists, convinced that the older theories of overthrust mechanics were completely inadequate, have developed a theory that internal fluid pressure in the pores of the rock strata might provide the answer.

The problem, of course, is to discover some mechanism for offsetting the tremendous frictional force which must be overcome if the thrust block is to slide. The frictional force is essentially the product of the weight of the thrust block and the coefficient of friction across the sliding plane. The presence of water along the plane, however, does *not* serve as a lubricant.

[1] *Ibid.*, p. 241.

[2] M. King Hubbert and Wm. W. Rubey: "Role of Fluid Pressure in Mechanics of Overthrust Faulting," *Bulletin of the Geological Society of America*, Vol. 70, February 1959, pp. 115-205.

Concerning the lubricating effect of water, Terzaghi has shown that water definitely is not a lubricant on rock materials and its presence, if anything, tends to increase the coefficient of friction.[1]

Neither is simple hydrostatic buoyancy of the water adequate. Water pressure on a submerged surface is the product of its density (approximately 62½ lbs. per cubic foot) and the depth below the free water surface. If water under pressure could somehow be admitted along the plane of incipient sliding, but not anywhere within the thrust block itself, then it is true that a buoyant force would be applied to the block which would offset in part the weight of the block. But this would be inadequate to allow the motion of really large thrust blocks since, even if the water surface were as high as or higher than the ground surface itself (which is rarely the case), the buoyant force would still be only about half the weight of the block, so that there would still be a tremendous positive friction force to overcome.

But here Hubbert and Rubey postulate a fluid under much more than hydrostatic pressure, pressure sufficient to provide a buoyant force equal substantially to the entire overburden of rock material! If this were actually the case, then the thrust block would be essentially floating and, therefore, could be moved laterally without having to overcome friction.

To account for such an anomalously high pressure, it is assumed that the water itself is compressed to a state of abnormal density. In support of this possibility, Hubbert points to measurements of abnormal fluid pressures occasionally obtained in deep oil wells and in certain laboratory tests. The physical explanation for such pressures is supposed to be the compressive action of sediments accumulating in a geosyncline, under conditions such that the entrapped water cannot escape as the pores in the sediment are reduced in volume by compaction. This phenomenon is quite possible on a laboratory scale and perhaps over the limited areas within which abnormal pressures have actually been measured in the field.

But it seems quite inconceivable that water compressed in this fashion could be applied continuously at all points throughout the extensive sliding plane of a great thrust block without the pressure somewhere being relieved. Surely, at some places over the many hun-

[1] *Op. cit.,* p. 129. Karl Terzaghi, the authority cited, is probably the world's leading authority on soil mechanics.

dreds of square miles of fault-line contact surface, fractures or folds would develop which would permit the compressed water to escape and thus to relieve the pressure. It is quite difficult to imagine that these terrifically high fluid pressures could be maintained over hundreds or thousands of square miles for millions of years while the strata undergo great distortion and thrusting, not to mention the grand assumption that such anomalous pressures could be developed over such a large area to begin with. The necessity of formulating such a theory of last resort in hope of salvaging the overthrust concept merely illustrates the utter physical implausibility of the concept.

Thus, we feel warranted in rejecting the whole concept of overthrusting, at least when applied on the scale of the so-called Lewis and Heart Mountain Thrusts and the many others of similar size and kind, such as the famous Matterhorn (Fig. 20) and Mythen Peaks in the Alps.[1] We do this for two perfectly sound scientific reasons: in the first place, there are many places where there are no field evidences of a physical nature that any such movements ever took place and, in the second place, all reasonable applications of engineering mechanics to the study of the phenomenon indicate that thrusting on the large scale required is highly unlikely and probably physically impossible.

We of course recognize that there are evidences of folding and fracturing along many supposed fault planes, and this may well indicate that there has been some motion of the upper and lower strata relative to each other. But this certainly does not prove that the upper strata have moved the many miles that would be required by the overthrust theory! Even slight motions would produce the indicated distortions. Similar folds and breccias are found along many bedding planes where the strata follow the standard order and so do not need to be "explained" as thrusts. They simply give evidence of the great stresses to which the strata were subjected during the uplifting processes following the Deluge. Naturally there would, in general, be greater evidence of stresses and strains along a bedding plane than elsewhere, because of the different elastic properties of the materials on the two sides of the plane.

But even if, for the sake of argument, we were to grant that some large overthrusts may actually have occurred, we would still insist

[1] See also Figs. 21 and 22 for two more examples of supposed overthrusts which give every outward appearance of having been deposited normally in their present positions.

Figure 20. THE MATTERHORN.

This famous Swiss mountain is only one of many in the Alps that are out of the standard geological order. The Matterhorn is supposed to have been thrust from some thirty to sixty miles away, over younger rocks, with subsequent erosion removing all evidence of its continuity with its source. The strata in the equally famous Mythen Peak of the Alps are, in ascending order, Eocene, Triassic, Jurassic and Cretaceous, and it was thought to have been pushed all the way from Africa into Switzerland!

that this would only be physically possible at all during or soon after the Deluge, when the strata were still relatively soft and plastic in their mechanical behavior and when the great forces necessary for overthrusting were at least feasible in terms of the post-Flood geologic adjustments that must have occurred. In either case, it is clear that the hypothesis of uniformity is completely inadequate when confronted with these numerous and extensive areas where the strata are in the "wrong" order!

SUMMARY

We have attempted in this chapter to consider the validity of the uniformitarian approach to historical geology. The all-importance of this principle in geologic interpretation is widely recognized and acknowledged; nevertheless we have seen that the principle is utterly inadequate to account for by far the greater part of the geologic phenomena.

The most important geologic processes are those of erosion, deposition, glaciation, diastrophism and volcanism. It is processes such as these which the uniformity concept asserts can explain the earth's stratified and massive rock formations. Our basic objection to this contention, however, is that the character and rates of activity of the processes cannot have been the same in the past as in the present. But the original enunciation of the uniformitarian doctrine by Hutton, Playfair and Lyell insisted also that the *rates* had never changed.

Lyell strongly opposed any appeal, in explanation of geologic phenomena, to violent "revolutions," i.e., catastrophes and deluges with periods of repose between. As a result of his observations, he was imbued with the conviction that *present causes solely have operated in the past.* More than that, he insisted that *they have always acted at the same rate.* This is the extreme form of the principle of uniformitarianism.[1]

Further study has convinced even uniformitarian geologists that this extreme form of the doctrine could not be valid. Too much evidence exists that the earth's formations cannot possibly be explained entirely in terms of present rates of these processes. Nevertheless, the principle of uniformity is still considered the basic geologic principle.

We have shown in this chapter that each of the important geologic

---

[1] O. D. von Engeln and Kenneth E. Caster: *Geology*, p. 25.

processes, without exception, must at some time or times in the geologic past, have acted with tremendously greater intensity than anything measured today. Present-day volcanic activity is not only quantitatively but qualitatively different from the volcanic phenomena of the geologic past that have produced the great dikes and sills, the batholiths and laccoliths, as well as the great lava fields and plateaus of the world, one of which covers an area of 300,000 square miles in South America. Similarly, modern diastrophic activity such as the earthquake is of apparently an entirely different order of magnitude from the tremendous earth movements of the past. The great faults and folds of the past are incomparably greater than earth movements of the present. The origin of the great mountain chains, which apparently have been uplifted from the sea bottom in the most recent geologic periods, is still a mystery. No satisfactory and generally accepted theory of orogeny has yet been devised, which fact in itself proves that modern diastrophic processes do not explain those of the earth's earlier history.

Glaciation is another modern process which is believed to have accomplished significant geologic work in historic times. But this process is assumed ·to have acted on a much greater scale in the immediate past (the Pleistocene), as well as on earlier occasions in geologic history, in order to account for certain widespread geologic phenomena such as tills and tillites. Not only are present rates of glaciation immensely milder than in the past but also present processes have been quite unable to account for these past increases in glacial activity. This also is evidenced by the fact that no satisfactory glacial theory has yet been propounded, although numerous attempts have been made.

The most important geologic process is sedimentation, including both erosion and deposition. The very basis of historical geology is the supposed sequence of the sedimentary rocks and their contained fossils. Erosion and deposition are of course very important present-day geomorphic processes. But once again, a study of the sedimentary rocks reveals that the sedimentary processes of the past must have been both quantitatively and qualitatively different from those of the present. The outstanding erosional feature of the past is the peneplain; the outstanding depositional feature is the geosyncline. Neither of these has any true modern counterpart, nor has any satisfactory

Figure 21. MIXING OF PLEISTOCENE AND CRETACEOUS STRATA.

theory of the development of either been devised. The same is true of most other sedimentary features.

Of special significance is the fact that modern sedimentary environments can rarely, if at all, be identified in the sedimentary rocks, at least with any certainty. Although uniformitarians may question this statement, it is substantiated by the fact that there have been so many different schemes advanced for classifying ancient sedimentary environments, none of them yet generally accepted. Only very rough classifications can be made, such as "marine," "deltaic," etc. One authority, although at great pains to develop an elaborate classification system of his own, says:

> Unfortunately, there are relatively few environments which can be positively identified in the rock record by our present state of knowledge.[1]

Fossil deposits are still harder to account for on the basis of uniformity. We have shown that some kind of catastrophic condition is nearly always necessary for the burial and preservation of fossils. Present-day processes are forming very few potential fossil deposits, and most of these are under conditions of rapid, sudden burial, which are abnormal. Nothing comparable to the tremendous fossiliferous beds of fish, mammals, reptiles, etc. that are found in many places around the world is being formed today.

And yet it is the fossils which are the basis of historical geology and the geologic time scale! It is the fossils which are considered to be the one sure proof of organic evolution, regardless of how they came to be buried. Nevertheless uniformity—modern processes—cannot legitimately account for the fossil deposits.

The importance of the fossils in the dating of the geologic strata cannot be overemphasized. It is remarkable that the vicious circle of reasoning in this procedure cannot be appreciated by paleontologists. The *fossils alone* are used to assign a geologic time to the rock stra-

[1] W. C. Krumbein and L. L. Sloss: *Stratigraphy and Sedimentation* (San Francisco, W. H. Freeman and Co., 1951), p. 254.

FIGURE 21.

The strata in this section of England are interpreted as Cretaceous (the Chalk) and Pleistocene glacial till. It is thought that the glacial action plucked great segments of the earlier Cretaceous strata and transported them as a great boulder, lifting them some 60 feet vertically, depositing them finally as a part of the till deposits of the glacial moraines. Note, however, the undisturbed condition of the chalk, with its horizontal lenses of flints. To all outward appearances, these strata were deposited normally, in vertical sequence.

Figure 22. "THRUST" PLANE.

tum, and yet this very sequence of fossils is said to constitute the greatest proof of organic evolution! The fact that the fossil evidence is the sole criterion of geologic dating has again been emphasized in a recent review by Jeletzky.

The more than amply proved and almost unanimously recognized impossibility of establishing any practically useful broadly regional or worldwide geologic time scale based on the physical-stratigraphic criteria alone for the vast expanse of pre-Cambrian time supplies conclusive proof that these phenomena are devoid of any generally recognizable geologic time significance.[1]

That is, Jeletzky says that the absence of fossils in pre-Cambrian strata has prevented any time sequence from being worked out for them. Therefore, it is evident that only fossils are adequate for this purpose. Furthermore, there are many contradictions in the fossiliferous rocks between the physical rock units and the time units as determined by the fossils. He says:

It is, indeed, a well established fact that the [physical-stratigraphic] rock units and their boundaries often transgress geologic time planes in most irregular fashion even within the shortest distances.[2]

The fossils and their presumed evolutionary sequence, therefore, provide the sole basis for division of the rocks into time units, which have no necessary correlation at all with the stratigraphic or physiographic units. Jeletzky also emphasizes that even the various radioactivity methods of geologic dating have not provided, and cannot provide, a geologic time criterion of equal validity or usefulness with the fossils.[3]

And yet we have seen that not only must most of the fossiliferous rocks have been deposited under conditions inconsistent with the principle of uniformity but that the strata as dated by the fossils are filled with numerous anomalies and contradictions.

One receives the impression from geological textbooks that the

[1] J. A. Jeletzky: "Paleontology: Basis of Practical Geochronology," *Bulletin of the American Association of Petroleum Geologists,* Vol. 40, April 1956, p. 684.

[2] *Ibid.,* p. 685.

[3] *Ibid.,* pp. 688-91.

FIGURE 22.

Here is shown another thrust plane, again essentially horizontal and looking very like a normal bedding plane. This is in Montana, the upper strata (Ch) being Mississippian limestone and the lower strata (Kk) being Cretaceous shales and sandstones.

strata are essentially harmonious everywhere, with the oldest on the bottom, each stratum succeeded in turn by one representing the next period. Of course this is not so, and everyone familiar with the facts recognizes that it is not so. The geologic time series is built up by a hypothetical superposition of beds upon each other from all over the world.

If a pile were to be made by using the greatest thickness of sedimentary beds of each geologic age, it would be at least 100 miles high. . . .

It is, of course, impossible to have even a considerable fraction of this at one place. The Grand Canyon of Colorado, for example, is only one mile deep. . . . By application of the principle of superposition, lithologic identification, recognition of unconformities, and reference to fossil successions, both the thick and the thin masses are correlated with other beds at other sites. Thus there is established, in detail, the stratigraphic succession for all the geologic ages.[1]

This frank statement makes the method by which the geologic time scale was built up quite plain. Since we have already noted that lithologic identification is unimportant in establishing the age of a rock, it is clear the "fossil successions" constitute the only real basis for the arrangement. And this means, in effect, that organic evolution has been implicitly assumed in assigning chronological pigeon-holes to particular rock systems and their fossils.

The geologist utilizes knowledge of organic evolution as preserved in the fossil record, to identify and correlate the lithic records of ancient time.[2]

And yet this succession of fossil organisms as preserved in the rocks is considered as the one convincing proof that evolution has occurred! And thus have we come round the circle again.

But even this carefully erected system is found to have numerous contradictions in it. Numerous fossils have been found grossly out of place in the time scale, despite all its built-in safeguards. Furthermore, many creatures supposedly primitive have persisted to the present day, including many which apparently skipped all the way from very early periods to the present without leaving any traces in the intervening periods.

It is not at all uncommon for the smaller fossils on which rock identification is commonly based to be found out of place in the ex-

[1] O. D. von Engeln and Kenneth E. Caster: *Geology,* pp. 417-18.
[2] *Ibid.,* p. 423.

pected sequences. Such anomalies are usually explained as simple "displacements."

Because of their small size they are easily transported by a variety of geologic and biologic agents and may be displaced either vertically or horizontally from their environments of life or from their place of entombment.

Reworking of microfossils has been known for a long time, and although the phenomenon is quite common, it need not impair or deter the widespread use of micropaleontological data in geological interpretations, provided the nature of the phenomenon is recognized and understood.[1]

Which, being interpreted, means that when fossils are not found in the stratum to which they have been previously assigned by evolutionary theory, it must be assumed that they have somehow been displaced subsequent to their original deposition. The indiscriminating manner in which such agencies of displacement are assumed to act is indicated by the following:

Vertical displacement, either from older to younger, or from younger to older zones, may also involve environmental mixing.[2]

And the rock systems themselves are often found in anomalous relations in the field. It is extremely common to find so-called "disconformities," which are those unconformities (strata with missing ages, supposedly caused by erosion during those ages) which have parallel bedding between the early and recent strata, with no outward evidence that the two were not deposited successively (see Figs. 23 and 24). The deceptiveness of these unconformities is indicated by Twenhofel, as follows:

An unconformity separating the oldest Pre-Cambrian from the latest Pleistocene may have the same physical appearance as one between the latest Pleistocene and the middle Pleistocene. The fossils of the strata bounding an unconformity are the only indicators of time value, and these are not always decisive for determinations within narrow limits. A nonconformity [i.e., an unconformity with non-parallel bedding] may represent a

[1] Daniel J. Jones: "Displacement of Microfossils," *Journal of Sedimentary Petrology,* Vol. 28, December 1958, p. 453.

[2] *Ibid.,* p. 455. H. S. Ladd gives a striking example of this: "A core from the depths of the Pacific . . . contained a mixed assemblage of Recent, middle Tertiary, Paleocene, and Cretaceous foraminifera." (*Treatise on Marine Ecology and Paleoecology,* Geological Society of America Memoir 67, 1957, Vol. II, p. 40).

(Photo by Chas. Schuchert)

Figure 23. A "DECEPTIVE CONFORMITY," OR PARACONFORMITY.

This is a typical example of an extremely common, yet quite paradoxical, phenomenon, namely the perfectly conformable superposition of a younger bed upon a much older bed, with many intervening geological ages entirely missing. The Jeffersonville limestone, of lower Middle Devonian age, is here resting quite normally upon the Louisville limestone, of Middle Silurian age. The significant thing is that these formations are separated by more than 3000 feet of strata in other parts of the Appalachian trough, and therefore it must be assumed that many millions of years elapsed between them, although they look as though they must have been laid out in quick succession. This phenomenon has been variously called a "disconformity," a "deceptive conformity," and, more recently, by C. O. Dunbar and John Rodgers, a "paraconformity." (*Principles of Stratigraphy,* New York, Wiley, 1957, p. 119).

longer time than a disconformity, as the event of deformation is involved, but it by no means follows that such is invariably the case.[1]

But these anomalies are more or less trivial compared to the numerous cases in which "old" formations are found resting con-

[1] W. H. Twenhofel: *Principles of Sedimentation* (2nd Ed., New York, McGraw-Hill, 1950), p. 562.

formably on "young" formations. These phenomena are found almost everywhere in hilly or mountainous regions and have been attributed to "thrust-faulting." The concept is that great segments of rock strata have been somehow separated from their roots and made to slide far over adjacent regions. Subsequent erosion then modifies the transported "nappe" so that the young strata on top are removed, leaving only the older strata superposed on the stationary young rocks beneath. There are various modifications of this concept, but all are equally difficult to conceive mechanically. As we have seen, many show little or no actual physical evidence of such tremendous and catastrophic movement.

In the light of such frequent flagrant contradictions to the established geologic time sequences, in addition to the arbitrary methods and circular reasoning by which the scale itself has been established, and also in addition to the innumerable evidences of catastrophe, rather than uniformity, as the basic principle in the deposition and modification of the geologic strata, the writers feel warranted in contending that the data of geology do not provide valid evidence against the historicity of the universal Deluge as recorded in the book of Genesis. It is thus legitimate to attempt a new interpretation of these data which will be in harmony with the Biblical account of Creation and the Flood.

The geologic time scale is an extremely fragile foundation on which a tremendous and unwieldy superstructure of interpretation has been erected. Dr. E. M. Spieker, Professor of Geology at Ohio State University, has recently admitted:

Does our time scale, then, partake of natural law? No. . . . I wonder how many of us realize that the time scale was frozen in essentially its present form by 1840. . . ? How much world geology was known in 1840? A bit of western Europe, none too well, and a lesser fringe of eastern North America. All of Asia, Africa, South America, and most of North America were virtually unknown. How dared the pioneers assume that their scale would fit the rocks in these vast areas, by far most of the world? Only in dogmatic assumption—a mere extension of the kind of reasoning developed by Werner from the facts in his little district of Saxony. And in many parts of the world, notably India and South America, it does not fit. But even there it is applied! The followers of the founding fathers went forth across the earth and in Procrustean fashion made it fit the sections they found,

Chattanooga sh.

Pegram ls.

Lego ls.

Waldron sh.

Laurel ls.

(Photo by Chas. Schuchert)

Figure 24. DOUBLE PARACONFORMITY.

even in places where the actual evidence literally proclaimed denial. So flexible and accommodating are the "facts" of geology.[1]

Had the above charges been made by George McCready Price or some other modern opponent of uniformitarian geology, they would have been indignantly discounted as the rantings of an ignorant fundamentalist! But the fact is that Dr. Spieker is such a thorough-going uniformitarian that his purpose in thus exposing the weakness of basic geological theory is primarily to deny that any revolutions or other geologic events of worldwide significance ever occurred and, therefore, that the boundaries between the various systems are meaningless. That is, he insists that there is no actually identifiable boundary between the Cretaceous and Tertiary, for example, or between the Cambrian and Ordovician, or between any other two supposedly adjacent systems.

To this contention we would certainly agree, but the same deficiencies in the basic character of the geologic time-scale that warrant Spieker in denying the reality of its supposed divisions also warrant us in denying the reality of its supposed sequences!

In the next chapter we shall make an exploratory attempt to re-interpret the actual data of geology, seeking a system which is both harmonious with the Biblical record and free of the innumerable anomalies and contradictions of the present uniformitarian system. We conclude this chapter with a further quotation from Spieker, emphasizing once again that the entire geologic time-scale is based squarely and solely on paleontology, which means on the assumption of organic evolution:

> And what essentially is this actual time-scale—on what criteria does it rest? When all is winnowed out, and the grain reclaimed from the chaff, it is certain that the grain in the product is mainly the paleontologic record and highly likely that the physical evidence is the chaff.[2]

[1] Edmund M. Spieker: "Mountain-Building Chronology and Nature of Geologic Time-Scale," *Bulletin American Association of Petroleum Geologists,* Vol. 40, August 1956, p. 1803.
[2] *Ibid.,* p. 1806.

FIGURE 24.

In this Tennessee quarry are exposed two major paraconformities, above and below the Pegram limestone, which is lower Middle Devonian. The Chattanooga shale above is upper Devonian and the Lego limestone below is Middle Silurian. Again there is no physical indication whatever of any substantial time lapse between the deposition of these various strata.

Chapter VI

A Scriptural Framework for Historical Geology

INTRODUCTION

The uniformitarian geologists of the nineteenth century, rejecting the Biblical testimony of deterioration and catastrophe and all the geological implications thereof and accepting instead the philosophy of evolutionary naturalism, built their system of historical geology upon a foundation of sand. The result, as we have seen in the preceding chapter, is what Dr. Robin S. Allen called "the present deplorable state of our discipline,"[1] a pseudoscience composed (as the geologists Rastall, Spieker, *et al* have themselves pointed out) of a patchwork of circular reasoning, Procrustean interpretations, pure speculation and dogmatic authoritarianism—a system purporting to expound the entire evolutionary history of the earth and its inhabitants, yet all the while filled with innumerable gaps and contradictions.

But we do not say these things in a critical vein nor with specific personalities in mind. We feel that the orthodox geologist's adherence to the uniformity principle is only rarely attributable to an anti-Christian bias. Rather he is the product of a particular background, conditioned by education and group pressure to think always in terms of evolution and uniformity. Many geologists are sincerely religious, feeling more or less satisfied that these concepts are basically harmoni-

[1] See page 170.

212

ous with theism and perhaps even with the Bible, although very rarely do they actually publish such opinions.

Nor are these criticisms meant to apply to geology as a whole, but rather only to the uniformitarian interpretation of historical geology. The sciences of mineralogy, petrology, geophysics, mining geology, petroleum geology, structural geology, seismology, geochemistry, marine geology, petrography, sedimentation and ground-water geology are all branches of geology and are true sciences in every sense of the word. Almost as much could be said of the sciences of geomorphology and stratigraphy, although much speculation necessarily enters into these disciplines, and even of paleontology in its descriptive aspects. Historical geology is only a small and economically unimportant aspect of the study of geology as a whole and is *the only aspect with which we take issue.* A complete reorientation of historical geology would be quite possible without any serious effects relative to the other branches of geology at all.

And of course there is no quarrel with the data of even the historical geologists, but only with the interpretations of those data. As we have seen, the data on which historical geology has been based are almost entirely paleontological and the interpretive framework has been that of uniformity and evolution. The previous chapter has shown some of the serious weaknesses of this framework, leading to the inference that nothing would really be lost by attempting to organize the paleontologic and other geological data on an entirely new basis.

This, we believe, can be done most effectively by means of the clear statements and legitimate implications of the Biblical revelation. After all, any real *knowledge* of origins or of earth history antecedent to human historical records can only be obtained through divine revelation. Since historical geology, unlike other sciences, cannot deal with currently observable and reproducible events, it is *manifestly impossible* ever really to *prove,* by the scientific method, any hypothesis relating to pre-human history.

Because it is highly important for man to understand the nature of his origin, as well as that of the earth on which he dwells, and because of the impossibility of his ever really *knowing* about these matters otherwise, it is eminently reasonable that his Creator would in some way reveal to him at least the essentials concerning them. Christians and Jews have for many centuries believed that this revelation is given in what is known as the book of Genesis ("Beginnings"), and indeed there is no serious rival claimant to such a revelation anywhere else in the religious books of mankind.

Consequently, there is ample warrant, both spiritually and scientifically, for seeking to build a true science of earth history on the framework revealed in the Bible, rather than on uniformitarian and evolutionary assumptions. This should be done, not with the attitude of trying to make the Bible accounts fit into the data and theories of science but rather of letting the Bible speak for itself and then trying to understand the geological data in the light of its teachings.

THE SCRIPTURAL DIVISIONS OF GEOLOGIC HISTORY

There is no need to suppose, of course, that the Noachian Deluge, which has occupied most of our attention in this book, produced all the geologic strata. On the contrary, the Bible plainly implies that there are at least five great epochs of history, each of which has produced substantial segments of the geological formations.

The Initial Creation Itself

"In the beginning," the Bible says, "God created the heavens and the earth" (Genesis 1:1). This initial act of creation quite evidently included the structure and materials of at least the earth's core and some sort of crust and surface materials. The first description given of its appearance is that of water ("the deep") covering its surface and of a dense shroud of darkness (Genesis 1:2) enveloping it. It seems reasonable that, even if the earth's creation was accomplished as an instantaneous act, its internal heat and the waters on its face would immediately have begun to perform works of profound geological significance.

The Work of the Six Days of Creation

Especially on the third day was a tremendous amount of geological work accomplished. On that day, the Genesis account tells us that dry land was made to appear above the surface of the waters. This can only mean a great orogeny, as the rocks and other materials of the primitive earth were uplifted above the waters. This process would necessarily have been accompanied by great erosion and redeposition of surface materials as the waters flowed down into the new basins. On the same day, the record says, God made vegetation of all kinds to appear, implying that there was now a uniform mantle of fertile soil over the surface (Genesis 1:9-13). The fourth day witnessed the establishment of the sun and moon in their functions with respect to the earth. Since the sun now provides all the energy received by the earth for its geological processes, this event also has profound geological implications. Undoubtedly there were innumerable other creative and developmental processes taking place during the six days, as the entire earth was being fitted as a wonderfully harmonious "dominion" for man to "subdue" (Genesis 1:28).

The Antediluvian Period

With the fall of man, a new order of things ensued, not only in God's spiritual economy with respect to man but also with respect to the earth itself, which was "cursed for man's sake" (Genesis 3:17, 5:29). The whole creation was delivered into the bondage of corruption (i.e., "decay"), groaning and travailing in pain together (Romans 8:21,22). The antediluvian earth had mountains (Genesis 7:20), rivers (Genesis 2:10) and seas (Genesis 1:10) and so must have experienced geological activities somewhat like those of the present era. On the other hand, there are implications that very significant differences existed as well. Mention is made in Genesis 1:7 of a division of the waters covering the earth at the time of creation, into two portions, separated by an expanse of atmosphere in which birds were to fly (Genesis 1:20) and in which light from the sun, moon and stars was to be refracted and diffused to give light on the earth (Genesis 1:17). The waters "above the firmament" seem to imply more than our present clouds and atmospheric water vapor, especially since Genesis 2:5 implies that during this time rainfall was not experienced on the earth. These upper waters were therefore placed in that position by divine creativity, not by the normal processes of the hydrologic cycle of the present day. The upper waters did not, however, obscure the light from the heavenly bodies and so must have been in the form of invisible water vapor. Such a vast expanse of water vapor would necessarily have had a profound effect on terrestrial climates and therefore on geological activity.

The Deluge

It has been demonstrated, we believe, in earlier chapters, that the Deluge was a global catastrophe and, therefore, must have had a global cause and produced worldwide geological effects. It is clearly the greatest physical convulsion that has ever occurred on the earth since the creation of life itself, and in fact all but obliterated everything living on the face of the earth! There is no escaping the conclusion that, if the Bible is true and if the Lord Jesus Christ possessed divine omniscience, the Deluge was the most significant event, geologically speaking, that has ever occurred on the earth since its creation. *Any true science of historical geology must necessarily give a prominent place in its system to this event.*

The Modern Post-Deluge Period

With the conclusion of the Flood epoch, God promised that no more such earth-shaking aqueous cataclysms would ever be visited on the earth as long as it remained (Genesis 8:22). In general, uniform processes of nature would henceforth prevail; thus the geological dogma of uniformity can, with certain limitations, be applied to the study of this period. However, even here, the principle must be sufficiently elastic to accommodate numerous minor disturbances recorded in Scripture and perhaps implied in ancient mythologies, as well probably as many others of which the only records are those in the geologic deposits themselves. It is likely that a large proportion even of present geological work is accomplished during brief, intense periods of earth activity, in floods, earthquakes, volcanic eruptions, and similar events.

All the earth's geological features must have been formed during some one or more of these periods. It should be possible, at least in a general way, to determine even at present what formations and phenomena are attributable to each of the various periods, and this will be the goal of the present chapter. It is realized, of course, that a really detailed reorientation of all the multitudes of geologic data that have been accumulated by thousands of geologists for more than a century is entirely beyond the scope of this volume, or of many such volumes. Such could, and should, occupy the undivided attention of many specialists for many years.

But first the attention of such specialists must be drawn to the problem and its importance. They must be persuaded that the older approach of uniformity is sterile and has led up a blind alley of hopeless paradoxes and contradictions and, therefore, that a new approach is timely and necessary. They must also first be convinced that a genuine divinely-given testimony concerning terrestrial and human origins is philosophically both possible and reasonable, and even necessary, and that we actually have such a testimony in the Bible, especially in the early chapters of Genesis. This divine record gives a basic framework within which to interpret earth history, and they must be persuaded that this will be the only sound basis of a true historical geology.

The writers hope, perhaps naively but sincerely, that this preliminary study will engage the attention of such potential workers and persuade them to undertake further, more extensive studies into these problems. The impetus for such investigations would be more than just the motive, though sufficiently worthy in itself, of pure scientific knowledge. It might well be possible eventually to reconstruct the nature of the antediluvian earth, with its associated climatology and its inhabitants, both human and animal. A detailed delineation of the processes employed, first in the period of Creation and later in the period of the Deluge, would lead to a much fuller knowledge of the nature of the earth itself and the physical phenomena associated with it. The nature of the earth's geological future could much better be elucidated, especially in the light of Biblical eschatology, since the Flood is frequently cited in Scripture as foreshadowing the great future destruction and renovation of the earth at the time of the second coming of Christ. Perhaps most important of all, the realization by mankind that the rocks of the earth everywhere bear eloquent witness to the power and holiness of Almighty God and to His certain ultimate intervention and termination of the affairs of men and nations might well serve a mighty evangelistic and purifying purpose in the world!

We gladly recognize that the detailed suggestions given below are tentative and may require much revision after further study. They are intended only to serve as a stimulus to such further study, as well as to show at least one possible way of understanding all valid geologic data in conformity with full acceptance of a literal Creation and universal Deluge.

THE BEGINNING OF CREATION

The Origin of the Solar System

First we shall attempt to discern, from the Biblical and geological records, something of the nature of the earth at its original creation and how much of the earth's present structure is attributable directly to this event. There are quite a few extant theories of the earth's origin. It is not our purpose to discuss these here, except to say that no one of them is generally accepted. Each has its own adherents, but each also has numerous uncertainties and difficulties. After a careful review of all the modern theories of the origin of the solar system, including the earth, Sir Harold Spencer Jones, of the Royal Greenwich Observatory, concludes:

> The problem of formulating a satisfactory theory of the origin of the solar system is therefore still not solved.[1]

The Origin of the Universe

With reference to the larger problem of explaining the origin of the universe as a whole, somewhat the same situation is encountered. A number of theories have been advanced, but all of them encounter serious objections. The Harvard astronomer, Harlow Shapley, after reviewing the two more important types[2] of theories now being advocated, says:

> Both hypotheses have plenty of trouble ahead of them and a paucity of observations behind them. Their main value is the demonstration of the fertility of the human imagination and the bravery of the uninhibited scientist who insists on asking "How come?"[3]

[1] H. S. Jones: "The Origin of the Solar System," in *Physics and Chemistry of the Earth*, (New York, McGraw-Hill, 1956), p. 15.

[2] The rapid synthesis theory and the continuous creation theory associated especially with the names of George Gamow and Fred Hoyle, respectively.

[3] H. Shapley: "Cosmography," *American Scientist*, Vol. 42, July 1954, p. 484. More recently, this judgment has been reiterated by Margaret and Geoffrey Burbridge, astronomers at Yerkes Observatory, who say: "Clearly, therefore, at the present time no cosmological arguments can be adduced in favor of one or another of the theories of the origin of the elements" ("Formation of Elements in the Stars," *Science*. Vol. 128, August 22, 1958, p. 389).

Of course, even if a satisfactory theory which fits all the data is ultimately worked out, either for the origin of the universe or for that of the earth only, it still would not have been proved that this was actually the way it was done. This is another of those problems which can never be completely solved by unaided human ingenuity. It is not amenable to the scientific method, which implies reproducibility of experimental results. It was a once-for-all event, never repeated and not observed by man. Therefore the only real knowledge of the mode of origin must be by means of divine revelation.

And this revelation simply says that "In the beginning God created the heaven and the earth" (Genesis 1:1). Although secondary processes are not precluded by this verse, the most obvious meaning derivable from it would be that God instantaneously, by divine omnipotence, called the universe, and particularly the earth, into being. The same is implied in Psalm 33:6: "By the word of the Lord were the heavens made; and all the host of them by the breath of His mouth." Not only is this the most obvious meaning of these passages but there is nothing whatever in science or theology to prevent us from accepting it in just this light!

We do not press this point, of course, as other interpretations are perhaps possible and because it is not essential to our present aim. We must insist, however, that if this initial creation was accomplished by means of secondary processes, they were *creative* processes— processes involving the actual creation of matter and energy—and not those of the present day which are essentially deteriorative processes, always accompanied by a "running-down" of the available energy or an over-all increase in "entropy." Thus it is impossible to deduce from present rates and processes the manner in which the earth was originally created.

The Primeval Earth

The earth has a radius of about 3,959 miles. Of this only the top 20 to 25 miles, down to the so-called "Mohorovočić Discontinuity" (after the scientist who first found evidence of its existence in 1909), comprises the crust. Below this is the mantle, extending to a depth of about 1,800 miles, and the core, whose radius therefore is about 2,160 miles.

Obviously, man can learn little or nothing by direct observation about the deep interior of the earth. Most of what is believed about the nature of the mantle and core, as well as the deeper crust, is inferred from characteristics of seismic waves.[1] It has long been supposed that the core consists primarily of molten iron, mixed with nickel; but a prominent alternative theory supposes that the extremely high pressures in that region cause whatever matter is there to assume an entirely different physical state from that of ordinary matter. The mantle seems to consist of several indistinctly defined layers of rock, also of uncertain composition. The rocks in this zone seem most probably to be predominantly silicates, rich in iron and magnesium, but this is uncertain, as is the question of the exact physical state of the materials. Deep-focus earthquakes originate in the mantle, and the earth's magnetic field probably originates from phenomena in the core.

Two other facts about the interior regions, about which there is little question, are that the densities of the materials increase with depth and that the temperature increases with depth to a certain point and then apparently remains essentially constant throughout the core at a temperature of the order of magnitude of $2,500°$ C.[2] Presumably these characteristics must date either from the initial creation or from the six-day period of creative activity.

The core and mantle are probably essentially the same today as when first created. The materials of the crust, on the other hand, give much evidence of intricate and extensive changes. There is a possibility that the afore-mentioned Mohorovočić Discontinuity marks the lower limit of the orogenic activity of the third day of creation. It is a worldwide discontinuity and so must have a global cause. However its nature is still uncertain.

The question as to whether the Mohorovočić Discontinuity is evidence of chemical changes in the rocks of the crust and mantle, or only of a physical phase change is still unanswered.[3]

It seems probable that the great internal heat resulted in intense chemical and physical activity throughout the earth at that time. The

[1] K. E. Bullen: "The Deep Interior," in *The Earth and Its Atmosphere,* D. R. Bates, Editor, (New York, Basic Books, Inc., 1957), pp. 31-47.

[2] J. Verhoogen: "Temperatures Within the Earth," *American Scientist,* Vol. 48, June 1960, p. 153.

[3] G. G. Lill and A. E. Maxwell: "The Earth's Mantle," *Science,* Vol. 129, May 22, 1959, p. 1408.

present density stratification may be a result of the heavier materials quickly gravitating toward the earth's center. At the same time, the lighter materials rose irregularly and sporadically to the surface, both solid materials to form the continental blocks and the water and dissolved materials to form the oceans. Something like this process has been suggested by Rubey[1] and is now widely accepted, although of course in terms of long periods of time.

The earth's crust may likewise have been built up by emission of rock materials from below the Mohorovočić Discontinuity, with resultant crustal shortening and orogenic upheavals. This is basically the theory of continent formation recently developed by the Canadian geophysicist, J. Tuzo Wilson. Thus, the Mohorovočić Discontinuity may represent the base level of the isostatic adjustments and continent-building processes of the third day of creation. Wilson says:

> The fact that volcanoes emit lava as well as steam and other gases suggests that the continents as well as the oceans and the atmosphere may have been formed by volcanic activity. This would go a long way toward explaining the irregularity of the crust.
>
> If this happened, it follows that the Mohorovočić Discontinuity represents the original surface of the Earth. Since this original surface is now overlain by an average thickness of 15 km. of crust, it must have shrunk or been reduced in radius by that amount. The emission of the crust would therefore have produced about 100 km. shortening in the circumference of the original surface which would be available to cause mountain building.[2]

On the other hand, it is just as reasonable to say that the core and mantle simply were created, in essentially their present form. Perhaps these are the "foundations of the earth," of which the Bible often speaks (e.g., Jeremiah 31:37, Isaiah 48:13, etc.). It is questionable whether man will ever be able to observe directly the nature of these foundations[3] or the processes that take place there, but it is probable that they exert great influence upon many of the geological phenomena at the surface, such as diastrophism, volcanism, terrestrial magnetism, etc., and so have real importance for the understanding of these processes.

[1] W. W. Rubey: "Geologic History of Sea Water," *Bulletin Geological Society of America,* Vol. 62, 1951, pp. 1111-1147.

[2] J. Tuzo Wilson: "Geophysics and Continental Growth," *American Scientist,* Vol. 47, March 1959, pp. 14, 15.

[3] However, a project for drilling a hole through the ocean bottom into the mantle is currently being promoted! See Lill and Maxwell, *op. cit.*

THE SCIENTIFIC BASIS OF CREATION

The First and Second Laws of Thermodynamics

The most important thing to recognize in connection with the events recorded in Genesis 1 as taking place during the six days of creation is that these were days of *creation*. The two most basic and certain of all laws of modern physical science are the first two laws of thermodynamics. The first law of thermodynamics is the law of energy conservation, affirming that although energy can be converted from one form to another, the total amount remains unchanged—energy is neither being created nor destroyed at the present time. The second law states that, although the total amount remains unchanged, there is always a tendency for it to become less available for useful work. That is, in any closed mechanical system in which work is being accomplished through energy conversions, the "entropy" increases, where entropy is essentially a mathematical formulation of the non-availability of the energy of the system.

The importance and universality of these laws is emphasized by the Harvard physicist, P. W. Bridgman:

> The two laws of thermodynamics are, I suppose, accepted by physicists as perhaps the most secure generalizations from experience that we have. The physicist does not hesitate to apply the two laws to any concrete physical situation in the confidence that nature will not let him down.[1]

It is not too much to say that these two laws provide the very foundation upon which the great superstructure of modern science and technology has been erected.[2] All the various geological processes as well as all other physical and biological processes operate in accordance with these principles. In none of them is any energy or

---

[1] P. W. Bridgman: "Reflections on Thermodynamics," *American Scientist*, Vol. 41, October 1953, p. 549.

[2] The physicist R. B. Lindsay, Dean of the Brown University Graduate School, says: "Thermodynamics is a physical theory of great generality impinging on practically every phase of human experience. It may be called the description of the behavior of matter in equilibrium and of its changes from one equilibrium state to another. Thermodynamics operates with two master concepts or constructs and two great principles. The concepts are *energy* and *entropy,* and the principles are the so-called first and second laws of thermodynamics. . . ." ("Entropy Consumption and Values in Physical Science," *American Scientist*, Vol. 47, September 1959, p. 376).

matter (matter may be regarded as one form of energy) being created. But during the six days of creation, both matter and energy *were* being created. Still more significantly, this newly-created matter and energy were being organized into increasingly complex and highly energized systems, in exact contradistinction to the universal tendency toward disorganization and de-energization experienced at the present time. The Princeton biologist, Harold Blum, says:

> A major consequence of the second law of thermodynamics is that all real processes go toward a condition of greater probability. The probability function generally used in thermodynamics is *entropy*. . . . Thus orderliness is associated with low entropy; randomness with high entropy. . . . The second law of thermodynamics says that left to itself any isolated system will go toward greater entropy, which also means toward greater randomness and greater likelihood.[1]

"Randomness," of course, is synonymous with disorder, disorganization, disarrangement. And this is an absolutely universal rule of nature at the present time, so far as scientific observation can show.

The Unique Processes of Creation

But during the period of Creation, God was introducing order and organization and energization into the universe in a very high degree, even to life itself! *It is thus quite plain that the processes used by God in creation were utterly different from the processes which now operate in the universe!* The Creation was a unique period, entirely incommensurate with this present world. This is plainly emphasized and reemphasized in the divine revelation which God has given us concerning Creation, which concludes with these words:

> And the heavens and the earth were *finished,* and *all* the host of them.

[1] Harold Blum: "Perspectives in Evolution," *American Scientist,* Vol. 43, October 1955, p. 595. Lindsay says: "Increase in entropy means a transition from a more orderly state to a less orderly state. . . . In any naturally occurring process, the tendency is for all systems to proceed from order to disorder." (*Op. cit.,* p. 382). And yet the evolutionist, Julian Huxley, says: "Evolution in the extended sense can be defined as a directional and essentially irreversible process occurring in time, which in its course gives rise to an increase of variety and an increasingly high level of organization in its products. Our present knowledge indeed forces us to the view that the whole of reality *is* evolution—a single process of self-transformation." ("Evolution and Genetics," in *What is Science?,* ed. by Jas. R. Newman, New York, Simon and Schuster, 1955, p. 278).

And on the seventh day God *finished* His work which He had made; and He *rested* on the seventh day from *all His work* which He had made. And God blessed the seventh day, and hallowed it; because that in it He *rested* from *all* His work which God had created and made.[1]

In view of these strong and repeated assertions, is it not the height of presumption for man to attempt to study Creation in terms of present processes?

Here is the basic fallacy of uniformitarianism in geology. It may be fairly reasonable to use the uniformity principle as a key to decipher geologic history that has taken place since the *end* of the Creation. But when it is used, as it actually is, to attempt to deduce the entire history of the Creation itself (calling it "evolution"), it is no longer legitimate. The geologic record may provide much valuable information concerning earth history *subsequent* to the finished Creation (which Creation includes that of "heaven and earth, the sea, and all that in them is," as summarized in the fourth Commandment in Exodus 20:11), but it can give no information as to the processes or sequences employed by God *during* the Creation, since God has plainly said that those processes no longer operate—a fact which is thoroughly verified by the two universal laws of thermodynamics!

The Entropy Principle and Evolution

Blum, impressed with the universality of the entropy principle in nature and yet believing that the world and all living things have developed by means of the supposed universal principle of evolution, has attempted in a profound and influential work[2] to harmonize and even essentially to equate entropy and evolution. But this is an impossible task, because really the one is itself the negation of the other. Creation (or what biologists imply by "evolution") actually has been accomplished by means of creative processes, which are now replaced by the deteriorative processes implicit in the second law. The latter are probably a part of the "curse" placed upon the earth as a result of the entrance of sin (Genesis 3:17), the "bondage

[1] Genesis 2:1-3.
[2] H. F. Blum: *Time's Arrow and Evolution,* (Princeton, N. J., Princeton University Press, 1951).

of decay" to which it has been "subjected" by God for the present age (Romans 8:20-22).[1]

Blum himself seems intuitively to sense the impossibility of his thesis and therefore of the entire evolutionary hypothesis, although he of course cannot bring himself to such an impasse, as he would regard it. Toward the end of his book, he recognizes the problem, but then simply shelves it:

We cannot think of irreversibility of evolution in terms of the relatively minor fluctuations and chance events connected with mutations and natural selection, but must deal in terms of overall changes, in the direction of greater entropy, that baffle the imagination.

"But," says a reader at this point, "by setting up the problem in this way, you have made the answer implicit in the argument, and have attempted to prove that there is no controversion of the second law of thermodynamics merely by denying the possibility of such a controversion. Your statement has been made so inclusive that it cannot be denied, but certainly you cannot believe you have proven that the second law of thermodynamics applies to evolution, only by setting up a system the magnitude of which cannot be measured."

True enough. But the important thing is the converse of this. That is, in order to deny the applicability of the second law these magnitudes would have to be measured, and until this is done the failure of the law cannot be proven. As was pointed out earlier in the book, the principal reason for accepting the second law of thermodynamics is that it has always worked wherever it has been possible to make the necessary measurements to test it; we assume therefore that it holds where we are unable to make such measurements.[2]

We present such an extended quotation because Blum, more than most other modern evolutionary biologists, has faced seriously the implications of the entropy principle in biological evolution. Most evolutionists have simply ignored the problem or have blandly asserted that the second law is refuted by the fact of evolution. But, as Blum insists, this second law of thermodynamics has always proved valid wherever it could be tested.[3] He bravely proceeds, therefore, to

---

[1] "All experience points to the fact that every living organism eventually dies. This is a process in which the highly developed order of the organism is reduced to a random and disorderly collection of molecules. We are reminded that we are 'dust' and to 'dust' we ultimately return" (R. B. Lindsay, *op. cit.*, p. 384).

[2] *Ibid.*, p. 202.

[3] R. B. Lindsay says: "The most careful examination of all naturally occurring processes (i.e., those in which external influences are not allowed to intervene) has

attempt to reconcile it with that with which it is utterly irreconcilable, the assumption of universal developmental evolution! Needless to say, he fails utterly. The most he can say is:

> If all things tend continually toward a condition of greater randomness, which would seem to represent a tendency toward increasing uniformity, how can complexity increase even in small parts of a system? Certainly if the tendency toward greater randomness flowed along smoothly in all things, at a uniform rate, the resulting course of events would be a most monotonous one. The earth is the interesting place it now is, because this is not true.[1]

But the basic disharmony between evolution and "devolution" is not to be disposed of simply by pointing to small systems which temporarily receive external stimuli retarding or apparently reversing their normal tendency toward deterioration. The almost infinite accumulation of improbabilities in the theory of total evolution is nothing less than an absolute denial of the second law of thermodynamics—despite the fact that it has been always verified experimentally wherever tested!

The marvel is that neither Blum nor apparently other evolutionary biologists (or geologists) seem able to see that the difficulty is not with the second law of thermodynamics but with the assumption of universal evolution, for which there has never yet been offered any genuine, experimental, laboratory proof! A leading biologist, Dobzhansky, not only admits this lack of proof but is affronted that anyone should expect it!

> These evolutionary happenings are unique, unrepeatable, and irreversible. It is as impossible to turn a land vertebrate into a fish as it is to effect the reverse transformation. The applicability of the experimental method to the study of such unique historical processes is severely restricted before all else by the time intervals involved, which far exceed the lifetime of any human experimenter. And yet it is just such impossibility that is demanded by antievolutionists when they ask for "proofs" of evolution which they would magnanimously accept as satisfactory.[2]

The evidences of micro-evolution, which Dobzhansky and others

only served to confirm our confidence in the inexorable over-all increase in the entropy of the universe" (*op. cit.*, p. 379).

[1] *Ibid.*, p. 205.

[2] Theodosius Dobzhansky: "On Methods of Evolutionary Biology and Anthropology," *American Scientist*, Vol. 45, December 1957, p. 388.

commonly cite, are not only irrelevant but are themselves denials of genuine evolution, in the sense of natural processes tending toward greater order and complexity. Rather, these chromosome and gene "mutations" are themselves almost always deteriorative rather than progressive and so constitute further verification of the universal entropy principle. This fact is admitted by no less an authority than H. J. Muller, perhaps the world's outstanding worker in the field of gene mutations and their supposed evolutionary significance:

It is entirely in line with the accidental nature of natural mutations that extensive tests have agreed in showing the vast majority of them to be detrimental to the organism in its job of surviving and reproducing, just as changes accidentally introduced into any artificial mechanism are predominantly harmful to its useful operation. According to the conception of evolution based on the studies of modern genetics, the whole organism has its basis in its genes. Of these, there are thousands of different kinds, interacting with great nicety in the production and maintenance of the complicated mechanism of the given type of organism. Accordingly, by the mutation of one of these genes or another, any component structure or function, and in many cases combinations of these components, may became diversely altered. Yet in all except very rare cases the change will be disadvantageous, involving an impairment of function.[1]

The plain facts of the situation, therefore, are that evolution has been simply *assumed* as the universal principle of change in nature, despite the fact that there is no experimental evidence supporting it and despite the still more amazing fact that universal experience and experimentation have demonstrated this universal principle of change to be its very opposite: namely, that of deterioration! Truly, this is one of the most astounding paradoxes to be found in all the history of scientism!

And the whole difficulty arises from man's *refusal* to accept God's emphatic statement that the creation of the world and of its living creatures was accomplished by processes no longer in operation. A real understanding of origins requires, as we have repeatedly emphasized, divine revelation. God in grace has provided this revelation, but men have refused to believe it, in effect making God a liar. No wonder they ultimately arrive at contradictions and irreconcilables in their reasonings!

[1] H. J. Muller: "How Radiation Changes the Genetic Constitution," *Bulletin of the Atomic Scientists,* paper prepared for the U. N. Conference on Peacetime Uses of Atomic Energy, at Geneva, 1955, Vol. 11, November, 1955, p. 331.

THE GEOLOGIC WORK OF CREATION WEEK

Therefore, we must approach a study of the work of the six days of Creation strictly from the perspective of Scriptural revelation, and not at all from that of a projection of present natural processes into the past. It is precisely this sort of illegitimate projection which has led to the theory of evolution and to the various theological devices that have been conceived for harmonizing it with the Biblical revelation. Since God's revealed Word describes this Creation as taking place in six "days" and since there apparently is no contextual basis for understanding these days in any sort of symbolic sense, it is an act of both faith and reason to accept them, literally, as real days.[1]

The First Day

As far as the earth itself is concerned, this work consisted essentially of molding the primitive materials—now presumably represented mainly in the core and mantle—into physical and chemical forms suitable for habitation and use by man and other forms of life. These reactions were initiated by the introduction of light[2]—the most basic and all-pervasive form of energy—to the surface of the earth. This light, however, was not that of the sun as presently constituted, the "making" of which occurred only on the fourth day.

What physical activity and chemical reactions were stimulated by this impulse of light energy, in connection with the earth's heat and its primeval elements, it would be pure speculation to try to say. It seems only reasonable that much of such activity then took place, particularly in the materials near the surface which now form the deeper crust, materials which everywhere give evidence of intense primeval activity—motion, deformation, pressure, metamorphism, etc. It is possible that many of those rocks now called Archaeozoic received their characteristics largely during this time. These rocks, also known as the "basement complex" apparently underlie

---

[1] For a brief summation of Biblical evidence that these "days" are intended to be understood literally, see "Creation and Deluge," by Henry M. Morris, *His Magazine,* January 1954, pp. 6-10, 19-23. See also, Louis Berkhof, *Systematic Theology* (rev.; Grand Rapids: Wm. B. Eerdmans Pub. Co., 1953), pp. 152-157, and R. F. Surburg, "In the Beginning God Created," in *Darwin, Evolution, and Creation* (Ed. by P. A. Zimmerman, St. Louis: Concordia Publ. House, 1959), pp. 57-64.

[2] Genesis 1:3.

all other crustal rocks and are almost or entirely composed of igneous and metamorphic rocks, in extreme heterogeneity. These crystalline rocks have roots which are as yet inaccessible to man and are separated at their surface by a worldwide unconformity from the sedimentary rocks that have been superimposed upon them at some later time or times. O. D. von Engeln and K. E. Caster say of this universal hiatus:

> *This is the truly universal break* [italics theirs]. Besides the places where it is exposed or visible in a rock section, the upper surface of the basement complex is found to be the floor wherever deep drilling or seismic sounding has penetrated to the bottom of the sedimentary blanket.[1]

Concerning their nature, they say:

> The main thing to be said about the Archeozoic is that the rocks which comprise its systems are largely a jumble of igneous intrusives and of steeply dipping schists and gneisses, some of which, like the intrusives, have no known base.[2]

The Second Day

On the second day of Creation, the waters covering the earth's surface were divided into two great reservoirs—one below the firmament and one above, the firmament being the "expanse" above the earth now corresponding to the troposphere.[3] The mechanism whereby this result was accomplished, together with any side effects, has not been revealed. Whether terrestrial heat was instrumental or extraterrestrial forces of some kind or whether solely due to creative fiat, we do not know. It is at least possible that further crustal disturbances occurred and also that the waters below the firmament were in continuous intense motion, pounding and grinding and mixing the elements in the superficial materials.

The Third Day

Then, on the third day, came the first appearance of "dry land." The waters under the firmament were gathered together into one

---

[1] O. D. von Engeln and K. E. Caster, *op. cit.*, p. 664.
[2] *Ibid.*, p. 673.
[3] According to Gen. 1:20, the birds were created to fly in the "open firmament of heaven."

common bed as the lands under them sank. In other parts, the lands rose and a great continent or continents appeared (Genesis 1:9, 10). Thus is implied the first great "orogeny" or "mountain birth." This seems to have been accomplished, at least in part, by differential sorting of the primeval surface materials in accordance with their weights. Materials of greater density gathered together and weighted down the crust beneath them, causing a sinking. Simultaneously this compression caused a lateral squeezing of the lighter materials outward and then upward, perhaps in many cases through igneous emissions, to form the continents. At the conclusion of the process, the heavy materials with their superimposed weights of water were in balance with the greater thicknesses of lighter materials elsewhere.

This principle is now known by geophysicists as the principle of isostasy, meaning "equal weights," and is quite basic in the study and interpretation of geology and geophysics.

(God) hath measured the waters in the hollow of His hand, and meted out heaven with the span, and comprehended the dust of the earth in a measure, and weighed the mountains in scales and the hills in a balance.[1]

It is obvious that this great uplift could have been, and probably was, accompanied by intense distortion of the crust. The factor of heat probably again played an integral part in the whole action. Also as the movements began and continued, the waters began to flow into the newly-formed basins and of course initiated erosion and deposition of sediments on a vast scale. It seems reasonable that many of the deeper sedimentary rocks may have been formed at this time, especially those now attributed to the Proterozoic Era.

The Proterozoic Era is thought to be the period between the Archeozoic and the Cambrian. It is also known by the term "Algonkian." It is marked by non-fossiliferous rocks, quite commonly typical sedimentaries except for this lack of fossils. As noted before, it is separated by a profound unconformity from the Archeozoic Rocks below it, although quite often the latter are also found either at the surface or else directly below some fossil-bearing stratum, with the Proterozoic absent. This great unconformity at the top of the Archean rocks has, until recently, been attributed to a tremendously long period of erosion. This is very unlikely, if not impossible, however, because such a lengthy period of universal erosion must have produced

[1] Isaiah 40:12.

somewhere great thicknesses of corresponding sediments, and these have *never been found*.

It is much more likely that the Archean rocks were truncated in this way by a brief, intense period of erosion in connection with the activities of the first three days of Creation. The rocks of the Proterozoic, of course containing no genuine fossils since life had not yet been introduced onto the earth, perhaps were then in part deposited during the orogeny of the third day. The essential equivalence in time of the Archeozoic and Proterozoic rocks is recognized by Wilson:

> These Proterozoic rocks, although little altered, are always younger than the metamorphosed Archaean rocks upon which they rest, but they may be older than Archaean rocks elsewhere. Archaean and Proterozoic are types of rocks and do not represent just two eras of time. Rocks of either type may be of any Precambrian age.[1]

It is significant that these rocks also are separated from the fossil-bearing rocks by a great unconformity in most cases.

We have already learned that a profound and generally widespread unconformity separates the Archeozoic and Proterozoic rocks in North America. Another unconformity commonly marks the bottom of the Cambrian system.[2]

On the other hand, there are a number of important localities where the transition from Proterozoic to Cambrian is *not* marked by an unconformity of a physical nature but rather by a disconformity, the only evidence of the change being fossiliferous. In other locations, notably in Glacier National Park, as we have seen, a thickness of some two miles of so-called Proterozoic strata is superimposed upon Mesozoic strata! This, of course, has been attributed to a vast overthrust, but we have already pointed out the essential impossibility of this explanation.

Evidently, at least from the perspective of a Biblical framework for geology, many so-called Proterozoic strata were actually formed at the same time as supposedly younger fossiliferous strata, whereas many were formed at essentially the same time as the Archaean rocks. The main criterion for recognition of the Proterozoic rocks,

---

[1] J. Tuzo Wilson: "Geophysics and Continental Growth," *American Scientist,* Vol. 47, March 1959, p. 21.

[2] W. J. Miller: *Introduction to Historical Geology,* (6th Ed., New York, Van Nostrand, 1952), p. 110.

unless they are found deposited between systems which are evidently Archean below and fossiliferous above, is that they be non-crystalline and non-fossil bearing. If crystalline, they would be called Archeozoic; if fossiliferous, they would be identified as Cambrian or later, depending on the contained fossils.

On the other hand, there seems no reason why sediments could not have been deposited at any later time but without fossils in them, depending simply upon their particular source areas and depositional histories. It is reasonable to postulate for our purposes, therefore, that Proterozoic rocks not separated by a genuine unconformity from fossil-bearing rocks vertically above them must have been deposited in similar times and manners to the latter, whereas there is at least a good possibility that Proterozoic rocks which do exhibit such an unconformity at their tops may have been laid down during the Creation period.

But another feature of great significance now appears in the Creation record. On the same day on which the lands were uplifted above the waters, the account tells us that land plants of all types appeared.

And God said, Let the earth put forth grass, herbs yielding seed, and fruit trees bearing fruit after their kind, wherein is the seed thereof, upon the earth: and it was so.[1]

All of this, together with the uplift of the lands, was accomplished on the third day. There is no way of accounting for this, if one is going to accept the revelation as meaning what it says, except in terms of God's omnipotence and creativity. But unless God is finite (and this is an impossible contradiction in terms) there is no reason to question that He could do these things in just the way they are described. We are unable to say, of course, how it was accomplished, or by what processes, since, as we have already shown, the processes used in the Creation were necessarily different from those which we can observe and study at the present time.

CREATION OF "APPEARANCE OF AGE"

One thing, however, is very significant. Plants, in order to continue to grow in the present economy, must have a soil, water, light, chemical nutrients, etc. The account has mentioned water and light, al-

[1] Genesis 1:11.

though in a somewhat different physical context than now provided, but the soil and nutrients must also be available. As now formed, a soil requires a long period of preparation before becoming able to support plant growth. But here it must have been created essentially instantaneously, with all the necessary chemical constituents, rather than gradually developed over centuries of rock weathering, alluvial deposition, etc. Thus it had an appearance of being "old" when it was still new. *It was created with an "appearance" of age!*

This, of course, was also true with the plants which were created at this time. Similarly with the fishes and birds created on the fifth day and with man and the land animals and insects created on the sixth day. Each was made "full-grown" and placed in an environment already perfectly adapted to it.[1] This fact of rapid, almost instantaneous, attainment of maturity is pointed out with special emphasis in the case of the first man, who is said to have been directly formed by God out of the same elements as are found in the earth (Genesis 2:7) but then endued with the breath of life, and of the first woman, fashioned by God out of man's side[2] (Genesis 2:21,22).

This tremendous truth of a "grown creation" cannot be overemphasized. We are not of course told all the details of Creation and its description. Enough is revealed, however, so that we should know beyond any doubt that at the end of the six days the Creation of "heaven and earth, the sea, and all that in them is" was complete and perfect: "very good," as God pronounced it.[3] Everything was in harmony, with each of God's creatures placed in an environment perfectly suitable to it.

Modern Rejection of This Biblical Doctrine

Acceptance of this simple fact of a genuine Creation somehow seems extremely difficult for modern man. Even in ancient times, philosophers were continually devising varied and sundry schemes of evolution, explaining how the world might have gradually developed from primeval chaos into its present state of high organization and complexity. This may perhaps be a faint reflection of the actual

---

[1] See also our discussions of this point below, pp. 344-346, and 356-357.

[2] The word translated "rib" [Hebrew *tsela*] in this passage appears some 20 times in the Hebrew Old Testament and is nowhere else given this translation. It usually means "side," although other usages are possible.

[3] Genesis 1:31.

Creation revelation, according to which God in six days did build up the universe from an initial formless state into a primeval state of high perfection. But the great error has been modern man's refusal to recognize that this original Creation was *complete* and that modern natural processes are *not* the continuation of Creation.

But modern man rebels at this suggestion, desiring to push the divine Creator as far back in time as possible and to conceive Him as being as little concerned with His Creation as possible. The concept of a Creation and a Creator, in any vital sense of the words, is assiduously avoided[1] in all scientific literature, with only very rare and very apologetic exceptions. Organic evolution is all but universally accepted today as the sufficient explanation for all forms of life, including men, as well as the evolution of life itself from inorganic compounds and even also of the physical universe. The most absurd improbabilities are considered more probable than the alternative of real creation. For example, George Wald, Professor of Biology at Harvard, in discussing the extreme complexity of even the simplest living organisms and the almost infinite improbability that such systems could ever arise spontaneously from non-living systems, yet confesses:

> One has only to contemplate the magnitude of this task to concede that the spontaneous generation of a living organism is impossible. Yet here we are—as a result, I believe, of spontaneous generation.[2]

If one wonders how such a careful and brilliant scientist as Wald could bring himself to believe in something which he himself calls "impossible," the answer is found in another statement of his:

> When speaking for myself, I do not tend to make sentences containing the word God; but what do those persons mean who make such sentences? ... What I have learned is that many educated persons now tend to equate their idea of God with their concept of the order of nature.[3]

This attitude of course renders absolutely impossible any recourse to supernatural creation at any point of cosmic history. So Wald says, in passing, as it were:

[1] For a remarkable example of the low esteem in which most scientific writers hold anything savoring of theism, see the article "Teleology in Science Teaching," by A. J. Bernatowicz (*Science*, Vol. 128, Dec. 5, 1958, pp. 1402-1405).

[2] George Wald: "The Origin of Life," in *The Physics and Chemistry of Life*, by the Editors of *Scientific American*, Simon and Schuster, 1955, p. 9.

[3] George Wald: "Innovation in Biology," *Scientific American*, Vol. 199, September 1958, p. 101.

. . . the only alternative to some form of spontaneous generation is a belief in supernatural creation. . . .[1]

All of which seems to be an up-to-date commentary on a well-known Biblical passage describing early man and his drift into polytheistic pantheism.

> For the invisible things of him since the creation of the world are clearly seen, being perceived through the things that are made, even his everlasting power and divinity; that they may be without excuse: because that, knowing God, they glorified him not as God, neither gave thanks; but became vain in their reasonings, and their senseless heart was darkened. Professing themselves to be wise, they became fools, and changed the glory of the incorruptible God for the likeness of an image of corruptible man, and of birds, and four-footed beasts, and creeping things.[2]

The "Steady-State" Cosmology

Nor does the evolutionary philosophy deal only with life and living organisms. The denial of true creation extends into the inorganic realm, encompassing eventually all the elements of the physical universe. The extreme example of this is the so-called "steady-state" cosmology, which is the principle of uniformitarianism carried to its ultimate extreme. This concept is fairly recent, attributed mostly to the British astronomer Fred Hoyle, but has rapidly attained a tremendous following among scientists and philosophers everywhere.

This theory is often called (really miscalled) the "continuous creation" theory, because its key feature is the concept of the continual evolution (not creation) of matter out of nothing, somewhere in the vast universe!

Hoyle describes the philosophy of this theory as follows:

> This idea requires atoms to appear in the Universe continually instead of being created explosively at some definite time in the past. There is an important contrast here. An explosive creation of the Universe is not subject to analysis. It is something that must be impressed by an arbitrary fiat. In the case of a continuous origin of matter on the other hand the creation must obey a definite law, a law that has just the same sort of logical status

---

[1] *Ibid.*, p. 100. And yet we now have the spectacle of "creationists" advocating spontaneous generation! (W. R. Hearn and R. A. Hendry in "The Origin of Life," Ch. 3 in *Evolution and Christian Thought Today*, Ed. by R. L. Mixter, Grand Rapids, Eerdmans Publ. Co., 1959, pp. 53-70).

[2] Romans 1:20-23.

as the laws of gravitation, of nuclear physics, of electricity and magnetism.[1]

The extreme uniformitarianism of the theory is even more evident when he says:

> The old queries about the beginning and end of the universe are dealt with in a surprising manner—by saying that they are meaningless, for the reason that the Universe did not have a beginning and it will not have an end.[2]

It is obvious that the concept of a Creator-God and a real Creation have no place in this interpretation of the universe. It is also obvious that the basic reason for replacing the concept of Creation with that of an eternal "steady-state" is not scientific at all, but purely the desire to conform all things in the universe to man's understanding of present physical processes. Herbert Dingle, a British specialist in the philosophy of science, has noted this:

> So far as I can judge, the authors of this new cosmology are primarily concerned about the great difficulty that must face all systems that contemplate a changing universe—namely, how can we conceive it to have begun? They are not content to leave this question unanswered until further knowledge comes; all problems must be solved now. Nor, for some reason, are they content to suppose that at some period in the distant past something happened that does not continually happen now. It seems to them better to suppose that there was no beginning and will be no ending to the material universe, and therefore, tacitly assuming that the universe must conform to their tastes, they declare that this must have been the case.[3]

The "Eternal Oscillation" Cosmology

However, the most prominent alternate theory, that of a single period of explosive evolution of the elements and the stars that occurred some several billions of years ago from an initial superdense state of the universe, is also purely evolutionary and naturalistic. This initial state is not conceived as a time of divine creation at all, but rather as one stage in a continually oscillating universe, eternally fluctuating between periods of expansion, as at present, and collapse

---

[1] Fred Hoyle: *Frontiers of Astronomy*, (New York, Harper's, 1955), pp. 317-318.
[2] *Ibid.*, p. 321.
[3] Herbert Dingle: "Science and Modern Cosmology," *Science*, Volume 120, October 1, 1954, p. 519.

into the superdense condition. The most prominent advocate of this theory is the physicist-astronomer George Gamow. He says:

> Thus we conclude that our universe has existed for an eternity of time, that until about five billion years ago it was collapsing uniformly from a state of infinite rarefaction; that five billion years ago it arrived at a state of maximum compression in which the density of all its matter may have been as great as that of the particles packed in the nucleus of an atom (i.e., 100 million million times the density of water), and that the universe is now on the rebound, dispersing irreversibly toward a state of infinite rarefaction.[1]

Thus there is no more room in this theory for a genuine divine Creation than there is in the steady-state theory. But again, this is not because the scientific evidence demands such a conclusion. Gamow himself admits that his hypothetical formulation of an eternal oscillation is purely metaphysical and has no objective scientific basis.

Thus from the physical point of view we must forget entirely about the pre-collapse period and try to explain all things on the basis of facts which are no older than five billion years—plus or minus five per cent.[2]

Importance of the Doctrine of a "Grown Creation"

We see, therefore, that when one decides to reject the concept of real Creation, there is no scientific stopping-point short of what amounts to atheism. Not only the various types of living creatures but even life itself, and then everything in the physical universe from the simplest atom to the greatest galaxy, must be incorporated into the evolutionary hypothesis! One searches in vain for the acknowledgment of God and His creative power in all these theories. Everything can be "scientifically" explained; what need for a Creator?

But the conviction of Wald, Hoyle and other scientists that evolution is the explanation of all things obviously arises from outside the domain of verifiable science. It is, in fact, much more a faith or belief, than is creationism. It is a belief exercised against all the evidences of the most basic and best-validated scientific laws. The revealed fact of creation, on the other hand, is at least very strongly

---

[1] George Gamow: "Modern Cosmology," in *The New Astronomy*, Edited by Editors of *The Scientific American*, (New York, Simon and Schuster, 1955), p. 23.
[2] *Ibid.*, p. 24.

supported by the law of causality,[1] by the first and second laws of thermodynamics, and by other basic truths of demonstrable science.

Men complain, however, that God would be dishonest to create things with an appearance of age. "How could a God who is Truth," they say, "cause things to look as though they were old and had come into their present form by a long process of growth when actually they had just been created? This is deceptive and therefore impossible. God would not lie."

This sort of reasoning, though it has often been propounded, is entirely unworthy of fair-minded, reasonable men, especially scientists! *It is essentially an affirmation of atheism,* a denial of the possibility of a real Creation. If God actually created anything at all, even the simplest atoms, those atoms or other creations would necessarily have an appearance of *some* age. There could be no *genuine* creation of any kind, without an initial appearance of age inherent in it. It would still be possible to interpret the newly-created matter in terms of some kind of previous evolutionary history. And if God could create atomic stuff with an appearance of age—*in other words, if God exists!*—then there is no reason why He could not, in full conformity with His character of Truth, create a whole universe full-grown.

Obviously, if He did this, there would be no way by which any of His creatures could deduce the age or manner of Creation by study of the laws of *maintenance* of His Creation. This information could only be obtained, correctly, through God Himself revealing it! And if God reveals how and when He created the universe and its inhabitants, then to charge God with falsehood in creating "apparent age" is presumptuous in the extreme—even blasphemous. *It is not God Who has lied, but rather man who has called Him a liar, through rejection of His revelation of Creation as given in Genesis and verified by the Lord Jesus Christ!*

But if we are willing to accept in faith the account of Creation as

[1] The law of cause and effect, which is the basis of the so-called scientific method, affirms that like causes produce like effects and that every effect must have an adequate cause. No effect can be quantitatively greater than or qualitatively divergent from its cause. Thus, regarding the personality of man as an effect, his intelligence requires a Cause possessed of intelligence, his power of choice implies a Cause possessed of volition, his moral consciousness must be explained in terms of a Cause possessed of morality. Similarly, the intelligibility of the physical universe implies a Designer, and so on. Thus the law of causality, though admittedly not philosophically impregnable, is at least strong circumstantial evidence of the existence of a great First Cause, a personal Creator-God.

simple, literal truth, then we immediately have a most powerful tool for understanding all the facts of geology in proper perspective. We can study the data in terms of the concept that the minerals, the rocks, and their various combinations were being brought together during the six days of Creation by unique creative processes into forms eminently and perfectly suitable for man's habitation and dominion. Of course, this original form is now much masked by virtue of the subsequent entrance of sin, decay and death into the Creation, with all their tremendous ramifications. Not only mankind but also "the whole Creation" has been delivered into the "bondage of decay" and has ever since been "groaning and travailing together in pain" (Romans 8:21,22). Recognition of these basic facts will, we are convinced, ultimately lead to a far more satisfactory and scientific explanation of the observed geological field relationships than any evolutionary synthesis can ever do.

THE WORLD THAT THEN WAS

How long it was between man's creation and his fall, the Bible does not say. In any event, it is very unlikely that any of the fossil-bearing geologic strata are attributable to that period. For fossils plainly tell of death and suffering. Although the sentence of death was specifically pronounced only on man and on the serpent used by Satan as the vehicle of temptation, the most obvious implication is that this curse on the master of creation extended likewise to his dominion. This fact is also strongly implied by the New Testament expositions of the Fall. Paul says: "By *man* came death" (I Corinthians 15:21) and in another place, "By *one man,* sin entered into the world, and death by sin" (Romans 5:12). Similarly, in Romans 8:20: "The *creation* was subjected to vanity." As already noted, most of the fossil deposits give evidence of sudden burial and therefore betoken catastrophe of some kind. The whole appearance of the fossiliferous rocks seems completely out of harmony with the system of creation which God so many times pronounced as "very good." Therefore, we feel compelled to date all of the rock strata which contain fossils of once-living creatures as subsequent to Adam's fall![1]

It seems likely, furthermore, that relatively few of these strata, if

[1] The significance of the Edenic curse for paleontology is discussed in more detail in Appendix I.

any, can be dated during the period between Adam's fall and the Deluge. This is primarily because geologic activity seems to have been very mild during that time and because such deposits as may have been formed then were most likely reworked during the Flood.

The conclusion that the period was probably one of relative inactivity geologically is supported by several teachings of the Scriptures, among them the following:

(1) "Waters Above the Firmament"

As we have seen, these waters apparently existed in the form of a great vapor canopy around the earth, of unknown but possibly very great extent. As vapor, it was quite invisible but, nevertheless, would have had a profound effect on terrestrial climate and meteorological processes.

The most immediate and obvious of these effects would be to cause a uniformly warm temperate climate around the earth. Such water vapor as is present in the atmosphere today has this specific effect of regulating the earth's temperature. The inferred antediluvian vapor envelope would have produced this result in much greater degree, with a larger percentage of the sun's incoming radiant energy being absorbed and retained and uniformly distributed over the earth than at present, both seasonally and latitudinally. This effect in turn would largely inhibit the atmospheric circulations which characterize the present troposphere and which are caused basically by temperature differentials between points of different latitudes and topographies. The constant battle of "fronts" would be mostly absent, so that antediluvian climates were not only warm but also without violent windstorms.

The physics and meteorology of such a vapor canopy, and its maintenance in the antediluvian atmosphere, may be difficult to delineate in detail; even today very little is known about the *present* upper atmosphere, its contituents and physical behavior. Much of the activity stimulated by the International Geophysical Year, in fact, including the artificial satellite program, has been directed to the end of finding out more about this region. It is known, however, that the region above about 80 miles is very hot, over 100° F and possibly rising to 3000° F,[1] and is in fact called the thermosphere for this reason. High temperature, of course, is the chief requisite for retaining

[1] D. R. Bates: "Composition and Structure of the Atmosphere," *The Earth and Its Atmosphere*, (New York: Basic Books, Inc.), 1957, pp. 104-105.

a large quantity of water vapor. Furthermore, it is known that water vapor is substantially lighter than air and most of the other gases making up the atmosphere. There is thus nothing physically impossible about the concept of a vast thermal vapor blanket once existing in the upper atmosphere.

It is known, of course, that nuclei of condensation, particularly salt particles from the breaking waves on the ocean,[1] are now necessary to cause water vapor in the present atmosphere to condense even at low temperatures, but it is likely that such nuclei were not present in the primeval canopy, since a high degree of atmospheric turbulence would be required for their elevation into the canopy. After water droplets are formed, they still must coalesce into large particles to fall as rain (otherwise, they remain suspended in the sky as clouds), and the mechanics of this process is still very incompletely understood. Although we can as yet point to no definite scientific verification of this pristine vapor protective envelope around the earth, neither does there appear to be any inherent physical difficulty in the hypothesis of its existence, and it does suffice to explain a broad spectrum of phenomena both geological and Scriptural.

(2) No Rainfall Before the Flood

This fact is specifically alleged in Genesis 2:5,6, as follows:

". . . for Jehovah God had not caused it to rain upon the earth: and there was not a man to till the ground; but there went up a mist from the earth, and watered the whole face of the ground."

This verse is applied specifically to the initial completed Creation, but there is no mention made of any change in this meteorological phenomenon after the Fall, so it evidently continued until the time of the Deluge. This inference is supported also by the fact that the rainbow is mentioned as a new sign from God to man after the Flood, implying strongly that rain as we know it and the subsequent rainbow were experienced for the first time then (Genesis 9:11-17).

The process of evaporation from both land and water surfaces apparently is implied in the "mist"[2] going up from the earth. However,

---

[1] A. H. Woodcock: "Salt and Rain," *Scientific American*, Vol. 197, October 1957, pp. 42-47.

[2] The suggestion has recently been made that the "mist" was actually a river. But the same Hebrew word is used also in Job 36:27, where it necessarily means "mist" or "vapor." It is quite different from the regular Hebrew word for "river," which

with atmospheric turbulence largely absent, the large movements of air masses and their contained water vapor, such as characterize present climates, were prevented. Also, the lapse rate (vertical decrease of temperature with elevation above the ground surface) was probably small due to the effect of the canopy, so that vapor would tend to recondense and precipitate as a light mist soon after its evaporation. Since the deposition of sediments is conditioned upon their precedent erosion by water or wind and since these elements evidently acted in a uniformly gentle manner, it follows that there could have been very little geological work accomplished during this period.

(3) Little Volcanic or Tectonic Activity

This is inferred from the fact that the "breaking-up of the fountains of the great deep" (Genesis 7:11), which implies this sort of activity, was one of the immediate causes of the Deluge; therefore, it must have been restrained previously. The phrase "the great deep" is used in Scripture to refer both to the waters of the ocean (e.g., Isaiah 51:10) and subterranean waters (Psalm 78:15). The one word "deep" (Hebrew *t^ehôm*) is also often used to refer to both types of terrestrial waters. The primeval deep of Genesis 1:2 was, as we have seen, segregated into waters above and below the firmament, so that these waters, in whatever location, are evidently intended by subsequent references to the deep. Presumably great portions of the waters were entrapped below the crust and in pockets within the crust during the first three days of Creation. Because of the high temperatures and pressures, they undoubtedly were very effective solvents, creating either chemically-rich crustal waters or water-rich magmas.

It seems, however, that these were either completely or in large measure imprisoned during the antediluvian period, perhaps steadily building up temperatures and pressures until, finally, the crust gave way at some point of weakness. Yielding of the crust at even one point, with resultant escape of magmas and water or steam would then lead to earth movements causing further fractures until, as the Scriptures portray so graphically, "the same day were all the fountains of the great deep broken up" (Genesis 7:11). Truly this was a

is used several times in the same chapter. (e.g., Genesis 2:10, etc.). Furthermore, it has been recognized and translated as "mist" by virtually all standard translations (KJV, ASV, RSV, etc.)

gigantic catastrophe, beside which the explosion of the largest hydrogen bomb, or of hundreds of such bombs, becomes insignificant!

Thus, the Biblical record implies that the age between the fall of man and the resultant Deluge was one of comparative quiescence geologically. The waters both above and below the firmament were in large measure restrained, temperatures were equably warm, there were no heavy rains nor winds and probably no earthquakes nor volcanic emissions. Probably a larger ratio of land surface to water surface existed than at present, but the atmosphere was maintained at a comfortable humidity by the low-lying "mist" rising from an intricate network of "seas" (Genesis 1:10) and mildly-flowing "rivers" (Genesis 2:10-14) evidently fed partially or largely by gentle springs.

GEOLOGIC EVIDENCES OF ANTEDILUVIAN CLIMATE

Universally Warm Climate

The most significant of these Biblical inferences is that of a universally warm climate, with ample moisture for abundant plant and animal life. It is significant that fossil remains everywhere in the world and throughout the geologic column testify to just such a condition. The fossiliferous rocks have been divided into geological "ages" in the uniformitarian system, and it is significant that practically all of these "ages" are inferred from the organic and physiographic character of the deposits to have been universally mild and warm. Speaking of the Mesozoic Era, the age of the great reptiles, Colbert says:

> Many lines of dinosaurs evolved during the 100 million years or more of Mesozoic history in which they lived. . . . In those days the earth had a tropical or sub-tropical climate over much of its land surface, and in the widespread tropical lands there was an abundance of lush vegetation. The land was low and there were no high mountains forming physical or climatic barriers.[1]

The more "recent" Cenozoic Era consists usually of the deposits nearer the surface and containing mammalian fossils or large per-

[1] E. H. Colbert: "Evolutionary Growth Rates in the Dinosaurs," *Scientific Monthly*, August 1949, Vol. 69, p. 71. W. J. Arkell says, of the Jurassic Era: ". . . a fairly rich flora of temperate facies flourished within or near both the Arctic and Antarctic Circles, in East Greenland and Grahamland" (*Jurassic Geology of the World*, New York, Hafner Publ. Co., 1956, p. 615).

centages of modern marine forms. The topmost deposits, attributed to the Pleistocene, are not typical of the rest and are probably in part to be dated subsequent to the Deluge. This may also be true of some of the Pliocene strata, although most of them are like the lower Tertiary strata.[1] The earlier epochs, from the Eocene through the Miocene, apparently had similar climates to those of the Mesozoic (Cretaceous, Jurassic and Triassic).

It (the Miocene) was also a time of world-wide climates; after the Miocene, climates became diversified and have remained so ever since.[2]

The climate of the Oligocene was definitely warm in comparison with that of the Miocene which followed it, and far warmer than the climate of the modern world. But the preceding Eocene was even warmer than the Oligocene. In the Eocene, subtropical heat was experienced in Greenland.[3]

The same situation is encountered in the great thicknesses of Paleozoic and Proterozoic rocks. With respect to the Cambrian, Miller says:

. . . the climate of Cambrian time was not essentially different from that of comparatively recent geological time, but . . . climatic conditions were then much more uniform over the earth than now. Considerable limestone formations of Cambrian age at high latitudes indicate strongly that they were there deposited in relatively warm or temperate waters.[4]

Similarly, of the subsequent Ordovician, he says:

The very extensive Ordovician seas, allowing a much freer circulation of waters between low and high latitudes, no doubt helped to keep the climate of the earth more uniform then than at the present time.[5]

And of the next period, the Silurian:

The general distribution and character of the rocks and their fossil content point to more uniform climatic conditions than those of today. Fossils in the Arctic Silurian rocks are not essentially different from those of low latitudes.[6]

[1] Gustaf O. S. Arrhenius notes, concerning the paleotemperatures indicated in oceanic sediments: "The cooling of the deep water body to the near-zero temperature now prevailing is recorded at the Pliocene-Pleistocene transition." ("Sedimentation on the Ocean Floor," in *Researches in Geochemistry*, ed. by P. H. Abelson, New York, John Wiley and Sons, 1959, p. 18).

[2] O. D. Von Engeln and K. E. Caster: *Geology*, p. 441.
[3] *Ibid.*, p. 451.
[4] W. J. Miller: *An Introduction to Historical Geology*, (6th Ed., New York, Van Nostrand, 1952), p. 116.
[5] *Ibid.*, p. 131.
[6] *Ibid.*, p. 143.

For the sake of completeness, even at the risk of monotony, we must continue with the other great periods. Of the Devonian, von Engeln and Caster say:

In the case of the Devonian, such evidence is indicative of a world-wide mild climate.[1]

The Carboniferous Era includes both the Pennsylvanian and the Mississippian, and the evidence is still the same.

As for the earlier Paleozoic periods, the character and distribution of Mississippian fossils rather clearly prove absence of well-defined climatic zones like those of today.[2]

It is in the Pennsylvanian strata that the coal formations are found at their richest. A universal warm, moist climate alone explains the evidence.

The environmental conditions of the Pennsylvanian appear to have been ideal for coal formation. A moist, warm climate throughout the year provided luxuriant, unceasing vegetative growth.[3]

The Supposed Permian Glaciation

The story is thus the same in practically all the strata. Except for the supposed glacial formations of the Pleistocene and, to a lesser extent, of the Pliocene, the only portion of the fossiliferous strata in which phenomena such as described above do not clearly apply is that of the Permian. It has been thought that many Permian strata in Africa and South America are of glacial origin. Permian strata elsewhere, however, betray the usual marks of temperate or tropical climates.

Even in those Permian (or Permo-Carboniferous transitional) strata which are thought to be of glacial origin, there are intercalated strata present which must have come from a warm climate, for example, extensive coal beds. The European stratigrapher, Maurice Gignoux, has described the remarkable similarity of the Permian sequences from Africa, India, Australia, Madagascar and Brazil, as follows:

In all the countries of the southern hemisphere which we have just

[1] O. D. von Engeln and K. E. Caster, *op. cit.*, p. 596.
[2] Miller, *op. cit.*, p. 169.
[3] von Engeln and Caster, *op. cit.*, p. 562.

studied, the same history may be reconstructed. The Carboniferous ends with a great glacial development, not confined to mountain valleys but extending over immense spaces and thus comparable to the Quaternary ice caps of the northern hemisphere. Immediately after the disappearance of the glaciers and throughout the Permian, these regions were colonized by the *Glossopteris* flora and nourished an abundant population of reptiles, as diversely adapted as present day mammals.[1]

This remarkably extensive glaciation is anomalous and difficult to explain, occurring as it did so near the equator and also largely near sea level. Gignoux believes the only possible explanation is the theory of continental drift, previously advocated strenuously by Wegener, du Toit and others, according to which the southern continents, and possibly others as well, were once parts of one great continental mass, since broken and drifted apart.

This theory of course bears quite hard on the uniformist concept, and so is rejected by most geologists. Opik, for example, says:

The interpretation of these changes was for long bedeviled by the possibilities of polar wandering and continental drift. . . . Alfred Wegener and his followers actually tried to explain in such a purely mechanical manner all paleoclimatic changes; the succession of warm and cold periods was ascribed to the transplantation of the same locality from the tropics to the Arctic circle and back again. . . . It has now been proved that during the past 100 million years, the relative positions of the poles and the continents were essentially the same as at present.[2]

Recent studies on faunal distributions in the Permian strata in both hemispheres seem to prove that the relative position of the poles and the continents was the same as now and, therefore, that neither continental drift nor polar wandering can explain the anomalous Permian glacial age.

The faunal boundary parallels the earth's present equator and, if truly caused by temperature, precludes the possibility of changes in the position of the poles with respect to the major land masses of the northern hemisphere. Also precluded is the possibility that the crust or mantle has shifted its position relative to the core.[3]

---

[1] Maurice Gignoux: *Stratigraphic Geology,* Translated from the 4th French Edition by Gwendolyn G. Woodford, (San Francisco, W. H. Freeman & Co., 1955), p. 245.

[2] Ernst J. Opik: "Ice Ages," in *The Earth and Its Atmosphere,* edited by D. R. Bates, (New York, Basic Books, Inc., 1957), p. 154.

[3] Francis G. Stehli: "Possible Permian Climatic Zonation and Its Implications," *American Journal of Science,* Vol. 255, November 1957, p. 617.

However, neither Stehli nor Opik nor apparently anyone else has been able to offer a satisfactory alternate explanation for the peculiar Permo-Carboniferous "ice age." Opik acknowledges the impasse as follows:

> We have to conclude the temperature there was at an arctic level. How this could happen in a region which at present is within the tropics, stretching between 17° and 24° northern latitude, is one of the greatest geological puzzles we are confronted with.[1]

Perhaps the difficulty, however, is that the evidences for the supposed "ice-age" have been misunderstood. The most characteristic indicators of ice action are believed to be tillites and striations, and these are the features which have been held to prove Permian glaciations. Tillites are hardened tills, which are non-sorted aggregations of gravel, sand and some boulders, in a clay matrix. Striations are longitudinal scratches, presumably formed by the overriding ice sheet in contiguous rocks. But there are many agencies besides ice which can produce these features. A recognized authority on sediments and sedimentary rocks says:

> Every chaotic deposit with large blocks embedded in a clayey matrix is not a tillite and great caution should be exercised in discriminating between true tillite and other materials which resemble it.[2]

Similarly, R. F. Flint, the glacial geologist, says:

> Absence of stratification and lack of size sorting, the two most obvious characteristics of till, are by no means confined to till but are shared with a number of other deposits with which till is sometimes easily confused.[3]

With respect to striations, he says:

> Thus it appears that under suitable conditions striations can be made by any flowing or floating heavy mass.[4]

Space does not permit a detailed discussion of these points, but

[1] *Ibid.*, p. 156.
[2] F. J. Pettijohn: *Sedimentary Rocks.* (2nd Ed., New York, Harper, 1957), p. 275.
[3] R. F. Flint: *Glacial and Pleistocene Geology,* (New York, Wiley, 1957), p. 122.
[4] *Ibid.*, p. 58. R. H. Dott of Wisconsin University has recently pointed out that: "Absolute criteria for distinction of sliding from glacial processes are difficult to discover . . . Both produce very poor sorting of clasts; both can conceivably produce faceting and striation of pebbles . . . clearly most ancient "tillites" and glacial periods must be regarded with suspicion until critically reanalyzed." ("Tillite or Subaqueous Slide," *Program Abstracts,* 1959 Meeting of Geological Society of America).

it is evident that these and other assumed indicators of glacial action may also be produced by many agencies other than ice, and therefore they are not at all necessary evidences of glaciation. Especially, in such a geologic cataclysm as the Bible describes the Deluge to be, it is easy to visualize the possibility of some great volcanic or turbidity current type of phenomenon centered over the southern hemisphere which produced these widespread conglomerates and striations, without any glacial action necessary at all. This is all the more reasonable in view of the associated coal deposits, often intercalated between conglomerate strata, as well as other deposits of definitely non-glacial origin. One such deposit is described as follows:

> In the southeastern quadrant of Australia and in Tasmania, tillites are interbedded with some 2000 feet of Permian sediments, partly marine, partly continental in origin, which include, also, a bed of coal.[1]

It would seem that by far the most reasonable way of understanding such deposits as these would be in terms of catastrophic diluvial action, with currents flowing from different directions and containing different sediments.

The Permian glacial deposits, so-called, have been found in Africa, South America, Australia and India. The deposits extend down to sea level and seem to have been spread out more or less radially from a center somewhere along the equator. How such a great ice-sheet could be formed in such a location seems impossible to conceive. Accordingly, attempts have been made to locate Permian glacial deposits in other areas, but unsuccessfully. Some of the greatest and most complete Permian sequences in the world are found in northern Mexico and the southwestern United States, as verified by the following:

> The area contains one of the most complete representations of the Permian system known. . . .[2]

The Permian beds in southwestern United States are a great complex of reef structures and, since corals are only active in tropical or subtropical waters, no one has suggested that glacial deposits are located here. However, in the Mexican beds, many supposed tillites have been found and attributed to glaciation.

---

[1] von Engeln and Caster, *op. cit.,* p. 537.

[2] N. D. Newell, J. K. Rigby, A. G. Fisher, A. J. Whiteman, J. E. Hickox, and J. S. Bradley: *The Permian Reef Complex of the Guadalupe Mountains Region, Texas and New Mexico,* W. H. Freeman & Co., San Francisco, 1953. p. 6.

Recent studies by Norman Newell, of the American
Natural History, an authority on Permian stratigraph
proved this interpretation, however. Regarding the extent oi the ucus,
he says

> The succession in which the conglomerates lie is noteworthy as one of
> the most fully represented and best-documented sequences of Permian
> rocks in North America.[1]

After examining the evidences quite thoroughly, Newell concludes:

> These Mexican boulder beds and volcanic rocks most probably are sub-
> marine slide deposits that accumulated in a stagnant basin adjacent to ac-
> tive volcanoes fringed with growing reefs.[2]

And then he makes the following very important general observation:

> Submarine slide deposits are much more abundant in the stratigraphic
> record than are tillites, and stratigraphers are becoming increasingly alert
> to their significance.[3]

We would therefore predict that it is only a question of time before
the very similar phenomena in the southern hemisphere will also be
recognized as of non-glacial origin.

This means, then, that all the fossiliferous sediments, comprising
the entire geologic column above the Proterozoic[4] or even the Archeozoic in places, give virtually unanimous testimony that "the world
that then was" was one of mild climate, essentially uniform throughout the world. The standard geological references, of course, speak
of these strata in terms of chronological ages and, in these terms, we
would say that the strata indicate that the earth's climate has always,
at least until the most recent geologic epochs, been basically warm
and uniform, with only mild seasonal and latitudinal variations. If
one thinks of the strata as having been largely deposited catastrophi-
cally, especially during the Deluge, then their testimony is of a single
antediluvian era having such a climate.

[1] N. D. Newell: "Supposed Permian Tillites in Northern Mexico Are Submarine
Slide Deposits," *Bulletin, Geological Society of America,* Vol. 68, November 1957,
p. 1569.

[2] *Ibid.,* p. 1572.

[3] *Loc. cit.*

[4] Supposed glaciations in Pre-cambrian times rest upon even more equivocal evidence than that of the Permian and may thus be similarly rejected.

Explanations of Climatic Change

In either case, here again is a great difficulty for uniformitarian geology—how to account for such a remarkable state of things in terms of the present very non-uniform climates, with such extremes of heat and cold. As von Engeln and Caster say concerning the Jurassic system, for example: "This universal tropicality is difficult to explain."[1]

Theories of past climatic change, attempting to explain both the glacial periods and the periods of universal warmth, have been many and varied. Dr. C. E. P. Brooks lists some three dozen or more different theories that have been propounded at one time or another.[2] These theories have involved such things as the passage of the solar system through regions of space filled with cosmical dust or gas, the precession of the equinoxes, tidal variations, warm springs, wandering poles, drifting continents, orogenic phenomena, changing land-sea distributions, shifting ocean currents, changes in solar radiation, atmospheric carbon dioxide, volcanic dust in the atmosphere, changes in atmospheric circulation, change in the obliquity of the ecliptic, and numerous other factors.

There is obviously no need here to discuss all of these theories. Many of them attempt to explain glacial climates but do not account for the much more significant universal warm climate indicated by all the sedimentary strata. Some would explain how a certain region could experience alternating periods of heat and cold but do not account for the *worldwide* warm climate. Probably most authorities now favor either the concept of changing distributions of land and sea or that of changing quantities of solar radiation. Brooks favored the former:

The conclusion to which we are brought, therefore, is that moderate changes in the land and sea distribution, such as have occurred frequently enough in geological times, are amply sufficient to bridge the gap between

---

[1] *Op. cit.*, p. 491. W. J. Arkell says: "The infrequency of glacial episodes and especially the rarity of fossil tills in Arctic regions indicate that if, in fact, the poles have always been approximately where they are now, the warm state of the earth in the Jurassic was normal and our present condition, with polar ice caps, is exceptional" (*Jurassic Geology of the World*, New York, Hafner Publishing Co., 1956, p. 618).

[2] C. E. P. Brooks: *Climate Through the Ages* (McGraw-Hill, New York, 2nd Edition, 1949), pp. 384-386.

non-glacial and glacial climates, or between warm and cold geological periods, and that extraneous aids, such as variations of solar radiation or changes in the astronomical climate, while possible causes, are not necessary conditions.[1]

But obviously any calculations which attempt to deduce the warming effect of such hypothetical changes are necessarily highly speculative, and it is very difficult to see how the important latitudinal differences in quantity of effective incoming solar energy (which constitute the basic reason for our present range of terrestrial climates) could ever be offset merely by changed patterns of land and sea. Accordingly, most present-day climatologists believe the only really competent agent for worldwide climatic change must be worldwide change in available solar energy.

For example, Dr. H. E. Landsberg, Director of the Office of Climatology of the U. S. Weather Bureau, in a recent review of these questions, states:

> There is, of course, a much underrated relation between the oceanic heat (or cold) reservoir and the climatic fluctuations on land. However no *quantitative* consideration has as yet demonstrated that these could account for the observed, and evidently recurring, phenomena of major ice epochs.[2]

And, by the same token, Landsberg implies that this type of mechanism is also inadequate to explain the worldwide warm climate preceding the Pleistocene.

Since solar radiation provides the energy, not only for heating the earth's atmosphere but also for practically all the physical and biologic processes that go into the production of a regional climate, it would surely seem most reasonable to conclude that it must be the basic cause of any such worldwide phenomenon as the universal warm climate we have been describing. Thus, as Landsberg says:

> Sooner or later most considerations get back to the question of changes in the solar radiation. Some astrophysicists contend that there are simply none of the magnitude required for major climatic changes. Others equally stoutly maintain that nuclear refueling processes on the sun actually call for periodic substantial changes in solar energy output.[3]

---

[1] *Ibid.*, p. 157.
[2] H. E. Landsberg: "Trends in Climatology," *Science*, Vol. 128, October 3, 1958, p. 756.
[3] *Ibid.*

It is occasionally argued that more solar radiation might actually lead to an ice age. But again quoting Landsberg:

It is, however, more logical to assume that increases in radiation cause warmer conditions, such as once prevailed in the Tertiary, and that decreases in radiation produce ice ages of the Pleistocene type.[1]

Similarly, Arkell, discussing the worldwide warm climate of the Jurassic, says:

All things considered, therefore, the most probable explanation of the warm temperature of the Jurassic is that which depends on receipt of more solar radiation . . .[2]

Probably the most authoritative compendium of evidence and opinion on this subject currently available is found in a symposium[3] edited by Harlow Shapley, bringing together studies of meteorologists, astronomers, anthropologists, geologists and other specialists interested in past climatic changes.

Dr. Kirtley Mather, reviewing the book, summarizes:

Their conclusions seem to indicate that meteorological conditions are secondary rather than primary causal factors; the real causes of difference in climate, as contrasted with changes in weather, must be found in the variations in output of solar radiation. Here the emphasis is placed upon the short-wave ultraviolet emission rather than variation of the effective black-body radiation of the sun.[4]

Thus are climatologists and others becoming more and more convinced that the only adequate way to explain worldwide climatic changes must somehow be in terms of changes in the only factor which controls climate on a worldwide basis, namely, solar radiation.

However, this apparently necessary conclusion still does not describe the cause of the necessary changes in solar radiation. In fact, there is no evidence for such variation at all. As the astronomer, Fred Hoyle, says:

There is neither theoretical nor observational evidence that changes take

[1] *Ibid.*

[2] W. J. Arkell: *op. cit.,* p. 617.

[3] Harlow Shapley (Ed.): *Climatic Change* (Cambridge, Mass., Harvard University Press, 1954), 318 pp.

[4] Kirtley F. Mather: Review of *Climatic Change, American Scientist,* Vol. 42, April 1954, p. 309.

place in the radiation of the sun, however . . . in support of this it is certain that variations in the sun's radiation from year to year are very small at the present time.[1]

The "Greenhouse Effect"

But of course it is not necessary for there to be an actual change in the sun's output of radiant energy in order for there to be a significant change in the amount of solar energy utilized on the earth in the process of atmospheric heating and other physical processes. All that is necessary is for there to be a change in the heat-absorbing and reflecting qualities of that atmosphere, and this could be accomplished by relatively minor changes in its composition. This is because of the "greenhouse effect" of the atmosphere. Harold Blum gives a cogent description of the key factors in this effect:

The principal atmospheric absorber for the entrant sunlight is water vapor, absorption by ozone being a minor factor qualitatively; the other gases are virtually transparent. Absorption of the outgoing radiation from the earth is again largely due to water vapor, with CO_2 and ozone playing lesser roles. . . . The part absorbed tends to warm the atmosphere, and just as the warm glass of the greenhouse tends to raise the temperature of the interior, the water vapor tends to raise that of the earth's surface below it. This surface, or any object on it, is constantly exchanging radiation with the water vapor in the atmosphere, so the temperature of the surface is closely dependent upon the amount and temperature of this vapor.[2]

These three constituents of the atmosphere—water vapor, ozone, and carbon dioxide—therefore, supply the blanketing effect whereby the sun's radiation becomes effectively available for the maintenance of physical and biological processes on the earth. The most important of these components, by far, is water vapor. Nevertheless, significant changes in the atmospheric proportion of any one or more of the three could produce significant changes in terrestrial climates. More attention has been given to possible variations in carbon dioxide content than either of the others, since this proportion is presumably related to the amount of biologic activity on the earth's surface and therefore is more subject to variation.

[1] Fred Hoyle: *Frontiers of Astronomy* (New York, Harper's, 1955), p. 6.
[2] Harold K. Blum: *Time's Arrow and Evolution* (Princeton University Press, 1951), p. 57.

Dr. Gilbert Plass, of the Office of Advanced Research of Aeronutronic Systems, Inc., has studied the effect of carbon dioxide probably more intensively than any other individual. He says:

Calculations show that a 50-percent decrease in the amount of carbon dioxide in the air will lower the average temperature of the earth 6.9 degrees Fahrenheit. We can be reasonably sure that such a sharp drop in temperature would cause glaciers to spread across the earth.[1]

Plass also gives corresponding quantitative data for the effect of heavier concentrations of CO_2 in producing warm climates; for example, he calculates that if the carbon dioxide content were quadrupled, and in balance with the carbonates on the earth's surface and in the oceans, then the earth's average temperature would be 12.5 degrees Fahrenheit higher than at present.[2]

Of course, this is all quite speculative, but is at least cognizant of the fact that worldwide climatic changes require changes in the effective solar radiation, and a change in the CO_2 content of the atmosphere is a possible means of effecting such changes. With respect to ozone, on the other hand, it is hard to conceive of a means whereby the ozone content of the upper atmosphere could be substantially changed, since it is formed by the reactions of the incoming ultraviolet light with the oxygen in the upper air. Presumably, neither of these latter quantities is likely to change significantly, except for short times.

Since water vapor is the most important of these three gases in producing the greenhouse effect, it would seem reasonable that any substantial change in the earth's climate must somehow be related to changes in the water vapor content of the atmosphere. More water vapor would create a warmer and more uniform climate; less vapor would cause a colder and more sharply zoned climate. Fred Hoyle, among other outstanding meteorologists and astronomers, has recognized this probability:

Evidently then an ice-age would arise if the greenhouse effect of our atmosphere were destroyed or seriously weakened. This would happen if the concentrations of those gases of the atmosphere that are responsible for blocking the infra-red radiation were appreciably reduced. The gas of main importance in this respect is water vapor. The question therefore arises as to how the amount of water vapor in the atmosphere might be

---

[1] Gilbert N. Plass: "Carbon Dioxide and Climate," *Scientific American*, Volume 201, July 1959, p. 42.
[2] *Ibid.*, p. 47

systematically reduced, especially the amount at a height of some 20,000 feet above the ground. In this may lie the answer to the riddle of the ice ages.[1]

Hoyle's suggested mechanism for thus drying out the atmosphere is to postulate the passage of the earth through a region in space filled with meteoric particles which could serve as nuclei of condensation. His reason for limiting this activity to the region of 20,000 feet is as follows:

Now conditions are often operative in the atmosphere, say at a height of about 20,000 feet, where a considerable concentration of water vapor exists that does not fall as rain because there is no way of forming large water drops out of the vapor—and only drops of an appreciable size can form as rain. The arrival from above of a large number of meteoric particles might well produce a drastic change in such a situation, since water drops would immediately tend to condense around the particles. If the concentration of the water vapor were large enough, rain would probably fall.[2]

Hoyle's discussion was mainly concerned with trying to explain the ice ages, but it is clear that the same line of reasoning could lead to an explanation for the uniform warm climate. If a great mass of water vapor had once existed in the atmosphere at an altitude sufficiently high to inhibit condensation about atmospheric dust or salt particles, the greenhouse effect would obviously have been materially strengthened and a warm, substantially uniform climate would have been the result, all over the world.

The Antediluvian Vapor Blanket

The geophysical evidence thus leads us first to recognize that there must have been a worldwide warm climate in pre-Pleistocene times (that is, from our viewpoint, in antediluvian times), that this climate could only have been caused by an increase in the effective amount of solar radiation retained on the earth's surface, but that this was most likely *not* due to an actual increase in radiation from the sun but rather to an increase in the radiation-absorption capacities of the atmosphere, and finally that the most likely means of accomplishing this result would have been through a substantial increase in the water vapor content of the upper atmosphere.

[1] Fred Hoyle, *op. cit.,* p. 8.
[2] *Ibid.,* p. 9.

And this, of course, is exactly what we have seen the early chapters of Genesis to imply, in the references to the "waters above the firmament." We feel warranted, therefore, in suggesting such a thermal vapor blanket around the earth in pre-Pleistocene times as at least a plausible working hypothesis, which seems to offer satisfactory explanation of quite a number of Biblical references and geophysical phenomena. The detailed physics of this inferred antediluvian atmosphere is bound to be uncertain as yet, especially in view of the fact that so little is known about even the present atmosphere, but there seems to be no inherent physical difficulty with the concept.

There is no question that a vapor blanket of indefinitely great extent could be supported by the lower atmosphere, since water vapor weighs only 0.622 times as much as dry air[1] for the same conditions. Furthermore, the amount of vapor that could be maintained in any given volume of space in the vapor blanket would not be significantly affected by the presence or absence of air or other gases in the region.

Practically speaking, the maximum amount of water vapor that can exist in any given space is a function of temperature and is independent of the coexistence of other gases. When the maximum amount of water vapor for a given temperature is contained in a given space, the space is said to be *saturated*. The more common expression "the air is saturated" is not strictly correct.[2]

In the present atmosphere, the stratosphere is quite cold. However, above the stratosphere, the temperature becomes quite warm, well above even the boiling-point of water, so that it would be possible to sustain a tremendous amount of invisible water vapor in the region above the stratosphere, if it somehow were placed there. These high temperatures in the upper atmosphere remain high both day and night, so that there would be no possibility of vapor condensation at night.

There appears to be no night-day effect in atmospheric temperatures, since the grenade-sound experiments were conducted at night while most of the telemetered pressure measurements were in daytime firing.[3]

[1] R. K. Linsley, M. A. Kohler, and J. L. H. Paulhus: *Hydrology for Engineers* (New York, McGraw-Hill, 1958), p. 15.

[2] *Ibid.*, p. 14.

[3] Fred L. Whipple: "Results of Rocket and Meteor Research," *Bulletin of the American Meteorological Society*, Vol. 33, January 1952, p. 25.

Dr. Fred Whipple, the Harvard astronomer, who wrote the above quotation, was referring to two independent sets of measurements of upper atmosphere temperatures, conducted by different investigators using different methods, one in the daytime and one at night, which he said gave *"excellent* agreement."[1]

It may also be possible that the vapor blanket could have been in the upper troposphere, *below* the stratosphere. The additional water vapor would have warmed not only the earth's surface but also the atmosphere more uniformly.

An increase of water vapor . . . would raise the temperature of the earth's surface . . . and would increase the temperature of the air at a height of four or five miles more than that at the surface, and so lessen the decrease of temperature with height.[2]

If the canopy were located at a high elevation in the lower atmosphere, not only would the increased temperatures at that level permit its maintenance but, as Fred Hoyle pointed out,[3] condensation nuclei would not rise to that level. And regardless of temperature, water vapor cannot condense unless nuclei of condensation are available.

Condensation does not begin until the water vapor has a suitable surface on which to condense. The surface of condensation is called a *nucleus of condensation,* and the process of introducing these surfaces into a vapor phase is called *nucleation. . . .*

All evidence to date points to sea salt as being the principal nucleus of condensation, with sulfurous and nitrous acids playing a secondary role.[4]

As a matter of fact, it would seem that the vapor blanket could possibly be substantially lower than 20,000 feet without being precipitated. Since the atmospheric temperatures would be very much more uniform than at present, both vertically and latitudinally, there would be very little atmospheric turbulence. Consequently the higher levels of the troposphere would be virtually free of salt particles and other potential condensation nuclei. Thus such a vapor canopy could be maintained indefinitely, until something happened to mix it with the cold gases of the stratosphere and to supply meteoric or other particles for nucleation.

[1] *Ibid.*
[2] C. E. P. Brooks: *Climate Through the Ages* (2nd Ed., New York, McGraw-Hill, 1949), p. 115.
[3] See p. 255.
[4] John C. Johnson: *Physical Meteorology* (New York, Wiley, 1954), pp. 206-207.

When finally that "something" happened, whatever it was—possibly the passage of the earth through a meteorite swarm or the sudden extrusion of large amounts of volcanic dust into the air—the vapor blanket was condensed and precipitated. As the Scripture describes it, "the flood-gates of heaven were opened," and torrents of rain fell all around the earth for forty days and forty nights!

OVERFLOWED WITH WATER

We have seen that most of the earth's crust, up to and including some of the Proterozoic strata, was probably formed during the period of Creation. Also, there must have been a primeval mantle of soil supporting the luxuriant plant life of the antediluvian earth. During the relatively brief period between the Fall and the Deluge, however, probably few deposits were formed, and those that were formed were most likely swept away by the waters of the Flood, together with the original soils and other unconsolidated materials. And it is highly probable that many of even the primeval crustal rocks were broken up, swept away, mixed and eventually redeposited by the tremendous hydrodynamic forces of the floodwaters, as well as by the volcanic and other phenomena accompanying them.

For one thing seems absolutely certain, if the Biblical record of the Flood is true, as we strongly affirm it to be; the Noachian Deluge was a cataclysm of absolutely enormous scope and potency and must have accomplished an immense amount of geologic work during the year in which it prevailed over the earth. There seems no reasonable alternative to either rejecting the Bible account as of no historical value whatever or else acknowledging the fact that many of the earth's present rock strata must have been produced by the Flood! We have already shown that the Bible quite clearly and emphatically teaches the historic fact of a global Flood, and it should be immediately obvious that if such a global Flood ever occurred, it must have been the greatest geomorphic agent acting on the earth since Creation itself! Anyone who can conceive of a worldwide flood as being "tranquil"[1] and geologically impotent, should as easily be able to equate east with west and black with white!

[1] See discussion, pp. 97-106.

The Destructive Power of Modern River Floods

Even the relatively trivial floods of modern experience exert tremendous erosive and tractive forces. Sir Cyril S. Fox, Director of the Geological Survey of India and a man of long experience with floods and their effects, says:

The astonishing power exerted by a flood of rushing water, both in scouring and in transporting material, is rarely fully appreciated even today.[1]

Sir Cyril quotes from a striking account of floods in northeast India:

P. D. Oldham has given a brief description of the carrying power of flood streams in the Cherrapunji (Assam) region, which is subject to heavy rain. He wrote: ". . . the water had risen only thirteen feet above the level at which it had stood a few days previously; the rush was tremendous—huge blocks of rock measuring some feet across were rolled along with an awful crashing, almost as easily as pebbles in an ordinary stream. In one night a block of granite, which I calculated to weigh upwards of 350 tons, was moved for more than a hundred yards; while the current was actually turbid with pebbles of some inches in size, suspended almost like mud in the rushing stream. . . ." In that region there now is practically no soil on the Cherrapunji plateau, and it is also noticeable that water carrying much mud in suspension (and its increased density therefrom) carries larger stones than clear water, for equal velocities.[2]

One must visualize flood action like this, not in a limited locale but worldwide, not for a few days or hours but continuing for weeks and months, to appreciate the character of the Biblical Deluge. On the other side of the world, from Utah, comes an account of another modern flood:

On this area the 1930 floods destroyed houses, broke in the east wall of the schoolhouse, and deposited debris to a depth of several feet, including boulders of all sizes up to 20 tons in weight. Some larger boulders were moved about 1000 feet from the canyon's mouth down a 4° gradient. Several of these weigh from 75 to 100 tons each, and two, previously mentioned, weigh 150 and 210 tons respectively. The deep gorges freshly excavated for the full length of the flooded canyons are no less impressive than the flood depositions in the valley. Cuts were made in typical canyon fill—

---

[1] Cyril S. Fox: *Water* (New York, Philosophical Library, 1953), p. xiv.
[2] *Ibid.,* p. 70.

in places to a depth of 70 feet. Long, continuous stretches of bedrock were exposed on the bottom of the channels. The canyon fill consisted of debris brought from further upstream by running water, and of materials collected from the adjacent canyon slopes. Included were boulders ranging up to 50 feet in diameter.[1]

A graphic impression of the powers of flood waters is obtained from such photographs as in Figure 25. As far as the ordinary smaller materials—sands and silts and clays—are concerned, rivers in flood stage normally excavate their beds to tremendous depths, carrying vast quantities of sediment along in suspension or along the bed, to be redeposited downstream when the flood subsides. The action of the great Colorado River of the western United States is not untypical:

> From the above description it is clear that when the Colorado River was in flood it was acting on the solid rock of its bed down to a depth of over 120 feet from the top of the flood water, but that as the current subsided it first filled up the inner and deep canyon and then covered the rock platform, thus giving no idea of the violence of its section in depth, where it could flush with great force more than 115 feet of sand-filled cuttings. Without such proofs few engineers would be inclined to believe that silting follows sand movements down to depths of 50 and 100 feet below normal bed level at each time of high flood.[2]

If this kind of activity occurs during present-day floods, what must have been the tremendous quantities of sediment eroded and transported when rain poured forth over all the earth for at least forty days without stopping! Lest anyone should object that the heavy stands of antediluvian vegetation may have prevented serious erosion by the floodwaters, we cite the following from the Yale conservationist, Dr. Paul Sears:

> It is often said that deforestation causes floods. This is a half-truth. Water flows faster, and in greater amounts, off of cleared land than off of forested land—up to a certain point. When rainfall exceeds the critical amount, especially on shallow soils, such as we have in New England, not even forests will hold it back.[3]

---

[1] R. W. Bailey, C. L. Forsling, and R. J. Becraft: "Floods and Accelerated Erosion in Northern Utah," U. S. Dept. of Agric. Misc. Publ. 196, 1934, p. 9.

[2] Cyril S. Fox, *op. cit.*, p. 111.

[3] Paul B. Sears: "Natural and Cultural Aspects of Floods," *Science*, Vol. 125, April 26, 1957, p. 807.

Not only would the great volumes of water have eroded the river beds to great depths but with long-continued soaking and pounding, with the ground everywhere saturated and weakened, sooner or later the vegetation would have been uprooted from the soil and borne away, leaving no protection at all for the exposed soils.

Destructive Power of Ocean Waves

And it must not be forgotten that the flood damages were due not only to the torrential rains pouring from the skies. There were also great volcanic upheavals, evidently unleashing vast amounts of juvenile waters and creating profound disturbances in all the earth's seas and waterways. Great tidal waves undoubtedly were generated in prodigious numbers, as the imprisoned waters progressively escaped through crustal fractures all around the earth, when "the fountains of the great deep were broken up."

Even the action of ordinary waves and littoral currents can, over relatively short periods of time, accomplish tremendous amounts of sedimentary work along coast lines, when something happens to change the sediment balance normally existing.

Any unusual conditions, whether natural or man-made, may upset the balance in such a way that what has been a very stable beach may quickly show significant erosion or accretion. For example, the hurricanes that at times sweep the Atlantic and Gulf Coasts of the United States frequently produce pronounced changes on the affected beaches.[1]

Obviously the onset of the Noachian Flood would have presented profoundly "unusual conditions" and would have immediately attacked the antediluvian beaches. And the destructive effect of ordinary storm waves is trivial compared to that of tidal waves or tsunamis, such as must have occurred with great frequency and complexity during the Deluge Period. Speaking, however, of ordinary waves, King says:

Waves are seldom more than twenty-five feet high; but violent storms may raise them to sixty feet, and there are unverified reports of even greater heights. . . . The immense striking power of a wave cannot be realized until it hits an object that cannot float with it. Waves striking the shore of Tierra del Fuego can be heard for twenty miles. Spray from a storm

[1] J. M. Caldwell: "Beach Erosion," *Scientific Monthly*, Vol. 69, October 1949, p. 432.

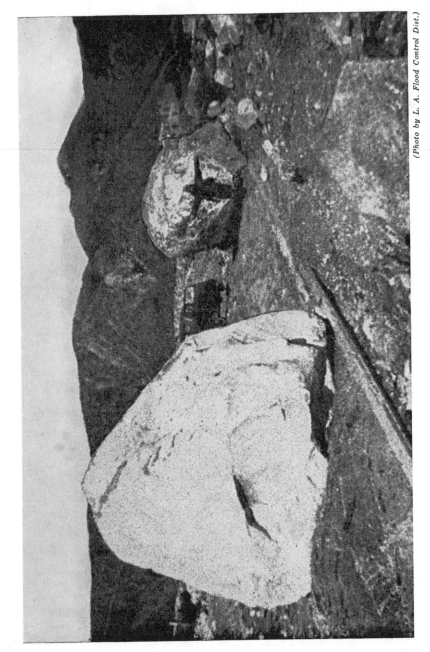

(Photo by L. A. Flood Control Dist.)

Figure 25. FLOOD DEBRIS NEAR LOS ANGELES.

wave has been hurled to the top of a lighthouse nearly 200 feet above sea level. The force of waves striking the shore can be measured, and has been found to reach three tons per square foot.[1]

The immense erosive power of such forces should be obvious. Thornbury graphically describes these powers as follows:

> Waves, particularly storm waves and tsunamis, are the most important agents of marine erosion. Smaller waves, such as those associated with surf, may carry on attrition of material and minor amounts of abrasion, but, just as a stream during a single flood may do more geologic work than it will for months or years at low-water stage, so storm waves during a short period may effect more change than ordinary waves will in months. . . . The enormous force exerted by breaking waves is attested by recorded movements of masses weighing many thousands of pounds. Air in joints and cracks is suddenly compressed and acts as if a wedge were suddenly driven into them. Recession of the water is accompanied by a sudden expansion of air with explosive force. This driving of water into cracks not only exerts great mechanical stress but in soluble rocks may greatly accelerate solution.[2]

Willard Bascom, a leading oceanographer, tells of wind-generated waves exceeding 100 feet in height and describes some examples of the immense destructive forces that storm waves can develop.

> At Cherbourg, France, a breakwater was composed of large rocks and capped with a wall 20 feet high. Storm waves hurled 7,000 pound stones over the wall and moved 65-ton concrete blocks 60 feet. . . . At Wick, Scotland, the end of the breakwater was capped by an 800-ton block of concrete that was secured to the foundation by iron rods 3.5 inches in diameter. In a great storm in 1872 the designer of the breakwater watched in amazement from a nearby cliff as both cap and foundation, weighing a total of 1350 tons, were removed as a unit and deposited in the water that the wall was supposed to protect. He rebuilt the structure and added a larger cap

[1] Thomson King: *Water* (New York, Macmillan Co., 1953), p. 49.
[2] W. D. Thornbury: *Principles of Geomorphology* (New York, Wiley, 1954), p. 432.

FIGURE 25.

Further evidence of the transporting capacity of flood waters is shown in this picture, indicating boulders and debris deposited in a residential area following a rainstorm in the San Gabriel Mountains. Measurements of erosion and debris production in this area have revealed magnitudes of up to 100,000 cu. yds. of debris eroded and redeposited from each square mile of the watershed, in a single brief flood! ("Control of Flood Debris in San Gabriel Area," by Paul Baumann, *Civil Engineering*, Vol. 14, April 1944, p. 144).

weighing 2600 tons, which was treated similarly by a storm a few years later.[1]

Probably the most destructive of all waves is that form of tidal wave known as the tsunami. Actually, these are not true tidal waves, although commonly called so, but are caused by submarine earthquakes, volcanic eruptions or slides. They have been known to attain velocities of 400 or more miles per hour and heights of 130 feet[2] and to travel extraordinary distances. The great Krakatoa earthquake, in the East Indies in 1883, created immense waves at least 100 feet high and traveling up to 450 miles per hour inundating neighboring islands and drowning nearly 40,000 people. A tsunami from this quake was still two feet high as it passed Ceylon and nine inches high at Aden beyond the Arabian Sea! In 1946, a tsunami originating in a quake in the Aleutian Island region traveled 470 miles per hour across the Pacific, creating a 19-foot high "tidal" wave on the shores of Hawaii, with great destruction. A wave that swept across the Bay of Bengal in 1876 left 200,000 people dead.[3]

Even more recently, tsunamis generated by the destructive Chilean earthquakes of 1960 have demonstrated once again the power available in this type of wave. A news account states:

> The disastrous series of earthquakes that struck Chile late in May has brought death and destruction to countries on the perimeter of the entire Pacific. In the wake of the earthquakes, great tidal waves—up to 50 ft. high and traveling at jet speeds of 525 miles an hour—caused extensive damage to Pacific ports, from Japan to California and from Alaska to New Zealand. The waves that wrecked the coastal villages of Japan a third of the way around the world were 32 ft. high. In both Japan and Hawaii, which was struck by four waves, there was serious loss of life and extensive property damage.[4]

And it is just this most destructive of all types of waves which must have been produced during the Biblical Flood by the "breaking-up of the fountains of the great deep"! Furthermore, this break-up, with all its attendant destructiveness, apparently continued from the first

---

[1] Willard Bascom: "Ocean Waves," *Scientific American,* Vol. 201, August 1959, p. 80.

[2] P. H. Kuenen: *Marine Geology* (New York, Wiley, 1950), p. 80.

[3] Willard Bascom, *op. cit.,* pp. 81-83.

[4] "Chile Earthquake Spreads Disaster Around the World", *Civil Engineering,* Vol. 30, July 1960, p. 88.

day of the Flood (Genesis 7:11) through the same period[1] as the great rains from heaven, until both were stopped by God (Genesis 8:2).

Sedimentation and Fossilization During the Flood

The picture then is of awesome proportions. The vast "waters above the firmament" poured forth through what are graphically represented in the Scriptures as the "floodgates of heaven," swelling the rivers and waterways and initiating the erosion and transportation of vast inland sediments. At the same time, waters and probably magmas were bursting up through the fractured fountains of the great subterranean deep. In the seas, these "fountains" not only belched forth their waters and volcanic materials, but the corresponding earth displacements must have been continually generating powerful tsunamis.

This tremendous complex of forces, diastrophic and hydrodynamic, must beyond any question have profoundly altered the antediluvian topography and geology of the earth's crust. Powerful currents, of all directions and magnitudes and periods, must have been generated and made to function as agents of immense eroding, transporting, and depositional potency. Under the action of this combination of effects, almost any sort of deposit or depositional sequence becomes possible and plausible. An immense variety of sediments must finally have been the result, after the Flood had run its course.

And yet, in spite of the complexity of physical agencies involved and the resulting variety of formations and sediments, certain general semblances of order might be anticipated in the deposits when the waters abated. The creatures of the deep sea bottoms would universally be overwhelmed by the toxicity and violence of the volcanic emanations and the bottom currents generated thereby and would in general be mixed with the inorganic materials simultaneously dislodged from the bed, transported and eventually redeposited on the bed.

In similar fashion, the fish and other organisms living nearer the surface would subsequently be entrapped by either materials washing down from the land surface or the shallow coastal sea bottoms or by materials upwelling from the depths. Again these sediments would be

---

[1] Both the rains and upheavals apparently continued for at least 150 days. See discussion, pp. 4, 9, 127.

transported and redeposited either on the sea bottom or occasionally on top of other sediments already laid down.

On the land, the raging rivers would carry great quantities of detritus seaward, occasionally entombing animals or reptiles, together with great rafts of vegetation. These would normally be deposited finally in some more or less quiescent reach of stream or finally in the sea on top of other deposits or perhaps on the exposed bottom itself.

As far as land animals and man were concerned, their greater mobility would have enabled most of them to escape temporarily to higher ground as the waters rose, only occasional individuals being swept away and entombed in the sediments. Eventually, of course, the floodwaters overtook even those who had fled to the highest elevations, but in most cases these men and animals would not be buried but simply drowned and then carried about by the waters on or near the surface until finally decomposed by the elements. Certain spectacular exceptions to this rule might occur when groups of animals, huddled together in a cave on some hillside or on a summit, were swept away by a sudden, sediment-laden wave of water to be buried en masse at another place.

Even after the first forty days, when the greatest of the rains and upheavals diminished, the Scriptures say that the waters "prevailed" upon the earth for one hundred and ten days longer. This statement—together with what one might infer from the prevalent unique meteorologic conditions during that period, with a universal ocean still reacting to the great dynamic imbalance so recently imposed on the earth—would certainly imply that extensive hydraulic and sedimentary activity continued for a long time, with many earlier flood deposits perhaps re-eroded and reworked. Some sediments may well have been transported and deposited several times before reaching their final resting-place.

EMERGENCE OF THE LANDS

New Atmospheric Movements

And now the Bible account speaks of a tremendous wind (Genesis 8:1). This was evidently no ordinary wind, as its purpose and result are said to have been to cause the waters to "return from off the earth." Although it would certainly very materially have accelerated the evaporation process, it is quite evident that evaporation alone could never return all the water that had fallen during the forty days back to the skies, not to mention the juvenile waters that had poured forth through the fountains of the great deep. The only way in which land could now appear again would be for a tremendous orogeny to take place. Mountains must rise and new basins must form to receive the great overburden of water imposed upon the earth. This process is described in Psalm 104:5-9.[1]

Prior to the Flood, the earth's protective canopy of water vapor had maintained a global climate of essentially uniform temperature. Since temperature differentials are the chief cause of wind movements and storms, we may infer that storms and strong winds, as well as strong rains, were unknown before the Flood. But with the condensation and precipitation of the canopy, the protection was removed. Air masses near the poles began to cool and those near the equator to heat more intensively, and soon a great complex of atmospheric motions began.

Even today, meteorologists are uncertain about the nature of the atmospheric circulation and its components, so that it would only be speculation to attempt to describe the winds as they developed for the first time on the water-shrouded globe. This, as well as the fundamental importance of the temperature differentials is indicated by Starr:

> But control of the weather and climate now looks even more difficult than had been thought. A complex of random, unmanageable processes seems to govern our weather patterns. To effect any general change would require nothing less than altering the Equator-Pole heat differential or the rate of the earth's rotation.[2]

But it does appear reasonable to conclude that the new temperature differentials then being established would result in terrific winds all over the globe, with the major component being from the poles toward the equator with much evaporation and subsequent re-precipitation. And such winds would again initiate violent waves on the universal ocean[3] with renewed sedimentary action in many places.

---

[1] See page 122.

[2] Victor P. Starr: "The General Circulation of the Atmosphere," *Scientific American*, Vol. 195, December 1956, p. 45.

[3] The height and spacing of wind-generated waves increase with the wind speed and the "fetch length;" that is, the open, unrestricted nautical distance along which the wind can blow across the water surface. (See C. L. Bretschneider: "Hurricane De-

Isostatic Readjustments

Presumably before the Flood, the earth's crust was in a state of general equilibrium, although the great pressures of the fluids locked within the "great deep" made it a *precarious* state of equilibrium. The principle of isostasy ("equal weights") requires that, at some datum level deep in the crust, pressures due to superincumbent materials be everywhere constant in order for crustal equilibrium to be maintained. Thus, regions of high topography must be regions of low density and vice versa. Probably there were no very substantial regional differences in land densities before the Flood, and correspondingly no very large regional differences in elevation. Mountains were relatively low and ocean beds relatively shallow as compared with present conditions.

But with the Deluge, several factors combined to destroy the antediluvian geophysical equilibrium. Great masses of water and other materials were ejected from below the surface. On the other hand, equally or more voluminous masses of sediments were formed and deposited in great beds, possibly often corresponding to what are now called geosynclines. A general redisposition of the prediluvian topography took place, placing the crust for a time in a state of isostatic instability.

The details of what must have taken place remain to be worked out and probably cannot be deduced at this time. Intense compressive stresses must have been generated in the crust, as previous surface materials began to settle into the voids left by the escaping magmas and water.[1] The less competent and less dense, newly-deposited sediments would have been easily deformed and uplifted under the action of such forces. The heavier simatic materials would tend to sink, forming deep basins, the lighter materials therefore rising and forming the continents.

sign Wave Practices," *Journal of the Waterways and Harbors Division of the American Society of Civil Engineers,* Vol. 83, Paper 1238, May 1957, p. 3). With a boundless ocean and a sudden great air movement from the poles to the equator, unimpeded by frictional resistance afforded by land surfaces, the potential wave size during this period would seem to be enormous.

[1] J. T. Wilson says: "It is believed that contraction of the earth due to its emission of lava and volcanic gases provides a tentative theory for the building of mountains and continents which is capable of explaining more of the details of these features than any other theory yet proposed" ("Geophysics and Continental Growth," *American Scientist,* Vol. 47, March 1959, p. 23).

The trigger mechanism that set in motion the forces of isostatic readjustment may well have been the great wind, with the gigantic waves and strong currents certainly generated thereby, as the Biblical accounts (Genesis 8:1-3 and Psalm 104:5-9) seem to imply. In any event, whatever the precise nature of the cause or causes, the process by which the lands were uncovered, the mountains rising and the basins sinking, is said to have begun on the seventeenth day of the seventh month (see discussion above, pp. 5-7). By the first day of the tenth month "were the tops of the mountains seen" (Genesis 8:5).

It is needless to point out that, during this period of orogeny, once again great quantities of erosion and deposition of sediments took place. Especially predominant would have been the phenomenon of turbidity flows. The newly-deposited sediments were still relatively soft and unconsolidated, and the imposition of new gradients and currents over them when the lands began to rise would have immediately induced scouring action on a large scale. The mixture of water and mud thus formed would, in flowing downslope, itself cause tremendous submarine erosion and ultimate redeposition. The great sedimentary competency of these turbidity currents, or density currents as they are also called, has only been appreciated in recent years but has been adequately demonstrated both by field data and laboratory studies.

> When large volumes of sediment start to slide downslope, it is thought that, in many cases, the mass of sediment becomes mixed with water to form a density current. . . . Laboratory and theoretical studies, largely by Kuenen, a Dutch geologist, have shown that the concept of density currents is valid. . . . The Grand Banks earthquake of 1929 apparently triggered off a great slide which rapidly became mixed with bottom water to become a density current. This current then flowed downslope at speeds up to 50 miles per hour and, for 13 hours, broke submarine telegraph cables successively, downslope, out to a distance of 300 miles. The current ran out onto the abyssal plain a distance of 600 miles, where it deposited sediments up to one meter in thickness.[1]

With the appearance of the lands and the going-forth of Noah and the other inhabitants of the Ark, the Flood period proper may be said to have ended. But it must not be thought that the present balance

[1] Edwin L. Hamilton: "The Last Geographic Frontier, the Sea Floor," *Scientific Monthly*, Vol. 85, December 1957, p. 298. Also see B. C. Heezen: "The Origin of Sub-Marine Canyons," *Scientific American*, Vol. 195, August 1956.

between the earth's various hydrological and physiographic factors was attained immediately. Undoubtedly effects of these profound changes in the earth's surface and atmosphere were felt for centuries and perhaps are still being felt in some degree. Some of these probable after-effects of the Flood will be outlined in a later section.

We have briefly sketched some of the inferences that can be derived from the Biblical record of the Deluge itself, as to the nature of the geologic action accompanying it. That it was a tremendous event, absolutely without parallel in all the earth's geologic history, with sedimentation and fossilization on a scale never approached before or since, seems an inescapable conclusion if the Bible is a reliable witness, as we of course insist that it is.

THE ORDER OF THE STRATA

These deductions are subject to test at a large number of points. Some of these shall be considered now in the light of actual geologic field data, with a view to establishing the general adequacy of the Scriptural framework for organizing and harmonizing the geological data. Obviously a very substantial portion of the earth's crustal geology must be explained in terms of the Flood, if the Bible record be true.

For example, the most obvious implication of the Bible account is that a very large part of the fossiliferous deposits of the earth must be associated either with volcanism or aqueous action, especially the latter. The vast extent of such sedimentary deposits is indicated as follows:

About three-fourths, perhaps more, of the land area of the earth, 55 million square miles, has sedimentary rock as the bedrock at the surface or directly under the cover of mantle-rock. . . . The thickness of the stratified rocks ranges from a few feet to 40,000 feet or more at any one place. . . . The vast bulk of the stratified rocks is composed of shallow-water deposits.[1]

This is exactly to be expected if the waters of a universal Flood ever covered the earth. Similarly, we have already called attention to the wide geographic distribution of recent volcanic deposits, both over the lands and on the ocean beds, just as the Bible account would imply.

[1] von Engeln and Caster, *op. cit.*, p. 129.

Tectonic Origin of Continental Blocks

Another Biblical inference is that the continental blocks rose rapidly, geologically speaking, relative to the ocean basins. That is, the continental shelves, which mark the boundaries between the continental and oceanic blocks, must have been formed tectonically rather than through sedimentary action of some sort. This also seems confirmed by the physical evidence.

The theory that the continental slopes have achieved their present form as a result of fault slippage at the contact of the continental blocks with the oceanic blocks of the earth's crust seems to accord with more observed facts than do other theories.[1]

Sequence of Stratified Beds

But now we must consider the all-important question of the sequence of deposition of these stratified beds. This supposed order has been made the basis of the accepted system of geochronology and historical geology. It is the backbone of the theory of organic evolution, with its purported display of gradual development of all forms of creatures from simple beginnings, through the various geological ages, as shown in the fossils contained in the sedimentary rocks. Thus, the very plainest testimony to the great Event in which the "world that then was, being overflowed with water, perished" (II Peter 3:6) has been transformed instead into a supposed rock record of gradual organic evolution!

We have already noted, however, at some length, that this record proves extremely fragmentary and contradictory upon closer examination. It has been shown that the supposed divisions between the various systems are more often than not non-existent. We have pointed out that anything approaching the complete geologic column is never found at any one place on the earth's surface, but only one or a very few systems at most. Even those that *are* found at a given locality quite commonly have one or more important systems missing, as compared with the standard column, often without any physiographic evidence that the supposed intervening period of ero-

[1] J. V. Trumbull, John Lyman, J. F. Pepper, and E. M. Thompson: *"An Introduction to the Geology and Mineral Resources of the Continental Shelves of the Americas,* U. S. Geological Survey Bulletin 1067, 1958, p. 25.

sion or non-deposition ever really occurred. And it is not at all un-usual for strata to be found completely out of the approved order, with "old" strata resting conformably on top of "young" strata. And all of this, as we have repeatedly emphasized, bears extremely hard on the theory of uniformity and the geologic ages.

But it is just what one would expect in the light of the Biblical record! In some areas would be deposited one assemblage of sedi-ments, and in other areas entirely different assemblages depending on the source areas and directions of the depositing currents. Thus, in the tremendous complex of flows and waves and sediments with their entrapped organisms, a variety of different types of sedimentary rocks would even be laid down directly on the crystalline basement. Again quoting Dr. Spieker, of Ohio State:

> Further, how many geologists have pondered the fact that lying on the crystalline basement are found from place to place not merely Cambrian, but rocks of all ages?[1]

This seems to be a rhetorical question, because neither Spieker nor anyone else seems to attempt to answer it. It seems incapable of satis-factory explanation on the basis of orthodox geology, although Spie-ker seems somehow to think it to be evidence of extreme uniformity of geologic process in space and time. Actually, of course, it is per-fectly consistent with the Flood record.

It is interesting to note, in passing, that even if the Cambrian rocks were accepted as actually the oldest of the fossil-bearing strata, the problem of evolution would still be far from solved. As Ladd says:

> Most paleontologists today give little thought to fossiliferous rocks older than the Cambrian, thus ignoring the most important missing link of all. Indeed the missing Pre-Cambrian record cannot properly be described as a link for it is in reality, about nine-tenths of the chain of life: the first nine-tenths.[2]

[1] E. M. Spieker: "Mountain-Building Chronology and Nature of Geologic Time-Scale," *Bulletin, American Association of Petroleum Geologists,* Vol. 40, August 1956, p. 1805.

[2] H. S. Ladd: Ch. I, "Introduction," in *Treatise on Marine Ecology and Paleoe-cology,* Vol. II, Geological Society of America Memoir 67, 1957, p. 7. Similarly, T. N. George says: "Granted an evolutionary origin of the main groups of animals, and not an act of special creation, the absence of any record whatsoever of a single member of any of the phyla in the Pre-Cambrian rocks remains as inexplicable on orthodox grounds as it was to Darwin." ("Fossils in Evolutionary Perspective," *Science Progress,* Vol. XLVIII, Jan. 1960, p. 5).

Early Burial of Marine Creatures

Of course, in localities where more than one system is found exposed or revealed by well-logging or other means, it is frequently found that the lowermost strata are those containing the simpler (and therefore supposedly more ancient) organisms, usually marine organisms. This, however, does not at all evidence evolution, as commonly claimed, but rather testifies quite plainly that these marine creatures were, as would be expected, deposited first and deepest in the Deluge sediments. Two factors combine to make this a general, though by no means inviolable, rule. The sea-bottoms, both deep and shallow seas, would have been first affected by the breaking-up of the fountains of the great deep. This inference is corroborated by the fact that those strata found usually lowest in the column are marine strata, containing marine organisms. With reference to the Cambrian strata, supposedly the oldest fossiliferous strata:

At least 1500 species of invertebrates are known in the Cambrian, *all marine,* of which 60% are trilobites and 30% brachiopods.[1]

The same could largely be said of the Ordovician, Silurian, and Devonian periods, as far as their fauna are concerned, although there are evidences of continental-type flora in the latter. It is not until the Permo-Carboniferous is reached, well up in the geologic column, that the first land animals are encountered.

Hydrodynamic Selectivity of Moving Water

The other factor tending to insure the deposition of the simple marine organisms in the deepest strata is the hydrodynamic selectivity of moving water for particles of similar sizes and shapes, together with the effect of the specific gravity of the respective organisms.

The settling velocity of large particles is independent of fluid viscosity; it is directly proportional to the square root of particle diameter, directly proportional to particle sphericity, and directly proportional to the difference between particle and fluid density divided by fluid density.[2]

[1] Maurice Gignoux: *Stratigraphic Geology,* Translated from the 4th French Edition by Gwendolyn G. Woodford, (San Francisco, W. H. Freeman & Co., 1955), p. 46.

[2] W. C. Krumbein and L. L. Sloss: *Stratigraphy and Sedimentation,* (San Francisco, W. H. Freeman and Co., 1951), p. 156.

These criteria are derived from consideration of hydrodynamic forces acting on immersed bodies and are well established. In other words, moving water (or moving particles in still water) exerts "drag" forces on those bodies, which depend on the above factors. Particles which are in motion will tend to settle out in proportion mainly to their specific gravity (density) and sphericity. It is significant that the organisms found in the lowest strata, such as the trilobites, brachiopods, etc., are very "streamlined" and are quite dense. The shells of these and most other marine organisms are largely composed of calcium carbonate, calcium phosphate and similar minerals, which are quite heavy—heavier, for example, than quartz, the most common constituent of ordinary sands and gravels. These factors alone would exert a highly selective sorting action, not only tending to deposit the simpler (i.e., more nearly spherical and undifferentiated) organisms nearer the bottom of the sediments but also tending to segregate particles of similar sizes and shapes, forming distinct faunal stratigraphic "horizons" with the complexity of structure of the deposited organisms, even of similar kinds, increasing with increasing elevation in the sediments.

It is not unlikely that this is one of the main reasons why the strata give a superficial appearance of "evolution" of similar organisms in successively higher strata.[1] Of course, these very pronounced "sorting" powers of hydraulic action are really only valid statistically, rather than universally. Local peculiarities of turbulence, habitat, sediment composition, etc., would be expected to cause local variations in organic assemblages, with even occasional heterogeneous agglomerations of sediments and organisms of a wide variety of shapes and sizes. But, on the average, the sorting action is quite efficient and would definitely have separated the shells and other fossils in just such fashion as they are found, with certain fossils predominant in certain horizons, the complexity of such "index fossils" increasing with increasing elevation in the column, in at least a general way.

[1] That the appearance of evolution of even such an important index fossil as the trilobite is really only superficial is evident from the recent presidential address of C. J. Stubblefield before the Geological Society of London. Describing the origin of the various groups of trilobites as "cryptogenetic,". he says: "The classification of trilobites has attracted much attention, with far from conclusive results. . . . A well-authenticated phylogeny of the trilobite class is still elusive." (*Quarterly Journal of the Geological Society of London*, Vol. 115, Dec. 1959, p. 146).

Higher Mobility of the Vertebrates

It is reasonable also, in the light of the Flood record, to expect that vertebrates would be found higher in the geologic column than the first invertebrates. Vertebrates in general possess much greater mobility, and this factor, together with their pelagic habitats, would normally prevent their being entrapped and deposited in the deepest sediments. The simplest vertebrates, the ostracoderms, are first found, and only sparingly then, in Ordovician strata. Fishes are found in profusion in the Devonian, often in great sedimentary "graveyards," indicating violent deposition, and often in fresh-water deposits. It is obvious that fish do not normally die and become fossilized in such conditions as these but usually are either destroyed by scavengers or float on the surface until decomposed. The whole aspect of the fossil fish beds bespeaks violent burial in rapidly moving deltaic sediments.

The source of these masses of sediments in which the marine vertebrates were entombed is largely continental in nature. This, for example, is true of the most famous of the Devonian fish beds, those of the Old Red Sandstone of Great Britain and the corresponding Catskill Mountain formations in the United States. The character of these deposits seems explicable only in terms of torrential streams carrying vast quantities of sediment entering the ancient lakes or seas of the areas and overwhelming and burying fish and other aquatic creatures by the hundreds of thousands. All of this is easily understood in light of the Biblical Deluge but is hard to account for in any other fashion!

Burial of Land Animals and Plants

In other localities, and perhaps somewhat later in the period of the rising waters of the Flood, in general, land animals and plants would be expected to be caught in the sediments and buried; and this, of course, is exactly what the strata show. Of course, this would be only a general rule and there would be many exceptions, as currents would be intermingling from all directions, particularly as the lands became increasingly submerged and more and more amphibians, reptiles and mammals were overtaken by the waters. One would certainly not expect to find, in any one locality, a continuous series of all the possible types of strata; the actual deposits would depend on the local circumstances of current direction and sediment source areas and the manner in which these changed during the course of the Flood period.

In general though, as a statistical average, beds would tend to be deposited in just the order that has been ascribed to them in terms of the standard geologic column. That is, on top of the beds of marine vertebrates would be found amphibians, then reptiles and finally birds and mammals. This is in the order: (1) of increasing mobility and therefore increasing ability to postpone inundation; (2) of decreasing density and other hydrodynamic factors tending to promote earlier and deeper sedimentation, and (3) of increasing elevation of habitat and therefore time required for the Flood to attain stages sufficient to overtake them. The order is exactly what is to be expected in light of the Flood account and, therefore, gives further circumstantial evidence of the truthfulness of that account; in no sense is it necessary to say that this order is evidence of organic evolution from one stage into the next. And the fact that, although this order is generally to be expected, it is found to have many exceptions, both in terms of omissions and inversions, is also certainly to be expected in terms of Deluge events but is extremely difficult to account for logically in terms of evolution and uniformity.

It is in the Permian and Carboniferous, near the top of the Paleozoic strata, that remains of land animals are first encountered. This, therefore, marks an important stage in the onset of the Deluge waters, when the smaller and less agile of the amphibians and reptiles were overtaken and swept into the Deluge sediments.

It is probable that this fact is somehow connected with the fact that the Permo-Carboniferous rocks are those in which have been found the extensive conglomerates and striations that have been mistaken for glacial deposits. In essence this horizon represents that at which continental and oceanic sediments began to meet and commingle on a large scale. We have already shown that the ice age interpretation of these Permian deposits is inadequate; the Permian, like the other strata, indicate a worldwide warm climate. As Newell says:

The Permian of western Texas lies within what may well have been simply a pantropical province. The lack of well-defined latitudinal zonation in the boreal faunas of higher latitudes, on the other hand, suggests prevailingly mild climates well into Arctic regions. Permian faunas of the Southern Hemisphere are not particularly illuminating with respect to climatic zonation. . . .[1]

Formation of Coal Beds

It is also at this stage that we begin to encounter the vast coal measures. We have already mentioned the tremendous numbers of coal beds that exist all around the world and in most parts of the geologic column, implying unimaginably great accumulations of metamorphosed vegetable matter, and we have pointed out the utter inadequacy of the uniformitarian subsidence theory to account for these beds. The physical evidence plainly and emphatically demonstrates the fact that the coal seams are water-laid deposits, in which great agglomerations of plants were rafted down on the surface of the Deluge rivers, then conveyed back and forth on the shifting currents until finally brought to rest in some basin of deposition, to be followed by a reacting current from another direction bearing non-organic materials perhaps, then another current with a load of plant debris, and so on. The only evidences cited in favor of the peat-bog theory of coal formation, such as the upright trunks, the stigmaria, etc., can, as we have seen, equally well or better be interpreted as resulting from the nature of the rafts of vegetation being floated into their final place of deposition by flood waters. Dr. Heribert-Nilsson, after an extensive discussion of the physical and biological aspects of the coal seams and the two theories for their formation, the autochthonous (growth in place) theory and the allochthonous (water-transported) theory, concurs:

A steady autochthonous formation of the coal seams is just as improbable as was an autochthonous formation of the strata with mixed faunas and floras. This difficult situation makes it necessary to look for allochthonous processes of immense magnitude and world-wide effects.[2]

This conclusion is doubly significant in that Dr. Heribert-Nilsson, who is a botanist and paleobotanist of wide ability and long experi-

---

[1] N. D. Newell, J. K. Rigby, A. G. Fischer, A. J. Whiteman, J. E. Hickox, and J. S. Bradley: *The Permian Reef Complex of the Guadalupe Mountains Region, Texas and New Mexico,* (San Francisco, W. H. Freeman and Co., 1953), p. 185.

[2] N. Heribert-Nilsson: *Synthetische Artbildung,* p. 1198.

ence, was not attempting to defend or expound a Flood theory of geology in coming to his conclusions but was literally driven to such a conclusion by the weight of the evidence. He has attempted to explain some of these things in terms of repeated cataclysms after the manner of Cuvier, but it is obvious that his conclusion as to the manner of coal formation fits in perfectly with the Biblical Deluge.

The question may be raised as to whether the plant remains, even if water-laid in the manner supposed in the allochthonous theory, could have been metamorphosed into coal in the relatively brief period of time since the Flood. Somehow, the impression prevails that immense ages would be necessary for coal to form, even after the materials had been deposited.

This opinion is unsound, however, since the details of the carbonization process are as yet very imperfectly understood.

Consideration of sources of energy for the metamorphic processes that convert plant residues into high-rank coals leads to the conclusion that neither bacteria, hydrostatic head, nor localized high temperatures were the geologically active agencies.[1]

Thus, although bacterial activity, pressure and temperature have been generally assumed as the agents for converting peat-bog residues into coals, recent studies have demonstrated their inadequacy. Apparently the most likely agent is the application of shearing forces,[2] and these would have been quite high during the post-Deluge period of tectonic re-adjustment.

Nor would they require long ages to do the work. Stutzer has noted:

Petzoldt (1882) describes very remarkable observations which he made during the construction of a railway bridge at Alt-Breisach, near Freiburg. The wooden piles which had been rammed into the ground were compressed by overriding blocks. An examination of these compressed piles showed that in the center of the compressed piles was a black, coal-like substance. In continuous succession from center to surface was blackened, dark-brown, light-brown and finally yellow-colored wood. The coal-like substance corresponded, in its chemical composition, to anthracite, and the blackened wood resembled brown coal.[3]

[1] Irving A. Breger: "Geochemistry of Coal," *Economic Geology*, Vol. 53, November 1958, p. 823.

[2] *Ibid.*

[3] Otto Stutzer: *Geology of Coal*, (Transl. from the German, by A. C. Noe, University of Chicago Press, 1940), pp. 105-106.

Stutzer also described various experiments which had, with some degree of success, attempted to synthesize coal in the laboratory, through application of various stresses. For these and other reasons, Moore, the American coal geologist, says:

From all available evidence it would appear that coal may form in a very short time, geologically speaking, if conditions are favorable.[1]

And we submit that conditions for its formation have never been so favorable, before or since, as during the Deluge period!

The "Mesozoic" Strata and the Dinosaurs

Proceeding higher in the geologic column (though not always, or even usually, higher in actual formational superposition), we come to the extensive Mesozoic strata, including the Triassic, Jurassic and Cretaceous systems. The "index fossils" for these strata are again marine organisms, especially the ammonites. Again there are many different kinds of these and of the other characteristic marine creatures of the period, and apparently they fall into large numbers of more or less distinct "horizons," which have been used as a basis for inter-regional and even inter-continental correlation. It is probable that these zones of similar assemblages can be explained on much the same basis as the zones of similar assemblages of trilobites and brachiopods in the Paleozoic strata.

The supposedly equivalent continental strata of the Mesozoic contain probably the most interesting of all fossils, those of the great dinosaurs. The question of the sudden extinction of these powerful creatures that supposedly ruled the earth for so long is still one of the great mysteries of uniformitarian paleontology. Various theories have been suggested, such as destruction by volcanoes, changes in environments, eating of dinosaur eggs by increasing numbers of mammals, some sort of dinosaur disease epidemic, etc.

These are some of the theories that have been advanced to explain the sudden extinction of dinosaurs throughout the world. Each theory will explain the death of some dinosaurs in some places but attempts to apply any of them, or combinations of them, to worldwide extinction have failed. This dinosaur story is like a mystery thriller with the last pages torn out.

[1] E. S. Moore: *Coal* (2nd Ed., New York, Wiley, 1940), p. 143.

A most important part is missing. That is true and the paleontologist knows it. He also knows the riddle will probably never be solved.[1]

Or at least it never will be solved as long as paleontologists insist on a uniformitarian explanation! The Biblical Deluge is a quite adequate solution.[2]

Another mystery connected with the dinosaurs is the number of great dinosaur graveyards found in various parts of the world. The entombment of such numbers of such great creatures literally demands some form of catastrophic action. One such location, the Dinosaur National Monument, in Utah and Colorado, in the Morrison formation of the Jurassic, for example, has yielded remains of more than 300 dinosaurs of many different kinds.

The quarry area is a dinosaur graveyard, not a place where they died. A majority of the remains probably floated down an eastward flowing river until they were stranded on a shallow sandbar. Some of them, such as the stegosaurs, may have come from far-away dry-land areas to the west. Perhaps they drowned trying to ford a tributary stream or were washed away during floods. Some of the swamp dwellers may have mired down on the very sandbar that became their grave while others may have floated for miles before being stranded.[3]

One could hardly ask for a better description of the way in which these great reptiles were overwhelmed, drowned and buried by the Deluge waters. As far as changes within the dinosaur lines were concerned, the most conspicuous was the tendency for each group to "evolve" from small ancestors to large descendants. Dr. Colbert, probably the chief authority on dinosaurs, says:

It is interesting to note that giantism was achieved independently by various separate lines of dinosaurian evolution. Time and again in the collective history of these reptiles a phylogenetic line had its beginning with small animals and very quickly progressed to animals of large or even huge size.[4]

[1] J. M. Good, T. E. White, and G. F. Stucker: "The Dinosaur Quarry," U. S. Government Printing Office, 1958, p. 26.

[2] If representative dinosaurs were taken on the Ark (presumably young ones), then it is likely that their final extinction is accounted for by the sharp changes in climate after the Flood. On the other hand, some may have persisted for a long time, possibly accounting for the universal occurrence of "dragons" in ancient mythologies.

[3] *Ibid.*, p. 20.

[4] Edwin H. Colbert: "Evolutionary Growth Rates in the Dinosaurs," *Scientific Monthly*, Vol. 69, August 1949, p. 71.

It is not clear how much of this tendency has been inferred from actual fossil position in successive strata, but to the extent that it is based on objective field evidence, it would seem merely to result from the abilities of the larger and more mature animals to escape the floodwaters longer. This is exactly what one would expect to find, in general, in the dinosaurian sediments of the Deluge.

THE FINAL FLOOD DEPOSITS

Tertiary Stratigraphy

The Tertiary Period is popularly known as the age of mammals, because of the large numbers of mammalian fossils found in these strata. However, as with the Paleozoic and Mesozoic Eras, the divisions of the Tertiary and its stratigraphy are based primarily on marine deposits and marine organisms. The basic method of subdivision was established in a rather remarkable manner:

Sir Charles Lyell first divided the Tertiary into Eocene, Miocene, and Pliocene on the basis of percentages of living species represented in each series, there being very few in the earliest and a very large percentage in the latest series. Later the Oligocene was added by combining some of the uppermost Eocene with some of the lowermost Miocene. The still later term "Paleocene" is used by some geologists to represent a separate epoch of the Cenozoic, and by others to indicate the earliest part of the Eocene epoch.[1]

Thus the original divisions of the presumably most recent deposits were based squarely upon what amounts to the assumption of organic evolution. The chief index fossils of the Tertiary are the marine protozoa known as Foraminifera, which occur in almost innumerable species and have been found in strata all the way from the earliest Paleozoic and still exist in abundance in the present oceans.

Certain species of these small shelled animals are believed to have been rather universally distributed geographically in rather limited zones stratigraphically, which lends them an apparent validity as index fossils. Actual correlations, however, are usually made only within the range of a particular oil field or some such limited area.

[1] W. J. Miller: *An Introduction to Historical Geology* (New York, Van Nostrand, 1952), p. 359.

In their discussion of index fossils, von Engeln and Caster indicate the importance attributed to Foraminifera for identification purposes in these rocks.

> In the more recent Mesozoic, especially, and Cenozoic rocks, great dependence is modernly placed on the Foraminiferal microscopic single-cell forms, in almost innumerable species, which like the graptolites were free-floating and experienced rapid evolutionary changes. Their minute shells, properly identified, serve accordingly as index fossils to beds of only limited thickness.[1]

Recent studies, however, have cast grave doubt upon the validity of foraminiferal dating, based as it is upon the different shell forms of the "innumerable species" of these small animals. It seems now that the most gross differences in shell form can be produced by members of any one species and thus do not show either evolution or necessary differences in chronology at all. Dr. Langenheim, of the Museum of Paleontology of the University of California, says:

> Inasmuch as fossil foraminifera are of preeminent economic importance, the work of Arnold (1953, 1954) with *Allogramia laticollaris* has special interest to paleontologists. Arnold has made a complete study of the life history of this living foraminifer and has discovered, among other things, great morphologic variation within laboratory cultures. . . . Inasmuch as these forms mimic most of the basic plans of foraminiferan test morphology, it may be deduced that specific and generic concepts based on shell shape —which includes all fossil foraminifera—are based on insecure biologic criteria. . . . *Any given body form or chamber arrangement apparently must be potentially derivative from almost any ancestral type* [italics are ours]. This, of course, is of fundamental importance and indicates that a critical reevaluation of foraminiferan micropaleontology is in order.[2]

In other words, if we understand the implications of these studies correctly, any single species of foraminifer can yield tests essentially identical with those of any other species. Perhaps instead of the "innumerable species" of foraminifera there is only one! Of course, this is an overstatement, but the general implication seems valid.

But what about the apparently well-worked-out and widely applicable techniques of micropaleontological dating based on foraminifera? It seems now that the well-defined faunal zones do not actually

---

[1] von Engeln and Caster, *op. cit.,* p. 436.

[2] R. L. Langenheim, Jr.: "Recent Developments in Paleontology," *Journal of Geological Education,* Volume 7, Spring 1959, p. 7.

represent evolutionary changes, but nevertheless the zones are still there. The answer apparently is that these zones, as we have been contending all along, are due strictly to the hydrodynamic sorting action of the flood waters and sediments in which they were deposited.

The original method of subdivision of the Tertiary, that of percentages of living and extinct organisms, especially mollusks, as worked out by Lyell on the basis of the fossils found in the Paris basin,[1] is of course no longer considered definitive, but the basic terminology and divisions still persist. The Paleocene, Eocene, and Oligocene strata are now identified mainly as associated with the large foraminifera known as nummulites, of which there are many species, but the main stages of these epochs are now divided and correlated primarily on the basis of fish and mammalian faunas in equivalent strata. The same is true of the Pliocene and Miocene, in which the nummulites are no longer so predominant.

It is significant that the Tertiary deposits are usually found in more or less isolated patches, rather than in great continuous sheets as so often is true of the Paleozoic and Mesozoic beds. There are notable exceptions, however, sometimes occurring in great geosynclines. It is likely that the Tertiary deposits represent in most cases the later stages of the Deluge activities, as they are usually found either on or near the surface and superimposed over Mesozoic and/or Paleozoic strata. However, it must be recognized that in some instances Tertiary strata are found lying directly on basement rocks and sometimes found in as hard and crystalline a state as any of the presumably more ancient rock systems and even are found lying beneath these supposedly older rocks in the case of the so-called thrust faults. In these cases they are classified as Tertiary primarily because of the more "modern" fossil assemblages found in them but more likely represent either areas where these particular groups of organisms happened to be deposited earlier in the Flood chronology than they were at other localities, or else were redeposited there after earlier deposits at the sites had been removed by some of the later periods of erosion during the Flood. In the more typical cases, the Tertiary rocks must represent some later stage in the Deluge phenomena, the details of which remain to be worked out.

[1] L. S. Stamp: "Tertiary," article in *Encyclopedia Britannica*, Vol. 21, 1956, p. 973.

Mammals As Index Fossils

Fossil mammals, however, are now considered the chief indicators of the various stages of the Tertiary, despite frequent popular text-book claims as to the worldwide provenance of marine index fossils. This is noted by the expert stratigrapher, Gignoux:

> Mammals are much more independent of local conditions than marine animals. They are also valuable for establishing correlations between widely separated basins, for the species and even the genera succeed each other in rapid succession. In the Nummulitic, and elsewhere in the Tertiary, the mammalian faunas provide the only truly exact criterion for the distinction of stages.[1]

Gignoux is primarily interested in European stratigraphy, but he points out the rather remarkable procedure by which the European and American Tertiary deposits have been correlated:

> All these [American central states] formations are sometimes extremely rich in mammalian bones, so that a scale of mammalian faunas can be established, absolutely independent of the American marine faunas. But this scale can be paralleled with the European mammalian faunas and, in that way, with our marine stages. The latter being correlated with the marine fauna of the New World, it is evident that American stratigraphers can thus correlate their continental faunas and their marine stages; a curious example of a singularly indirect method of correlation.[2]

It must not be surmised from the above, however, that these mammalian deposits are precisely identified and correlated on this worldwide basis.

Notice, moreover, that the chronology of mammalian faunas, like that based on marine faunas, is valuable only within certain geographic limits.[3]

The foregoing recital of past and present criteria for subdividing the Tertiary era seems to illustrate quite clearly our contention that the orthodox concepts of historical geology are almost entirely subjective in character, based squarely on the assumption of the fact of organic evolution. The variously correlated stages and even epochs are not at all based on the evidence of physiographic superposition,

---

[1] Maurice Gignoux: *op. cit.*, p. 471.
[2] *Ibid.*, p. 538.
[3] *Ibid.*, p. 558.

but rather on the paleontologic contents of the deposits, interpreted almost entirely in terms of assumed evolutionary development.

It is significant that the most important paleontologic evidences of evolution are found in the Tertiary strata. One need only mention such famous phylogenetic series as those of the horse and the elephant to illustrate this fact. As in the case of the dinosaurs of the Mesozoic, so here the main feature of these presumed evolutionary series is that of an increase in size in the course of the ages. This phenomenon of evolutionary size increase has been considered to be so universal that it has been called "Cope's Law." Yet, as the paleontologist Simpson says:

Increase in body size is very common, a stock example being the change from eohippus to the modern horse. The phenomenon is perhaps sufficiently usual to be a rule, but the rule has many exceptions. Even in the horse family, several evolving lines became smaller rather than larger. The apparent extent of this rule has been exaggerated by students who thought it absolute and who insisted that because an earlier animal was larger than a later relative therefore it was not ancestral to the latter.[1]

Whatever may be the actual field evidences of increasing size with increasing elevation in the strata, they can once again be most easily explained in terms of greater mobility of the larger, stronger animals, and therefore their generally greater ability to retreat from the rising floodwaters and to escape being caught in the swollen streams rushing downward from the hills. There would be many exceptions to this, of course, and that is just what the strata tend to show, according to Simpson.[2]

More commonly, however, the various animals in the series (and even the classic horse series contains only a relatively small number of distinct forms, with little indication of any sort of *gradual* change between forms) are not found superposed in the strata at any one location or adjacent locations, but rather are found on the surface at scattered points around the world with the phylogenetic series then being constructed mainly on the basis of evolutionary presup-

[1] George Gaylord Simpson: "Evolutionary Determinism and the Fossil Record," *Scientific Monthly*, Vol. 71, October 1950, p. 265.

[2] To whatever extent Cope's "Law" may have applied during the formation of the fossiliferous strata, it appears that its trend is now reversed! Practically all modern plants and animals, including man, are represented in the fossil record by larger specimens than are now living, (e.g., giant beaver, saber-tooth tiger, mammoth, cave bear, giant bison, etc., etc.).

positions as to the possible relationships between these various creatures. The series thus constructed is thereupon submitted as proof positive for the evolution of the modern horse!

Uplifts of the Pliocene

It is probable that many of the later Tertiary beds, those attributed to the Miocene and Pliocene epochs, represent the deposits made during the time when the "mountains were rising, and the valleys sinking," in the final weeks of the Deluge activities. This may also be true of some of the supposed Pleistocene deposits.

The uplifts of the Pliocene are especially noteworthy and are indicated both by present beds of pre-Pliocene strata now found at high elevations and by Pliocene inter-montane deposits of such character as to demonstrate deposition by swollen streams rushing from newly-uplifted mountains.

The North American uplift is referred to as the Cascadian revolution. However, it affected not only the Cascade Mountains after which it is named but the whole of the mountain country from the Rocky Mountains westward. The diastrophism was largely epeirogenic rather than orogenic. Mountains were raised 5,000 to 10,000 feet vertically by faulting (Sierra Nevada) and upwarping (Rockies), not by folding. The Andes of South America were similarly affected, likewise the Appalachian region. Great volcanic activity was an accompaniment of this upheaving in many localities. . . .

The Pliocene upheavals of other parts of the world are referred to as developments of the Alpine revolution because they got conspicuous expression in the Alps. . . . The Himalayas acquired much of their height in the Pliocene. Pliocene and Pleistocene diastrophism is perhaps the greatest and most widespread that the earth has known since Pre-Cambrian times.[1]

Thus, these uplifts constituted truly a worldwide phenomenon, for which, as we have already pointed out, geologists have no satisfactory explanation on uniformitarian principles. But this is just what the account of the Biblical Deluge would lead us to expect in the strata and harmonizes perfectly with it. Of course, the only real basis of distinction between the earlier and later Tertiary deposits is paleontological, so that many of the physiographic evidences of uplift are also

[1] von Engeln and Caster, *op. cit.*, p. 439.

discernible in the supposed earlier Tertiary beds, the Paleocene, Eocene and Oligocene. Thus, the entire Tertiary period seems to be characterized to a considerable extent by orogenic phenomena, as well as extensive volcanism. In general, the record of the entire Tertiary and early Quaternary, especially in the continental deposits, can be reasonably interpreted as preserving the record of the last phases of the Flood, including both the final deposits attributable to the original onset of the floodwaters and also the deposits and geomorphic phenomena related to the rising of the lands and sinking of the basins that terminated the inundation. On the other hand, it may well be found eventually that some deposits originally ascribed to the Tertiary period, as well as to the Pleistocene, are actually Recent (i.e., post-Deluge) deposits. Particularly may this be true in those deposits which are relatively unconsolidated. No generalizations on this point are advisable at present; each deposit must be considered on its own local evidence.

Continuing Abnormal Conditions

But the termination of the Deluge proper, occupying a period of a little more than a year (as measured between the times Noah and his family entered and left the Ark), did not by any means mark the termination of the abnormal hydrologic and geomorphic phenomena. Almost unimaginably profound changes had taken place in the entire domain of terrestrial energetics. The precipitation of the antediluvian vapor canopy instituted a new hydrologic cycle, as well as a new cycle of seasons. A larger proportion of the earth's surface was now taken up in ocean basins and water surface areas. The pre-diluvian topography was completely changed with great mountain chains and deep basins now replacing the formerly gentle and more nearly uniform topography. Removal of the protective canopy around the earth permitted development of extreme latitudinal variations of temperature, with resulting great air movements and established climatic zones. Removal of the canopy also permitted the earth's atmosphere to be penetrated by much larger amounts of radiation of various types and perhaps also by inter-planetary gas or dust. Isostatic adjustments of the rocks and water and other materials near the earth's surface were profoundly disturbed and altered.

And it is obvious that these and other geophysical changes associated with the Flood could not have been completely accomplished and stabilized for centuries.

POST-DELUGE GEOLOGIC ACTIVITY

Freezing of Arctic Soils

The lowering of the temperature of the polar latitudes as the vapor canopy condensed and precipitated would have had immediate and important climatologic reactions. However, the initially warm temperature of the water in the polar seas, together with its continuing turbulent state, sufficed to prevent its freezing for a period of unknown, but substantial, duration. Undoubtedly the first water actually to freeze would have been that mixed in with the sediments being deposited in these regions, cut off, as it were, from the warmer temperatures and the turbulent agitation of the free water in the open seas. Thus must have been formed, at some intermediate or late stage in the Deluge period, those vast stretches of permanently frozen soils in the Arctic and sub-Arctic known as "permafrost."

Embedded in these frozen mucks of the Arctic are large numbers of fossil mammals, apparently trapped and in some cases partially frozen before the soft parts had decayed.

The extensive silty alluvium, now frozen, in central Alaska contains a numerous mammal fauna. . . . Freezing has preserved the skin and tissue of some of the mammals. The faunal list includes two bears, dire wolf, wolf, fox, badger, wolverine, saber-tooth cat, jaguar, lynx, woolly mammoth, mastodon, two horses, camel, saiga antelope, four bisons, caribou, moose, stag-moose, elk, two sheep, musk-ox and yak types, ground sloth, and several rodents. The number of individuals is so great that the assemblage as a whole must represent a rather long time [*sic*].[1]

That these mammals and the freezing of the alluvium now containing them represents a rather sharp change of climate is quite obvious:

The time of inception of permafrost remains, nevertheless, unknown. The fossil record . . . implies that in earlier Cenozoic time there could have been no permafrost in the Arctic region . . . the areas of former ice sheets bears no evident relation to the distribution of permafrost.[2]

[1] R. F. Flint: *Glacial and Pleistocene Geology* (New York, Wiley, 1957), p. 471.
[2] *Ibid.*, p. 204. J. K. Charlesworth says: "Vast herds of mammoth and other

Siberian Mammoth Beds

The richness of the Siberian mammoth deposits in the permafrost defies description. Although uniformitarian writers consistently understate the extent and abundance of these beds, even their admissions are significant:

> In this connection the extinction of the woolly mammoth in northern Eurasia should be mentioned. In Siberia alone some 50,000 mammoth tusks have been collected and sold to the ivory trade, and there are rare occurrences of whole animals preserved in frozen ground. These finds have fostered many tales of great catastrophes, for which there is no factual support.[1]

Perhaps a little less restrained estimation of the character of these deposits may be gleaned from the following:

> A certain amount (of ivory) is furnished by the vast stores of remains of prehistoric animals still existing throughout Russia, principally in Siberia in the neighborhood of the Lena and other rivers discharging into the Arctic Ocean. The mammoth and mastodon seem at one time to have been common over the whole surface of the globe. In England tusks have been dug up—for instance at Dungeness—as long as 12 feet and weighing 200 pounds. The Siberian deposits have been worked now for nearly two centuries. The store appears to be as inexhaustible as a coalfield. Some think that a day may come when the spread of civilization may cause the utter disappearance of the elephant in Africa, and that it will be to these deposits that we may have to turn as the only source of animal ivory.[2]

And the Arctic Islands north of Siberia have been described as even more densely packed with the remains of elephants and other mammals, as well as dense tangles of fossil trees and other plants, so much that the entire islands seem to be composed of organic debris. No wonder these things have "fostered tales of great catastrophes"; the wonder is that uniformitarians could possibly offer any other explanation in any seriousness! There is most certainly no modern par-

animals (the New Siberian Islands in the far north of Asia have yielded mammoth, woolly rhinoceros, musk ox, saiga antelope, reindeer, tiger, arctic fox, glutton, bear and horse among the 66 animal species) required forests, meadows and steppes for their sustenance, . . . and could not have lived in a climate like the present, with its icy winds, snowy winters, frozen ground and tundra moss the year round." (*The Quaternary Era*, Vol. II, London, Edward Arnold Co., 1957, p. 650).

[1] *Ibid.*, p. 470.

[2] Article, "Ivory," in *Encyclopedia Britannica*, Vol. 12, 1956, p. 834.

allel entombment of elephants or any other kind of mammal taking place anywhere in the modern world. It may not be quite clear as yet whether these deposits were made directly during the Deluge period or soon after, or both,[1] but it seems fairly evident that the extermination of such immense hordes of animals and their interment in what has ever since been frozen soil must be somehow explained in terms of the events accompanying just such a universal aqueous catastrophe as the Bible describes.

A remarkable recent study of these Arctic phenomena attributes them to violent catastrophes associated with the shifting of the earth's crust. The convulsions postulated by Ivan Sanderson in his theory make our visualization of the Deluge seem quite uniformitarian by comparison. For example:

A sudden mass extrusion of dust and gases would cause the formation of monstrous amounts of rain and snow, and it might even be so heavy as to cut out sunlight altogether for days, weeks, months or even years if the crustal movements continued. Winds beyond anything known today would be whipped up, and cold fronts of vast lengths would build up with violent extremes of temperature on either side. There would be forty days and nights of snow in one place, continent-wide floods in another, and roaring hurricanes, seaquakes and earthquakes bringing on landslides and tidal waves in others, and many other disturbances.[2]

Sanderson attributes the quick-freezing of those mammoths that have been preserved whole to the descent of great "blobs" of chilled

---

[1] It has occasionally been suggested that the ocean waters would have remained warm for too long a period to allow for the preservation of the soft parts of the animals, the inference being that they must have perished in some other catastrophe centuries later. However, it is doubtful that post-diluvian Siberian climates could ever have supported such vast hordes of animals.

The animals that perished in the Flood did not, of course, have to float around on the Arctic Ocean for months, but were quickly buried in the depositional silts of the flood waters. The entrapped waters in these sediments, cut off from the warm waters of the open ocean, froze rapidly, forming the "permafrost," the permanently frozen soils and subsoils of the Arctic lands, and it was in these that the mammals and other animals of the region were buried. As Charlesworth says: "The frozen mammoths are found on the timbered banks of rivers and in a soil that nearly always contains fragments of trees. Bacterial decay was hindered by the cold climate and by quick interment in fine silts" (*op. cit.,* p. 649).

On the other hand, most of the animals *did* suffer decay and thus may have been exposed for some time prior to burial. ". . . putrefaction however seems to have started immediately after the animal's death and before burial despite the small precipitation of the time." (*Ibid.*). Also, many mammoths and mastodons certainly lived during the first centuries *after* the Flood as well, before finally becoming extinct or modified to their present forms.

[2] Ivan T. Sanderson: "Riddle of the Frozen Giants," *Saturday Evening Post,* January 16, 1960, p. 83.

volcanic gases, first shot up towards the stratosphere, then rapidly falling and expelling the ground air violently outward radially. Others were overcome by the intense winds and' floods, their bones commingled with hosts of other animals as now found in Alaska and other places.

This is exactly the state of affairs we find in Alaska, where the mammoths and other animals, with one or two significant exceptions, were all literally torn to pieces while still fresh. Young and old alike were cast about, mangled and then frozen. There are also, however, other areas where the animals are mangled, but had time to decompose before being frozen; and still others where they decomposed down to bones and were then either frozen or not. Beyond these again, there are similar vast masses of animals, including whole families or herds, all piled together into gulleys and riverbeds and other holes, but where only bones remain.[1]

It is interesting that the same author thirteen years previously had written on the same subject, and at that time had followed the usual uniformitarian viewpoint that the mammoths had fallen into holes and gulches or had drowned in river floods, and that the reason for their extinction was a low birth rate! Further study, however, has convinced him that such explanations were wholly inadequate, and he has been driven to the geologically heretical concept of catastrophism as the necessary answer. Rather than return to Biblical catastrophism, however (he had previously written: "The Biblical theory that the Deluge was the agency by which these animals were killed was in due course demolished by simple logic and modern rationalization"[2]), he has sought a naturalistic explanation in terms of Hapgood's recent shifting-crust theory, previously referred to.[3]

At any rate, it is transparently obvious that catastrophism of a very high order is alone sufficient to account for such things as these.

The greatest riddle, however, is when, why and how did all these assorted creatures, and in such absolutely countless numbers, get killed, mashed up and frozen into this horrific indecency?[4]

We submit that the answer to the riddle must be found in terms of the Genesis Flood.

[1] *Loc. cit.* Sanderson is a field zoologist and author of numerous volumes on wild life.
[2] Ivan T. Sanderson: "The Riddle of the Mammoth," *Saturday Evening Post*, December 7, 1946.
[3] See above, p. 141, note #3.
[4] Sanderson, *op. cit.* (1960), p. 82.

THE GLACIAL PERIOD

Onset of the Ice Age

And now begins another aftermath of the Deluge, of tremendous significance. As the modern cycle of evaporation, atmospheric turbulence and vapor transportation, and condensation and precipitation became established, snow began to fall, quite possibly for the first time in earth's history. As we have already seen, there is strong evidence that the climate of the entire world prior to the Flood was uniformly mild and pleasant. This snow, falling primarily in the arctic and antarctic regions, was of course derived via the hydrologic cycle from the waters which only recently were covering the earth. Great amounts of snow also accumulated in the mountains which had just been uplifted.

In this way, large amounts of water were removed from the oceans and stored in the polar regions in the form of great ice caps, which in some instances are believed by glacial geologists to have attained the immense size of continental ice sheets thousands of feet thick and thousands of square miles in area. This agency thus combined with the agency of orogeny to cause the retreat of the globe-encircling waters off the continents.

We need not discuss here the evidences for and against the idea that such ice sheets have actually existed in recent geologic times. They constitute the primary characteristic of what is called the Pleistocene Epoch, and are universally accepted by modern geologists. Since the onset of a cold period is also strongly implied by our deductions from the Biblical description of the Deluge, we do not take issue with the accepted uniformitarian geology at this point.[1]

[1] This is not to say that we necessarily exclude other possible explanations of the evidences for supposed continental ice sheets. As pointed out previously (pp. 245-249), many of the evidences for ice sheets such as tills, striations, etc., can be interpreted as well or better in terms of catastrophic diluvial action. This could easily be true of other supposed glacial features such as kames, eskers, erratic boulders, etc. as well.

Glacial geologists have never answered the cogent criticisms of Sir Henry Howorth, President of the Archaeological Institute of Great Britain near the close of the nineteenth century, who amassed a tremendous amount of evidence that most of the supposed ice-sheet deposits may have been formed by a great flood sweeping down from the north. See especially his works, *The Glacial Nightmare and the Flood,*

However it seems that uniformitarianism is a singularly inadequate term to describe a system of geology that must interpret its presumably *most recent and plainest records* in terms of such a tremendous and uniquely catastrophic event as that of a great complex of continental ice sheets! The present is thus *not* the key to even the most immediate geologic past; our present valley glaciers and even the ice caps of Greenland and Antarctica are hardly to be compared with the supposed ice sheets of the Pleistocene.

Ice-Age Theories

As evidence that the Ice Age constitutes a catastrophe that is utterly inexplicable in terms of present processes, one need only recall again the fact that there are dozens of hypotheses that have been advanced attempting to explain its cause and mechanism; all have had grave defects and none has yet been generally accepted. Probably the most widely adopted theory at present is the "solar-topographic" hypothesis of the Yale glacial geologist, Dr. R. F. Flint. This theory explains the glaciations in terms of the worldwide mountain uplifts at the close of the Tertiary, combined with assumed fluctuations in incoming solar radiation. But Flint admits, after setting forth at some length his hypothesis:

> However, changes in the composition and turbidity of the atmosphere and changes in the earth's axis and orbit may have been factors.[1]

In other words, all sorts of non-uniform causes may be or must be invoked to provide a sufficient explanation. New theories appear in the literature fairly frequently, but each in turn seems quickly to be demolished by the ensuing criticisms.

The Biblical Deluge, however, obviously offers an eminently satisfactory explanation. The combined effect of the uplift of the conti-

Vols. I and II, 1895, and *Ice or Water*, Vols. I and II, 1905, both published in London by Sampson Low, Marston Searle, and Risington, but now out of print.

Howorth was not defending Genesis, in which he was not a believer, but only was concerned to show the scientific inadequacy of the glacial theory. It is perhaps illuminating to record the experience of one of the authors several years ago in the library of the University of Minnesota's outstanding Department of Geology. Howorth's massive work *Ice or Water* was found on the shelves and was borrowed for study . . . the first time in the forty-odd years of its residence there that it had ever been checked out or (judging from the numerous page-pairs still not cut apart from each other) even opened!

[1] Flint, *op. cit.*, p. 509.

nents and mountain-chains and the removal of the protective vapor blanket around the earth could hardly have failed to induce great snow and ice accumulations in the mountains and on the land areas near the poles. And these glaciers and ice caps must have continued to accumulate and spread until they reached latitudes and altitudes at which the marginal temperatures caused melting rates in the summers adequate to offset accumulation rates in the winters.

The total amount of water locked up in these great glaciers during their greatest extent is not known as yet, but it may have been very great. The main evidence of this fact is in the greatly lowered sea levels of the Ice Age. In the past decade a large amount of evidence has been amassed to show that ocean levels were at least 400 feet lower than at present,[1] possibly much more, as shown by such features as the continental shelves, sea-mounts, submerged canyons and terraces, etc.

The Flood and the Glacial Period

It has been argued that, once an ice sheet got started, it would probably grow rapidly and extensively.[2] This would perhaps be possible in the years immediately following the Deluge. An abundant supply of moisture, strong polar winds, lowered polar temperatures due both to removal of the thermal vapor blanket and probable dense accumulation of volcanic dust particles in the atmosphere, newly uplifted mountains, essentially barren topography of the denuded lands: all these and possibly other factors could have contributed to the rapid accumulation and growth of the ice sheets. These factors are all legitimately deduced from the record of the Flood and would be quite sufficient to explain the Ice Age. The catastrophic nature thereof, however, will of course be unacceptable to many geologists.

Although extraordinary or even catastrophic events may have caused the ice ages and their oscillations, it is nevertheless true that the ideal theory ought [*sic*] to fit within the framework of uniformitarian principles.[3]

[1] Richard J. Russell: "Instability of Sea Level," *American Scientist,* Vol. 45, Dec., 1957, pp. 414-430.

[2] C. E. P. Brooks, *Climate Through the Ages* (2nd Ed., McGraw-Hill, 1949), pp. 31-45.

[3] W. L. Stokes: "Another Look at the Ice Age," *Science,* Vol. 122, October 28, 1955, p. 815.

Nevertheless the Flood theory satisfactorily meets the requirements for a Glacial Age mechanism.

The ideal theory must be prepared to explain simultaneous glaciations over the entire earth. . . . Last but not least, the theory must explain the greatest paradox of all—the evidence of cold and ice existing and increasing simultaneously with conditions that favored accelerated evaporation and precipitation.[1]

In general, the various aspects of glacial and Pleistocene geology as commonly held by geologists are quite in harmony with our deductions from the Biblical accounts. Some of the larger and more indurated formations attributed to the Pleistocene in the non-glaciated areas are perhaps best grouped with the later Tertiary deposits, as formed during the last stages of the Flood, with the effects of uplift involved. But most of the so-called Pleistocene deposits can be accepted as post-Deluge, associated with the continental glaciers[2] or with the equivalent events in unglaciated regions, and can be accepted substantially as interpreted by glacial geologists.

It may be objected that a Flood-induced glaciation does not account for the four glacial stages which are quite generally accepted as composing the entire Pleistocene Glacial Epoch. Glacial geologists believe that each of the four stages was separated by a warm period comparable to that of the present, or perhaps even warmer. A glaciation such as we have envisioned as brought on by the Deluge would more likely be one event, not four separate events. In fact, it is uncertain what could have terminated the Ice Age at all, once it got started.

The Theory of Multiple Glaciations

It is admitted that it is difficult to account for the four stages on the basis of our present explanation. But it is also true that it is equally difficult to account for the four stages on the basis of any of the other glacial theories that have been devised. The usual recourse

---

[1] *Ibid.*, p. 815.

[2] On the other hand, the supposed ice-sheet deposits may have been largely formed by extensive floods caused by the abnormal meteorologic and hydrologic conditions resulting from the Deluge, persisting perhaps for many years. However, except for the time-factor, the standard geological concept of continental glaciation does not appear to conflict with Scripture, so we accept it as at least a working hypothesis.

is simply to attribute it all to fluctuations in solar radiation, but this is obviously entirely speculative. The most recent authoritative evaluation of the subject by Opik, admits this:

> More difficult is the question of the succession of several glaciations during one glacial epoch. The phenomenon seems to be of great complexity, corresponding to a perpetual variation of solar radiation according to various cycles and amplitudes, of which perhaps the sunspot cycle is one.[1]

Even more recently, Opik, who is an astronomer rather than a geologist, says:

> These fluctuations seem to be worldwide and have been most difficult to understand. My own guess is that they represent a kind of "flickering" of the disturbance in the sun—like a candle flame blown by the wind.[2]

If fluctuations in solar radiation provide the correct explanation for the glacial maxima and minima during the Ice Age, they can do so as well for the Flood theory as for any other. In either case, there must have been some worldwide event to bring on the first glacial maximum, making effective the solar fluctuations which presumably had been operating in the same way previously without causing the glaciations. The Flood provides just such an explanation.

The Evidence for Only One Glaciation

As a matter of fact, the reason that it is so difficult to account theoretically for the four glacial stages may be simply that they never existed. It should not be thought that the evidence for the three earlier stages is the same as that for the last. The latter is found in nearly all the present surface features of the topography in the glaciated regions—the moraines, the drumlins, eskers, striations and grooves, etc. But these are found only in connection with the supposed last glacial maximum and its retreat, the so-called Wisconsin stage.

The earlier stages—in retrograde order, the Illinoian, Kansan and Nebraskan—are evidenced mainly by a deposit of "gumbotil," supposedly a very mature and weathered clay soil containing small stones. It is explained that these gumbotils are the weathered rem-

---

[1] Ernst J. Opik: "Ice Ages," in *The Earth and Its Atmosphere*, edited by D. R. Bates, (New York, Basic Books, Inc., 1957), p. 172.
[2] Ernst J. Opik: "Climate and the Changing Sun," *Scientific American*, vol. 198, June 1958, p. 89.

nants of former till deposits (a till is an unstratified deposit of gravel, sand and clay which is considered evidence of glacial origin). The apparent depth of leaching of carbonates in these soils has been used as the chief basis of estimating their age of formation.

Not only are the earlier tills usually devoid of any of the typical glacial formations characterizing the last one, but also the latter shows no evidence of gumbotil formation as in the earlier ones. As Flint says:

> As indicated in Chapter 12 the strongly differentiated mature soils, represented in this region· by gumbotils and ferretos, are not developed in Wisconsin drift but do occur in Illinoian, Kansan and Nebraskan drift.[1]

This is strange if the early and recent drifts actually represent the same type of deposit, because there has certainly been enough time since the deposition of the Wisconsin drift to develop a mature soil on it. As a matter of fact, few, if any, localities show evidence of more than two drifts; the four or more have been built up by superposition from various localities. Most places show no evidence at all of an earlier drift than the Wisconsin.

In Europe, although again four glacial stages are commonly accepted now, the evidence is not unequivocal and there have been a number of glacial geologists who have demurred. As Gignoux admits:

> So some German geologists, knowing their country very well, have held the opinion that the withdrawals separating two successive stages were very unimportant and there was no proof of the existence of several glacial periods. These monoglacialists believed the glacier had one maximum and was stationary with small oscillations in detail, then began to retreat spasmodically and the climate did not become similar to the present until after this retreat, in post-glacial times.[2]

The evidence for the several glacial stages has been primarily those of the supposed weathered tills underlying fresh tills. Also at some locations strata containing flora and fauna from warm climates have been found between two till deposits, and this is held to be evidence of a warm interglacial period. There have also been attempts to correlate series of ancient river terraces with the respective glacial

[1] Flint, *op. cit.*, p. 335.
[2] Maurice Gignoux: *Stratigraphic Geology* (San Francisco, W. H. Freeman, 1955), p. 626.

stages. However, all of these factors can be explained on other grounds than large-scale glacial fluctuations.

The length of time required to weather fresh material and develop a soil profile is quite unknown. Seldom if ever is there found in any one vertical sequence more than one apparently mature soil other than that on the surface, and there is no reason to insist that it took a long time to form.

Nor has it been possible to estimate the time required for the development of any given soil. Indirect evidence suggests that some kinds of soils can develop to maturity within periods of a few hundred years and possibly even within much shorter periods but truly quantitative methods are mostly still in the future.[1]

Many factors influence the character and rapidity of soil profile development, such factors as nature of parent material, climate, drainage, rainfall, topography, vegetation, micro-organisms, etc. As Hunt and Sokoloff have noted:

Deep soils representing the residual effect of rock weathering are commonly attributed to considerable absolute age, but the age is probably one of the least important of all the factors that must have controlled the development of so deep and mature a profile as characterizes this soil. . . . Given favorable moisture and temperature conditions and appropriate animal and vegetable life to accelerate biochemical activity, it is not at all difficult to visualize rather rapid rock decomposition and deep soil development.[2]

With respect to the ancient soil profiles represented by the gumbotils and similar fossil soils, the depth of leaching of carbonates from these soils, as compared with the depth in recent soils, has been the main criterion used to determine the age of the soils. The highly speculative nature of this procedure should be obvious, but it is emphasized by the following:

The depth of leaching of carbonates in soils has been widely used for estimation or comparison of age of Pleistocene deposits in areas of temperate, humid climate. Leaching is influenced by many factors, such as time, climate, vegetation, surface topography, permeability and carbonate content of the material, and so forth.[3]

[1] R. F. Flint: *Glacial and Pleistocene Geology* (New York, Wiley, 1957), p. 210.
[2] C. B. Hunt and V. P. Sokoloff: *Pre-Wisconsin Soil in the Rocky Mountain Region*, U. S. Geological Survey Professional Paper No. 22, 1949, pp. 117-118.
[3] Aleksis Dreimanis: "Depths of Leaching in Glacial Deposits," *Science*, Vol. 126, August 30, 1957, p. 403. With respect to leaching of carbonates, it is obvious that

It is obvious that any method comprising so many variables, most of which are unknown, can hardly be used to determine precise chronologic data. Yet this is the main method by which the age of the Pleistocene Epoch has been estimated. As Flint says:

In summary: weathering and soil development have constituted the chief basis for estimates of the duration of major units of the Pleistocene epoch.[1]

In general, we feel the conclusion may be justified that the supposed earlier, weathered tills and other soils beneath the last glacial deposits really represent either deposits made in the last stages of the Deluge or else deposits made in the early stages of the oncoming glaciation. It is also possible that the ice sheets may have made numerous minor advances and retreats within a relatively short span of years. At both the edges and the snout would always have been large meltwater streams and lakes, actively reworking the true glacial deposits.

Nor do we need to require a complete destruction of the ice sheet in order to account for intervening strata containing warm climate fauna and flora. It is more probable that one would find a mixture of warm and cold climate organisms fairly near the ice sheet. The cold climate inhabitants would of course have been driven south by the advancing ice, but there is no reason to suppose the periglacial climate was so modified as to cause a displacement of the temperate zone inhabitants too.

If, then, the temperatures of the polar climates decreased, as it would appear, a total of 25° F, does it follow that those of the remainder of the continent diminished to the same extent at the maximum period? The evidence, scanty as it is, seems to indicate otherwise.[2]

Our supposition that a mixture of warm and cold climate types would be found in the zone bordering the ice sheet is borne out by several studies of Pleistocene paleontology.

the amount of carbonates initially present will have a determinative effect. Richard S. Merritt and Ernest H. Muller have shown that: "Under the control of initial carbonate content, depth of leaching varies as much within a single drift as it does across a drift border. Depth of leaching alone, without knowledge of variation of carbonate content, may prove an unreliable criterion of relative age of drift-sheets." (*American Journal of Science*, Vol. 257, Summer, 1959, p. 478).

[1] Flint, *op. cit.*, p. 292.
[2] Lawrence S. Dillon: "Wisconsin Climates and Life Zones in North America," *Science*, Vol. 123, February 3, 1956, p. 167.

If it is true today that the boundaries of the life zones and biotic provinces cannot be too sharply drawn, it would seem that this is doubly true for the last period of maximum glaciation. At least in the eastern half of the continent all available data point to a curious intermixing of boreal elements such as spruce with the present floral components, even in the southernmost parts of the United States, except Southern Florida.[1]

The same phenomenon is exhibited by the mammalian fossils of the Ice Age. The most prolific source of these materials in this continent has been the famous Cumberland Bone Cave in Maryland. Concerning these finds, a recent writer says:

> The accumulation of bones must have been gradual, although all the animals are pre-Wisconsin in age. The diversity of type indicates that widely varying climate zones must have existed during the time of deposition. This has led to much speculation and has given evidence of more radical changes in environmental conditions than had been originally suspected.[2]

Of course, such an inference is not at all necessary. The data can all be better explained in terms of more or less abnormal climatic conditions existing for a relatively brief period, in which fauna from varying habitats would have been forced to live together for a time in the same general environment. Discussing other like indications of the Wisconsin stage fauna, Dillon concludes:

> Hence there is no good evidence that severe polar conditions existed within the United States except in close proximity to the glaciation.[3]

Thus, it is not necessary to conclude that a stratum containing warm climate fauna or flora between two tills represents a long, warm inter-glacial period. It may represent either a brief and short retreat of the ice sheet or an aqueous deposit from a stream or lake (or an aeolian deposit in the case of loess beds) with source fairly near the glacier itself.

The picture that is beginning to emerge, then, is of one great glaciation brought on by the events associated with the Great Flood. The spreading ice sheets fanned out over areas which, recently emerged from the flood waters, had probably as yet little vegetation,

---

[1] *Ibid.*, p. 174.

[2] Bro. G. Nicholas: "Recent Paleontological Discoveries from Cumberland Bone Cave," *Scientific Monthly*, Vol. 76, May 1953, p. 301.

[3] Lawrence S. Dillon, *op. cit.*, p. 172.

and so were easily subject to tremendous erosion. Great quantities of newly-hardened rock materials were plucked up and carried along by the ice, eventually being deposited in some sort of moraine, then probably reworked by marginal streams in many cases. The glacier undoubtedly waxed and waned a number of times, permitting a great variety of deposits to be formed along its margins, but there is no real justification for inferring long inter-glacial periods.

Except relatively near the ice edges, the climate was not materially affected, so that floral and faunal populations of considerable variety could exist reasonably near. It was only as the ice sheet finally began its permanent retreat that the kinds of organisms now adapted best to cold climates began to separate from those more fitted for temperate climates. In the temperate and especially in the sub-tropical latitudes (where most of Biblical and other early peoples enacted their histories) very little influence of the glaciers would have been felt, with the probable exception of higher average precipitation than now occurs, and of the relatively lower sea level.

This intimation of only *one* great glaciation has received very recently support from intensive studies made during the International Geophysical Year. A preliminary notice gives the following information:

A paper to be presented at the December meeting of AAAS in Washington, D. C., will include a proposal for a wholly new concept of ice age history. Full treatment of this subject will be presented in the future.

Deposits formerly attributed to four or five separate Pleistocene glaciations, both in America and Europe, are deposits of a single glaciation.

Normal retreat of the borders of the icecap permitted the Leverett Sea to expand into the valleys of southern New England and the lower Hudson Valley, and in the Mississippi basin, over the whole area of the so-called Nebraskan, Kansan, and Illinoian glaciations, so that an immense ice-marginal body of water was formed, extending from Ohio to Montana and from the Gulf of Mexico to the Wisconsin driftless area. Iceberg-rafted erratic stones and boulders became grounded on the submerged topography of northern Kentucky, southwestern Missouri, and eastern Iowa (the so-called "Iowan" stage). Gumbo clays, until recently interpreted to be weathered tills, were deposited within the expanse of the sea-level waters, along with driftwood and other organic material heretofore interpreted to be "interglacial" deposits. Immense kames and eskers were built by subglacial rivers emerging from beneath the ice-border under water. . . . Reduction of the ice age to "unity" shortens geologic history and nullifies the present meaning of the terms *Nebraskan, Kansan, Illinoian, Wisconsin,* and the several "inter-glacials." Ice age history appears to have been influenced or regulated far less by climatic changes and moraine building than by the intermittent character of the great land movements which continue to the present. There is urgent need in America and Europe for a tectonic chronology of the ice age, based on transatlantic correlation of marine stages and simultaneous timing of the continental uplifts.[1]

If this concept is accepted, and it certainly seems to be supported by much evidence, there must be a revolution in geological thought. One may anticipate therefore a great deal of resistance to it! Nevertheless, the evidence is there, and it obviously correlates with the concept of post-Deluge effects which we have been advocating.

We have not the space here to explore more of the ramifications of the various glacial theories and the numerous correlative studies that relate thereto. It appears in general that the concept of one great ice advance (which can be legitimately inferred from the Deluge events) is supported by many independent lines of evidence, not only from the glacial deposits but also from former lowered sea levels, former lower ocean temperatures[2] and other evidences of cold climates at low latitudes. However, the evidence for more than one glaciation, whether in the Pleistocene, the Permian, the pre-Cambrian, or any other geologic system, is utterly inadequate. As just seen, evidences for multiple Pleistocene glaciations are now being seriously reconsidered by even the orthodox geologists and, as pointed out earlier, evidences for pre-Pleistocene glaciations are of an entirely different sort from those of the recent Ice Age and can be interpreted quite as well in terms of aqueous or other geomorphic agents, harmonizing quite well with the concept of catastrophic deposition during the Deluge period.

Further study is necessary to delineate the extent and character

[1] Richard J. Lougee: "Ice-Age History," *Science,* Vol. 128, November 21, 1958, p. 1290. J. K. Charlesworth, though he favors the multi-glacial hypothesis, gives an extensive discussion of the arguments advanced in the past for a single glaciation, including a quite lengthy bibliography of writings of mono-glacial geologists, especially in Europe (*The Quaternary Era,* Vol. II, London, Edward Arnold Co., 1957, pp. 911-914). Lougee's suggestion, therefore, is not merely a current aberration. Lougee is Professor of Geomorphology in the Graduate School of Geography at Clark University and is also Secretary of the Commission on Terrace Studies Around the Atlantic for the International Geographical Union. He is currently writing a book on his proposed tectonic chronology of the glacial period.

[2] Cesare Emiliani: "Ancient Temperatures," *Scientific American,* Vol. 198, February 1958, pp. 54-63.

of deposits formed *since* the Ice Age, particularly in the non-glaciated regions. As a general rule, it seems likely that most of the deposits which have been popularly designated as Tertiary deposits can be attributed to the waning action of the Deluge and subsequent uplifts; those commonly designated as Pleistocene usually can be attributed to the Ice Age or shortly before or after the Ice Age; and, finally, those designated as Recent can actually be accepted as having been formed after the retreat of the Ice.

However, there are bound to be exceptions to this general rule, perhaps many of them, and each deposit must be considered on its own merits. Many Pleistocene and Recent deposits give evidence of catastrophic formation such as might have been attributed to the Deluge itself, but which, in view of their stratigraphic and other aspects, must rather be attributed to a post-Deluge catastrophe of some sort. Furthermore, there is as yet no really satisfactory explanation of what caused the Ice Age to end. Nor of course is there any really meaningful indication, geologically speaking, as to how long it lasted.

THE END OF THE ICE AGE

Sudden Warming of Climate

Such geophysical and paleontological evidence as has been brought to bear on the subject does indicate that the glacial age ended rather suddenly. Both the evidence of foraminiferal types (different species inhabit cold waters and warm waters) and oxygen isotope composition in the carbonate of their shells (the ratios of these isotopes is also dependent upon water temperature) unite in indicating a somewhat sharp change from glacial to temperate conditions.[1]

The data indicate a rather sudden change from more or less stable glacial conditions to postglacial conditions.[2]

Other lines of evidence, such as a sudden change from deposition of sand to silt in the Mississippi delta and a rapid desication of

[1] *Ibid.*
[2] D. B. Ericson, W. S. Broeker, J. L. Kulp, and G. Wollin: "Late-Pleistocene Climates and Deep-Sea Sediments," *Science*, Vol. 124, August 31, 1956, p. 388.

pluvial lakes, all dated more or less simultaneously,[1] point to the same conclusion. Richard J. Russell, an authority on Mississippi Basin geology and recent president of the Geological Society of America, says:

> In summary, shoreline irregularity and the alluvial filling of valleys in-
> *f*icate a recent general rise of sea level. Comparatively small areas of deltas
> and topographic instability along coasts, which is evidenced by rapid ad-
> vance of delta fronts and anomalous features such as Sapanca Lake, sug-
> gest that the rise in sea level has been rapid.[2]

Still more recently, geologists from Columbia's Lamont Geological Laboratories, have noted the recency (geologically speaking) of this sudden warming of the earth's temperatures:

> From the evidence listed above it is clear that a major fluctuation in
> climate occurred close to 11,000 years ago. The primary observation that
> both surface ocean temperatures and deep sea sedimentation rates were
> abruptly altered at this time is supplemented by evidence from more local
> systems. The level of the Great Basin lakes fell from the highest terraces
> to a position close to that observed at present. The silt and clay load of
> the Mississippi river was suddenly retained in the alluvial valley and delta.
> A rapid ice retreat opened the northern drainage systems of the Great
> Lakes and terrestrial temperatures rose to nearly interglacial levels in
> Europe. In each case the transition is the most obvious feature of the
> entire record.[3]

It is obvious, from our previous discussion of the radio-carbon dating assumptions, that the 11,000-year date must be too high, so these worldwide events clearly date from about the time of the Flood and its after-effects. Neither was this warming of the earth a gradual process occupying thousands or millions of years.

Evidence from a number of geographically isolated systems suggests that the warming which occurred at the close of Wisconsin glacial times was extremely abrupt.[4]

It seems there must have been a rather abrupt warming of the

[1] *Ibid.*

[2] Richard J. Russell: "Instability of Sea Level," *American Scientist,* Vol. 45, December 1957, pp. 419-420.

[3] Wallace S. Broeker, Maurice Ewing and Bruce C. Heezen: "Evidence for an
Abrupt Change in Climate Close to 11,000 Years Ago," *American Journal of
Science,* Vol. 258, June 1960, p. 441.

[4] *Ibid.,* p. 429.

climate in order for the glaciers to melt and the oceanic temperature to change as rapidly as the evidence indicates. This again argues for some sort of explanation outside the scope of doctrinaire uniformitarianism. It is possible to speculate that some new tectonic activity, perhaps a sudden change in either continental or marine topography or possibly new volcanic activity, or even perhaps extra-terrestrial encounters with cometary bodies or the like may have been the trigger mechanism.

However, it appears that the Flood events, and particularly the associated atmospheric changes, can once again suggest a cause adequate to explain this event also. Terrestrial climates, as already shown, are now largely conditioned by the constituents of the atmosphere.

Most of the incident solar energy is contained in the visible radiation which can penetrate right through the atmosphere. The earth re-emits the energy it receives from the sun, but being a much cooler body it does so mainly in the infra-red region of the spectrum. Infra-red radiation is strongly absorbed by water vapour, carbon-dioxide and ozone. These constituents therefore act like the glass of a greenhouse—they trap the outgoing energy. The effect is of the utmost importance for without it the mean surface temperature would be lower by almost 40 degrees Centigrade and life could not exist.[1]

These three constituents—water vapor, ozone and carbon dioxide—must have been present in large amounts in the antediluvian atmosphere. The first we have already discussed, in connection with the inferred vapor canopy, the "waters above the firmament." Ozone would have been formed by reaction of the sun's ultra-violet radiation with molecules of oxygen and of water vapor, as at present.[2] The amount of carbon dioxide in the atmosphere is a function of the amount of carbon-producing and carbon-extracting mechanisms on the earth's surface. Through the process of photosynthesis, carbon dioxide is taken out of the air and used in plant growth, then returned to the air through the processes of expiration, decay, excreta,

---

[1] D. R. Bates: "Composition and Structure of the Atmosphere," in *The Earth and Its Atmosphere*, D. R. Bates, Ed., (New York, Basic Books Inc., 1957), p. 111.

[2] However, the "equilibrium amount" of ozone in the atmosphere depends also on the temperature of the atmosphere, so that the location of the antediluvian ozonosphere may have been different from the present. See R. A. Craig: *The Observations and Photochemistry of Atmospheric Ozone*, (Boston, American Meteorological Society, 1950).

burning, etc. Also, the waters of the ocean exchange carbon dioxide with the atmosphere, the amount increasing as the surface temperature increases. The formation of carbonates in rocks and shells, as well as their weathering out and return to the atmosphere, also enter into the cyclic balance. The amount in the antediluvian atmosphere must have been very high, in order to maintain equilibrium with the large amounts of plant life, the large amount of continental relative to oceanic areas, and the large amount of carbonate-fixing organisms in the seas. The effect of this large carbon dioxide and ozone concentration in the antediluvian atmosphere augmented the effect of the vapor canopy in maintaining the global greenhouse effect and in shielding the earth from harmful short wave length radiation coming from the sun and outer space.

With the Flood, these balances were all profoundly modified. The vast areas of plants were buried, and their carbon content was concentrated in coal seams. Extensive bodies of organic materials were converted into petroleum hydrocarbons. Great thicknesses of carbonate rocks were formed. The Deluge precipitated the atmospheric ozone and carbon dioxide, in all probability, along with the condensed water vapor, temporarily partially denuding the atmosphere of these constituents.

Atmospheric Carbon Dioxide

The lowering of the atmospheric temperature after the Flood, as a result of these atmospheric changes, especially in higher latitudes, certainly supplies a potent mechanism for initiating glaciation of continental magnitudes. The carbon dioxide remaining in the air would support only limited plant life, as compared with the luxuriant pre-Flood stands and, therefore, only limited animal life as well.

However, in time, there is no doubt but that the shielding effect of the thermal blanket would have been at least in part restored. The ozonosphere would have soon formed in essentially its present character, once the new hydrologic cycle was established and more or less stabilized. More important, as plants and animals began to grow again and gradually to multiply, their life processes would gradually restore carbon dioxide to the atmosphere, approaching the balance that has in general characterized present times. Along with this, carbon dioxide equilibrium between ocean and atmosphere required gradual discharge of the gas from the ocean into the air; further, volcanic sources undoubtedly yielded a certain amount to the atmosphere. And all of this in turn would have caused a gradual rise in terrestrial temperatures, probably at an accelerating rate.

The importance of carbon dioxide in the atmosphere as a determiner of temperature has recently been subjected to a great deal of study, especially in connection with the International Geophysical Year program. The most immediate reason for this interest is the possibility that carbon dioxide is again being added to the atmosphere in large amounts, due to the burning of coal and oil.

A coordinated effort is being made by scientists at Scripps, Woods Hole, Lamont, the University of Washington, and Texas A & M to gain an understanding of the CO_2 (carbon dioxide) content of the atmosphere and oceans.

Man, in his burning of fossil fuels and denudation of the land surface, may be performing a gigantic geophysical experiment in which the CO_2 cycle is being influenced. It is thought we may be increasing the CO_2 input into the atmosphere by 70% in 40 years, although it is not certain how much of this may be absorbed by the oceans. A substantial increase in CO_2 content in the air would trap more of the earth's radiated heat and cause a warming of temperatures.[1]

One might think from this that the destruction of plant and animal life on the earth's surface by the Deluge would likewise have enriched the air with CO_2, rather than reduced it. However, most of the organic matter was evidently trapped in the sediments and buried. But undoubtedly many of the higher animals must have floated on the waters after death, finally decaying, and thereby have contributed to the atmospheric reservoir of carbon dioxide. Likewise much plant life also must have decayed on the surface without burial. There is no doubt therefore that, in view of the sparsity of living organisms on the earth in the early years after the Flood, there was an excess of carbon dioxide over that necessary to support whatever life might be able to grow. And as the (much reduced) continental areas began to be repopulated by both plant and animal life and as sea water gave up a portion of its excess CO_2 into the atmosphere, it is highly probable that the CO_2 content of the atmosphere began to increase and thereby terrestrial temperatures likewise.

Another factor may also have been involved. We have seen that a

---

[1] "Oceanography Program: First Twelve Months," *I.G.Y. Bulletin,* National Academy of Sciences, pub. in *Trans., Amer. Geophysical Union,* Vol. 39, October 1958, p. 1016.

great amount of volcanic activity occurred during the Flood. This activity, which is evidenced by the tremendous amounts of volcanic rocks found associated with the strata of all the geologic systems, must have released an indefinitely large amount of carbon dioxide gas. Much of this was released beneath the waters and probably contributed chemically to the formation of the extensive carbonate rock deposits. But also much may have been released above the ground and added to the atmospheric carbon reservoir. In addition, after the Flood, although the high intensity of volcanic activity was restrained, there continued to be much more activity than occurs at present, as witnessed by the large amount of post-Pleistocene lava and ash beds that have been found.

Although the volcanic eruptions thus may have made a substantial contribution to the post-Deluge increment of CO_2 in the air, this effect was undoubtedly masked and more than offset for a time by the fine dust that was also discharged into the air by the volcanic actions. This volcanic dust served to reduce the "insolation" (the amount of solar energy reaching the earth's surface), whereas the effect of CO_2 and water vapor is to prevent the escape of heat radiated back from the earth's surface. In fact, the volcanic dust discharged into the air by the intense volcanic activity near the beginning of the Pleistocene has been one of the main theories advocated as an explanation of the glacial age. It may well have been a contributing factor, along with the removal of the thermal blanket by the Flood, to the initiation of the actual glaciation. Dr. Wexler, of the U.S. Weather Bureau, one of the chief advocates of this theory, estimates that the solar radiation reaching the ground may be reduced by as much as 20 per cent by volcanic dust after a severe eruption.[1]

However, it would have remained in the air only a few years at most. Speaking of the dust produced by the most prolific volcanic explosion of modern times, that of Krakatoa in the East Indies, the biochemist Asimov says:

Pretty nearly all that dust had settled back to earth after two years.[2]

[1] H. Wexler: "On the Effects of Volcanic Dust on Insolation and Weather," *Bulletin of the American Meteorological Society,* Vol. 32, January 1951, p. 12.
[2] Isaac Asimov: "14 Million Tons of Dust Per Year," *Science Digest,* Vol. 45, January 1959, p. 34. See also Wexler, *op. cit.,* p. 10, who says the effect lasted three years.

The Krakatoa dust caused a definite lowering of temperatures for two or three years but had no particular effect after that. The much more extensive volcanic activity of the Deluge and post-Deluge periods would probably have reduced temperatures for somewhat longer periods but at best only for a few years. This effect likely contributed to the initiation of the Ice Age, but the greater cause was the loss of the earth's thermal blanket.

But the carbon dioxide contributed by the volcanoes remained after the dust had settled and combined with that already present and gradually being added by biological and oceanic exchange mechanisms to cause a gradual warming of the temperature of the earth.

One particular biological mechanism may have acted to contribute an abnormally large amount of carbon dioxide, namely the development of bogs. These are not the same as the familiar coastal salt marshes but may form on uplands as well as low areas. The cool, moist conditions of the proglacial regions would have been unusually well suited for the development of boglands. Dr. E. S. Deevey, Director of the Geochronometric Laboratory at Yale, in a recent study on bogland areas describes them as follows:

> Bogs are found in the drier interiors of continents as well as near the oceans but they require some rainfall—deserts have few bogs. If the rainfall is great enough and the summers are cool enough for trees to grow on the uplands of a region, bogs may be expected in the lowlands. Bogs in rainy areas may be more sodden than a tropical rain forest, but the rain water they soak up contains few salts and other nutrients. Only plants that partake sparingly of nutrients, like the shrubs and perennials of arctic barrens and cold steppes, can survive in a bog.[1]

But these plants can grow rapidly, and bogs can and have spread rapidly. The present peat bogs of the world are of great extent, in spite of great areas that have been drained or burned.

> George Kazakov, a Russian peat expert now living in this country computes that there are 223 billion dry tons of peat available on earth, more than half of it in the U.S.S.R.[2]

The significance of large amounts of peat vegetation, in fairly close proximity to the ice sheets, is that they could have had a material

---

[1] E. S. Deevey, Jr.: "Bogs," *Scientific American,* Vol. 199, October 1958, p. 115.
[2] Deevey, *op. cit.,* p. 120.

influence on the accumulation of carbon dioxide in the air over the ice sheet, and probably over the whole world. As Deevey says:

> So large a supply of combustible carbohydrate, delicately poised between growth and destruction, can seriously affect the earth's carbon balance.[1]

Deevey is also mostly concerned about the possibility of our present climate becoming warmer due to the addition of carbon dioxide to the atmosphere. His point is that the initial warming, due to incremental carbon dioxide from fossil fuels, may have triggered the oxidation of the world's peat.

> The warming of the world's climate since the last century may well have set a slow fire to the peat, simply by favoring surface oxidation by soil bacteria . . . it is not impossible that the carbon dioxide added to the earth's atmosphere may have come mainly from peat and humus.[2]

If this is considered a serious possibility now, it seems that it could very well have been a material factor in the warming of the climate toward the close of the ice age. It would have taken some decades or centuries for extensive bogs to develop around the ice, and it is likely that some other factor, such as volcanic carbon dioxide, increased atmospheric ozone, or carbon dioxide from biological mechanisms in general would have initiated the warming. But this in turn may then have begun to oxidize the peat already developed and caused an accelerated warming which in effect finally brought a relatively sudden termination to the Ice Age.

Whatever may have been the detailed processes which initiated and terminated the great glaciations, it seems evident that the Great Flood provides an abundantly adequate ultimate explanation thereof.

Certain of the above concepts as to the effect of carbon dioxide on the antediluvian and glacial climates are supported by the studies of Dr. Gilbert Plass of Johns Hopkins University, whose work is sponsored by the Office of Naval Research, and probably the greatest present authority on the subject. He says, for example:

> There is some interesting evidence which suggests that the carbon dioxide content of the atmosphere was once much larger than at present. It is known that plants grow more luxuriantly and rapidly in an atmosphere that has from five to ten times the normal carbon dioxide amount. In fact, carbon dioxide is sometimes released in greenhouses in order to

[1] *Ibid.*
[2] *Ibid.*

promote growth. Since plants are perfectly adapted to make maximum use of the spectral range and intensity of the light that reaches them from the sun for photosynthesis, it seems strange that they are not better adapted to the present carbon dioxide content in the atmosphere. The simplest explanation of this fact is that the plants evolved at a time when the carbon dioxide concentration was considerably higher than it is today and that it has been at a higher level during most of the ensuing time. Higher temperatures than today during most of the earth's history would have resulted from this higher carbon dioxide content. In fact the geological evidence shows that warmer climates than today have existed for at least nine-tenths of the time since the Cambrian period.[1]

Dr. Plass explains the initiation of glaciation largely in terms of depletion of atmospheric carbon dioxide due to fixation of so much carbon in the coal and oil deposits, much as we have envisioned, except for the different concepts of time and manner of burial.

This loss (of CO_2 from the air) is relatively minor today. On the other hand it would be especially large during a period such as the Carboniferous when there were extensive marshes and shallow seas. At the end of the Carboniferous the atmospheric carbon dioxide content may have been reduced to a very low level because of the tremendous quantities that had been used in the newly formed coal and oil deposits.[2]

However, he is at somewhat of a loss to explain the end of the glaciation, the only suggestion being that the amount of rock weathering is reduced during a glacial period, thereby reducing the amount of CO_2 extracted from the atmosphere to form carbonates. Such a mechanism would take ages to become effective, if ever, it would seem. Cutting down the amount of CO_2 taken from the air might inhibit further spread of the glacier but would hardly cause its retreat.

RESIDUAL EFFECTS OF THE DELUGE PERIOD

Continuing Volcanic and Tectonic Disturbances

Glaciation was only one of the after-effects of the Deluge, though undoubtedly the most spectacular. Although the Pleistocene Epoch is

[1] G. N. Plass: "Carbon Dioxide and the Climate," *American Scientist,* Vol. 44, July, 1956, p. 313.
[2] *Ibid.,* p. 310.

generally thought of as the Glacial Period, there is much evidence of continuing catastrophic activity of other kinds.

The Pleistocene was an Ice Age only in certain regions. Sub-crustal forces were also operative; signs of Pleistocene vulcanicity and earth movements are visible in all parts of the world.[1]

Evidently the tectonic and volcanic disturbances which played such a large part in the initiation of the Flood, as well as in the uplift of the land at its close, continued with only gradually-lessening intensity for many centuries thereafter.

The Pleistocene indeed witnessed earth movements on a considerable, even catastrophic, scale. There is evidence that it created mountains and ocean deeps of a size previously unequalled—a post-Tertiary age has been proved for at least one deep-sea trench, its movement being greater than for any other corresponding period of geological time. . . . Faulting, uplift and crustal warping have been proved for almost all quarters of the globe.[2]

All of which points up once again the remarkable fact that the earth's *most recent* geological formations (except for those corresponding to periods of human recorded history) must be interpreted in such cataclysmic terms as continental glaciations, intensive volcanism and perhaps previously unequalled diastrophism. The Pleistocene deposits are presumably the least altered and most easily read of all the geological data, and yet they can be interpreted only in such a non-uniformitarian context as this! The geological axiom about the present being the key to the past does not seem to apply, therefore, to even the most recent past.

And from the viewpoint of Biblical catastrophism, this makes it very difficult to determine precisely which deposits were laid down in the Deluge proper and which are attributable to the disturbed centuries after the Flood. This difficulty parallels the problem that geologists encounter in trying to fix the exact limits of the Pleistocene Epoch. The Pliocene deposits, on the one hand, and the Recent, or Holocene, deposits on the other, appear to grade more or less imperceptibly into the Pleistocene.

The boundary between Pleistocene and Recent is as ill-defined as that between Pleistocene and Pliocene.[3]

[1] J. K. Charlesworth: *The Quaternary Era*, Vol. 2, (London, Edward Arnold, 1957), p. 601.
[2] *Ibid.*, p. 603.
[3] *Ibid.*, p. 1515.

But this is exactly what we would expect, in light of the Biblical implications concerning the character and extent of the Deluge. Although the Flood subsided enough so that Noah and the animals could disembark from the ark after only one year, the profoundly disturbed and altered hydrological and isostatic balances of the earth undoubtedly continued to manifest themselves in what might be called residual catastrophism for many centuries at least.

Enclosed Lake Basins and Raised Beaches

There is strong evidence, for example, that much more water once filled the lakes and flowed in the rivers of the earth than is true at present. This is the picture revealed by the raised beaches and terraces found all over the world, as well as the evidence that desert regions were once well-watered. With respect to enclosed lake basins, the American limnologist, G. E. Hutchinson of Yale University, says:

> Almost all the drainage basins of the closed lakes of the world bear, above the modern lake level, raised beaches which clearly testify to high lake levels at a previous time; Bonneville and Lahontan are only two of the more dramatic examples.[1]

Lake Bonneville, mentioned by Hutchinson, was a great lake that once covered much of Utah, the present Great Salt Lake being one of its small remnants. It still shows at least four distinct strand lines, the highest and oldest being about 1,000 feet above the present level of Great Salt Lake and covering an area of almost 20,000 square miles.[2] Lake Lahontan, mostly in Nevada, has three major strand lines and covers some 8,400 square miles,[3] with only a few insignificant relict lakes left of it at present. This entire region, now the most arid part of the United States, once was covered with an abundance of lakes and other features of a relatively humid climate. Lake Tahoe, in California, was 655 feet above its present remnant and probably connected with Lake Manley, which occupied the present site of Death Valley.

---

[1] G. Evelyn Hutchinson: *A Treatise on Limnology*, Vol. 1 (New York, Wiley, 1957), p. 238.
[2] W. D. Thornbury: *Principles of Geomorphology* (New York, Wiley, 1954), p. 417.
[3] *Ibid.*, p. 418.

In addition to the two immense lakes (i.e., Bonneville and Lahontan), about seventy other Pleistocene lakes of much smaller size, nearly all of tectonic origin, are known in the basin-and-range area.[1]

The same phenomenon is found in other parts of the world. Thornbury says:

> There are many examples outside the United States of similar lake expansions during pluvial glacial times. Lake Texcoco in Mexico was at least 175 feet higher than it is now; Lake Titicaca in South America was 300 feet higher; the Dead Sea was 1400 feet higher, and as many as 15 abandoned strand lines have been observed around it; the Caspian Sea was at least 250 feet higher and was apparently confluent with the Aral Sea to the east and the Black Sea to the west; lakes in Kenya Colony and Abyssinia, in Africa, were greatly expanded, as was Lake Eyre in Australia.[2]

Even in the world's greatest deserts, such as the Sahara, an abundance of testimony exists that the climate in fairly recent times was more humid. Ewing and Donn attempt to use this fact as support for their own theory of ice age causes:

> The effect of the Pleistocene conditions of moisture in presently arid areas is second in importance only to the contemporaneous glaciation in higher latitudes. The major desert areas, which are today uninhabited barren wastes, although they occupy a very large part of the temperate zones, were formerly fertile, well-watered lands. These areas, which were often covered by very large lakes, include the Sahara and Arabian deserts, the desert of central Asia, and the Australian Kalahari, the North American, the Atacama, and the Patagonian deserts.[3]

It is common, as evident from the above quotations, to attempt to relate the glaciations in the higher latitudes with the pluvial conditions in the lower latitudes. This is not as easy as it might appear, however, and there have been numerous theories attempting to explain climatologically why glaciation and pluviation should be contemporaneous. But as Flint says:

> The fundamental causes evidently lie in the atmospheric circulation pattern, but they are still in the realm of theory.[4]

[1] G. E. Hutchinson, *op. cit.*, p. 17. Flint, in his *Glacial and Pleistocene Geology* (New York, Wiley, 1957, pp. 228-229), lists 119 lakes, instead of 70.

[2] Thornbury, *op. cit.*, p. 418.

[3] M. Ewing and W. L. Donn: "A Theory of Ice Ages," *Science*, Vol. 127, May 16, 1958, p. 1161.

[4] Flint, *op. cit.*, p. 224.

Charlesworth similarly summarizes an extended discussion of pluviation as follows:

Much work still remains to be done to free the pluvial theory of grave internal troubles regarding the number of events, their degree of severity and their contemporaneity.[1]

It is quite reasonable, on the other hand, to explain many or most of these raised beaches around enclosed lake basins in terms of the gradually retreating Flood waters. At the termination of the Deluge year, the uplift of the lands resulted in a continental topography of much higher relief than before the Flood, and this rugged topography included many of these interior basins, in which large amounts of water were trapped. In most cases, however, these high levels could not be maintained by the local precipitation, so that over the years the lakes gradually dried up. This process was intermittent, owing to changing meteorological conditions and perhaps also to occasional regional uplifts still occurring; each period of meteorologic and tectonic stability resulted in the formation of another strand line.

Evidence of pluviation and high lake levels is even stronger in the regions supposedly covered by continental glaciers, but presumably these are all to be attributed to glacial meltwaters, glacier-dammed streams, and similar factors related to the ice sheets. Whatever the explanation, whether in terms of glacial effects or retreating Flood waters, or both, it is abundantly plain that waters from some source occupied extensive areas which are now dry land and produced many and varied aqueous erosional and depositional features. Most of the thousands of lakes now found in the northern states of this country are believed to be remnants of glacial lakes formed by the great ice sheet. Similar phenomena are found in other countries.

The beds of thousands of extinct glacial lakes are known to be scattered over the glaciated area. . . . Among the best criteria for the recognition of these extinct glacial lakes are distinct beaches, and typical, flat-topped, delta deposits, formed by inflowing streams.[2]

Similarly, former shore lines, both lacustrine and marine, are found

[1] Charlesworth, *op. cit.*, p. 1139.
[2] W. J. Miller: *An Introduction to Historical Geology* (6th Edition, New York, Van Nostrand, 1952), pp. 466-467.

(Photo by U.S. Air Force)

Figure 26. MARINE TERRACES.

Coastal terraces, such as these on the coast of New Guinea, are found around all the continents. Each terrace indicates a former stand of the sea, the oldest being the highest. Although attempts have been made to explain these by eustatic changes in sea level associated with glacial melting, the most obvious explanation is in terms of intermittent uplift of the lands after the Deluge period. Similar terraces are also found around lakes and along rivers.

around the borders of existing bodies of water in the glaciated regions in large numbers.

Raised marine shorelines extend to elevations hundreds of feet above sea level around the borders of glaciated North America, but it is not generally known that they preserve a record of uplift of the earth's crust which amounts to a history of postglacial time. . . . In the region of former Glacial Lake Agassiz, the Glacial Great Lakes, New England, Labrador, and Arctic Canada, there are raised marine or raised lacustrine shorelines, or both . . .[1]

The Glacial Great Lakes, for example, covered an immensely greater region than even their present large remnants. The great complexity of the old lake deposits and erosional features has made their history difficult to decipher, and as a result a very complicated sequence of events is believed to have occurred before the present Great Lakes were more or less stabilized.

Their history has been worked out by tracing topographic features that mark positions of former lake levels and outlets. Such features include: wave-cut cliffs and associated features such as arches and caves; beaches and associated bars; lacustrine deposits; dunes back of former shore lines; and spillways or outlets cut across bedrock or glacial deposits, which are today occupied by underfit streams, and exhibit accumulations of peat or muck in abandoned channels.[2]

It is evident that these features could also be explained in terms of large water bodies remnant from the Flood, pluvial climates persisting after the Flood for a time, and continuing intermittent uplift of the lands. It may be that the difficulty of unraveling Great Lakes history has been in part due to the neglect of this very factor of the Flood. We recognize, however, that much evidence exists in favor of the glacial explanation of the lakes, and we see no necessary reason to question it from the Biblical point of view. In either case, whether the water came directly from the retreating Deluge waters or only indirectly from them by way of the great ice sheet to which they contributed, it is clear that in the very recent geologic past, both in glaciated and non-glaciated regions, a much greater part of our present continents was covered by water than at present!

[1] Richard J. Lougee: "A Chronology of Postglacial Time in Eastern North America," *Scientific Monthly*, Vol. 76, May 1953, p. 259.
[2] W. D. Thornbury, *op. cit.*, p. 405.

Raised River Terraces

And this is true not only of the huge Pleistocene and post-Pleistocene lakes. The rivers of the world universally give evidence of having once carried much larger volumes of water than do their present remnants. This is evidenced both by the raised river terraces nearly always found along their courses and by the extensive deposits of alluvium along their floodplains. These terraces are so common that an entire terminology has been developed attempting to categorize them in different types on the basis of their assumed evolution.[1]

Many streams are actually called "underfit" streams, because the valleys they traverse are much too large to have been constructed by them.

If a stream, or more correctly the size of the stream meanders, is too small for the size of the valley, the stream is said to be *underfit;* if too large, it is referred to as *overfit.* It is difficult to cite examples of overfit rivers, or streams with floodplains too small for the size of the stream. Hence there may well be a question whether overfit streams exist. . . . The underfit condition can persist indefinitely; hence many examples of such streams exist.[2]

Similarly, there are many examples known of former stream channels that are now completely dry. Some of these of course have resulted from shifting of channels, but many others were evidently formed by streams that no longer exist, except perhaps in greatly reduced volume as sub-surface streams. These are especially common in the glaciated regions and of course are usually attributed to formation by glacial meltwaters. But they are also found in the non-glaciated regions. In addition, sand and gravel deposits are found in many places that indicate the former existence of great rivers whose valleys now are buried by the later glacial deposits. A notable example of this phenomenon is the so-called Teays River, which once coursed across the continental United States nearly from the Atlantic to the present Mississippi, where it debouched into a far northerly embayment of the old Gulf of Mexico. This was truly a mighty river in every sense of the word.

[1] C. A. Cotton: *Geomorphology* (New York, Wiley, 4th Ed., 1946), pp. 240-250.
[2] Thornbury, *op. cit.,* p. 156.

It was this valley that Tight long ago recognized as the abandoned course of a great river. Thick beds of sand and gravel, including water-worn boulders up to twelve inches or more in diameter, lie upon the valley floor. Many, composed of rocks quite dissimilar to the bedrock of the valley, show unmistakably that they were washed by river action from the bedrock region of the Blue Ridge. Only a great and powerful river could have accomplished this.[1]

This great river probably represented a channel developed by the retreating Flood waters in response to the uplifting of the present Appalachian region. With its huge load of sand and gravel and boulders it could have scoured out its great channel rapidly and also carried an immense amount of alluvial materials to initiate the formation of the Mississippi delta region.

With its great network of tributaries, it helped carve the landscape of a large portion of the continent. The amount of sediment—mud, silt, sand, and pebbles—which it eroded and carried to the sea must have been tremendous. The sea into which it poured those sediments was the long narrow arm of the Gulf of Mexico. This long seaway, from southern Illinois to New Orleans, has been completely filled, and the great delta now juts far into the Gulf proper.

. . . It seems evident that the greater bulk of the delta was built by the Teays, with the Mississippi adding only the latest portions. Hence, the immense delta, more appropriately, might be called the delta of the Teays.[2]

Glacial geologists believe that the continental glaciers then buried the Teays and other such streams under a thick deposit of till and completely changed the surface drainage pattern when they retreated.

But it is the present valleys and rivers which appear to give the strongest witness to the former existence of much larger rates of river flow than now.

In a stream valley, the width of the channel occupied by the current may be only a small fraction of the width of the valley floor. Further, the banks of the channel are regularly low compared to the height of the valley sides. In a word, valleys commonly appear to be far too large to have been formed by the streams that utilize them. A first thought is to infer that the stream was once a much greater current. This almost always proves to

---

[1] Raymond E. Janssen: "The Teays River, Ancient Precursor of the East," *Scientific Monthly*, Vol. 77, December 1953, p. 309.

[2] *Ibid.*, p. 311.

be an unreasonable conclusion because no evidence can be found that a larger volume of drainage was ever available.[1]

If, as indicated, the reason for rejecting the plain indication of a former much greater stream flow is merely the lack of a source of the required waters, we would suggest for consideration once again the waters of the Flood, which in response to the uplift of the lands and subsidence of the ocean beds, required to be rapidly and powerfully transported to the sea. Furthermore, the rainfall of the early post-diluvian times must have been much greater in most places than it is now.

Similarly, the former higher levels and volumes of stream run-off are shown by the raised river terraces, but in like manner this evidence is commonly explained away as caused by various complicated processes of geomorphic evolution.

> Most stream valleys, other than very small ones, on which sufficient data are available contain remnants of dissected fills of alluvium, some of which form terraces.[2]

Although Flint characteristically understates the case, it is nevertheless true that most large stream valleys are both deeply filled with alluvium and exhibit well developed raised terraces more or less paralleling their present slopes. These conditions are, of course, exactly what would be expected on the basis of the Biblical descriptions of the tectonically-induced retreat of the waters after the Flood. Nevertheless, they are commonly explained on a strictly uniformitarian basis. Thus, old river terraces are attributed to gradual formation of a flood-plain by "lateral planation"; that is, by the meandering of the river back and forth across its valley, gradually eroding the valley sides and smoothing out the valley floor; then, "rejuvenation" of the river somehow takes place, so that it begins a downcutting action, leaving its former flood-plain perched above its new level as a raised terrace. Thus, in the words of Cotton:

> The side-to-side swinging of a meander belt or broadly braided river bed which takes place while alternate, or meander-scar, terraces are in course of development implies movement across the valley down slip-off slopes, either smooth or minutely terraced. Sloping terraces which might be remnants of these slopes, if they occur at all, are rare. Most known

---

[1] O. D. von Engeln and K. E. Caster: *Geology*, pp. 256-257.
[2] Flint, *op. cit.*, p. 217.

terraces are remnants of the approximately horizontal floors of meander belts or wide river beds.[1]

It is plain that there is little actual evidence of this extensive lateral corrasion of streams, especially when cutting through bedrock. Alluvial streams, such as the lower Mississippi, of course have a wide meander belt, but they are cutting into an alluvial fill which had already been deposited by earlier flows of greater magnitude, so that the flood plain itself is basically a plain of deposition rather than erosion.

If rivers that flow across floodplains many times wider than their meander belts are observed, it will be found that in relatively few places are the streams actually against and undercutting the valley sides. This suggests at least that there may be a limiting width of valley flat beyond which lateral erosion becomes insignificant.

The valleys of many, if not most, of the world's large rivers are so deeply filled with alluvium that it may seem inappropriate to consider their floodplains as veneers over bedrock valley flats. The alluvial fills in such valleys as those of the Mississippi, Missouri, and Ohio in places are several hundred feet thick.[2]

Thus, the lateral corrasion hypothesis of river terrace formation appears to be mainly a uniformitarian assumption rather than an actual present geomorphic process. Nevertheless, the above author still insists that:

Although the present floodplains of most of our great rivers are much more than alluvial veneers over an erosional bedrock surface, the fact still remains that floodplains many miles wide could not have been built up through aggradation had not the rivers previously by lateral erosion opened up wide valleys.[3]

The Mississippi and its terraces have been studied probably more than any other stream and, although a complex history has been deduced for it, the evidence strongly refutes the notion that its broad valley could ever have been eroded by lateral planation. Russell, long a student of Mississippi delta geology and now Dean of the Graduate School at Louisiana State University, says:

Broad flood plains are characteristic of most rivers leading to the sea.

[1] Cotton, *op. cit.*, p. 250.
[2] Thornbury, *op. cit.*, pp. 131-132.
[3] *Ibid.*, pp. 132-133.

For many years these were explained on an erosional basis. The rivers were pictured as having cut down their valleys to a base-level established by the sea, after which their energies were directed toward lateral corrasion, or valley widening. The alluvium of flood plains was thought of as a thin veneer, resting on laterally planed bedrock. Within more recent years, however, the alluvium of many of these flood plains has been penetrated by borings, which in practically all cases reveal valley fill which is many times deeper than the deepest pools scoured along the river beds. In the case of the Lower Mississippi Valley the character of the bedrock topography which underlies the alluvium is comparatively well known, and contains river trenches several hundred feet deep, while the river is rarely over sixty feet and in no case as much as 200 feet deep.[1]

That these extensive alluvial deposits, not only in the delta region, but also along the continental shelves, required a tremendous river to erode and transport and finally deposit them seems as obvious as anything could well be. By all odds, the most reasonable explanation of these things is that one or more great streams initiated by the post-Deluge uplifts, and perhaps later augmented by glacial melting, laid down these alluvial fills after carving the great valley, and then, in response to intermittent uplift toward the north, left the present raised terraces. The terraces all tend to converge as they approach the Gulf, the oldest terrace being the highest and, therefore, reflecting the period of greatest discharge. Furthermore, the terraces are as difficult to explain in terms of former higher sea levels as in terms of lateral corrasion, although some theorists have attributed their elevation to "inter-glacial" warm periods when the "base level" was higher. Again quoting Russell:

Most of the evidence in favor of higher sea levels is provided by terrace and shoreline features which now occupy elevated positions. But the alternative possibility exists that continental margins and interiors have actually risen positively. If there were freshly created shoreline features widely distributed along maritime coasts at some comparatively uniform level, such as 200 feet, the argument that today's sea level represents a lowering by that amount would be strong. On the other hand, if shoreline features stand at a variety of elevations, the suggestion is fairly conclusive that elevation has resulted from the differential elevation of rising land masses. The latter appears to be the case. . . . That interglacial seas at times may have exceeded today's stands is possible, but not by the differences of level suggested by positions of higher terraces, for many of these

[1] Richard J. Russell: "Instability of Sea Level," *American Scientist*, Vol. 45, December 1957, p. 417.

surfaces are located well above the level which would be established if all continental ice should melt.[1]

Thus the height of the terraces can only be explained in terms of intermittent uplift processes such as terminated the Deluge period, and the width of the valleys and their great depth of alluvial fill can only reasonably be explained in terms of great swollen rivers plunging rapidly toward the sea.

This evidence from the most thoroughly explored continental shelf on earth refutes the physiographers' lateral-corrasion hypothesis for the Lower Mississippi Valley and an erosional explanation for the shelf. A deeply alluviated major valley leads to a deeply blanketed shelf. The flatness is depositional in both cases.[2]

Further proof that the rivers formerly carried much larger quantities of water is found in the great size of their original channels as cut out of the bedrock.

As has already been stated, the bed widths of the filled channels are some ten times those of the present channels in the same localities. . . . The whole of the present annual precipitation, with no loss to percolation or evaporation, could similarly have been run off in no more than five days. It is therefore necessary to postulate a former precipitation greater, and probably considerably greater, than that which is now recorded.[3]

Mention should also be made of the old marine shore lines that are now found around all the world's sea coasts. As we have noted, these raised beaches are found so universally that they have been considered the chief evidence of eustatic variations in sea level.

In various parts of the world elevated strand lines and terraces exist which are believed to have had a marine origin. If these were local phenomena, their positions above sea level could be explained as the result of local diastrophism, but they are so world-wide in extent that they seem to be related to eustatic rise in sea level rather than to local uplift.[4]

Glacial geologists have long been intrigued with the idea of cor-

[1] Russell, *ibid.*, pp. 427-428. See Fig. 26 for an example.

[2] Richard J. Russell: "Geological Geomorphology," *Bulletin of the Geological Society of America*, Vol. 69, January 1958, p. 4.

[3] G. H. Dury: "Contribution to a General Theory of Meandering Valleys," *American Journal of Science*, Vol. 252, April 1954, p. 215. Theory, model tests, and field observations all demonstrate that there is a definite limit to the width of a stream's meander belt, and this is always much less than the width of the alluvial plane on which it flows. See "Basic Aspects of Stream Meanders," by Gerard Matthes (*Transactions of the American Geophysical Union*, Vol. 22, Part III, 1941, pp. 632-636).

[4] Thornbury, *op. cit.*, p. 410.

relating these old beaches with the supposed inter-glacial warm periods when the ice sheets had melted and filled the oceans to a higher level. But, in spite of intense study directed to this end, such correlation has proved quite elusive.

Finally, if we can follow continuously a system of terraces all along a river valley and see them united on the one hand with moraines, on the other with ancient shores, the whole problem of correlation is solved. . . . Unfortunately, and contrary to expectation, it is extremely difficult to follow fluviatile terraces continuously from the region of moraines as far as former marine shores.[1]

One is warranted, therefore, in suspecting that the multi-glacial hypothesis may perhaps be wrong after all. Although the old marine shorelines are found around all the continents, they could reflect universal continental uplift processes just as well as higher sea levels. In fact their irregularity, their varying number from place to place and the great elevation of some of them strongly favor the former explanation, as Russell pointed out.

Evidence of Former Lower Sea Levels

On the other hand, there *does* appear to be much evidence of a former *lower* sea level. The topography of the continental shelves, the irregularity of coast lines, the great submarine canyons, the seamounts, similarities between faunas of now-separated areas, and many other factors seem to indicate that they were formed at least in part at a time when the sea level was relatively lower by several hundred feet than it is at present.

The continental shelves themselves are evidence of a former lower sea level, since their edges mark the true boundaries between ocean basins and continental blocks. The continental shelf extends out as much as 750 miles, with an average width of about 42 miles,[2] and descends gradually to a maximum depth of from about 300 feet to about 1500 feet, with a mean depth of about 430 feet. Beyond the shelf, the continental slope then descends to the ocean depths. As already noted, most evidence favors the view that the continental blocks were uplifted (or the ocean basins subsided, or both) by a great fault along the continental slope.

---

[1] Maurice Gignoux, *op. cit.,* p. 611.
[2] F. P. Shepard: *Submarine Geology* (New York, Harper's, 1948).

This of course accords quite well with the Biblical implication that the uplift of the lands, coincident with the subsidence of the ocean basins, marked the terminus of the universal inundation caused by the great Flood. This uplift (or fault slippage along the edge of the granite blocks of the continents) was intermittent, largely being completed during the Flood year but evidently continuing on a lesser scale for many centuries to come. The present continental shelf could well define the edge of the oceans as they developed during the glacial period. The best calculations for the depth of ocean lowering during the Pleistocene due to the water locked in continental ice sheets seem to be of the same order of magnitude as the average depth (about 430 ft.) of the edge of the shelf.[1] With the melting of the ice sheets, the oceans rose to their present level and, with minor fluctuations, have remained at that level since.

The ocean basins can thus be characterized as overfull—water not only fills the ocean basins proper, but extends out over the low margins of the continents.[2]

There is even some evidence of a past lowering of sea level to much greater depths than that of the continental shelf.[3] These evidences include the great depth of some of the submarine canyons and some of the flat-topped sea-mounts (for both of which there is strong evidence for formation above sea level) and the many fresh-water and shallow-water deposits found in recent years in deep-sea sediments. The nature of these deposits is actually very inadequately known as yet, so that any judgment as to their significance is undoubtedly premature. The general feeling among geologists at present is that these features can best be explained in terms of localized subsidence of the sea floor, in some cases, and turbidity currents in others. These concepts, of course, are perfectly in keeping with our understanding of post-Deluge phenomena. On the other hand, if convincing evidence should eventually be forthcoming that the sea level actually *was* several thousand feet lower than at present, as some of these data seem to indicate, then it would appear that the only logical explanation of such lowering would be simply that there was

[1] J. K. Charlesworth, *op. cit.,* pp. 1354-1355.
[2] J. V. Trumbull, John Lyman, J. F. Pepper, and E. M. Thompson: *An Introduction to the Geology and Mineral Resources of the Continental Shelves of the Americas,* U. S. Geological Survey Bulletin 1067, 1958, p. 11.
[3] See pp. 124-126 and 409-412.

no more water in the ocean at that time—in other words, that must have been the antediluvian sea level! It is obvious that the immense amount of missing water involved in this amount of lowering could not have been frozen in a great ice sheet, and there seems no other way of explaining where it could be.

Most marine geologists today think that the sea floor has subsided, but there is a small minority who think that perhaps the ocean volume increased enough to explain most of the relative sinking of the seamounts. If the latter idea is correct, something on the order of a 30 percent increase in the volume of the oceans must have occurred during the last 100 million years.[1]

This interesting alternative reveals something of the impasse faced by uniformitarianism here. The 100-million-year date, of course, is based on the fact that the deposits of coral and foraminifera on the seamounts have been assigned to the late Cretaceous or early Tertiary. But the significant thing is that these data can only be interpreted as due either to great and unexplained subsidence or to a great and unexplained addition of water to the ocean.

For some reason that is not known, probably having to do with isostatic adjustment or subcrustal forces, the whole great undersea range sank and, initially, sank fast enough to kill the reef coral when the coral dropped below its life zone in the upper waters.[2]

And if the second alternative is chosen, that of a relatively sudden increase of 30 per cent in the volume of the ocean, the compelling question of the source of this water must be faced, and this few geologists can bring themselves to do! But the problem becomes simple if the existence of the antediluvian "waters above the firmament," precipitated at the time of the Deluge, is accepted.

SUMMARY AND CONCLUSION

In this chapter, we have made a preliminary attempt to re-orient the data of historical climatology and geology in order to correlate them with the basic Biblical outline of creation, the Flood and other aspects of the earth's early history. This has been done through the perspective of full confidence in the accuracy, perspicuity and lu-

---

[1] Edwin L. Hamilton: "The Last Geographic Frontier: the Sea Floor," *Scientific Monthly*, Vol. 85, December 1957, p. 305.
[2] *Ibid.*, p. 303.

cidity of the Scriptural records, regarding them as constituting a divine revelation from God Himself.

Although there may be considerable latitude of opinion about details, the Biblical record *does* provide a basic outline of earth history, within which all the scientific data ought to be interpreted. It describes an initial Creation, accomplished by processes which no longer are in operation and which, therefore, cannot possibly be understood in terms of present physical or biological mechanisms. It describes the entrance into this initial Creation of the supervening principle of decay and deterioration: the "curse" pronounced by God on the "whole creation," resulting from the sin and rebellion of man, the intended master of the terrestrial economy, against his Creator.

The record of the great Flood plainly asserts that it was so universal and cataclysmic in its cause, scope and results that it also marked a profound hiatus in terrestrial history. Thus the Creation, the Fall, and the Flood constitute the truly basic facts, to which all the other details of early historical data must be referred.

Within this basic framework we have attempted to re-interpret the basic data of historical geology and other pertinent sciences, which at present are popularly interpreted in a context of uniformitarianism and evolutionism. We have tentatively suggested a categorization of the various geologic strata and formations in terms of the Biblical periods of earth history, although retaining as far as possible the terminology of the presently accepted geological periods.

Thus, it seems most reasonable to attribute the formations of the crystalline basement rocks, and perhaps some of the Pre-Cambrian non-fossiliferous sedimentaries, to the Creation period, though later substantially modified by the tectonic upheavals of the Deluge period. The fossil-bearing strata were apparently laid down in large measure during the Flood, with the apparent sequences attributed not to evolution but rather to hydrodynamic selectivity, ecologic habitats, and differential mobility and strength of the various creatures.

An undetermined amount of the strata, particularly in the upper levels, may have been reworked and redeposited during the later stages of the Deluge, as a result of the great epeirogenic (continental uplift) processes which ended the universal inundation. These processes and the hydrologic abnormalities accompanying them evidently continued with gradually-lessening intensity for many centuries after the Flood. Thus, many of the geologic strata, especially those attributed to the Pleistocene, may actually have been laid down after the Flood, although related to residual catastrophism caused by the Flood.

And indeed it is in the depth of the waters that almost all the stratigraphic series which we have described were built up: torrential waters spreading over the deserts and accumulating there prodigiously thick sediments, lagoonal waters on coastal plains in process of sinking, marine waters dispersing afar the muds and sands.[1]

The Flood itself appears to have been due to a combination of meteorologic and tectonic phenomena. The "fountains of the great deep" emitted great quantities of juvenile water and magmatic materials, and the "waters above the firmament," probably an extensive thermal atmospheric blanket of water vapor, condensed and precipitated torrential rains for a period of forty days.

We realize that such a thorough reorganization of the geologic data raises many questions and must be subject to modification and revision in many details. Nevertheless, we believe that this type of analysis comes much more realistically to grips with all the basic data than does the commonly accepted theory of uniformitarianism.

But the latter theory will undoubtedly die hard, mainly because it is the chief bulwark of evolutionism, and evolution is the great "escape mechanism" of modern man. This is the pervasive philosophic principle by which man either consciously or sub-consciously seeks intellectual justification for escape from personal responsibility to his Creator and escape from the "way of the Cross" as the necessary and sufficient means of his personal redemption.

Numerous objections will, therefore, be raised to our exposition of Biblical-geological catastrophism, most of them ostensibly on the basis that various types of deposits and geologic phenomena are difficult to reconcile with Biblical chronology. Such problems as posed by radio-activity age measurements, great beds of evaporites, fossil varved lake beds, superposed beds of fossil forests, slowly accumulating sea-bottom oozes, and many like phenomena seem superficially to require a longer period for their formation than can be allowed within the Biblical framework of chronology.

Therefore, the next chapter will deal with representative problems

---

[1] Maurice Gignoux, *op. cit.*, p. 652.

of this sort and will attempt to show that the data actually at hand in such cases can be understood quite satisfactorily in terms of Biblical catastrophism. But, in the last analysis, it is likely that on questions so fundamental and basically emotional and spiritual as these, each man will continue to believe as he "wants" to believe. We can only show that those who want to believe the Bible can do so in full confidence that the actual data of geology are consistent with such a belief, even though the apparent weight of scholarly opinion for the past century has been on the side of those who want to believe otherwise.

The words of Dr. Leonard Carmichael, Secretary of the Smithsonian Institution, in the Phi Beta Kappa address at the 1953 meeting of the American Association for the Advancement of Science are worth noting in this connection:

> It has been said that no intellectual discoveries are more painful than those which expose the pedigree of ideas.[1]

He then traces the genesis of modern scientific naturalism, with its ultimate fruition in Fascism and Communism.

> There can be no doubt, however, that the special methods of science as such, especially in the past 15 decades, have themselves been important factors in promoting social change. Certainly in the second half of this period—that is, since the rise and acceptance of the Darwinian point of view in evolution—a wholly naturalistic and positivistic attitude toward the physical and organic world, including man, has become an intellectual commonplace.
>
> Except for occasional writers who seemed out of step with their times, or clergymen or professional religious philosophers, naturalism, or the reign of law as it has been called, became for a time the generally accepted view of most academic leaders in the Western World. This point of view had not previously characterized all great scientists. Such a giant in logic as Sir Isaac Newton saw no inconsistency between a thoroughly scientific cosmology and great reverence for the dogmas and customs of the orthodox Christian tradition.[2]

The decision between alternate theories does not therefore depend only on the scientific data but is ultimately a moral and emotional

---

[1] Leonard Carmichael: "Science and Social Conservatism," *Scientific Monthly*, Vol. 78, June 1954, p. 373.
[2] *Ibid.*, p. 375.

decision. Dr. Barrington Moore, senior research fellow at the Russian Research Center at Harvard University, has said:

Few people today are likely to argue that the acceptance of scientific theories, even by scientists themselves, depends entirely upon the logical evidence adduced in support of these theories. Extraneous factors related to the philosophical climate and society in which the scientist lives always plays at least some part.[1]

We therefore urge the reader to face up to the fact that the actual data of geology *can* be interpreted in such a way as to harmonize quite effectively with a literal interpretation of the Biblical records and then also to recognize the spiritual implications and consequences of this fact.

[1] Barrington Moore, Jr.: "Influence of Political Creeds on the Acceptance of Theories," *Scientific Monthly,* Vol. 79, September 1954, p. 146.

Chapter VII

Problems in Biblical Geology

INTRODUCTION

We have attempted in the preceding chapter to outline a system of historical geology which will explain all the actual data in a more comprehensive and consistent fashion than the evolutionary and uniformitarian framework which has been in vogue for the past hundred years. This proposed system finds its basic rationale in a frank recognition of the uniquely revelatory character of the Judaeo-Christian Scriptures. Beginning with the realization that a uniformitarianism based on *present* processes not only has not but *cannot* provide a scientifically correct explanation of early geophysical and biologic history, we recognize that any *genuine knowledge* of these matters must necessarily come by way of some form of divine revelation.

The unique claim of the Bible, supported by the testimony of Jesus Christ Himself, and of nineteen hundred years of Christian history, that it embodies this revelation is more than adequate warrant for us to base a proposed framework for geologic history on the facts recorded therein. Accordingly, an attempt has been made to determine how the actual data of geology and paleontology can be understood in full harmony with these revealed facts, especially with the fact of a genuine Creation and the fact of a great world-destroying Deluge. We submit that the data, at least in broad outline as presented in the preceding chapter, have been shown thus to harmonize quite remarkably with the Biblical record. Such a demonstrated harmony does not of course indicate any particular insight or originality possessed by the writers but only gives testimony to the veracity and perspicuity of the inspired accounts in the Bible.

It is certainly recognized that not all questions have been answered or all problems resolved. A complete reorientation of all the enormous accumulations of pertinent data and interpretations would take not a few hundred pages, but several large volumes at least, and would require the intensive efforts of a great number of specialists trained in the various areas of geology and geophysics. But the Biblical framework can at least point the way for such studies, and it provides the basic key with which all such problems *can* be ultimately resolved.

This chapter can only deal with some of the major aspects of some of the major problems. But if it has indeed been shown that the general features of the geological data all harmonize with the Biblical outline, and if it can now be shown that the major apparent difficulties in this system can likewise be resolved and understood in these terms, then it is reasonable to conclude that the smaller problems can also be eventually solved by further study.

METHODS AND RESULTS OF GEOCHRONOLOGY

By all odds, the most important and serious of these problems is that of time. There are many lines of geological evidence apparently implying that the earth and its various crustal formations are immensely older than a straightforward Biblical system of interpretation can allow. The latter, as we have seen, involves a relatively recent Creation and Deluge as the cause of most of the earth's geologic features.

There are many different ways by which geologists have attempted to measure the absolute age of the earth and its various formations and deposits. In each such method, some physical or chemical process is found whose present rate of activity can be measured. The total accumulation of the product of the process must also be measured. It is a simple matter of mathematics then to calculate how long the process must have been in operation in order to have produced its present results. Some of the processes which have been used as supposed geologic chronometers involve the influx of sodium and other chemicals into the ocean and into lakes from rivers, the erosion of gorges or other areas by running water or wind or glaciers, the building of deltas or other sedimentary deposits, the growth of chemical deposits in soils or caves or other places, the weathering of rocks, the accumulation of annual bands in trees or lake beds or other entities whose appearance may be affected by seasonal changes, the escape of terrestrial gases into the atmosphere, the efflux of connate waters through volcanism to the earth's surface, and various other like processes. There are also various astronomic chronometers that have been used to determine absolute age, most of them based on the rate of expansion of the universe and its various component parts and on the velocity of the light coming from distant galaxies. The most important geologic chronometers are of course those based on the phenomenon of radioactivity. Various chemical elements are in some degree radioactive, disintegrating continuously into another element or isotope. The rate of disintegration can be measured and if a mineral containing measurable quantities of both the parent and daughter elements is found and analyzed, then a relatively simple mathematical computation will yield the time period during which the daughter element has apparently been accumulating by the process. The most important of these radioactivity methods involve the disintegration of uranium and thorium into radium, helium, and lead; of rubidium into strontium, and of potassium into argon and calcium. Of a somewhat different type is the radiocarbon method, based on the formation of radioactive elements of carbon in the atmosphere by cosmic radiation and their subsequent decay to the stable carbon isotope.

There is no question that the vast majority of these geochronometers have given estimates of geologic age immensely greater than any possible estimate based on Biblical chronology. The radioactivity estimates, in particular, (except the radiocarbon method) usually yield age values measured in hundreds of millions of years and some up to three billions of years.

But the accuracy and significance of any or all such measurements are of course based entirely upon the accuracy with which the measurements can be made and the assumptions which enter into their interpretation. Far too little account has been taken of the limitations which these factors impose.

THE LEAD AGE METHODS

Experimental Difficulties

Consider, for example, the various methods based on disintegration of uranium and thorium into lead. Each of the parent elements disintegrates by some process through a certain chain of elements and isotopes until it reaches a stable condition. Geochronological use of these facts requires very accurate measurements of the amounts of the various elements of the chain present in the mineral and also very accurate knowledge of the respective decay constants. The techniques for these determinations are exceedingly difficult and subject to large error.

Although radioactivity measurements of geologic age have been widely accepted for some fifty years and have been responsible for the wide acceptance of an age for the earth measured in billions of years, it is now generally admitted that most of the work done before 1950 was quite misleading, mainly because of defective measurements or interpretations of the measurements. One of the main workers in this field, Dr. L. T. Aldrich, says:

Between this classic pioneer work (i.e., the discovery of the several uranium and lead isotopes about 1930) and 1950, only a handful of mineral ages were accurately determined. The reason for this was primarily the requirements that the mineral contain one percent or more of uranium and/or thorium, so that the chemical determinations of these two elements and the daughter element, lead, could be made by the standard techniques of analytic chemistry. Even for such minerals, serious errors of analysis were very common.[1]

Partly because of the inadequacies of the measurements, most of the ages published in the literature were discordant and therefore rejected.

It was found during this pioneering period that the three ages derived from the radioactive series of uranium and thorium on the same mineral were often discordant, and in fact the geologic time scale given by Holmes [i.e., by Arthur Holmes, the leader in the development and popularization of the radioactivity methods] is based in part on discordant ages which are very difficult to interpret unambiguously.[2]

[1] L. T. Aldrich, "Measurement of Radioactive Ages of Rocks," *Science*, Vol. 123, May 18, 1956, p. 871.

[2] *Ibid*. Gordon Gastil has recently reminded his colleagues: "Attempts to measure mineral age began soon after the discovery of natural fission. During each decade since then, analysts have discarded most of the age determinations made in the

Original Lead

A more important reason for the errors in the earlier published ages was the neglect of the factor of original lead in the mineral. Obviously, if some of the lead in the sample was non-radiogenic, then the computed age would be too large by an indefinite amount, unless the "common" lead were first determined and eliminated from the calculation. This is verified by Knopf:

The contaminating lead would make the calculated age too great, and it must be allowed for. To make the proper correction, especially if the correction is a considerable one, an isotopic analysis of the common lead that had been deposited in the same district and at the same time as the radioactive mineral must be used. The necessity for this rigorous requirement has only been recognized within the past several years.[1]

Since measurement techniques have been highly refined in recent years and since common lead corrections on the above basis are now made in most computations,[2] these criticisms are not particularly serious at present. But it is well to be reminded of the history of the radioactivity method. Its proponents 20 and 30 years ago were maintaining its finality and the validity of its estimates of absolute time as dogmatically as do its present-day expositors, even though the vast majority of their calculations are now known to have been quite wrong. It may be that currently accepted results will one day have to be rejected as well, for reasons yet unrecognized.

Leaching

Other possible sources of error are known to exist, of course, and have often been used as the basis for rejecting measurements which

preceding one." ("The Distribution of Mineral Dates in Time and Space," *American Journal of Science*, Vol. 258, Jan. 1960, p. 4).

[1] Adolph Knopf, "Measuring Geologic Time," *Scientific Monthly*, November 1957, Vol. 85, p. 230.

[2] However, recognition of supposed common lead contamination depends on detection of lead of atomic weight 204 in the mineral. Ore lead contains a small amount of this isotope along with larger but varying amounts of 206, 207, and 208 atomic weights. Each of the latter isotopes can also be produced radiogenically. However, the all-important amount of 204 lead is quite difficult to determine accurately. As G. R. Tilton points out: "It should be realized that the Pb 204 abundance is the least accurately known of all the isotopic abundances for the leads" ("Interpretation of Lead-Age Discrepancies," *Transactions, American Geophysical Union*, Vol. 37, April 1956, p. 225.)

seemed incapable of harmony with the accepted chronology. Hahn indicates one possibility:

> It may be that part of the lead was leached out; then the age determined would be too low. However, it is also possible that uranium was removed; then relatively too much lead would be found, and the age determined would be too high. It follows that reliable lead values can be expected only from specially selected, dense mineral samples that are weathered as little as possible.[1]

The serious probability of significant uranium leakage is clearly shown by the following:

> Most igneous rocks also contain uranium in a form that is readily soluble in weak acids. Hurley (1950) found that as much as 90 percent of the total radioactive elements of some granites could be removed by leaching the granulated rock with weak acid. . . . Larsen and Phair (in Faul, 1954, p. 80) note that 'commonly, as much as 40 percent of the uranium in most fresh-appearing igneous rocks is readily leachable.' "[2]

The seriousness of these defects is also pointed out by Faul:

> Countless determinations have been made by this method, but it was found that the premises on which the method rests are not valid for most uranium minerals. There is definite evidence of selective uranium leaching by acid waters, and it is now known that most radioactive minerals contained some lead when they were formed. As a result, most of the early lead:uranium age determinations are questionable.[3]

Lead Isotope Methods

Several auxiliary methods have been devised with the uranium series, in order to attempt to obviate some of these difficulties. Each involves ratios of two of the elements in the disintegration series. Each seems to have certain advantages and applications, but each also has quite definite disadvantages. For example, concerning the series which proceeds from the uranium 238 isotope to the lead 206 isotope (the numbers refer to atomic weights). Faul says:

> The chief disadvantages are that hexavalent uranium is readily leached

---

[1] Otto Hahn, "Radioactive Methods for Geologic and Biologic Age Determinations," *Scientific Monthly,* Vol. 82, May 1956, p. 258.

[2] M. R. Klepper and D. G. Wyant, *Notes on the Geology of Uranium,* U. S. Geological Survey Bulletin 1046-F, 1957, p. 93.

[3] Henry Faul, *Nuclear Geology* (New York, John Wiley & Sons, 1954), p. 282.

and that radon 222, which forms in the decay of uranium 238, has a half-life of 3.82 days and, being gaseous, might escape from the system.[1]

Uranium 235 decays through a different series to lead 207 but is present in such infinitesimal amounts as to curtail its usefulness seriously. It also is subject to uranium leaching, though not so much to radon leakage. Both methods are also subject to lead enrichment or removal during geologic time.

Deficiency of lead could be due to the loss of lead itself or escape of some intermediate member of a decay chain. . . . no satisfactory solution to the actual cause of apparent lead deficiency has yet been found. . . .[2]

It may be noted in passing that these apparent lead deficiencies found in so many minerals have been adjudged deficient primarily because the calculated ages turned out to be discordantly low.

Another method consists of comparing the relative amounts of the two lead isotopes, 206 and 207, which are present in the mineral, since these have been produced at different rates through different decay chains. This method has in recent years been considered as one of the most reliable. But:

Actually, the method is subject to several errors. Loss of radon 222 raises the lead:lead ratio and the calculated age. A rather large error may be introduced by the uncertainty in the composition of the original lead. This error may exceed the measured value when dealing with younger uranium minerals containing even small amounts of original lead, as clearly recognized by Holmes when the method was first proposed. Presence of old radiogenic lead (formed in a prior site of the parent uranium) may cause great error. Instrumental errors in mass spectrometry may yield consistently high apparent proportions of lead 204 and lead 207. Redistribution of elements by renewed hydrothermal activity may be a serious source of error in all lead methods.[3]

Radiogenic Lead Contamination

One of the above-named sources of error may be particularly significant. Although it is common now to attempt to allow for con-

[1] Faul, *op. cit.*, p. 294.
[2] L. H. Ahrens: "Radioactive Methods for Determining Geologic Age," in *Physics and Chemistry of the Earth*, ed. by Ahrens, Rankama, & Runcorn, (New York, McGraw-Hill, 1956, pp. 49-50).
[3] Faul, *op. cit.*, p. 295.

tamination by original common lead by assuming that the presence of lead 204 in the mineral indicates such contamination, it appears also quite possible that many, or most, such minerals might equally well contain some contaminating radiogenic lead from some other source; if so, the age computation would of course be too high by a quite unknown amount. The possibility of this type of phenomenon occurring is indicated by a recent study at the University of Toronto:

There are some leads that have been referred to as anomalous which have isotope ratios that do not, at first sight, seem to participate in this regularity. We believe that additional amounts of radiogenic lead have been added to these leads, at or about the time of final mineralization. That is, an anomalous lead is simply an ordinary or non-anomalous lead which has been further altered.[1]

The above authors were concerned about the fact that too much radiogenic lead was present in certain supposedly ancient lead ores to harmonize with the theory that "common" lead has been uniformly enriched during geologic time with increments of radiogenic lead as evidenced by the larger proportion of lead isotope 204 in older common leads. These anomalous leads show less 204 lead than should be present according to the theory. The really significant thing, however, is that it is thereby evident that radiogenic lead can contaminate any uranium-lead bearing mineral to an unknown amount and thereby make any age determination on it meaningless.

That such contamination of ordinary lead deposits by radiogenic lead is far from rare is indicated by the following:

True ordinary leads are probably derived from below the crust, and anomalous leads are derived in turn from these by variable radiogenic contamination in the crust. Thus ordinary and anomalous leads form a series rather than two distinct groups. It is likely, furthermore, that no absolutely ordinary leads occur on the earth's surface, as all have probably received at least minute radiogenic contamination in coming from the mantle.[2]

Thus, as Boyle recognizes:

The ratio of the lead isotopes in deriving their lead from such rocks is,

[1] R. M. Farquhar and R. D. Russell: "Anomalous Leads from the Upper Great Lakes Region of Ontario," *Transactions, American Geophysical Union,* Vol. 38, August 1957, p. 552.
[2] R. L. Stanton and R. D. Russell: "Anomalous Leads and the Emplacement of Lead Sulfide Ores," *Economic Geology,* Vol. 54, June-July 1959, p. 606.

therefore, neither a measure of the age of the deposits nor the age of the sedimentary host rocks but is rather a function of the complex geochemical processes through which the lead may have passed.[1]

In spite of the necessarily unknown amount of radiogenic contamination of all lead deposits, the theory that common leads have been *uniformly* enriched by gradual accumulations of radiogenic lead during geologic time has been made the basis of probably the most important present geologic estimate of the total age of the earth's crust, leading to a figure of the order of five billion years. As Harrison Brown claims:

> Thus solely on the basis of the isotopic composition of common leads we can say that the age of the earth probably lies somewhere between 3.1 and 5.6 billion years.[2]

This sort of calculation, though containing numerous unverifiable assumptions, has been widely accepted and circulated, but there are many who remain unconvinced. After a rather lengthy and impelling criticism of the method, especially on the basis of its very subtle and speculative assumptions, a triad of authors (one from California Institute of Technology, one from Carnegie Institute in Washington, one from Chicago University), concludes:

> In view of the evidence for extensive mixing, it would seem contrary to the facts to postulate differing frozen lead-uranium ratios that have existed for billions of years. The requirements of the assumptions in the ore lead method are so extreme it is unlikely that it should give a correct age.[3]

It would seem, therefore, that it is quite possible for any lead deposit or any mineral containing lead (including the uranium minerals on which most age-estimates have been based) to contain substantial though unknown amounts of antecedent radiogenic lead. This would necessarily make all such age-estimates too high by an unknown amount.

From these examples it is readily apparent that the amount of accumu-

[1] R. W. Boyle: "Some Geochemical Considerations on Lead Isotope Dating of Lead Deposits," *Economic Geology,* Vol. 54, Jan.-Feb. 1959, p. 133.

[2] Harrison Brown: "The Age of the Solar System," *Scientific American* Vol. 196, April 1957, p. 86.

[3] C. Patterson, G. Tilton, and M. Inghram: "Age of the Earth." *Science,* Vol. 121, January 21, 1955, p. 74.

lated radiogenic lead contributed to a deposit is the deciding factor in age determinations and must be known before any age can be assigned to a deposit.[1]

Other Methods

Still other methods have been used to some extent, for example, the thorium-lead 208 ratio. As Aldrich says, however:

The two uranium-lead ages often differ from each other markedly, and the thorium-lead age on the same mineral is almost always drastically lower than either of the others.[2]

Apparently a satisfactory explanation of this conflict is not yet available:

Most of the ages obtained by the lead:thorium method disagree with the ages of the same minerals computed by other lead methods. The reasons for this disagreement are largely unknown.[3]

Another method is the lead 210 method, lead 210 being a particular stage in the decay series leading to lead 206. The ratio of lead 206 to lead 210 is used to compute the age of the mineral. But as Faul says:

Unfortunately, the lead 210 method is subject to similar errors as the lead:uranium and lead:lead methods, owing to loss of constituents of the radioactive series of leaching or emanation.[4]

The very light gas, helium, is a product of the disintegration of uranium and thorium, along with lead, and helium measurements in minerals have long been used as indices of age. The method has had many ups and downs in the favor of geophysicists, due to experimental difficulties and the presumed ease of helium leakage. In a recent review of the present status of all the various radioactivity methods, Dr. Adolph Knopf concludes:

Because of such uncertainties about the helium age determinations, the method has again fallen into nearly complete disuse.[5]

---

[1] Boyle, *op. cit.,* p. 135.
[2] L. T. Aldrich: "Measurement of Radioactive Ages of Rocks," *Science,* Vol. 123, May 18, 1956, p. 872.
[3] Henry Faul: *Nuclear Geology* (New York, John Wiley & Sons, 1954, p. 295.)
[4] *Ibid.*
[5] Adolph Knopf: "Measuring Geologic Time," *Scientific Monthly,* Vol. 85, Nov. 1957, p. 228.

Discordant Ages

After listing all the various requirements for successful determination of an age by the lead method, Rankama says:

No radioactive minerals have been analyzed that satisfy all these requirements. Consequently, errors are liable to creep into the calculated lead ages. In particular, the alteration of radioactive minerals is the cause of errors in the age values. Even the freshest-looking minerals usually have gained or lost small quantities of the pertinent nuclides.[1]

In view of all the sources of error in the various uranium-thorium series methods, it is small wonder that *most age measurements have been found hopelessly discrepant and have been rejected.* Only those few minerals which give agreement by more than one method are now considered really reliable, and these are so few and far between that at least some of *these* apparent agreements can be explained on the basis of pure chance.

It appears that the best criterion for a reliable age determination is the agreement of age values calculated from the lead 207-lead 206, lead 206-uranium 238, and lead 207-uranium 235 ratios, even though the lead 208-thorium 232 age may be discordant. This happy situation occurs in the case of some pegmatitic radioactive minerals, and in the case of a few pitchblendes, but seems to be the exception rather than the rule.[2]

THE RUBIDIUM METHOD

In addition to all the difficulties encountered in these methods, they have been of limited usefulness because of the extreme rarity of uranium and thorium minerals, especially in fossiliferous rocks. Consequently, much attention has been given in the past decade to the development of methods involving the radioactive isotopes of the alkali metals, rubidium and potassium. These are much more common, and the potassium minerals especially are commonly found in sedimentary rocks.

One of the main workers in the development of the rubidium-strontium method has been Dr. Otto Hahn. The main question about

[1] Kalervo Rankama: *Isotope Geology* (New York, McGraw-Hill, 1954), p. 379.
[2] National Research Council: "Report of the Committee on the Measurement of Geologic Time," 1957, p. 4.

the method has been the lack of agreement concerning the disintegration rate of rubidium. Hahn says:

> For this method, however, a knowledge of the transformation rate of rubidium into strontium is necessary. The final decision regarding the half-life has yet to be made.[1]

Ahrens, another leading worker in this field, gives a list of different determinations of the half-life of rubidium as made by various scientists, showing a variation all the way from 48 to 120 billion years.[2] A further limitation is the very small amount of strontium present and the fact that much of this may be non-radiogenic.[3]

THE POTASSIUM METHODS

Potassium was proved about ten years ago to decay by two different processes into calcium and the gas argon. Because of the wide incidence of potassium minerals in sedimentary rocks, this has seemed to be a potentially very fruitful geochronologic device. Again, there are serious difficulties, however. As Wetherill says:

> The two principal problems have been the uncertainties in the radioactive decay constants of potassium and in the ability of minerals to retain the argon produced by this decay.[4]

Although the decay rates are still a matter of considerable uncertainty, the more serious problem is that of argon loss. Potassium is found mainly in feldspars and micas, and it is believed, on the basis of comparative age measurements with other methods, that the feldspars in general must have lost about half of their radiogenic argon through emanation from the mineral. It is maintained, however, that the micas in general are able to retain most of the argon. But again Wetherill admits:

> In view of the fact that fairly low retentivities sometimes occur even in the case of mica, measurement of the potassium-argon age of a mica does not give a completely trustworthy value of the age.[5]

[1] Otto Hahn: "Radioactive Methods," *Scientific Monthly*, Vol. 82, May 1956, p. 261.
[2] L. H. Ahrens: *Physics & Chemistry of the Earth* (New York, McGraw-Hill, 1956, p. 54.)
[3] Hahn, *op. cit.*, p. 262.
[4] G. W. Wetherill: "Radioactivity of Potassium and Geologic Time," *Science*, Vol. 126, September 20, 1957, p. 545.
[5] *Ibid.*, p. 549.

Thus, as we examine one by one the various radioactivity methods for measuring geologic age we find that each encounters many serious problems in it use—enough to cast grave doubt on the reliabiltiy of any age computed from it. The potassium-calcium method is even less reliable than the potassium-argon method, owing to the fact that radiogenic calcium (of atomic weight 40) is impossible to distinguish from other calcium 40 which is commonly found present in potassium minerals. Hahn says:

> Unfortunately, calcium 40 is the most frequent partner of the regular mixed element calcium. Therefore, only in very old potassium minerals, nearly completely free of calcium, is it possible to find through extremely accurate mass spectroscopy the very small shift in the isotope ratio of calcium, and thus use the activity of the potassium for age determination.[1]

THE SIGNIFICANCE OF THE RADIOACTIVITY DATA

It thus becomes evident that age measurements by radioactivity are not nearly so precise nor so reliable as most writers imply. The great variety of possible experimental errors and physical alterations in the quantities being measured have all combined to produce such a high degree of statistical scatter in the results of the computations, especially when compared with the geochronological implications of the associated stratigraphy, that the great majority of the measurements have had to be rejected as useless for the desired purpose. Relatively, only a handful has been acceptable.

But of course it will be answered that, even though experimental errors may be important, the measurements are still sufficiently accurate to give in most cases ages of at least the right order of magnitude. For example, a measurement indicating an age, say of one billion years, could hardly be in error by more than a factor of 10, and this would still give a hundred million years, nothing remotely comparable to the few thousand years implied by the Bible. Furthermore, it will be maintained that even though any given age measurement may be completely erroneous due to leaching or emanation or some other effect, there are many cases now known where the age estimate has been checked by two or more different methods, independently. It would seem improbable that the elements concerned would have each been altered in such a way as to continue to give

[1] Otto Hahn, *op. cit.*, p. 261.

equal ages; therefore, such agreement between independent measurements would seem to be strong evidence that alteration had not occurred and that the indicated age is therefore valid.

We reply, however, that the Biblical outline of earth history, with the geologic framework provided thereby, would lead us to postulate *exactly this state of the radioactivity evidence!* We would expect radiogenic minerals to indicate very large ages and we would expect different elements in the same mineral, or different minerals in the same formation, to agree with each other! The fact that so many calculations *fail* to agree or to fall into proper place in the stratigraphic sequence is strong testimony that uniform processes do *not* constitute the norm in earth history. The great number of "discordant ages," of "anomalous leads," and the like, testify to the intense mixing activity of the Deluge and other catastrophic geologic events.

This may appear to many to be a surprising assertion, but a little consideration should suffice to show its validity. The whole problem revolves about the basic assumptions implicit in all the radioactivity methods of measurement. In addition to the problems of measurement and alteration already discussed, there are two basic assumptions always present. One is that all of the identified radiogenic isotope has been derived from the parent isotope by radioactive disintegration. The other is that the rate of disintegration has always been the same as at present. Both these assumptions are absolutely necessary in order to obtain any kind of meaningful age measurement. *But neither assumption can possibly be valid if the Bible account is true!* They implicitly deny the two divinely revealed facts of a genuine Creation and at least one great discontinuity in the uniform processes of nature at the time of the Deluge.

THE FACT OF A "GROWN" CREATION AND "APPARENT AGE"

We have already shown[1] that the Bible quite plainly and irrefutably teaches the fact of a "grown" Creation—one with an "apparent age" of some sort, analogous to the "apparent age" of a mature Adam at the first instant of his existence.[2] This Creation must have included

[1] See page 218-19, 223-24, and 232-35.
[2] The uniqueness of Adam and Eve's creation (see also p. 456) is emphasized in the New Testament: "For Adam was first formed, then Eve" (I Tim. 2:13), ". . . for the man is not of the woman, but the woman of the man" (I Cor. 11:8). Similarly,

all the chemical elements already organized in all the organic and inorganic chemical compounds and mixtures necessary to support the processes of the earth and of life on the earth. These processes include the phenomena of radioactivity. It is perhaps possible that only the parent elements of the radioactive decay chains were originally created, but it is eminently more harmonious with the whole concept of a *complete* Creation to say that all the elements of the chain were also created simultaneously, most likely in a state of radioactive equilibrium.

This means that, with each mineral containing a radioactive element, there were also at the original Creation all of the daughter elements in the decay series, including some of the final stable end-product. Such a concept is undoubtedly shocking to the mind of a consistent uniformitarian, but there is nothing impossible or unreasonable about it. In fact, short of denying the existence of any Creator or original Creation at all, one must logically come to some place in the long chain of secondary causes where *something* was created. If so, that something, at the instant of its creation, must have had an "appearance of age." And the only way we could then determine its "true age" would be through divine revelation. An "apparent age" might of course be deduced for that something on the basis of any processes of change which were observed in connection with it, but this would not be the *true* age.

And this is exactly the situation we find in connection with these radioactive elements and with many other geochronometers. It is eminently reasonable and consistent with the basically efficient and beneficent character of God, as well as with His revelation concerning the fact, that He would have created the entire universe as a complete, operational, functioning mechanism. The grossly cruel and wasteful processes of an almost interminable evolution leading up to man's arrival as its goal, as usually envisioned by uniformitarians, (or at least by theistic uniformitarians), are on the other hand utterly inconsistent with the character and wisdom of God! It is therefore not ridiculous after all, but perfectly reasonable, to suppose that the radiogenic elements, like all other elements, were created directly by God.

most of the Biblical miracles stress true creative activity, in which the time factor is immensely compressed: for example, the transformation of water into wine (John 2:10), creation of "apparent age" in other words.

The obvious question then arises as to whether the "apparent ages" of the minerals so created, as indicated by the relative amounts of "parent" and "daughter" elements contained therein, would all be diverse from each other or whether they would all exhibit some consistent value; and if the latter, what value of apparent age might be implied.

In the absence of specific revelation, it seems impossible to decide this question with finality. However, it is more satisfying teleologically, and therefore more reasonable, to infer that all these primeval clocks, since they were "wound up" at the same time, were also set to "read" the same time. Whatever this "setting" was,[1] we may call it the "apparent age" of the earth, but the "true age" of the earth can only be known by means of divine revelation.

VARIATIONS IN THE DECAY RATES

Supposed Invariability

But this is not the only assumption in age calculations. Regardless of whether or not the original mineral was "set" to read a certain finite time at the instant of its creation, we still could not know for certainty what this original condition had been, since we cannot know to what extent the rate of decay has varied since that time.

It is possible, of course, to measure or estimate the decay rates as they exist now for each of the radioactive series and for each stage in the series, and this has been done. As we have seen, considerable question still exists as to the proper value for many of these decay constants, but the values of all the important ones are known to at least the right order of magnitude. And of course the claim is made that these decay rates never change and that it is, therefore, legitimate to use them in the computation of ages. Extremes of temperature, pressure, physical state, chemical combination, etc. have been applied to the radioactive elements without any significant indication of resulting changes in the disintegration constants. It is claimed

---

[1] It is interesting to note that Peter, when discussing the duration of terrestrial history, emphasizes as significant the fact that: "One day is with the Lord as a thousand years" (II. Peter 3:8), thus stressing the time-transcendent nature of God. Perhaps God has also emphasized this truth in His physical creation, by means of "setting the clocks" of natural processes to read such tremendous ages as they appear to do. Yet the Biblical revelation of *actual* human and earthly history indicates a relatively ephemeral existence, beginning only some eight to ten thousand years ago.

that no past change in terrestrial environments, as conceived accord ing to uniformitarian principles, could have been outside the scope of these laboratory studies. It is, therefore, maintained that the decay rates have never changed.

There is nothing basically inviolable about these decay rates, how-ever. This is proved by the fact that it *has* been found possible to change some of them at least slightly, in the laboratories.

Experiments with decay of two artificial isotopes thought to be the most sensitive to change in atomic structure (beryllium 7 and an excited state of technetium 99) have shown that the decay rate can be changed, but the change is extremely small.[1]

These changes were due to changes in the chemical compounds of which the elements were a part, but similar small changes in certain decay rates can be effected by pressure.[2]

The Decay Processes

There are several types of radioactive disintegration that are known to occur in nature. Alpha-decay consists of the emission of nuclei of atoms of helium 4 from nuclei of heavy atomic weight. This is the type of decay initiating the uranium and thorium series, whose disintegration results finally in lead and helium with several inter-mediate elements in the chain. Beta-decay consists of the emission from the nucleus of a beta-particle (an electron) and a neutrino; this is the decay process involved in the formation of strontium 87 from rubidium 87 and of calcium 40 from potassium 40. A third type of decay is the capture of an orbital electron by the nucleus, accompanied by the emission of X-rays. The formation of argon 40 from potassium 40 is of this kind. A fourth kind of decay is nuclear fission, by which the nucleus splits into two discrete parts. This is the action of the atomic bomb, but it also occurs in nature. The uranium 235 isotope is subject to fission by free neutrons in the earth, from whatever source. Uranium 238 and thorium 232 undergo a process of spontaneous fission, whereby occasional atoms, under the pressure of high internal proton charge, spontaneously break into two parts. In this process, the main products are the rare gases xenon and krypton, along with neutrons and other particles.

[1] Henry Faul: *Nuclear Geology,* p. 10.
[2] *Ibid.*

Each of these processes is interpreted essentially as a statistical process, with the particular rate of decay being a probability function related to the type of process and the element concerned. Each is known to be related to the structure of the atomic nucleus and the various nuclear forces and particles. But, although the intensive research devoted to modern nuclear physics has yielded a tremendous amount of information about the various nuclear particles and reactions, most of these formulations are still largely empirical, with very little basic understanding of *why* the nucleus behaves as it does. As Beard has said:

We comprehend quite well *what* nuclear structure is; but as yet we are only beginning to see *why* it is.[1]

Similarly, George Gamow, who has made many significant contributions to nuclear physics, including in particular the present interpretation of the alpha-decay process, in a recent review points out:

Although experimental studies of these new particles reveal new and exciting facts about them almost every month, theoretical progress in understanding their properties is almost at a standstill.[2]

Alpha-Decay and the Potential Barrier

With respect to the alpha-decay process, which is the most important process from the standpoint of geologic time measurement, the best theoretical explanation developed to date is Gamow's suggestion, formulated in terms of wave mechanics and statistical probabilities. According to this concept, although the energy of the alpha-particle is apparently too small to permit it to escape from the "nuclear potential barrier" of energy surrounding the nucleus, nevertheless it has a certain small probability of doing so.

According to classical mechanics, the incoming or outgoing nuclear particles can pass the potential barrier only if their kinetic energy is larger than the maximum height of the barrier. Experimental evidence shows, however, that this is definitely not so. An example is represented by a uranium nucleus, which has a radius of 9×10^{-13} cm. and is surrounded by a potential barrier 27 Mev high. Since the alpha-particles that escape from

[1] David B. Beard: "The Atomic Nucleus," *American Scientist,* Vol. 45, Sept. 1957, p. 342.
[2] George Gamow: "The Exclusion Principle," *Scientific American,* Vol. 201, July 1959, p. 86.

uranium in the process of its natural decay have an energy of only 4 Mev, it is difficult to understand how they get out across the barrier at all. . . . It turns out, in fact, that the wave mechanics of a particle permit it to do things that would be completely prohibited in classical mechanics. . . . Using wave mechanics, we can calculate that the chances of getting through are about 1 in 10^{38}.[1]

The symbol Mev stands for a "million electron volts," an electron-volt being the energy imparted to a single electron when it is accelerated by a one-volt electric potential. (Similarly, Kev stands for "thousand electron-volts, Bev for billion electron-volts, etc.). The probability of escape of an alpha-particle through the energy barrier erected by the high nuclear forces in the atom depends on the relation between the energy of the particles and that of the barrier, and these factors vary in some incompletely-understood manner from one nuclear species to another. The nearer the energy of the alpha-particles to that of the barrier, the more probable is the escape of any single particle, and, therefore, the more rapid the general decay of the nucleus. Thus, the "decay constant" of any given radioactive element depends on the relative energies contained in its nucleus.[2]

External Energy Sources

Herein lies the reason for the apparent constancy of these decay rates. The energies are so high that any ordinary external energy source, whether physical or chemical, is of entirely too low an order of magnitude to have any effect.

After Rutherford became completely persuaded that the radioactive decay of heavy elements is due to the intrinsic instability of their atomic nuclei, his thought turned to the possibility of producing the artificial decay of lighter and normally stable nuclei by subjecting them to strong external forces. True enough, it was well known at that time that the rates of radioactive decay are not influenced at all by high temperatures or by chemical

[1] George Gamow: *Matter, Earth, and Sky* (Englewood Cliffs, N. J., Prentice-Hall, Inc., 1958), pp. 341-342.

[2] Thus: "In general, it can be said that this probability is greater, the larger the energy of the alpha particle relative to the top of the barrier, and the smaller the "thickness" of the barrier at the point corresponding to the given energy value. . . . It follows, therefore, that the greater the energy of the alpha particle in a radioactive atom, the more likely is it to be found outside the nucleus" (Samuel Glasstone: *Sourcebook on Atomic Energy,* 2nd Ed., New York, D. Van Nostrand & Co., 1958, pp. 173-174).

interactions, but this could be simply because the energies involved in thermal and chemical phenomena are much too small as compared with the energies in the nuclear disintegration phenomena.[1]

Rutherford proceeded to bombard his nuclei with high-energy alpha-particles, and the whole subsequent history of nuclear physics has demonstrated the possibility of penetrating the nucleus, through the potential barrier, provided only that a source of sufficiently high energy is used.

It is, therefore, evident that the basic decay relationships could be changed if something were done to change the relationship between the energy of the alpha-particles in the nucleus and the nuclear forces creating the potential barrier. Although the exact nature of these forces is still uncertain, it seems evident that some external source of sufficiently high energy level would be required. Pressures, temperatures, chemical reactions, ordinary radiations are all inadequate, and therefore the decay rates seem to be constant. Nevertheless, if an environment of high-energy radiation could be imposed on the elements, it seems certain that the balances, and therefore the decay phenomena, would be altered.

Such an environment may be difficult, or impossible, to impose in the laboratory, and in any case it supposedly could not have been produced at any time in the earth's past history as a geologic environment and so could have had no influence on the decay constants.

But this is an entirely gratuitous assumption. Such an environment *does* exist, right now, in the earth's upper atmosphere, where a great variety of radiations, including particles of fantastically high energies, exist in profusion. If any very substantial part of this radiation has ever in the past been able to penetrate to the lower atmosphere and into the earth's crust, it *must* have had some substantial effect on the radioactive decay rates of the unstable atomic nuclei. And, in view of the Biblical record of the Creation and the Flood, it seems likely that a large amount of this radiation may have reached the earth's surface during the creation before the establishment of the earth's thermal vapor blanket and during the Flood, immediately after its dissipation and before the development of the present atmospheric regime.

[1] George Gamow: *Matter, Earth, and Sky,* 1958, p. 330.

Cosmic Radiation

Of particular interest in this connection are the intensely powerful cosmic rays. The character of these rays is indicated by the following:

> To begin with, primary cosmic radiation, that is, the rays as they exist in space, is composed of atomic nuclei traveling with speeds so enormous as to approach that of light (186,000 miles per second).[1]

The rays are mainly nuclei of atoms, of many of the chemical elements, especially hydrogen and helium but also including heavier elements. The energies of these particles are tremendous, ranging from one billion to over a billion billion electron volts, far beyond the capacities of our largest man-made accelerators (compare the 27 million-electron-volt energy barrier in the uranium atom!). The tremendous energy of this radiation, as it enters the upper atmosphere and collides with air atoms, results in the formation of a secondary stream of charged particles in great variety.

Before these particles (i.e., the primary cosmic radiation) can reach the earth's surface they must pass through the atmosphere. The blanket of air covering our planet is heavier than many realize—equivalent to a layer of water thirty-four feet thick. Even the tremendous energy of the primary cosmic rays is not sufficient to enable them to get through this much matter unchanged. However, the debris resulting from their collisions with air atoms does reach the surface of the earth and in fact has been detected several hundred feet underground. This debris, in addition to the protons and neutrons of which the struck atoms are composed, includes mesons, unstable particles associated with nuclear structure that are not very well understood at present, gamma rays, like those given off by radium, only more penetrating, and positive and negative electrons.[2]

Although comparatively little of the cosmic radiation actually reaches the earth's surface at present, that part which does reach it gives intimation of the tremendous energy that certain of its particles contain.

The extraordinary penetrating power of cosmic rays is shown, in the first place, by their ability to pass through the earth's atmosphere, the ab-

[1] Arthur Beiser: "Where Do Cosmic Rays Come From?", *Scientific Monthly*, Vol. 77, August 1953, p. 76.
[2] *Ibid.*, p. 76.

sorptive power of which for ionizing radiations is approximately equivalent to one meter thickness of lead. But that is not all. The rays have been detected underground and under water at distances equivalent to 1400 meters of water below the earth's surface. Only particles with many billions of electron volts of energy could have penetrated to such depths.[1]

The portion of the cosmic radiation reaching the earth's surface seems to consist predominantly of highly energetic mesons, along with some neutrons, electrons, protons and photons. Mesons are particles intermediate in mass between electrons and protons, which decay very rapidly into electrons.

The question arises as to what effects might be produced on the earth's surface if a substantial part of this "hard component" of the cosmic radiation, rather than only a very insignificant part, could reach the earth. It is doubtful whether this question can be answered on the basis of present knowledge, since such an environment is not producible, even in the largest accelerators.[2]

But it does seem highly probable that such an environment, which must have reached the earth's surface to at least some degree both during the first day of the creation and during the Deluge period and possibly at other times as well, would have had a marked effect on such radioactive elements in particular. The bombardment of these atoms, which are basically unstable anyway, by large amounts of various kinds of particles of extremely high energy could hardly fail to have added to their instability. Or, to put it in another way, the addition of large amounts of external energy into the atomic nucleus would have supplied the needed energy for alpha particles or other groups to overcome the energy barrier normally retaining most of them within the nucleus.

This means that it is not only possible, but highly probable, that the disintegration rates of radioactive elements would have been much higher than at present during at least these two periods of earth

[1] Samuel Glasstone: *Sourcebook on Atomic Energy* (2nd Ed., New York, Van Nostrand, 1958), p. 562.

[2] "It is not only astrophysicists who are interested in superenergetic cosmic-ray particles. Students of the fundamental constitution of matter would very much like to know what happens when one of these particles strikes an atomic nucleus. . . . Experiments at lower energies such as are available from existing accelerators—indeed, from any accelerator yet envisaged—give no hint as to the behaviour of matter at the fantastically high energies of which we have been speaking." (Bruno Rossi: "High-Energy Cosmic Rays," *Scientific American*, Vol. 201, Nov. 1959, p. 145).

history. However, there seems to be no way on the basis of present knowledge by which the magnitude of this increase in rates[1] can now be determined.

The Van Allen Radiation Belt

There may also have been other sources of radiation and energy during these periods. The mere fact that the quantity of actively radioactive material in the earth must originally have been greater than at present would have been one such environmental factor. Also, one of the results of the artificial satellite studies in the higher atmosphere has been to reveal a belt of very high incidence of corpuscular radiation.

This abnormal radiation was found above the level about 450 miles high. The evidence is that:

. . . the great radiation belt around the earth consists of charged particles, temporarily trapped in the earth's magnetic field. . . . These studies, in connection with other results of the IGY (the cosmic ray work, in particular), begin to relate a variety of atmospheric and spatial phenomena in an exciting and meaningful way, suggesting that major advances are in process of being made and formulated.[2]

These radiation belts contain far more radiation than that due to the incidence of the cosmic rays.

Above some 1000 km. (this transition altitude being longitude and latitude dependent) the intensity of radiation increased very rapidly with increasing altitude, in a way totally inconsistent with cosmic ray expectations.[3]

As Dr. J. A. Van Allen, the man chiefly responsible for the discovery of these radiation zones, says:

[1] The postulated environment would probably produce a variety of nuclear transmutations in addition to accelerating the disintegration of uranium, thorium, etc. The various elements in each decay chain would also be affected. It is thus not strictly correct to speak of a simple increase in decay rate as resulting from such an environment. However, the net effect is the same . . . namely, an increase in the ratios of "daughter" to "parent" elements in each series.

[2] Hugh Odishaw: "International Geophysical Year," *Science*, Vol. 128, December 26, 1958, p. 1609.

[3] James A. Van Allen, Carl E. McIlwain, and George H. Ludwig: "Radiation Observations with Satellite 1958E*," *Journal of Geophysical Research*, Vol. 64, March 1959, p. 271.

Up to the points at which the counter jammed, it showed counting rates more than 1,000 times the theoretical expectation for cosmic rays. From the rate of increase and the length of the periods of jamming, we judged that the maximum count probably went to several times this level.[1]

The many and diversified electrical and magnetic phenomena in and around the earth's upper atmosphere are thus extremely interesting, but as yet little understood. Just how they all interact with each other at present, or how they may have acted in the past is not known. It is plain, however, that there is an abundance of rays and charged particles of high energies which, if any substantial portion could reach the earth's surface, would undoubtedly produce very significant changes in many geophysical processes and phenomena, certainly including those of radioactivity.[2]

We conclude, therefore, that a time measurement based on the principle of radioactive decay is in itself quite inconclusive. It is, in the first place, quite reasonable to believe that both parent and daughter elements in each radioactive chain were created at the beginning, probably in "equilibrium" amounts. The amount of originally created radiogenic end-product in each chain is uncertain; it is likely, however, that homologous amounts were created in all such minerals so that all such elements would, when created, give an "appearance" of the same degree of maturity or of age. Furthermore, the intense environmental radiation present in the upper atmosphere could well have resulted in much higher decay rates for the radioactive elements at one or more times in the past.

Thus, by the end of the Creation period, each radioactive mineral would very likely contain a sizeable amount of its radiogenic daughter, though actually but a few days old! Again, at the time of the Deluge, it seems reasonable that the increased radioactivity in the environment would have speeded up all decay processes by some unknown amount. Therefore, even in the relatively rare cases where the radioactive mineral was not disturbed excessively during the in-

---

[1] James A. Van Allen: "Radiation Belts Around the Earth," *Scientific American,* Vol. 200, March 1959, p. 44.

[2] A highly radioactive environment such as postulated mav, in addition to accelerating the decay of certain elements, have formed artificial radioactive elements, with various decay rates. The fact that these have not been found in nature may mean either that they just have not *yet* been found, or else that their initial decay rates were also higher than at present and they have substantially vanished by now. It is only the elements with very long half-lives that have survived the accelerated decay periods.

tense geologic upheavals of the Creation and Deluge periods, the relative amounts of parent and daughter elements would still be entirely incapable of yielding a valid record of *true* age, since neither the original amount of radiogenic material nor the changes in past decay rates can now be determined. The only thing reasonably certain is that the present decay rate and present amount of daughter element, if applied in a uniformitarian computation, must result in an age-estimate immensely too great!

AGREEMENT OF AGES FROM DIFFERENT METHODS

It might appear at first that these strictures do not invalidate an estimated age which is based on two or more independent calculations with different materials. Uranium and thorium are often found together in the same mineral, for example, and although calculations of the age are usually discordant, they occasionally agree. With respect even to the case of a mineral containing only uranium, Brown says:

Now there are four different ways we can compute the age of the mineral; namely, from (1) the ratio of lead 206 to uranium 238, (2) the ratio of lead 207 to uranium 235, (3) the ratio of lead 206 to lead 207, and (4) the ratio of helium to uranium. Ideally, all four of these ages should agree, and no estimate can be considered trustworthy unless at least two independent methods (i.e., two of the first three here) agree. But, unfortunately, complicating factors often produce discrepancies in evaluating a given sample.[1]

There is even more commonly disagreement between uranium and thorium ages, but again there is occasional agreement.

As more and more evidence was gathered, the lead method began to carry conviction. There could be little doubt when pure thorium minerals associated in the same rocks with pure uranium minerals gave the same absolute age.[2]

There are now known even a few cases where there is agreement between ages obtained by the lead method, the rubidium method, and/or the potassium method.

[1] Harrison Brown: "The Age of the Solar System," *Scientific American*, Vol. 196, April 1957, p. 82.
[2] O. B. Muench: "Determining Geologic Age from Radioactivity," *Scientific Monthly*, Vol. 71, November 1950, p. 300.

There is good reason to present the state of progress at this time, since the newer techniques have already provided an indication of their usefulness and simplicity in providing potassium-argon and rubidium-strontium ages that agree for rocks for which the two indicated uranium-lead ages disagree. These measurements have also shown that rubidium-strontium and potassium-argon ages can be made to agree with concordant uranium-lead ages by a suitable choice of half-lives for potassium 40 and rubidium 87. The values so found lie within the large range of values for these two constants, which have been obtained by direct laboratory counting experiments.[1]

Creation of Accordant "Apparent Ages"

But this kind of agreement is exactly what is to be expected on the basis of our deductions as to the past history of the radioactive elements, as originally created and as possibly subject during the Creation and Deluge periods to accelerated rates of decay. If any of the radiogenic elements were actually and truly created at the beginning, as seems eminently reasonable, it is most consistent with the perfect, "very good" character of the original Creation to infer that these different radiogenic elements were created in homologous quantities. That is, if two or more such elements were to be included in the same created mineral or group of minerals, their relative amounts would have been the same as their relative rates of origin by radioactive disintegration from their respective "parents." Furthermore, it is most likely that, if these parents were also created in juxtaposition in the same minerals with them, they and each member of their respective decay chains would have been created and present in their so-called "equilibrium" amounts as now governed by the individual decay rates of the members in the chain.

Skeptics will of course be immediately inclined to discard such a deduction as quite unscientific, in virtue of its being by its very nature unverifiable scientifically. And of course this is true to a degree, since no human experimenter can duplicate or even study processes of creation which are no longer going on. But as a matter of fact the assumption of uniformity is equally unverifiable scientifically as far as past history is concerned. It is only uniformitarian presupposition that decides the assumption of uniformity to be more reasonable than that of original creation!

[1] Lt. T. Aldrich: "Measurement of Radioactive Ages of Rocks," *Science*, Vol. 123, May 18, 1956, p. 871.

The writers strongly deny that it is unscientific to postulate a primeval and genuine creation. The two great universal principles of thermodynamics—energy conservation and deterioration—inexorably witness to the scientific necessity of original creation. Nor is it unscientific to accept the Biblical revelation, verified as it has been in countless ways, especially by the testimony of the Lord Jesus Christ Himself, as a true and reliable record of that which man cannot discover without such revelation, namely the events and order of the Creation.

All of this leads to the conclusion that, if it had been possible to make a radioactive time-estimate from these minerals *immediately after their creation* by the same methods as are now in use, they would have indicated some finite age for the earth, and this age, whatever it may have been, would have been the same for each of the different radiogenic elements in the mineral association. *This is the most reasonable conclusion possible on the assumption of a genuine primeval creation as recorded in Genesis.*

Concordant Changes in Decay Rates

Consider also the probable effect on the relative rates of radioactivity of the different elements during times when the environment was more radioactive than at present, such as on the first day of the Creation week and during the period of the Deluge. Each element of course has at present a definite value for its "half-life" or rate of disintegration. Whatever may be the fundamental nature and cause of these respective decay processes, it is likely that each would be affected roughly *proportionately* by any environmental factor potent enough to affect them at all. For example, if the higher incidence of cosmic radiation during any period were such as to have, say, doubled the rate of decay of uranium into lead, it is most probable that it would also have approximately doubled the rate of decay of thorium and that of rubidium and of other radioactive elements. Each rate would have been increased by a factor of the same order of magnitude, since each was subject to the same constant incidence of radiant energy.[1]

---

[1] Since uranium and thorium have decay chains consisting of several different elements, each with a different half-life, the assumption of simple proportional increase is an over-simplification. The resulting increase of each respective daughter-parent ratio may not be exactly in accordance with our assumption but it should be so qualitatively at least.

And this of course means that, if the particular minerals were left undisturbed, they would continue to yield roughly "accordant" ages, though these ages would now be apparently higher than they appeared at the time of Creation. Similarly, during the Flood period, each decay rate would have been speeded up in the same ratio, so that the individual elements would continue to give "accordant" ages. Finally, at the present date, still assuming this to be one of the relatively rare cases where the minerals have remained comparatively undisturbed through all the vicissitudes of geomorphic history, the suite of minerals would still give accordant ages, but the age so indicated would obviously be much greater than the true age since its creation!

This can all be illustrated by a somewhat simplified[1] algebraic calculation which will demonstrate the principles involved. Consider that we have at hand two distinct radiogenic elements, whose rates of production by decay from their parents are denoted by R and cR, with c being the constant ratio of these two production rates to each other. During any specific time interval T, the amounts of the two radiogenic elements produced are therefore $R(T)$ and $cR(T)$. Thus, the total amounts generated in the given time are in the same ratio c as their rates of generation.

If these elements existed also as a result of direct creation, it is reasonable to assume that they existed in these same proportions. Say, then, that their initial amounts are represented by quantities of A and cA, respectively. Now, if at some time the incidence of environmental radiation is increased, both rates will be increased in roughly these same proportions; assume that both are multiplied by a factor k and that the increased rates persist throughout a length of time T'. Prior to this period, the normal rates applied and persisted, say, for a time $T°$, and following this period they applied again for a time of $T*$.

The total quantity of the first element that would now be measured would therefore be: $A + R(T°) + k(R)(T') + R(T*)$. The total quantity of the second element would be: $cA + cR(T°) + k(cR)(T') + cR(T*)$.

---

[1] This discussion is not meant to be an exact exposition of radiogenic age computation; the relation is mathematically more complicated than the direct proportion assumed for the illustration. Nevertheless, the principles described are substantially applicable to the actual relationship.

Now, if these total quantities of the two elements are each used to make an age-estimate, their respective normal decay rates would of course be used, since it is commonly assumed that these rates could never have been different. Accordingly, the two ages would be calculated as follows:

(1). $T = \dfrac{A + R(T°) + k(R)(T') + R(T^*)}{R} = A/R + T° + k(T') + T^*$

(2). $T = \dfrac{cA + cR(T°) + k(cR)(T') + cR(T^*)}{cR} = A/R + T° + k(T') + T^*$

Obviously, these two age-estimates agree perfectly, and might therefore be thought to verify each other and demonstrate the validity of both computations. As a matter of fact, however, each is too large, since the true age of each is only $T° + T' + T^*$. Each is too high by the amount: $A/R + (k-1)(T')$. The numerical value of this excess depends upon the initial amount present A and on the rate increase factor k, and neither of these quantities is known nor evidently can ever be determined. Therefore, it is concluded that it is impossible to make a really certain age determination unless it is known beyond any question that the term A is zero and the factor k is 1, or perhaps some other known values.

Nor does the fact that two or more apparently independent age-estimates agree prove that the computations are valid and the age correct! The foregoing analysis shows that this result is to be expected *regardless* of whether or not the decay rates had changed in the past, and therefore it proves nothing except that the mineral under examination had probably not been disturbed and its component parts segregated since its original formation.

This apparent agreement is really the only evidence that might be offered to prove that the rates had *not* varied in the past, as we have already shown. But now we have shown that it does not necessarily prove this at all. Therefore, radioactivity age estimates cannot legitimately be used as *proof* of the age of the earth or of any formation in it!

Pleochroic Halos

Someone may object that it has been proved that the disintegration rate of uranium has never changed during past geologic time, since the size of the so-called "pleochroic halos" is the same in strata of all ages. These halos are spherical zones of discoloration produced in rocks around radioactive nuclei by the ionizing powers of the alpha particles emitted from the nucleus. The distance to which these particles can penetrate before they are stopped depends on their energy of emission, and this in turn is believed to control the normal rate of decay, high rates corresponding to large ranges.

The range of the alpha-particles depends, however, not only on the decay rate of the radioactive nucleus but also upon the nature of the material in which it is enclosed, the denser the material, the shorter the range. For this reason, this particular argument is usually limited only to the halos surrounding nuclei of uranium or thorium in a matrix of mica. The argument goes that, for this type of halo, the radius is always the same, and therefore that the disintegration rate must always have been the same.

There is some reason to question this assertion, however. Nearly all the studies that have been made on this subject were made by Joly, about 1907, and G. H. Henderson, in 1934. Others have simply referred to their work and interpreted it as proving the constancy of the decay rate. Joly, however, had himself concluded that the decay rate had changed.

Joly's study of pleochroic halos in micas of various geological ages brought out a variation of the radii of halos of presumably the same radioactive origin, the older being apparently the longer. His suggestion of varying rate of disintegration of uranium at various geological periods would, if correct, set aside all possibilities of age calculation by radioactivity methods. Fortunately, enough evidence has been found of correct radii for the different geologic periods and sufficient variation in the same period that one is forced to look for a different explanation of such variations as were observed by Joly.[1]

Although this statement explicitly denies that the halos indicate different decay rates, as thought by Joly, it does admit that there is quite a bit of variation in the halo radii, and therefore the claim that they always show the same radii is clearly unwarranted. The most that can be claimed is that they exhibit a rather wide statistical fluctuation about a mean value—which is itself microscopic in size!

More recent studies by a consulting metallurgist, Dr. Roy M. Allen,

[1] A. F. Kovarik, in *The Age of the Earth,* Adolph Knopf, Editor, Bulletin 80, National Research Council, 1931, p. 107.

confirm this variation in radii, together with the difficulty of truly meaningful measurement of them. Among various conclusions regarding the variability in character and occurrence of these halos, the following is of particular interest:

The extent of the halos around the inclusions varies over a wide range, even with the same nuclear material in the same matrix, but all sizes fall into definite groups. My measurements are, in microns, 5, 7, 10, 17, 20, 23, 27, and 33. Joly's figures correspond with these except he does not include the smaller sizes and does include 39 (38-40) which I have not run across. Halos sometimes show two, or even three definite rings or zones, indicating the presence of more than one radioactive element, each with its own specific alpha-ray path.[1]

In view of these observations made by a very careful scientist, it appears that the oft-reiterated claim about the constancy of the radius may be invalid. Therefore, there remains no actual evidence that the decay rates may not have been different at some time or times in the past than they are at present.

But even if there should turn out to be at least a statistical constancy of the halo radii, this does not mean that the past rates are the same as present rates. According to our hypothesis, all rocks are of essentially the same age, so that the fact that pleochroic halos have about the same radius in all of them is exactly what would be expected. They were all formed at about the same time; therefore, the same decay rates, whether constant or changing, have continually occurred in all of them. Furthermore, it seems unlikely that even a substantial increase in the decay rate would cause any measurable change in the halo radius. The latter is determined mainly by the extremely short-lived elements in the decay chain, for these have the longer ranges. It does not seem necessary to conclude that an acceleration of the first stage in the decay process—the expulsion of helium atoms from the uranium nucleus—would thereby accelerate all other stages in the chain individually. But even if it did, the increase in alpha particle range corresponding to increase in expulsion energies becomes vanishingly small as the energies increase, and this factor would prevent any very substantial increase in the radius.

This argument, however, is not infallible, because according to the bilo-

---

[1] Roy M. Allen: "The Evaluation of Radioactive Evidence on the Age of the Earth," *Journal of the American Scientific Affiliation* (December 1952) p. 18.

garithmic form of the law of Geiger and Nuttall a considerable variation in the decay constant will produce a very small change in the range of the alpha-particle.[1]

Thus, we conclude that a statistical constancy of the halo radii in rocks of various "ages" proves nothing about the decay rates.

SUPPOSED CORRELATION OF RADIOACTIVITY AND STRATIGRAPHIC AGES

Extent of Agreement

There is still the claim to be faced that the radioactivity age-estimates agree in general with the geological ages assigned to the strata on the basis of paleontology and stratigraphy. That is, the "absolute ages" deduced from radioactivity measurements for various positions in the geologic time scale fall into proper position, so that strata deemed young on the basis of paleontology give young radioactivity ages, paleontologically old strata yield higher ages, etc. On this basis, a scale of absolute time has been worked up for the entire geologic column and, in various forms, has been published in many, many books and periodicals. For example, Arthur Holmes, probably the most prolific of all writers and workers in this field, said long ago in the famous National Research Council symposium on geochronology:

In attempting to build up a time scale it is clear that we have to steer a difficult course through a maze of data of very variable quality, guided in some places by atomic weight evidence, in others by series of accordant ratios, but in far too many by a subjective weighing of probabilities. Nevertheless, although only a few points can be fixed with precision into the geological column, and the total assemblage of data is too confused to permit detailed accuracy, it is remarkable how consistently the most probable ratio for each of the various suites falls into its proper place and order as judged by geological age.[2]

A major reason for the supposed concordance between the radioactivity and paleontological time scales is evident from this remarkable quotation: the time estimates which agree with the pre-judged

---

[1] Kalervo Rankama: *Isotope Geology* (New York, McGraw-Hill, 1954), p. 109.
[2] Arthur Holmes, in *The Age of the Earth,* Adolph Knopf, Editor, Bulletin 80, National Research Council, 1931, p. 431.

proper order are accepted, the others are rejected! The latter are supposed to have been altered in some way since deposition and therefore unacceptable, the criterion for postulating alteration being this lack of agreement. This sort of "subjective weighing of probabilities" is quite convenient, but hardly constitutes compelling proof.

But it will be objected that the above was written almost thirty years ago; great masses of data have been accumulated since then from radioactive minerals from all parts of the world and all parts of the geologic column. Listen, then, to the recent words of Adolph Knopf (who was also editor of the symposium cited above) in a recent review of the data:

An urgent task for geology is to determine, in years, the length of the eras, periods, and "ages" (time spans of the stages) and, eventually of the zones. Not a single one of them—eras, periods, and ages, let alone zones— has yet been reliably determined. This statement is possibly surprising in view of the fact that almost any modern writer can produce a geologic timetable that gives precise datings and lengths of the eras and systems and even of some of the smaller subdivisions. . . . These figures have been obtained in various remarkable ways. Ultimately, however, they are tied to three dates based on atomic disintegration: 60 million years, the age of the pitchblende at Central City, Colorado; 220 million years, the age of the pitchblende at St. Joachimstal, Bohemia; and 440 million years, the age of the uranium-bearing shale at Gullhogen, Sweden. The age of the Swedish shale is the only one of these that is paleontologically controlled. . . . All other absolute ages have been derived from the three radioactive tie points by interpolation based on thicknesses of strata or by "reasoned guesses" . . .[1]

Now, herein is a marvelous thing! Consider what *science* has proved! All the world of learning and scholarship has been driven to accept the *fact* of universal evolution as the basic principle and philosophy controlling everything, despite the testimony of both Scripture and the demonstrated truths of energy conservation and degradation, because of the supposed overwhelming weight of scientific evidence. When one goes to the geneticist to see such evidence, he is shown only micromutations and is directed to the geologist for evidence of historical evolution on the broader scale. The geologist then points to a series of time-rock units, which has been erected on the assumption of organic evolution, despite the evidence of many

[1] Adolph Knopf: "Measuring Geologic Time," *Scientific Monthly*, Vol. 85, November 1957, p. 227.

exceptions and contradictions in the series, and which even at best still contains essentially the same gaps that the genetic evidence shows. Although most of these rocks show evidence of rapid, catastrophic formation, he maintains that radioactivity has provided him with a scale of absolute time that proves that they are in the proper order and that the times are so immense as to provide for all the statistical improbabilities that evolution demands. And when we inquire into the nature of the radioactive evidence that proves such wonderful things, we learn that out of the hundreds and hundreds of such measurements that have been made on rocks from every geological age and from all parts of the world, after winnowing out all those with discordant ratios, with anomalous amounts of component elements, or that disagree with the paleontological dating, there are *three* (three!) that form the basis of the time-scale and that all others are interpolated therefrom by "reasoned guesses," based mainly on relative thicknesses of strata.

And of these three datings, only one is considered adequately dated paleontologically. That one, the Cambrian shales of Sweden containing nodules of uranium called "kolm," has long been the pride and joy of geochronologists. But it also is highly questionable. Knopf says:

> The isotopic composition of the radiogenic lead in the kolm was determined by Nier, in 1939, and yielded the very disconcerting result that the age, based on Lead 206-Uranium 238, is 380 million years, whereas that based on Lead 207-Lead 206 is 770 million years. Now Nier, it must be recalled, regarded the figure given by the Lead 207-Lead 206 ratio as being the least subject to error and hence the most reliable. For the kolm, however, the figure 770 million years was clearly too large.[1]

However, instead of rejecting this as discordant, the discrepancies have been compromised and the age recorded as 440 million years, on the assumption that some of the radon gas formed as one stage in the decay series had escaped, thus causing too small an amount of radiogenic lead to be produced.[2] Note that there is no *proof* that this was actually the case; it merely was an assumption which provided a means of reconciling the discrepancy and arriving at an age

---

[1] Knopf, *op. cit.*, p. 234.

[2] *Ibid.* More recent measurements on this material, by J. C. Cobb and J. L. Kulp, indicate that "preliminary measurements of radon leakage show room-temperature radon loss to be of an order of magnitude less than that needed to explain the discordance" ("Age of the Swedish Kolm," *Bulletin of the Geological Society of America*, Vol. 68, Dec. 1957, p. 1711).

that seemed appropriate for the paleontological stratum in which the mineral was found.

And this date, deduced by so devious and questionable an analysis, is considered the best and most reliable of all the hundreds and perhaps thousands of dates that have been obtained from the radioactivity measurements on the earth's post-Precambrian strata!

Still more recently, Henry Faul concludes that only the Colorado pitchblende is at all acceptable:

> Of the five points on which Holmes based his time scale, only one (Laramide) can be included now. The stratigraphically unimpeachable "Swedish Kolm" from the alum shale does not present a closed system, and all attempts to establish an age for it have failed. The stratigraphic limits on Holmes' remaining three points are too vague to make them useful.[1]

With regard to the device of interpolating dates for other geologic horizons from thicknesses of strata, Knopf says:

> As long ago as 1936 the conclusion had been reached by Twenhofel [the outstanding authority on sedimentation] that estimates of time based on thicknesses of strata "are hardly worth the paper they are written on," and he presents detailed evidence in support of this revolutionary concept.[2]

Thus, the general inadequacy of the radioactivity geochronometric data for paleontologic dating is indicated by Teichert:

> The literature contains few age determinations (perhaps no more than one) on syngenetic radionuclides from paleontologically defined stratigraphic units, and almost all radioactive age determinations are made on igneous, hydrothermally introduced, or secondarily transported minerals that cannot as a rule be referred to a precisely defined place in the stratigraphic succession. At present, no coherent picture of the history of the earth could be built on the basis of radioactive datings.[3]

On the other hand, we do recognize, of course, that in spite of the high degree of confusion and inconsistency in much of the radio-

[1] Henry Faul: "Geologic Time Scale," *Bulletin, Geological Society of America*, Vol. 71, May 1960, p. 640.

[2] Knopf, *op. cit.*, p. 228.

[3] Curt Teichert: "Some Biostratigraphical Concepts," *Bulletin of the Geological Society of America*, Vol. 69, January 1958, p. 102. Henry Faul says: "When we now attempt to construct a time scale by reasonable interpolation between these points, it becomes obvious that the available data are still too few, too poor, and internally inconsistent" (*Op. cit.*, p. 642).

activity age data, there does seem to be a certain rough tendency for some degree of correlation between paleontologic and radioactivity relative ages. The bulk of these measurements have been made on Pre-Cambrian strata, of course, and although there are many flagrant exceptions, most of the values so obtained do indicate ages greater than 500,000,000 years, which is now assumed to be about the beginning of the Paleozoic Era.[1] Similarly, a number of age estimates obtained on the fossiliferous strata, especially as obtained within the last few years by the Potassium-Argon method, exhibit rough trends parallelling the traditional order of the geologic column.

Thus, although we insist that the case in favor of the accepted geologic time-scale has been made to appear much stronger than it is by this dubious process of accepting those data which support it and rejecting those which contradict it, there still seems to remain enough evidence of correlation to indicate some basic physical phenomenon which has operated in such fashion as to cause apparently higher proportions of radiogenic materials in the "older" strata, that is, those which were usually deposited earlier and deeper than the others.

Cause of the Apparent Limited Agreement

But again, isn't this tendency only what is to be expected on the basis of the events inferred from Scripture to have transpired during the periods of the Creation and the Flood? At the time of the primal Creation, each of the radioactive parent elements was created in place at various points throughout the crust. As we have already indicated, it is reasonable that there would also be associated with each parent atom an "equilibrium amount" of its various daughters. But we must allow for the probability that there were intense crustal disturbances and adjustments during the first days of the Creation period. It is probable also that certain amounts of non-radiogenic lead, helium, argon and other of the elements associated with the disintegration chains were created initially, independently of the equilibrium amounts established in association with radioactive parents. During

---

[1] However, Henry Faul says: "K/Ar and Rb/Sr determinations on intrusive rocks of the Paleozoic era almost always give ages greater than the numerical ages predicted by the currently accepted time scale. . . . The results show that one may begin to think of fairly drastic revision in the Paleozoic time scale." ("Doubts of the Paleozoic Time Scale," *American Geophysical Union Program Abstracts,* May 1959, p. 42.)

the later Creation stages, as well as during the Deluge, there would be abundant opportunity for mixing of the "common" isotopes and their sister "created radiogenic" isotopes, as well as with the "actually radiogenic" isotopes which began to form immediately after the creation of the parents.

Some such mixing process as this is envisaged by Faul, who says:

It is very likely that "primordial lead," or the lead that was made with all the other elements at the time of nucleogenesis, was well mixed. When the earth's crust was formed, the primordial lead was frozen into rocks that also contained uranium and thorium in various ratios to lead.[1]

Therefore, it would be expected that those radioactive minerals found in the rocks of the shields and other Pre-Cambrian formations would yield many different age values, though in general most of them would be very high. This is exactly what is found.

With regard to the sedimentary strata, as well as the igneous intrusions found in them, together with the other fossiliferous volcanic rocks, these we believe were largely formed during the Deluge, as outlined in the preceding chapter. The materials for these rocks were derived from the primitive crustal rocks in large part, although there must undoubtedly have been a primitive soil created as well to support the first life-forms, and these materials also were eroded and redistributed by the flood waters. Mixing of radiogenic and non-radiogenic isotopes must have been even more intensive during the Flood period than during the Creation period.

As a general rule, those radioactive minerals nearest the surface would be subject to the greatest degree of mixing during the Flood, since they would have been those first eroded by the torrential rains and swollen streams. This would have had the effect of "diluting" the radiogenic component of such minerals, making those near the surface appear to be relatively "younger" than those further below the surface. Furthermore, both during and after the Deluge, those minerals nearer the surface and in the lighter, less consolidated sediments, would be much more likely to lose their gaseous components (e.g., argon from the potassium minerals, radon and helium from the uranium) than those in the denser, deeper rocks. This, too, would have the effect of making the radioactive minerals in the surface rocks appear to be younger than those below. Obviously, with all

[1] Henry Faul: *Nuclear Geology* (New York, John Wiley & Sons, 1954), p. 297.

the intense mixing involved, the inferred orders would represent only rough trends rather than inviolable rules, and this is exactly the state of things encountered in the present strata.

Also, there are many radioactive minerals found in the igneous intrusions in the sedimentary strata, which we have inferred to be associated with outpourings from the "fountains of the great deep" during the Flood. These radioactive minerals would also, in general, contain smaller relative amounts of radiogenic elements because of the greater mixing and diffusive action associated with the intrusion and would therefore, when deposited, read "younger" ages than those in the true Pre-Cambrian strata.

Further discussion of other aspects of the radioactivity age estimates does not appear necessary here. The important features of these data are all now seen to be explainable in terms of the phenomena and activity associated with the Creation and the Deluge. It is not at all necessary to interpret them as teaching the immense ages hitherto inferred therefrom. In fact the gross and entirely unwarranted assumptions on which they are based (especially uniformity and denial of any true creation), in contrast to the sound basis in Holy Scripture upon which the assumptions in our interpretation are based, justify the assertion that the latter is actually much better oriented scientifically than the former.

ASTRONOMIC METHODS OF AGE MEASUREMENT

Nor do we need to consider at length the various other methods that have been used for estimating the age of the earth and the universe. We can say in general that they are based on much more extreme assumptions and on much flimsier empirical evidence than are the radioactivity methods. For example, a commonly heard claim is that the rate of expansion of the astronomic universe is such as to indicate a time since the beginning of the expansion of about five billion years, a time which is thought to be compatible with radioactivity evidence as to the age of the earth's crust. But, as the astronomer, Dr. T. S. Jacobsen of the University of Washington says:

. . . the current estimates for the expanding universe, whether on the old or the new time scale, are very far from being in any sense factual. While it is true that the Hubble constant enters into the computation of the "age," McVittie has stressed that a factor depending upon the model, a pure guess that the present radius of curvature is about 100 times the original Einstein radius, and an assumption of the average density of matter in the observed universe (an estimate which is still uncertain within a factor of 1000 according to some observational astronomers) all enter into the computation of the age. In addition to these uncertainties, we do not know that the nebulae have always moved at their present constant speeds. Accelerations and decelerations with time are at present being considered as possibilities. The result is that we know nothing certain about the age of the universe.[1]

A common opinion is that the very distance of the far galaxies testifies that the universe must be billions of years old. Since these galaxies are known to be some few billion light-years away, by definition it has taken that number of years for their light to reach us; therefore they are at least that old, so the argument goes.

But this contention of course again begs the question. It constitutes an implicit denial that the universe could have been created as a functioning entity. If creation has occurred at all (and the two principles of thermodynamics require this) then it is reasonable that it would have been a *complete* creation. It must have had an "appearance of age" at the moment of creation. The photons of light energy were created at the same instant as the stars from which they were apparently derived, so that an observer on the earth would have been able to see the most distant stars within his vision at that instant of creation. There is nothing unreasonable either philosophically or scientifically in this, although it does contradict the uniformitarian assumption.

Even apart from this factor, it is not commonly realized how many esoteric assumptions enter into even such apparently simple concepts as the speed of light and the geometric nature of the universe. To illustrate, a recent theory rather vigorously advocated by some astrophysicists strongly questions the constancy of the velocity of light in space and time, as well as the generally accepted Einsteinian nature of the universe. These writers regard the universe much more realistically as a Euclidian universe (3-dimensional, as in our everyday experience) and the velocity of light as constant with respect to its source, rather than with respect to any observer as Einstein does. Among the implications of this thesis the following is most interesting:

[1] T. S. Jacobsen: Review of "Space, Time, and Creation," by M. K. Munitz, appearing in *Science*, Vol. 128, September 5, 1958, p. 527.

In essence, therefore, the method of this paper leaves astronomical space unchanged but reduces the time required for light to travel from a star to the earth.[1]

Or, more specifically, and rather surprisingly:

The acceptance of Riemannian space allows us to reject Einstein's relativity and to keep all the ordinary ideas of time and all the ideas of Euclidean space out to a distance of a few light years. Astronomical space remains Euclidean for material bodies, but light is considered to travel in Riemannian space. In this way the time required for light to reach us from the most distant stars is only 15 years.[2]

We do not propose to evaluate this theory but only to point out that all cosmological theory is still highly speculative. The very fact that such a theory can be developed and seriously considered demonstrates that astronomy has nothing really *definite* as yet to say about the age of the universe. And this is entirely aside from the really much more fundamental issue of the reality of a genuine Creation!

There are many other geochronometers that have been suggested and utilized to a certain extent, but each is based on the typical uniformitarian assumptions, and none have been as widely and intensively developed as have those already discussed. Each of them has grave deficiencies and is admittedly less reliable than the radioactivity methods which we have already analyzed and reinterpreted.

THE RADIOCARBON DATING OF RECENT DEPOSITS

We must give some consideration, however, to one more particular method, namely the radiocarbon method of dating. This tool has become quite widely used and accepted in recent years and is important to our study since it professes to supply absolute dates for events within the past 30 or 40 thousand years. This of course covers the apparent periods of Biblical history, as well as more recent dates, and so bears directly upon the question of the Flood and other related events.

The method was first developed by W. F. Libby in 1946. Since that time, literally thousands of such measurements have been made, by workers in many different laboratories, and a great variety of archaeo-

[1] Parry Moon and Domina Eberle Spencer: "Binary Stars and the Velocity of Light," *Journal of the Optical Society of America,* Vol. 43, August 1953, p. 639.
[2] *Ibid.,* p. 635.

logical and Recent geological datings have been obtained. The formation of radiocarbon (that is, Carbon 14, the radioactive isotope of ordinary carbon) from cosmic radiation was first discovered, however, by Serge Korff, an authority on cosmic rays. Describing the Carbon 14 dating method which has resulted, Korff says:

Cosmic ray neutrons, produced as secondary particles in the atmosphere by the original radiation, are captured by nitrogen nuclei to form the radioactive isotope of carbon, the isotope of mass 14. This isotope has a long half-life, something over 5500 years. By the application of some very well thought-out techniques, Libby and his colleagues have actually not only identified the radiocarbon in nature, but have also made quantitative estimates thereof. Since this carbon in the atmosphere mostly becomes attached to oxygen to form carbon dioxide, and since the carbon dioxide is ingested by plants and animals and is incorporated in their biological structures, and further, since this process stops at the time of the death of the specimen, the percentage of radiocarbon among the normal carbon atoms in its system can be used to establish the date at which the specimen stops metabolizing.[1]

Assumptions in the Method

There is no doubt that this constitutes a very ingenious and powerful dating tool, provided only that the inherent assumptions are valid. Kulp lists the assumptions as follows:

There are two basic assumptions in the carbon 14 method. One is that the carbon 14 concentration in the carbon dioxide cycle is constant. The other is that the cosmic ray flux has been essentially constant—at least on a scale of centuries.[2]

To which we might add the assumption of the constancy of the rate of decay of the carbon 14 atoms, the assumption that dead organic matter is not later altered with respect to its carbon content by any biologic or other activity, the assumption that the carbon dioxide content of the ocean and atmosphere has been constant with time, the assumption that the huge reservoir of oceanic carbon has not changed in size during the period of applicability of the method, and the assumption that the rate of formation and the rate of decay of

[1] Serge A. Korff: "The Origin and Implications of the Cosmic Radiation," *American Scientist,* Vol. 45, September 1957, p. 298.

[2] J. L. Kulp: "The Carbon 14 Method of Age Determination," *Scientific Monthly,* Vol. 75, November 1952, p. 261.

radiocarbon atoms have been in equilibrium throughout the period of applicability. Every one of these assumptions is highly questionable in the context of the events of Creation and the Deluge.

But it is maintained that the method has been verified beyond any question by numerous correlations with known dates. Here an observation by Libby himself is interesting and in point:

> The first shock Dr. Arnold and I had was that our advisors informed us that history extended back only 5000 years. We had thought initially that we would be able to get samples all along the curve back to 30,000 years, put the points in, and then our work would be finished. You read books and find statements that such and such a society or archaeological site is 20,000 years old. We learned rather abruptly that these numbers, these ancient ages, are not known; in fact, it is at about the time of the first dynasty in Egypt that the last historical date of any real certainty has been established.[1]

It is obvious, therefore, that any genuine correlation of the radiocarbon method with definite historical chronologies is limited only to some time after the Flood and Dispersion. The major assumptions in the method are evidently valid for this period, but this does not prove their validity for more ancient times, the periods in which we would infer that the assumptions are very likely wrong and therefore the datings also wrong.

Attempts to apply the carbon 14 method to earlier datings have, in fact, been called in serious question by geologists for entirely different reasons than our own. Charles B. Hunt, who is recent president of the American Geological Institute, has cautioned:

> In order that a technique or discipline may be useful in scientific work, its limits must be known and understood, but the limits of usefulness of the radiocarbon age determinations are not yet known or understood. No one seriously proposes that all the determined dates are without error, but we do not know how many of them are in error—25%? 50%? 75%? And we do not know which dates are in error, or by what amounts, or why.[2]

Hunt emphasizes particularly the danger of contamination of the sample by external sources of carbon, especially in damp locations.

[1] W. F. Libby: "Radiocarbon Dating," *American Scientist*, Vol. 44, January 1956, p. 107.
[2] Charles B. Hunt: "Radiocarbon Dating in the Light of Stratigraphy and Weathering Processes," *Scientific Monthly*, Vol. 81, November 1955, p. 240.

The sharp reduction in previously estimated dates for the close of the glacial period (a date which had been estimated mainly on the basis of counts of varved clays presumably laid down by the retreating ice sheet) has been a source of much argument among Pleistocene geologists as to the relative merits of the varve method (which gave a date of over 20,000 years) and the radiocarbon method (which gave a date of about 11,000 years). The American specialist in varve chronologies, Dr. Ernst Antevs, has sharply criticized the radiocarbon method, as a result:

In appraising C 14 dates, it is essential always to discriminate between the C 14 age and the actual age of the sample. The laboratory analysis determines only the amount of radioactive carbon present. . . . However, the laboratory analysis does not determine whether the radioactive carbon is all original or is in part secondary, intrusive, or whether the amount has been altered in still other irregular ways besides by natural decay.[1]

A conference on radiocarbon dating held in October, 1956, resulted in the following conclusions about the reliability of the method:

Local variation, especially in shells, can be highly significant. Possible variations in the size of the exchange reservoir under glacial climates are unimportant. The most significant problem is that of biological alteration of materials in the soil. This effect grows more serious with greater age. To produce an error of 50 per cent in the age of a 10,000 year old specimen would require the replacement of more than 25 per cent of the carbon atoms. For a 40,000-year-old sample, the figure is only 5 per cent, while an error of 5000 years can be produced by about 1 per cent of modern materials. Much more must be done on chemical purification of samples.[2]

The problem of atmospheric contamination by fossil fuels has also come in for some consideration, since the burning of coal and oil during the past century and more has added measurably to the amount of carbon dioxide in the carbon cycle. A recent study on the quantitative aspect of this factor concludes:

. . . it follows that atmospheric carbon dioxide has probably been diluted to the extent of about 3½ percent with carbon dioxide from the combustion of fossil fuels. The radiocarbon evidence indicates, on the basis of a comparison of the radiocarbon assays of old, historically dated marine

[1] Ernst Antevs: "Geological Tests of the Varve and Radiocarbon Chronologies," *Journal of Geology,* March 1957, p. 129.

[2] F. Johnson, J. R. Arnold, and R. F. Flint: "Radiocarbon Dating," *Science,* Vol. 125, February 8, 1957, p. 240.

shells from the Atlantic coast with the assays of their modern counterparts, that there has been a perceptible dilution of shallow oceanic carbonates with dead carbon from fossil fuels. The limited data available suggest that the extent of dilution is possibly one to two per cent.[1]

This means that the standard figures as to present content of carbon dioxide in the exchange reservoir of carbon, on which radiocarbon age calculations are based, are incorrect with respect to conditions under which older specimens were formed and have since been decaying. Although this might be corrected approximately by modifying the standard to one before the Industrial Revolution, the following caution is also in order:

Since completion of the present list, a careful study has been made of a series of samples of known age. It was found that the activity of radiocarbon in the atmosphere was going up and down even before the Industrial Revolution.[2]

This particular correction, however, is only of the order of a few hundred years for most computed dates, so apparently is negligible for the purposes of our studies. Much more important are the effects of the aforementioned assumptions in the method,[3] when viewed in the light of the probable events occurring during and immediately after the Flood.

CARBON 14 AND THE DELUGE

Antediluvian Radiocarbon Proportions

Prior to the Flood, it is highly probable that the ratio of ordinary carbon to radiocarbon in the atmosphere was much higher than at

---

[1] H. R. Brannon, A. C. Daughtry, D. Perry, W. W. Whitaker, and M. Williams: "Radiocarbon Evidence on the Dilution of Atmospheric & Oceanic Carbon," Transactions, *American Geophysical Union*, Vol. 38, October, 1957, p. 650.

[2] H. deVries and H. T. Waterbolk: "Groningen Radiocarbon Dates III," *Science*, Vol. 128, December 19, 1958, p. 1551.

[3] Another important source of error is the assumed contemporary assay, the initial concentration of radiocarbon in the material, which can be seriously diluted by old carbon in the environment at the time the organism was living, thus making the computed radiocarbon age too high. "Any error in the choice of the value of the contemporary assay results in an error of the radiocarbon age. . . . The error in age is approximately 80 years for an error in contemporary assay of one percent and is proportionately more for larger errors in contemporary assay." (W. W. Whitaker, S. Valastro, Jr., and Milton Williams, "The Climatic Factor in the Radiocarbon Content of Woods," *Journal of Geophysical Research*, Vol. 64, August 1959, p. 1023).

present, mainly because of the global semi-tropical climate and the vast amounts of plant life found around the world. This effect would have been augmented by the smaller amount of carbon sustained in the ocean then than now, since the oceans were smaller and the land areas larger before the Flood. And it is possible that it would be still further augmented by the shielding effect of the thermal vapor canopy, which would have inhibited the formation of radiocarbon in the high atmosphere. All of these factors would have reduced the ratio of radiocarbon to ordinary carbon to a much smaller fraction than now obtains.

Another possible effect of the vapor canopy is very interesting. In addition to the formation of Carbon 14 from nitrogen in the atmosphere by cosmic-ray neutrons, these neutrons also react with deuterium (heavy hydrogen, the hydrogen isotope in heavy water), which would undoubtedly have been present in substantial amounts in such a canopy, to form tritium, a still heavier isotope of hydrogen. Tritium is unstable and decays rapidly by beta decay to an isotope of helium, He 3. But it turns out that there is too much He 3 in the atmosphere to be accounted for by this process operating at present rates during geologic time. The cosmic ray authority, Korff, suggests the following solution of the problem:

There are two factors which would tend to increase the amount of tritium. One of these is that the intensity of cosmic radiation, and hence the rate of production of neutrons might have been higher at some time in the geologic past. . . . The second possibility invoking action in the past assumes that at a time when the earth was warmer the atmosphere contained much more water vapor, and (the process of generating tritium from deuterium) might have been operating at a much higher rate than at present.[1]

The vapor canopy thus not only provides an explanation for the present excess of atmospheric Helium 3 but also implies that the proportion of cosmic ray neutrons reacting with nitrogen to form radiocarbon would be smaller by the amount reacting thus with the hydrogen. This factor combines with the others mentioned to assure that the per cent of radiocarbon in the carbon dioxide of the antediluvian atmosphere must have been much smaller than at present. Therefore

[1] Serge A. Korff: "Effects of the Cosmic Radiation on Terrestial Isotope Distribution," *Transactions, American Geophysical Union,* Vol. 35, February 1954, p. 105.

the radioactivity of living organisms ingesting this carbon dioxide would have been much smaller than that of organisms living at present.

Thus, antediluvian organic matter probably would now have little or no radioactivity if preserved as fossils, even though they may actually have been buried by the Flood only a few thousand years ago. Although present radiocarbon activity seems to indicate measurements will detect radioactivities from matter perhaps as much as 70,000 years old, such indications are based upon the assumption of uniformity. This stricture is considered quite serious by Dr. G. N. Plass, who is a specialist in investigations dealing with atmospheric carbon dioxide:

> All calculations of radiocarbon dates have been made on the assumption that the amount of atmospheric carbon dioxide has remained constant. If the theory presented here of carbon dioxide variations in the atmosphere is correct, then the reduced carbon dioxide amount at the time of the last glaciation means that all radiocarbon dates for events before the recession of the glaciers are in question.[1]

Postdiluvian Radiocarbon Proportions

With respect to plants and animals living after the Flood, the loss of the earth's canopy would tend to increase the per cent concentration of Carbon 14 in the carbon dioxide of the atmosphere, since the rate of formation of Carbon 14 atoms would be accelerated by the loss of the canopy. On the other hand, the influx of carbon into the atmosphere from the intense volcanism during and after the Deluge period must have greatly augmented the carbon dioxide content of the atmosphere and oceans as well, probably more than offsetting the increase in C-14, at least for some time.

Furthermore, the equilibrium condition between generation and decay of radiocarbon, which has to be assumed in making any age calculation by this method, would obviously not be applicable for quite a long time after the Deluge. Although there quite probably was a marked increase in rate of formation of Carbon 14 atoms at the time of the Deluge due to the greater effectiveness of the cosmic radiation in this process after the precipitation of the vapor canopy, it

---

[1] Gilbert N. Plass: "Carbon Dioxide and the Climate," *American Scientist*, Vol. 44, July 1956, p. 314.

would necessarily have taken many years for the total amount of radiocarbon to have built up a reservoir of such size that the numbers of atoms being created and dissipated were equal. And this would mean that organisms living in these early years and centuries after the Flood would have received a proportionately smaller amount of radiocarbon into their systems than those living in later times. Especially in the few hundred years immediately after the Flood, during the time when mixing of the atmospheric, oceanic, and biologic carbon was first being accomplished, would this be true. In his definitive book on the subject, Libby says:

> If one were to imagine that the cosmic radiation had been turned off until a short while ago, the enormous amount of radiocarbon necessary to the equilibrium state would not have been manufactured and the specific radioactivity of living matter would be much less than the rate of production calculated from neutron intensity.[1]

The obvious conclusion is that plants and animals living in the early centuries after the Flood would have much less radioactivity than would be assumed on the basis of present rates and therefore would appear to be older than they are.

The specific radioactivity increased as time went on, approaching the present equilibrium rates. That is why radiocarbon dates for the last four thousand years seem to show a generally good correlation with historically verified chronology, although there are many discrepancies and a large margin of error the farther back in time comparisons are made. But for earlier dates, the specific radioactivity in the terrestrial environment becomes progressively smaller as one goes back in time. Therefore, when material older than, say, about four thousand years is analyzed now for radiocarbon, it would certainly be found that the activity was low and, if the age were then calculated on the basis of present equilibrium conditions and rates, it would necessarily be measured to be too old, with the amount of error increasing progressively with the age of the material.

Therefore, the Deluge and associated events adequately explain the data from Carbon 14 studies, accounting for the agreement with historically dated recent events but at the same time indicating that the earlier unverified datings must be too high, as one would infer from the Biblical records.

[1] W. F. Libby: *Radiocarbon Dating* (Chicago, University of Chicago Press, 1955). p. 7.

Consequently, all of the more important of the data from radioactivity methods of geochronometry harmonize perfectly with the Biblical records and inferences associated with the Creation and the Flood. Space does not warrant discussion of all the methods that have been used or suggested, but only those which have been considered the most important and best established. It would be possible by similar analyses to show the essential harmony of the data from these other subsidiary methods (e.g., the ionium method, the varve chronologies, thermoluminescence, etc.) with the Biblically established facts of a genuine recent Creation and universal Deluge.

These events must be dated only some few thousands of years ago according to the Bible, and the evidence that has been brought against this testimony has now been shown rather to harmonize quite satisfactorily with it. In fact, it would seem highly probable that no method of geochronometry could be devised that would permit determination of dates earlier than the Flood, since all such processes, whether geological or meteorological, would almost certainly have been profoundly disturbed and altered by the events of that global cataclysm. The Scriptural description is that "the world that then was, being overflowed with water perished" (II Peter 3:6), and the context shows that this statement comprises the geological earth and the atmospheric heavens! The only possible way in which men can *know* the age of the earth is by means of divine revelation!

CONTRADICTIONS IN GEOCHRONOLOGY

Even aside from the Biblical testimony against the radioactivity age estimates for the earth and its formations, there are numerous evidences in geology itself against the validity of these tremendous time durations. The currently accepted figure for the age of the earth as deduced from radioactivity of uranium and other elements is about five to six billion years,[1] with the solidification of the crust dated about 4½ billion years ago.

But there are many geological processes which appear to be at least as suitable for geochronometric purposes as the phenomena of radioactivity and which give much lower estimates than this. None of these is sufficiently precise for accurate measurements, and all in-

[1] G. P. Kuiper: "Origin, Age, and Possible Ultimate Fate of the Earth," in *The Earth and Its Atmosphere*, D. R. Bates, Ed. (New York, Basic Books, Inc., 1957), p. 14-16.

volve the same sort of unlikely assumptions as the radioactivity methods, but they are nevertheless sufficiently meaningful to cast very serious doubt on the reliability of the radioactivity estimates.

Meteoritic Dust

One of these lines of evidence is derived from the study of meteorites and comets, of which there are large numbers in our solar system. A tremendous amount of meteoritic material falls each year on the earth. Estimates vary widely, but the most careful studies have been made by Hans Pettersson of the Swedish Oceanographic Institute.

Pettersson calculated that the total quantity of dust of meteor origin in the atmosphere, up to a height of 60 miles, amounts to 28,600,000 tons. . . . half the total—14,300,000 tons of such dust—settles to earth each year and 14,300,000 tons of new dust must enter the atmosphere.[1]

The significance of this large amount of meteoritic dust, in terms of the supposed great age of the earth, is noted by Asimov as follows:

Of course, this goes on year after year, and the earth has been in existence as a solid body for a good long time, for perhaps as long as 5 billion years. If, through all that time, meteor dust had settled to the earth at the same rate it does today, then by now, if it were undisturbed, it would form a layer 54 feet thick over all the surface of the earth.[2]

Obviously, no layer of meteoritic dust of any appreciable thickness, certainly not 54 feet, is found around the earth's surface, although some indications of such a layer have been found on the ocean bottoms.

Pettersson and Rotschi have found good evidence from the peculiar nickel content of deep sea deposits both in the Atlantic and the Pacific Ocean that several thousand tons per day of meteoritic material are accumulated by the earth.[3]

The absence of this meteoritic dust layer on the earth's surface

[1] Isaac Asimov: "14 Million Tons of Dust Per Year," *Science Digest*, Vol. 45, Jan. 1959, p. 34. Pettersson confirms this: "If meteoritic dust descended at the same rate as the dust created by the explosion of the Indonesian volcano Krakatoa in 1883, then my data indicate that the amount of meteoritic dust landing on the earth every year is 14 million tons." ("Cosmic Spherules and Meteoritic Dust," *Scientific American*, Vol. 202, February 1960, p. 132).

[2] *Ibid.*, p. 35.

[3] F. L. Whipple, in *Advances in Geophysics* (Academic Press, Inc., 1952), p. 131.

cannot be reasonably accounted for in terms of crustal mixing processes, as Asimov claims. This type of material is composed mostly of iron, with large amounts of nickel and other relatively rare components of the earth's crust, and these elements are not found in sufficient abundance to correspond to the amount supposedly accreted by meteoritic showers. For example, the average nickel content of meteorites is of the order of 2.5 percent, whereas nickel constitutes only about 0.008 percent of the rocks of the earth's crust.[1] Thus, about 312 times as much nickel per unit volume occurs in meteorites as in the earth's crust. This means that the 54 ft. thickness of meteoritic dust would have to have been dispersed through a crustal thickness of at least 312 x 54 ft., or more than three miles, to yield the present crustal nickel component percentage, even under the impossible assumption that there was no nickel in the crust to begin with! Similar calculations could be made for cobalt and other important constituents of meteorites, all testifying that there simply *cannot* have been meteoritic dust falling on the earth at present rates throughout any five billion years of geologic time!

Similar calculations indicate that enormous quantities of iron would have accumulated on the surface from meteoritic matter during geologic time. Iron is the most abundant element in the meteorites and is also abundant in the earth's crust.

Can this surface iron be, not the earth's original substance, but at least in significant part, the accumulated meteoric dust of ages? According to my calculations, the dust would account for all the iron in the upper 1½ miles of the earth's solid crust, which certainly accounts, too, for all the iron we've managed to dig up.[2]

But does anyone actually think that all the iron in the upper 1½ miles of crust was derived from meteoritic dust? Such a proposition seems out of reason, on its face. Yet this is the strange conclusion to which we are led if meteorite dust has been falling on the earth for anything like five billion years.

Meteorite Radioactivity

It is interesting that radioactivity age calculations made on meteorites are similarly very contradictory.

[1] Pettersson, *op. cit.,* p. 132.
[2] Isaac Asimov, *op. cit.,* p. 35.

By examining the helium content of several meteorites, Paneth arrives at ages ranging from 60 million to 7 billion years. . . . Reexamining the evidence, Bauer arrives at a common age of about 60 million years for the meteorites examined by Paneth. This would give us thus a lower limit for the age of the meteorites and also for the age of the universe.[1]

It has been difficult for astronomers and geologists to accept such a "small" age for the meteorites in terms of any of the classical theories of the origin of the solar system. More recent and much more subtle calculations have been invoked to "reconcile" the discrepancy.

When that is done, the age of the stony meteorites since solidification is found. The result is about 4.6 thousand million years.[2]

Thus, merely by changing the method of calculation, one can increase the age of a meteorite from 60 to 4600 million years! The latter calculation was made by the potassium-argon method, the first by the helium isotope method.

Tektites

The special type of glassy meteorites known as tektites is still more difficult to interpret. These are found in various localities in the form of what seem to have been showers of the particles.

In contrast to these great ages, the estimated argon ages of tektites (Suess, *et al.*, 1951; Gerling and Yaschenko, 1952) are only one million to ten million years. Gerling and Yaschenko regard this as evidence against a cosmic origin for tektites.[3]

Nevertheless, as Stair, in a summary of the evidence, says:

Although some investigators believe that these glass bodies are of terrestrial origin, the preponderance of evidence seems to point to a cosmic source as the origin.[4]

The significant feature about the relatively small ages indicated for the tektites is that they seem to be smaller than those of some of the terrestrial strata in which they are deposited.

[1] D. Ter Haar: "The Age of the Universe," *Scientific Monthly*, Vol. 77, October 1953, p. 177.
[2] G. P. Kuiper, *op. cit.*, p. 15.
[3] L. H. Ahrens: "Radioactive Methods for Determining Geological Age," in *Physics and Chemistry of the Earth* (New York, McGraw-Hill, 1956), p. 60.
[4] Ralph Stair: "Tektites and the Lost Planet," *Scientific Monthly*, Vol. 83, July 1956, p. 4.

Each of the major occurrences is thought to be one shower. Those in Czechoslovakia are weathering out of Miocene strata; those in Texas, first described by the writer, are thought to be weathering out of Eocene strata; and those in Australia may be Recent.[1]

Another significant fact, difficult to reconcile with uniformitarianism, is that the tektites are apparently not found in any strata earlier than Tertiary.

Neither tektites nor other meteorites have been found in any of the ancient geological formations.[2]

This, of course, is hard to reconcile with the generally accepted uniformitarian concept that meteorites have been falling on the earth at essentially present rates throughout some five billion years of geologic time. True meteorites, in fact, have apparently not been found in any but Recent deposits.

It is only the meteorites that escape decomposition in passage through the atmosphere that can possibly be recognized. There probably are many of these, and in the deep sea, where the rate of deposition is extremely slow, cosmic particles may rate high in the sediments as compared to places where other sediments are abundant. No meteorites have ever been found in the geologic column.[3]

Disintegration of Comets

The origin and age of comets is even more obscure than that of meteorites. Fred Whipple, who has contributed more to the theory of cometary phenomena than most other modern astronomers, says:

We are still left quite in the dark as to the ultimate origin of comets. Where was the factory in which they were made located, and when did the sun acquire this magnificent assemblage of quite trivial bodies, whose combined total mass, in spite of their vast extent, is probably less than that of the earth?[4]

The interesting thing about the comets is that they seem to be disintegrating continuously. A number of them have broken up and dissi-

---

[1] Virgil E. Barnes: "Tektites," *Geotimes*, Vol. I, No. 12, 1957, p. 6.

[2] Ralph Stair, *op. cit.*, p. 11.

[3] W. H. Twenhofel: *Principles of Sedimentation* (2nd Ed., New York, McGraw-Hill, 1950), p. 144.

[4] Fred L. Whipple: "Comets," in *The New Astronomy* (New York, Simon and Schuster, 1955), p. 207.

pated within the period of human observation. Evidently all the known comets can be expected to break up and vanish within a time which is geologically very short. Fred Hoyle notes this.

It has been estimated that the break-up of many comets is taking place at such a rate that they will be entirely disrupted within a million years. It is an immediate inference that these comets cannot have been moving around the Sun as they are at present for much longer than a million years, since otherwise they would already have been broken up.[1]

Since comets are very definitely a part of the solar system, the natural inference would be that the maximum age of the comets would also be the maximum age of the solar system, the two having come into existence at approximately the same time. Hoyle avoids this by assuming that the comets did not begin their breaking-up until less than a million years ago! Whipple and most others avoid this conclusion by assuming that there is a gigantic reservoir of "hibernating" comets far out on the edges of the solar gravitational field, almost to the nearest stars. This theory is attributed to Ernst Opik and Jan Oort.

Oort postulated that the cometary cloud may contain as many as 100 billion comets very few of which come as close to the sun as the planets. Occasionally, however, the random passage of a star disturbs the motions of some comets sufficiently to make them swing into the sphere of gravitational attraction of Jupiter or another major planet. In this way comets are taken one by one from the "deep freeze" of the solar swarm and are pulled into relatively short-period orbits. Their hibernation period over, they become active and disintegrate into gas and meteoric particles during a few hundred or few thousand revolutions around the sun.[2]

There is not the slightest observational basis for this strange theory, nor, as Whipple pointed out, any acceptable theory as to the origin of this hypothetical swarm of hibernating comets. Its only rationale is the need for some escape from the apparent cometary testimony to the youthfulness of the solar system.

[1] Fred Hoyle: *Frontiers of Astronomy* (Harper and Brothers, New York, 1955), p. 11.
[2] Whipple: *op. cit.*, p. 201-202. See also L. F. Biermann and Rhea List: "The Tails of Comets," *Scientific American*, Vol. 199, October 1958, p. 44.

Atmospheric Helium

Another type of geophysical chronometer indicating an anomalously youthful age of the earth is the accumulation of radioactively derived gases in the atmosphere. The most important of these, of course, is radiogenic helium, which as we have already pointed out, is derived from the disintegration of uranium and thorium in the earth's crust. Some of this radiogenic helium, of course, escapes and eventually finds its way to the surface, where it is then added to the atmosphere.

But it has been realized for many years that there is not nearly enough helium in the atmosphere to correspond to the supposed age of the earth and the rate of escape of helium from the crustal rocks into the atmosphere.

It may be reasonably supposed that the entire atmospheric supply of Helium-4 is of radioactive origin. Goldschmidt, considering the known helium content of the atmosphere and the known concentrations of uranium and thorium series in primary rocks, concludes that all the atmospheric helium would have been produced in the course of 2 billion years from 2 kilograms per square centimeter of primary rock. This represents about 1.3% of the total amount of primary rock that has been eroded and, which, therefore, might have been expected to have delivered its helium to the atmosphere.[1]

This implies that the true maximum age for the earth on the basis of helium production would be only 1.3% of 2 billion, or 26 million years. And even this is impossibly high because it neglects any primary atmospheric helium and any formerly higher radioactive decay rates, as well as helium that may have made its way to the surface from non-denuded rocks.

The method used for avoiding this conclusion is to assume that the excess helium generated in the past has somehow attained the "escape velocity," overcoming gravity and escaping from the atmosphere completely. This requires that the temperatures in the exosphere (the outermost portion of the atmosphere) must be extremely high.

H. Petersen, F. A. Lindemann and others have shown that the amount

[1] G. E. Hutchinson: "Marginalia," *American Scientist,* Vol. 35, January, 1947, p. 118.

of helium released from radio-active rocks during the geological life of the earth exceeds the amount now in the atmosphere. Assuming Stoney's mechanism to be responsible for the loss of helium that must have occurred, L. Spitzer deduced that the temperature at the critical level is either about 1800 degrees Centigrade or, though usually less, is occasionally more— perhaps for 2 per cent of the time is 2300 degrees Centigrade; and even greater values may be required, for Mayne has recently concluded that the amount of helium released and lost is far greater than has been supposed. Some theorists find the high temperature mentioned difficult to accept.[1]

No independent evidence of such high temperatures yet exists. In other words, instead of accepting the obvious conclusion from the helium content of the atmosphere that the earth's age must be much less than usually believed, it is rather deduced that the exosphere temperatures must be sufficiently high to permit helium to escape, regardless of how extreme this requirement may be.

Salt in the Sea

Still another evidence of terrestrial youth is found in geochemical analyses of ocean waters. The salts and other chemicals in the sea are being continually augmented, through the process of land denudation and river transportation of the materials of erosion to the sea. Under the assumption that the ocean originally contained none of a specific element and that the rate of supply has always been the same as at present (neither assumption, of course, valid), it is possible to obtain a maximum age for the ocean, and therefore presumably of the earth, on the basis of the measured quantities and rates existing today.

The most common chemicals in ocean water are, of course, sodium and chlorine, the contituents of ordinary table salt, sodium chloride. Sodium averages 10.8 and chlorine 19.6 parts per thousand in ocean water,[2] on the average. In average river water these proportions are only 0.0085 and 0.0083 parts per thousand, respectively.[3] Oceans constitute about 315,000,000 cubic miles of water volume and rivers

---

[1] D. R. Bates: "Composition and Structure of the Atmosphere," in *The Earth and Its Atmosphere* (New York, Basic Books, Inc., 1957), p. 107.

[2] A. S. Pearse and Gordon Gunter: "Salinity," Ch. 7 in *Treatise on Marine Ecology and Paleoecology*, Vol. I, Geological Society of America Memoir 67, 1957, Tables I, II. Sodium and chlorine of course occur in many other compounds in the ocean besides that of sodium chloride.

[3] *Ibid.*

about 50,000 cubic miles.[1] Of the latter, about 8200 cubic miles annually run off to the seas and are replenished by rainfall. The maximum age of the ocean, as determined from its sodium content is thus computed as $\dfrac{(10.8)(315,000)}{(.0085)(8.2)}$, or about 50 million years. The corresponding chlorine calculation yields about 90 million years. Both are obviously vastly less than 5 billion years!

Attempts to make direct estimates of the age of the ocean on the basis of its salt content meet with difficulty. Those based on the amount of sodium in the sea and present rate of erosion put the age at only about fifty million years, a figure that was once accepted as the age of the earth. This figure is only a fraction of that now attributed to the oldest sedimentary rocks, the formation of which depended upon the existence of oceans and continents.[2]

The usual way of attempting to sidestep this difficulty is to assume a large amount of "cyclic" sodium, etc.—material that has somehow been precipitated on the lands and re-eroded and re-transported, perhaps several times. Of such cyclic sodium there is no definite measure, but even the most generous estimates are inadequate to explain the profound discrepancies.

However it is not thought that the total salt which has been carried into the oceans and has (i) remained there, (ii) been cyclic, (iii) is in rock salt and salt water in the strata can alter the estimate to much more than 200,000,000 years.[3]

This appears to be the maximum figure that can possibly be allowed for the age of the ocean on the basis of its most important chemical constituent.[4] But it should be obvious that this is impossibly high because it involves the absurd assumption that the ocean contained no sodium to begin with! Modern marine biologists and oceanographers are, on the other hand, convinced that the salinity of the ocean has always been about as it is now.

[1] Sir Cyril S. Fox: *Water* (New York, Philosophical Library, 1952), p. xx.

[2] Harold F. Blum: *Time's Arrow and Evolution* (Princeton, N. J., Princeton University Press, 1951), p. 53.

[3] Sir Cyril S. Fox, *op. cit.,* p. 27.

[4] Other chemicals in the ocean give even shorter age estimates, when calculated on a similar basis. See, for a more extended discussion of this subject, a booklet by D. J. Whitney: *How Old Is the Earth?* (Malverne, N. Y., Christian Evidence League, n.d.). Also, by the same author, *The Face of the Deep* (New York, Vantage Press, 1955), p. 27-36).

It seems reasonably certain that the salinity of the ocean has remained both quantitatively and qualitatively constant within quite narrow limits since the Cambrian.[1]

Indeed there is no reason to doubt that the oceans as great basins of salt water were already present in pre-Cambrian times.[2]

The net result of these considerations would seem to be, quite plainly, that the oceans of the world must be extremely youthful. Both paleo-biological[3] and geochemical considerations seem to require that the ocean has always been nearly as saline as at present but that it is continually becoming more saline year by year. This process cannot have been going on for very long.

Juvenile Water

As a matter of fact, there is some basis for believing that the water of the ocean has itself come out of the earth by volcanic emanations in the form of steam and that this process, as well, cannot have continued for a period as long as the supposed age of the lithosphere. It is not ordinarily appreciated what tremendous amounts of juvenile water (that is, water reaching the surface of the earth for the first time) are poured out on the earth's surface every time a volcano erupts. It is hard to obtain accurate data, of course; probably the

---

[1] G. Evelyn Hutchinson: "Future of Marine Paleoecology," in *Treatise on Marine Ecology and Paleoecology*, Vol. II, Geological Society of America Memoir 67, 1957, p. 684.

[2] C. S. Fox, *loc. cit.*

[3] In connection with the salinity of the ocean, a supposed difficulty with the Deluge record has been imagined by some writers, who say that the mixing of salt and fresh waters in a universal Flood would have been fatal to marine creatures accustomed to saline waters and to lacustrine and river fish used to fresh waters. That multitudes of water inhabitants were killed in the Deluge is certain, but there is no reason to suppose the change to have been sudden enough or sharp enough to prevent adaptation of at least some individuals out of each group to their altered environment. The change at the Deluge would, for some time at least, have been to decrease the salinity of most waters and, as Black points out: "Gunter (1942) found that for every fresh-water fish that has been taken in sea water in North America, nine species of marine fish have been taken in fresh water. It seems to be easier for fishes to adapt themselves to excess water than to excess salt" (Virginia S. Black, in *The Physiology of Fishes*, New York, Academic Press, 1957, p. 195). An interesting note in *Science* (Vol. 121, May 27, 1955) describes sharks and sawfish, both marine creatures, found in a fresh water mountain lake 20 miles inland and 500 feet above sea level in western Dutch New Guinea. All fish must be adaptable to at least a certain range of salinities, so it is not unreasonable that some individuals of each kind would be able to survive the gradual mixing of the waters and gradual change in salinities during and after the Flood.

best are those that were obtained on the famous Mexican volcano, Paricutin, during the period 1943-52 of its most active life.

If the proportion of water to total solids had been nearly constant throughout the period of activity of the Volcano, the total weight of water expelled would have amounted to some 39 million metric tons—the approximate weight of a body of water about six kilometers square by one meter deep.[1]

The U.S. Geological Survey personnel making these measurements and studies on Paricutin were of the opinion that all of this water was truly juvenile water. Although there are various theories, most volcanologists now believe this to be true of at least most and probably all of the water expelled from volcanoes.

Until the turn of the present century many geologists considered lava to get its water by seepage from ocean bottoms. Now generally discarded, this view has been replaced by a startling proposal. Volcanic water, say numerous analysts, comes from 'primary constituents'—that is, the original matter from which the planet was formed.[2]

The Paricutin water described above can be computed as, on the average, about 1/1000 of a cubic mile per year. In view of the fact that there are some 400 or 500 active volcanoes on the continents of the world with several times that number known to have been active in the recent geologic past, we feel it is not unreasonable to guess that the average annual activity of volcanoes in the world has been such as to produce at least one cubic mile of juvenile water each year. Probably this is a gross under-estimate, in view of the tremendous amounts of igneous rocks on and near the surface of the earth which, whatever their method of formation may have been, were certainly accompanied by the expulsion of tremendous amounts of entrapped waters.

It is also known that there are many active volcanoes on the ocean bottom, and there have been many more in the past. Obviously, the number and production of these is almost entirely unknown, but both must be very great. In view of all these factors, we feel that a figure of one cubic mile of water per year, on the average throughout

[1] Carl Fries, Jr.: "Volumes and Weights of Pyroclastic Material, Lava, and Water Erupted by Paricutin Volcano, Michoacan, Mexico," *Transactions, American Geophysical Union*, Vol. 34, August 1953, p. 615.
[2] Gary Webster: "Volcanoes: Nature's Blast Furnaces," *Science Digest*, Vol. 42, November 1957, p. 7.

geologic time is a bare minimum estimate of the increment of water added to the ocean.

Since the ocean now contains approximately 315,000,000 cubic miles of water (about 340,000,000 cubic miles if all the water in the earth's crust and atmosphere, rivers, lakes, etc., is added), a simple calculation[1] will yield a figure of 315 to 340 million years as the maximum possible age of the earth, even on the assumption that all the water in the ocean has originated through volcanic action! Once again, this is far less than 4 or 5 billion years.

And of course all this completely ignores the revelation of the initial condition of the created Earth in Genesis 1:2, which describes it as *covered* with water. Furthermore, it ignores the account of the Deluge, when great volumes of juvenile water were caused to gush forth through the breaking-up of the "fountains of the great deep" and when great volumes of water entered the ocean through the dissipation of the primeval atmospheric vapor blanket.

Crustal Accretion

But, even more amazingly, volcanic action can account for the entire crust of the earth itself in terms of this kind of calculation. That is, if the earth is as old as claimed, emission of volcanic materials at present rates would have produced a volume of material equal to or greater than the volume of rock in all the continents of the world! This is the basis of J. T. Wilson's remarkable theory that the earth's crust has developed in just this way.

The emission of lava at the present rate of 0.8 km.^{3}/year throughout the earth's history of 4.5×10^9 years or even for the 3×10^9 years since the oldest known rocks were formed would have poured out lava of the order of 3×10^9 km.^{3} on the Earth's surface. This corresponds approximately to the volume of the continents (about 30 km. x 1.1×10^8 km.^{2}). A slightly higher rate of volcanism in the early stages of the Earth would allow for the emission of the oceanic crust as well.[2]

---

[1] A somewhat similar analysis has been made the basis for the now widely-held opinion among geologists that the ocean has indeed been derived by just this method. See W. W. Rubey: "Geologic History of Sea Water," *Bulletin, Geological Society of America*, Vol. 62, pp. 1111ff. However, for reasons indicated, we believe Rubey and others have grossly over-estimated the time involved.

[2] J. Tuzo Wilson: "Geophysics and Continental Growth," *American Scientist*, Vol. 47, March 1959, p. 14.

Surely the idea that all the rock and soil materials of all the earth's crust have been built up by volcanic emissions during geologic time is no less strange in terms of traditional uniformitarianism than is the Deluge theory. Although, as we have emphasized, volcanic lavas are of great extent over the earth's surface, they nevertheless constitute a relatively small proportion of all rocks. Wilson's supposition is that the granites and other rocks were originally lavas which have since been eroded and metamorphosed from their original condition. This theory is quite speculative, of course, and has not yet attracted any great following. Nevertheless, the arithmetical calculations lead to such a conclusion.

In fact, more realistic calculations would show that the continents could have been derived by volcanic action in much less time than 4.5 billion years. This figure was based on an average lava emission of 0.8 km.^{3}/year. But this latter figure was taken from work by Sapper, which in turn was based on lava flows since 1500 A.D.[1] But it is apparent that this rate must be much less than the average rate during geologic time in view of the vastly greater extent of volcanic activity in the past than in the present. Even on the basis of present activity, however, this seems low. The materials (lava and ash) derived from Paricutin during its ten years of activity were over 2000 million cubic meters in volume,[2] which therefore averaged 0.2 cubic kilometers per year. Thus, only *four* such volcanoes would produce Wilson's 0.8 cubic kilometers per year. If, as we have surmised, the minimum average figure should be at least 1,000 volcanoes, then the above estimate of age would be reduced from 4.5 billion to less than 20 million years. And this on the assumption that *all* the earth's crust developed uniformly in this manner!

We have now discussed a number of lines of evidence that seem plainly to show that the estimate of 4 or 5 billion years for the age of the earth must be much too great. Such diversified processes as the fall of meteorites, the break-up of comets, the influx of dissolved chemicals into the ocean, the escape of helium into the atmosphere, the growth of the ocean, and the growth of continents by volcanism, all give ages much less than this. And this is on the basis of the geologist's own principle of uniformity! Obviously, in terms of the revealed facts of an initial grown Creation and the great discontinuity

[1] *Ibid.*
[2] Fries, *op. cit.*, p. 611.

in all natural processes at the time of the Deluge, even these latter ages must be immensely too large.

Just how much too great is as impossible to determine by scientific calculation as it is to determine the *true* age of the earth by any of the radioactive minerals. Once again we emphasize that the only *certain* basis of prehistoric chronology must come by way of divine revelation. This revelation, in the Bible, records a Creation and subsequent universal Flood, both occurring only a few thousand years ago! And nothing in true science can possibly negate this; nor, in fact, when the data are rightly understood, does it even seem to do so.

POST-DELUGE CHRONOLOGY

It may be possible, however, to deduce means of measuring the time *since* the close of the Deluge phenomena. Except for a period of adjustment to the present normal, it is undoubtedly true that uniform processes have predominated in nature since that time, although we cannot exclude the occasional effects of later lesser catastrophes. This period of adjustment to present rates after the intense activities of the Deluge period does, however, preclude the use of many of these processes for age measurements except for much more recent times, as we have pointed out in the case of the radiocarbon method.

As a matter of fact, men already have at least an approximate chronological framework for post-Deluge history, recorded in the Bible. The traditional Biblical date for the Deluge, as computed in the Ussher chronology, has been about 2350 B.C. (or some 4,300 years ago). There are, of course, various lines of evidence in the Bible itself which militate against the strict-chronology interpretation of the genealogy of Genesis 11:10-26.[1] But although the Biblical text does not appear to speak unequivocally as to the date of the Flood, it does give strong witness that this date is on the order of magnitude of only some several thousands of years ago.

And it is very significant that such extra-Biblical information as can be obtained on post-Deluge chronology—whether from archaeological, biological, anthropological, or other sources—all concur in pointing to a time some several millenniums ago from which the present order of things seems to date.

[1] See Appendix II, pp. 474-489.

Tree Rings

One valuable natural chronometric device is the common tree and its annual growth rings and their patterns. Both living and dead trees can be used in this science, known as dendrochronology, by matching sequences of ring patterns between living trees and beams cut from contemporary trees and these with still earlier beams, etc. The ring patterns are, of course, determined mainly by temperature and precipitation variations from year to year. It might be possible theoretically to extend this chronology back, step by step, using fossil wood, indefinitely. But, as Flint says:

The study of the annual growth rings of trees has yielded a record that extends back through the last 2000-3000 years.[1]

More significantly, it is well known that the oldest living things are trees. Many of the giant sequoias are known to be over 3000 years old and, except for unusual catastrophe, seem to be immune to disease and pest attack. A remarkable fact is that these still-living trees seem to be the original trees that grew in their present stands. Note the following very interesting observation:

Perhaps the most intriguing of the unanswered questions regarding longevity in conifers has to do with *Sequoia gigantea* trees, which, some believe, may enjoy perpetual life in the absence of gross destruction, since they appear immune to pest attack. . . . Pertinent also is the well-known fact that standing snags of this species, other than those resulting from factors of gross destruction, are unknown. Does this mean that shortly preceding 3275 years ago (or 4000 years ago, if John Muir's somewhat doubtful count was correct) *all* the then living giant sequoias were wiped out by some catastrophe?[2]

The dendrochronological laboratory at the University of Arizona recently discovered a stand of still older trees in the White Mountains of California, a group of bristlecone pines. Their discoverer says:

Only recently we have learned that certain stunted pines of arid highlands, not the mammoth trees of rainy forests, may now be called the oldest living things on earth.

---

[1] R. F. Flint: *Glacial and Pleistocene Geology* (New York, Wiley, 1957), p. 292.
[2] Edmund Schulman: "Longevity Under Adversity in Conifers," *Science,* Vol. 119, March 26, 1934, p. 399. Of course, no actual evidence of catastrophe was noted, but only the remarkable absence of evidence of any trees of a generation previous to those now growing.

Microscopic study of growth rings reveals that a bristlecone pine tree found last summer at nearly 10,000 feet began growing more than 4,600 years ago and thus surpasses the oldest known sequoia by many centuries . . . Many of its neighbors are nearly as old; we have now dated 17 bristle-cone pines 4,000 years old or more . . .[1]

Since these, as well as the sequoias and other ancient trees, are still living, it is pertinent to ask why these oldest living things apparently have had time to develop only *one* generation since they acquired their present stands at some time after the Deluge. There is no record of a tree, or any other living thing, being older than any reasonable date for the Deluge.

Origin of Postdiluvian Civilizations

In the last analysis, the only really reliable recorder of time is man himself! In any kind of natural process that might be used to determine past time, there is always the possibility that the rates may have changed as well as uncertainty regarding its initial condition. It is absolutely impossible to know beyond question that such and such a formation or deposit has an age of so many years, unless that age is supported by reliable human records of some kind.

And it is, therefore, highly significant that no truly verified archaeological datings antedate the time of about 3000 B.C. or even later. Larger dates are of course frequently ascribed to various localities and cultures, but they are always based on radiocarbon or other geological methods rather than written human records. There are numerous extant chronologies that have been handed down from various ancient peoples, and it is bound to be significant that none of them yield acceptable evidence that the histories of these or other peoples antedate the Biblical date for the Deluge.

The Bible pictures the dispersal of post-diluvian man from the geographical areas implied also by archaeology and secular history. The most ancient peoples leaving historical records were, of course, the inhabitants of the Tigris-Euphrates valley, the Nile Valley of Egypt, and other near-Eastern areas. This correlates perfectly with the Bible records, which picture the centrifugal movement of tribes out from the first kingdom of Babylon (Babel, Genesis 11:9).

---

[1] Edmund Schulman: "Bristlecone Pine, Oldest Living Thing," *National Geographic Magazine,* Vol. 113, March 1958, p. 355.

The archaeological testimony is confirmed further by botanical studies. A systematic agriculture was, of course, necessary for the existence of stable and civilized communities and so would be one of the best indices of the beginnings of post-diluvian cultures. The following from a Danish scientist is therefore significant:

Thus, we may conclude from present distribution studies that the cradle of Old World plant husbandry stood within the general area of the arc constituted by the western foothills of the Zagros Mountains (Iraq-Iran), the Taurus (southern Turkey), and the Galilean uplands (northern Palestine), in which the two wild prototypes occur together. We may conclude, further, that wheat played a more dominant role than barley in the advent of plant husbandry in the Old World."[1]

It is remarkable how many different lines of evidence of a historical nature point back to a time around 3000 B. C. as dating the beginning of true civilization. There have been theories and speculations about earlier periods, but nothing concrete. With reference to Egypt, H. R. Hall, the Egyptologist, states:

We think that the First Dynasty began not before 3400 and not much later than 3200 B.C. . . . A. Scharff, however, would bring the date down to about 3000 B.C.; and it must be admitted that his arguments are good, and that at any rate it is more probable that the date of the First Dynasty is later than 3400 B.C. than earlier.[2]

Even this date is very questionable, as it is based mainly upon the king-lists of Manetho, an Egyptian priest of about 250 B.C., whose work has not been preserved except in a few inaccurate quotations in other ancient writings. As George A. Barton, of the University of Pennsylvania pointed out long ago:

The number of years assigned to each king, and consequently the length of time covered by the dynasties, differ in these two copies, so that, while the work of Manetho forms the backbone of our chronology, it gives us no absolutely reliable chronology. It is for this reason that the chronological schemes of modern scholars have differed so widely.[3]

Other scholars think that some of Manetho's lists may actually rep-

[1] Hans Helbaek: "Domestication of Food Plants in the Old World," *Science*, Vol. 130, August 14, 1959, p. 365.

[2] H. R. Hall: Article, "Egypt: Archaeology" in *Encyclopedia Britannica*, 1956, p. 37, Vol. 8.

[3] George A. Barton: *Archaeology and the Bible* (Philadelphia, American Sunday School Union, 1941), p. 11.

resent simultaneous dynasties in upper and lower Egypt, which would still further reduce the date of the beginning of the period. The length of the pre-Dynastic period is quite unknown, but there is no necessary reason to regard it as more than a few centuries at most.

In Babylonia, the earliest peoples leaving written monuments were the Sumerians, who were later displaced by the Semitic Babylonians. These people likewise are dated about this time.

Dr. Samuel Noah Kramer, Research Professor of Assyriology at the University of Pennsylvania says:

> The dates of Sumer's early history have always been surrounded with uncertainty, and they have not been satisfactorily settled by tests with the new method of radiocarbon dating. . . . Be that as it may, it seems that the people called Sumerians did not arrive in the region until nearly 3000 B.C.[1]

The Egyptians and Babylonians were presumably of Hamitic and Semitic derivation, as were most of the other tribes who settled in Africa and Asia. The Japhetic peoples, on the other hand, according to the Table of Nations of Genesis 10 (which Dr. William Foxwell Albright regards as "an astonishingly accurate document"[2]), migrated largely into Europe, where they became the so-called Aryan peoples, peoples of the language stocks known as Indo-European. Recent linguistic studies have indicated that these languages radiated from a common center, probably in central Europe. Dr. Paul Thieme, Professor of Sanskrit and Comparative Philology at Yale, in discussing this evidence, says:

> Indo-European, I conjecture, was spoken on the Baltic coast of Germany late in the fourth millennium B.C. Since our oldest documents of Indo-European daughter languages (in Asia Minor and India) date from the second millennium B.C., the end of the fourth millennium would be a likely time anyhow. A thousand or 1500 years are a time sufficiently long for the development of the changes that distinguish our oldest Sanskrit speech form from what we construct as Indo-European.[3]

Since the above date was based somewhat heavily on geopaleonto-logical data, it is likely that it is too high even as it stands.

---

[1] S. N. Kramer: "The Sumerians," *Scientific American*, Vol. 197, October 1957, p. 72.

[2] W. F. Albright: "Recent Discoveries in Bible Lands," article in *Young's Analytical Concordance*, (New York, Funk & Wagnals, 1955), p. 30.

[3] Paul Thieme: "The Indo-European Language," *Scientific American*, Vol. 199, October 1958, p. 74.

Studies of ancient agricultures in Europe, based mainly on pollen analyses and radiocarbon datings, point to similar conclusions:

> The main results of the age determinations is that the oldest agricultures in Switzerland (Older Cortaillod culture) and in Denmark (younger Ertebolle culture and A-earthen vessel) started almost simultaneously, about 2740-90 B.C. and 2620-80 B.C., respectively.[1]

The same story could be repeated at other places if space permitted. For example, in China, the earliest historical cultures date from somewhat later than this time. The anthropologist, Ralph Linton, says:

> The earliest Chinese date which can be assigned with any probability is 2250 B.C., based on an astronomical reference in the *Book of History*.[2]

The worldwide testimony of trustworthy, recorded, history[3] is therefore that such history begins about 3000 B.C. and not substantially earlier. This is indeed surpassingly strange if men actually have been living throughout the world for many tens or hundreds of thousands of years! But on the other hand, if the Biblical records are true, then this is of course exactly the historical evidence we would expect to find. And it is pertinent to mention, in passing, the worldwide incidence of flood legends, which we have discussed in an earlier chapter. It is not at all unreasonable to conclude that the clear testimony of all recorded human history points back to the stark reality of the great world Deluge, which remade the world in the days of Noah.

Population Statistics

The statistics of human populations give further support to this intimation. Ever since the famous studies of Malthus, it has been known that human populations (applied to animal populations by the first Charles Darwin, in developing his theory of evolution by natural selection) have tended to increase geometrically with time. That is,

[1] J. Troels-Smith: "Neolithic Period in Switzerland and Denmark," *Science,* Vol. 124, Nov. 2, 1956, p. 879.

[2] Ralph Linton: *The Tree of Culture* (New York, Alfred A. Knopf Publishing Company, 1955), p. 520.

[3] A period of duration undetermined as yet of course lies between the Flood, the dispersion at Babel, and these beginnings of recorded history. See Appendix II, pp. 474-489.

the world population tends repeatedly to double itself at equal increments of time. In a recent and alarming study presented at the Lac Beauport Conference, a modern Darwin calls attention to the very real danger of overpopulation in the present world in our time. He says:

The central doctrine which has influenced me is that of Malthus, who 160 years ago gave his theory that there was a natural tendency for man, like any other animal, to increase by geometrical progression . . .[1]

This means that, if the time for the population to double itself is called T, then starting from an initial population of two people, after T years there would be four people, after twice T years there would be eight people, after $3T$ years sixteen people, and so on. At any time $n(T)$ after the start of this process, the total population of the world would be two multiplied by itself n times or two raised to the nth power, $(2)^n$. The total time required to attain this population is $n(T)$, but this can be determined only if the time increment T and the exponent n are known. The latter is easily found by equating 2^n to the present world population, which is about 2½ billion people. This calculation gives a value of n of slightly over 31. Since the value $n=1$ corresponds to the initial human pair, it is obvious that the starting population of one man and one woman has gone through slightly more than thirty "doublings."

The value of T, the time increment for one doubling, is less certain. But the following data will suggest the most reasonable basis for estimating it:

At the time of the birth of Christ, there presumably were from 250 to 350 million persons on this planet. Some 700 years later, there was about the same number—say 300 million—a long slow decline in total population having been followed by a compensating increase.

It took roughly 950 more years, namely, until 1650, for this 300 million to double to 600 million. But then it took only 200 years, from 1650 to 1850, for the next doubling up to 1200 million, or 1.2 billion. From 1850 to 1950, in only 100 years, the earth's population doubled again, to about 2.4 billion.[2]

Obviously the figures given for world populations prior to the mod-

[1] Sir Charles Darwin: "Population Problems," Bulletin of the *Atomic Scientists*, Vol. 114, October 1958, p. 322.

[2] Warren Weaver: "People, Energy, and Food," *Scientific Monthly*, Vol. 78, June 1954, p. 359.

ern period are only guesses, since no one has any real knowledge of the populations of America, Africa, Asia, etc., during those centuries. The 1650 figure is the first one with any degree of validity. From 1650 to 1950, therefore, the population increased from 600 million to 2400 million, representing two doublings in 300 years, or a value for *T* of 150 years. This figure is undoubtedly too low, however, being influenced by the very rapid population growth of the past century. The latter is even more spectacular at present, increasing at a rate which would permit the next doubling to occur in 65 years. However, this is not typical and is attributable almost entirely to advances in medicine and sanitation.

It is fallacious to think that booming birth rates are responsible for this speed-up. Actually, birth rates have declined in many countries. Falling death rates account for most of the spectacular growth.[1]

All things considered, it would seem that the period from 1650 to 1850 is one that would be about as typical as any for one doubling, although accuracy of the figures then was not what it has been in more recent years. One could split the difference between the previous 150-year figure and this 200-year figure and estimate that the most likely value of *T* is about 175 years. This value, multiplied by the 30 doublings, leads us back to about 3300 B. C. as the time of the birth of Noah's first son!

It could not be maintained, of course, that this calculation is completely rigorous, but it certainly is reasonable—far more so than to say that the population has been doubling itself since a hypothetical beginning several hundred thousand years ago. Added to all the other evidence for the beginning of the present order of things on the earth after the Deluge several thousand years ago, this further testimony is quite impressive.[2]

[1] Robert C. Cook: "The Population Bomb," *Bulletin of the Atomic Scientists,* Vol. 12, October 1956, p. 296.

[2] Philip M. Hauser, Head of the Department of Sociology at Chicago University, has recently noted: "World population growth averaged 1 percent per year between 1930 and 1940 . . . One hundred persons multiplying at 1 percent per year, not over the period of 200,000 to 1 million years of man's occupancy of this globe but merely for the 5000 years of human history, would have produced a contemporary population of 2.7 billion persons per square foot of land surface of the earth!" ("Demographic Dimensions of World Politics," *Science,* Vol. 131, June 3, 1960, p. 1641).

ANTEDILUVIAN LONGEVITY AND RADIATION

One must also reckon with the probability that population increase rates in the early centuries after the Flood, as well as those before the Flood (when "men began to multiply on the face of the earth" as recorded in Genesis 6:1), may have been abnormally high, owing to the great longevity of mankind at the time. According to the records, men lived 900 years or more before the Flood! One of the strongest evidences of the validity of these figures is the fact that, after the Flood, the ages of the patriarchs exhibit a slow but steady decline from that of Noah, who lived 950 years, through Eber, who lived 464 years; Abraham, who died at 175 years; Moses, who died an old man at 120 years; to the familiar Biblical 70 year life-span (Psalm 90:10), which is very close to where we have returned today. Large early post-diluvial populations are also intimated by the Table of Nations in Genesis 10 and the account of the dispersion in Genesis 11. Thus, these early high rates of doubling would more than counterbalance whatever evidence there may be of slower rates during the first 1,500 years after Christ.

Effect of Canopy on Longevity

And, incidentally, the declining life-span after the Flood seems to fit in perfectly with our concept of the dissipation of the earth's protective blanket during the Flood. As we have noted, this canopy of water vapor (with probably also large amounts of carbon dioxide and ozone augmenting the effect) provided a warm, pleasant, presumably healthful environment throughout the world. Perhaps the most important effect of the canopy was the shielding action provided against the intense radiations impinging upon the earth from space. Short wave-length radiation, as well as bombardment of elementary particles of all kinds, is known to have damaging effects—both somatic and genetic effects—on organisms and this is generally true for all types of radiations.

Somatic Effects of Radiations

With respect to somatic (non-hereditary) effects, research is only very recently bringing to light some of the damage that can be done by radiation. It is now common knowledge, of course, that large doses of radiation can be fatal, and this is one of the most feared aspects of possible nuclear warfare. But even small amounts, if long-continued, may well be very harmful. Cancer and leukemia, among others, are possibilities that are being seriously studied.

Statistical studies on life-spans as affected by radiation intensities are very pertinent to our present discussion. Austin Brues, Director of the Biological and Medical Research Division of the Argonne National Laboratory, says:

> Such experiments have shown that a single dose of radiation which does not kill an animal within the period of acute radiation sickness may tend to shorten life. . . . Studies using radiation may lead to an understanding of this most universal, but least understood, fact about life, the aging process.[1]

Dr. Shields Warren, a specialist in cancer research, also writes in this vein:

> There is much evidence that overdoses of radiation lead to premature aging. Both animal experiments and observations of the life spans of radiologists indicate that a dose of 1000 roentgens received over a long period of time may well shorten the life span about 10 percent. Data on the longevity of more than 82,000 physicians indicate that the average length of life of those not known to have had contact with radiation in the period of 1930 through 1954 was 65.7 years as against an average life span of 60.5 years for the radiologists. Not only is leukemia more prevalent among those exposed, but death from causes such as heart disease and arteriosclerosis also appears to come at an earlier age. In fact, radiologists succumbed at an earlier average age to practically every type of disease, indicating that the damage done to the body is widespread in its influence.[2]

Similarly, George Beadle, Nobel laureate for his work in biochemical genetics and head of the Biology Department at California Institute of Technology, writes:

> In experimental animals, the mouse for example, sublethal doses of radiation appreciably reduce the life span. It is almost certain that this also

[1] Austin M. Brues: "Somatic Effects of Radiation," *Bulletin of the Atomic Scientists,* Vol. 14, January 1958, pp. 13-14.
[2] Shields Warren: "Radiation and the Human Body," *Scientific Monthly,* Vol. 84, January 1957, p. 5.

occurs in man. Most investigators agree that there is no threshold below which ionizing radiation has no effect on living matter.[1]

If such effects can be observed in a short lifetime as a result of artificial radiations, it is certainly possible that much greater effects on longevity would have been produced over the millenniums by the natural background radiation.

Genetic Effects of Radiations

Even more significant than these somatic effects, however, are the genetic effects of radiation, which injure not only the individual receiving the first exposure but also his descendants as well. As pointed out previously, radiations are the chief cause of "mutations," permanent, hereditary, changes in the genetic structure of the germ cell. In fact, as the pioneer worker in this field and still one of its leading authorities, Dr. H. J. Muller, says:

> Radiation is in fact the only type of agent yet known to which human beings are likely to be exposed in quantity sufficient to cause any considerable production of mutations in them.[2]

And the nature of these mutations is practically always—perhaps unqualifiedly always, so far as the laboratory evidence goes—harmful!

> Mutations and mutation rates have been studied in a wide variety of experimental animals and plants, and in man. There is one general result that clearly emerges: almost all mutations are harmful. The degree of harm ranges from mutant genes that kill their carrier, to those that cause only minor impairment. Even if we didn't have a great deal of data on this point, we could still be quite sure on theoretical grounds that mutants would usually be detrimental. For a mutation is a random change of a highly organized, reasonably smoothly functioning living body. A random change in the highly integrated system of chemical processes which constitute life is almost certain to impair it—just as a random interchange of connections in a television set is not likely to improve the picture.[3]

It may be noted once again, in passing, that these mutations pro-

[1] George W. Beadle: "Ionizing Radiation and the Citizen," *Scientific American,* Vol. 201, September 1959, p. 224.

[2] H. J. Muller: "Radiation Damage to the Genetic Material," *American Scientist,* Vol. 38, January 1950, p. 38.

[3] James F. Crow: "Genetic Effects of Radiation," *Bulletin of the Atomic Scientists,* Vol. 14, January 1958, pp. 19-20.

vide very poor evidence of progressive organic evolution, since they always, or practically always, make the carrier less fit to survive in the struggle for existence—but the remarkable and amazing fact is that practically all geneticists insist that this is the process by which all organic life has gradually developed from primitive beginnings! Muller, for example, says:

According to this conception, all the adaptations of living things must have arisen through the survival and reproduction of those mutations which happened to give by-products favorable for gene continuance, or, as we say, for life. But mutations are found to be of a random nature, so far as their utility is concerned. Accordingly, the great majority of mutations, certainly well over 99 per cent, are harmful in some way, as is to be expected of the effects of accidental occurrences. These harmful mutations, however, eventually die out naturally, because of the lower ability to live, or the lower *viability*, of the individuals containing these mutated genes. On the other hand, the very few mutants that happen to have by-products favorable for life must tend to survive and to multiply. In this way living things have evolved, becoming more complexly and adaptively organized in the course of ages.[1]

The non-evolutionist finds it exceedingly difficult to contemplate with any patience such reasoning as this, which thus blandly equates *plus* with *minus,* deterioration with progress! As a matter of fact, only the rare gross mutations tend to die out naturally, as Muller himself says. The great majority of them are only slightly harmful and continue to survive. Their descendants also survive, perhaps with additional mutations, and the net result is *bound* to be an over-all deterioration of the species. This undoubtedly is why the fossil record reveals living creatures before the Flood, of all kinds, to be larger and better equipped than their modern descendants! Dr. Crow, one of the present authorities on radiation mutations and Chairman of the Department of Medical Genetics at the University of Wisconsin, emphasizes this aspect of the subject:

One might think that mutants that cause only a minor impairment are unimportant. But this is not true for the following reason: A mutant that is very harmful usually causes early death or sterility. Thus the mutant gene is quickly eliminated from the population. . . . Since minor mutations can thus cause as much harm in the long run as major ones, and occur

[1] H. J. Muller, *op. cit.,* p. 35.

much more frequently, it follows that most of the mutational damage in a population is due to the accumulation of minor changes.[1]

It is interesting now to read on every hand alarming statements warning against the genetic damage that will accrue to future generations as a result of nuclear testing through this very medium of radiation-induced mutations, when for years these same authorities have been insisting these mutations in the past have been the cause of the great evolutionary progress of organic life through the ages. The eminent Committee on Genetic Effects of Atomic Radiation, brought together by the National Academy of Sciences and composed of sixteen of the nation's top geneticists and radiologists (men like Muller, Weaver, Crow, Glass, Beadle, Wright and others) in its summary report, makes some revealing statements:

Many will be puzzled about the statement that practically all known mutant genes are harmful. For mutations are a necessary part of the process of evolution. How can a good effect—evolution to higher forms of life—result from mutations practically all of which are harmful?

First of all, it is not mutations which, of themselves, produce evolution, but rather the action of natural selection on whatever combination of genes occur. . . . Nature had to be rather ruthless about this process. Many thousands of unfortunate mutations, with their resulting handicaps, were tolerated, just so long as an advantageous mutation could be utilized, once in a long while, for inching the race up slightly to a better adjustment to the existing conditions. The rare creature with an advantageous combination of genes was better fitted to survive and displace his less favored companions, and thus evolution was served, even though there were thousands of tragedies for every success.[2]

It is at least marvelous that many who profess to believe the above philosophy of history profess also to believe in the God of the Bible, One who does not create confusion, One who is concerned about the birds of the air and the lilies of the field, who notes with concern the falling of each sparrow, One who could truthfully pronounce His completed Creation "very good"!

[1] J. F. Crow, *op. cit.,* p. 20. Crow says in another place: "The process of mutation also produces ill-adapted types. The result is a lowering of the average fitness of the population, the price that asexual, as well as sexual, species pay for the privilege of evolution" ("Ionizing Radiation and Evolution", *Scientific American,* Vol. 201, September 1959, p. 156).

[2] Committee on Genetic Effects of Atomic Radiation: "Genetic Effects of Atomic Radiation," *Science,* Vol. 123, June 29, 1956, p. 1159.

Decrease in Life-Span after Precipitation of Canopy

But to return to the question of antediluvian longevity, it surely is quite reasonable in view of what is known about the somatic and genetic effects of radiations to infer that, over the centuries since the Flood, the accumulation of these effects in man in particular has resulted in gradual deterioration and decreasing life-span.[1] Especially marked must have been the effect in the centuries *immediately* after the Flood, in view of the precipitation of the earth's vapor blanket, which previously had filtered out practically all the environmental radiation which is now found in our troposphere. Little has been done as yet on the subject of the effect of these "natural" radiations, but such information as is available clearly indicates that their effect is similar to that of artificial radiations. It is quite possible that most spontaneous mutations are ultimately attributable to the natural radiation in the environment; that is, the sun's ultra-violet rays, cosmic radiation products, radiocarbon, etc. The committee concurs that these spontaneous mutations are also harmful:

Like radiation-induced mutations, nearly all spontaneous mutations with detectable effects are harmful.[2]

Before the Flood, therefore, everything was conducive to physical health and longevity. Equable temperatures, freedom from environmental radiations, and other factors attributable to the vapor canopy all contributed to this effect. Nevertheless, sin and death and the curse were also realities then as much as now.

After the Flood, the canopy was precipitated, its protective effects largely removed, and then began a long decline in general health and longevity, only partly offset in recent decades by advances in medicine and public health engineering. Much of this decline, as well as other effects we have already discussed, can undoubtedly be attributed to the greatly increased incidence of radiation upon the earth's surface and upon its inhabitants. Probably during and immediately after the Flood this increase was very sharp; the present equilibrium

---

[1] Other suggested causes for declining longevity are changes in diet and inbreeding. See Arthur Custance: *Longevity in Antiquity*. Doorway Papers, No. 2, Privately printed, Ottawa, 1957.

[2] *Ibid.*, p. 1160.

was gradually established by the inauguration of the present hydrologic cycle.

The possibility of past changes in mutation rates due to changed cosmic and other environmental radiation has already been noted by others.

There were probably periods of vastly increased cosmic radiation intensity in the history of the earth, and the resulting increase in the rate of mutations could have been responsible for far reaching evolutionary changes.[1]

And from what we have seen the evolutionary effect of such mutations to be, it is obvious that any such period or periods of increased radiation must have caused widespread biologic deterioration. And this, of course, is what the Bible teaches the general history of the human race to have been.

We conclude, therefore, that post-diluvian history as recorded in the Bible is quite satisfactorily vindicated, both as to its nature and as to its duration, by all true historical and archaeological records and data and by not a few lines of genuine scientific evidence.

FORMATIONS IMPLYING SLOW DEPOSITION

The greatest objection that has been offered to the concept of geological catastrophism, especially on such a scale as envisioned in the Deluge, is that many formations appear to be of such character as to have required long ages in their construction, much longer than the Biblical chronology can allow. We have already seen how most of the formations, however, do give real evidence of catastrophic formation—especially those deposits containing large numbers of fossils, as well as all igneous deposits and a great many water-laid deposits. Also, we have shown how the radioactivity and other methods of supposed absolute chronometric significance can be understood in terms of the Biblical outline.

Nevertheless, there are a number of special types of deposits which, although they may not yield absolute time estimates, do give superficial appearance of requiring great ages to form. Space only permits brief examination of a few of these, but it can be said that it is again quite possible to interpret these also in terms of the framework of Biblical geology.

[1] B. Peters: "Progress in Cosmic Ray Research Since 1947," *Journal of Geophysical Research,* Vol. 64, February 1959, p. 156.

Deposition and Lithification

Many types of sedimentary deposits are said to be explainable only in terms of long periods of time. It is natural to think that great thicknesses of water-laid rock beds, perhaps thousands of feet thick, must have taken ages to form. But this is reckoning in uniformitarian terms. It is not difficult to see how they could be formed in a short period, if the aqueous and sedimentary activity were intense enough, as it undoubtedly was during the Deluge. Even apart from this surpassingly important discontinuity in uniform processes, it is now generally recognized that sedimentary thicknesses are no criterion of duration of deposition. As Pettijohn says:

The rate of sedimentation shows extremely wide variations from place to place at the present time. It is virtually impossible to determine an average rate of sedimentation for the present; it is more difficult to do so for past times.[1]

In connection with the formation of sedimentary rocks, it has been maintained that great ages would be required for the compaction and solidification of the sediments. Kulp[2] says that the lithification of muds requires a superposed body of sediment at least a mile in depth to squeeze out the pore water and provide enough pressure to bring about solidification. He says that any sedimentary rock now appearing at the earth's surface must at some time in its history have had at least a mile of sediment on top of it, which has since been eroded away.

But this of course assumes that vertical pressure is the sole factor affecting compaction and lithification, whereas it is really only one of many:

The amount and rate of compaction depend on the porosity of the original sediment, on the size and shape of the particles, on the rate of deposition and thickness of the overburden, and on the factor of time.[3]

To these might be added the important factor of the ease of egress of the pore water. With the uplift of the sedimentary beds toward the

---

[1] F. J. Pettijohn: *Sedimentary Rocks* (2nd ed. New York: Harper, 1957), p. 688.

[2] J. L. Kulp: "Flood Geology," *Journal, American Scientific Affiliation*, Jan. 1950, p. 4.

[3] W. C. Krumbein & L. L. Sloss: *Stratigraphy and Sedimentation,* (San Francisco, Freeman, 1951), p. 217.

close of the Deluge, much of the contained water would quite rapidly drain out simply by gravity flow. With respect to the process of lithification, little is known about it as yet except that it can take place quite rapidly under some conditions and that it bears no necessary relation to time. Twenhofel says:

Time is a factor, but not the deciding one, and sands, clays, and silts of the Cambrian are known that are as nearly unindurated and little cemented as they were on the days of deposition. . . . On the other hand, some Pleistocene outwash deposits are known that have become fairly well lithified.[1]

The process of lithification is included in the broad band of phenomena known as diagenesis, which includes all normal changes that sediments undergo after their deposition. Lithification is usually the end-product of these changes. Diagenesis grades into, but does not include, metamorphism. Many chemical processes are included in the concept, all of which would be abetted tremendously by the circumstances obtaining during the Deluge.

Water is the main agent of diagenesis, and organic matter is an auxiliary.[2]

With an abundance of organic matter available, not to mention water, it is thus obvious that conditions after the Deluge would be highly favorable to rapid initiation of diagenetic processes, with resultant early lithification.

It seems, rather, that diagenesis sometimes follows sedimentation so closely that it begins while the deposit is still on the sea bottom.[3]

Various cementing materials are used, especially quartz and calcite. The methods by which these materials are introduced into the sediments are not definitely known, however, despite the importance of the subject to the understanding of the whole problem of formation of sedimentary rocks.

The problems of *how* and *when* sands become cemented and the source of the cementing material are still unresolved. . . . Other cements, the carbonates, for example, pose problems similar to those of silica.[4]

Perhaps these mysteries could be resolved if they were approached

[1] W. H. Twenhofel: *Principles of Sedimentation,* (2nd Ed., New York, McGraw-Hill, 1950), p. 279.
[2] Z. L. Sujkowski: "Diagenesis," *Bulletin, American Association of Petroleum Geologists,* Vol. 42, November 1958, p. 2694.
[3] *Ibid.,* p. 2697.
[4] F. J. Pettijohn: *Sedimentary Rocks,* pp. 656, 659.

not on the basis of uniformity with present processes but were envisioned in terms of rapid deposition of great masses of sediments mixed with various chemicals and organic matter; Deluge conditions quite obviously afford an ample source of silica, calcite, and other cementing materials.

The problem of lithification of sediments is, therefore, not at all a serious one for Biblical geology. Rather, it is highly consonant with the whole character of the catastrophic action attending deposition of the Deluge sediments to infer that the processes of compaction, cementation, drying, etc. leading to final lithification could have been accomplished quite rapidly.

Coral Reefs

Other types of sedimentary deposits which have been conceived as longtime accumulations can also be otherwise explained. For example, the great coral reefs, which appear to represent the accumulations of the calcium carbonate remains of the coral organisms over aeons of time could just as well have been formed in relatively short periods. The total mass of material in a reef is a function not only of time but also of numbers of the multiplying reef-building corals.

There is little direct evidence relating to the vertical rate of growth of coral reefs, but such as is available is compatible with the hypothesis of fairly rapid growth.

Little has been discovered of the growth rate of reefs by direct measurement. Sluiter found that a new reef established in Krakatau after the eruption of 1883 had grown to a thickness of 20 cm. in 5 years, or 4 cm. per year. Other investigators have estimated reef growth at 0.1 to 5 cm. per year.[1]

This rate of growth could certainly account for most of the coral reef depths found around the world even during the few thousand years since the Deluge. But it is also possible that many coral reefs are of deceptive thickness.

Many colonies of reef corals are round and with little or no wear become perfect boulders. When such boulders are transported, an appreciable percentage of them will come to rest in 'position of growth,' whether they be moved a mile across a reef flat or a mile down a seaward talus slope. Even elongated or slablike colonies may end their journey right side up.[2]

[1] Ph. H. Kuenen: *Marine Geology*, (New York, Wiley, 1950), p. 421.
[2] H. S. Ladd: "Paleoecological Evidence," Ch. 2 in *Treatise on Marine Ecology and Paleoecology*, Geological Society of America Memoir 67, Vol. 2, 1957, p. 35.

Particularly during the Flood, the extensive reefs formed in the warm waters of the antediluvian seas would have been eroded and re-deposited, often giving the appearance now of an ancient reef of great extent. In any case, it is evident that it is possible to explain coral reef formation, whether ancient or modern, in terms of Biblical geochronology.

Deep-Sea Sediments

Similarly, it has been claimed that the unconsolidated sediments of the deep sea floor accumulate at extremely slow rates and that their great thicknesses must, therefore, represent immense spans of time. However, evidence is recently indicating both that these thicknesses are not as great as imagined and that the ocean bottom is subject to too many disturbances to permit any kind of gradual undisturbed accumulation.

The thickness of unconsolidated sediments on the ocean floor is much less than was anticipated in view of the probable great age and permanence of the great ocean basins. Why this is so is an unsolved problem at the present time.[1]

That the oozes of the deep sea floor are not in an environment of perpetual calm is proved by the fact that ripple marks have been found on them.

A feature of immediate interest was the fact that ripple marks, long considered evidence of shallow-water deposition by land geologists, were found in the deep sea. Two remarkable photographs taken on the top of Sylvania Seamount in the Marshall Islands area established the fact that the soft, *Globigerina* ooze between the manganese-coated boulders was definitely rippled. Recently Carl J. Shipek of the Navy Electronics Laboratory has found well-defined ripple marks down to a depth of about 6000 feet.[2]

It may be uncertain whether ripples require shallow water or not, but hydraulically it is certain that they at least require substantial motions of the water above them, and this fact militates strongly against any assumption that the oozes have been settling calmly in static water over great periods of time.

[1] Edwin L. Hamilton: "The Last Geographic Frontier: the Sea Floor," *Scientific Monthly*, Vol. 85, Dec. 1957, p. 296.
[2] *Ibid.*, p. 311.

But there is evidence of much greater activity than mere ripple-forming currents over great portions of the deep ocean. Somehow even *fresh-water* deposits have been formed, and that *recently* in many such areas. In analyzing the deep-sea cores obtained by the Swedish Expedition of 1947-48, in the Atlantic Ocean particularly, a surprising fact was discovered:

> One of the most interesting observations was the unexpected presence of many fresh-water diatoms in certain cores taken by the expedition's ship *Albatross* parallel to the coast line of equatorial Africa at a great distance off the coast. . . . The novelty of the present observations lies in the constant occurrence of fresh-water diatoms in Atlantic deepsea cores, the large number of individuals, and the relatively great variety of species. More than 60 fresh-water species, belonging to various ecological groups, were observed: plankton and benthonic forms, species typical for habitats rich in nutrients and even for some poor in nutrients, most forms being common cosmopolites—that is, species of world-wide distribution.[1]

The presence of fresh-water organisms in deep-sea deposits can mean one of only two things: either the originally fresh-water deposits have been moved into the deep ocean by some kind of strong currents or other disturbances or else the present sea-bottom was once a continental area which has since sunk thousands of feet to its present position.

Similarly, there are numerous places in the deep ocean where shallow-water sediments are found. Speaking of the cores taken in the supposedly ancient and undisturbed sediments of the deep ocean floor, Hamilton says:

> The surprising result has been the discovery that there is, in many areas, only a superficial carpet of the expected deep-sea sediment and that under this thin carpet there is an alternation of thin layers of sediments which could have come only from shallower water.[2]

Referring to recent discoveries of the Woods Hole and Lamont Geological Observatory deep-sea expeditions, Parker Trask remarks:

> Many of these cores show interstratified layers of sand. Some of these sand layers are in many thousand feet of water and are remarkably well sorted. Similar sand bodies have been reported by investigators of Scripps

---

[1] R. W. Kolbe: "Fresh-Water Diatoms from Atlantic Deep-Sea Sediments," *Science,* Vol. 126, November 22, 1957, p. 1053.

[2] E. L. Hamilton, *op. cit.,* p. 298.

Institution of Oceanography in water off the coast of southern California. The origin of these sand bodies has not been satisfactorily explained.[1]

We have already pointed out the evidence of the great amount of volcanic and tectonic activity on the deep sea floor, as well as the capacity of submarine turbidity currents to move large masses of sediments great distances along the ocean floor. The lesson so obviously to be learned from all these facts is that the sea bottom is not the quiet, inactive place it has been thought for so long to be, but rather can and does experience frequent and varied disturbances of such intensity as to bring shallow-water and even fresh-water deposits down into the deepest depths. This can mean only that any supposed method of geochronometry based on the supposedly slow, regular deposition of deep-sea (or shallow-sea) oozes or other sediments is basically unreliable. One can never be sure in any given situation that the particular deposit has not been disturbed or that the deposition rate has been constant.

In fact, it is doubtful that even such a semi-uniformitarian process as turbidity currents can explain some of the phenomena. Continuing his consideration of the fresh-water diatoms found two miles deep in the mid-Atlantic, Kolbe says:

> Even if we should accept the faint possibility of a turbidity current flowing from the African coast and dumping its load of fresh-water diatoms at a distance of 930 km. from this coast, it remains to be explained how it was possible for this current not only to carry its load such a distance but, at the same time, to climb uphill more than 1000 m. before dumping the load on top of a submarine hill.[2]

These phenomena not only demonstrate the meaninglessness of any evidence for great ages of time that might be inferred from the deep-sea sediments but actually demonstrate once again the barrenness of the principle of uniformity as the determinative basis of historical geology.

Some geologists are beginning to recognize this fact. In the 1958 annual Sigma Xi address at the Virginia Polytechnic Institute, Dr. Kenneth Landes, Chairman of the Department of Geology at the University of Michigan, said among other things:

---

[1] Parker D. Trask: *Recent Marine Sediments*, (Tulsa, 2nd Ed., Society of Economic Paleontologists and Mineralogists, 1955), p. xix.

[2] R. W. Kolbe: "Turbidity Currents and Displaced Fresh-Water Diatoms," *Science*, Vol. 127, June 1958, p. 1505.

Can we, as seekers after truth, shut our eyes any longer to the obvious fact that large areas of sea floor have sunk vertical distances measured in miles? Why not accept this, and devote the cerebral horsepower now being wasted on futile attempts to explain away the truth to finding out the mechanism which produces these drastic sea-level changes?[1]

Evaporites

Another type of sedimentary deposit that may seem difficult to compress into a short span of time is found in the great beds of so-called "evaporites." These consist mainly of salt, gypsum, and anhydrite (calcium sulphate) beds. The term "evaporite" is applied to these deposits because it is believed that they were formed by long-continued evaporation from inland seas or lakes containing saline water. A supposed modern example is the Dead Sea, where the evaporation rate is very high (about 120 inches annually) and where the water continually entering the lake has no other outlet than evaporation. The Dead Sea, of course, is known to have an extremely high concentration of chemicals of various kinds as a result, and it is believed that this process, if continued over long ages, would produce beds of evaporites such as are found in many places in the geologic column. But, at present rates, this process would obviously require hundreds of thousands of years to produce such beds as are actually found in the strata.

As usual, the difficulty here is the indiscriminate application of the uniformity principle. It is assumed that an evaporite bed must have been completely formed in some such kind of environment as is to be found in the present world and by rates of evaporation that can be measured at present. But there is always the possibility that the evaporite bed was formed by transportation from some previous location, where it may have existed since the Creation. And there is also the possibility that it may have been formed by intense application of heat for evaporation of large quantities of water in a short time rather than ordinary solar heat acting over a long time.

One of the most important types of evaporite deposits is the salt dome. These structures are often associated with petroleum and so have important economic implications. Their tremendous size is indicated by the following:

[1] Kenneth K. Landes: "Illogical Geology," *Geotimes,* Vol. III, March 1959, p. 19.

The salt core generally stands vertical or nearly vertical and has a roughly circular or oval horizontal section, measuring from 1000 ft. to two miles or so in diameter. It extends downward several thousand feet. In North America wells have penetrated salt more than 3000 ft. without going out of it, and there are reasons for believing that the plugs in Europe extend downward 15,000 and even 20,000 ft.[1]

It would seem the height of absurdity to imagine that these huge thicknesses of salt had been built up by evaporation of standing water. It would require complete evaporation of a body of sea water about 8000 ft. deep to produce a depth of only 100 ft. of salt! Nevertheless, evaporation or other precipitation from solution was considered for a long time to be the proper explanation for such beds. However, a much more realistic interpretation is now generally accepted.

Although many theories have been proposed to explain the origin of these salt domes, the view most commonly supported in America until the early 1920's was that the salt was deposited from ascending waters. However serious objections to this theory have been presented. In Europe, where the domes are often laid bare to considerable depths by erosion, and where, consequently, a more certain idea of their structure and origin is obtainable, geologists came to believe that the salt was thrust upward into the sediments like a punch, principally by mechanical means, assisted by the ordinary processes of granulation and recrystallization supposed to accompany the development of schistosity in metamorphic rocks.[2]

It is commonly supposed that the salt in these domes was originally deposited as an evaporite in some deep-lying horizontal stratum, whence it was forced up by action of great pressure or temperature. But no actual field evidence of such extensive beds has yet been discovered. As noted above, the domes seem to extend down to unknown depths. In terms of Biblical geology, it would seem reasonable to attribute these original salt beds to the activities of the Creation period, with the intrusions forming the salt domes being associated with the other volcanic and tectonic activity during the Deluge period. Pettijohn says:

Although several theories have been advanced to explain salt domes,

[1] F. H. Lahee: *Field Geology* (5th ed., New York, McGraw-Hill, 1952), pp. 190-191.
[2] *Ibid.*, p. 192.

they are now generally regarded as intrusive bodies of salt. They are therefore a tectonic structure. . . .[1]

And if tectonic activity can suffice to explain these most spectacular of the various types of evaporites, there seems to be no reason why it cannot also explain, at least in part, many of the others. As a matter of fact, the principle of uniformity has been quite unsuccessful in accounting for the more extensive evaporites of all kinds, as well as for the salt domes.

Writers usually talk about desert lakes, marginal salt pans, lagoons, and the like as examples of modern environments analagous to the great beds of evaporites in the geologic column. We do not question, of course, that some Recent deposits may be explained in this way. For example, in arid regions, there are many playas (broad, shallow, ephemeral lakes), with significant salt deposits resulting from evaporation of the intermittent waters in the lake. But these are trivial and constitute no problem.

The great salt and gypsum beds of economic importance, on the other hand, cannot be explained in such terms as these. The only two environments that have been considered as possible explanations of such great beds as the Michigan salt beds, the Permian anhydrite beds of Texas and New Mexico, and others are the marginal lagoon and the relict sea. Either, in order to explain the great thicknesses that are actually found, would require not only evaporation but also continuing subsidence of the bed of the lagoon or relict sea. No comparable modern example of such activity can be demonstrated.

With regard to the lagoonal theory of evaporite origin, Twenhofel says:

> No lagoonal evaporites are known in the older parts of the geologic column. . . . A Miocene salt deposit in Wieliczka, Galicia . . . may be considered the oldest known example of a lagoonal deposit.[2]

But this stricture eliminates all the larger evaporite beds from consideration, as they are attributed to far older strata than Miocene. That leaves the relict sea—by which is meant a basin formerly freely connected with the ocean but which is now nearly isolated and, therefore, gradually drying up.

It is the considered opinion that the great deposits of evaporites in the

[1] F. J. Pettijohn: *op. cit.*, p. 480.
[2] W. H. Twenhofel: *op. cit.*, pp. 501-502.

geologic column were deposited in relict seas. The general features of these evaporites and the associated sediments indicate that deposition did not take place in very deep water, but, as the sequences of sediments are hundreds and even thousands of feet in thickness, it follows that the basins subsided as the sediments accumulated.[1]

There are a few bodies of water at the present time which can be considered as relict seas, such as the Caspian Sea, the Salton Sink, Lake Baikal, etc. But none of these has produced evaporites at all comparable in scope to those in the older strata! In fact, it seems quite impossible for a relict sea in itself ever to produce the great thicknesses of salt that are actually found in the older strata. Thus Pettijohn says:

> Relict seas seem incapable of producing the thick salt deposits for reasons given above; a continued influx of marine waters is required to maintain the precipitation of salt.[2]

As noted above, tremendous depths of water are indicated to account for the deposits; or else, there must be continuing subsidence together with a continued influx of marine waters into the relict sea. There is no place in the world today where this combination of features is found; hence there must again be added to the uniformitarian principle a sizeable increment of pure imagination to account for the great salt and gypsum beds. Many ingenious schemes have been devised, attempting in some way to account for the data.

The multiple-basin hypothesis, for example, postulates a succession of connected basins. The waters flow from the sea through the successive basins and become progressively more saline. In a second or third basin, perhaps, halite might be precipitated without a subjacent deposit of anhydrite or gypsum. Because this concept, however, requires a most complex arrangement of basins and concentrations, it is an improbable one. Fractional crystallization can be accomplished in a simpler manner. King (1947), for example, has advanced an ingenious explanation for the thick anhydrite deposits of the Permian Castile formation of Texas and New Mexico [the largest of all the evaporite deposits]. He postulates deposition in a semi-isolated sea into which normal sea water flowed through a somewhat restricted channel. The concentrated brine of the Castile sea tended to sink to the bottom and in part return, by a sort of reflux action, to the

[1] *Ibid.*, p. 504.
[2] F. J. Pettijohn: *op. cit.*, p. 484.

sea. The salinity achieved was sufficient to precipitate calcium sulfate but not sodium chloride.[1]

The latter theory has many more ramifications, involving numerous discrete deposits brought about by the influx-reflux action. We need not consider it in detail; the significant point about all this, of course, is that modern processes do *not* account for the beds as they are found, and therefore some kind of hypothesis must be developed which proposes to account for the facts in some measure. One of the difficult facts to reconcile is that the order of deposition of various salts by evaporation out of standing sea water is not the same as found in the stratigraphic evaporite beds.

Detailed experiments on evaporation of sea water were carried out over a hundred years ago by Usiglio, obtaining the order of precipitation of various salts at various temperatures and conditions. But:

Although the order observed by Usiglio agrees in a general way with the sequence found in some salt deposits, many exceptions are known. Also, many minerals known from salt beds did not appear in the experimentally formed residues. The crystallization of a brine is very complex, and depends not only on the solubility of the salts involved but also upon the concentration of the several salts present and the temperature. . . . Inasmuch as many evaporite deposits show marked exception to the above requirements, simple evaporation of sea water did not occur, and either the parent brine was not formed from sea water or the evaporation took place under special conditions that will explain the anomalies.[2]

Modern writers are gradually coming to the opinion that even the stratified evaporite beds are very largely the result of metamorphic processes rather than simple sedimentation and evaporation. K. B. Krauskopf, of Stanford University and Secretary of the Geochemical Society, says concerning the older idea:

Further investigation showed that this simple picture was inadequate, and during the past 50 years both chemists and geologists have tried to work out the necessary modifications. . . . Probably most geologists would now agree with Borchert's conclusion that the Stassfurt beds [the chief type locality of the traditional evaporite interpretation] look like a simple depositional sequence only by accident, and that other processes besides

<hr />

[1] *Ibid.,* pp. 484-485.
[2] *Ibid.,* p. 483.

deposition from an evaporating brine must be invoked to explain their origin.[1]

Similarly, Greensmith writes:

As more fundamental data on stratified evaporites accumulate in current literature, it becomes demonstrably more apparent that their status as sediments is declining. Whereas they could once be grouped in their entirety as rocks formed by sedimentary processes, there is little doubt that some, if not the majority, could now be quite logically grouped as resulting from metamorphism.[2]

In view of the difficulties encountered by uniformitarianism in attempting to explain the great evaporite beds and the need to postulate either some special kind of brine which does not now exist or else some special conditions of evaporation and metamorphism that are not known to exist at present, perhaps it is not too presumptuous to suggest that these unusual brines may have been generated during the volcanic upheavals accompanying the Deluge and that unusual conditions of vaporization and separation of precipitates may likewise have been caused by the locally high temperatures accompanying these same upheavals. The details of such reactions may be difficult to decipher at present, at least without considerable further study, but it does appear that the catastrophic environmental factors associated with the Flood provide a more satisfactory framework within which to develop a satisfactory hypothesis than does the alternate procedure of pure speculation!

Cave Deposits

A different form of evaporite which is popularly believed to require long periods of time for formation is the familiar stalactite or stalagmite found in limestone caverns. These are formed by the evaporation of lime-bearing waters percolating through the cavern roof. Obviously, the rate of such cave travertine formation depends mainly on the rate of percolation of the source water. The fact that this rate may be very slow at present certainly does not mean it has always been so. Thornbury says:

[1] Konrad B. Krauskopf: Review of *Ozeane Salzlagerstatten,* by Hermann Borchert, (Berlin, Borntraeger, 1959), *Science,* Vol. 130, July 17, 1959, p. 156.
[2] John T. Greensmith: "The Status and Nomenclature of Stratified Evaporites," *American Journal of Science,* Vol. 255, October 1957, p. 593.

Various attempts have been made to estimate the rate of formation of cave travertine, but so many variable factors affect the rate of deposition that it is doubtful if cavern ages arrived at by this method are accurate.[1]

The caverns themselves are believed by most cave geologists to have been formed by solution of the limestone rock at a time when the rocks were saturated. With the gradual lowering of the water table, it is obvious that percolating waters would for some time be still quite plentiful, only gradually lessening in amount. Thus, the rate of formation of stalactites and stalagmites would be rapid at first, gradually leveling off to present rates.

Even under modern conditions, it is quite possible for these formations to develop rapidly. The speleologist Hendrix says, for example:

How long does it take for a stalactite to grow? Many people, impressed by repeated statements of the extreme duration of geologic time, have made statements to the effect that it takes dripstone practically forever to grow appreciably. However there is more than a little evidence that growth is considerably rapid. First of all, stalactites are found in man-made tunnels that are only a few years old. . . . Second, certain conditions are so favorable to dripstone growth that as much as several cubic inches a year may be deposited in a single stalactite. . . . Third, there are many examples of large stalagmites growing on blocks of stone that have fallen from cave ceilings.[2]

Consequently, to attribute great lengths of time to the formation of such cave deposits is not only unnecessary but unreasonable as well.

Buried Forests

Another important type of sedimentary phenomenon that seems at first to require much longer periods of time than the Bible would allow is found in cyclically repeated deposits, each cycle of which seems to require a certain more or less measurable time in which to be formed. An often-quoted example is a succession of buried forests on Amethyst Mountain in the northwestern part of Yellowstone National Park. J. L. Kulp discusses these as follows:

In Yellowstone Park there is a stratigraphic section of 2000 ft. exposed

---

[1] Wm. D. Thornbury, *op. cit.,* p. 338.
[2] Charles E. Hendrix: *The Cave Book* (Revere. Mass.: Earth Science Publ. Co., 1950), p. 26.

which shows 18 successive petrified forests. Each forest grew to maturity before it was wiped out with a lava flow. The lava had to be weathered into soil before the next forest could even start. Further this is only a small section of stratigraphic column in this area. It would be most difficult for flood geology to account for these facts.[1]

There are similar phenomena to be found at other places, but this case seems to be the most spectacular and the most difficult to reconcile with Biblical catastrophism. But actually such volcanic deposits surely represent catastrophic conditions themselves! They form a part of the great complex of volcanic formations blanketing the Pacific northwest and, as we have already pointed out, represent a state of things for which there is no modern parallel at all. Extensive volcanism was undoubtedly associated with the Deluge and such volcanic deposits are only to be expected in the Deluge strata. These in the Pacific northwest are mostly attributable to the later stages of the Deluge and perhaps post-Deluge events, since they are commonly dated as Tertiary or even sometimes Quaternary.

Why, then, is it not legitimate to explain such buried forests as largely allochthonous instead of autochthonous? We have already seen this to be most reasonable in the somewhat analogous case of the coal seams. That is, the cyclical deposits represent an oscillation of sedimentary deposits of water-transported trees and other vegetation with intermittent volcanic ash or lava flows.

In the case of Amethyst Mountain and Specimen Ridge, cited above, the appearances certainly do not indicate normal forest growths. Arnold says:

> On the slopes of Amethyst Mountain 15 successive forests are exposed, one above the other, and each is separated from the next one above or below by a few inches or feet of ash.[2]

Many of these trees are prostrate and in various positions; those that are upright apparently remained in that position due to the weight of their root system and attached soil as they were rafted into their final burial place. A diagrammatic sectional sketch of the exposure along Specimen Ridge, as shown by Miller,[3] (see Fig. 27) originally taken

---

[1] J. L. Kulp: "Flood Geology," *Journal of the American Scientific Affiliation,* January 1950, p. 10.

[2] C. A. Arnold: *An Introduction to Paleobotany* (New York, McGraw-Hill, 1947), p. 24.

[3] W. J. Miller: *An Introduction to Historical Geology* (New York, Van Nostrand, 1952), p. 485.

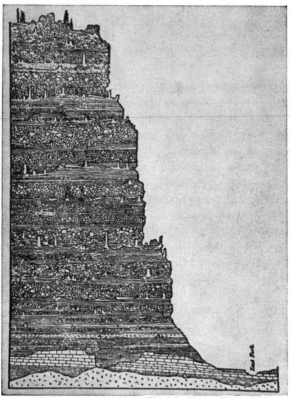

(Sketch by Holmes, U.S. Geol. Survey)

Figure 27. BURIED "FORESTS" IN SPECIMEN RIDGE.

This is a schematic representation of the succession of petrified tree layers on Specimen Ridge in Yellowstone Park, which have been interpreted as a sequence of forests which grew *in situ,* only to be overwhelmed in turn by a shower of volcanic materials. But it seems far more reasonable to interpret the tree layers as sedimentary strata, washed into place by a succession of strong currents interspersed with flows and volcanic showers from another direction.

from a U.S. Geological Survey Report, certainly gives the impression of this kind of origin, although it undoubtedly has been somewhat "schematized" to make it look like what the growth-in-place concept would require. The so-called petrified forests are in reality only stumps; there are no limbs or fossil foliage as one would expect if the complete trees had suddenly been inundated by a shower of volcanic fragments and ash. Neither are the root systems complete; only occasional trees remain upright and show some parts of the root system still attached.

The stumps give every appearance of having been in some manner sheared off by some overwhelming force (possibly tsunami-driven debris), then uprooted and transported and sorted out from other materials and then suddenly buried beneath a volcanic shower. Then came another wave of sediment and stumps (several layers of sediment, however, appear to be without any stumps), possibly resulting from the tsunami generated by the preceding eruption, then another volcanic shower, and so on. The whole formation, as does the volcanic terrain all over the Yellowstone region and the Pacific northwest, literally proclaims catastrophic deposition!

VARVED DEPOSITS

One other cyclic form of sedimentary deposit will be briefly discussed, namely the so-called "varved clays." These varves are banded sediments, each band usually quite thin with color grading from light to dark. Each varve has been interpreted as an annual deposit, the light-colored portion representing coarser deposits presumably formed during the summer months and the darker portion representing winter deposition, all on the bed of a former lake. If this interpretation is valid, varves can be used not only as qualitative indices of time duration but as actual measures of years during which the deposit was being formed. This is the basis of the "varve chronology" for the glacial and post-glacial periods in particular, now largely displaced by the C-14 method.

Difficulties in Varve Interpretation

There are several important difficulties with the varve method, however, one of which is the impossibility of knowing that the bands actually represent annual layers. Many other phenomena could produce such bands; for example, variation in flow and sediment burden of the stream or streams feeding the lake. Any brief flooding discharge into the lake would cause an initial layer of larger-sized particles followed by gradual settling of the finer particles, and this would give the appearance of a lamination. And there are other causes. As Pettijohn says:

> The cause of such laminations are variations in the rate of supply or deposition of the different materials. These variations might result from changes in the quantity of silt, clay, or calcium carbonate, or organic matter in the sea water or to changes in the rate of accumulation of these materials. Such variations have been attributed to the fortuitous shift in the depositing currents, to climatic causes (especially cyclical changes related to diurnal or annual rhythms), and also to aperiodic storms or floods.[1]

Obviously, not all—if any—of these factors are necessarily annual in character, and it would certainly be a very difficult task to determine for certain that a given bed of laminated clays actually had been laid down as annual varves.

The same kind of doubts have been expressed by many geomorphologists. This is pointed out by Thornbury:

> There has been criticism of this method of arriving at estimates of Pleistocene chronology. In the first place, it involves a great deal of interpolation and extrapolation, which introduce possible errors. Secondly, there is some question as to whether varves actually are annual deposits. Deane (1950) from his study of the varves in the Lake Simcoe region of Ontario was led to doubt seriously that varves represent yearly deposits and was more inclined to think that they represent deposits of shorter lengths of time.[2]

Not only is there doubt about the yearly nature of the varves, but an even more important question has to do with correlation of deposits from place to place. For, at any one exposure, there is no great number of varves, but the supposed chronology is built up by correlation and superposition of varves at any number of successive exposures. Flint also recognizes the dangers in this procedure:

> However, research on rhythmites in Denmark showed the common occurrence of laminations within a single couplet. These were ascribed to the redeposition of sediment after it had been stirred up by storms in shallow lakes. . . . Because the De Geer chronology interprets storm laminations as varves, Danish geologists do not accept the part of the chronology that antedates the moraines. Similar minor laminations have been identified in Germany and in Britain.

[1] F. J. Pettijohn: *op. cit.,* p. 163.
[2] W. D. Thornbury: *Principles of Geomorphology* (New York, Wiley, 1954), p. 404.

Rhythmites belonging to a segment of the same period were studied in Finland by Sauramo, who showed that correlation based on thickness alone could lead to error and developed a more conservative method akin to that of ordinary stratigraphic correlation . . .

The correlation of rhythmites, as described above, depends on the judgment of the person who matches the curves, and therefore it is not wholly objective. The literature does not report any attempt at independent correlation by several persons. A positive result from such objective testing would inspire confidence in the method.[1]

The highly doubtful significance of any varve chronology has been demonstrated plainly in recent years by its general rejection by geologists when the newer radiocarbon method was found to be contradictory to it. The radiocarbon dates for the glacial period proved to be much smaller than the varve counts had indicated but have now been quite generally accepted. Actually, as we have already seen, it is very likely that the radiocarbon dates themselves are much too large, except in the past few thousand years, so that this proves quite emphatically that the varves are either not annual deposits or that it is impossible to correlate them from place to place. In a work appearing even before the advent of the radiocarbon method, Flint had indicated the low esteem most geologists had for the varve method when he said:

Even the varve correlation made by De Geer and Antevs through the very short distance between Denmark and southern Sweden was severely criticized on the ground that the implied relative dates of the several Danish deposits concerned are in complete conflict with the stratigraphic evidence.

The whole matter of the reliability and usefulness of varve correlation is at present in an unsatisfactory state. Largely because it has been subjected to an inadequate amount of criticism and discussion, most geologists have no definite opinions on it.[2]

Thus, it is concluded that the varved clays of the Pleistocene glacial lakes offer no problem to the chronology of Biblical geology. The varves were deposited, either annually or at shorter intervals, within the post-Deluge period.

[1] R. F. Flint: *Glacial and Pleistocene Geology* (New York, Wiley, 1957), p. 297.
[2] R. F. Flint: *Glacial Geology and the Pleistocene Epoch* (New York, Wiley, 1947), p. 397.

Green River Formation

An apparently more serious difficulty is encountered in connection with the laminated deposits, supposedly annual varves, encountered in connection with deposits earlier than the Pleistocene. These deposits, according to our interpretation, must be accounted for in terms of the Flood itself, which occupied only *one* year and, therefore, cannot possibly represent a long succession of annual layers. The most important such formation, by far, is the Green River formation, which has been dated as Eocene, and which consists of great thicknesses of thinly-laminated shales. The importance of this formation, as well as a succinct description thereof, is given below:

To obtain criteria by which laminated rocks believed to be built up of varves can be proved to be actually varved is the present urgent task of geology. The most thorough study of rocks thought to be varved are the Green River shales of Eocene age in Wyoming and Colorado. . . . The shales are very thinly layered; and each layer consists of two laminae, one of which contains considerably more carbonaceous matter than the other. The paired laminae are interpreted as representing the sediment laid down during one year, in short, a varve, an interpretation which is strengthened by the fact that the varves fluctuate in thickness in a cycle corresponding to the sunspot cycle. The varves average less than 1/2000 of a foot in thickness, and as the Green River shales are 2,600 feet thick, the time represented by their accumulation is about 6 million years.[1]

The uncertain tone of the above evaluation is evidence enough that the supposed annual character of the Green River laminations is far from clear. Apparently the only real study that has ever been made of this well-known formation from this viewpoint is one made over thirty years ago by Bradley.[2] All later writers who refer to these layers as being examples of pre-Pleistocene varves do so on the authority of this one study. But in the study itself, only two very inadequate reasons are given for believing the layers to be annual.

One is a calculation purporting to show that the amount of sediment in the formation is of the same order of magnitude as the prob-

[1] Adolph Knopf, "Time in Earth History," in *Genetics, Paleontology, and Evolution*, ed. by Jepsen, Mayr, and Simpson, (Princeton, N. J., Princeton Univ. Press, 1949), p. 4.

[2] W. H. Bradley: "The Varves and Climate of the Green River Epoch," U. S. Geological Survey Professional Paper 158, 1929, pp. 87-110.

able amount of erosion from the ancient drainage basin contributing to the lakes whose beds are supposed to form these shales. But obviously anything so hypothetical as a calculation involving a watershed of entirely speculative extent, slope, character, erosibility and drainage characteristics, all taken as a basis for estimation of average rates of erosion—a type of calculation which almost everyone now admits to be nothing but rank guesswork—can hardly warrant so far-reaching a conclusion as that the accumulation of the formation required about 6 million years!

The other reason for concluding the laminations to be annual varves was their similarity of appearance to the varved clays of the Pleistocene and, to a lesser extent, banded sediments found in certain modern lakes. This is the old principle of uniformity again! The resemblance, however, is largely superficial (see Fig. 28). The Pleistocene varves are much thicker than the Green River laminations (which average less than 6/1000 of an inch in thickness) and reflect glacial melt-water deposition, whereas the Green River shales are denoted mainly by a cyclic repetition of organic and inorganic matter. The organic layers are quite rich petroleum deposits, and these oil shales are now being extensively investigated as a potential source of oil of great importance. Obviously, no modern lake deposits, although some of them (relatively few, actually) do show faint laminations in their bottom sediments, can possibly be held to be equivalent to these tremendously extensive deposits of rich oil shales.

Actually, the origin of these, as well as other, oil-bearing shales is still largely a matter of uncertainty.

Geologically, the origin of oil shale is obscure. The general belief seems to be that it was formed during millions of years of successive deposits of plant and animal life, mixed with sand and clay, at the bottoms of quiet lakes and lagoons.[1]

Obviously, there must be a considerable degree of uncertainty in the "general belief" in order to warrant such an equivocal judgment as this.

With respect to the Green River shales, in particular, several factors make it highly doubtful that they could possibly represent annual varved layers. For one thing, they are entirely too thin and uniform

[1] F. L. Hartley and C. R. Brinegar: "Oil Shale and Bituminous Sand," *Scientific Monthly*, Vol. 84, June 1957, p. 276.

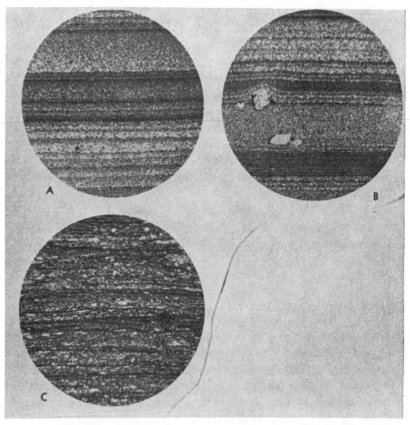

(Photo by William Schmidt)

Figure 28. COMPARISON OF BANDING EFFECTS.

Specimens A and B are argillites (indurated clays) and the laminations have been interpreted as annual varves. Specimen C is from the Green River oil shales, whose laminations have also been attributed to seasonal (though non-glacial) varves. The black bands in the latter are organic matter. The resemblance to other supposed varved deposits is superficial at best.

and extend over too wide an area to have been deposited in a normal lake bed. No matter how calm a lake may be ordinarily, occasional storms stir up the bottom sediments, and occasional river floods dump into the lake large quantities of sediment, which would then settle out on the lake bottom in an essentially graded series. To imagine that such an extensive lake, fed as it must have been by many rivers, could continue so impossibly quiet and inactive and undisturbed for six million years is somewhat ridiculous.

The Green River shales are also rich in fossils, a fact which is hard to reconcile with the supposed quiet manner of its formation. Miller observes:

The Green River formation is a fresh-water lake deposit composed largely of evenly stratified soft shales as much as 2000 feet thick. Many fossils, including fishes, insects, and plants occur in it.[1]

How does one explain, for example, a dead fish lying on the bed of a lake for about two hundred years while the slowly accumulating sediments gradually cover it and then fossilize it? Where does this happen in modern lakes?

Other significant features include the extensive deposits of volcanic ash mingled with the shales and the almost complete absence of any graded bedding in the oil-rich shales such as would be normally encountered in any lake-bottom sediment. Also, there is evidence of brecciated conditions in many parts of the formation. All of these features are described by Bradley,[2] and all of them seem difficult to harmonize with the postulated character of the beds.

We feel quite warranted in concluding, therefore, that the supposed annual, lacustrine, character of the laminations of the Green River oil shales is an entirely inadequate hypothesis. Therefore, some other explanation must be sought for the banding, and since the uniformitarian explanation is seen to be faulty, it is justifiable to seek an explanation in terms of the Biblical outline.

The absence of graded bedding in the shales is significant. If the individual layers had been deposited by simply settling to the bottom of a quiescent lake, it seems certain that each layer would be marked by a gradual decrease in particle size with increasing elevation. The laminations are marked strictly by thin layers of black organic-rich matter, and the location and frequency of these seem quite irregular.

The detailed manner of deposition may be hard to deduce at this time, owing to the catastrophic nature of the environmental factors during the Deluge. The only certain conclusion, from the very nature of the deposits, would seem to be that they could not have been formed as cyclic varves as claimed. A possible plausible explanation might be in terms of a vast sedimentary basin formed by the gradual uplift of the land surrounding it, in the later stages of the Deluge period. A complex of shallow turbidity currents, carrying the still soft surface sediments and organic slime from the surface of the rising lands would then enter the basin, mingle, and deposit their loads. Slight changes in velocities or compositions of the turbidity currents would account for much of the laminated appearance of the central deposits, although it is possible that the accumulation of the organic matter into a succession of thin seams was also partly caused by later physico-chemical factors affecting the sedimentary mass. The general appearance of the Green River formation as a whole seems consistent with this sort of concept.

Bradley . . . showed that the Green River formation is an extensive sedimentary body with thicknesses ranging to 2,000 feet. The predominant sediment is marl, with varying amounts of organic matter. The organic marl grades into oil shale which occupies the central portion of the deposit. Saline deposits occur to a thickness of 800 feet. The marginal shore deposits include sandstone, shale, algal limestone, and oolites.[1]

Other Causes of Lamination

Of course, this oil shale problem is only one aspect of the general problem of the origin of petroleum, which is one of the most important geological problems yet awaiting solution. In any case, these and other banded deposits need not be explained as annual deposits at all or even chronologically cyclic deposits in many cases. Various types of chemical reactions are known to be capable of producing this type of phenomenon. R. L. Handy says:

A third school of thought is that the bands represent a cyclic precipitation, or so-called diffusion banding or Liesegang phenomenon. Reacting solutions of chemicals do this if over-saturation is required for the reaction to start. The reaction starts, uses up all the chemicals in the vicinity, and makes a band; then it won't start again until the same point of over-saturation is again reached farther down or farther out.[2]

This description applied specifically to banding in soils, but the same kind of phenomenon can occur in any chemical-rich, water-bearing sediments. The Green River formation, in addition to its rich organic content, certainly is rich in chemicals and minerals of many kinds.

---

[1] W. C. Krumbein and L. L. Sloss: *Stratigraphy and Sedimentation* (San Francisco, W. H. Freeman and Co., 1951), p. 204.

[2] R. L. Handy: *Screenings from the Soil Research Lab*, publ. by Iowa Engineering Experiment Station, Ames, Iowa, Vol. 3, Mar.-April, 1959, p. 4.

These lacustrine beds are characterized by an extraordinary mineralogy, such as complex silicates of sodium, barium, calcium, boron, titanium, and niobium, and many complex carbonates. These include remarkable minerals, some unique to the Green River, . . . and others, found elsewhere only in pegmatite or igneous environment . . . and besides there are many more extremely rare or otherwise noteworthy species.[1]

Laboratory studies have also verified the formation of various types of bands by such chemical reactions. One example is reported by Vallentyne:

It has been shown above that periodic red bands are formed in reduced lake sediments rich in iron, if those sediments are exposed to air at room temperature in the laboratory . . . If the bands do form in lake sediments in situ, then there is of course the possibility that they may be confused with some types of varves.[2]

ORIGIN OF OIL AND MINERAL DEPOSITS

Uniformitarian geology is frequently defended on the ground that it has worked so well in leading to the discovery of economically important deposits of petroleum and metals. It is maintained that it *must* be basically correct, or else it could not have served so well as a guiding philosophy in economic geology.

But two replies can quickly be given to this sort of statement. In the first place, it has apparently *not* worked very well, as the discovery of valuable deposits of *any* kind is hardly on anything approaching a fully scientific basis as yet. In the second place, such techniques as have actually been found helpful in exploration do not really depend on the historical aspects of geology at all but only on recognition of the structural and sedimentary markers that experience has shown are associated with such deposits.

Uniformitarianism and Petroleum Geology

Petroleum geology is an excellent case in point. The high importance of this discipline in the whole spectrum of geological science is indicated by the following:

[1] Charles Milton: "Green River Mineralogy," *Geochemical News*, 1959. For detailed analysis of the minerals in this formation, see Charles Milton and H. P. Eugster, "Green River Mineral Assemblages," in *Researches in Geochemistry*, ed. by Philip H. Abelson (New York, Wiley, 1959), pp. 118-150.

[2] J. R. Vallentyne: "A Laboratory Study of the Formation of Sediment Bands," *American Journal of Science*, Vol. 253, Sept. 1955, p. 550.

More than half the geologists in the world work directly for oil companies, and the support for many geologists in academic and government employment comes from petroleum.[1]

Thus, with most of the world's geological brainpower being expended on those aspects of geology concerned with oil and gas accumulations, one would expect that evolutionary historical geology would find its most productive application in this field—*if* it is really valid.

In spite of the immense size of the oil industry, however, and while freely granting that oil geologists make a very substantial and almost indispensable contribution to this industry, it is nevertheless true that oil discovery is still not very efficient scientifically. The following comment points up a few of the pertinent statistics, coming as it does from one of the country's leading petroleum geologists:

> Oil is getting harder to find. The high risks inherent in the research for oil are unusual in the business world. Statistics show that only one wildcat well in nine discovers oil or gas; only one in 44 proves to be a profitable venture; only one in 427 discovers a field of 25 million barrels; and only one in 991 finds a real payoff—a major pool with 50 million or more barrels.[2]

It could not be claimed that Biblical geology in its present state of development would lead to more effective results than uniformitarian geology in the search for oil fields, but it could hardly be much *less* effective! It might at least be worth some serious consideration on the part of oil geologists to see whether or not it could yield any real economic value.

As yet, in fact, uniformitarian geology has not been able to develop even a generally acceptable theory as to the origin of oil or its basic source material. A recent review of the problem opens with:

> Although much progress has been made in the past decade, a generally acceptable understanding of the origin of oil is still lacking. Insight into the mechanism of the migration of oil has proved to be even more elusive.[3]

Levorsen has elaborated more fully on this uncertain state of the science:

[1] Parke A. Dickey: "100 Years of Oil Geology," *Geotimes,* Vol. III, No. 6, 1959, p. 6.

[2] R. D. Sloan: "The Future of the Exploration Geologist," *Geotimes,* Vol. III, No. 1, 1958, p. 6.

[3] E. G. Baker: "Origin and Migration of Oil," *Science,* Vol. 129, April 3, 1959, p. 871.

While agreement is nearly complete on the organic source of petroleum, there are wide differences of opinion on the process by which it was formed and on the nature of the organic matter from which it was derived . . . Further differences of thought arise when an attempt is made to explain the transformation of organic source material into petroleum. Heat and pressure, bacterial action, radioactive bombardment, and catalytic reactions—each has its proponents as the chief source of energy responsible for the conversion.[1]

It is apparent that once again, and in this most important (both economically and in numbers of geologists concerned) of all geological disciplines, the principle of uniformity has proved impotent. Although some use is made of micropaleontology in correlation of oil-bearing strata, its economic applicability is almost entirely local. That is, geologists can identify a given formation from two or more well logs by the microfossils contained in the cuttings and thus orient the log with respect to some plane of interest, but this can only be done on a local scale within the confines of the given formation. The process has virtually *no* value or significance for regional correlations.

Even on the local scale, the miscrofossils are not nearly so important as other factors revealed by the well logs. In one of the newest and most comprehensive texts on petroleum geology, running to over 700 pages,[2] the words "micropaleontology" or "microfossil" do not even appear in the 35-page index. Although the subject is mentioned at occasional places in the book, it is only *mentioned*, the very silence bespeaking the relative inutility of the method in petroleum exploration. We have already called attention to Bucher's plaintive remark in this connection:

Professional geologists working in the petroleum industry are apt to lose sight of the importance of fossils, for within the confines of one oil field and even one sedimentary basin, bed tracing by lithologic characters and by electric logging makes fossils appear superfluous.[3]

Thus it hardly seems that evolutionary geology, as based on the assumed sequence of fossils, can lay claim to spectacular success in the field of petroleum geology; the latter would certainly not be ad-

[1] A. I. Levorsen: *Geology of Petroleum* (San Francisco, W. H. Freeman & Co., 1954), p. 476.

[2] Levorsen, *op. cit.*

[3] Walter H. Bucher: "International Responsibilities of Geologists," *Geotimes*, Vol. I, No. 3, 1956, p. 6.

versely affected by a reorientation of basic geological philosophy in the direction of catastrophism and quite possibly would be materially benefited.

Stratigraphic Occurrence of Oil

One important fact accounts in large measure for the difficulty in explaining the origin and geological history of oil, namely that oil has been found in rocks of practically all geologic ages except the Pleistocene. It is a feature essentially common to all the stratified rocks and, therefore, cannot be easily located by means of the usual stratigraphic and paleontologic criteria for identifying rocks. This fact also gives strong testimony that such a universal phenomenon as oil, found as it is in all the rock systems, must have a universal explanation. The conditions of its formation must have been essentially the same everywhere. Rather than supporting thereby the concept of uniformity in time, this fact seems rather to evidence the fact of uniformity of manner of origin and formation and thereby to imply one global event which somehow brought about the genesis of all the great oil reservoirs of the earth's crust! This universal occurrence of petroleum is indicated by Cox, as follows:

> Petroleum occurs in rocks of all ages from the Cambrian to the Pliocene inclusive, but no evidence has been found to prove that any petroleum has been formed since the Pliocene, although sedimentation patterns and thicknesses in Pleistocene and Recent sediments are similar to those in the Pliocene where petroleum has formed.[1]

We would suggest that there must be a connection between the fact that Pleistocene and Recent sediments are post-Diluvian and the fact that in these only has no petroleum deposit been found. Otherwise the reason for this fact is quite mysterious.

> The apparent absence of formation of petroleum subsequent to the Pliocene must be explained in any study of the transformation of organic material into petroleum.[2]

A very few oil deposits have been noted in both pre-Cambrian and

---

[1] Ben B. Cox: "Transformation of Organic Material Into Petroleum Under Geological Conditions," *Bulletin, Amer. Assoc. Petroleum Geologists*, Vol. 30, May 1946, p. 647.

[2] *Ibid.*

Pleistocene deposits, but these are known to have migrated into them after earlier formation and deposition in other sedimentary rocks. The absence of oil in Pleistocene rocks is all the more mysterious in view of the fact that some petroleum hydrocarbons have been found in Recent sediments,[1] indicating that long ages are *not* required for the formation of such hydrocarbons. At the same time, these hydrocarbons are definitely *not* petroleum, which evidently requires special conditions of some kind before it will form.[2]

About all that is definitely known is that petroleum occurrences seem to have no particular relation to particular stratigraphic sequences or to structural forms. Neither the paleontologic history nor the deformational history appears to bear any necessary relation to actual oil deposits.

Reservoir rocks that contain petroleum differ from one another in various ways. They range in geologic age from pre-Cambrian to Pliocene, in composition from siliceous to carbonate, in origin from sedimentary to igneous, in porosity from 1 to 40 percent, and in permeability from one millidarcy to many darcies.

There is a wide variation also in the character of the trap that retains the pool. The trap may have been formed as the result of causes that are entirely structural or entirely stratigraphic, or from any combination of these causes . . . The geologic history of the trap may vary widely—from a single geologic episode to a combination of many phenomena extending over a long period of geologic time. Pools trapped in limestone and dolomite reservoir rock, for example, have the same relations that pools trapped in sandstone rocks have to such things as the reservoir fluids, oil-water and oil-gas contacts, and trap boundaries. Yet the chemical relations of the reservoir rock and the effects of solution, cementation, compaction, and recrystallization are quite different in sandstone and carbonate reservoirs.[3]

[1] P. V. Smith, Jr.: "The Occurrence of Hydrocarbons in Recent Sediments from the Gulf of Mexico," *Science,* Vol. 116, October 24, 1952, pp. 437-439.

[2] W. E. Hanson says: "Although hydrocarbons form an important part of the organic fraction of recent sediments, crude oil as we know it has not formed in these sediments even well beyond the zone of major bacterial activity." ("Some Chemical Aspects of Petroleum Genesis," *Researches in Geochemistry,* ed. by P. H. Abelson, New York, John Wiley and Sons, 1959, p. 114).

[3] A. I. Levorsen: *op. cit.,* pp. 523-524.

Formation of Petroleum Deposits

The most immediately apparent conclusion from all this is that the accumulation of petroleum into traps must have occurred *after* all, or practically all, the strata were laid down, since they are apparently entirely independent of the particular type of rock but are, nevertheless, similar to each other in hydraulic characteristics. The main feature that all such deposits have in common is that of being associated with water:

> Nearly every petroleum pool exists within an environment of water—free, interstitial, edge, and bottom water. This means that the problem of migration is intimately related to hydrology, hydraulics, and ground-water movement.[1]

Another extremely important fact is that apparently all petroleum is organic in origin. There have been inorganic theories of origin in the past, but the accumulated evidence now is overwhelming that petroleum has an organic basis.

> Early ideas leaned toward the inorganic sources, whereas the modern theories, with few exceptions, assume that the primary source material was organic.[2]

The exact nature of the organic material has been as yet quite unsettled, but there seems little doubt that the vast reservoirs of organic remains, both plant and animal, in the sedimentary rocks constitute a more than adequate source.

Although the details are not clear, the Deluge once again appears to offer a satisfactory explanation for the origin of oil, as well as the other stratigraphic phenomena. The great sedimentary basins being filled rapidly and more or less continuously during the Flood would provide a prolific source of organic material, together with whatever heat and pressure might have been needed to initiate the chemical reactions necessary to begin the transformation into petroleum hydrocarbons. Of course, not all organic debris deposited during the Flood was converted into oil; apparently certain catalysts or other chemicals were also necessary, and where these were present, it was possible for oil to form.

[1] *Ibid.*, p. 523.
[2] *Ibid.*, p. 476.

Recent studies indicate that certain dilute soap solutions seem to be associated with petroleum formation, in that these can act as solubilizers for the hydrocarbons in the deposited sediments which, when further diluted with water, permit the dissolved hydrocarbons to appear as discrete oil droplets.

Thus, it would seem that crude oil originates during the compaction of a sedimentary basin by virtue of the fact that sediment hydrocarbons dissolve in waters containing natural solubilizers and then come out of solution as oil droplets. The composition of crude oil as now understood is consistent with this hypothesis.[1]

Different specific types of solution mechanisms appear to account for the different types of crude oils. Constituents for the solubilizers would certainly be available at many places during the Deluge, especially in areas of heavy organic deposition of marine animal remains.

This process of oil formation implies, too, that oil was formed over wide areas, rather than in the relatively limited locations in which it is found.

Such a mechanism would lend credence to the suggestion that the source beds of petroleum are not necessarily unique accumulations of hydrocarbons in a limited area but, rather, may generally be coincident with the area from which water is expressed into the porous strata that eventually form the reservoirs.[2]

This hypothesis is quite new and may not stand the test of further investigation, but it is based on an impressive research study. In any case, the general picture of vast organic remains, somehow dissolved and transformed chemically into petroleum hydrocarbons, then eventually reprecipitated as oil, is basically valid and harmonizes well with the concept of catastrophic burial and dissolution during the Deluge.

The process of gradual accumulation into oil pools and reservoirs is, then, from here on basically a hydraulic problem. The oil droplets, by buoyancy, tend to rise up through the surrounding water and thus gradually to accumulate at the upper surface of the water. The extent of this transportation and the amount accumulated will depend on the hydraulic gradients and permeabilities of the containing strata.

[1] E. G. Baker: "Origin and Migration of Oil," *Science,* Vol. 129, April 3, 1959, p. 874.
[2] *Ibid.*

This, of course, has nothing to do with the fossil contents of the strata and very little to do with the tectonic history of the region, except to the extent that particular formations which are either permeable or impermeable, as the case may be, may have been distorted in some way.

Rapid Formation of Petroleum Pools

These hydraulic processes have been continuing since the Deluge, gradually concentrating the oil that was formed at that time, or soon after, into traps. But there is no reason at all to think that these processes may have required long ages of time to be accomplished. As already seen, even under some modern conditions, petroleum hydrocarbons can be formed rather quickly.

More recently a school of thought has developed which believes that oil formation may begin soon after deposition of the organic matter in the sediments . . . One of the surprising results of this study has been the discovery of liquid hydrocarbons in Recent sediments from the Gulf of Mexico.[1]

Similarly, the traps that form the pools need not have taken long to form. Although no primary oil deposits are found in Pleistocene strata, it *has* been shown that certain of the traps found in earlier strata were actually formed during Pleistocene time, which as we have seen is, in our framework, post-Deluge.

An example is the Kettleman Hills pool in California; the oil and gas of this pool are in the Miocene Temblor formation, but the fold that forms the trap cannot be earlier than Pleistocene, for the Temblor formation fold is parallel to the Pleistocene rocks at the surface of the ground. This places the accumulation in late Pleistocene or post-Pleistocene time . . . An illustration of the short time for a pool to adjust itself to a change in conditions may be seen in the tilting of the Cairo pool in Arkansas. The tilt occurred within a period of 10-12 years; if it had gone on for a few years more, at the same rate, the oil would probably have moved completely out of the trap. Thus the time it takes for oil to accumulate into pools may be geologically short, the minimum being measured, possibly, in thousands or even hundreds of years.[2]

[1] P. V. Smith, Jr.: "Occurrence of Hydrocarbons in Recent Sediments from the Gulf of Mexico," *Science*, Vol. 116, October 24, 1952. p. 437.

[2] A. I. Levorsen: *op. cit.*, p. 524.

There is thus no reason to reject the Deluge as a possible framework for formation of the great oil deposits of the world. Especially is this so since the uniformitarian hypothesis and the evolutionary framework of geological ages have been shown to be largely irrelevant to the actual practice of petroleum exploration. The character of petroleum deposits, and such information as has been accumulated regarding the origin and migration of oil, harmonize quite well with the Deluge hypothesis.

Origin of Ore and Mineral Deposits

And if petroleum geology has developed essentially independently of historical geology, this development is even more true of economic geology, which is the study and development of commercial ore and mineral deposits. Ores of all kinds may be found in rocks of all geologic ages, nearly always associated with igneous intrusions. Thus, historical geology can be of no real aid in locating such deposits. Neither is the origin of ore bodies any better understood than the origin of petroleum deposits.

There is so much honest difference of opinion among geologists, regarding the mode of formation of ore deposits, that any attempt at setting forth conclusions regarding the subject is bound to conflict with other opinions.[1]

This great difference of opinion is itself the strongest evidence that any sort of consistent uniformitarianism is unsuccessful in accounting for metalliferous deposits or in locating such deposits.

The predominant group of theories explains most ore veins as originating in cooling magmas which have intruded themselves into the strata with gaseous or aqueous solutions carrying the metals upward through fissures or "pipes" until they are precipitated out in ore form. But as von Engeln and Caster have pointed out this concept encounters serious problems:

The awkward thing to explain about the mechanics of vein formation is how there can be at one and the same time a passageway for the ascending solutions and a fissure completely filled and even enlarged by the minerals that the solutions deposit.[2]

[1] R. S. Walker & W. J. Walker: *Origin and Nature of Ore Deposits*, (Authors, Colorado Springs, 1956), p. viii.
[2] O. D. von Engeln & K. E. Caster: *op. cit.*, p. 163.

As far as is known, nothing of this sort has been observed to happen in the present era or even in the Pleistocene. The formation of ore deposits is seemingly a phenomenon that occurred in the past, independently of the particular geological stratum and by means of agencies which are not understood now but which most likely were catastrophic in character, associated with volcanism.

> . . . mineralization is not a rare phenomenon nor a vagary of Nature, as is sometimes assumed, but is, instead, a common geological process, almost invariably accompanying volcanic activity as a final phase thereof, while it is probably an attendant feature of most igneous intrusions within the uppermost four miles of the Earth's Crust.[1]

Although ore formation is little understood and uniformitarian approaches to its understanding have proved mostly sterile, it would seem that its universality in both geographic location and supposed geologic time, its almost invariable association with igneous activity, and its apparently catastrophic manner of deposition are most easily visualized in our basic Deluge framework. During the Flood, as we have seen, volcanic activity of all sorts continued globally during most of the Flood period, and therefore volcanic rocks are now found throughout the world and throughout the geologic column. Formation of mineral deposits of great extent and variety was undoubtedly possible during the Flood and can best be understood in this context. Of course, the very extensive pre-Cambrian ores may well be attributed to the Creation period itself in many cases.

Although there is much yet to be learned about the earth's great oil and mineral deposits, it is surely obvious that the evolutionary concept of historical geology is of little practical utility in their discovery and exploitation. Such as is known about the character of these deposits and their formation fits equally well or better into the framework of Biblical geology. It simply is incorrect to assert that such success as has been attained by the disciplines of petroleum and economic geology is evidence of the validity of orthodox historical geology.

MODERN SIGNIFICANCE OF THE GENESIS FLOOD

We have obviously not attempted to solve all the difficulties that may be encountered in our proposed Biblical reorientation of his-

---

[1] Walker and Walker, *op. cit.*, p. 336.

torical geology. However, we have made a serious attempt to select the most difficult problems for treatment, and it is hoped that even these have been shown to be amenable to satisfactory explanation in terms of Biblical geology.

Bankruptcy of Uniformitarianism

The present widely accepted system of uniformitarianism in historical geology, with its evolutionary basis and bias, has been shown to be utterly inadequate to explain most of the important geologic phenomena. Present rates and processes simply *cannot* account for the great bulk of the geologic data. Some form of catastrophism is clearly indicated by the vast evidences of volcanism, diastrophism, glaciation, coal and oil and mineral deposits, fossilization, vast beds of sediments, and most of the other dominant features of the earth's crust. When this fact is once recognized, it can then be seen that even the supposed evidences of great geologic age can be reinterpreted to correlate well with the much more impelling evidences of violent and rapid activity and formation.

But if present processes cannot be used to deduce the earth's past history (and this fact is proved not only by the failure of geological uniformity but even more by the impregnable laws of conservation and deterioration of energy), then the only way man can have certain knowledge of the nature of events on earth prior to the time of the beginning of human historical records, is by means of divine revelation. And this is why the Bible record of Creation and the Flood immediately becomes tremendously pertinent to our understanding, not only of the early history of the earth but also of the purpose and destiny of the universe and of man.

We have, therefore, sought to show how the outline of earth history provided by the early chapters of Genesis, as well as by the related passages from other parts of the Bible, actually provides a scientifically accurate framework within which all the verified data of geology and geophysics fit together remarkably well. The great Deluge of Noah's day is seen to account for a large portion of the sedimentary rocks of the earth's crust and indirectly for the glacial and other surface deposits which resulted from the change in earth climates at the time of the Flood. The reader may judge for himself whether the evidence truly warrants this reorientation of geological philosophy. We hope, of course, that he will really *consider* the evidence and not be disposed to reject it strictly on the basis of the fact that "authorities" may not approve!

Importance of the Question

But many may thoughtlessly wonder what difference it makes, whether or not the Flood was really a global Flood or whether it actually produced many of our present rock strata or whether indeed the world and its inhabitants came about by a process of evolution or not. Even many Christians allege that these are unimportant questions, not affecting Christian faith one way or the other.

However, these are *not* mere academic questions. Though it may be possible for the careless to treat them as such, a little serious consideration should show that they are profoundly important and that one's convictions about them may have deep influence upon his whole philosophy of life and, therefore, perhaps even on his ultimate destiny.

The Two Basic Philosophies

There are really only *two* basic philosophies or religions among mankind. The one is oriented primarily with respect to God, the Creator, of Whom and by Whom and for Whom are all things. Man is a creature of God, among the highest of His creatures but nevertheless utterly dependent upon and responsible to Him. Man's disobedience to His Creator has resulted in universal loss of fellowship with God, and this condition manifests itself in all forms of sin and in pain and death, even being reflected in the inharmonious relationships in the rest of the animate and in the inanimate creation. Salvation from this lost condition of man and his world has required the direct intervention of God Himself, in the form of man in the person of the Lord Jesus Christ, whose atoning death on the Cross of Calvary was the terrible price of redemption! But with the full price of redemption and regeneration and restoration thus provided by God in Christ, salvation then becomes available freely to all men to be received "by grace through faith" entirely apart from man's works. This, of course, is the essence of Christianity—or, at least, *Biblical* Christianity.

The other basic philosophy is oriented primarily with respect to man. This system, appearing in an almost infinite variety of forms, supposes that man is inherently capable of acquiring by his own efforts all he needs in this present life and in any possible life to come. The emphasis is always on man's own works or his reason or his religious duties or something else that *he* does to bring about his own improvement and ultimate salvation. The idea of God is perhaps accommodated somewhere in the system but always as a Being more or less limited in His activities or decisions. He is often conceived primarily in pantheistic terms, essentially identical with the universe and even with man himself as the highest entity thus far evolved.

And the underlying dynamic of this philosophy is the concept of evolution! The idea of development, of growth, of progress, of improvement appeals to man's pride and ambition and so finds abundant manifestation in all the many religious and philosophic systems of man, be these ancient idolatries or primitive animism or modern existentialism or atheistic communism! All of these center around man and his works, as do all other religions except Biblical Christianity! The idea of evolution did not originate with Charles Darwin, by any means; men have always conceived in some way or another the idea of man's identification with Nature and his dependence upon it for his own existence. Whatever gods there be have also been visualized as arising (evolving) out of some sort of primeval stuff or chaos. In early cosmologies this concept seems sometimes connected also with the competing concept of a divine Creator, indicating even in those times a conflict between the two fundamental systems.

Theistic Evolution Rejected

The prominent historian of science, Dr. Charles Gillispie of Princeton, remarks concerning the philosophy of Lamarck, one of the evolutionary predecessors of Darwin:

> M. de Lamarck was the last representative of that great school of naturalists and general observers who held sway from Thales and Democritus right down to Buffon. He was the mortal enemy of the chemists, of experimentalists and petty analysts, as he called them. No less severe was his philosophical hostility, amounting to hatred, for the tradition of the Deluge and the Biblical creation story, indeed for everything which recalled the Christian theory of nature.[1]

[1] C. C. Gillispie: "Lamarck and Darwin in the History of Science," *American Scientist*, Vol. 46, December 1958, p. 397.

And, of course, all the prominent founders of the modern theory of evolution—Darwin, Huxley, Spencer, Haeckel, and others—were firm opponents of the entire Biblical view of the world and of man. By and large, this is also true *today* of the present leaders of evolutionary thought,[1] although it is true that there are many people who have tried to harmonize evolution and Christianity in their own personal philosophies. But the light esteem in which such a concept as theistic evolution is held by the real *leaders* of evolutionary philosophy and research is indicated by the following from the geneticist Goldschmidt:

> Another type of evolutionary theory hardly deserves to be mentioned in a scientific paper. This is the mystical approach, which hides its insufficient understanding of the facts behind such empty words as creative evolution, emergent evolution, holism, and psycho-Lamarckism. . . . The biologist does not receive any constructive help from such ideas and is forced to ignore them.[2]

In addition to genetics, the other science which has been most directly concerned with evolution is that of paleontology, which has in fact provided the one genuine class of evidence that evolution on any large scale may actually have occurred, through its study of the fossils. One of the world's outstanding paleontologists, Dr. George Simpson of Harvard University, delivers himself on the subject of these theistic theories of evolution as follows:

> The fossil record definitely does not accord with . . . the concept of orthogenesis or more broadly with overtly or covertly non-materialistic theories like those of Driesch, Bergson, Osborne, Cuenot, du Nuoy, or Vandel.[3]

This opinion, written ten years ago, is now held apparently more emphatically than ever by Simpson. In an important address given in connection with the Darwinian Centennial Convocation and the

[1] For example, C. D. Darlington, Sherardian Professor of Botany at Oxford, says: "We owe it to (Darwin) that the world was brought to believe in evolution; we ought to be duly grateful and leave it at that . . . Here is a theory that released thinking men from the spell of a superstition, one of the most overpowering that has ever enslaved mankind . . . We owe to the *Origin of Species* the overthrow of the myth of Creation . . ." ("The Origin of Darwinism," *Scientific American,* Vol. 200, May 1959, pp. 60, 66.)

[2] R. B. Goldschmidt: "Evolution, as Viewed by One Geneticist," *American Scientist,* Vol. 40, January 1952, p. 85.

[3] G. G. Simpson: "Evolutionary Determinism and the Fossil Record," *Scientific Monthly,* Vol. 71, October 1950, p. 264.

annual meeting of the American Association for Advancement of Science at the University of Chicago, Simpson said:

Evolution is a fully natural process, inherent in the physical properties of the universe, by which life arose in the first place and by which all living things, past or present, have since developed, divergently and progressively . . . Organisms diversify into literally millions of species, then the vast majority of those species perish and other millions take their places for an eon until they, too, are replaced. If that is a foreordained plan, it is an oddly ineffective one . . . A world in which man must rely on himself, in which he is not the darling of the gods but only another, albeit extraordinary, aspect of nature, is by no means congenial to the immature or the wishful thinkers . . . Life may conceivably be happier for some people in the other worlds of superstition. It is possible that some children are made happy by a belief in Santa Claus, but adults should prefer to live in a world of reality and reason.[1]

At the same convocation, the internationally-famous British biologist, Sir Julian Huxley, said:

In the evolutionary pattern of thought there is no longer need or room for the supernatural. The earth was not created; it evolved. So did all the animals and plants that inhabit it, including our human selves, mind and soul, as well as brain and body. So did religion.[2]

Probably the most significant thing about these remarks of Simpson and Huxley, and many others that were to the same effect at this significant Darwinian "worship service," was that evidently none of the more than 2,000 leading scientists that were present, from all over the world, raised any public objections to these sentiments. The general commitment of the world intellectual community to this type of philosophy is well known to all who are at all conversant with modern scientific literature.

Evolution, Communism and Humanism

In this country with its Christian culture and traditions, true atheistic evolution has never been able to gain a great following, even among scientists, although it is certainly true that a large majority of the leaders in biology, paleontology, and such fields, even in this

[1] George Gaylord Simpson: "The World Into Which Darwin Led Us," *Science,* Vol. 131, April 1, 1960, pp. 969, 973-974.
[2] Associated Press dispatch, November 27, 1959.

country, have completely rejected true Biblical Christianity in favor of the evolutionary view of the world. In other countries, the real implications of evolution have been more readily recognized and acknowledged, and this is especially true in Communist countries, where it is the backbone of the whole scientific structure of Communistic philosophy.[1] The outstanding biologist and geneticist, Dobzhansky, who formerly lived in Russia, says:

> Marx recommended rather different methods, which he believed to be somehow deducible from Darwin's discoveries. He proposed to acknowledge his indebtedness by dedicating *Das Kapital* to Darwin—an honor which Darwin politely declined.[2]

The famous funeral oration over the body of Karl Marx, delivered by Engels, stressed the evolutionary implications of Communism. He said:

> Just as Darwin discovered the law of evolution in organic nature, so Marx discovered the law of evolution in human history.[3]

Although Communism is the most dangerous and widespread philosophy opposing Christianity today, there are many others. And the significant thing is that all of them are basically man-centered with some form of evolutionary philosophy undergirding them. And such a man-centered, evolutionary philosophy is becoming ever more powerful all over the world in every area of life. This viewpoint dominates the United Nations Organization, and all the various "One-World" movements. Its thesis is succinctly stated by Dr. H. J. Muller, as follows:

> The foregoing conclusions represent, I believe, an outgrowth of the thesis of modern humanism, as well as of the study of evolution, that the primary job for man is to promote his own welfare and advancement, both that of his members considered individually and that of the all-inclusive group, in due awareness of the world as it is, and on the basis of a naturalistic, scientific ethics.[4]

These "scientific" ethics, envisioned by the intellectual elite, no

---

[1] For an enlightening discussion of the influence of evolution on communist and other modern philosophies, see Conway Zirkle: *Evolution, Marxian Biology, and the Social Scene* (Philadelphia, University of Pennsylvania Press, 1959, 527 pp.).

[2] Th. Dobzhansky: "Evolution at Work," *Science*, Vol. 127, May 9, 1958, p. 1091.

[3] Otto Ruhle: *Karl Marx* (New York, New Home Library, 1943), p. 366.

[4] H. J. Muller: "Human Values in Relation to Evolution," *Science*, Vol. 127, March 21, 1958, p. 629.

longer derive their basis from Christian doctrine and from Scripture. Their basis is simply in what their proponents decide is best for the "greatest good for the greatest number" and is thus thoroughly secularized.

The observer who is not already identified with one of the contending theological parties can see clearly that the moment a theology is to be used to yield ethical prescriptions, these rules of conduct are obtained by deliberations in whose outcome secular aims and thought are every bit as decisive as in the reflections of secular ethicists who deny theism. And the perplexity of ethical problems is not lessened by the theological superstructure. I therefore cannot see in what sense theism can be held to be logically necessary as an axiomatic basis for ethics.[1]

Evolution and Education

The theory of evolution, with its mechanistic philosophy and humanistic ethics, has actually permeated not only the biological sciences but also the physical sciences and social sciences even in this country. The social sciences, especially, have become almost completely dominated by the evolutionary perspective. And these disciplines with their more immediate impact on actual human relationships and conduct through modern sociology, psychology, economics, psychiatry, criminology—all of which are almost completely organized now in terms of evolutionary concepts—have had far greater influence on modern society than most people realize.

Especially important is the influence the evolutionary philosophy and ethics have had on our educational system. Not only is organic evolution either assumed or openly taught throughout the curriculum of the public schools of our country, it is the very foundation of the whole educational philosophy upon which our modern system of "progressive education" is built. The major architect of the system is everywhere acknowledged to be John Dewey, whose great Schools of Education at the University of Chicago and Columbia University have had unparalleled influence in molding the educational system and philosophy of our nation's schools. His biographer says of him:

The starting-point of his system of thought is biological: he sees man as an organism in an environment, remaking as well as made. Things are to

[1] Adolf Grunbaum: "Science and Ideology," *Scientific Monthly,* Vol. 79, July 1954, p. 18.

be understood through their origins and their functions, without the intrusion of supernatural considerations.[1]

Before he became so influential, Dewey made abundantly clear his thorough commitment to the evolutionary system and ethic, as follows:

There are no doubt sufficiently profound distinctions between the ethical process and the cosmic process as it existed prior to man and to the formation of human society. So far as I know, however, all of these differences are summed up in the fact that the process and the forces bound up with the cosmic have come to consciousness in man . . . We have, however, no reason to suppose that the cosmic process has become arrested or that some new force has supervened to struggle against the cosmic.[2]

This idea that Evolution (personified) has finally come to consciousness in man and that Man is the paramount agent now in its further development has had tremendous influence throughout the world, and amounts to nothing less than a deification of Man! This enthronement of Man, and forced abdication of God are the ultimate goal of all non-Christian or anti-Christian systems—a great super-system of humanistic evolutionary pantheism.

Biblical Christianity and Evolutionary Philosophy

Yet, despite the tremendous influence exerted by the theory of evolution in almost every aspect of American life and education (even leavening the modern theological systems of most of the major Christian denominations), its more vocal advocates continue to complain that it is not sufficiently understood or applied. They protest at its illogical emasculation through incorporation into theological and moral philosophical systems. A recent work[3] by the prominent evolutionary biologist, Oscar Riddle, for example, is a 400-page indictment of organized religion for obstructing the adequate teaching of biology by harnessing evolution to theism!

But if evolutionists have cause to object to religionists attempting to accommodate their theory to religious concepts, even more do Bible-believing Christians have cause to reject such an attempted har-

[1] Will Durant: Article "John Dewey," in *Encyclopedia Britannica*, Vol. VII, 1956, p. 297.
[2] John Dewey: "Evolution and Ethics," *The Monist*, Vol. VIII (1897-1901), reprinted in *Scientific Monthly*, Vol. 78, February 1954, p. 66.
[3] Oscar Riddle: *The Unleashing of Evolutionary Thought* (New York, Vantage, 414 pp., 1955).

mony from their viewpoint. Not only is the hypothesis of evolution primarily an attempt to account for all things, man included, apart from God as well as an attempt to glorify man in place of God but its whole character is squarely opposed to that of Biblical Christianity. The Bible teaches a perfect Creation, followed by a Fall and subsequent deterioration, requiring the intervention of God Himself, in Christ, to bring about redemption and salvation. Evolution postulates a gradual progress from crude beginnings through innate forces, to higher and higher levels of achievement and complexity. Vannevar Bush has reminded us that:

> The assumption of Darwin and Spencer that all evolution must be progress was of course only an assumption. But it was generally accepted by most of their contemporaries despite the criticism of Huxley in his later years. In the generally hopeful temper of the late nineteenth century the whole Spencerian dogma was eagerly taken up, with or without its claims of reason, by all classes of people in England and the United States. The prevailing mood of our society before the first World War was one of complacent expectation that all things would improve perpetually. Retrogression, at least, was unthinkable.[1]

Similarly, the morality of evolution, which assumes that progress and achievement and "good" come about through such action as benefits the individual himself or the group of which he is a part, to the detriment of others, is most obviously anti-Christian. The very essence of Christianity is unselfish sacrifice on behalf of others, motivated by the great sacrifice of Christ Himself, dying in atonement for the sins of the whole world! It is highly unlikely, if not inconceivable, that an all-powerful, all-wise, all-holy God would institute two such fundamentally contradictory systems in the world. The two systems certainly exist, as already stressed, but God can be the Author of only one of them. The other must have its source in the pride and selfishness of man and ultimately in the pride and deception of the great adversary, Satan himself.

The Scientific Weakness of the Evolutionary Hypothesis

And the remarkable thing is that, despite its widespread acceptance as the scientific explanation of origins and processes, there is such a small amount of actual scientific evidence in favor of it! There is cer-

[1] Vannevar Bush: "Science and Progress?", *American Scientist,* Vol. 43, April 1955, p. 243.

tainly no evidence of any genuine evolution occurring in our present experience.

Organic diversity is an observational fact more or less familiar to everyone. . . . If we assemble as many individuals living at a given time as we can, we notice at once that the observed variation does not form any kind of continuous distribution. Instead, a multitude of separate discrete distributions are found. In other words, the living world is not a single array of individuals in which any two variants are connected by unbroken series of intergrades, but an array of more or less distinctly separate arrays, intermediates between which are absent or rare.[1]

And with respect to present processes of change, especially genetic mutations, we have already seen that these are practically always processes of deterioration and seldom if ever produce any real progress in evolution.

Although the living matter becomes adjusted to its environment through formation of superior genetic patterns from mutational components, the process of mutation itself is not adaptive. On the contrary, the mutants which arise are, with rare exceptions, deleterious to their carriers, at least in the environments which the species normally encounters. Some of them are deleterious apparently in all environments. Therefore the mutation process alone, not corrected and guided by natural selection, would result in degeneration and extinction.[2]

All the real evidence from present species and their variation supports perfectly the Biblical revelation that God created all living things "after their kinds." There is no evidence of present-day biological change, except within small limits.

And so evolutionists must say that, even though mutations are almost always harmful, the very few that *may* be helpful are acted upon by natural selection and preserved and that, in the course of the great ages of geologic time, these favorable changes gradually accumulate to bring about true progress in evolution.[3]

---

[1] Th. Dobzhansky: *Genetics and the Origin of Species* (New York, Columbia University Press, 1951), pp. 3, 4.

[2] Th. Dobzhansky: "On Methods of Evolutionary Biology and Anthropology," *American Scientist*, Vol. 45, December 1957, p. 385.

[3] The gymnastics of logic involved in this interpretation are perhaps unintentionally revealed by James F. Crow, when he says: "The general picture of how evolution works is now clear. The basic raw material is the mutant gene. Among these mutants most will be deleterious, but a minority will be beneficial. These few will be retained by what Muller has called the sieve of natural selection. As the British statistician R. A. Fischer has said, natural selection is a 'mechanism for gen-

Strategic Role of Historical Geology

And for their proof that this is so, they point triumphantly to the fossil record of former life on the earth. The fossils are supposed to show the actual record of evolutionary change over the ages. Thus the geneticist Goldschmidt says in this vein:

Fortunately there is a science which is able to observe the progress of evolution through the history of our earth. Geology traces the rocky strata of our earth, deposited one upon another in the past geological epochs through hundreds of millions of years, and finds out their order and timing and reveals organisms which lived in all these periods. Paleontology, which studies the fossil remains, is thus enabled to present organic evolution as a visible fact . . .[1]

But when one asks for details he is told, for example, by the paleontologist Simpson:

In spite of these examples, it remains true, as every paleontologist knows, that *most* new species, genera, and families, and that nearly all categories above the level of families, appear in the record suddenly and are not led up to by known, gradual, completely continuous transitional sequences.[2]

Dr. Dwight Davis, Curator of Vertebrate Anatomy in the Chicago Museum of Natural History, also recognizes these "gaps" in the record.

The sudden emergence of major adaptive types as seen in the abrupt appearance in the fossil record of families and orders, continued to give

erating an exceedingly high level of improbability.' It is Maxwell's famous demon superimposed on the random process of mutation. Despite the clarity and simplicity of the general idea, the details are difficult and obscure." ("Ionizing Radiation and Evolution," *Scientific American,* Vol. 201, September 1959, p. 142). With regard to the "beneficial minority" of mutations, he later says: "There can be little doubt that man would be better off if he had a lower mutation rate. I would argue, in our present ignorance, that the ideal rate for the foreseeable future would be zero." (*Ibid.,* p. 160.)

[1] Richard B. Goldschmidt: "An Introduction to a Popularized Symposium on Evolution," *Scientific Monthly,* Vol. 77, October 1953, p. 184. Historically the rise of uniformitarian geology was a necessary precursor to the development and acceptance of evolution. Loren Eiseley says: "Darwin and Wallace were Lyell's intellectual children. Both would have failed to be what they were without the *Principles of Geology* to guide them." ("Charles Lyell," *Scientific American,* Vol. 201, August 1959, p. 106.)

[2] G. G. Simpson: *The Major Features of Evolution* (New York, Columbia U. Press, 1953), p. 360.

trouble. The phenomenon lay in the genetical no-man's land beyond the limits of experimentation. A few paleontologists even today cling to the idea that these gaps will be closed by further collecting . . . but most regard the observed discontinuities as real and have sought an explanation.[1]

The "explanations" are always highly speculative, involving concepts of "explosive evolution," continental migrations, macromutations, and the like. Davis is willing to admit:

> But the facts of paleontology conform equally well with other interpretations that have been discredited [sic] by neobiological work, e.g., divine creation, etc., and paleontology by itself can neither prove nor refute such ideas.[2]

Simpson and Davis were concerned primarily with gaps in the fossil record of animals. Regarding plant fossils, the paleobotanist Arnold says:

> It has long been hoped that extinct plants will ultimately reveal some of the stages through which existing groups have passed during the course of their development, but it must be freely admitted that this aspiration has been fulfilled to a very slight extent, even though paleobotanical research has been in progress for more than one hundred years. As yet we have not been able to trace the phylogenetic history of a single group of modern plants from its beginning to the present.[3]

Thus, the fossil record, no less than the present taxonomic classification system and the nature of genetic mutation mechanisms, shows exactly what the Bible teaches—namely, clear-cut "kinds" of organisms, each perhaps including numerous "sub-kinds" with unbridged gaps between. But evolutionists persist in believing in evolution, since the only alternative is creation! And the only real

[1] D. Dwight Davis: "Comparative Anatomy and the Evolution of Vertebrates" in *Genetics, Paleontology and Evolution*, ed. by Jepsen, Mayr and Simpson, (Princeton, N. J., Princeton University Press, 1949), p. 74. Darwin apologized for the weakness of the paleontological evidence for evolution in his day, hoping that these gaps would be closed by further field studies of fossils. But the gaps are still there, after another century of intensive paleontological investigations. The Professor of Geology at the University of Glasgow says: "There is no need to apologize any longer for the poverty of the fossil record. In some ways it has become almost unmanageably rich, and discovery is out-pacing integration. . . . The fossil record nevertheless continues to be composed mainly of gaps" (T. N. George: "Fossils in Evolutionary Perspective," *Science Progress*, Vol. XLVIII, Jan. 1960, pp. 1, 3).

[2] *Ibid.*, p. 77.

[3] C. A. Arnold: *An Introduction to Paleobotany* (New York, McGraw-Hill, 1947), p. 7.

scientific justification for such a position is the dogma of uniformitarianism, which insists that all things must be explained in terms of *present* processes. The supposed great expanse of geologic time, necessarily implied by uniformitarianism with its fossil time-indices for each age, *does* give some semblance of plausibility to the concept of gradual evolution over the ages.

The Prophetic Testimony of Scripture

And this is where the testimony of the Biblical Deluge becomes so important! For if the Bible record is true, most of the strata could not have been deposited over long ages of time under uniformitarian conditions but were laid down in the course of a single year under catastrophic conditions. The last refuge of the case for evolution immediately vanishes away, and the record of the rocks becomes a tremendous witness, not to the operation of a naturalistic process of Godless development and progress but rather to the holiness and justice and power of the living God of Creation!

And this is what the Flood was meant to be as far as its testimony to post-diluvian man is concerned. Jesus Christ pointed back to the great Flood as a reminder of God's power over the world and as a foreshadowing of His future great intervention in judgment on a sinful and rebellious world in the last days (Matthew 24:37-39). One may refer also to such passages as Luke 17:26,27, Hebrews 11:7, I Peter 3:20, and II Peter 2:5 for ample evidence that the New Testament writers regarded the Flood as a historical event of tremendous testimonial importance to modern man!

Especially pertinent and incisive is the remarkable passage found in II Peter 3:3-10 (A.V.), which we quote again, in entirety, because of its intense relevance to this situation:

Knowing this first, that there shall come in the last days scoffers, walking after their own lusts, and saying, Where is the promise of his coming? for since the fathers fell asleep, all things continue as they were from the beginning of the creation.

For this they willingly are ignorant of, that by the word of God the heavens were of old, and the earth standing out of the water and in the water: Whereby the world that then was, being overflowed with water, perished:

But the heavens and the earth, which are now, by the same word are kept in store, reserved unto fire against the day of judgment and perdition of ungodly men.

But, beloved, be not ignorant of this one thing, that one day is with the Lord as a thousand years, and a thousand years as one day. The Lord is not slack concerning his promise, as some men count slackness; but is long-suffering to usward, not willing that any should perish, but that all should come to repentance.

But the day of the Lord will come as a thief in the night; in the which the heavens shall pass away with a great noise, and the elements shall melt with fervent heat, the earth also and the works that are therein shall be burned up.

Here again the Flood is used as a type and warning of the great coming worldwide destruction and judgment when the "day of man" is over and the "day of the Lord" comes. But the prophet is envision-ing a time when, because of an apparent long delay, the "promise of his coming" is no longer treated seriously. It is to become the object of crude scoffing and intellectual ridicule. It will be obvious to "think-ing men" in such a day that a great supernatural intervention of God in the world, as promised by Christ, is scientifically out of the ques-tion. That would be a miracle, and miracles contradict natural law!

And how do we know that miracles and divine intervention contra-dict natural law? Why, of course, because our experience shows and our philosophy postulates that "all things continue as they were from the beginning of the creation"! This is what we call our "principle of uniformity," which asserts that all things even from the earliest be-ginnings can be explained essentially in terms of present processes and rates. Even the Creation itself is basically no different from pres-ent conditions, since these processes are believed to have been oper-ating since even the *"beginning* of the creation." There is no room for any miracle or divine intervention in our cosmology; therefore, the concept of a future coming of Christ in worldwide judgment and purgation is merely naive!

Or so they say. "For . . . they *willingly* are ignorant of" two things! One is a *real* Creation. The heavens and earth were established "by the word of God" not by uniformitarian processes! Second, this first heavens (that is, the atmospheric heavens) and the first earth *per-ished,* being "overflowed with water."

Recognition of these two great events of history would immediately brand as false the great system of evolutionary pantheism. These events proclaim as from a mountaintop the fact of a personal Creator-God, vitally and directly concerned with His creation, whose "long-suffering" will one day be exhausted and who will then bring this present earth to a fiery end in atomic distintegration!

And as we have seen, the evidence of the reality of these great events, the Creation and the Deluge, is so powerful and clear that it is only "willing ignorance" which is blind to it, according to Scripture!

Thus do the Creation (as attested to not only by Scripture but by the two great laws of thermodynamics) and the Genesis Flood as indelibly recorded in human histories and in the rocks of the earth constitute the paramount scientific negation of all man-centered philosophy and religion for those who will accept it for what it is.

And, according to the Biblical writer, there is a great and final personal challenge in this testimony. To the man whose faith is centered in himself or his particular society, relying upon his own works for whatever salvation he seeks, the message is one of "coming to repentance" while there is time, since "God is long-suffering and not willing that any should perish." "For God so loved the world, that he gave his only begotten Son, that whosoever believeth in him should not perish, but have everlasting life" (John 3:16).

To the Christian the admonition is, as recorded in II Peter 3:11 (A.V.):

Seeing then that all these things shall be dissolved, what manner of persons ought ye to be in all holy conversation and godliness.

And the final word, as given in the last verses of the chapter, II Peter 3:17,18:

Ye therefore, beloved, seeing ye know these things before, beware lest ye also, being led away with the error of the wicked, fall from your own stedfastness. But grow in grace, and in the knowledge of our Lord and Saviour Jesus Christ. To him be glory both now and forever. Amen.

Appendix I

Paleontology and the
Edenic Curse

INTRODUCTION

If the concept of a universal Flood since the appearance of man on the earth is difficult to reconcile with uniformitarian geology, it must be confessed that the Biblical doctrine of the Fall is even more irreconcilable with this scientific hypothesis. But there is a much closer connection between the Biblical doctrines of the Fall and the Flood than the mere fact that neither can be harmonized with uniformitarian views of the earth's history. The really important connection between them consists in the explanation which a universal Flood provides for the laying down of the fossiliferous strata *since* the time of Adam; for once the full implications of the Edenic curse are understood, it will be seen that only within the framework of a supernatural catastrophism can a satisfactory explanation be given for these fossils. To put the issue into its sharpest delineations, a literal interpretation of the Fall demands as its corollary a thorough-going Biblical catastrophism; and the doctrine of the Flood can be fully understood only in the light of the Fall and the Edenic curse.

Uniformitarian paleontology, of course, dates the formation of the major fossiliferous strata many scores and hundreds of millions of years before the appearance of human beings on the earth. It assumes that uncounted billions of animals had experienced natural or violent

454

deaths before the Fall of Adam; that many important kinds of animals had long since become extinct by the time God created Adam to have dominion over every living creature; and that long ages before the Edenic curse giant flesh-eating monsters like Tyrannosaurus Rex roamed the earth, slashing their victims with ferocious dagger-like teeth and claws.

But how can such an interpretation of the history of the animal kingdom be reconciled with the early chapters of Genesis? Does the Book of Genesis, honestly studied in the light of the New Testament, allow for a reign of tooth and claw and death and destruction before the Fall of Adam? If not, we have further compelling reasons for questioning the uniformitarian scheme of reading the rocks and at the same time strong encouragement for finding in the great Genesis Flood the true explanation for fossil formations in the crust of our planet.

ANTHROPOLOGY AND THE FALL

In the face of such clear-cut passages as Romans 5:12-21 and I Corinthians 15:21-22, few who accept the Bible as the Word of God will deny that Adam's sin and fall introduced *spiritual* and *physical* death into the human race. In the Romans passage we learn that "through *one man* sin entered into the world, and death through sin; and so death passed upon all men, for that all sinned . . . by the trespass of *the one* many died . . . the judgment came *of one* unto condemnation . . . by the trespass of *the one,* death reigned through *the one* . . . through *one trespass* the judgment came unto all men to condemnation . . . through the *one man's* disobedience the many were made sinners. . . ." And if such Biblical testimony were regarded as insufficient to settle the matter, we are told also in the Corinthians passage that *"by man* came death" and *"in Adam* all die."

The Bible further teaches that all human beings have descended from one human pair (Gen. 3:20, "Eve . . . was the mother of *all living";* Acts 17:26, "he made of *one* every nation of men to dwell on all the face of the earth") and that these first human beings were created directly by God wholly apart from any evolutionary development of man's body from animal forms. Theistic evolutionists readily admit that man's soul and spirit were created directly by God. But the non-evolutionary origin of Adam's body can also be easily demonstrated from the Scriptures.

In the first place, the Lord Jesus Christ stated that "he who made them from the beginning made them *male and female"* (Matt. 19:4, cf. 1:27). But would not supposed animal ancestors have been male and female already? In the second place, Genesis 2:21-23 clearly indicates that Eve came out of Adam and not from the animal kingdom by some evolutionary process. This is confirmed by the Apostle Paul: "the man is not of the woman; but *the woman of the man"* (I Cor. 11:8). If Eve received her body in this purely supernatural way out of Adam's side, why should anyone postulate an evolutionary development for Adam's body? Such a view would be completely inconsistent. In the third place, the Bible teaches that Adam's body was made "of the dust of the ground" (Gen. 2:7), not of evolved animal forms. Louis Berkhof explains:

> Some theologians, in their eagerness to harmonize the teachings of Scripture with the theory of evolution, suggest that this may be interpreted to mean that God formed the body of man out of the body of animals, *which is after all but dust.* But this is entirely unwarranted, since no reason can be assigned why the general expression "of the dust of the ground" should be used after the writer had already described the creation of the animals and might therefore have made the statement far more specific. Moreover, this interpretation is also excluded by the statement in Gen. 3:19, "In the sweat of thy face shalt thou eat bread, till thou return unto the ground: for out of it wast thou taken: for dust thou art and unto dust thou shalt return." This certainly does not mean that man shall return to his former animal state. Beast and man alike return again to the dust. Eccl. 3:19-20. Finally, we are told explicitly in I Cor. 15:39 that "All flesh is not the same flesh: but there is one flesh of men, and another flesh of beasts."[1]

Finally, the phrase "man became a living soul" (Gen. 2:7) cannot permit the thought of evolutionary development. A Christian anthropologist summarizes the argument as follows:

> Genesis 1:21 states that God created every "living creature" (*nephesh hayah*) which the waters brought forth, and verse 24 states that "God said, Let the earth bring forth the living creature" (*nephesh hayah*) ". . . of the earth." Then Genesis 2:7 states, "And the Lord God formed man . . . and man became a living soul" (*nephesh hayah*) presumably for the *first*

[1] Louis Berkhof, *Systematic Theology* (2nd ed.; Grand Rapids: Wm. B. Eerdmans Pub. Co., 1941), p. 184.

time. So it would certainly seem from this that man was not derived from any pre-existing line of *nephesh hayah,* or living creatures.[1]

In the light of this Biblical revelation concerning the origin of Adam and Eve, Christians must insist upon the *essential unity*[2] and the *supernatural, non-evolutionary creation*[3] of the human race. Otherwise, there could be no such thing as human sin or eternal salvation through the blood of Jesus Christ (Rom. 6:23; Heb. 2:9,14; I John 1:5-2:2).

It is well known that some of the most "ancient" human skulls have practically the same capacity as those of modern man; while many human remains have been buried in such a manner as to indicate belief in the after-life.[4] Did such men have eternal spirits? Did they commit sin? To these questions the Christian must give an affirmative answer, for God "made of *one* every nation of men to dwell on all the face of the earth" (Acts 17:26) and that one was *Adam.*

What are we to say, then, concerning the Fall and the modern science of physical anthropology? We say, on the basis of overwhelming Biblical evidence, that every fossil man that has ever been discovered, or ever will be discovered, is a *descendant* of the *supernaturally created* Adam and Eve. This is absolutely essential to the entire edifice of Christian theology, and there can simply be no true Christianity without it. With only a few exceptions,[5] American evan-

---

[1] James O. Buswell, III, "A Creationist Interpretation of Prehistoric Man," Chapter X in *Evolution and Christian Thought Today,* edited by Russell L. Mixter (Grand Rapids: Wm. B. Eerdmans Pub. Co., 1959), p. 186. Buswell observes: "The theistic evolutionist, if he allows man to have arisen from a non-human form, is obliged to inject some action or other upon his physical body in addition to giving him a soul, in order to make that body perfect and not subject to death. To me this is simply an additional and unnecessary complication of hypotheses to which Occam's razor (entities must not be unnecessarily multiplied) could well be applied." *Loc. cit.*

[2] See Benjamin B. Warfield, "On The Antiquity and The Unity of The Human Race," Chapter IX in *Biblical and Theological Studies,* edited by Samuel G. Craig (Philadelphia: The Presbyterian & Reformed Pub. Co., 1952), pp. 238-261.

[3] See Oswald T. Allis, "The Time Element in Genesis 1 and 2," *Torch and Trumpet,* VIII, No. 3 (July-August, 1958), pp. 16-18.

[4] See A. L. Kroeber, *Anthropology* (New York, Harcourt, Brace and Co., 1948), pp. 112-115, 625.

[5] Such exceptions include several prominent representatives of the so-called "new evangelicalism," such as Cordelia Erdman Barber, "Fossils and Their Occurrence," Chapter VIII in *Evolution and Christian Thought Today,* p. 151; and Dr. Edward John Carnell, Professor of Apologetics at Fuller Theological Seminary, *The Case For Orthodox Theology* (Philadelphia: The Westminster Press, 1959), p. 95. For example, Dr. Carnell says: "The Genesis account implies an act of immediate creation, but the same account also implies that God made the world in six literal days;

gelicals have been willing to part company with evolutionary anthropology along these lines. But why? Certainly not because Christians have carefully studied the pros and cons of various theories of the origin of man and have concluded that the Biblical view is the most consistent with the "facts." No one ever arrives at a world-and-life view by such a purely inductive method. The true reason why Christians have been willing (with some exceptions, of course) to take their stand upon a Biblical anthropology, in opposition to an evolutionary anthropology is that they enjoy a vital spiritual relationship with Jesus Christ and accept His authority. It was none other than the Son of God Himself who taught Christians to accept the historical accuracy of the Old Testament in general (Matt. 5:18, Luke 16:17, 18:31, 24:25,44, John 10:35) and the Book of Genesis in particular (Matt. 19:4, 23:35, 24:37-39, Luke 17:29,32). Standing upon this infallible foundation, the Christian is perfectly confident that modern scientific theories (colored as they are by the presuppositions of finite and fallible men) cannot possibly constitute the final word on the subject of the origin and early history of man. And beyond that, he is perfectly sure that when all the evidence is in, his faith in the Son of God and in the verbally inspired special revelation of God will be found to have led him to an accurate knowledge and understanding of these vitally important matters.[1]

THE ANIMAL KINGDOM AND THE FALL

Now if the Christian has spiritually compelling reasons for insisting that the science of anthropology be interpreted in the light of Biblical revelation, what should be his attitude toward the science of

and since orthodoxy has given up the literal-day theory out of respect for geology, it would certainly forfeit no principle if it gave up the immediate-creation theory out of respect for paleontology. The two seem to be quite parallel . . . If God was pleased to breathe his image into a creature that had previously come from the dust, so be it." Although he does not personally subscribe to theistic evolution, Bernard Ramm insists that it is not essentially antichristian and should be viewed with tolerance. *Op cit.,* pp. 280-293.

[1] It has often been maintained that God has given us two revelations, one in nature and one in the Bible and that they cannot contradict each other. This is certainly correct; but when one subconsciously identifies with natural revelation his own interpretations of nature and then denounces theologians who are unwilling to mold Biblical revelation into conformity with his interpretation of nature, he is guilty of serious error. After all, special revelation supersedes natural revelation, for it is only by means of special revelation that we can interpret aright the world about us.

paleontology? What do the Scriptures teach concerning the relationship between the human race and the animal kingdom? Have animals as well as man been affected by the Fall, or has the animal kingdom continued for countless ages, even before the creation of Adam, in its struggle for existence against a multiplicity of hostile forces?

The Bondage of Corruption

The first passage of Scripture which we must examine in this connection is Romans 8:19-22.

For the earnest expectation of the creation waiteth for the revealing of the sons of God. For the creation was subjected to vanity, not of its own will, but by reason of him who subjected it, in hope that the creation itself also shall be delivered from the bondage of corruption into the liberty of the glory of the children of God. For we know that the whole creation groaneth and travaileth in pain together until now.

It was at the time of the Edenic curse of Gen. 3:17-19 that "the creation was subjected to vanity" by God. This "vanity" (of which the Book of Ecclesiastes speaks so eloquently) is further described as "the bondage of corruption," which is the explanation for the fact that "the whole creation groaneth and travaileth in pain together until now." This passage teaches very clearly that some tremendous transformations took place in the realm of nature at the time of the Edenic curse; and therefore any scientific theory which purports to explain the history of life on this planet without taking into full account the effects of the Fall upon the realm of nature must be rejected.

Adam's Dominion Over Animals

But there are other passages besides Romans 8:19-22 which indicate rather clearly that the Edenic curse had far-reaching effects upon nature, including the animal kingdom. In Genesis 1:28, for example, we are told that God gave to Adam "*dominion* over the fish of the sea, and over the birds of the heavens, and over every living thing that moveth upon the earth." This is the dominion of which we read in Psalm 8:6-8.

Thou makest him to have dominion over the works of thy hands; thou hast put all things under his feet: all sheep and oxen, yea, and the beasts of the field, the birds of the heavens, and the fish of the sea, whatsoever passeth through the paths of the seas.

It was on the basis of such God-constituted *dominion* that Adam "gave names to all cattle, and to the birds of the heavens, and to every beast of the field" (Gen. 2:20). Likewise Christ, the last Adam, exercised *dominion* "over the fish of the sea" when He commanded a fish in the Sea of Galilee to take a shekel of silver into its mouth, and to take hold of Peter's hook (Matt. 17:27) and when He commanded 153 fishes to move into the disciples' nets (John 21:6-11; cf. Luke 5:4-7).

Daily experience teaches us that dominion *of this kind* is no longer being exercised by the human race over the animal kingdom. Something drastic has taken place in man's relationship to the animal kingdom since the days of the Garden of Eden. The subservience and instant obedience of all classes of animals to the will of man has been transformed into a fear and dread of man that often brings with it violence and destruction.

As a matter of fact, the New Testament interprets the eighth psalm as referring to a relationship that is not now in force. After quoting Psalm 8:4-6, the author of Hebrews comments:

For in that he subjected all things unto him, he left nothing that is not subject to him. *But now we see not yet all things subjected to him.* But we behold him who has been made a little lower than the angels, even Jesus . . . (Heb. 2:8-9).

Since Psalm 8 refers primarily to man as originally constituted by God, and not to Christ, the author of Hebrews seems to be saying that even though we do not see man at the present time exercising his constituted dominion over the animal kingdom and the rest of nature, we do at least see *one* member of the human race, "even Jesus," who even *now* exercises such dominion and that through *Him* redeemed men shall at last regain all that they lost in Adam, and much more besides, thus bringing into final fulfillment the statements of the eighth psalm.[1]

The fact that the animal kingdom is not at the present subject to man's dominion is further confirmed by the terms of God's covenant with Noah after the Flood. Notice the contrast between this cove-

[1] See the standard commentaries on this passage in Hebrews, such as those by Henry Alford, Franz Delitzsch, B. F. Westcott, Albert Barnes, and R. C. H. Lenski.

nant and the statement of Genesis 1:28, which we have already examined. In Genesis 9:2,5, God said to Noah and his family:

The fear of you and the dread of you shall be upon every beast of the earth, and upon every bird of the heavens; with all wherewith the ground teemeth, and all the fishes of the sea, into your hand are they delivered . . . and surely your blood, the blood of your lives, will I require; at the hand of every beast will I require it . . .

Let it be noted that "the fear of you and the dread of you" cannot be understood as the equivalent of "dominion" in Genesis 1:28, because here we are specifically told that beasts will be capable of shedding "the blood of your lives." An illustration of how the shedding of human blood would be required "at the hand of every beast" is found in Exodus 21:28: "And if an ox gore a man or a woman to death, *the ox shall be surely stoned,* and its flesh shall not be eaten." Such a possibility, of course, cannot be imagined in the case of the first Adam before the Fall or the Last Adam during His earthly ministry! No animal could have harmed them, because God put all things under their feet.

Vegetarian Diet Before the Fall

One of the clearest texts in the Old Testament on the transformation of animal characteristics after the Fall is that which describes the diet which God ordained for animals before the Fall. Before the Edenic curse, this was God's provision for the food of animals: "to every beast of the earth, and to every bird of the heavens, and to every thing that creepeth upon the earth, wherein there is life, *I have given every green herb for food:* and it was so" (Gen. 1:30). Under such conditions, there could have been no carnivorous beasts on earth before the Fall; for the animals to which God gave "every green herb for food" included "every beast of the field" and "every thing that creepeth upon the earth, wherein is life."

In discussing the important question of death in the animal kingdom in relation to the Fall, Dr. Edwin Y. Monsma, Professor and Head of the Department of Biology at Calvin College, makes the following observations:

The eating of herbs, seeds, and fruits implies the death of these plant parts from a biologist's point of view because they all contain living protoplasm. But there is no indication here of destructive and natural death of whole living organisms nor of the carnivorous habit upon which so many animals are dependent at present. Indeed, nowhere in the Scriptures is there any indication of natural or accidental death before the fall of man. Even immediately after the fall the natural processes which culminate in death seemed to work much more slowly than they do now, as is evident from the great age of men during the antediluvian period. Reformed scholars have generally been of the opinion that the Bible gives no evidence of death among animals before the fall but rather that the opposite is true.[1]

Some of the greatest Reformed thinkers of modern times have insisted that this is the Biblical view of the animal kingdom as originally constituted by God. For example, Abraham Kuyper, founder of the Free University of Amsterdam, concluded:

> Also wild beasts were not originally created as carnivores. That is substantiated by the fact that they came to Adam without devouring him. Their carnivorous condition can be explained out of the curse alone. At present we distinguish between vermin, predators, and domestic animals, but that difference is. not derived from creation. Then the green herb was the food of all animals.[2]

In the Stone Lectures of 1930, delivered at Princeton Theological Seminary, Valentine Hepp, Professor of Theology at the Free University of Amsterdam, made the following significant statement:

> Whether it is correct to say that before the fall organic life used up its life-power is a question. But we may never believe that any organic being could have suffered death by violence before the fall . . . the dumb fossils . . . cannot be placed as petrifactions within the hexaemeron [the six days of creation].[3]

Numerous Lutheran scholars have been led by Genesis 1:30 to adopt a similar position, but the following statement by H. C. Leupold may be considered as representative:

---

[1] Edwin Y. Monsma, *If Not Evolution, What Then?* (Published by the author, 1955) p. 32.

[2] Abraham Kuyper, *Dictaten Dogmatiek* (Kok, Kampen), II, 91-92. Quoted by Monsma, *op. cit.,* p. 33.

[3] Valentine Hepp, *Calvinism and the Philosophy of Nature* (Grand Rapids: Wm. B. Eerdmans Pub. Co., 1930), pp. 185-187. See also Geerhardus Vos, *Biblical Theology* (Grand Rapids: Wm. B. Eerdmans Pub. Co., 1948), p. 50; and Louis Berkhof, *Systematic Theology* (2d ed; Grand Rapids: Wm. B. Eerdmans Pub. Co., 1941), p. 670. Albertus Pieters, *op. cit.,* p. 59, cites G. C. Aalders, Professor of Old Testament at the Free University of Amsterdam, as finding this significance in Genesis 1:30 also.

In brief, this verse is an indication of the perfect harmony prevailing in the animal world. No beast preyed upon the other. Rapacious and ferocious wild beasts did not yet exist. This verse, then, indicates very briefly for this chapter what is unfolded at length in chapter two, that a paradise-like state prevailed at creation.[1]

Now it cannot be objected that this is a mere argument from silence and that animals may very well have been constituted by God in such a way that they could eat each other as well as "every green herb for food"; for in Isaiah 11:6-9 we are given God's picture of *ideal conditions* in the animal kingdom, not only with respect to relationships between animals and men, but also between the various kinds of animals:

And the wolf shall dwell with the lamb, and the leopard shall lie down with the kid; and the calf and the young lion and the fatling together; and a little child shall lead them. And the cow and the bear shall feed; their young ones shall lie down together; and the lion shall eat straw like an ox. And the sucking child shall play on the hole of the asp, and the weaned child shall put his hand on the adder's den. They shall not hurt nor destroy in all my holy mountain . . . (Isa. 11:6-9; cf. 65:25).

Now if this is God's ideal plan for the animal kingdom, it is quite impossible to assume that the Bible allows for the existence of carnivorous beasts, violence, and death before the Fall; for the creation account ends with the statement that "God saw everything that he had made, and, behold, it was very good."

Even commentators who do not hold to the concept of a literal future millennial age on the earth insist that this prophecy of Isaiah indicates the kind of conditions that existed on the earth before the Fall. For example, John Calvin states:

He describes the order which was at the beginning, before man's apostasy produced the unhappy and melancholy change under which we groan. Whence comes the cruelty of beasts, which prompts the stronger to seize and rend and devour with dreadful violence the weaker animals? There would certainly have been no discord among the creatures of God, if they had remained in their first and original condition. When they exercise cruelty towards each other, and the weak need to be protected against

[1] H. C. Leupold: *Exposition of Genesis* (Columbus: Wartburg Press, 1942), pp. 98-99. See also John Theodore Mueller, *Christian Dogmatics* (St. Louis: Concordia Pub. House, 1934), p. 184; and Keil, *op. cit.*, pp. 65-67, for additional supporting arguments.

the strong, it is an evidence of the disorder (*ataxias*) which has sprung from the sinfulness of man . . . if the stain of sin had not polluted the world, no animal would have been addicted to prey on blood, but the fruits of the earth would have sufficed for all, according to the method which God had appointed (Gen. 1:30).[1]

Similarly, Oswald T. Allis considers Isaiah's prophecy to be specially significant in this connection. In commenting on Genesis 1:30, he writes:

That originally the food of man and of the animals was, and under ideal conditions will be, vegetarian is clearly taught here and suggested by Isaiah 11:9, 65:25. Many of the so-called carnivora are largely or wholly vegetarians. It was after the Fall and the Flood that the eating of flesh was permitted to man.[2]

Some have objected that vast structural changes would have been involved in making an herbivore into a carnivore and that such a transformation would have been tantamount to a creation of new Genesis "kinds" after the termination of the Creation Week.[3] But this is surely an exaggeration of the facts. Isaiah says that *lions* (not some totally new kind of animal) will eat straw like oxen; *wolves* will dwell with lambs; *leopards* will lie down with kids; *bears* will feed with cows; and *deadly serpents* will be pets for children.

The Edenic Curse and Structural Changes

In order to clarify this problem in our thinking, let us consider two examples of specific structural and organic changes that occurred as a direct result of the Edenic curse, according to the third chapter of Genesis, which did not involve "an entirely new creation" or the loss of identity in the creatures involved.

The first case for consideration is that of the serpent, which is introduced in Genesis 3:1 as being "more subtle than any beast of the field which Jehovah God had made." Presumably, the serpent was possessed of four legs like other "beasts of the field." But the fact that Satan had used this creature as an instrument for deceiving Eve

---

[1] John Calvin, *Commentary on the Book of the Prophet Isaiah*, trans. William Pringle (Grand Rapids: Eerdmans Pub. Co., 1948), I, 383-384.

[2] Oswald T. Allis, *God Spake By Moses*, p. 13. See also Keil, *op. cit.*, p. 65.

[3] See Albertus Pieters, *op. cit.*, p. 55; Edward Hitchcock, *op. cit.*, p. 81; and Brian P. Sutherland, "The Fall and its Relation to Present Conditions in Nature," *Journal of the American Scientific Affiliation*, Vol. II, No. 4 (Dec., 1950), p. 15.

brought the curse of God upon the instrument as well as upon the deceiver himself.[1]

From the earliest times it has been recognized as a psychologically valid principle of pedagogy that sub-human creatures which have been used as instruments of sin be included in the punishment of the offender. Biblical examples of this are found in Genesis 6:7, 7:21; Exodus 21:28; Leviticus 20:15, 16; Joshua 7:24, and elsewhere.

But the important thing to notice, so far as our discussion is concerned, is not *why* the serpent was punished as the instrument of Satan but *how* it was punished. Observe carefully the wording here: "cursed art thou above all cattle, and above every beast of the field; *upon thy belly shalt thou go,* and dust shalt thou eat all the days of thy life" (3:14). Surely to be deprived of limbs involved far greater structural transformations in this creature than would have been involved in changing herbivores into carnivores, and the serpent's transformation took place after the Creation Week. C. F. Keil concludes:

> If these words are not to be robbed of their entire meaning, they cannot be understood in any other way than as denoting that the form and movements of the serpent were altered, and that its present repulsive shape is the effect of the curse pronounced upon it, though we cannot form any accurate idea of its original appearance.[2]

The force of this analogy as an argument for the general transformation of the animal kingdom at the time of the Fall may be judged by the efforts which some uniformitarians have exerted to escape from its clear implications. For example, Edward Hitchcock wrote:

> The sentence pronounced upon the serpent for his agency in man's apostasy seems, at first view, favorable to the opinion that animal natures experienced at the same time important changes; for he is supposed to have been deprived of his limbs, and condemned henceforth to crawl upon the

---

[1] Herman Bavinck's note on the fall of Satan is helpful here: "In Genesis 1:31 it may well be that it is said of the whole work of creation and not of the creation of the earth alone that God saw what He had made, and, behold, it was very good. If so, the rebellion and the disobedience of the angels must have taken place after the sixth day of creation." *Our Reasonable Faith* (Grand Rapids: Wm. B. Eerdmans Pub. Co., 1956), p. 221.

[2] Keil, *op. cit.,* p. 99. Bernard Ramm completely misses the point by asking, "Are we to believe . . . that the sharp claws of the big cats and the magnificent array of teeth in a lion's mouth were for vegetarian purposes only?" *Op. cit.,* p. 335; cf. p. 209. The point is that such specialized structures appeared for the first time after the Edenic curse.

earth, and to make the dust his food. But is it the more probable interpretation of the passage, which makes the tempter a literal serpent, or only a symbolical one? . . . Hence the probability is, that an evil spirit is described in Genesis under the name of a serpent. This conclusion is supported by other parts of Scripture where the tempter is in several places declared to be "the devil," "the old serpent," and "the great dragon."[1]

How similar to this are the allegorizing techniques of modern Barthian theology, even Hitchcock would have been surprised to learn. But here again, the student of Scripture must make an all-important choice between authorities; for uniformitarian theories of paleontology cannot long survive in an atmosphere of consistent Biblical hermeneutics and exegesis.

However, there is yet another instance of physical changes in living organisms that took place as a direct result of the Edenic curse. It is the case of Eve, to whom God said: "I will greatly multiply thy pain and thy conception; in pain thou shalt bring forth children . . ." (Gen. 3:16). In the light of this verse, it would be precarious indeed to argue that the Edenic curse was confined to purely moral and spiritual realms; for we are clearly told here that an important *change* took place in Eve's body. Whereas she would have borne children without pain before the Fall in accordance with the Edenic command to "be fruitful and multiply" (Gen. 1:28), the very structure of her body was now altered by God in such a way that childbirth would be accomplished henceforth by severe pain. While it is true that this case does not prove a similarly drastic change in the animal kingdom at the time of the Fall, it serves as an important illustration of how God could have introduced significant changes in the physical make-up of His creatures without at the same time eradicating their identity and producing thereby newly created "kinds."

THE PLANT KINGDOM AND THE FALL

Turning our attention now from the animal kingdom to the plant kingdom, we read of further important effects of the Edenic curse: "Cursed is the ground for thy sake; in toil shalt thou eat of it all the days of thy life; thorns also and thistles shall it bring forth to thee; and thou shalt eat of the herb of the field; in the sweat of thy face shalt thou eat bread, till thou return unto the ground . . ." (Gen. 3:17-19).

[1] Hitchcock, *op. cit.*, p. 82.

Once again, it becomes evident that uniformitarianism can find no place in its scheme of things for such a transformation of nature at the time of the Fall; and, therefore, its advocates have been compelled to eliminate this curse from the text of Scripture by various stratagems of exegesis and logic. A recent example of such an effort may be found in the following statement by Bernard Ramm:

> Part of man's judgment was that he was turned out of that park and into the conditions prevalent in the rest of the creation . . . Ideal conditions existed only in the Garden . . . Outside of the Garden of Eden were death, disease, weeds, thistles, thorns, carnivores, deadly serpents, and intemperate weather. To think otherwise is to run counter to an immense avalanche of fact. Part of the blessedness of man was that he was spared all of these things in Paradise, and part of the judgment of man was that he had to forsake such a Paradise and enter the world as it was outside of the Garden, where thistles grew and weeds were abundant and where wild animals roamed and where life was only possible by the sweat of man's brow.[1]

The principal objection to this approach to the problem is that it lacks a single shred of Scriptural support in its favor and runs counter to an immense avalanche of revelation. Let it be carefully noted that the text in question reads: "Cursed is *the ground* for thy sake . . . thorns and thistles *shall it bring forth to thee.*" This is certainly an opposite concept from that advocated by Dr. Ramm and others of like persuasion, who presumably could wish that the author of Genesis had written the verse in the following manner: "Cursed art thou from the Garden; from henceforth shalt thou be removed to the thorns and thistles." But the Bible states that *the earth outside of the Garden* had to be cursed by God before it could bring forth thorns and thistles *for Adam's sake.* Uniformitarians insist that the earth has experienced such conditions for hundreds of millions of years and thus did not need to be cursed by God subsequent to the appearance of man in order to become overrun with thorns and thistles.

But in opposition to this view, we not only have the testimony of Romans 8:19-22 but also an important statement by Lamech, the father of Noah. Speaking many centuries after the Edenic curse, Lamech looked upon his new-born son with a hope implanted in his heart by the Lord Himself that Noah would somehow be instrumental in bringing to men a measure of release from the awful drudgery and toil of life:

[1] Ramm, *op. cit.*, pp. 334 f., cf. p. 209.

This same [Noah] shall comfort us in our *work* and in the *toil* of our hands, *which cometh because of the ground which Jehovah hath cursed.* (Gen. 5:29).

Now if this statement be not robbed of all its meaning, it indicates rather conclusively that the earth *outside* of the Garden of Eden had experienced a stupendous transformation as a result of the Fall. As a matter of fact, it implies quite clearly that the Flood was to bring a measure of relief from the bitter effects of the Edenic curse. For these reasons, among others, Christians have been entirely justified in thinking of the whole earth before the Fall in terms of Edenic conditions.

THE BALANCE OF NATURE AND HARMONISTIC THEODICY

One argument that has frequently been advanced against the concept of an herbivorous animal kingdom before the Fall is that such an arrangement would have thrown the cycles of nature out of balance. It is claimed that no other balance of nature than the one with which we are familiar can be imagined, for it is necessary that certain types of creatures be devoured by others to prevent the earth from being overpopulated. Albertus Pieters expresses the argument as follows:

So far as we can see now, the existence of carnivorous beasts (including insect-eating birds) is necessary to preserve the "balance of nature." Without insectivorous birds, insect life would soon destroy vegetation, and even apparently harmless little animals like rabbits may become a scourge if there are no foxes and other carnivora to keep their numbers in check, as was abundantly illustrated in Australia some years ago. This "balance of nature" is essential to the perfection of God's creation and we are not to reckon it a blemish or an afterthought.[1]

But who are we to say that God is limited to the "balance of nature" which now prevails in the earth? Even if Edenic conditions had persisted for centuries, could not God have prevented the overpopulation of the earth with insects, fish, and other animals through a different means than by mutual extermination? Such reasoning reminds us of the pessimistic and fatalistic views of Thomas Robert

[1] Albertus Pieters, *op. cit.,* p. 57.

Malthus (1766-1834), who "proved" that a certain number of people simply *had* to starve to death or be killed in wars each year to prevent the earth from being overpopulated. After all, God *can* take care of His creatures, and mutual extermination does not happen to exhaust the possible methods at His disposal.

The human mind has a wonderful capacity (in its fallen state) for interpreting God's ways in its own finite terms and limiting the Supreme Being to its own little world of experience. Notice, for example, in the quotation cited above how the author leaps from his own present experience of things to the formulation of a law by which God must presumably operate in every age:

> *So far as we can see now,* the existence of carnivorous birds and beasts (including insect-eating birds) is necessary to preserve the "balance of nature" . . . *This "balance of nature" is essential to the perfection of God's creation.*

Edward Hitchcock, one of the outstanding uniformitarian apologists of the last century, committed the same logical fallacy when he wrote:

> It would require an entirely different system in nature from the present, in order to exclude death from the world. To the existing system it is as essential as gravitation, and apparently just as much a law of nature . . . The conclusions from all these facts and reasonings are, that death is an essential feature of the present system of organized nature; that *it must have entered into the plan of creation in the divine mind originally, and consequently must have existed in the world before the apostasy of man.*[1]

Actually, however, there is a very dangerous principle involved in this type of reasoning. By denying that the Fall and the Edenic curse had anything to do with the "bondage of corruption" under which the whole creation now travails in pain, these scholars are driven logically to the position of ascribing the conditions of evil which we see around us, so far as the realm of nature is concerned, to the hand of the Creator. Bernard Ramm states this position quite clearly:

> The universe must contain all possible ranges of goodness. One of these grades of goodness is that it can fail in goodness . . . If there were nothing corruptible, or if there were no evil men, many good things would be missing in this universe. The lion lives because he can kill the ass and

[1] Hitchcock, *op. cit.*, pp. 77f. Italics are ours.

eat it. Avenging justice could only be praised if there were injustice; and patient suffering could be a virtue only in the presence of injustice . . . Bacteria destroy the carrion of the earth for Nature's own good, but unfortunately the same bacteria can kill a living creature . . . The entire system of nature involves tigers and lions, storms and high tides, diseases and parasites. It is part of our probation to learn how to capture or control the tiger and the lion . . . If we fail in this probation innocent and sinful suffer alike. The baby dies of infection and the mother of fever; the young man of appendicitis and the prophet of pneumonia.[1]

It is quite astonishing to see how closely this philosophy of nature fits Professor Berkouwer's description of the "harmonistic theodicy" of the Stoics and of the German philosopher Leibnitz (1646-1716). In this type of theodicy,[2] which Professor Berkouwer vigorously opposes, the attempt is made to demonstrate that the world as we *now* see it is *the best possible world*. He sets forth the view as follows:

We must view everything in the world as part of the whole, part of the cosmic unity. We shall then discover that there is in all things a pre-established harmony. Naturally, we still hear some dissonant notes within the harmony, but these are not essential . . . If we keep the interrelationship of things continually before us, we shall, says Leibnitz, learn to recognize God's goodness in creation. We shall then no longer allow evil and suffering to form a stumbling block to our faith in the righteousness of God's government . . . Evil is inherent in the nature and structure of this world. It functions as an accessory to the whole, as an atonality which is blended into the beautiful harmony of the cosmos.[3]

It is true that Dr. Ramm would not want to trace human sin back to God; but he does refer with approval to Thomas Aquinas' idea that "if there were no evil men, many good things would be missing in this universe,"[4] which is dangerously close to that. This whole uniformitarian philosophy of nature richly deserves, in our opinion, the severe judgment pronounced by Berkouwer:

[1] Ramm, *op. cit.*, pp. 93-95. Ramm is here paraphrasing the "plenitude of being" concept of Augustine and Aquinas, which he attempts to qualify by adding the ingredients of divine probation and judgment. But it is difficult to see, from the standpoint of uniformitarianism, how "probation" and "judgment" could be expected to shine through the disharmonies of nature before Adam and Eve fell into sin, and especially in the supposed millions of years of animal life on earth before their creation.

[2] A "theodicy" is a vindication of the justice of God in permitting evil to exist.

[3] G. C. Berkouwer, *The Providence of God* (Grand Rapids: Wm. B. Eerdmans Pub. Co., 1952), pp. 256f.

[4] Ramm, *op. cit.*, p. 94.

This theodicy rests principally on a relativizing of sin. God's goodness shines only as the grim clouds of sin and evil are dispelled . . . Recall, in contrast, how the Scriptures speak of sin as having "entered into the world" (Romans 5:12), as "enmity against God" (Romans 8:7). The basic error of this theodicy is its fundamental assumption that reason can find a proper place for sin in creation . . . a fundamental failure to appreciate the awful reality of sin, suffering, and death. Oversimplification typifies it, and the self-evidency of this oversimplification has contributed to modern man's profound distrust of every attempt at a theodicy.[1]

Thus, Christian scholars who attempt to fit uniformitarian paleontology into the framework of Genesis are not only forced into the use of unsound principles of hermeneutics and exegesis but also are in danger of stumbling into the quicksands of rationalistic philosophy. Surely, this is too high a price to pay for the perpetuation of a mere scientific theory!

To be sure, Dr. Ramm seeks to evade the force of Genesis 1:31 by the rather dubious observation that "God did not say that creation was perfect, but that it was good."[2] Nevertheless, we feel that another writer has penetrated to the heart of that text when he says:

What does this mean? . . . the original creation is considered as having been free from sin and its effects. There were no destructive forces at work; no disease, no sudden death, no animals preying upon others, no violent storms or destructive floods. The destructive forces which we see in nature are in the Bible traced back to the fall of Adam. It is because of the sin of man that nature has become disruptive. *Any other view has its source in the rationalism of modern thinking which considers pain and suffering, death and destruction as natural aspects of creation.*[3]

SUMMARY AND CONCLUSION

Living in an age of science and materialism, the church of Jesus Christ finds itself now faced with some of the most perplexing problems of theology and apologetics in its entire history. There is increas-

[1] Berkouwer, *op. cit.,* pp. 257ff.

[2] Ramm, *op. cit.,* p. 93.

[3] Monsma, *op. cit.,* p. 42. Italics are ours. In the light of the entire discussion above, it is disappointing to see the following statement by N. H. Ridderbos (the successor of Dr. G. Ch. Aalders in the field of Old Testament studies at the Free University of Amsterdam): "When did death make its appearance? . . . Would not animals have died apart from the fall? Was man carnivorous before the fall? . . . We cannot avoid the question whether there is not a conflict with utterances like those of Genesis 1:31, 3:14ff., Romans 8:19ff. It cannot be denied that on the basis

ing evidence from every side that the modern mind, characterized by dogmatic claims to finality in the realms of metaphysics and epistemology, has little patience with those who insist upon finding the criteria for ultimate truth within the covers of a supernaturally-inspired Book.

Perhaps the most obvious clash between these two world-views is in the field of anthropology, where modern science, because of its materialistic presuppositions, is forced to establish a continuous genealogy between man and the lower forms of life. But most evangelical scholars, recognizing the immense importance of the doctrines of Creation and the Fall so far as the plan of salvation is concerned, have been willing to part company with evolutionary anthropologists on this question and have insisted that the Genesis account of the creation of Adam and Eve be interpreted literally.

When we come to the question of the animal kingdom in relation to the Fall, however, we discover a much greater hesitancy on the part of such scholars in taking a united stand in opposition to the claims of uniformitarian paleontology. They seem to have been overawed, to a large extent at least, by the unanimous voice of modern paleontologists to the effect that death and violence reigned in the animal kingdom for hundreds of millions of years before the appearance of man on the earth.

But the Scriptures contain powerful testimonies to the contrary. For example, Romans 8:19-22 speaks of the stupendous transformation experienced by the entire creation, when, at the time of the Fall and as a result of the Edenic curse, it entered into a "bondage of corruption" from which it still longs to be delivered. This is strikingly confirmed by what we read in Genesis 1:28 of the original "dominion" which man exercised over God's creation and by the inspired commentary on Psalm 8 which is provided for us in Hebrews 2:8-9. Further support for this doctrine is found in the terms of the Noahic Covenant, in Isaiah's prophecy of ideal conditions in the animal

---

of these texts we form for ourselves a picture of conditions before the fall which is different from that offered by natural science. Must we then reject the results of natural science in this respect? We cannot answer too quickly in the affirmative. Cannot the world have been very good in the eyes of God even though there were catastrophes and though there was what we humans would call cruelty?" *Is There a Conflict Between Genesis 1 and Natural Science?* (Grand Rapids: Wm. B. Eerdmans Pub. Co., 1957), pp. 70-71. For a refutation of the entire "framework hypothesis" of Ridderbos, see Paul A. Zimmerman, ed., *Darwin, Evolution, and Creation* (Saint Louis: Concordia Publishing House, 1959), pp. 63-64.

kingdom, in the cursing of the serpent, the inflicting of birthpangs upon the woman, and the cursing of the ground. So powerful, in fact, are these Biblical evidences that many of the greatest modern theologians have been willing to incur the intense opposition of modern uniformitarians rather than attempt to mold the text of Scripture into conformity with current scientific theories.

But those evangelical scholars who *have* been willing to allow uniformitarian theories to shape their thinking concerning origins have not only been forced to reinterpret these Biblical passages but also have found it necessary to construct a system of "harmonistic theodicy" to explain how the present balance of nature could be characterized by God as "very good." Dr. Berkouwer has shown that such a philosophy of nature is both shallow and unscriptural. It neither satisfies the human heart nor fits the Biblical world-view.

In conclusion, we find ourselves faced with an important alternative. We must accept either the current theories of paleontology, with an inconceivably vast time-scale for fossils before the appearance of man on the earth, or we must accept the order of events as set forth so clearly in the Word of God. Both views cannot be true at the same time, any more than can a Biblical anthropology and an evolutionary anthropology be true at the same time. But if the "bondage of corruption," with all that such a term implies for the animal kingdom, had its source in the Edenic curse, then the fossil strata, which are filled with evidences of violent death, must have been laid down *since* Adam. And if this be true, then the uniformitarian time-table of modern paleontology must be rejected as totally erroneous; and a Biblical catastrophism (centering in the year-long, universal Deluge) must be substituted for it as the only possible solution to the enigma of the fossil strata.

Genesis 11 and the Date of the Flood

GENESIS 11 NEED NOT BE INTERPRETED AS A STRICT CHRONOLOGY

One of the greatest objections to the concept of a geographically universal Deluge in the minds of some scholars today is the fact that there are no historical or archaeological evidences for such a vast catastrophe during the third millennium B.C. (this date being obtained by adding the years of patriarchal maturity given in the Massoretic Text of Genesis 11) or even the fourth millennium B.C. (according to the years given in the Septuagint). Near Eastern cultures apparently have a rather continuous archaeological record (based upon occupation levels and pottery chronology) back to at least the fifth millennium B.C., and it seems impossible to fit a catastrophe of the proportions depicted in Genesis 6-9 into such an archaeological framework. But there are several important reasons for questioning the validity of the strict-chronology interpretation of Genesis 11.

(1) The Number of Years Are Not Totalled

If the list of names and ages in Genesis 11 has been given to us for the purpose of constructing a pre-Abrahamic chronology, it is rather strange that Moses failed to give the *total* number of years from the Flood to Abraham. Of course, it may be objected that he expected the reader to do his own totalling and, therefore, did not add unnecessary words. But Moses took nothing for granted in the reader's ability to add just *two* numbers in the life of each antediluvian patriarch (Gen. 5) in order to ascertain their total life-spans! If the time-span of the *whole* period was one of the important reasons for giving the genealogy, how simple it would have been to give the total, as he did in Exodus 12:40 for the time of Israel's sojourn in Egypt!

(2) *The Name and Years of Cainan Do Not Appear in the Hebrew Text*

Another reason for questioning Ussher's chronology for Genesis 11 is the evidence that not all the post-diluvian patriarchs are listed in our present Hebrew text. For in Luke's genealogy of Mary, the name "Cainan" appears between "Shelah" and "Arphaxad" (Luke 3:36). The Septuagint translation of Genesis 11 places the name "Cainan" in the same position that Luke does. It is possible, of course, to hold that the name "Cainan" was a later insertion into the Septuagint text and that it did not appear in the original manuscript of Luke. The problem is admittedly a complex one, but for the sake of brevity, we shall simply state our conclusion: the Septuagint *does* give us the full list of *names* as they appeared in the original Hebrew text; but since the *years* for these patriarchs as given in the Septuagint are obviously false, we have no way of determining how old Cainan was at the birth of his first son.[1] Thus, this one omission, even if there are no others, makes it impossible to fix the date of the Flood.

(3) *Genesis 5 and 11 Are Perfectly Symmetrical in Form*

The fact that Cainan should be included in Genesis 11 has greater implications than might appear at first glance; for the addition of his name puts the genealogies of Genesis 5 and 11 into perfectly sym-

[1] C. Robert Fetter ("A Critical Investigation of 'The Second Cainan' in Luke 3:36" Winona Lake, Indiana: Grace Theological Seminary, unpublished critical monograph, 1956), lists the following texts and versions which omit the name of Cainan: (1) all the passages in the Hebrew text (Gen. 10:24; 11:12-13; I Chron. 1:18, 24); (2) the Samaritan Pentateuch; (3) I Chron. 1:24 in the Septuagint; (4) the Targums of Jonathan and Onkelos; (5) the Syriac Version; (6) the Latin Vulgate; and (7) Codex Bezae on Luke 3:36. But those which *do* mention Cainan are: (1) nearly all the Greek manuscripts of Luke 3:36; (2) the Septuagint of Gen. 10:24,

metrical forms. In each case, there are *ten* patriarchs listed, with the *tenth* patriarch having *three* important sons:

1. Adam		1. Shem	
2. Seth		2. Arpachshad	
3. Enosh		3. Cainan	
4. Kenan		4. Shelah	
5. Mahalalel		5. Eber	
6. Jared		6. Peleg	
7. Enoch		7. Reu	
8. Methuselah		8. Serug	
9. Lamech		9. Nahor	
10. Noah		10. Terah	
(Shem, Ham, Japheth)		(Abram, Nahor, Haran)	

Now this symmetrical arrangement is of great importance in enabling us to determine one important purpose of these genealogies; for a study of the closest parallel to this phenomenon in Scripture, namely, that of the three groups of fourteen names in the first chapter of Matthew, reveals the purposely symmetrical character of such an arrangement of names, possibly as an aid to memorization. If it be objected that in our arrangement of the two lists of patriarchs Shem's name appears twice, it is sufficient to answer that Matthew lists David twice in his arrangement of names too. And even if the name of Cainan were not in the original text, the genealogies of Genesis 5 and 11 would still be symmetrical: Adam to Noah, ten generations; and Shem to Abram, ten generations. These facts may well indicate that it is not necessary to press the numerical data of these chapters into a strict chronology.

(4) *Information Is Given Concerning Each Patriarch Which Is Irrelevant to a Strict Chronology*

Genesis 5:6-8 states that "Seth lived a hundred and five years and begat Enosh: and Seth lived after he begat Enosh eight hundred and

---

11:12-13, and I Chronicles 1:18; (3) the Book of Jubilees; and (4) Demetrius of the 3rd century B.C., according to Polyhistor and Theophilus of Antioch. Apart from the question of Cainan's inclusion in Genesis 11, the Septuagint numbers for the years of the patriarchs at maturity are not trustworthy. The purpose of these translators was apparently not so much to stretch the chronology as it was to make the lives of the patriarchs more symmetrical by having their first born sons after they were 100 years old. "A simple glance at these numbers is sufficient to show that the Hebrew is the original." William Henry Green, "Primeval Chronology," *Bibliotheca Sacra*, XLVII, No. 186 (April, 1890), p. 302.

seven years, and begat sons and daughters: and all the days of Seth were nine hundred and twelve years: and he died." Now if the purpose of this genealogy was to provide us with a chronology, all we would need to have is this: "Seth lived a hundred and five years and begat Enosh." But the additional facts which are provided concerning each patriarch indicate that the purpose of these genealogies was more than simply chronological. Their major purpose was to show us how faithfully God guarded the Messianic line (Gen. 3:15; 9:26) even in ages of universal apostasy (Gen. 6:1-12; 11:1-9); to impress upon us "the vigor and grandeur of humanity in those old days of the world's prime";[1] to demonstrate the fulfillment of the curse of Genesis 2:17 by the melancholy repetition of the phrase "and he died"; to show by the shorter life spans of postdiluvian patriarchs and by the omission of their total years of life the tightening grip of the Edenic curse upon the human body; and to make "the record end in terms of the command of 9:1, which was so vitally important in view of the Flood," by omitting the words "and he died" in the genealogy of Genesis 11.[2] Since, therefore, so many pedagogical purposes are evident in these two genealogies that have nothing to do with the actual length of the overall period, it is unnecessary to press them into a rigid chronological system.

(5) The Postdiluvian Patriarchs Could Not Have Been Contemporaries of Abram

If the strict-chronology interpretation of Genesis 11 is correct, *all* the postdiluvian patriarchs, including Noah, would still have been living when Abram was fifty years old; *three* of those who were born before the earth was divided (Shem, Shelah, and Eber) would have actually outlived Abram; and *Eber,* the father of Peleg, not only would have outlived Abram, but would have lived for two years after Jacob arrived in Mesopotamia to work for Laban!

On the face of it, such a situation would seem astonishing, if not almost incredible. And the case is further strengthened by the clear and twice-repeated statement of Joshua that Abram's "fathers," including Terah, were idolaters when they dwelt "of old time beyond

---

[1] Benjamin B. Warfield, *Biblical and Theological Studies,* edited by Samuel G. Craig (Philadelphia: The Presbyterian & Reformed Publishing Co., 1952), p. 244.

[2] Oswald T. Allis, *The Five Books of Moses* (Philadelphia: The Presbyterian & Reformed Pub. Co., 1943), p. 263.

the River" (Joshua 24:2, 14, 15). If all the postdiluvian patriarchs, including Noah and Shem, were still living in Abram's day, this statement implies that they had all fallen into idolatry by then. This conclusion is surely wrong, and therefore the premise on which it is based must be wrong. Consequently, it seems that the strict-chronology view must be set aside in order to allow for the death of these patriarchs long before the time of Abram.

(6) The Bible Implies a Great Antiquity
For the Tower of Babel

If we accept 2167 B.C. as the year of Abram's birth,[1] the Flood must have occurred in the year 2459 B.C. and the judgment of the Tower of Babel between 2358 and 2119 B.C. (the lifetime of Peleg) according to the strict-chronology interpretation.

When we turn to the Genesis account of Abram's journeys, however, we discover the international scene to have been quite different from that suggested by the above-mentioned dates for the Flood and the judgment of Babel. Abram is certainly not depicted as one of the early pioneers from the land of Shinar who migrated to western territories that were only beginning to be settled 200 years after the judgment of Babel. Quite to the contrary, the Bible implies that the world of Abram's day, with its civilizations and cities, was ancient already; and we are left with the unmistakable impression that its peoples had long since been divided "after their families, after their tongues, in their lands, in their nations" (Gen. 10:5, 20, 31).

As we follow Abram in his wanderings, from Ur of the Chaldees to the land of Canaan, filled to overflowing with "the Kenite, and the Kenizzite, the Amorite, and the Canaanite, and the Girgashite, and the Jebusite" (Gen. 15:19-21); and then follow him down into the land of Egypt with its Pharoah and its princes (12:15); and then see him going to Lot's rescue in the vicinity of Damascus after Lot and other captives from the five Cities of the Plain had been deported by the kings of Shinar, Ellaser, Elam, and Goiim (14:1-

---

[1] According to Edwin R. Thiele (*The Mysterious Numbers of the Hebrew Kings* [Chicago: University of Chicago Press, 1951]), 931 B.C. was the date of the division of the kingdom at the death of Solomon. Following I Kings 6:1 and Exodus 12:40, we arrive at 1877 B.C. for the entrance of Jacob into Egypt. Since Jacob was 130 years old at this time (Gen. 47:9), he was born in 2007 B.C. Isaac was 60 when Jacob was born (Gen. 25:26), and Abraham was 100 when Isaac was born (Gen. 21:5). Therefore, Abraham was born in 2167 B.C.

16); and then see him being met by a priest-king of Salem (14:18); and later see him coming into contact with a Philistine king (20:2) and Hittite landowners (23:2-20), we cannot help but feel that the judgment of God upon the Tower of Babel must have occurred many centuries before the time of Abram.[1]

This impression is confirmed by Jeremiah (47:4) and Amos (9:7), who inform us that the Philistines came into Canaan, not from Shinar but rather from the west from Caphtor, which is the island of Crete. And Moses tells us that before the Philistines ever came to Canaan from Caphtor, the southwestern section of Canaan had been occupied by the Avvim (Deut. 2:23). Thus, the Bible implies that Babel was judged long before 2358 B.C.

(7) The Messianic Links Were Seldom Firstborn Sons

Within the genealogy of Genesis 11 there are additional indications that we are dealing with something other than a chronology. One of these is found in the statement of Genesis 11:26—"And Terah lived seventy years, and begat Abram, Nahor, and Haran." Taking this statement at face value, one might well conclude that Terah became the father of triplets in his seventieth year (even as his grandson Isaac became the father of twins in his sixtieth year), Abram being the firstborn of the triplets. We are somewhat astonished, however, to discover upon further investigation that Abram was *not* the firstborn of the three and that Terah was *not* seventy, but rather one hundred and thirty years old when Abram was born!

In Genesis 11:32 we read that "the days of Terah were two hundred and five years: and Terah died in Haran"; while in 12:4 we find that "Abram was seventy and five years old when he departed out of Haran." Thus, if Abram left Haran to go to Canaan after Terah's death, Abram must have been born when his father was 130 years old. The possibility of Abram's leaving Terah in Haran sixty years before Terah finally died is excluded by Stephen's statement that "from thence, when his father was dead, God removed him into

---

[1] Byron C. Nelson, *Before Abraham* (Minneapolis: Augsburg Pub. House, 1948), p. 100, points out that Genesis mentions 26 cities in Canaan alone during the days of Abraham. Seven of these are said to have had kings. Presumably the five cities of the Plain, at least, had been in existence there so long that their cup of iniquity was already full to overflowing (cf. Gen. 15:16).

this land, wherein ye now dwell" (Acts 7:4).[1] In the light of these considerations, we may paraphrase Genesis 11:26 as follows: "And Terah lived seventy years and begat the first of his three sons, the most important of whom (not because of age but because of the Messianic line) was Abram."

It is quite possible that only a small number of the patriarchs listed in Genesis 11 were firstborn sons. A comparison of 11:10 with 5:32 and 8:13 suggests that Shem was not. A comparison of 11:10 with 10:22 suggests that Arpachshad was not. And we have already seen that Abram was not. Actually, *not one* of the Messianic ancestors in Genesis, whose family background is known in any detail, such as Abel, Seth, Abram, Isaac, Jacob, Judah, and Perez, was a firstborn son. The year of begetting a first son, known in the Old Testament as "the beginning of strength," was an important year in the life of the Israelite (Gen. 49:3, Deut. 21:17, Psa. 78:51, and Psa. 105:36). It is this year, then, and not necessarily the year of the birth of the Messianic link, that is given in each case in Genesis 11. Thus we have clear evidence for the possible addition of a limited number of years from the lives of some of these patriarchs to the total of years from the Flood to Abraham.[2]

---

[1] F. F. Bruce, in his *Commentary on the Book of Acts* (Grand Rapids: Wm. B. Eerdmans Pub. Co., 1955), pp. 146-147, attempts to sidestep the problem by adopting the view that Stephen was using a Greek text of Genesis 11:32 that gave Terah's age at death at 145 (like the Samaritan Pentateuch). The serious implications of such a view may be seen in the more recent statement of Everett F. Harrison, "The Phenomena of Scripture," in *Revelation and the Bible*, edited by Carl F. H. Henry (Grand Rapids: Baker Book House, 1958), p. 249: "Does inspiration require that a Biblical writer should be preserved from error in the use of sources? Presumably when Stephen asserted that Abraham left Haran for Canaan after his father's death (Acts 7:4), he was following a type of Septuagintal text such as Philo used, for the latter has the same statement (*Migration of Abraham*, 177). The Hebrew text of Genesis will not permit this, since the figures given in Genesis 11:26, 32 and 12:4 demand that Terah continued to live for 60 years after Abraham left Haran." The principal objection to the interpretation we have advocated is that Abraham would not have staggered at the thought of a 100-year-old man begetting a son if his own father was 130 when he was born (Gen. 17:17, Rom. 4:19). But it should also be remembered that Abraham did not think it impossible to beget a child by Hagar when he was 86 (Gen. 16:16) or to beget children by Keturah when he was over 140 (Gen. 25:1, cf. 23:1, 25:20). Even as Isaac experienced a serious failing in health 43 years before he died (27:1), so also Abraham may have failed in health by the time he was 99. In response to his renewed faith in God and in God's promise (Rom. 4:19), his body, which was "now as good as dead," must have been renewed by God to live out the remaining 75 years and to beget many more children (Gen. 25:1-7). Thus, the emphasis of Genesis 17:17 may well be the physical condition of Abraham and Sarah at this particular period in their lives, and not so much their actual age. R. C. H. Lenski, in *The Interpretation of the Acts of the Apostles* (Columbus:

(8) *The Term "Begat" Sometimes Refers to Ancestral Relationships*

Such terms as "begat" and "the son of," which in English imply a father-son relationship, sometimes have a much wider connotation in the Bible. In Matthew 1:8, we read that "Joram *begat* Uzziah," but three generations are omitted. In I Chronicles 26:24, we are told that "Shebuel the son of Gershom, the son of Moses, was ruler over the treasures" in the days of David. Here we have 400 years of generations skipped over between Shebuel and Gershom. But the most interesting case of all, in our opinion, is to be found in Exodus 6:20. Here we read that "Amram took him Jochebed his father's sister to wife; and she bare him Aaron and Moses: and the years of the life of Amram were a hundred and thirty and seven years." Now anyone reading this statement as it stands by itself would be forced to conclude that Aaron and Moses were the actual sons of Amram and Jochebed; for the text clearly states that "she bare him Aaron and Moses," and immediately following this we are given the number of the years that Amram lived, in a manner strikingly similar to that of the genealogy of Genesis 5. So it is with profound amazement that we turn to Numbers 3:17-19, 27-28, and discover that in the days of Moses, "the family of the *Amramites*," together with the families of Amram's three brothers (Izhar, Hebron, and Uzziel), numbered 8,600! Unless we are willing to grant that the first cousins of Moses and Aaron had over 8,500 living male offspring, we must admit that Amram was an *ancestor* of Moses and Aaron, separated from them by a span of 300 years! In the light of this, it is significant that the

---

Lutheran Book Concern, 1934), p. 259, concludes his discussion of the problem as follows: "Aside from the inspiration by which Stephen spoke and Luke wrote, it does seem that in the simple matter of adding a few figures, Stephen (Philo too) would not have made such palpable errors. The real motive lying behind these claims that discrepancies exist in the account is the denial of the inspiration and inerrancy of the Scriptures."

[2] John Urquhart, *How Old Is Man?* (London: James Nisbet & Co., 1904), pp. 101ff., suggested that since Abram was born near the half-way mark of the period between the birth of Terah's first son and the time of Terah's death, the same situation might have been true, on the average, for the other postdiluvian patriarchs as well. By averaging the two extreme possibilities, he arrived at 1668 years as the probable interval between the Flood and the birth of Abram. If, as we pointed out above (note 1, page 478), Abram was born in 2167 B.C., this would date the Flood at 3835 B.C. But Urquhart did not take into consideration the possible ancestral usage of the term "begat."

names of the actual parents of Moses and Aaron are not recorded in the narrative of Exodus 2:1-10.[1]

Keeping in mind this remarkable and enlightening example of how the Jews compiled their genealogies, we turn our attention once again to Genesis 11. Taking as a case for special study the central section of that genealogy, we read in verses 16-19:

And Eber lived four and thirty years, and begat Peleg; and Eber lived after he begat Peleg four hundred and thirty years, and begat sons and daughters. And Peleg lived thirty years, and begat Reu: and Peleg lived after he begat Reu two hundred and nine years, and begat sons and daughters.

For at least two reasons, this section of the postdiluvian patriarchal genealogy is unusual and calls for careful consideration. First, we find here a sudden drop in the life-span of the patriarchs that is unparalleled in the entire genealogy. Until the time of Eber, no postdiluvian patriarch is said to have lived less than 433 years. But now, without any explanation, the life-span drops to 239 years and never exceeds that number again! This represents a permanent drop in life-span of 45%, as opposed to the 23% drop from Shem to Eber.

The second peculiarity about this section is that it contains the name of Peleg, of whom it is said (in 10:25) that "in his days was the earth divided." It has been generally conceded by Old Testament scholars that this explanation has reference to the judgment of Babel, at which time "Jehovah scattered them abroad from thence upon the face of all the earth" (11:8, cf. 10:25). But it is difficult to understand why it should be said only of *Peleg,* that "in his days was the earth divided," if, on the assumption that Genesis 11 is a strict chronology, Noah, Shem, Arpachshad, Shelah, and Eber (and probably Cainan) were still living throughout the entire lifetime of Peleg.

All of this leads us to submit the following proposition: at least in *this* section of Genesis 11, if not in other sections, we have warrant for assuming that the term "begat" is to be understood in the ancestral sense. From the fact that there is a sudden and permanent drop in the life-span between Eber and Peleg and also from the fact

[1] See John D. Davis, *A Dictionary of the Bible* (4th ed., rev.; Philadelphia: The Westminster Press, 1929), p. 195.

that Peleg is the only patriarch who is recorded as having lived at the time of the judgment upon Babel, we feel justified in assuming that Peleg was a distant *descendant* of Eber.

Now the objection might be raised at this point that Genesis 10:25 cannot allow for such a view; for in that passage we read that "unto Eber were born two sons: the name of the one was Peleg; for in his days was the earth divided; and his brother's name was Joktan." How, then, could Peleg be a distant descendant of Eber, if we are told in this passage that Eber had two sons of whom one was Peleg? Would not such a statement preclude the possibility of a merely ancestral relationship?

Indeed, this would be a serious objection, were it not for our parallel case in Exodus 6:20. There we found that *two sons were born unto Amram*. But from the third chapter of Numbers we also discovered that Moses and Aaron were only two of 8,600 living descendants of Amram's father. Now the very same thing could be true of Genesis 10:25, where we read that *two sons were born unto Eber*. By analogy with Exodus 6:20, then, it seems quite possible that Peleg and Joktan were only two of the many living descendants of Eber at the time of God's judgment upon Babel.

In summarizing the arguments of this entire discussion, we may say that the lack of an overall total of years for the period from the Flood to Abraham, the absence of Cainan's name and years in the Hebrew text, the symmetrical form of the genealogies of Genesis 5 and 11, the inclusion of data that are irrelevant to a strict chronology, the impossibility of all the postdiluvian patriarchs being contemporaries of Abraham, the Biblical indications of a great antiquity for the judgment of Babel, the fact that the Messianic links were seldom firstborn sons, and the analogy of "begat" being used in the ancestral sense allow the existence of gaps of an undetermined length in the patriarchal genealogy of Genesis 11.

GENESIS 11 CANNOT BE STRETCHED
BEYOND CERTAIN LIMITS

The strict-chronology interpretation of Genesis 11 has been shown to be unnecessary for various reasons. Thus, it seems Biblically possible, or even probable, that the Flood occurred several millennia before Abraham. But what is to be said for the view that is gaining new popularity in evangelical circles, that Genesis 11 (as well as Genesis 5) allows for gaps totalling *scores or hundreds of thousands of years* and that the Flood (as well as the creation of Adam) must be dated in harmony with the time-table of uniformitarian anthropology?[1]

According to A. L. Kroeber, Upper Paleolithic cultures in Europe and the Near East, such as the Aurignacian, Solutrean, and Magdalenian, are to be dated between about 25,000 and 8,000 B.C., while Lower Palaeolithic cultures such as the Chellean, Acheulian, and Mousterian, are to be dated from several hundred thousand years B.C. to about 25,000 B.C. Even if the most conservative estimates of modern anthropologists are accepted, we are still asked to think in terms of a hundred thousand years of human history at the very least. Kroeber comments on this shorter chronology:

If we allot 25,000 of this to the Mousterian, we have left 75,000 for the continuous Chellean-Acheulian bifacial-core tradition. This is a long time . . . a dozen times longer than the whole of documented, authentically datable human history. And what do we know to have happened in this time? Essentially just one thing: the improvements from roughed Chellean core flints to evener, symmetrical Acheulian ones. That is, the technological tradition remained basically unchanged: it stood still except for some degree of refinement of finish. That is surely a tremendous lot of cultural stationariness to have lasted so long, in comparison with the changeability that characterized later prehistory and all history. No doubt development was indeed exceeding slow at the beginning; all the evidence points that way. Yet if we accept the most recently alleged chronology, with the Pre-

---

[1] Christians who have been calling for an acceptance of the vast antiquity of the human race as postulated by modern anthropologists include Russell L. Mixter, "Man in Creation," *Christian Life* (October, 1961), p. 26; Marie Fetzer in "A Christian View of Anthropology," *Modern Science and Christian Faith* (Wheaton, Ill., 1950), p. 183; Bernard Ramm, *The Christian View of Science and Scripture* (Grand Rapids, 1954), pp. 314-315, 327-328; James O. Buswell, III, "The Creation of Man," *Christian Life*, XVIII, No. 1 (May, 1956), p. 17; Jan Lever, *Creation and Evolution* (Grand Rapids, 1958), pp. 171-177; Henry W. Seaford, Jr., "Near-Man of South Africa," *Gordon Review*, IV, No. 4 (Winter, 1958), pp. 165-192; and Edward John Carnell, *The Case for Orthodox Theology* (Philadelphia, 1959), pp. 96-97. There are three schools of thought concerning the date of the Flood among Christians who accept the anthropological time-table. Those who believe the Flood was geographically universal tend to date the Flood several hundred thousands years ago. Those who believe it destroyed all men but was geographically local (e.g., James O. Buswell III) would date it from about 15,000 to perhaps 100,000 years ago. Those who believe it only destroyed part of the race (e.g., Bernard Ramm) would tend to date it less than 10,000 years ago. In other words, the more catastrophic the Flood is conceived to have been, the more remote it must have been if the human race is as old as modern anthropologists claim.

Crag tools as preglacial, then our 75,000 years of Chellean-Acheulian nondevelopment are stretched into 400,000, which certainly is an added strain on the credibility we have to extort from our imagination. Even 4000 years without basic change in methods of human living is really wholly beyond our experience to conceive. *Perhaps once we get beyond comparable historical experience, we are lost anyhow, as critical minds, and we might as well trust to faith in an authority that claims a lot as in one that claims less.*[1]

Those who have no ultimate authority or standard of revealed truth to appeal to may well rest content with such speculations. But how can Genesis 11 be made to harmonize with such a scheme of things? Are we to grant that the assumptions which underlie modern anthropological dating schemes are basically valid and put Adam, the Flood, and the Tower of Babel hundreds of thousands of years before Christ? For several reasons, we believe that Christians cannot with consistency allow for such datings.

The Analogy of Biblical Chronology

To stretch the genealogy of Genesis 11 to cover a period of over 100,000 years is to do violence to the chronological framework of all subsequent Bible history and prophecy. Approximately 2,000 years covers the history of the Church up to the present. Before Christ's first coming, the history of Israel covered a period of 2,000 years; and after Christ's second coming, according to Revelation 20, there will be another 1,000 years of earth-history before the commencement of the eternal state (amillennialists do not even allow for these final 1,000 years). The incongruity of insisting upon 100,000 years between Noah and Abraham, while granting that the entire history of redemption from Abraham to the eternal state may be only four or five thousand years, becomes obvious.

To be sure, it was by means of Biblical analogies that we were able to find possible gaps in the genealogy of Genesis 11. But the

---

[1] A. L. Kroeber, *Anthropology*, p. 654. Italics are ours. More recently, Harry L. Shapiro (ed.), *Man, Culture, and Society* (New York: Oxford Univ. Press, 1956), p. 49, calls attention to "the immense space of time between the first appearance of man and the beginnings of written records . . . a period of perhaps some 1,000,000 years duration at a conservative estimate." On July 17, 1959, L. S. B. Leakey discovered what he claims to be "the oldest known stone tool-making man yet found." He has named him *Zinjanthropus boisei,* and dates him about 500,000 years ago. *Antiquity,* XXXIII, No. 132 (December, 1959), pp. 285-287.

point we now wish to emphasize is that *those very analogies serve also to limit our time-scale for Genesis 11*. The gap between Amram and Moses was 300 years, not 30,000. And the gap between Joram and Uzziah in Matthew 1:8 was 50 years, not 5,000. On the basis of the analogy of Biblical chronology, therefore, we maintain that it is very hazardous to assume a period of 100,000 years between the Flood and Abraham.

The Dating of the Tower of Babel

But the matter becomes even more serious when we discover that not all of the postdiluvian patriarchs can be used to cover this supposed 100,000 years which elapsed between the Flood and Abraham. As we have pointed out previously, the judgment of Babel occurred in the days of Peleg, the sixth patriarch listed after Noah. The centrality of the human race and its linguistic unity (Gen. 11:1-2), coupled with the magnitude of the building project at Babel (Gen. 11:4), presuppose a fairly high degree of civilization. That God's judgment upon Babel took place not more than a millennium after the Flood is suggested by the fact that the world's population was still confined to one comparatively small area of the earth at that time.[1] Of course, those who are seeking a harmonization between Genesis and the time-table of uniformitarian anthropologists would be perfectly willing to grant a comparatively short period between the Flood and God's judgment of Babel anyway, for they are looking for ample time *since* the confusion of tongues at Babel to explain the distribution of mankind to the ends of the earth in terms of the uniformitarian time scheme.

[1] That the antediluvians scattered abroad much more quickly than the postdiluvians is suggested by at least two considerations. First, such passages as Gen. 4:14-16, 6:1, and 6:11 indicate that the earth was filled with people long before the Flood (see above, pp. 28-33). Secondly, the early postdiluvians are said to have built their city and tower "lest we be scattered abroad upon the face of the whole earth" (Gen. 11:4), presumably with the experience of antediluvian humanity in mind. The Biblical emphasis upon their refusal to be scattered strongly implies a contrary situation in the antediluvian world, as well as a direct disobedience of God's command to "replenish the earth" (9:1). That the judgment of Babel could have occurred as much as 1,000 years after the Flood is suggested by two further considerations. First, the analogy between Genesis 10:25 and Exodus 6:20 (as discussed above, pp. 481-483) shows that Peleg could have been a distant descendant of Eber. Secondly, the fact that Peleg *alone* is singled out as the patriarch in whose days the earth was "divided" (a reference to the judgment of Babel) permits us to assume that Noah, Shem (who lived for half a millennium after the Flood), Arpachshad, Shelah, and Eber had died long before the birth of Peleg and therefore before the judgment of Babel.

But this would mean that we have eliminated half of the post-diluvian patriarchs before the "stretching process" really begins in earnest! Since Terah is obviously the actual father of Abram, we are left with only Reu, Serug, and Nahor, as the patriarchal links during the 100,000 years that supposedly elapsed between the Flood (and the Tower of Babel) and Abram. And the very place where we found the clearest possibility for a gap in the genealogy of Genesis 11, namely, between Eber and Peleg, was *before* the Tower of Babel! Thus, the obvious proximity of the first five postdiluvian patriarchs to the time of the Flood makes it all the more difficult to imagine a vast period of time elapsing between the judgment of Babel and the birth of Abraham.

The Patriarchs and the "Old Stone Age"

Even if we dismiss the incongruity of allowing only a few centuries between the Flood and the Tower of Babel and then pressing 100,000 years or so into the period from Babel to Abraham, we are still faced with the staggering problem of explaining how our three "link" patriarchs—Reu, Serug, and Nahor—are to be related to the various stone-age cultures that anthropologists assign to the vast ages of time that supposedly preceded the rise of civilization. May we think of Reu and Serug as savage, illiterate cave-dwellers of the Chellean period and Nahor perhaps as a primitive hunter of the Acheulian period whose flints were more even and symmetrical than those of his ancestors? Or are we to suppose that in some tiny pocket of civilization, nearly swamped by an ocean of savagery, an unbroken chain of saintly men[1] perpetuated the Messianic line of Shem and handed down the knowledge of the one true God for scores of thousands of years? If Babel was judged 100,000 years before Abraham, how can we explain the close connection between the sons of Noah and the various national and language groups of Genesis 10? And if

---

[1] To be sure, the case of Terah (Joshua 24:2) proves that not all links in the Messianic chain had to be saints, any more than in the case of some of the links which are named in Matthew 1. But we must insist that the Messianic line remained in fairly close contact with men who were saints and that these links, without exception, were civilized men. It would be unbiblical to allow for any period of human history with *no* human witnesses to the truth of God; and the very existence of a Messianic *line* (even though only a few of the names are mentioned in Scripture) would seem to presuppose some sort of a written record, which in turn presupposes at least a tiny pocket of civilization in the Near East from Babel onward.

tens of thousands of years separated Abraham from his post-Babel ancestors, how can we explain the fact that there are evidences in Assyrian records of the existence of towns in Mesopotamia whose names correspond to those of Peleg (Paliga), Reu, Serug (Sarugi), and Nahor (Nakhiri or Nakhur)?[1] The absurdity of attempting to harmonize Genesis 11 with the time-table of uniformitarian paleoanthropologists should be apparent to those who ponder these and similar questions.

The Babylonian Flood Tradition

The most serious limitation on the stretching of Genesis 11, in the opinion of some scholars, is that which is imposed by the Flood traditions of many nations, especially that of Babylon. So remarkable are the similarities between the Genesis account of the Flood and that which is recorded in the Gilgamesh Epic that most archaeologists insist on deriving the former from the latter. Christian scholarship, on the other hand, unanimously asserts that Genesis gives us God's inspired record of that great catastrophe, while the Babylonian epic was handed down by oral and written tradition for many centuries, showing by its gross polytheism the serious corruption of the original facts with the passing of time.

Now the problem, simply stated, is this: How could certain details of the story of the great Flood have been more or less accurately handed down from one primitive stone-age culture to another, purely by oral tradition, for nearly 100,000 years, to be finally incorporated into the Gilgamesh Epic? That such could have happened for four or five thousand years is conceivable. That it could have happened over a period of nearly 100,000 years is quite inconceivable. The Gilgamesh Epic alone, rightly considered, administers a fatal blow to the concept of a 100,000 B.C. Flood.[2]

---

[1] Cf. Merrill F. Unger, *Archaeology and the Old Testament*, pp. 112-113.

[2] James O. Buswell, III, in a review of Bernard Ramm's volume, *The Christian View of Science and Scripture*, challenged his statement (quoted above, p. 37) that Genesis and Babylonian parallels demand a comparatively recent date for the Flood (*Journal of the American Scientific Affiliation*, VII, No. 4, December, 1955, p. 5). To this, Ramm replied, "Believe that common oral tradition was handed down for 5,000 years so that the Babylonians received it, or what you will. The parallels between Genesis and Babylonian materials is too close to be sheer accident or verbal coincidence." (*Loc. cit.*, p. 6). For further discussions of the Babylonian Flood account, see above, pp. 37ff., and pp. 49ff.

CONCLUSION

A careful study of the Biblical evidence leads us to the conclusion that the Flood may have occurred as much as three to five thousand years before Abraham. Some evangelical scholars, seeing the possibility of gaps in the genealogy of Genesis 11, have urged an acceptance of uniformitarian and evolutionary dating schemes for early man, with the Flood occurring more than 100,000 years ago. But the analogy of Biblical chronology, the obvious proximity of the judgment of Babel to the Flood, and the problem of Reu, Serug, and Nahor make it highly improbable that such an extended postdiluvian chronology can be allowed. This improbability approaches impossibility when we consider the oral traditions of the Flood which have been incorporated into such documents as the Gilgamesh Epic of Babylonia.

Evangelical scholars who feel the necessity of bringing Genesis 11 into conformity with current paleoanthropological timetables should realize the full implications of such harmonization efforts. It would seem to us that even the allowance of 5,000 years between the Flood and Abraham stretches Genesis 11 almost to the breaking point. The time has come when those who take the testimony of God's infallible Word with seriousness should begin to look with favor upon the efforts of those who are examining and exposing the unwarranted assumptions and false presuppositions of uniformitarianism as it applies to the dating of early man.[1]

[1] The assumptions which underlie Carbon 14 dating methods are discussed above, pp. 43-44; 370-379. Also, see pp. 296-303 on the theory of multiple glaciations; and pp. 417-418 for the dating of cave deposits. Among those who are advocating a relatively recent date for the universal Flood are R. Laird Harris, "The Date of the Flood and the Age of Man," *The Bible Today*, XXXVII, No. 9 (June, 1943), p. 579; Joseph P. Free, *Archaeology and Bible History* (Wheaton, Ill.: Van Kampen Press, 1950), pp. 18, 21; J. Barton Payne, *An Outline of Hebrew History* (Grand Rapids: Baker Book House, 1954), p. 20; and Merrill F. Unger, *Unger's Bible Dictionary* (Chicago: Moody Press, 1957), p. 202.

Index of Subjects

Aaron, 481, 483

Abel, 26, 480

Abraham (Abram): not contemporary with postdiluvian patriarchs, 476-78; date of birth, 478 and n; contacts with old civilizations, 478-79; not Terah's firstborn son, 479-80, 481n; physical condition at Isaac's birth, 480n

Acapulco Trench: 'living fossil' found in, 178

Acheulian culture, 484-85

Adam: creation of, 21, 233, 344 and n, 456-57; longevity of, 23; descendants of, 26, 28, 475; fall of, 454-55, 465, 467, 470n, 471; date of creation of, 484-85. See also Evolution; Fall

Africa: human fossils found in, 31, 485n; human migrations to, 45-47, 48n; flood traditions in, 48n, 53n; animals travelled to Ark from, 63; marsupials in, 82

Agate Springs (Nebraska): bone bed in, 161 (Fig. 8)

Age: of universe, 237; true as distinct from apparent, 345-46, 346n, 355. See also Dating, geologic

Aging: accelerated by radiations, 400-1

Agriculture, origin of: in Near East, 394; in Europe, 396

Alaska: land bridge to, 64, 86n; fossil graveyards in, 156, 288, 291

Aleutian Islands: earthquakes and tsunamis in, 264

Alligator: fossil remains of, 157

Allochthonous processes: explain most fossil deposits, 159; and origin of coal beds, 277-78

Allogramia laticollaris: in foraminiferal studies, 282

Alpha-decay: in radioactive disintegration, 347-49, 360-62

Alps: Pliocene uplift of, 128, 286

Amazon: vegetation rafts from, 85n; tides at mouth of, 101

America: human fossils in, 31; Indians in, 37, 40; not affected by Egyptian famine, 56, 60; animals travelling to Ark from, 63; marsupials in, 82-83. See also Central America; North America; South America

Amethyst Mountain: buried forests in, 418-21, 420 (Fig. 27)

Ammonites: index fossils of Mesozoic era, 279

Amorites: related to Abraham, 38, 42; flood traditions of, 42; in Abraham's day, 478

Amphibians: excluded from Ark, 68-69; hibernation of, 71

Amram (ancestor of Moses and Aaron), 481, 483, 486

Andaman Islands: Negritoes in, 47

Andes: Pliocene uplift of, 128, 286

Animals: domesticated varieties in Ark, 12; destruction by Flood, 12-14; number in Ark, 69; hibernation of not necessary before Flood, 73; brought to Ark by God, 74-76; cared for in Ark by God, 74-76, 103-4; universal distribution from Ararat, 79-86; creation of, 233; violent death of, before Fall, 454-55; herbivorous before Fall, 461-465, 465n

Anomalous leads: geochronological significance of, 338

Antarctic coal deposits, 162. See also Coal beds

Anteaters: problem of migration from Ararat, 80; marsupial variety of, 81; monotreme variety of, 82

Antediluvian period: mountains of, 4, 6-7, 57-58, 61-62, 77, 215; geography and topography of, 61-62, 83; climate of, 73; characteristics of, 215, 239-43

Antediluvians: depravity of, 17-20, 30; destruction of, 17-23

Antelope: fossil remains of, 158

Anthropology: in relation to the Flood (xix); in relation to distribution of mankind since Flood, 44-54; limita-

491

beakhead fossils in, 176, 177 (Fig. 12); coelecanth fossils in, 178; underlying pre-Cambrian strata, 185-91; "overthrust" on Pleistocene strata, 202 (Fig. 21); overlain by Mississippian strata, 204 (Fig. 22); warm climate indicated by, 244; characteristic fossils of, 279

Crete (Caphtor), 479

Crocodiles: and the Ark, 71

Crossopterygii: fossil fish, 177-78

Crust, accretion of: significance for geologic dating, 389-91

Cubit: length of, 10

Cumberland bone cave: fossil deposits in, 158; climatic mixing in fossil types, 300

Curse, Edenic. *See* Edenic curse

Cush: Hamites in, 46 and n

Cushites: dark skin of, 46n

Cyclical deposits: succession of buried forests, 418-21, 420 (Fig. 27); varved sediments, 421-29, 426 (Fig. 28); causes of lamination, 422, 428-29

Cyclothems: hypothetical sequence of coal formation, 162-63

Darwinian Centennial Convocation, 117, 442-43

Dating, geologic: held in suspension by authors, 84n; uniformity assumption implicit in, 124; geologic time-table, 132-34, 133 (Fig. 5); dependent upon paleontologic data, 169-70; based on fossils and evolution, 203, 205-7, 211, 281, 284-86; order of stratified beds, 270-87; use of depths of leaching in glacial deposits, 297-98; 298n; radioactivity methods, 333-43; paleontologic and radioactivity methods compared, 362-66, 365n; cause of apparent stratigraphic correlation with radioactivity dates, 366-68; astronomic methods, 368-70; contradictions with accepted results, 378-91; meteoritic dust method, 379-80, 379n; meteorite age-estimates, 380-81; age-estimates for tektites, 381-382; disintegration of comets, 382-83; atmospheric helium method, 384-85; oceanic chemical changes, 385-87, 386n; influx of juvenile water, 387-89; by rate of crustal accretion, 389-91; tree-ring method, 392-93; varve chronology, 421-23

Day-age theory: attempted harmonization with uniformitarian geology, 116

Days of creation. *See* Creation, days of

Dead Sea: former extent of, 314; salt content of, 413

Death: entrance into world, 239, 471; in animal kingdom before Fall, 454-55

Death Valley: remnant of Lake Manley, 313

Decay, radioactive: supposed invariability of rates, 346-55; various processes of, 347-48; the "potential barrier," 348-50, 349n, 352; effect of external energy sources, 349-55; 352n, 353n, 354n; possible effect of Van Allen radiation belts, 353-54, 354n; concordant changes in rates, 357-59, 357n, 358n; pleochroic halos, 359-62

Deccan Plateau (India); volcanic deposits in, 127

"Deep, the great": at initial creation, 214; nature and extent of, 242. *See also* "Fountains of the great deep"

Deep-sea sediments: formation and extent of, 409-10; reveal shallow-water deposits, 410-11

Deluge. *See* Flood

Dendrochronolgy, 392-93

Deposition: environments of, 145-47, 146n; in geosynclines and fluviatile plains, 147-50, 150n; factors affecting, 406

Deserts, former fertility of, 314

Detachment thrusts, Heart Mountain, 180-84. *See also* Overthrusts

Deterioration, biologic: stimulated by radiations, 401-3, 403n; caused by mutations, 448 and n

Devonian period: "living fossils" of, 178; warm climate of, 244; marine fossils of, 273, 275

Diagenesis, processes of: time required for, 407-8

Diluvium theory: origin of, 92-94, 97-98; collapse of, 98-99

Dinosaurs: and the Ark, 69n; fossil beds of, 161; fossil footprints of, 166-67, 167 (Fig. 9); footprints associated with human footprints, 173-75, 174n, 174 (Fig. 10); in Mesozoic era, 244; theories of extinction of, 279-80; possible survival after Flood, 280n; formation of fossil deposits by Flood, 280-81; not carnivorous before Fall, 455

Dinosaur National Monument (Utah and Colorado), 280

Disconformities: uniformitarian explanations for, 136; evidenced by missing

bottoms, 139-40; assumption of, in classification of sedimentary environments, 145-46; evidenced in most mountainous regions, 185; absent in antediluvian period, 242; at close of Deluge, 268-69, 271; influence on ice-age history, 302; postdiluvian, 312; in production of salt domes, 414

Tektites: age-estimates for, 381-82

Teleology: abhorred by modern scientists, 234 and n

Temperatures, ocean: change at end of ice age, 303-4

Terah, 24 (Fig. 3), 41, 476-79, 480n, 481n, 487 and n

Terraces, lake and marine: evidence of former higher water levels, 313-17, 316 (Fig. 26), 323-24

Terraces, river: evidence of former larger river flows, 318-20; depositional formation, 319-24

Tertiary period: fluviatile plains of, 149; warm climate of, 252; order of fossil deposits of, 281-86; strata represent later events in Flood, 283

Theology: importance of Flood to, xix; importance of Adam's creation to, 457; problems of, 471. *See also* Miracles; Revelation

Thermodynamics, two laws of: universal application of, xxi and note, 222-227, 222n, 225n

Thermoluminescence: method of geochronology, 378

Thermosphere: high-temperature zone in atmosphere, 240-41; possible vapor capacities of, 256

Thrust-faults. *See* Overthrusts

Tibetan plateau: vast uplift of, 151

Tidal waves. *See* Tsunamis

Tierra del Fuego: wave forces on, 261

Tigris River, 83n

Tillites: possible non-glacial origin of, 247 and n. *See also* Glacial period

Tower of Babel. *See* Babel

Tranquil theory: origin and weaknesses of, 97-106

Tree-ring dating: method and results, 392-93

Tree-trunks, fossil: found in coal beds 165

Triassic period: possible hail impression in New Jersey shales, 168; warm climate of, 244; characteristic fossils of, 279

Trilobites: possibly still living, 179 and

n; "index fossils" of Paleozoic strata, 273-74, 274n

Tritium: in antediluvian and postdiluvian atmospheres, 375

Tsunamis: generated during Flood, 122, 261, 264-65; tremendous power of, 264. *See also* Tectonic activity

Tuatara. *See* "Fossils, living"

Tunicates: species of, 68

Turbidity currents: relation to submarine canyons, 126; during post-Deluge uplifts, 269; indicated in deep-sea sediments, 411; possible evidence in Green River shales, 427-28

Turtles: fossil remains of, 157

Tyrannosaurus rex, 455

Uinta Mts. (Utah): superposed streams in, 150

Unconformities: at base of Proterozoic, 228; at base of Cambrian, 231

Underfit streams: evidence of former high flows, 318-23

Uniformitarianism: defined xx n, 200; "hyperorthodox" attitude toward, 36; assumed rather than proved, 77; hostile to Genesis Flood, 89-90, 113; rise of, 95-96; attempted harmonization of with Bible, 111-15; basis of historical geology, 117, 130-31, 137; bias of professional geologists toward, 119-20; invalidated by Flood, 123-34; inadequate to explain igneous rocks, 138-39; inadequate to explain past tectonic activity, 140-41; inadequate to explain past glacial activity, 143-44, 293-94; inadequate to explain sedimentary rocks, 145-46; inadequate to explain geosynclines, 147-48; inadequate to explain peneplains, 148; inadequate to explain fluviatile plains, 150; inadequate to explain vast uplifted areas, 151-53, 152 (Fig. 6); inadequate to explain incised meanders, 154-155, 155 (Fig. 7); inadequate to explain fossil deposits, 155, 157n, 158, 161, 168; inadequate to explain origin of coal beds, 162-65; inadequate to explain fossil tracks and impressions, 168; inadequate to explain assumed overthrusting, 172, 180-81, 181n, 184n; inadequate to explain mountain-building, 193; summary of inadequacies of, 200-203; basis of geologists' training, 212; post-Deluge applicability of, 216; not applicable to the Creation period, 224; in cosmology, 235-36; inadequate to explain mammoth deposits, 289-90; inadequate to explain sudden end of ice age, 305; inadequate for many post-Deluge deposits, 312; assumed in geochronology, 356-57; failure to account for meteorites and tektites, 382; inadequate to explain deep-sea sediments, 411; inadequate to explain evaporites, 414-17; inadequate to explain Green River varves, 426-28; unsuccessful in petroleum geology, 429-432, 437; inadequate to explain ore deposits, 437-38; inadequate to explain geologic data, 439; refuted by the facts of Creation and the Flood, 451-53

United Nations Organization: pervaded by evolutionist philosophy, 444

United States, U.S.S.R.: compared to size of Ark, 10n

Unity of human race, 455, 457

Universal terms used in limited sense, 21-22, 55-62

Universe: inadequate theories of origin of, 218-19, 218n, 236; geometric nature of unsettled, 368-70; time-scale implied in expanding, 368-69; astronomic methods of age determination, 368-70

Uplifts, continental: postdiluvian, 121-123, 126, 128; characterize strata of Pliocene and Pleistocene, 286-87; evidenced by river deposits, 319, 322-24. *See also* Mountain-building; Volcanism

Ur of Chaldees: "Flood stratum" at, 109-111, 111n, 112n; Abraham from, 478

Ussher's chronology, 117, 475

Utah: floods in, 259

Utnapishtim: the Babylonian Noah, 39, 40n

Van, Lake: supposed source of Flood, 59n

Van Allen radiation belts: nature and possible effects of, 353-54

Varved deposits: nature and interpretation of, 421-23; Green River formation, 424-28, 426 (Fig. 28)

Vapor, atmospheric water: in present atmosphere, 121, 121n; effect on climate, 254-55, 257; effect on warming climate, 305-6

Vegetarian diet: before the Fall, 461-64, 465n; in the Millennium, 463

Verbal inspiration of Bible, xx, 1, 118

Volcanic dust: possible condensation nuclei, 258

Volcanism: during Flood, 122-23, 268 and n; on sea floor, 127; extent of volcanic rocks, 126-27, 137-38, 139n; present igneous rocks not accounted for by uniformity, 201; theory of continental formation, 221; absence of in antediluvian period, 242; cause of tsunamis, 261, 264; addition of carbon dioxide to postdiluvian atmosphere, 307-9, 376; atmospheric dust possible factor in glaciation, 308-9; postdiluvian, 312; juvenile water source, 387-389, 389n; source of crustal materials, 389-90; associated with buried forests, 419-21, 420 (Fig. 27); effect on forming mineral and ore deposits, 437-38

Water: formerly smaller amount in oceans, 124-25; initial aspect of earth, 214; importance of in formation of most geologic deposits, 328. *See also* Flood, Genesis; Floods, river

Water, juvenile: significance for geologic dating, 387-89

"Waters above the firmament." *See* Canopy, antediluvian vapor

Waters, subterranean, 9, 242

Water vapor, atmospheric. *See* Vapor, atmospheric water

Waves, ocean: erosive power of, 261, 263; effect of surface winds, 267n

Whales: and the Ark, 68

White Mts. (California): Bristlecone pines in, 392

White Sands (New Mexico): giant human footprints at, 175

Wick (Scotland): wave erosion at, 263

Wind, postdiluvian: caused Flood to assuage, 77n; nature and cause of, 267, 269. *See also* Climatic change

"Windows of heaven," 9, 76. *See also* Canopy, antediluvian vapor

Wisconsin stage: supposed last glacial stage, 296-97, 300-2

Wolf: marsupial variety of, 81; in Millennium, 463-64

Wolverine: fossil remains of, 158

Worms: species of, 68-69, 69n

Yellowstone Park: petrified forests at, 166; buried forests at, 418-21, 420 (Fig. 27)

Index of Authors

508

Index of Scripture